Advanced Excel®
for Scientific Data Analysis

Robert de Levie

OXFORD
UNIVERSITY PRESS

2004

OXFORD
UNIVERSITY PRESS

Oxford   New York
Auckland   Bangkok   Buenos Aires   Cape Town   Chennai
Dar es Salaam   Delhi   Hong Kong   Istanbul   Karachi   Kolkata
Kuala Lumpur   Madrid   Melbourne   Mexico City   Mumbai   Nairobi
São Paulo   Shanghai   Taipei   Tokyo   Toronto

Copyright © 2004 by Robert de Levie

Published by Oxford University Press, Inc.
198 Madison Avenue, New York, New York 10016

www.oup.com

Oxford is a registered trademark of Oxford University Press

Library of Congress Cataloging-in-Publication Data
De Levie, Robert.
Advanced Excel for scientific data analysis / Robert de Levie.
   p. cm.
Includes index.
ISBN-13 978-0-19-517089-4; 978-0-19-517275-3 (pbk.)
ISBN 0-19-517089-X; 0-19-515275-1 (pbk.)
1. Chemistry, Analytic—Data processing. 2. Electronic spreadsheets. 3. Microsoft Excel
(Computer file) I. Title.
QD75.4.E4D43 2003
530'.0285—dc21   2003053590

Disclaimer
Neither the author nor the publisher of this book are associated with Microsoft Corporation.

While Oxford University Press takes great care to ensure accuracy and quality of these mate-
rials, all material is provided without any warranty whatsoever, including, but not limited to,
the implied warranties of merchantability or fitness for a particular purpose.

Excel and Visual Basic are either registered trademarks or trademarks of Microsoft Corporation in the United States and/or other countries. The product names and services are used
throughout this book in editorial fashion only and for the benefit of their companies. No such
use, or the use of any trade name, is intended to convey endorsement or other affiliation with
the book.

9 8 7 6 5 4 3

Printed in the United States of America
on acid-free paper

Preface

This book will take you, my reader, beyond the standard fare of Excel. This is why the title starts with the word "Advanced". This book is not a primer, and familiarity with Excel is presumed. You will learn how to make the spreadsheet do *your* bidding, not so much by prettying up its display, but by exploiting its considerable computational prowess to the fullest, and by adding to it with custom functions and custom macros where necessary. If Excel's built-in least squares facilities don't provide the covariance, don't handle statistical weights, don't supply orthogonal polynomials, or lack special tools for equidistant data, this book will show you how to make those tools. If Excel's fast Fourier transform routine is cumbersome, replace it, and go from there to perform time-frequency analysis. If you want to use the Runge-Kutta method, write a custom function to do so. If you need a deconvolution, there are several macros to perform it, in addition to the direct spreadsheet approach.

The focus of this book is on the *numerical analysis of experimental data* such as are encountered in the physical sciences. Data analysis is nowadays often performed with one of two approaches, least squares or Fourier transformation, which therefore form the core of this book, occupying chapters 2 through 6. Sometimes, theory does not furnish explicit expressions for our models, in which case the experiments must be compared with the results of numerical simulations, as briefly discussed in chapter 7. Then follows a short discussion of macros, while the final chapters round out the book with an annotated tour of its custom macros.

The material is illustrated with practical examples. In cases where the background of some of the methods used may be hard to find, short explanations have been included. Throughout this book, the objective is to make math a convenient scientific tool rather than an obstacle. You should know what a square root means, and have access to a tool (such as a table of logarithms, a slide rule, a calculator, or a computer) to find it, rather than have to learn (as yours truly once did) how to evaluate it by hand, with pencil and paper. That, incidentally, turned out to be a thoroughly useless skill, and was promptly forgotten. It is useful as well as intellectually satisfying to know how to design an engine, but it is not needed for safe driving. In the same sense, you need not know all theorems, conjectures, and lemmas underlying your mathematical tools in order to reap their benefits, as long as you understand what you are doing. Where math is displayed in this book, often at the beginning of a chapter or section, it is used as convenient shorthand for those who can read its precise, compact language, but it seldom requires you to execute the corresponding mathematical operation. In other words, you can skip the math if, otherwise, it would scare you away. On second reading, the math may not even look so frightening any more. At any rate, there are many more figures in this book than equations.

*****

Books are as much defined by what they are not as by what they are, and a prospective reader should know the score. This book offers no templates, since the idea is not to provide canned solutions but, instead, to illustrate how solutions can be created. While the macros listed in this book have a fairly general usefulness and applicability, they are primarily meant as examples, and you are encouraged to modify them for your own purposes, or to scavenge them for useful ideas and parts.

Furthermore, this book is neither an introduction to Excel or VBA, nor a text-book on the mathematical basis of scientific data analysis. There are already some good introductions to scientific uses of Excel on the market, and this book will build on them. There are also numerous books on VBA (which stands for Visual Basic for Applications, the computer language used in Excel custom functions and macros) that go into much more detail than could possibly be incorporated here, and many excellent books on statistics, on Fourier transformation, and on numerical simulation, the three main scientific applications discussed in the present book. Recommended books on each of these subjects are listed at the end of the relevant chapters.

What the present book offers instead is an attempt at synthesis of these various areas, illustrating how many numerical problems can be fitted comfortably in the convenient, user-friendly format of the spreadsheet. As such, this book should be suitable for use by any scientist already familiar with Excel. Because it retains its primary focus on science, it can also be used as the text for an introductory course in scientific data analysis, especially when combined with student projects.

While an effort has been made to make this book as broadly useful as possible, and to incorporate examples from different areas, my own background as a physical and analytical chemist will unavoidably show. Readers who are not chemists will still recognize the general, more widely applicable approach and features involved in many of these examples.

*****

Idiosyncratic notation has been kept to a minimum, with three exceptions. The notation 2 (3) 17 is used as convenient shorthand for the arithmetic progression 2, 5, 8, 11, 14, 17 (i.e., starting at 2, with increment 3, ending at 17). The linking symbol $\cup$ is used to indicate when keys should be depressed simultaneously, as in Alt$\cup$F11 or Ctrl$\cup$Alt$\cup$Del. (Since the linking sign is not on your standard keyboard, you will not be tempted to press it, as you might with a plus sign.) And the symbol $\varnothing$ will identify deconvolution, complementing the more usual symbol $\otimes$ for convolution.

*****

This book can be read at several levels. It can serve as a brief, illustrated introduction to least squares, Fourier transformation, and digital simulation, as used in the physical sciences. For those interested in simply using its macros (which provide a useful set of tools for solving a few standard scientific problems on a spreadsheet), it illustrates their modes of operation, strengths, and shortcomings. And for those who want the spreadsheet to solve other scientific problems, the fully documented macros can serve as examples and possible starting points for novel applications.

Here is how this book is organized. After the introduction, three chapters are devoted to least squares methods, used here almost exclusively as a data-fitting tool. Least squares methods are nowadays used routinely for describing experimental data in terms of model parameters, for extracting data from complex data sets, for finding their derivatives, and for a host of other manipulations of experimental data, and chapters 2 through 4 illustrate some of these applications. The guiding principle has been to relegate most of the mathematical manipulations to macros and, instead, to focus on how to use these tools correctly.

Then follows a chapter on Fourier transformation, a cornerstone of modern data analysis as well as of modern scientific instrumentation, and a companion chapter on methods for handling related problems, such as convolution, deconvolution, and time-frequency analysis. Next is a chapter on the numerical solution of ordinary differential equations. All of these can be, and are, valid topics of entire books and treatises, and we here merely scratch the surface and sniff their smells. The final chapters get the reader started on writing Excel macros, and provide a number of specific examples. Readers of my earlier book on this subject, *How to Use Excel in Analytical Chemistry*, Cambridge University Press, 2001, will of course find some inevitable overlap, although in the present volume I have restricted the topics to those that are of most general interest, and treated these in much greater depth.

Only relatively few owners of Microsoft Office realize that they have in Excel a modern, compilable, high-level language, VBA, ready to be used, a powerful computational engine raring to go, complete with the associated graphical tools to visualize the results. With so much power under the hood, why not push the pedal and see how far you can go?

*****

Numerous friends, colleagues, and students have contributed to this book, corrected some of its ambiguities, and made it more intelligible. I am especially grateful for invaluable help on many occasions to Bill Craig; for their many helpful comments, especially on the chapters on least squares, to Whitney King, Panos Nikitas, Carl Salter, and Brian Tissue; for commenting on the chapter on Fourier transformation to Peter Griffiths and Jim de Haseth; for valuable comments on deconvolution to Peter Jansson; for letting me use his elegant equidistant least squares macro to Philip Barak; and for sending me experimental data that are so much more realistic than simulations to Harry Frank, Edwin Meyer, Caryn Sanford Seney, and Carl Salter. I gladly acknowledge the various copyright holders for permission to quote from their writings or to use their published data, and I am grateful to William T. Vetterling of Numerical Recipes Software for permission to incorporate some programs from the *Numerical Recipes* in the sample macros. As always, my wife Jolanda helped and supported me in innumerable ways.

*****

This book was printed from files made on a standard personal computer. All text was written in Word; all figures (including those on the front and back cover) were made with Excel. Special graphing software was neither needed nor used. If so desired, you can read this book by restricting yourself to the passages printed in (relatively) large type, and the figures, even though that would be somewhat like learning to swim or ride a bicycle from a correspondence course. The only additional ingredient you will need for some of the exercises (in smaller print), apart from a computer with Excel version 5 or (preferably) later, is the set of custom macros in the Macro-Bundle, which can be downloaded as Word text files from the web site oup-usa.org/advancedexcel, and are listed in chapters 9 through 11. These macros are most conveniently accessible through an extra toolbar or, where viewing space is at a premium, as a menu item. The above web site also contains a SampleData file so that you need not type in the numerical values of the examples, and a SampleMacros file from which you can copy the macros and functions used in the exercises, and even a short GettingUpToSpeed exercise to help you recall your Excel skills. The software requirements are spelled out in section A.9

It is well-nigh impossible to write a book of this type and length without some typos and even outright errors, and the present volume is no exception. This second, corrected printing has benefited greatly from help from several careful readers, among them especially Prof. Panos Nikitas. Moreover, I have used this opportunity to add another macro, ColumnSolver. I will be grateful to receive further comments and suggested corrections at my e-mail address, rdelevie@bowdoin.edu, and I will keep posting corrections and updates on the web site of the book.

Copyright credits

The following copyright holders graciously provided permission to use data or verbatim quotes. Data from Y. Bard in *Nonlinear Parameter Estimation*, copyright © 1974, Academic Press, are used by permission. Data from L. M. Schwartz & R. I. Gelb are reprinted with permission from *Anal. Chem.* 56 (1984) 1487, copyright 1984 American Chemical Society. Likewise, data from J. J. Leary & E. B. Messick are reprinted with permission from *Anal. Chem.* 57 (1985) 956, copyright 1985 American Chemical Society. Data from R. D. Verma published in *J. Chem. Phys.* 32 (1960) 738 are used with permission of the American Institute of Physics. Data from W. H. Sachs are reprinted with permission from Technometrics 18 (1976) 161, copyright 1976 by the American Statistical Association, all rights reserved. Data from G. N. Wilkinson in *Biochem. J.* 80 (1961) 324 are reproduced with permission, © the Biochemical Society. Data from G. R. Bruce & P. S. Gill in *J. Chem. Educ.* 76 (1999) 805, R. W. Schwenz & W. F. Polik in *J. Chem. Educ.* 76 (1999) 1302, S. Bluestone in *J. Chem. Educ.* 78 (2001) 215, M.-H. Kim, M. S. Kim & S.-Y. Ly in *J. Chem. Educ.* 78 (2001) 238, are used with permission from the Journal of Chemical Education; Division of Chemical Education, Inc. Permission to quote data from E. S. Eppright et al., *World Rev. Nutrition Dietetics* 14 (1972) 269 was granted by its copyright holder, S. Karger AG, Basel. Data from the 2000 book *Modern Analytical Chemistry* by D. Harvey are reproduced with permission of The McGraw-Hill Companies. Finally, material from N. R. Draper & H. Smith in the 2nd edition of their book *Applied Regression Analysis,* copyright © 1998; from D. M. Bates & D. G. Watts, *Nonlinear Regression Analysis and Application,* copyright © 1988; and from K. Conners, *Chemical Kinetics, the Study of Reaction Rates in Solution*, copyright © 1990; is all used by permission of John Wiley & Sons, Inc.

About the author

Robert de Levie is the author of more than 150 papers in analytical and electrochemistry, of an early *Spreadsheet Workbook for Quantitative Chemical Analysis*, McGraw-Hill, 1992; of a textbook on the *Principles of Quantitative Chemical Analysis*, McGraw-Hill 1997); of an Oxford Chemistry Primer on *Aqueous Acid-Base Equilibria and Titrations*, Oxford University Press, 1999; and, most recently, of *How to Use Excel in Analytical Chemistry,* Cambridge University Press, 2001.

He was born and raised in the Netherlands, earned his Ph.D. in physical chemistry at the University of Amsterdam, was a postdoc with Paul Delahay in Baton Rouge LA, and for 34 years taught analytical chemistry at Georgetown University in Washington DC. For ten of those years he was the US editor of the *Journal of Electroanalytical Chemistry*. Now an emeritus professor, he lives on Orr's Island, and is associated with Bowdoin College in nearby Brunswick, ME.

Contents

3 *Further linear least squares*   98

6 *Convolution, deconvolution, and time-frequency analysis*   280

7 *Numerical integration of ordinary differential equations*   339

8 *Write your own macros*   377

9 *Macros for least squares & for the propagation of imprecision* 425

Chapter *1*

Survey of Excel

This chapter primarily serves as a brief refresher for those who have used Excel before, although it also contains some more advanced material that needed to be introduced here in order to be available in subsequent chapters. The novice user of Excel is urged first to consult a manual, or an introductory text, as can usually be found on the shelves of a local library or bookstore. Several such books are listed in section 1.18. A short 'getting up to speed' exercise is included in the web site.

The instructions in this book apply to versions starting with Excel 97, and can be used also (albeit sometimes with minor modifications) with the older versions Excel 5 and Excel 95. The instructions are primarily for Excel installed on IBM-type personal computers, but Macintosh users are alerted to the few commands that are different on their computers, while Table A.8 in the appendix compares the most useful instructions on both types of machines. Table A.9 lists the requirements necessary to get the most out of this book. Excel versions 1 through 4 used a different macro language, and are therefore *not* recommended in connection with this book. If you have such an early version, it is time to upgrade.

1.1 Spreadsheet basics

A spreadsheet is laid out as a page in an accountant's ledger, i.e., as a sheet with rows and columns. Because it is electronic rather than actual, the sheet can be (and often is) quite large, while only a small part of it is visible at any one time on the monitor screen. For that reason, the most important information is usually kept *at the top* of the spreadsheet, where it is easily found, rather than at the bottom of the columns, as would be common on paper.

The rows and columns define individual cells, denoted by a column letter and a row number. The top left-hand cell is A1, to its right is B1, below B1 is B2, etc. A cell can contain one of three different items: a label, a number, or an instruction. In the absence of contrary information, labels start with a letter, numbers with a digit, and instructions (i.e., formulas or functions) with the equal sign, =. When a cell contains an instruction, it will show the corresponding numerical result; the underlying instruction can be seen in the *formula window* in the formula bar when that particular cell is highlighted. At the same time, the cell address is shown in the *address window* in the same formula bar. Unless otherwise instructed, Excel displays labels as left-justified, and numbers as right-justified.

The most basic mathematical operations of a spreadsheet are listed in table A.1 of the appendix. Note that multiplication must use an asterisk, *, division a forward slash, /, and exponentiation a caret, ^. Numerous built-in functions are listed in tables A.2 through A.6 of that same appendix. And in section 1.11 you will see how to make your own, user-defined functions.

In general, copying instructions to another cell assumes *relative* addressing. This uses rules like those in chess, where the knight in one move can only reach squares with a given relative position, i.e., either 2 horizontal (sideways) plus 1 vertical (forwards or backwards), or 1 horizontal + 2 vertical, with respect to its starting point. Relative addressing can be overridden by using the dollar sign, that symbol of stability, in front of the column letter and/or row number, thereby making (that part of) the address *absolute*. The function key F4 conveniently toggles through the four possible permutations, say from A1 to \$A\$1, A\$1, \$A1, A1, \$A\$1, etc.

A highlighted cell or cell block has a heavy border surrounding it, and a *handle*, a little dark square, at its bottom-right corner. By highlighting two adjacent cells containing different numbers, and by then dragging the corresponding handle, one can conveniently generate a row or column of numbers in *arithmetic* progression.

***Exercise 1.1.1*:**
    (1) Place the numbers 0, 1, 2, and 3 in cells B3, B4, C3, and C4 respectively. Highlight the block B3:C4, grab its handle, and move it down or sideways. Note that one can drag only vertically or horizontally at the time, but can still make a block such as shown in Fig. 1.1.1 by dragging twice, e.g., first down and then, after momentarily releasing the handle, sideways (or vice versa). Note that this trick does not work for letters or other text, which is simply repeated. Try it.

The more general way to fill a row or column uses a formula that is copied. In the example of Fig. 1.1.1, the result shown could have been obtained by entering the value 0 in cell B3, the formula =B3+1 in cell B4, copying this to B5:B15, entering the instruction =B3+2 in cell C3, and copying this to the block C3:F15. While this takes slightly more initial effort, it is not restricted to arithmetic progressions, and is more readily modified, especially when the constant involved is specified in a separate cell, say C1, and referred to by absolute addressing, as in =B3+$C$1 for cell C3.

	A	B	C	D	E	F	
1							
2							
3		0	2	4	6	8	
4		1	3	5	7	9	
5		2	4	6	8	10	
6		3	5	7	9	11	
7		4	6	8	10	12	
8		5	7	9	11	13	
9		6	8	10	12	14	
10		7	9	11	13	15	
11		8	10	12	14	16	
12		9	11	13	15	17	
13		10	12	14	16	18	
14		11	13	15	17	19	
15		12	14	16	18	20	

Fig. 1.1.1: The square B3:C4 (here shown with gray background) as extended by dragging its handle sequentially in two directions.

In complicated mathematical expressions it is often convenient to use (easier to remember and easier to read) symbolic names rather than cell addresses. In Excel you can assign such names to constants, i.e., to parameters with an absolute address. The simplest method to assign names is to highlight the cell containing the constant to be named, and then to move the mouse pointer to the Name Box on the Formula Toolbar, click on the cell address, type the name, and press Enter (on the Mac: Return). You can also use the sequence Insert ⇒ Name ⇒ Define, and then type in the Define Name dialog box the desired name. If you want to restrict the name definition to a given sheet, use the latter method, and precede the name with that of the worksheet plus an exclamation mark, as in Sheet1!Ka1. You can then define Ka1 differently (or not at all) on the next page. Note that valid cell addresses (e.g., A2 or IV34) cannot function as names, but single letters (except R and C) and combinations such as BB, 4U, or A2B2C can.

1.2 Making 2-D graphs

Graphs form an integral part of science and technology, because well-designed visual images are often interpreted more readily than data sets. Excel makes it very easy to generate publication-quality 2-D graphs. In order to make a graph, we first must have something to show in it. Below we will use *simulated* data, generated with the Data Analysis ToolPak. If you cannot find Data Analysis listed under Tools, see section 1.7.1.

But first a brief technical excursion. In Excel, graphs are made of at least two largely independent blocks: the *chart* area, and the *plot* area. To these you can add other independent blocks, such as legends, labels, and other textboxes, which can be placed anywhere within the chart area. The data are shown in the plot area. The larger chart takes up the total space of the graph, and it contains the plot area plus the regions surrounding it. Thus, the chart surrounds the plot as a frame (and perhaps a mat) surrounds a painting. Axis labels and legends can be either inside or outside the plot area, but must be within the chart area. In this book, most chart borders have been deleted, but (with the exception of some 3-D plots in section 1.3) the plot borders have been retained.

Exercise 1.2.1:

(1) Enter the sequence 1, 2, 3, ... , 1000 in A1:A1000. From now on, such an arithmetic progression will be denoted by its first and last members and, within brackets, its increment, i.e., as 1 (1) 1000. In recent versions of Excel this is conveniently accomplished as follows: enter the starting value (here: 1 in cell A1), highlight it, then use Edit ⇒ Fill ⇒ Series and, in the resulting dialog box, specify Series in Columns, Type Linear, Step value: 1, Stop value: 1000, OK.

(2) Open the Data Analysis ToolPak with Tools ⇒ Data Analysis, then in the Data Analysis dialog box use the scroll bar and select Random Number Generation. In its dialog box, select Distribution: Normal (for Gaussian noise), click on the round 'option' or 'radio' button to the left of Output Range, click on the corresponding window, and enter N1:N1000 (it is easy to remember that we have synthetic *n*oise in column N), then click OK.

(3) In cell B1 enter the instruction =10+N1, then double-click on the handle of cell B1 to copy this instruction to B2:B1000. The newly copied column acquires the length to which the adjacent column is filled contiguously, and will not work when there are no adjacent, contiguously filled columns.

(4) With column B still highlighted, use Shift‿← (by simultaneously depressing the Shift and back arrow keys) to extend the highlighting to the two-column block A1:B1000, then use Insert ⇒ Chart, select XY(Scatter), pick your style of Chart sub-type (with markers and/or lines), and Finish. (In general do *not* use the Line chart, which assumes that all points are equidistant, i.e., that all *x*-values are equally spaced, regardless of whether or not this is true.)

(5) Click on the superfluous Legend box, and delete it. You should now have a graph such as Fig. 1.2.1.

By right-clicking (on the Mac, use Ctrl click instead) or double-clicking on the various components of the graph we can modify them; the most often modified elements are the function shown and its axes. Click on the data and try out some of the many options available in the Format Data Series dialog box. These include smoothing the curves using a cubic spline (Smoothed line under the Pattern tab) and, for multiple data sets, the use of a secondary axis (highlight the series, click on Format ⇒ Selected Data Series and, under the Axis tab, click on Secondary axis). Click on the numbers next to the horizontal axis, then change their font and size using the font and size windows on the formatting toolbar. Click on the vertical axis and try out some of the many options available in the Format Axis dialog box, including (under the Scale tab) using a logarithmic and/or reversed axis. Click on the plot background to get the Format Plot Area dialog box, or on the chart edge to find the Format Chart Area dialog box instead. Or, for more drastic changes, look under Chart, which appears in the Menu bar instead of Data when the graph is activated.

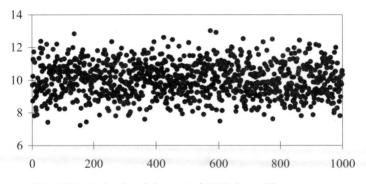

Fig. 1.2.1: A simulated data set of 1000 data with an average value of 10 and Gaussian noise with a standard deviation of 1.

Below we will import a label, calculate 9-point averages and their standard deviations, and display these as error bars.

Exercise 1.2.1 (continued):

(6) To compute averages and standard deviations of pairs of nine successive data points, deposit in cell C5 the instruction =AVERAGE (B1:B9), and in cell D5 the command =STDEV(B1:B9). Highlight the block C1:D9, and double-click on its handle. You will see the averages and corresponding standard deviations appear on rows 5, 14, 23, 32, 41, etc.

(7) In order to plot C1:C1000 versus A1:A1000, copy the graph you made for Fig. 1.2.1, and in that copy click on a data point. The columns A1:A1000 and B1:B1000 will now be outlined with color. Go to the top of cell B1, grab its colored edge when the mouse pointer is an arrow, and move it over to cell C1. This

will change the *y*-axis assignment of the graph, which will now show C1:C1000 vs. A1:A1000. Figure 1.2.2 shows what to expect.

(8) To add error bars, click on a data point, right-click (on the Mac: Ctrl⌣click) to get the Format Data Series dialog box, and select the Y Error Bars tab. Highlight the Display: Both, select Custom:, and in both windows type =Sheet1! D1:D1000 (assuming that your spreadsheet is called Sheet1, otherwise instead use whatever name shows on the tab below the working area of the spreadsheet). Compare with Fig. 1.2.3.

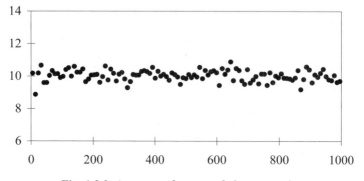

Fig. 1.2.2: Averages of groups of nine successive data points from the data shown in Fig. 1.2.1.

(9) If you want to see a smaller fraction of these data, copy the graph, and in the copy right-click (on the Mac: Ctrl⌣click) on it to change the appropriate range, and in the resulting Format Axis dialog box, under the Scale tab, change the Mi̲nimum and Ma̲ximum values, as well as the Ma̲jor and Mi̲nor units. Also change the *y* range, and the size of the markers.

(10) To enter text, click on the plot area of the graph so that the plot border (its inner framing) is highlighted. Type the text in the formula bar, then depress Enter (on the Mac: Return). The text will now appear in the graph in a text box, which you can move and shape with the mouse pointer. By passing over the text with the mouse key depressed, you can activate the text, then use F̲ormat ⇒ Text B̲ox ⇒ Font to change its appearance.

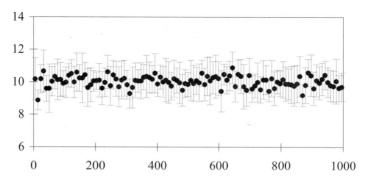

Fig. 1.2.3: The same data as in Fig. 1.2.2 with added (medium gray) error bars.

(11) To highlight a particular point, double-click on it (the mouse pointer changes into crossed double-pointed arrows) to see the options in Format Data Point, where you can change its appearance. A few examples are shown in Fig. 1.2.4; furthermore, color can also be used.

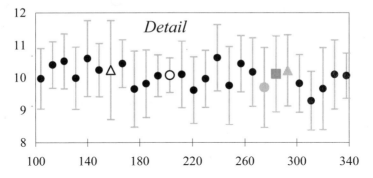

Fig. 1.2.4: Embellished detail from Fig. 1.2.3, with a few individual points highlighted with different markers (or, not shown here, colors).

Error bars can also be used to label specific features in graphs and spectra, see K. L. Lim, *J. Chem. Educ.* 79 (2002) 135.

The above examples involve a single function or data set. In order to introduce another data set with the same abscissa (horizontal axis), just highlight that set, copy it to the clipboard with Ctrl⏝c, click on the display area of the graph, and paste the data with Ctrl⏝v. To enlarge or reduce part of a data set displayed in a graph, click on a corresponding line and/or marker in that graph, then either change its range description in the formula box, or move the cursor to the input data and drag the now colored frames around the *x*- and *y*-values by their handles to surround the new ranges. Make sure that the *x*- and *y*-axes have the same lengths. No special action is needed when enlarging (or reducing) the data sets shown in graphs by inserting new rows (or deleting existing ones) inside existing data columns, or vice versa for new columns inserted or deleted inside rows of data.

When displaying more than one function in a single graph, it may be necessary to add a second ordinate (vertical axis) on the right-hand side of the plot. To do this, click on the particular data set in the graph that you want to associate with a second vertical axis, select its Format Data Series dialog box, and under the Axis tab select Secondary Axis.

Sometimes Excel places an axis somewhere in your graph (typically at *x* = 0 or *y* = 0) where you may not want it. If so, move it by selecting Format Axis and, under the Scale tab, change the C̲rosses at.

Some of these aspects are illustrated in exercise 1.2.2, which shows the use of two different axes by plotting the proton and hydroxyl ion concentrations as well as the pH as a function of the proton excess $\Delta = [H^+] - [OH^-]$. The plots for $[H^+]$ and $[OH^-]$ have two linear asymptotes, whereas that for pH has the typical shape of a titration curve.

Exercise 1.2.2:

(1) Here we illustrate the use of two different axes by plotting the proton and hydroxyl ion concentrations as well as the pH as a function of the proton excess $\Delta = [H^+] - [OH^-]$.

(2) Start a new spreadsheet, and in column A make a table of Δ with the values -0.05 (0.01) -0.01 (0.005) -0.005 (0.001) 0.005 (0.005) 0.01 (0.01) 0.05 where the numbers within brackets indicate the data spacing.

(3) In columns B, C, and D compute $[H^+] = \{\Delta + \sqrt{(\Delta^2 + 4 \times 10^{-14})}\}/2$ (assuming for convenience the value $K_w = 10^{-14}$), $[OH^-] = 10^{-14}/[H^+]$, and pH $= -\log[H^+]$.

(4) Highlight the data in columns A and B, and plot them in an XY graph. Select appropriate *x*- and *y*-scales.

(5) Highlight the data in column C, copy them with Ctrl∪c, then highlight the plot border, and paste the data of column C into the graph with Ctrl∪v. Select marker size and style, line thickness, and/or colors to distinguish the two curves.

(6) Again highlight the plot border, type the text of appropriate function labels, use Enter (Mac: Return) to place them in the graph, maneuver the mouse pointer over the text so that the pointer takes the shape of a capital I, move it to highlight the text, then use F<u>o</u>rmat ⇒ Text B<u>o</u>x to modify the appearance of the text, and finally move the pointer so that it becomes a cross, at which point you can drag the label to its final place.

(7) Likewise, highlight the data in column D, copy them, highlight the plot border, and paste the copied data in the graph. Now click on these data, right-click (Mac: Ctrl∪click), select F<u>o</u>rmat Data Series, and under the Axis tab specify the plot series as <u>S</u>econdary Axis.

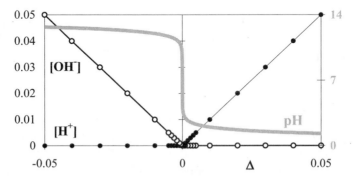

Fig. 1.2.5: Using two vertical axes. This rather complicated plot shows the values of $[H^+]$, $[OH^-]$, and pH $= -\log[H^+]$ as a function of the proton excess $\Delta = [H^+] - [OH^-]$. Gray is used here instead of color to identify the secondary (right-hand) scale and the corresponding curve.

(8) If, as in this example, the data in column D all fall outside the vertical range already established for the other data, replace one data point in column D by a temporary value (such as 0), and click on it to establish the secondary axis. Afterwards repair that point.

Use line width, marker type and size, and (if your final output can display it) color to emphasize important aspects, and to make your graph more intelligible. Resist the temptation to put too much information in a single graph: visual overload defeats the purpose of a graph. In fact, the information in Fig. 1.2.5 would be better illustrated in two separate graphs, one plotting $[H^+]$ and $[OH^-]$ vs. Δ, the other showing pH vs. Δ. The rule of thumb is: two is company, three is a crowd, unless the curves all belong to the same family. And do read the books by E. R. Tufte, especially *The Visual Display of Quantitative Information* (Graphics Press, P.O.Box 430, Cheshire CT, 1992) on the design of effective as well as visually pleasing graphical displays.

If you want to include details, use multiple panels or inserts; sometimes, a logarithmic scale will work. For example, the Fourier transform of the tidal data shown in Fig. 5.10.2 is displayed there as three panels with different vertical scales in order to show both the major peaks and the harmonics. An alternative, logarithmic plot of the same data is illustrated in Fig. 1.2.6 and conveys the same information in a single frame.

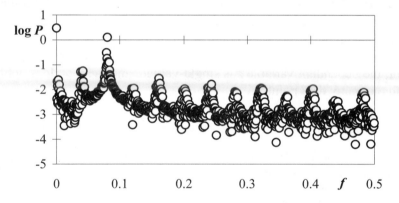

Fig. 1.2.6: The data in the three panels of Fig. 5.10.2 combined in a single, semi-logarithmic display, i.e., as the corresponding power spectrum.

It makes for a good-looking spreadsheet, and makes copying graphs into Word much easier, if you make sure that the graph is in register with the spreadsheet grid. To do this, highlight the chart area (by clicking on the region between the right edges of the plot and chart areas), move the mouse to a corner of the chart area, grab the double-sided arrow, and drag it to a cell corner while depressing the Alt key. Doing this with two diagonally opposed corners will align the graph with the cell grid.

Inserts are best made as independent graphs. After the insert is the way you want it, move it so that it is completely inside the area of the main graph, and adjust the scales, labels, and symbols to fit with the main graph. By highlighting the cell block *underneath* the main graph you can then lift both off simultaneously and, e.g., transfer them to a Word document, as described in section 1.6. This book contains several examples of inserts, such as Figs. 4.5.2 and 4.5.3.

1.3 Making 3-D surface graphs

The two-dimensional surface of a computer screen or a printed page cannot contain a truly three-dimensional image, but (as in a painting or photograph) it can give the *illusion* of a third dimension. That is what we mean by a 3-D graph. Excel cannot make general 3-D graphs, with arbitrarily spaced functions for all three axes. For complicated three-dimensional shapes, programs such as Mathematica, Maple, or AutoCad should be used. However, for one single-valued variable a 3-D surface graph can be made. It is really a three-dimensional form of Excel's Line plot, i.e., it assumes that the x- and y-values are *equidistant*, so that only the z-parameter (plotted vertically) can have arbitrary values. Moreover, you will have much less control over its appearance than Excel gives you for 2-D graphs. Still, such a graph will often make a reasonable 3-D plot as long as the independent coordinates x and y are both indeed equidistant, the dependent variable z is single-valued, and the plot does not contain too many data points.

> *Exercise 1.3.1*:
> (1) Open a spreadsheet, and enter the sequence 0 (0.2) 10 in both A2:A52 and B1:AZ1.
> (2) Deposit the instruction $=(1+\text{SIN}(\$A2*\text{SQRT}(B\$1)/\text{PI}()))/2$ in cell B2, and copy this to the area B2:AZ52.
> (3) Highlight the block A1:AZ52. Specifically include the x- and y-axes, which will be used automatically to calibrate the axes. Call the Chart Wizard with Insert ⇒ Chart, select Surface and its top-left Chart sub-type, then Finish. Double-click on the graph and position it where you want on the sheet. Click on the graph axes to select the label spacing. (In the example, for both axes, the number of categories (or series) between tick mark labels and the number of tick marks were set at 10.)
> (4) By rotating the graph we can select a different point of view. Click on a top corner of one of the vertical background panels when it shows the label "Corners". Grab the little square at the top front corner, and drag it to rotate the graph until it suits you.

(5) The resulting surface net has a color, which is one of the few attributes of a 3-D graph you can change. But even that is not easy, so pay attention. Click the plot to activate it. Select Chart ⇒ Chart Options, and under the Legend tab select Show Legend, and click OK. Now click on one of the colored boxes in the Legend box, then right-click (Mac: Ctrl click) to get the Format Legend Key (or start in the Formatting toolbar with Format ⇒ Selected Legend Key), and click on the colored marker specifying an area color. (In Fig. 1.3.1 we could also have selected the color white. Selecting None would have shown the surface as a transparent wire frame.) Changing the major unit on the vertical axis changes how many color bands are displayed. Exit with OK. Afterwards, you can click on the Legend box and delete the box; the selected color(s) will stay.

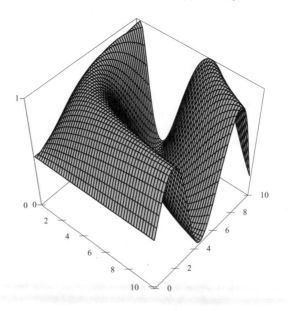

Fig. 1.3.1: A graph of the function $z = \frac{1}{2} + \frac{1}{2}\sin(x\sqrt{y}/\pi)$.

(6) In cell B2 now deposit instead the instruction =EXP(-5*(($A2-3)^2)) *EXP(-10*((B$1-6)^2))+0.7*EXP(-(($A2-7)^2))*EXP(-2*((B$1-4)^2))+0.5*EXP(-3*(($A2-2)^2))*EXP(-5*((B$1-3)^2)), and copy this to the area B2:AZ52. Your graph might look like Fig. 1.3.2.

(7) A fun picture is that of the Mexican or cowboy hat $z = 0.5\,[1 + \cos\sqrt{(x^2+y^2)}]$ illustrated in Fig. 1.3.3 for $-10 \le x \le 10$, $-10 \le y \le 10$ with all axes, legends, and borders colored white to make them invisible. The function is scaled to fit within the range $0 \le z \le 1$ in order to avoid lines where it crosses these boundaries. Make it, and play with it by moving the corner and thereby changing the point of view. Then, for precise control, use Chart ⇒ 3-D View, where you can numerically specify elevation, rotation, perspective, and height. In Fig. 1.3.3 all coordinate frames have been removed by clicking on them and then either removing them or coloring them white.

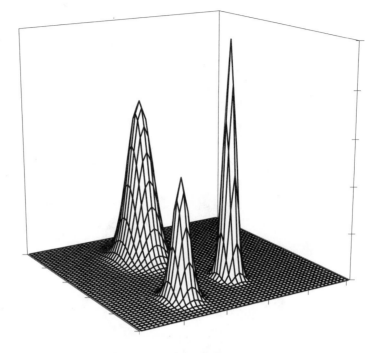

Fig. 1.3.2: A graph of three Gaussian peaks.

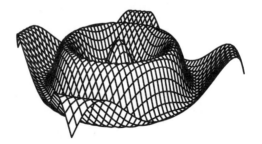

Fig. 1.3.3: The Mexican or cowboy hat, $z = \frac{1}{2}(1+\cos\sqrt{(x^2+y^2)})$, using the precise controls of Chart $\Rightarrow$ 3-D View. Top: Elevation 30, Rotation 70, Perspective 30, Height 100% of base.

You can control the line thickness of a 3-D line plot as follows. In the legend box, select the individual Legend Keys (the colored boxes to the left of the ranges), click on them, select Format Legend Key, then under Patterns select Border $\Rightarrow$ Custom $\Rightarrow$ Weight (and, if wanted, also Color). This is also where you can select an area color, such as the light gray in Fig. 1.3.1, or None as in Figs. 1.3.2 and 1.3.3.

1.4 Making surface maps

Maps provide an alternative way to visualize a single-valued, three-dimensional surface, especially when that surface contains much detail. Maps are most satisfactory when one must display a large number of data points, precisely the situation where the grid of Excel's 3-D line plots may become too dense. 3-D line plots and maps are, therefore, largely complementary tools. Either method works only for one single-valued parameter z (x, y).

Traditionally, maps use color and/or contour lines to provide the impression of a third dimension. Contour maps can be difficult and time-consuming to generate because they involve interpolation in the height data, but color (or even gray-scale) maps are relatively easy to make as long as there are enough data to define each pixel. Unfortunately, Excel has no built-in facilities for such maps.

As it turns out, it is possible to introduce color maps through a back door, because Excel has the option of using a picture as the background of a graph. While that may have been intended for company logos, there is nothing to prevent us from using it for our maps. We therefore generate a picture based on the information we want to plot, i.e., with a gray scale or colors representing the parameter values z, and then mount this picture in the frame of an x,y plot. The background picture then *is* the graph. The custom macro Mapper in the MacroBundle provides a gray scale as well as several color schemes to represent height. Moreover, once you understand how to write VBA (see chapter 8) you can easily modify Mapper's color schemes to your own liking.

Colors are coded in the RGB *additive* color scheme, in which all colors are represented in terms of three color components, *r*ed, *b*lue, and *g*reen, which roughly correspond to the maximum sensitivities of the three types of cones in the human retina. The additive color scheme is used in light projection and in television and computer monitors, which build the color sensation by adding light beams of different colors. In the additive system, red plus green yields yellow, while combining red, green, and blue colors in the right proportions leads to white. (The alternative, *subtractive* color scheme is based on light absorption and reflection of the remainder, rather than on light emission. It is based on pigments and dyes, typically yellow, cyan, and magenta, and is used in color printing as well as in painting. Adding its three components leads to black rather than white.)

Exercise 1.4.1:

(1) Open a spreadsheet, and enter the sequences –20 (0.4) 20 horizontally and vertically in, say, row 1 and column A.

(2) In cell B2 deposit the instruction for a modified Mexican hat, `=0.5*(1+ COS(SQRT($A2*$A2+B$1*B$1)))/(100+$A2*$A2+B$1*B$1)`, and copy this to the area B2:CX102.

(3) Call the macro Mapper0 and compare what you get with Fig. 1.4.1. Then try colors (with Mapper1 through 3), and other functions.

(4) Modify the axes to –50 (0.4) 50 horizontally and vertically, copy the same instruction to the area B2:IR251, again call Mapper, and compare with Fig. 1.4.2.

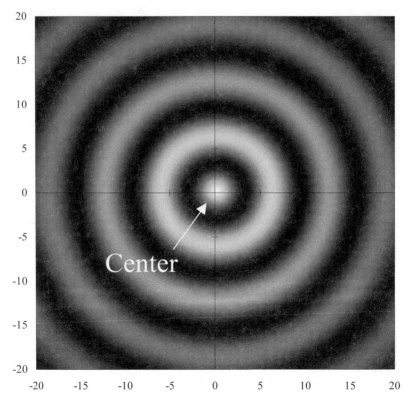

Fig. 1.4.1: The result of Mapper after step (3) of exercise 1.4.1, with super-imposed (white) text, and with a (white) arrow from the drawing toolbar.

Each RGB color is represented numerically by an integer with a value from 0 through 255. For example, black is (0, 0, 0), white is (255, 255, 255), pure red is (255, 0, 0), bright yellow is (0, 255, 255), while (180, 180, 180) gives a light neutral gray, etc. With three different colors to represent the single numerical value of each data point, there are many possible schemes to suggest height. Here we illustrate a gray scale, for which the values for R, G, and B are the same. More colorful schemes, such as that illustrated on the cover, are described in section 11.7. One such color scheme borrows from geographic maps (with the sequence black, blue, green, yellow, white), another from black body heat radiation (black, dark red, red, orange, yellow, white). It is not necessary to go from dark to light: one can, e.g., use the color sequence of the rainbow (from black via violet, blue, green, yellow, orange to red), which provides vivid pictures with great contrast but only a rather weak illusion of height.

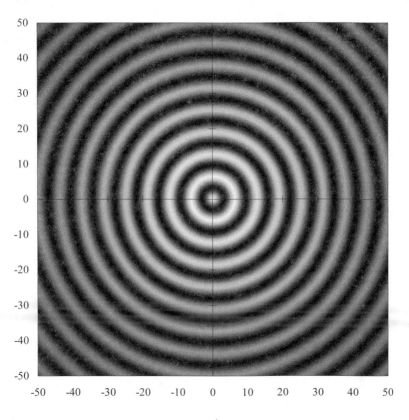

Fig. 1.4.2: The function $z = (1 + \cos\sqrt{(x2+y2)}) / (100 + x2 + y2)$, a variation on the cowboy hat, as represented (here in black and white) by Mapper.

Just as a 3-D graph, Mapper can only display one surface per graph. Color maps lack the illusion of perspective obtainable by rotating 3-D graphs, but they can provide better resolution, and better scales and legends, than Excel's 3-D graphs, and they can handle larger data arrays. They can be treated and modified like any other XY graph, and markers, curves, contour lines, and text boxes can all be added, see Fig. 1.4.1.

In applying Mapper, place in the bottom right-hand corner whatever features you want to display in the bottom right-hand corner of the graph, etc. And make sure that the axis labels are *to the left* and *on top of* the data, leaving an empty space at the top left corner.

1.5 Making movies

Excel has a (rather limited) capability to make movies, which will not challenge Hollywood, but on occasion may come in handy, if for no other reason than to break the monotony of a presentation. The Macro-Bundle contains a few demonstration macros (MovieDemo1 through 5) that illustrate how simple movements can be generated in an Excel graph. The trick is to make a computation that recalculates a number many times, and to force the screen to update after every recalculation. Here is a simple one.

Exercise 1.5.1:
   (1) Open a spreadsheet, enter the number 0 in cells A1 and B1, and enter the number 10 in A2.
   (2) Highlight the area A1:B2, and use Insert ⇒ Chart to make a corresponding graph. Click on the axis (which may show the label Value (X) Axis or Value (Y) Axis), right-click (Mac: Ctrl⌣click) to get Format Axis, and adjust both scales to have Minimum: 0 and Maximum: 10. Make sure that these values are not 'auto'matic (by turning off the top three check marks under Auto) because, in that case, the scale might change annoyingly as the movie plays. Moreover, for the duration of the show turn off the spreadsheet gridlines (with Tools ⇒ Options, View tab, Gridlines).
   (3) Make sure that the graph displays A2:B2 vs. A1:B1 (for a square input array, Excel automatically plots rows vs. columns), and show the individual point A1:A2 prominently with an individual marker, with large size and striking color. Your graph should now look like Fig. 1.5.1.

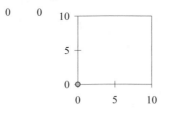

Fig. 1.5.1: The starting graph for MovieDemo1.

   (4) Call the custom macro MovieDemo1, which is part of the MacroBundle, and enjoy the show. The instructions for this macro are shown below, and can be downloaded from the SampleMacros file on the web site.

```
Sub MovieDemo1()

Range("A1") = 0
Range("A2") = 0
```

```
For i = 1 To 400
  Range("A1") = 10 - 0.05 * Abs(i - 200)
  Range("A2") = 10 * Exp(-0.001 * (i - 300) ^ 2)
  Application.ScreenUpdating = True
Next i

Range("A1") = 0
Range("A2") = 0

End Sub
```

(5) You should see the point trace a straight horizontal line on the way going, and a Gaussian peak on the way back.

Try the other MovieDemo macros of the MacroBundle. Figure out how they work (you may have to read chapter 8 first), then make your own. Use different markers and colors to enliven the display. Figures 1.5.2 through 1.5.5 illustrate the starting screens for these demos. Consult the heading comments of the MovieDemo macros for specific instructions on how to configure them, and where to place them. Have fun.

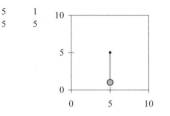

Fig. 1.5.2: The starting graph for MovieDemo2.

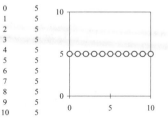

Fig. 1.5.3: The starting graph for MovieDemo3.

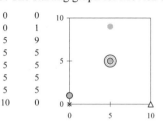

Fig. 1.5.4: The starting graph for MovieDemo4.

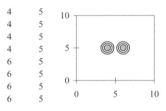

Fig. 1.5.5: The starting graph for MovieDemo5.

1.6 Printing, copying, linking & embedding

In order to print a spreadsheet, highlight the area you want to show, and print it. It may be helpful to add simulated spreadsheet axes (i.e., the letters A, B, C, ... across, the numbers 1, 2, 3, ... down), as was done in Fig. 1.1.1, because the grid parameters otherwise will not be shown. Some examples also display the instructions used, with the locations where they are used first, and the cells to which they are copied. By placing the most important information at the top left-hand corner of the spreadsheet, perhaps even including one or more thumbnail graphs, it is often sufficient to show only that part of a large spreadsheet.

Exercise 1.6.1:

(1) To simulate a horizontal (letter) row atop a spreadsheet, color a cell in the top row (e.g., gray-25% of the Fill Color icon on the Formatting toolbar), accent it (with all-around thin border), copy it to the other cells in that row, and fill the cells with centered capitals such as A, B, C, etc. For the vertical (number) column, use the same approach (with numbers instead of letters), and set its Column Width to 3 points (after highlighting the entire column by clicking on its true column heading, followed by right-clicking or, on the Mac, Ctrl‿clicking).

Charts use absolute addressing, and therefore keep referring to their original input data even when moved around or copied. To make compatible pictures it is often useful to copy one, and then modify its contents. This can be done by highlighting each individual curve, and either changing its address in the formula bar, or clicking on the curve and dragging the identifying data frames to their new spreadsheet positions.

Copying a spreadsheet to another sheet in the same spreadsheet book is straightforward, except that embedded figures will still refer to the data series on their *original* sheet. To make the graphs reflect the values on the copied sheet, highlight each series in turn, and adjust its sheet name in the formula bar.

There are two proper methods to import (part of) a spreadsheet into a Word document, *linking* and *embedding*. Embedding takes the part you select, and stores it permanently in the Word file. Linking instead estab-lishes a connection ('link') between the spreadsheet and the Word docu-ment, so that any subsequent changes in the spreadsheet will be reflected in its image in Word. Not only does linking update the image in Word automatically when you subsequently make a change in the Excel file, but it is also much more efficient in terms of storage requirements. Un-fortunately, in the experience of this author, linking has not always been reliable in Excel, and it may save you a lot of headaches to use embed-ding, provided that you can handle the resulting, huge data files. This is how you do it.

> **Exercise 1.6.2**:
> (1) Highlight a block of cells in a spreadsheet, or an embedded graph. Store it in the clipboard with Ctrl⌣c. Switch to the Word document, go to the place where you want to insert the graph, and make sure the corresponding line is formatted (F<u>o</u>rmat ⇒ <u>P</u>aragraph) with the line spacing Single or At least, the only two for-mats that have self-adjusting heights and can therefore accommodate the picture. Then use <u>E</u>dit ⇒ Paste <u>S</u>pecial, click on Microsoft Excel Worksheet Object, de-select Float over text, and click OK. This is how all figures in this book were im-ported into the text.

Because embedding can require large amounts of space, it is not very suitable for use in, e.g., e-mail attachments, or for storage on what, not so long ago, were called high-density (1.2 MB) diskettes. In such cases it may be better to send (or store) text and spreadsheets containing graphs as separate items. Alternatively, if both sender and receiver can handle these, use Zip disks, compact disks, or other high-capacity media, and/or use data compression. Excel files that are either linked or embedded re-tain their vector nature, i.e., they are stored as equations, and can be re-sized afterwards without loss of resolution. (Word2000 allows many ma-nipulations on embedded pictures, such as sizing, rotating, scaling, pic-ture placement and text wrapping, cropping, and control over contrast and brightness. Just double-click on the image, and select Format <u>O</u>b-ject.) All illustrations in this book were directly taken from Excel and embedded into Word, thereby preserving their original smoothness even if subsequently resized. This is the method of choice if publication-quality graphics are required.

Another option (if you have Adobe Acrobat, and only need to commu-nicate high-quality page *images*) is to compress the Word file with its embedded vector-based Excel graphs as a pdf file.

There are other ways to paste Excel images into Word that require much less memory, such as by using the PrintScreen button to capture an image, which can then be pasted into Word (possibly after manipulation in Paint), or by using Save as Web Page to generate a GIF image to be inserted into Word. These methods are not recommended, because they store the image as a bitmap, i.e., as a collection of pixels, which will show their discrete nature upon resizing. The resulting 'pixellation' has undeservedly given (vector-based) Excel graphics a bad name.

1.7 Setting up the spreadsheet

In this book we will use a number of auxiliary programs that come with Excel but that may not have been installed on your computer, e.g., if the software was installed using the 'typical' option. Any resulting omissions should be remedied before you start to use this book. Moreover, you will need to use MacroBundle, the package of macros specially developed for and discussed in this book, which can be downloaded freely from the web site of this book at oup-usa.org/advancedexcel. Below the various add-ins are listed, and ways to activate them.

1.7.1 Data Analysis ToolPak

The Data Analysis ToolPak contains many useful tools, including a random number generator, a data sampler, and many statistical tools such as anova, F-tests, and t-tests. It may already be part of your spreadsheet, so first check whether you find it in the menu under Tools, usually at or near the very bottom. (Excel 2000 has shortened menus that show only the most often used parts. The rest is still available, but you must either let the mouse pointer hover over that menu for a few seconds, or click on the chevron at the bottom of the menu to get the full display.) If it is not listed under Tools, check in the same menu list under Add-Ins; it (and the associated Data Analysis ToolPak – VBA) may just need to be activated there. Otherwise, in the Add-Ins dialog box, click on Browse, and locate the drive, folder, and file for the Analysis ToolPak add-in; it is usually located in the MicrosoftOffice\Office\Library\Analysis folder. Then run the Setup program to install it.

1.7.2 Solver

Solver is an add-in, automatically included in the Full installation, but left out with skimpier installation protocols. (Why this is done defies logic, because Solver is one of the most useful features of Excel, available also in Lotus1-2-3 and QuattroPro.) When you don't find it listed under Tools on the Excel main menu bar, get the Excel or Office CD, and install it.

The above lets you *use* Solver, but it doesn't allow you to *call* Solver from a macro, as is done, e.g., by the custom macros SolverScan and ColumnSolver discussed in chapter 4. To make such automatic calls of Solver possible requires the following additional action. First click on the Start button and, in the resulting menu, on Search, For Files or Folders ... (or Find ⇒ Files or Folders). In the Find: All Files dialog box, under the tab Name & Location, in the Name: window type Solver.xla, and, if necessary, enter Systemdisk[C:] in the Look in: window, activate Include subfolders, and click on Find now. Note down where Solver.xla is located. (If you have Microsoft Office, it most likely is in Systemdisk[C:], Program Files, Microsoft Office, Office, Library, Solver.) Exit the Find dialog box, which will bring you back to the spreadsheet, select the VBA editor with Alt◡F11 (on the Mac: Opt◡F11) where F11 is the function key labeled F11, then go to Tools ⇒ References, which will display the References – VBAProject dialog box. Click on Browse, and in the resulting Add Reference box select Files of type: Microsoft Excel Files (*.xls, *.xla). Now that you know where to find it, navigate your way to Solver.xla, and Open it. This will return you to the References – VBAProject dialog box, where you now use the Priority up button to bring it up, so that it is listed contiguously with the other, already activated add-ins. Click OK; from then on (i.e., until you re-load or upgrade Excel) VBA will know how to find Solver when called from a macro.

1.7.3 VBA Help file

Also check whether the VBA Help file has been activated and, if not, do so. This file provides help files specific to VBA.

MovieDemo4 in section 1.5 uses the VBA instruction `Volatile`, see section 11.5. How would you find out what it does? Since it operates only in VBA, the Excel Help file does not list it, but the VBA Help file does. Likewise, the VBA Help file includes extensive information on how to use Solver as a VBA-driven function, see sections 4.17 and 11.6, material you would otherwise have a hard time finding.

1.7.4 Additional macros

Users of this book should download the macros from my macro package MacroBundle. To do this, go to the web site www.oup-usa.org/advancedexcel and download the MacroBundle text file you can read with Word. The MacroBundle contains all the major macros listed in chapters 9 through 11, and used in this book. Near its top it describes how to place the MacroBundle (explanatory comments and all) in an Excel module. You may want to store a copy of this text file on your hard disk as a back-up.

1.7.5 Additional files

Two other files are provided in the web site with the MacroBundle. The SampleMacros file contains the exercise macros used in the text. By highlighting and copying a particular macro, and pasting it into the VBA module, the reader can avoid typing the macro, a convenience for those prone to typos. Likewise, the SampleData file contains external data used in some of the exercises, and therefore make it possible to do those exercises without having to retype the data.

1.7.6 Commercial tools

It is useful to know when to use a spreadsheet, and when to use more specialized software packages. Brief descriptions of a few examples of two different types of additional tools are given below: add-ins that, after installation, function as if they were part of Excel, and interfaces that make other products available through Excel.

An example of the first category is the set of 76 statistical routines provided by Numerical Algorithms Group (NAG) as its Statistical Add-Ins for Excel. These add-ins, specially made for Excel, might be a way around some of the documented deficiencies in Excel (see section 1.15), but to my knowledge they have not yet been tested against the NIST standards. Some of these routines overlap with functionality built into Excel (though perhaps at higher accuracy), while others significantly extend the power of Excel, such as the principal component and factor analysis routines. A free 30-day trial of the NAG add-in is available from NAG at extweb.nag.com/local/excel.asp, or from secondary freeware/ shareware distributors such as download.com, especially useful because the NAG site has had downloading problems with some browsers.

Examples of the second category are the interfaces between Excel and Maple and Mathematica, mathematics packages that can do both symbolic and numerical mathematics. Both certainly 'know' more math than most graduating math majors, and both have superb 3-D graphics. Maple includes its Excel add-on package in its basic software, whereas Wolfram Research requires its users to buy a separate Mathematica Link for Excel. These add-ons make Maple or Mathematica accessible through Excel, including their extensive collection of standard functions, and still more in their specialized packages that must be purchased separately. The user must buy (or have institutional access to) both Excel and Maple or Mathematica plus, in the case of Mathematica, the rather expensive link between them.

In order to access such functions once Excel, Mathematica, and the link between them have been installed, the Mathematica command on the spreadsheet must be wrapped in quotes and then identified as a Mathematica instruction, as in =Math("6!+8!"), which yields the sum of the factorials of 6 and 8 as 41040. This expression can be applied to the contents of, e.g., cells C16 and D18 respectively, with the command =Math ("#1!+#2!",C16,D18), and can then be copied to other places in the spreadsheet just like any other Excel function, using relative, absolute, or mixed addressing.

We have picked the above example because Excel also provides a factorial function, and the same result can therefore be obtained more easily as =FACT(C16)+FACT(D18). Of course, Maple and Mathematica have many more functions than Excel, and may be able to provide superior accuracy, which may make their links convenient for Excel users who also have access to one or both of these symbolic math packages.

It is also possible to embed Mathematica functions in Excel macros, and to manipulate Mathematica using Excel's VBA. Still, the software systems are so different, and their links are sufficiently non-intuitive, that many users having access to both may opt to keep and use them separately.

1.7.7 Choosing the default settings

In Excel, as in Windows, almost anything can be changed. It is useful to have *default settings*, so that one need not specify everything every time Excel is started. Moreover, to the novice, it is also helpful to have fewer (potentially confusing) choices. However, once you have become familiar with Excel, you may want to make changes in the default settings to make the spreadsheet conform to your specific needs and taste. Here are some of the common defaults, and how to change them.

By default, Excel displays the standard and formatting *toolbars*. Excel has many other toolbars, which can be selected with View ⇒ Toolbars. You can even make your own toolbar with View ⇒ Toolbars ⇒ Customize. An existing toolbar can be positioned anywhere on the spreadsheet simply by dragging the two vertical bars at its left edge (when it is docked in its standard place) or by dragging its colored top (when not docked).

Many aspects of the spreadsheet proper can be changed with Format ⇒ Style ⇒ Modify, including the way *numbers* are represented, the *font* used, cell *borders*, *colors*, and *patterns*.

Many Excel settings can be personalized in Tools ⇒ Options ⇒ General. Here one can specify, e.g., the number of *entries* in the *Recently used file list*, change the *Standard font* (e.g., from Arial to a more easily readable serif font such as Times New Roman) or perhaps use a different font *Size*. Here you can also set the *Default file location* (from C:\My Documents) and even define another *Alternate startup file location*.

Under the View tab (i.e., under Tools ⇒ Options ⇒ View) you can toggle the appearance of *spreadsheet Gridlines* on or off. Under the Edit tab (Tools ⇒ Options ⇒ Edit) you can (de)select to *Edit directly in the cell*, which allows you to edit in the cell (after double-clicking) rather than in the formula bar. Here you can also *Allow cell drag and drop* or disallow it, and specify whether and how to *Move selection after enter*, i.e., you might prefer the cursor to stay put rather than move down one cell after each data, text, or formula entry.

Excel does not make *back-up files* by default. If you wish to change this, use Files ⇒ Save As ⇒ Options or Files ⇒ Save As ⇒ Tools ⇒ General Options and select Always create backup. You can also automate periodic saves with Tools ⇒ Add-Ins by activating the Autosave Add-In.

When you print with the Print button on the Standard Toolbar, you use the default printing settings. File ⇒ Page Setup provides many alternatives, including *paper size* and *orientation*, as well as *margins*.

In Excel 97 and later versions, browse in Tools ⇒ Customize to see (and select) your Toolbars and their Commands. You can click on a command and then use the button to get its Description.

Likewise, in Excel 97 and beyond, the default setting for the graph type is accessible after you activate a chart to make the Chart menu available. Select Chart ⇒ Chart Type, and under Chart type pick your choice, XY(Scatter), and Set as default chart. Even better, you can define the format of the default chart. Say that you dislike the gray background and the horizontal gridlines that Excel puts in its XY plots. Make a graph the way you like it, e.g., with a white background (activate the plot area, select Format Plot Area, then select Area None or the white square) and without the gridlines (activate a gridline, right-click or, on the Mac, Ctrl⌣click, and select Clear). While the chart is still activated (so that the

Chart button is accessible in the menu toolbar) click on Chart ⇒ Chart Type, select the Custom Types tab, click on the User-defined option button, then on Add. In the next dialog box, specify its Name, give an (optional) Description, Set as default chart, and exit with OK. Then, the next time you highlight a block and invoke Insert ⇒ Chart you will get the selected format just by pushing the Finish button on step 1 of the Chart Wizard. Or, faster, highlight the area involved, and type Alt⌣i, Alt⌣h, Alt⌣f, or /⌣i, /⌣h, /⌣f (for Insert Chart Finish).

The menu bars and toolbars in Excel 2000 initially display only those items that you have used most recently; the others are out of view, even though they are still available by clicking on the chevron at the bottom of the menu, or by waiting a few seconds. If you don't like this feature, go to View ⇒ Toolbars ⇒ Customize, select the Options tab, and undo the checkmark for Menus show recently used commands first.

1.8 Importing data

Data copied from the Web may fit directly into Excel, or may squeeze into a single column (in which case they may *seem* to fit the spreadsheet columns, until you check what the formula bar shows for cells in the next column). Avoid the latter situation by first converting them into a text format, e.g., by importing them into WordPad (which has the extension .txt rather than the Word extension .doc), and by saving them as such in a directory or on your Desktop. Then open Excel, select File ⇒ Open, make sure that the Open dialog box deals With files of type: All files (*,*) so that .txt files show, and select the Notepad file. Because the data are now presented to Excel as a text file, the Text Import Wizard will appear, in which you can specify how to treat the file. Usually the data are either separated by commas *(comma-delimited)* or by empty spaces *(tab-delimited)*, and after you tell the Wizard what you want it will execute your wishes. Instead of File ⇒ Open you can use Data ⇒ Get External Data ⇒ Import Text File, which allows importation directly into your spreadsheet, and will remember the Text Import Wizard settings.

1.9 Error messages

Excel has a rather limited set of error messages, as listed in table A.7 of the appendix. On the other hand, Excel is very forgiving: it does not stop operating when asked to divide by zero or to take the square root or the logarithm of a negative number, but just labels those tasks as impossible, and then continues with those parts of the assignment it can do.

1.10 Troubleshooting Excel

Excel has two useful features to help you debug your spreadsheet. To check a formula, activate (i.e., click on) the cell that contains it, and then click on the corresponding formula in the formula box. Now the various terms in the formula will be colored, and the corresponding cells surrounded by frames of corresponding color. Even more powerful is activating the cell, and then calling Tools ⇒ Auditing ⇒ Trace Precedents, which will show what information flows into the cell. Likewise, Tools ⇒ Auditing ⇒ Trace Dependents shows how that information flows out of that cell. After use, reset with Tools ⇒ Auditing ⇒ Remove All Arrows.

1.11 Functions, subroutines & macros

Excel is quite powerful, and comes with many functions, but it cannot be all things to all people. Fortunately, it has extra flexibility built in, allowing the user to personalize it by adding custom-made functions and macros to do things Excel might otherwise find difficult or impossible to do. The language used for these is VBA, an adaptation of Visual Basic, a modern and quite powerful computer language that is used in all parts of the Microsoft Office suite. Moreover, VBA will accept (with perhaps some minor modifications) earlier code written in modern versions of Basic, including TurboBasic and QuickBasic. Consequently there is no need to reinvent the wheel when writing your own functions and macros, because you can often find such material in the literature. You must still provide the special adaptations to match the algorithm to the spreadsheet, but chapters 8 through 11 will help you with that.

Excel offers two custom-supplied procedures based on VBA: functions and subroutines. Of these, *functions* can only affect the *value* displayed in a *single* spreadsheet cell. Otherwise, functions are quite flexible: they can use many inputs, and they can call subroutines (as long as the end result only affects that single-cell output value). Just like the Excel-provided functions, custom functions can be copied to other cells.

An advantage of functions over subroutines is that they respond automatically to changing input information, so that they need not be activated or called, but update themselves whenever a parameter affecting them is entered or modified. (By inserting the instruction `Application.Volatile True` you can even make them respond to changes elsewhere on the spreadsheet.) Custom functions can be copied from one cell to another just as built-in Excel functions can. Custom functions will be used occasionally throughout this book.

Subroutines are not restricted to changing the output in a single spreadsheet cell, thus making them more powerful than functions. In general, both functions and subroutines have input parameters that are specified in the function or subroutine call. (The argument list cannot contain output parameters, which are simply left in the subroutine or macro.) A subroutine without any input parameters is called a *macro*. Macros can be called directly from the spreadsheet, but they cannot be embedded in spreadsheet cells, nor do they update automatically. Instead, macros must be called every time one wants to use them. We will encounter many examples of custom macros in this book, and we will look at them in detail in chapter 8. You can use these specific examples as starting points for writing *your own* functions, macros, and subroutines. The latter often work rather invisibly, upon being called by either a function, a macro, or another subroutine.

1.11.1 Custom functions

Functions can be placed in particular cells, in which case they can control the value displayed in those cells. The minimal function declaration in a cell contains its name followed by parentheses, as in =myOutput(). Inside the parentheses you may find one or more *arguments*, or none, as in the above example. If you type this instruction in a particular cell, without having defined its role, that cell will show the error message #NAME?.

You specify a function in a *module*. In Excel 5 and Excel 95, you open a module by clicking on the tab at the bottom of the spreadsheet, and then clicking on module. After that, you can switch between module and spreadsheet by clicking on their tabs, just as you would move between different sheets in a workbook. In other words, the module is treated as a worksheet without a grid. In Excel 97 and more recent versions, the module is hidden from view in the Visual Basic Editor. To open the more recent type of module, use Tools ⇒ Macro ⇒ Visual Basic Editor, then in the Visual Basic toolbar click on Insert ⇒ Module. Once you have established a module, you can toggle between it and the spreadsheet with Alt⌣F11 (Mac: Opt⌣F11).

The arguments (the material within the brackets following the function name) comprise the input data; they can be either numerical values, or addresses of individual cells or of cell ranges where information can be found. They are defined in the function by the order in which they appear in the function argument, not by their names. You can even specify *optional* input arguments.

The output of a function is restricted to the output of a single cell and to a single value. There is one exception to the latter rule: it is possible to have a single cell display (within curly brackets) an array as a string of numbers, separated by commas and/or semicolons. That is only of practical use for relatively small vectors or matrices.

A module can contain one or more functions, subroutines, macros, or combinations thereof, and it is usually easiest to keep them all together in one module.

  A simple function might be defined as

```
Function myOutput()
myOutput = 8.3
End Function
```

which accomplishes the trivial task of setting the cell value to 8.3, but shows the general structure: a first line defining the function by its name, a last line specifying the end of the function, and in between one or more statements including at least one that specifies the function value, tying the function name to an output. The output will most often be a value, but can also be a message (identified as such within quotation marks) as when the above statement is replaced by `myOutput = "abc"`.

The custom function will appear in the Paste Function dialog box (under Function category: User Defined, by Function name:) that you can access by clicking on the function icon f_x on the standard toolbar. If you do not want such a listing, specify the function name in the module as Private, as in `Private Function myOutput()`.

You will encounter custom functions throughout this book. A sometimes particularly useful aspect of functions is that they can be *recursive*, i.e., they can call themselves. Here is an example of a recursive function calculating *n!* that can be used by itself or be called by a macro.

```
Function Factorial(n)
MsgBox "n = " & n     ' optional display of n-values
If n <= 1 Then
   Factorial = 1
Else
   Factorial = n * Factorial(n - 1)
End If

Sub F()
' Demo of subroutine using a recursive function
Dim n As Integer
n = InputBox("n = ")
MsgBox "Factorial(" & n & ") = " & Factorial(n)
End Sub
```

1.11.2 Custom subroutines & macros

Subroutines are specified in the module by prefacing their name by Sub (instead of Function). You cannot enter a subroutine in a particular cell, but you can store it in a VB Editor module just like a macro. You can only call it with Tools $\Rightarrow$ Macro $\Rightarrow$ Macros or with Alt⌣F8 (Mac: Opt⌣F8), and by then using the resulting Macro dialog box) provided the subroutine has no input and output arguments. If it has arguments, it lives out-of-sight in a module, and can only be called by other procedures, i.e., by functions, macros, or other subroutines.

Macros are a most useful, special type of subroutines. As illustrated throughout this book, and described in chapters 8 through 11, they can be used for quite sophisticated mathematical operations. A fairly detailed look at them will be given in chapter 8. The important thing to remember about them here is that many problems have already been solved, and that their solution can be found in the literature. If it happens to be available in Basic you are in luck, because Basic (especially in one of its more modern forms) can be incorporated readily in VBA. Even if the program is in Fortran it is often readily transcribed. When the program is listed in the *Numerical Recipes* by W. H. Press et al., Cambridge University Press, 1986 (which can be read or copied free of charge from lib-www.lanl.gov/numerical/index.html or www.library.cornell.edu/nr/nr_index.cgi) you can find a corresponding Basic version in J. C. Sprott, *Numerical Recipes: Routines and Examples in Basic*, Cambridge University Press, (1991). Often the only modification such code requires is to make sure that it operates in double precision. Of course you will have to supply the code for connecting the macro with the spreadsheet, an aspect we will explore in chapter 8.

Keep in mind that custom macros are *not* self-updating, and therefore do not necessarily reflect the input information displayed on the spreadsheet. Can we make a macro self-updating? The literal answer to this question is "No", but an often applicable answer might be "Yes, if you are willing to convert the macro into a function." That means that you can trade the flexibility of the input and output formats of a macro for the convenience of automatic self-updating of a function. Such a trade-off might be useful if you deal repeatedly with input data of identical format, say with spectra generated by a given instrument under fixed instrumental settings. In that case you may want to make a spreadsheet into which the data are always entered in the same manner, and convert the necessary macros into corresponding functions. The Lagrange interpolation of section 1.12 illustrates that a function can indeed perform a rather complex operation, in this case a polynomial interpolation. Each function can only affect one single output value, but since functions can be copied to other cells, that need not be a constraint. Likewise, section 6.7 will illustrate how a function can be combined with the Excel-supplied macro Solver, in a case where a macro could not be used because Solver has no facility to call it.

1.12 An example: interpolation

Much of this book focuses on working with *experimental* data, i.e., with numbers that are not exact but that are to some extent uncertain, as the result of experimental 'noise' corrupting the underlying 'signal'. Such data require special methods to try to extract that signal, a problem addressed in the central chapters of this book. However, science is not about experimental numbers per se, but about their comparison with model theories. Consequently we must also be able to handle theoretical expressions, where noise is absent, and for which the methods therefore can be quite different.

In this section we will illustrate some approaches for dealing with noise-free data. This will also give us a first opportunity to practice with custom functions, and to illustrate what this book is all about: making the spreadsheet do the things *you* want it to do.

Interpolation is useful when we need to rescale a table of data, and even more so when we have a model theory that provides data $y = f(x)$ but instead we need those data in the form $x = g(y)$. The most common interpolation schemes use either polynomials or trigonometric functions. Below we will illustrate polynomial interpolation; for additional information and alternative algorithms see, e.g., chapter 25 by P. J. Davis & I Polonsky in the *Handbook of Mathematical Functions*, M. Abramowitz & I. A. Stegun, eds., Dover 1965, or chapter 3 of the *Numerical Recipes* by W. H. Press et al., Cambridge University Press 1986.

The prototype for polynomial interpolation of noise-free data is the Lagrange method. In order to find y for a given value of x by linear interpolation between the two adjacent points x_1, y_1 and x_2, y_2 (so that $x_1 \leq x \leq x_2$) we have

$$y = \frac{(x - x_2)\, y_1}{x_1 - x_2} + \frac{(x - x_1)\, y_2}{x_2 - x_1} \tag{1.12.1}$$

while, e.g., cubic interpolation between four adjacent points x_1, y_1 through

x_4, y_4 (preferably with two points on either side, i.e., with $x_1 \le x_2 \le x \le x_3 \le x_4$) is given by

$$y = \frac{(x-x_2)(x-x_3)(x-x_4)y_1}{(x_1-x_2)(x_1-x_3)(x_1-x_4)} + \frac{(x-x_1)(x-x_3)(x-x_4)y_2}{(x_2-x_1)(x_2-x_3)(x_2-x_4)}$$

$$+ \frac{(x-x_1)(x-x_2)(x-x_4)y_3}{(x_3-x_1)(x_3-x_2)(x_3-x_4)} + \frac{(x-x_1)(x-x_2)(x-x_3)y_4}{(x_4-x_1)(x_4-x_2)(x_4-x_3)} \quad (1.12.2)$$

and so on. Such Lagrange interpolation is readily handled with a custom function; the one illustrated here is based on an elegant example from E. J. Billo, *Excel for chemists*, 2nd ed., Wiley 2001, who in turn credits W. J. Orvis, *Excel for Scientists and Engineers*, Sybex 1993, 1996.

We should emphasize here that we can fit n data points *exactly* to a polynomial of power $n-1$, but that there is no assurance that this will be a good approximation for the underlying curve through those n points, which may or may not resemble a power series in x. In this latter, more significant sense the interpolation is *not* exact (even if it passes exactly through all n points), and this is readily verified by observing that the result obtained with Lagrange interpolation in general depends on the polynomial order used.

As our example we will apply cubic Lagrange interpolation to an acid-base titration curve, i.e., to the relation between the pH of a solution containing a fixed initial amount of, say, an acid, as a function of the volume V_b of added base. The general theory of such curves is quite straightforward when we *calculate* the volume V_b as a function of the proton concentration $[H^+]$, but not the other way around. In practice one does the opposite: one *measures* pH as a function of the added volume V_b of base. We therefore first calculate a table of V_b as a function of pH = $-\log[H^+]$, then interpolate this table in order to generate a second table of pH as a function of V_b. We will do so here for the simplest type of titration, viz. that of a single strong monoprotic acid (such as HCl) with a single strong monoprotic base (such as NaOH).

Exercise 1.12.1:

(1) Open a new spreadsheet, with 12 rows at the top for graphs, and in cells A13:A16 place the labels for the constants, K_w, V_a, C_b, and C_a. In A18:C18 enter the column headings pH, [H], and Vb.

(2) In B13:B16 deposit numerical constants for K_w, V_a, C_b, and C_a, such as 10^–14, 20, 0.1, and 0.1.

(3) In the column for pH, starting in cell A20, enter the values 1 (0.1) 12.9. In B20:B139 calculate $[H^+]$ as 10^–pH, and in C20:C139 the corresponding titrant

volume as $V_b = V_a (C_a - [H^+] + K_w/[H^+]) / (C_b + [H^+] - K_w/[H^+])$. This completes the first stage, calculating a table of data in A20:C139.

(4) Plot the resulting titration curve as pH vs. V_b. Note that it shows many points in the transition region, since the points are computed for equal increments in pH which, in that region, is a very steep function of V_b.

(5) Now make a second table in which the pH is listed at given (not necessarily equidistant) values of V_b. In cells E18 and F18 place two more column headings, Vb and pH respectively. Below the Vb heading, in cells E20:E49, enter the values 1 (1) 30. In cell F20 of the corresponding pH column enter the instruction =Lagrange($C$20:$C$139,$A$20:$A$139,E20,3), and copy it down to F139. The ranges $C$20:$C$139 and $A$20:$A$139 specify the X- and Y-ranges in which to interpolate, E20 is the X-value for which the interpolation is requested, and 3 denotes the order of the Lagrange polynomial used, here a cubic.

(6) Even though you have entered the function call, nothing will happen, because you have not yet specified that function. Do this as follows.

(7) Open a Visual Basic module as described earlier. For instance, in Excel 97 or later, use Tools ⇒ Macro ⇒ Visual Basic Editor, and then (in the new toolbar) Insert ⇒ Module.

(8) In that module enter the following code (either by typing or by copying from the SampleMacros file):

```
Function Lagrange(XArray, YArray, X, m)

' m denotes the order of the polynomial used,
' and must be an integer between 1 and 14

Dim Row As Integer, i As Integer, j As Integer
Dim Term As Double, Y As Double

Row = Application.Match(X, XArray, 1)
If Row < (m + 1) / 2 Then Row = (m + 1) / 2
If Row > XArray.Count - (m + 1) / 2 Then _
  Row = XArray.Count - (m + 1) / 2
For i = Row - (m - 1) / 2 To Row + (m + 1) / 2
  Term = 1
  For j = Row - (m - 1) / 2 To Row + (m + 1) / 2
    If i <> j Then Term = Term * _
      (X - XArray(j)) / (XArray(i) - XArray(j))
  Next j
  Y = Y + Term * YArray(i)
Next i
Lagrange = Y

End Function
```

(9) The =Match(*value, array, type*) function in Excel returns the relative position of the largest term in the specified array that is less than or equal to *value*. The array must be in ascending order, and the above definition is for *type* = 1. By preceding it with the instruction Application. we appropriate it as a VBA command.

(10) The function will work without the dimensioning statements, which are included here as part of good housekeeping practice. The same applies to the two comment lines, which are ignored by the computer but may serve the user.

(11) The two nested For ... Next loops generate the terms in the numerators and denominators of the Lagrange expression, such as those in (1.12.2).

(12) Note that Y need not be initialized: each time, the function starts afresh.

(13) For more information on functions and macros see chapter 8.

(14) Return to the spreadsheet with Alt‿F11 (Mac: Opt‿F11). There should now be data in F20:F49.

(15) Plot the pH (in F20:F49) as a function of V_b in (E20:E49). Note that there are now very few points in the transition region, for the same reason that the plot of V_b vs. pH has so many: near the equivalence point, the slope $d(\text{pH})/d(V_b)$ is quite high, and that of $d(V_b)/d(\text{pH})$ is correspondingly low.

(16) The top of the completed spreadsheet is shown in Fig. 1.12.1.

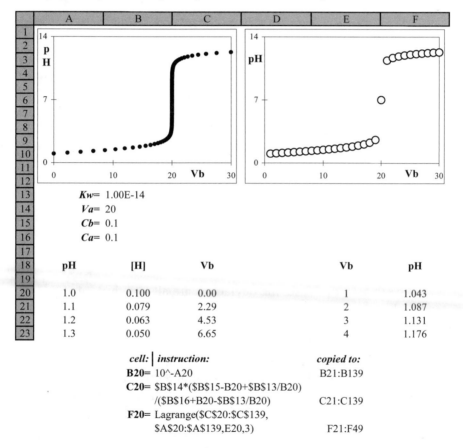

	A	B	C	D	E	F
13		Kw=	1.00E-14			
14		Va=	20			
15		Cb=	0.1			
16		Ca=	0.1			
17						
18	pH	[H]	Vb		Vb	pH
19						
20	1.0	0.100	0.00		1	1.043
21	1.1	0.079	2.29		2	1.087
22	1.2	0.063	4.53		3	1.131
23	1.3	0.050	6.65		4	1.176

cell:	instruction:	copied to:
B20=	10^-A20	B21:B139
C20=	$B$14*($B$15-B20+$B$13/B20)	
	/($B$16+B20-$B$13/B20)	C21:C139
F20=	Lagrange($C$20:$C$139,	
	$A$20:$A$139,E20,3)	F21:F49

Fig. 1.12.1: The top of the spreadsheet for interpolating in a table of V_b vs. pH (in columns C and A respectively) in order to generate a second table of pH as a function of V_b (in columns E and F). Note that the points in plot *a* are equidistant in pH (with $\Delta\text{pH} = 0.1$) while those in plot *b* have constant increments $\Delta V_b = 1$.

We already mentioned that a cubic Lagrange interpolation can be a fairly good approximation for this curve as long as the spacing between adjacent, computed data points is sufficiently small. In this particular case a closed-form solution for the pH as a function of titrant volume V_b is available, so that we can check the interpolation procedure. It is always useful to calibrate new software with a test for which the (exact) answer is known, because it provides an early indication of its reliability and, as a bonus, may alert you to possible problems.

Inversion of the expression used under (3) in exercise 1.12.1, $V_b = V_a \times (C_a - [H^+] + K_w/[H^+]) / (C_b + [H^+] - K_w/[H^+])$, yields

$$pH = -\log[H^+]$$

$$= -\log\left[\frac{C_a V_a - C_b V_b}{2(V_a + V_b)} + \sqrt{\frac{(C_a V_a - C_b V_b)^2}{4(V_a + V_b)^2} + K_w}\right] \qquad (1.12.3)$$

which will now be used to check the results obtained from the Lagrange interpolation.

Exercise 1.12.1 (continued):
(17) You can calculate the pH from (1.12.3) in one operation, or even the difference between it and the pH computed by Lagrange interpolation. Here we will use three steps, which requires simpler expressions but uses more spreadsheet real estate.
(18) In cell G20 calculate the quantity $(C_a V_a - C_b V_b)/(2(V_a + V_b))$ as =($B$16* $B$14-$B$15*E20)/(2*($B$14+E20)).
(19) In cell H20 compute the pH as =-LOG(G20+SQRT(G20^2+$B$13)).
(20) In cell I20 enter the instruction =H20-F20, and change the cell format to scientific with Format ⇒ Cells, Category: Scientific.
(21) Copy the instructions in cells G20:I20 down to row 49.

Notice that, in this case, the deviations are all less than $\pm 4 \times 10^{-4}$, i.e., smaller than the resolution of a pH meter (typically ± 0.01 pH unit, occasionally ± 0.001 pH unit), and therefore inconsequential. Verify that using a ten times smaller pH increment in column A (with a concomitant change in the ranges XArray and YArray in the function call) can reduce the errors by another three orders of magnitude. Increasing the polynomial order has a smaller effect, and can even be counter-effective, especially when the intervals are relatively large, in which case fitted curves of high order may swing wildly between adjacent points. Optimal results are usually obtained with a low-order polynomial interpolation of densely spaced data.

Now that we have converted a theoretical curve into one more like those encountered in the laboratory, we will make a short excursion to illustrate what we can do with it. First we will calculate the concentrations of the species of interest, $[H^+]$ and $[OH^-]$, and a useful, derived quantity, the proton excess $\Delta = [H^+] - [OH^-]$. Then we correct these for the mutual dilution of sample and titrant, and so obtain $[H^+]'$, $[OH^-]'$, and Δ'. Finally we will make the simulation more realistic by adding offset and random noise to the pH. In practical implementations, offset can usually be kept at bay by careful instrument calibration using standard buffers.

Exercise 1.12.1 (continued):

(22) In cell J18 place the heading [H], in cell J20 compute the proton concentration $[H^+]$ as `=10^-F20`, and copy this instruction down to cell J49.

(23) In cell K18 deposit the label [OH], in cell K20 calculate the corresponding hydroxyl concentration $[OH^-]$ as `=$B$13/J20`, and likewise extend this calculation downward to row 49.

(24) In L18 put the label Δ (type D, then highlight it and change the font to Symbol) for the *proton excess*, and in L20:L49 compute its value as $\Delta = [H^+] - [OH^-]$.

(25) Plot $[H^+]$, $[OH^-]$, and Δ as a function of V_b, see Fig. 1.12.2.

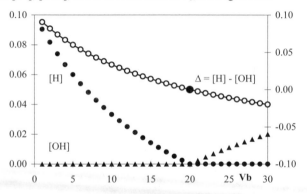

Fig. 1.12.2: The proton concentration $[H^+]$, the hydroxyl ion concentration $[OH^-] = K_w/[H^+]$, and (using the right-hand scale) the proton excess $\Delta = [H^+] - [OH^-]$, all as a function of the titrant volume V_b. In the latter curve the equivalence point at $\Delta = 0$ is highlighted.

(26) Adding titrant to sample clearly dilutes both. We can correct for this mutual dilution by multiplying $[H^+]$, $[OH^-]$, and Δ by $(V_a+V_b)/V_a$. Use three additional columns, M through O, one for $[H^+]' = [H^+] (V_a+V_b)/V_a$, one for $[OH^-]' = [OH^-] (V_a+V_b)/V_a$, and one for $\Delta' = [H^+]' - [OH^-]'$, then plot these, as in Fig. 1.12.3. Note that the quantities $[H^+]'$ and $[OH^-]'$ are directly proportional to the Gran plots (G. Gran, *Analyst* 77 (1952) 661) for this type of titration.

(27) The above are purely *theoretical* plots. They suggest that the equivalence point of the titration can be found simply by looking for that value of V_b where Δ' is zero. You could do this, e.g., by linear interpolation in the table for Δ' as a function of V_b for $\Delta' = 0$.

(28) We now make the transition to *practical* data analysis. In cell D13 deposit the label *offset=*, in cell D14 the label *na=*, and in cell P18 the heading "noise".

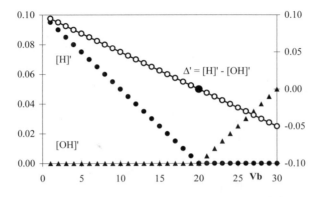

Fig. 1.12.3: The dilution-corrected proton concentration $[H^+]'$, hydroxyl ion concentration $[OH^-]'$, and proton excess Δ', all as a function of the titrant volume V_b. Note that Δ' is a linear function of V_b throughout the entire titration. The equivalence point, where $\Delta' = 0$, has been highlighted.

(29) In cells E13 and E14 enter corresponding values (0 for zero offset or noise, 0.05 for offset or noise of 0.05 pH unit, etc.), and in P20:P49 deposit Gaussian ('normal') noise of zero mean and unit standard deviation, using Tools ⇒ Data Analysis ⇒ Random Number Generation, Distribution: Normal, Mean = 0, Standard Deviation = 1, Output Range: P20:P49, OK.

(30) To the instruction in cell F20 now add the terms +$E$13+$E$14*P20, and copy this down to F49. Now experiment with non-zero values for either offset or noise.

(31) The effect of an offset a is to multiply $[H^+]'$ by $10^{(-a)}$, $[OH^-]'$ by $10^{(+a)}$, and Δ' by $10^{(-a)}$ before the equivalence point, and by $10^{(+a)}$ beyond it, and therefore leads to the slope changes shown in Fig. 1.12.4.

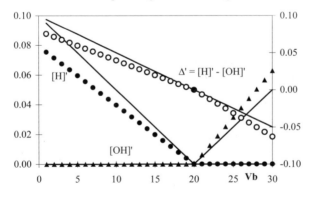

Fig. 1.12.4: The effect of a relatively small amount of pH offset (*offset* = 0.1) on the concentration parameters $[H^+]'$, $[OH^-]'$, and Δ'. Again, $[H^+]'$ and $[OH^-]'$ use the primary (left-hand) scale, while the secondary (right-hand) scale pertains to Δ'. For comparison, the lines are drawn for zero offset.

(32) Even though the titration curve may barely show the effect of added random noise, the corresponding concentration terms $[H^+]'$, $[OH^-]'$, and Δ' and analysis procedures relying on them may be affected strongly, because the exponentiation involved in the conversion from pH to $[H^+]$ greatly accentuates the noise, see Fig. 1.12.5.

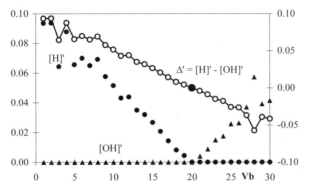

Fig. 1.12.5: The effect of a relatively small amount of random pH noise (with zero mean and standard deviation $s_n = 0.05$) on the concentration parameters $[H^+]'$, $[OH^-]'$, and Δ'.

It is straightforward to use formal mathematics to identify the zero crossing of Δ' in Fig. 1.12.3, but to do so in Fig. 1.12.5 is a different problem, because these data fit a straight line only approximately (even though most of the noise is at the extremes of the curve). Dealing with such more realistic data on a spreadsheet lies at the core of this book. For now, the latter part of this example merely illustrates what we can do by simulating an experiment, e.g., by visualizing how sensitive a proposed analysis method will be to the effects of offset (systematic, deterministic bias) and (random, stochastic) noise. More robust data analysis methods for titration curves will be described in section 4.3. Alternatively, the macro ColumnSolver of the MacroBundle can be used for perform the interpolation.

1.13 Handling the math

One way in which Excel facilitates computations is through its extensive collection of functions, ranging from search tools to sophisticated mathematical and statistical tools. Some of the most useful of these are listed in tables A.2 through A.4 of the appendix. Excel can also handle complex numbers, and matrices, as illustrated below. The corresponding functions are listed in tables A5 and A6 respectively of the appendix.

1.13.1 Complex numbers

Excel operations on complex numbers use text strings to squeeze the two components of a complex number into one cell. In order to use the results of complex number operations, one must therefore first *extract* its real and imaginary components, using IMREAL() and IMAGINARY(). Instead of *i* one can use *j* to denote the square root of −1 (which must then be *specified* as such), but one *cannot* use the corresponding capitals, *I* or *J*. Table A.5 in the appendix lists the complex number operations provided in Excel's Data Analysis ToolPak. VBA lacks a special data type for complex numbers, which are therefore best handled in terms of their real and imaginary components respectively, as in the Fourier transform macro described in section 10.1.

1.13.2 Matrices

Excel has several built-in functions for matrix operations: {}, TRANSPOSE, INDEX, MINVERSE, and MMULT.

Curly brackets {} around a set of numbers separated by commas and/or semicolons can be used to deposit an array. Highlight a block of cells 2 cells wide and 3 cells high, then type the instruction ={2,3;4,5; 6,7}, and deposit this instruction with Ctrl⌣Shift⌣Enter (on the Mac: Command⌣Return). This will deposit the numbers 2 and 3 in the top row, 4 and 5 in the middle row, and 6 and 7 in the bottom row of the block. Here commas separate matrix elements in the same row, while semicolons separate successive rows. Remember the order: first rows, then columns. As a memory aid, think of the electrical RC (resistor-capacitor) circuit or time constant: RC, first Row, then Column.

TRANSPOSE interchanges the row and column indices. Because transposing rows and columns is a common operation in, e.g., accounting, it is performed as part of the Edit ⇒ Paste Special operation. Select (i.e., highlight) the array to be transposed, and copy it to the clipboard (e.g., with Ctrl⌣c). Then select the top left corner (or the left column, or the top row, or the entire area) of where you want its transpose to appear, and use the keystroke sequence Edit ⇒ Paste Special ⇒ Transpose ⇒ OK. (Depending on your software, you may have to specify Values or Formulas before Transpose, or the generic All may just work fine.)

INDEX(*array,row#,column#*) yields the individual matrix element in a given array. Say that C4:E8 contains the data

$$\begin{array}{ccc} 0 & 4 & 8 \\ 1 & 5 & 9 \\ 2 & 6 & 10 \\ 3 & 7 & 11 \end{array}$$

then =INDEX(C4:E8,2,3) yields the answer 9, since it specifies the array element in row 2, column 3. You can also incorporate the array elements in the instruction, as in =INDEX({0,4,8;1,5,9;2,6,10;3,7,11},2,3), where the array elements in each row are enumerated one at a time, from left to right, separated by commas, while different rows are separated by semi-colons and are read from top to bottom. This instruction likewise yields the answer 9.

Function	Description and example

MINVERSE(*array*) The matrix inverse of a square array: when B3:C4 contains the data

$$\begin{array}{cc} 3 & 5 \\ 4 & 6 \end{array},$$

MINVERSE({3,5; 4,6}) = {−3, 2.5; 2, −1.5}

$$= \begin{vmatrix} -3 & 2.5 \\ 2 & -1.5 \end{vmatrix},$$

$$\text{MINVERSE(B3:C4)} = \begin{vmatrix} -3 & 2.5 \\ 2 & -1.5 \end{vmatrix}$$

MMULT(*array*) The matrix product of two arrays (where the number of columns in the first array must be equal to the number of rows in the second array): MMULT({3, 5; 4, 6},{−3, 25; 2, −1.5})

$$= \begin{vmatrix} 1 & 0 \\ 0 & 1 \end{vmatrix},$$

and likewise MMULT(B3:C4,E6:F7) = $\begin{vmatrix} 1 & 0 \\ 0 & 1 \end{vmatrix}$

when B3:C4 and E6:F7 contain the data $\begin{array}{cc} 3 & 5 \\ 4 & 6 \end{array}$

and $\begin{array}{cc} -3 & 2.5 \\ 2 & -1.5 \end{array}$ respectively.

Matrix inversion and matrix multiplication work only on *data arrays*, i.e., on rectangular blocks of cells, but not on single cells. To enter these instructions, first highlight the area where you want to place the result, type the instruction, and enter it with Ctrl⌣Shift⌣Enter (Mac: Command⌣Return). In the formula box, the instruction will show inside curly brackets to indicate that it is a matrix operation. Note that MINVERSE can only be used with square arrays, while for MMULT the number of columns in the first array must be equal to the number of rows in the second array.

In VBA, parameters dimensioned As Variant (as well as all undimensioned parameters) can represent arrays, when their specific sizes (# of rows, # of columns) are specified using a Dim or ReDim statement. Matrix manipulations can often be relegated conveniently to subroutines.

1.14 Handling the funnies

With its many built-in functions, Excel makes it easy to compute many mathematical expressions. Even so, we may sometimes need to help it along, especially when our calculations involve some of the mathematical 'funnies', such as $0/0$, $\infty - \infty$, ∞/∞, and $0 \times \infty$. Below we will explore some of these; once you see the approach you will know how to deal with similar problems you may encounter.

As a simple example, the convolution of a sine wave and an impulse function yields the sinc function, $\mathrm{sinc}(\omega t) = [\sin(\omega t)]/(\omega t)$. When ωt is zero, both the numerator and denominator are zero, suggesting that the value of $\mathrm{sinc}(0)$ might be undefined. But this is not the case, as is most readily seen by expanding $\sin(x)$ for $x \ll 1$ as $x - x^3/3! + x^5/5! - x^7/7! + \dots$ so that $[\sin(x)]/x = 1 - x^2/3! + x^4/5! - x^6/7! + \dots \to 1$ for $x \to 0$. If you encounter this problem in a spreadsheet, you can use the series expansion or, simpler, sidestep it by using a *very small* value instead of 0. Even if you take x as small as 10^{-300}, close to the smallest number it can represent, Excel will return 1 for $[\sin(x)]/x$. But for $x = 0$ you will get the error message #DIV/0! without a numerical result.

1.14.1 The binomial coefficient

There is an old birdwatcher's trick. When one person enters a blind, birds that have seen this will remember that someone went in until he or she comes out again. When two people enter, most birds will know that the blind is not yet empty after they see one of them emerge: $2 - 1 \neq 0$. But you can usually fool birds by having three enter, and two leave: apparently birds count zero-one-many, i.e., they cannot distinguish between 2 and 3. Birds can count, but only up to a limited number.

The same applies to computers, even though they can count a little further. But still, you may occasionally ask a computer to calculate $\infty -$ ∞, or ∞ / ∞, in which case it will come up short.

The binomial coefficient is most clearly associated with binomial statistics, but once in a while it crops up in seemingly unrelated scientific and engineering problems. For example, it occurs in the Gram functions used for equidistant least squares discussed in section 3.14.

The binomial coefficient is defined as

$$\binom{N}{n} = \frac{N!}{(N-n)! \, n!} \tag{1.14.1}$$

and should not give the spreadsheet any problems because Excel contains the factorial function (the instruction =FACT(3) will yield 6) and, at any rate, you can always evaluate a factorial from its definition, $N! = 1 \times 2 \times 3 \times 4 \times \cdots$. Perhaps so, but when you apply this to the binomial coefficient, you will quickly run out of luck.

Exercise 1.14.1:
(1) Start a spreadsheet with the label and value of n, two rows lower enter labels for N and the binomial coefficient, and in cell A5 start a column for $N = 0$ (1) 200.
(2) In B5 start the column for the binomial coefficient where $N = n$, by calculating it as $N! / (N–n)! \, n!$. For $n = 10$ you will do fine till $N = 170$; thereafter, even though the binary coefficient is still smaller than 10^{16}, the computer fails.
(3) Make a temporary third column in which you calculate $N!$ for the same range of N-values. At $N = 171$, $N!$ exceeds the maximum number the computer can represent (about 10^{207}), and this ruins the calculation of the much smaller binary coefficient.

Understanding what causes the problem is, of course, the most important part of fixing it. Obviously we should compute the binomial coefficient without explicitly calculating $N!$. We first note that the definition of $N!$ as a product makes it easy to compute it in logarithmic form, since

$$\ln(N!) = \ln(N) + \ln(N–1) + \ln(N–2) + \ln(N–3) + \ldots + \ln(2) + \ln(1)$$

will not exceed the numerical capacity of the computer.

Exercise 1.14.1 (continued):
(4) Re-label the third column as $\ln(N)$ and use it to compute $\ln(N!)$ by making cell C6 read =LN(A6), and by entering in cell C7 the instruction =C6+LN(A7). (We avoid cell C5 because $\ln(0)$ is not very useful.) Copy the instruction from cell C7 all the way down.

(5) In cells C1 and D1 enter the label and value respectively of $\ln(n!)$, which for $n < 170$ can be computed simply as =LN(FACT(B1)).

(6) Now use column D to compute the binomial coefficient. For example, for $n = 10$, deposit the instruction =EXP(C16-C6-$D$1) in row 16, and copy it all the way down. You now have the binomial coefficient for as far as the eye can see on the spreadsheet: for $N = 65531$ and $n = 10$ it has the value $4.02167227 \times 10^{41}$, a sizable number but no problem whatsoever for Excel.

1.14.2 The exponential error function complement

A function that appears in, e.g., problems of statistics, heat transport, and diffusion is the calculation of the exponential error function complement, $y = \exp[x^2] \, \text{erfc}[x]$. Excel provides both $\exp[x^2]$ and $\text{erfc}[x]$, and we therefore start out by simply multiplying them, as illustrated in exercise 1.14.2.

Exercise 1.14.2:

(1) In a spreadsheet enter columns for $x = 0$ (0.1) 10 and $y = \exp[x^2] \, \text{erfc}[x]$, the latter simply by calling the functions exp() and erfc() and multiplying them.

(2) Plot y versus x. There should be no problem as long as $x < 5$, while the computation obviously fails above $x = 6$. The open circles in Fig. 1.14.1.show what you should get.

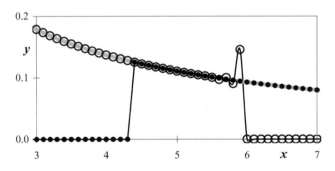

Fig. 1.14.1: Cobbling together a smooth function from two partially overlapping segments. Open circles: the product of $\exp(x^2)$ and $\text{erfc}(x)$. Solid circles: the output of the asymptotic series. Gray band: the result of switching from one to the other at $x = 5$. Only the region of switchover is shown.

Clearly we run into a problem for $x > 5$, where $\exp[x^2]$ becomes large while $\text{erfc}[x]$ tends to zero. This is the digital analog of the product $\infty \times 0$, as can be recognized by plotting both functions separately. For large values of x we therefore use an asymptotic expansion instead, in this case

$$\exp[x^2] \, \text{erfc}[x] \approx \frac{1}{x\sqrt{\pi}} \left\{ 1 + \sum_{m=1}^{\infty} (-1)^m \frac{1 \cdot 3 \cdot 5 \cdots (2m-1)}{(2x^2)^m} \right\} \qquad (1.14.2)$$

for $x \to \infty$. The problem therefore is two-fold: how to incorporate a computation such as (1.14.2) into a cell, and (because the asymptotic expansion fails for small values of x) how to switch smoothly from one to the other. The first problem will be addressed below by introducing a custom function.

Exercise 1.14.2 (continued):

(3) We first find a macro in which to write the custom function. Either use Alt⌣F11 (Mac: Opt⌣F11) or Tools ⇒ Macro ⇒ Visual Basic Editor. If you find a gray space, there is no module yet, and you therefore make one with Insert ⇒ Module. If a module already exists, go to the end.

(4) In the module, type (or copy from SampleMacros) the following lines:

```
Function EE(x)

Dim m As Integer
Dim sum As Double
Dim oldterm As Double, newterm As Double
m = 1
sum = 1
oldterm = 1

Do
   newterm = -(2 * m - 1) * oldterm / (2 * x * x)
   sum = sum + newterm
   oldterm = newterm
   m = m + 1
Loop Until Abs(newterm) < 0.00000001

ee = sum / (X * Sqr([Pi()]))

End Function
```

(5) The first line specifies the function by name, and within brackets indicates the name of the parameter(s) on which the function operates. The last line identifies the end of the custom function.

(6) The next three lines contain the dimension statements, which specify the nature of the variables used in the custom function. Note that the variable x should not be dimensioned, since the spreadsheet already knows its dimension, which (through the first line) is imported into the function together with its value. You can operate the function without the dimension statements, except when your module starts with the line `Option Explicit`, in which case they are required. However, it is good general programming custom to include dimension statements, which is why we will do so here. Empty lines have no meaning for the computer, and are inserted merely for greater readability.

(7) The next three lines *initialize* the calculation, i.e., they assign the relevant parameters their initial values.

(8) The heart of this custom function is the part between `Do` and `Loop until`, which forms a so-called *do-loop*. This loop executes a set of commands until a termination criterion is reached; here we use as such a criterion the requirement that the absolute value of the last-computed term is smaller than 10^{-8}. (The initial value of the function $\exp[x^2] \operatorname{erfc}[x]$, at $x = 0$, is 1.)

(9) Now we consider the terms summed in (1.14.2), which we can write as $T_1 = -1/2x^2$ for $m = 1$, $T_2 = -3T_1/2x^2$ for $m = 2$, $T_3 = -5T_2/2x^2$ for $m = 3$, and in general $T_m = -(2m-1)\ T_{m-1}/2x^2$. This is the logic behind starting with the parameter `oldterm` and using it to compute successive values of `newterm`.

(10) In the next line we then add the successive terms to sum, using the *assignment* symbol = to mean $\Leftarrow$, i.e., to replace the left-hand expression (`sum`) by that on the right-hand side (`sum + newterm`). Note that, unlike the expression in (1.14.2), `sum` already incorporates the term 1.

(11) Then we update `oldterm`, and increment m.

(12) Finally, outside the loop, we assign the value of ee to `sum` divided by $x\sqrt{\pi}$. Visual Basic does not have the rich assortment of functions that Excel has, and doesn't know what π means. Therefore we can either write out the value of π, or simply use the spreadsheet function. In the latter case we must place that function, `Pi()`, between square brackets: `[Pi()]`. Also note that the instruction for taking the square root in Visual Basic is `sqr`, not `sqrt`.

(13) Use Alt$\cup$F11 (Mac: Opt$\cup$F11) to switch back to the spreadsheet, and make a third column in which you use the custom function. For example, if your column containing the values of x starts in cell A3, in C3 deposit the instruction =EE(A3), and copy this down the length of columns A and B.

(14) Add the result obtained with this custom function to your graph.

Figure 1.14.1 illustrates what we have just calculated. Apparently, above $x = 5$ we are bitten by the dog, and below it scratched by the cat. So the final column takes the good parts of each calculation, and avoids their problems.

***Exercise 1.14.2 (continued)*:**
(15) In cell D3 deposit the instruction =IF(A3<5,EXP(A3^2)*ERFC(A3), EE(A3)). This reads as 'if A3 < 5, then use EXP(A3^2)*ERFC(A3), otherwise use EE(A3)', and apparently solves both problems.

(16) Plot this result; it should look like Fig. 1.14.1.

1.15 Algorithmic accuracy

Excel can do many things, but how well does it do them? This question is increasingly being asked of many types of software, as benchmarks (such as the Statistical Reference Datasets from the National Institute of Science and Technology) have become available to test them. A number of software packages, including Excel, have recently been tested, and readers of this book may be especially interested in tests of Excel such as those published by L. Knüssel, *Computational Statistics and Data Analysis* 26 (1998) 375, and B. D. McCullough & B. Wilson, *Computational Statistics and Data Analysis* 31 (1999) 27, or in broader comparisons such as given, e.g., by M. Altman & M. P. McDonald, *Political Science and Politics* 43 (2001) 68.

The basic problem with all programs (including Excel) that use a fixed number of *bi*nary uni*ts* ('bits') to represent data is that many non-integers cannot be represented exactly as binary numbers. For example, the binary representation of 1/10 is 0.00011001100110011001... , and an error is therefore made wherever it is truncated. (The binary number as shown is actually good to fewer than six significant figures, since its decimal value is 0.0999994... .) The resulting small errors can accumulate in complicated calculations, especially if those involve subtractions of numbers of near-equal magnitudes. Good software design tries to minimize such errors, but that is an area of competence that most scientists will have to leave to the specialists. The present author certainly makes no claims to such expertise, and his macros will no doubt confirm that.

There are several issues here. First and foremost, one wants the final results of a calculation to be correct rather than wrong. We will call this *absolute accuracy*. It would be optimal if software could let its user know when the computer cannot find the requested answer, rather than display the last result before the algorithm stopped. Knüsel lists several examples where Excel cannot find a result, and then does not give one, but instead displays the error message #NUM!. That is fine, even though one might wish the algorithm to yield the requested answer. It is equivalent to a teacher, or a politician, honestly answering "I don't know" if that is the case, regardless of whether the answer might be knowable.

Secondly, one would like only significant numbers to be displayed, or perhaps just one more, as a guard digit. We will call this *numerical accuracy*, and it requires elaborate software testing.

Algorithms incorporated in standard software packages often reflect a compromise between accuracy and execution speed, although one would hope that, with the increasing processing speeds, consistent accuracy will soon become the sole determining factor. But sometimes algorithms have been chosen consciously for speed, to the detriment of accuracy. While that might have been justifiable in the days of 1 MHz processors, it is of questionable value now that personal computers have clock speeds above 1 GHz. We will illustrate this in exercise 1.15.1 with an example taken from M. Altman & M. P. McDonald, *Political Science and Politics* 43 (2001) 681, which uses the population standard deviation given by

$$\sqrt{\frac{\sum (x - x_{av})^2}{n}} = \sqrt{\frac{\sum [x - (\sum x)/n]^2}{n}} \qquad (1.15.1)$$

which is mathematically (but *not* computationally) equivalent to

$$\sqrt{\frac{n\sum x^2 - \left(\sum x\right)^2}{n^2}} \qquad (1.15.2)$$

Use of (1.15.2) can be faster than that of (1.15.1) because (1.15.2) requires only a single pass through the data set, whereas one needs two passes (one to determine x_{av} first) for (1.15.1). On the other hand, (1.15.1) keeps better numerical accuracy for large values of x, because it computes the squares of the differences $x - x_{av}$ between the numbers x and x_{av}, rather than the difference between the usually much more extreme values of $\sum x^2$ and $(\sum x)^2$.

Exercise 1.15.1:

(1) In cells A3:A9 of a spreadsheet enter the values 1 (1) 7, either directly as 1, 2, 3, 4, 5, 6, 7, or with a 1 in cell A3, the instruction =A3+1 in A4, and copies thereof in cells A5:A9.

(2) In cell B1 enter the number 1000000, and in cell B3 the instruction =B$1+$A3. Copy this instruction down through B4:B9.

(3) In C1 deposit the instruction =10*B$1, and copy this to D1:F1.

(4) Highlight B3:B9, copy it, then highlight C3:F3 and paste. You now have entered the test data set.

(5) In cell B11 use =AVERAGE(B3:B9) to compute the average.

(6) In cell B13 place the instruction =B3-B$11, and copy this down through B14:B19.

(7) In B21 deposit =COUNT(B13:B19), in B23 =SQRT(SUMSQ(B13:B19)/B$21), and in B24 =STDEVP(B3:B9).

(8) Highlight B11:B24, copy it, highlight C11:F11, and paste. You should now have a spreadsheet that, apart from the few added notations in column A, resembles Fig. 1.15.1.

The built-in Excel function STDEVP fails when x contains more than 8 significant figures, predictable because squaring such a number requires more than 16 significant decimal digits in its computation, more than it has available. Interestingly, you can force Excel to compute the average (actually twice) by replacing STDEVP(*xRange*) by SQRT (COVAR(*xRange,xRange*)), which avoids the above problem because covar(*xRange,yRange*) = $(1/n) \sum (x - x_{av})(y - y_{av})$ cannot be written in terms of squares. Or, as illustrated below, you can write a function yourself to do better than Excel.

```
Function myStDevP(myRange)

Dim Count As Long      ' just in case Count exceeds 32K
Dim DifSq As Double, x As Double, xav As Double

' compute the average x-value, xav
```

```
x = 0
Count = 0
For Each Cell In myRange
  x = x + Cell.Value
  Count = Count + 1
Next Cell
xav = x / Count

' compute the standard deviation

DifSq = 0
For Each Cell In myRange
  DifSq = DifSq + (Cell.Value - xav) ^ 2
Next Cell
myStDevP = Sqr(DifSq / Count)

End Function
```

	A	B	C	D	E	F
1		1000000	10000000	100000000	1000000000	10000000000
2						
3	1	1000001	10000001	100000001	1000000001	10000000001
4	2	1000002	10000002	100000002	1000000002	10000000002
5	3	1000003	10000003	100000003	1000000003	10000000003
6	4	1000004	10000004	100000004	1000000004	10000000004
7	5	1000005	10000005	100000005	1000000005	10000000005
8	6	1000006	10000006	100000006	1000000006	10000000006
9	7	1000007	10000007	100000007	1000000007	10000000007
10						
11	AVERAGE	1000004.0	10000004.0	100000004.0	1000000004.0	10000000004.0
12						
13		-3	-3	-3	-3	-3
14		-2	-2	-2	-2	-2
15		-1	-1	-1	-1	-1
16		0	0	0	0	0
17		1	1	1	1	1
18		2	2	2	2	2
19		3	3	3	3	3
20						
21	COUNT	7	7	7	7	7
22						
23	eq.(1.15.1)	2	2	2	2	2
24	STDEVP	2	2	2.285714286	0	0

Fig. 1.15.1: A spreadsheet computation of the standard deviation of sets of seven large numbers. Comparison of the results on the two bottom lines suggests that the Excel function STDEVP fails when x has more than 8 significant figures.

Unfortunately, Excel does not alert the user to the fact that the numbers entered into this function are too large for it to function properly; instead it provides an incorrect result with the same aplomb as a correct answer. Computers do not blush, and neither does Excel. Yet, this is really a simple problem with a simple solution, which has haunted Excel at least since version 5, and still has not yet been fixed in Excel2002. You can readily verify the latter statements by consulting the Microsoft

Knowledge Base article Q 158071 on "XL: Problems with statistical functions and large numbers", http://support/microsoft.com. For the analysis of the problem, look up the Excel Help file for STDEVP, which gives the formula used. This problem affects not only the functions listed in note Q158071, such as StDev, LinEsT, LogEst, Kurt, and BinomDist, but also functions not listed there, such as the variance Var and the related functions VarA, VarP, and VarPA. A similar algorithm is used for the calculation of, e.g., R^2 in Trendline. On the other hand, do keep matters in perspective: how often in your lifetime do you expect to encounter computations involving numbers with eight or more significant digits? As long as you care only about their first seven digits, you might never know this problem exists.

x	F_{calc}	F_{exact}	x	F_{calc}	F_{exact}	x	F_{calc}	F_{exact}
-7.80	3.10862E-15	3.094E-15	-8.00	6.66134E-16	6.22E-16	-8.20	1.11022E-16	1.20E-16
-7.81	2.88658E-15	2.858E-15	-8.01	5.55112E-16	5.73E-16	-8.21	1.11022E-16	1.11E-16
-7.82	2.66454E-15	2.640E-15	-8.02	5.55112E-16	5.29E-16	-8.22	1.11022E-16	1.02E-16
-7.83	2.44249E-15	2.438E-15	-8.03	4.44089E-16	4.87E-16	-8.23	1.11022E-16	9.36E-17
-7.84	2.22045E-15	2.252E-15	-8.04	4.44089E-16	4.49E-16	-8.24	1.11022E-16	8.61E-17
-7.85	2.10942E-15	2.079E-15	-8.05	4.44089E-16	4.14E-16	-8.25	1.11022E-16	7.92E-17
-7.86	1.88738E-15	1.920E-15	-8.06	3.33067E-16	3.81E-16	-8.26	1.11022E-16	7.28E-17
-7.87	1.77636E-15	1.772E-15	-8.07	3.33067E-16	3.51E-16	-8.27	1.11022E-16	6.70E-17
-7.88	1.66533E-15	1.636E-15	-8.08	3.33067E-16	3.24E-16	-8.28	1.11022E-16	6.16E-17
-7.89	1.55431E-15	1.510E-15	-8.09	3.33067E-16	2.98E-16	-8.29	1.11022E-16	5.66E-17
-7.90	1.44329E-15	1.394E-15	-8.10	3.33067E-16	2.75E-16	-8.30	0	5.21E-17
-7.91	1.33227E-15	1.286E-15	-8.11	2.22045E-16	2.53E-16	-8.31	0	4.79E-17
-7.92	1.22125E-15	1.187E-15	-8.12	2.22045E-16	2.33E-16	-8.32	0	4.40E-17
-7.93	1.11022E-15	1.095E-15	-8.13	2.22045E-16	2.15E-16	-8.33	0	4.04E-17
-7.94	9.99201E-16	1.011E-15	-8.14	2.22045E-16	1.98E-16	-8.34	0	3.72E-17
-7.95	8.88178E-16	9.32E-16	-8.15	2.22045E-16	1.82E-16	-8.35	0	3.41E-17
-7.96	8.88178E-16	8.60E-16	-8.16	2.22045E-16	1.67E-16	-8.36	0	3.14E-17
-7.97	7.77156E-16	7.93E-16	-8.17	1.11022E-16	1.54E-16	-8.37	0	2.88E-17
-7.98	7.77156E-16	7.31E-16	-8.18	1.11022E-16	1.42E-16	-8.38	0	2.65E-17
-7.99	6.66134E-16	6.74E-16	-8.19	1.11022E-16	1.31E-16	-8.39	0	2.43E-17

Table 1.15.1: The answers F_{calc} obtained for the functions F =NormDist(x,0,1,1) or F =NormSDist(x) for various (admittedly rather extreme) values of x, and their correct values F_{exact}.

The cumulative standard Gaussian distribution, i.e., the area under the Gaussian distribution curve for zero mean and unit standard deviation, can be found in Excel with the instructions =NormDist(x,0,1,1) or NormSDist(x), where x denotes the probability. As can be seen in Table 1.15.1 the results for large negative values of x are 'quantized' in steps of about $1.11×10^{-16}$, and it would be preferable if they were provided to $±1×10^{-16}$ rather than with the extra, insignificant digits. Especially, it would be better if the answers for $x ≤ -8.30$ were to read, e.g., <1E-16. A similar but even more severe problem exists with its inverse functions NormInv(x,0,1) and NormSInv(x) which, according to their descriptions in the Index, are computed iteratively to within $±3×10^{-7}$, even though the result is displayed with 16 digits. Moreover, when NormDist or NormS-Dist becomes small, NormInv and NormSInv can blow up to quite ridiculous numbers.

In general, then, it is prudent to assume, in the absence of contrary evidence, that not all digits displayed by Excel functions and macros (including the custom macros used in this book!) are significant. Considering the uncertainties in the input data analyzed, this will often be unimportant (i.e., the standard deviations in the results will often be far larger than the computational errors of Excel), but it is still useful to keep in mind. When your results depend critically on more than the first 3 or 4 non-zero digits of the result, it is time to check the numerical precision of the method. Preferably it should be checked with non-integers that cannot be written exactly in binary notation, see S. D. Simon & J. P. Lesage, *Comp. Stat. Data Anal.* 7 (1988) 197. Testing with a number such as 0.375 would not be useful even though it is a non-integer, because 0.375 = 3/8 and is therefore represented exactly in binary format as 0.011.

Here is another issue. Chapter 4 describes many applications of the nonlinear least squares routine Solver, made by Frontline Systems Inc. and included in Excel as well as in Lotus 1-2-3 and in QuattroPro. While it is a well-designed and very useful tool, it is a good general precaution always to repeat Solver to see whether its answer is stable. Not infrequently, a second run of Solver starting from the just-obtained answer will produce a slightly improved result. It is not clear why Solver doesn't incorporate such a simple check itself.

Algorithms are continually debugged, refined, and made more robust, but available software packages may not always incorporate such improvements. By comparison with other makers of statistical software, Microsoft has not been very willing to improve its routines after its problems had been pointed out and acknowledged which, if nothing else, makes for poor public relations. Custom-made functions and macros (including those in this book) are also likely to contain errors that crop up only when algorithms are put under some duress. Yours truly will much appreciate your suggestions to improve his macros. As with anything else, user beware. For most applications, as long as your data are relatively few, and the number of significant figures needed is small, Excel will be fine, and the same applies to the custom macros presented here. But if you deal with complex problems, and especially when the results you obtain may have serious, practical consequences, calibrate your procedure with similar (but binary-incompatible) data for which you know the exact answer, and use other software packages for independent verification. This holds for Excel as well as for more specialized software programs. There are possible errors every step of the way: at sampling, at measuring, at data analysis, and at the final interpretation of the results, and it is best to know about them, and to keep them all as small as possible.

1.16 Mismatches between Excel and VBA

In this book we will first use macros, and then learn how to write them, at which point we will often switch back and forth between the spreadsheet and its macros. The language used in Excel macros is Visual Basic for Applications (VBA), an adaptation of Visual Basic which, in turn, is an evolutionary development of Dartmouth Basic (an acronym for Beginners All-purpose Symbolic Instruction Code) via Borland's Turbo Basic and Microsoft's QuickBasic. Along the way, Basic lost some of its less convenient features, such as line numbers and line interpreters, and became more like Fortran77 (for *For*mula *tran*slator), the successor to a computer language developed at IBM in the 1950s. In the meantime, Fortran has morphed into a much more powerful language with Fortran90 and Fortran95, but that is a different story.

Visual Basic was combined with Excel in version 5 (Excel 95), when both were already mature products. As in any marriage, both partners brought in their own characteristics, and they did not always match. Unfortunately, Microsoft has done little to soften the resulting conflicts, a few of which we will illustrate below.

Perhaps most annoying is the fact that VBA uses single precision arithmetic as its default, whereas Excel automatically computes everything in double precision. VBA must therefore be reminded to use double precision.

Another annoyance is that the order in which simple arithmetic operations are performed in Excel and VBA is not always the same. In Excel, negation comes before exponentiation, so that $-3^4 = 81$, whereas it is the other way around in VBA: $-3^4 = -81$. To avoid confusion and the resulting ambiguity it is therefore best *always* to use brackets when a minus sign is involved: $(-3)^4 = 81$ and $-(3^4) = -81$ in both Excel and VBA. Matters can get especially confusing when a negative sign is used all by itself, as in $=\exp[-(x-c)^2]$, which in Excel is therefore best coded as, e.g., `=EXP(-((A3-$B$1)^2))` or `=EXP(-1*(A3-$B$1)^2)` because `=EXP(-(A3-$B$1)^2)` will square (and thereby cancel) the first minus sign.

Here are some more beauties: in Excel, $\sqrt{x}$ must be coded as sqrt(*x*), in VBA as sqr(*x*). In Excel the sign of *x* is obtained with sign(*x*), in VBA as sgn(*x*). Both are a consequence of the three-letter codes used in VBA. In the same category you will find rand(*x*) in Excel, and rnd(*x*) in VBA, for a random number, and arctan(*x*) in Excel vs. atn(*x*) in VBA for the arc tangent. VBA rounds 0.5 to the nearest even integer, i.e., round (2.5,0) = 2 and round(–2.5,0) = –2, while the Excel function rounds up for *x* > 0 and down for *x* < 0, as in round(2.5,0) = 3, round (–2.5,0) = –3.

The worst offender in this category is perhaps the logarithm. In VBA, log(*x*) represents the *natural*, *e*-based logarithm, which in Excel (and in almost everyone else's nomenclature) is written as ln(*x*). VBA does not even have a symbol for the ten-based logarithm, so that it must be calculated as log(*x*)/log(10), in what everyone else would write as log(*x*) or ln(*x*)/ln(10). Excel, on the other hand, has no fewer than *three* ways to represent the ten-based logarithm of *x*: log(*x*), log(*x*,10), and log10(*x*). In Excel, log(3) yields 0.47712, but in VBA we find log(3) = 1.0986. However, in VBA we can refer to the spreadsheet function, as in Application.Log(3), in which case we obtain 0.47712, as illustrated in the function Logarheads. Go figure!

```
Function Logarheads(x)
MsgBox "Log(" & x & ") = " & Log(x) & " but" & Chr(13) & _
    "Application.Log(" & x & ") = " & Application.Log(x)
End Function
```

An additional set of problems is encountered outside the US, because Excel and VBA may provide different adaptations to languages other than American English. A case in point is the use of the decimal comma (rather than point) in most continental European languages. In the US versions of Excel and VBA, the comma is used as a general separator in both Excel and VBA, whereas a semicolon may be used as such in Europe. The macros described in this book may therefore have to be modified to run properly in such environments.

1.17 Summary

Excel is a powerful spreadsheet. It is primarily designed for business applications, and is marketed as such, which makes it both ubiquitous and affordable. Fortunately it incorporates many features that make it very useful for science and engineering, and its ability to accommodate custom functions and macros greatly extends its already considerable power to solve scientific data analysis problems.

That does not mean that we should try to do everything with Excel: just as no carpenter will go to the job with only one tool, no scientist should rely on just one type of data analysis software. For special problems, specialized software will often be required. For instance, Excel cannot handle very large data arrays, it has very limited capabilities for displaying three-dimensional objects, and it cannot do formal, closed-form mathematics. In all such cases, one should use more appropriate software. On the other hand, for many relatively mundane problems, Excel is eminently suited, because it combines general availability with transparency, ease of use, and convenient graphics. So, spread the sheet, and go for it.

1.18 For further reading

There are many introductory books on Excel, both for a general (often business-oriented) audience, and those specifically written for scientists and/or engineers. In the latter category we mention E. J. Billo, *Excel for chemists*, 2nd ed., Wiley 2001, which describes many useful shortcuts, and clearly lays out the differences between personal computers and Macs; S. C. Bloch, *Excel for Engineers and Scientists*, Wiley 2000, with its two most valuable chapters tucked away on the accompanying compact disk; B. S. Gottfried, *Spreadsheet Tools for Engineers Excel 2000 Version*, McGraw-Hill 2000, which like Bloch's book hardly mentions custom functions and macros; and W. J. Orvis, *Excel for Scientists and Engineers*, 2nd ed., Sybex 1996, despite its age still worthwhile.

The Microsoft manual provided with Excel is quite good; moreover, you have much information at your fingertips in the Help section. All Microsoft manuals can be consulted and searched on http://support. microsoft.com. For other books, go to your local bookstore, public library, college library, or (if you will not miss browsing) to a web-based bookseller.

For the graphical presentation of data, you may want to consult the beautiful books by E. Tufte, especially *The Visual Display of Graphical Information* (1992) and *Visual Explanations* (1997), available from Graphics Press, P.O.Box 430, Cheshire CT 06410 or from web booksellers. In general, the simpler and clearer the graph, the more impact it will have. For best effect, use color sparingly: moderation marks the master.

Chapter 2
Simple linear least squares

All experimental observations are subject to experimental uncertainty. We can often distinguish two types of such uncertainty, which is sometimes called 'error'. Measurements may be distorted systematically by interfering phenomena, instrumental distortion, faulty calibration, or any number of factors that affect their *accuracy*, i.e., how far from true they are. (Since the truth is not known, the amount of inaccuracy can at best be guessed.) Moreover, measurements may exhibit 'noise', because most experiments leave wriggle room for a multitude of small, seemingly random fluctuations in experimental conditions, amplifiers may magnify the effects of thermal fluctuations, read-out instruments may have limited resolution, etc. Such noise affects the reproducibility of the measurements, i.e., its *precision*. Even assuming that all experimental artifacts could be removed, many measured properties are inherently *stochastic*, i.e., have a small amount of randomness because of the discrete nature of mass (atoms, molecules) and energy (quanta). We seldom have or take the time and tools to analyze the sources of such noise, and they are often of little interest as long as they can be removed without seriously affecting the underlying information. Only rarely do they make the evening news, as when the margin of error in Votomatic vote counting machines exceeds the margin of votes for one presidential candidate over another.

In this and the next two chapters we will be mostly concerned with precision, i.e., with random fluctuations and their reduction or removal. This is no reflection on their relative importance vis-à-vis systematic sources of uncertainty, but merely of the fact that a useful theoretical framework exists for their treatment. Books can only teach what is known, a criterion that does not imply a value judgement regarding its relative importance. Chapter 6 will briefly discuss some known sources of systematic uncertainty, and their possible remedies.

Scientific experiments typically generate large volumes of data, from which one tries to extract much smaller amounts of more meaningful numerical information, in a process often called *data reduction*. This chapter will illustrate the method of least squares, one of the most widely used techniques for the extraction of such essential information from an excess of experimental data. Excel provides convenient facilities for least squares analysis; where necessary we will use additional tools to facilitate the application of this method.

Least squares analysis is based on a single Gaussian distribution of errors. We do not explain the basis for this or other statistical techniques, since that would require a text all its own, and a large number of those have already been written. But, whenever necessary, we will explain some of the more practical features of least squares methods, and highlight what choices the experimenter must make.

In order to keep the present chapter within reasonable length, we have split the discussion of linear least squares into two parts. In the present chapter we survey the simple applications of unweighted linear least squares methods to the proportionality $y = a_1x$ and to the straight line $y = a_0 + a_1x$. Chapter 3 will deal with its extensions to include polynomial, multi-parameter, and weighted linear least squares, while chapter 4 will cover nonlinear least squares.

2.1 Repeat measurements

When we make a measurement, we obtain a reading. When we repeat the measurement under what appear to be identical conditions, we will usually get a similar reading, but not necessarily an identical one. Apart from major identifiable changes (the power just went out) or unintentional ones (we transposed two digits when noting down the result), this is most likely caused by possible fluctuations in some uncontrolled parameters: the temperature may have drifted somewhat between measurements, someone may have opened a door and let in a draft, there may have been a glitch on the power line because an instrument in an adjacent room was turned on or the elevator motor just started, or for any number of other, often not readily identifiable reasons. The question then arises: which is *the* correct result? There is no general answer to that question, and we usually deal with it by making several repeat observations, and averaging the result, on the assumption that any experimental errors tend to 'average out'. This can indeed be expected for many errors that are essentially random, although some experimental errors (such as might result from, e.g., the presence of an impurity, or a slow increase in room temperature during the morning hours) can introduce a bias, i.e., they are systematic rather than random.

The *sample average* or *sample mean*, y_{av} or $\bar{y}$, of N equivalent observations is defined as

$$y_{av} = \frac{1}{N}\sum_{i=1}^{N} y_i \tag{2.1.1}$$

where the index i, running from 1 to N, identifies the individual observations y_i. (In many fields of science and technology the superscript bar has a special, field-specific meaning, and it is also difficult to use in Excel. We will therefore use the more explicit notation y_{av}.) We can also get an estimate of the likely statistical uncertainty in that result, such as its *standard deviation*

$$s = \sqrt{\frac{\sum_{i=1}^{N}(y_i - y_{av})^2}{N-1}} \tag{2.1.2}$$

or the associated *variance*

$$v = s^2 = \frac{\sum_{i=1}^{N}(y_i - y_{av})^2}{N-1} = \frac{\sum_{i=1}^{N}\delta_i^2}{N-1} \tag{2.1.3}$$

where the difference between the individual observation and its average value, $\delta_i = (y_i - y_{av})$, is called the *residual*.

Exercise 2.1.1:

(1) We use the data generated in exercise 1.2.1. This is a large data set, which we cannot possibly display legibly on a typical computer screen. On a sheet of paper, totals are typically placed at the bottom of columns, and carried forward to the top of the next page when necessary. In a spreadsheet, the columns can be very long, making the bottom of a column rather hard to find. It is therefore convenient to place totals and related derived quantities at the *top* of the spreadsheet. If there is no room at the top, make it (which is much easier to do in a spreadsheet than in a job) by, e.g., highlighting the top two cells containing the row labels, right-clicking, and then selecting Insert.

(2) In order to calculate the average, you could use (2.1.1) to calculate the average of the data in column B with the instruction =SUM(B3: B1003)/1000, but it is more convenient to use instead =AVERAGE(B3:B1003). If you don't know how long the column is, type =AVERAGE(, click on the top cell of the column (B3), then use Shift⌣End, Shift⌣↓ (or, in one command, Ctrl⌣Shift⌣↓), and Enter. In Excel 2000 you need not even enter the closing bracket.

(3) Likewise, in order to compute the standard deviation, you could use (2.1.2), make a new column containing the squares of the residuals, add them up, and divide by $N - 1$. But it is much easier to use the single command =STDEV(B3: B1003) instead.

The numbers we obtain for the average and standard deviation over a large number of data points are much closer to their 'true' value (which in exercise 2.1.1 we know to be 10 and 1 respectively, because these are synthetic rather than real data) than the averages and standard deviations for smaller subsets of these data. If we could take an infinite number of measurements, and the uncertainties would all be truly random, we would get their 'correct' values. But for a small number of observations, we must make do with the sample average and sample standard deviation. For a sample of N observations, the standard deviation of the mean is $\sqrt{N}$ smaller than the standard deviation of the individual measurements, i.e.,

$$s_{av} = s_i / \sqrt{N} \qquad (2.1.4)$$

A sometimes more realistic measure of the uncertainty in the mean is the *confidence interval* (or *confidence limit*), which is the standard deviation of the mean, y_{av} multiplied by a factor that reflects both the finite sample size and a specified 'confidence level'. The confidence interval is found with =CONFIDENCE(α, s, N) where α is the assumed imprecision, in %, $\alpha = 0.05$ for 5% imprecision, corresponding with a confidence of $1 - \alpha = 1 - 0.05 = 0.95$ or 95%; $\alpha = 0.01$ for a confidence of 0.99 or 99%, etc. The second parameter, s, is the standard deviation, and N counts the number of data points analyzed.

> **Exercise 2.1.1 (continued)**:
>
> (4) Calculate the 95% confidence limits of the first 9-point average of exercise 1.2.1 using the instruction =CONFIDENCE(0.05,D7,9), or =CONFIDENCE (0.05,D5,9) in case you did not insert the two additional lines at the top.

Note that the confidence intervals delineate the likely range of the *reproducibility* of the data, and have nothing whatsoever to do with how reliable or confidence-inspiring they are. The term 'confidence' would appear to have been chosen deliberately to blur the distinction between accuracy (i.e., how reliable a number is) and precision (how reproducible that number is when the measurement is repeated under the very same experimental conditions).

2.2 Fitting data to a proportionality

Say that we apply a constant current I to a resistor, and measure the resulting voltage difference V across its terminals. We will assume that Ohm's law applies, as it has been shown to do over many orders of magnitude. We could make a single measurement, and calculate the resistance R of the resistor from Ohm's law as $R = V/I$. We can repeat the measurement, and then analyze the resulting data as in section 2.1. But often it is more efficient to make measurements at several *different* currents, because we can then use the data also to test the applicability of the assumed proportionality. In this case we must fit the observations to a given *function*, here Ohm's law, $V = IR$.

In general, the resulting analysis is non-trivial, because the numerical values of *both V and I* will be subject to experimental uncertainties. Fortunately, one of them usually has a smaller uncertainty than the other. In that case it is reasonable to focus on the more uncertain parameter, the so-called *dependent* variable, the other being called the *independent* one, which we will then assume to be error-free. If the disparity between the uncertainties in the two variables is sufficiently large, this is often an acceptably small price to pay for a considerably simplified analysis.

Usually it will be clear from the type of measurements made which variable is the dependent one. In other situations, the choice is sometimes made merely for mathematical convenience. In any case, the experimenter must decide what *model* is the most appropriate to use in conjunction with the least squares method. Any least squares analysis depends on a model, and the choice of model is always a judgement call.

Below we will assume that the measurement of V is the more imprecise one, so that I will be taken as the independent variable. When we plot V versus I we expect to see data that, apart from the noise, fit to a straight line with a slope R passing through the origin of the graph. In order to extract the value of the resistance R from such data, we need to use the expression

$$R = \sum_{i=1}^{N} I_i V_i \left/ \sum_{i=1}^{N} I_i^2 \right. \tag{2.2.1}$$

or, in general, for the proportionality $y = a_1 x$,

$$a_1 = \sum_{i=1}^{N} x_i y_i \left/ \sum_{i=1}^{N} x_i^2 \right. \tag{2.2.2}$$

where, by convention, y is the dependent variable, and the index 1 for the slope a_1 is given for the sake of consistency with subsequent extensions. Equation (2.2.2) can be derived by minimizing the sum of squares of the residuals δ_i, which in this case are defined as $\delta_i = (y_i - a_1 x_i)$.

We can now define *two* standard deviations, where s_f characterizes the stochastic uncertainty (i.e., the imprecision) in the over-all *f*it of the data to the model *f*unction, and s_1 the resulting imprecision in the derived slope a_1. The corresponding expressions are

$$s_f = \sqrt{\frac{\sum\limits_{i=1}^{N}\Delta_i^2}{N-1}} = \sqrt{\frac{\sum\limits_{i=1}^{N}(y_i - a_1 x_i)^2}{N-1}} = \sqrt{\frac{\sum\limits_{i=1}^{N}x_i^2 \sum\limits_{i=1}^{N}y_i^2 - \left(\sum\limits_{i=1}^{N}x_i y_i\right)^2}{(N-1)\sum\limits_{i=1}^{N}x_i^2}}$$

$$(2.2.3)$$

and

$$s_1 = \frac{s_f}{\sqrt{\sum\limits_{i=1}^{N}x_i^2}} = \sqrt{\frac{\sum\limits_{i=1}^{N}x_i^2 \sum\limits_{i=1}^{N}y_i^2 - \left(\sum\limits_{i=1}^{N}x_i y_i\right)^2}{(N-1)\left(\sum\limits_{i=1}^{N}x_i^2\right)^2}}$$

$$(2.2.4)$$

Again, we could use the spreadsheet and (2.2.2) through (2.2.4) to compute a_1, s_f, and s_1 respectively, but Excel makes that unnecessary, because it has these operations already built-in.

2.3 LinEst

LinEst, for *linear estimator*, is the simplest (and most terse) least squares fitting tool Excel provides.

Exercise 2.3.1:

(1) First we make a set of mock data on which to practice. In cell A1, deposit the label a1 =, and in cell C1 the label sn =, where s_n denotes the *standard deviation* of the *noise*. In cells B1 and D1 place some associated values. (By left-justifying these, and right-justifying the associated labels, we make them easy to read as one unit.) Make A3, B3, and N3 contain labels for y, x, and noise respectively; why in this order will soon become clear. In B4:B10 deposit some x-values, such as 1 (1) 7, and in N4:N10 some Gaussian noise. (Use Tools ⇒ Data Analysis ⇒ Random Number Generation, select Distribution: Normal, activate Output Range, activate the corresponding window, enter N4:N10, then press OK or Enter. In order to keep the monitor screen uncluttered, we have put the noise out of sight, in column N.) In A4 place the instruction =$B$1*B4+ $D$1*N4, and copy it to A5:A10. The spreadsheet should now resemble Fig. 2.3.1, except for the specific numbers.

(2) Highlight an empty block, one cell wide and two cells high, such as E4:E5, type =LINEST(A4:A10,B4:B10,FALSE,TRUE) and enter this with the special instruction Ctrl⌣Shift⌣Enter, i.e., by holding down the Control and Shift keys before and while depressing the Enter key. This is necessary to let the computer know that you want to enter an instruction into a *block* of cells rather than in a single cell. The selected cell block will now contain, in its top cell, the value of the slope a_1, and directly below it the standard deviation s_1. Had you forgotten to hold down the Ctrl and Shift keys while depositing the LinEst instruction, you

would only have obtained the top answer, a_1. The arguments of LinEst are the ranges of the y- and x-values respectively, then the absence (0 or false) or presence (1 or true) of an intercept, and whether you want the associated statistics (again 0 or 1, for false or true respectively).

	A	B	C	D	E		N	
1	a1 = 2.3		sn = 0.2					
2								
3	*y*	*x*					*noise*	
4	2.2400	1					-0.3002	
5	4.3445	2					-1.2777	
6	6.9489	3					0.2443	
7	9.4553	4					1.2765	
8	11.7397	5					1.1984	
9	14.1466	6					1.7331	
10	15.6633	7					-2.1836	

Fig. 2.3.1: The spreadsheet with some test data. The instruction in cell A4, =$B$1*B4 +$D$1*N4, was copied to cells A5:A10. The normally out-of-view cells N4:N10 contain Gaussian ('normal') noise with zero mean and unit standard deviation.

(3) The value found for a_1 should be close to that in cell B1, but (because of the added noise) not quite match it. Check this by changing the value of s_n in D1 to 0. Then change s_n to a value larger than used earlier, and observe its effects.

(4) We will now, for once, verify that these numbers are indeed correct. In cells G3:I3 place the labels XX, XY, and YY respectively, in cell G4 the instruction =B4^2, in H4 the command =A4*B4, and in I4 =A4^2. Copy these down to G5:I10. In G12 deposit =SUM(G4:G10), and copy this to H12 and I12, so that these cells now contain the sums Σx^2, Σxy, and Σy^2 respectively. In cell G14 compute the value of a_1 using (2.2.2), as =H12/G12, in H14 calculate s_f as =SQRT((G12*I12-H12^2)/(6*G12)), see (2.2.3), and in I14 find s_1 as =H14/SQRT(G12), see (2.2.4). To guard against the possibility of taking the square root of a negative quantity in the instruction in H14 you might instead want to use =SQRT(ABS((G12*I12-H12^2)/(6*G12))).

(5) If you have made no mistakes, the values for a_1 and s_1 will be the same as those generated by LinEst. But where is the value of s_y? Go to cell D4, now highlight block D4:E8, and again type =LINEST(A4:A10,B4:B10,FALSE,TRUE) or the equivalent but somewhat shorter =LINEST(A4:A10, B4:B10,0,1). (Excel uses 0 for false, 1 for true.) Pressing Ctrl∪Shift∪Enter will yield the answer, and your spreadsheet should now resemble that in Fig. 2.3.2. You will find the value of s_f in cell E6. The other information: D6 contains the square of the correlation coefficient, D7 the value of the F-test, and D8 the 'regression' sum of squares; in column E you find, from top to bottom, the intercept a_0 (here zero by definition) and its standard deviation s_0 (not applicable here), the standard deviation of the fit s_f, the number of degrees of freedom $N–P$, and the 'residual' sum of squares. Unfortunately, this output is rather cryptic, since no labels are provided to tell you what is what. You can find that out by using Help $\Rightarrow$ Contents and Index, by then typing LINEST, and by clicking on the LINEST worksheet function.

(6) In summary, LinEst is convenient, compact, and cryptic. It allows you to select what statistical information you want to display. It updates automatically
when you change one of the y and/or x parameters, as long as they fall within the
ranges specified for them, here A4:A10 and B4:B10 respectively. But don't forget to deposit the LinEst instruction in the entire block you want (e.g., if you
want to see a_1, s_1, and s_f, select D4:E6), using Ctrl∪Shift∪Enter, otherwise you
will only see the value of a_1.

	A	B	C	D	E		N	
1	a1 = 2.3		sn = 0.2					
2								
3	*y*	*x*					*noise*	
4	2.2400	1		2.30584	0		-0.3002	
5	4.3445	2		0.0244	#N/A		-1.2777	
6	6.9489	3		0.99666	0.28868		0.2443	
7	9.4553	4		1792.08	6		1.2765	
8	11.7397	5		149.342	0.5		1.1984	
9	14.1466	6					1.7331	
10	15.6633	7					-2.1836	

Fig. 2.3.2: The spreadsheet of Fig. 2.3.1 with the results of LinEst in block D4:E8.

2.4 Regression

Regression is Excel's most extensive tool for least squares fitting of
data. It yields a large (some might say excessive) amount of statistical
information on the fit, as illustrated below. It can also generate useful
auxiliary graphs.

Exercise 2.4.1:

(1) The Regression routine in the Data Analysis Toolpak is somewhat more
user-friendly than LinEst, but may overload you with statistical information. You
get it with Tools ⇒ Data Analysis. (In case you do not find Data Analysis under
Tools, select Tools ⇒ Add-Ins, select both Analysis Toolpak and Analysis Tool-
pak-VBA, and exit with OK. If the Analysis Toolpak is not listed in the dialog
box, you may have to run the Setup program to install it from the original CD or
diskettes.) In the Data Analysis dialog box, use the scroll bar to the right of the
list to see items too far down the alphabet to be displayed, and double-click on
Regression. Another dialog box appears, in which you enter (by typing or pointing) the Input Y Range as A4:A10, and the Input X Range as B4:B10. Click on
Constant is Zero (for the zero intercept), and select a cell for the Output Range
next to or below your data, because the output block is large, and will overwrite
and erase any data in its way. Click OK. You will now find three sets of data, as
illustrated in Fig. 2.4.1. In the top set, labeled Regression Statistics, the correlation coefficient is listed as Multiple R, and s_f as Standard Error. In the second
block of ANOVA you will find the zero intercept and its non-applicable standard
deviation, and as X Variable 1 the values of a_1 and s_1. The data at the bottom
come with the two (optional) graphs discussed in the next paragraph.

SUMMARY OUTPUT

Regression Statistics	
Multiple R	0.998330163
R Square	0.996663115
Adjusted R Squa	0.829996448
Standard Error	0.288676399
Observations	7

ANOVA

	df	SS	MS	F	Significance F
Regression	1	149.3416561	149.3416561	1792.084172	1.38776E-07
Residual	6	0.500004381	0.083334063		
Total	7	149.8416605			

	Coefficients	Standard Error	t Stat	P-value	Lower 95%	Upper 95%	Lower 95.0%	Upper 95.0%
Intercept	0	#N/A	#N/A	#N/A	#N/A	#N/A	#N/A	#N/A
X Variable 1	2.30584072	0.024397609	94.5109313	9.45466E-11	2.246141878	2.365539561	2.246141878	2.365539561

RESIDUAL OUTPUT

Observation	Predicted Y	Residuals
1	2.30584072	-0.065887152
2	4.61168144	-0.267218073
3	6.917522159	0.031329302
4	9.223362879	0.231931829
5	11.5292036	0.210466445
6	13.83504432	0.311582302
7	16.14088504	-0.477602566

Fig. 2.4.1: The lavish output generated by Regression upon its application to the 7 data pairs in Fig. 2.3.1. As the intercept was set to zero, no corresponding statistical information for that intercept is available.

(2) Repeat the same analysis, but click on the square windows to the left of Line Fit Plots and Residual Plots. On pressing OK you will now see two graphs, illustrated in Fig. 2.4.2, which you can move around on the screen. You can also enlarge or reduce them, change their colors or other features, whatever, all by dragging and clicking. Figure 2.4.3 shows them after some adjustments to emphasize data rather than labels, and to distinguish more clearly between data *points* and fitted *line*.

(3) Note that the Regression routine in the Analysis Toolpak is a macro, and needs to be invoked every time the input information is changed. On the other hand, LinEst is a function, and updates automatically whenever the input changes.

Like much of the work of Galton, the founder of the eugenics movement, the term "regression" is quite misleading, and will not be used here other than to refer to the Excel macro of that name. To quote K. A. Brownlee from his *Statistical Theory and Methodology in Science and Engineering*, 2nd ed., Wiley 1965 p. 409:

"Galton observed that on the average the sons of tall fathers are not as tall as their fathers, and similarly the sons of short fathers are not as short as their fathers; i.e., the second generation tended to regress towards the mean. But if we look at the data the other way round, we find that on average the fathers of tall sons are not as tall as their sons and the fathers of short sons are not as short as their sons, so the first generation tends to regress towards the mean. It seems implausible that both statements can be true simultaneously, so this phenomenon has been called the regression fallacy."

Clearly, if we select the *tallest* individuals of one generation, and compare them with the *averages* of the generation before and after them, then *both* their fathers *and* their adult sons on average will be smaller, as long as the average size remains constant. We should not compare a biased (tallest) subset with an average, or be surprised that the two differ. The term "regression" implies movement back towards something, in this case 'regression to the mean', a directionality that simply isn't there.

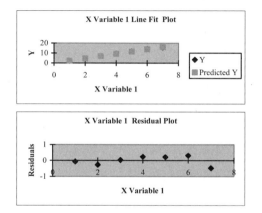

Fig. 2.4.2: Two plots produced by Regression upon its application to the data in Fig. 2.3.1.

2.5 LS

For reasons that will become clear later in this chapter, we also provide a *custom* least squares macro, LS, for *l*east *s*quares. It comes in two flavors: LS0 fits data to a line through the origin, while LS1 allows for an arbitrary intercept, and will therefore be discussed in section 2.7.

The input format of LS0 requires that the dependent data y and independent data x be placed in two contiguous, adjacent columns. The left-hand column must contain the dependent variable y, the right-hand column the corresponding independent x-values. In order to use LS0, highlight the data in the two adjacent columns (without including their labels) and call the macro. This will provide the slope a_1 in bold italics in the column for x, directly below the data, underneath it the standard deviation s_1 in italics, and below that the standard deviation of the fit, s_y.

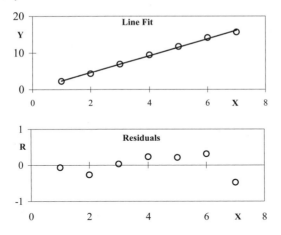

Fig. 2.4.3: The plots of Fig. 2.4.2, cleaned up by re-scaling, deleting background color, moving labels inside the graph, and representing measured data by points, the assumed function by a curve.

Exercise 2.5.1:

(1) Start again with the layout of Fig. 2.3.1. Highlight the two columns of data (in this example, block A4:B10) and then call LS0.

(2) If you want to display the standard deviation of the fit, s_y, answer the input box affirmatively. The spreadsheet should now resemble Fig. 2.5.1.

	A	B	C	D	E		N	
1	a1 = 2.3		sn = 0.2					
2								
3	*y*	*x*					*noise*	
4	2.2400	1					-0.3002	
5	4.3445	2					-1.2777	
6	6.9489	3					0.2443	
7	9.4553	4					1.2765	
8	11.7397	5					1.1984	
9	14.1466	6					1.7331	
10	15.6633	7					-2.1836	
11	*Coeff.:*	2.3058						
12	*St.Dev.:*	0.0244						
13		0.2887						

Fig. 2.5.1: The spreadsheet after using LS0.

Whether we use LinEst, Regression, or LS0, it is usually good practice to make a plot of the experimental data (as points), and add to that graph the computed line. For noisy data it is also advisable to calculate and plot the corresponding residuals, because a systematic trend in the deviations may reveal a flaw in the model used. Regression will make these plots automatically when you ask for them; with LinEst and LS0 you must make them yourself. In all cases the results should look like those in Fig. 2.4.3.

2.6 Trendline

When we already have made a graph of the data to be fitted, Trendline is a very convenient tool to determine the unknown parameters, though not the associated imprecision estimates.

Exercise 2.6.1:

(1) Trendline is simpler, but also more limited, than the above approaches. It requires that you have a *graph* of the data. Therefore, first make a graph of *y* vs. *x* on the spreadsheet, using Insert ⇒ Chart and the Chart Wizard. If you bypass step 2 of the Chart Wizard, you will obtain a graph of *x* versus *y*. In that case, first exchange the positions of the *x*- and *y*-columns.

(2) Click on the data in the graph to highlight them, right-click, and select Add Trendline. (Alternatively, after highlighting the data, click on Chart ⇒ Add Trendline.) In the dialog box select Type Linear, and under Options activate both Set intercept = 0 and Display equation on chart. Click OK. The equation for *y* will now appear in the graph, together with a line representing it. You can click on the line and change its color, thickness, etc.; likewise, you can move the equation around and, e.g., change its font.

(3) Trendline automatically updates as you change any or all of the data in the graph, but it cannot fit to part of a curve, nor can it provide any statistical estimates beyond the square of the correlation coefficient r_{xy}, which in this context is mostly a non-informative feel-good parameter. Compare your results with Fig. 2.6.1.

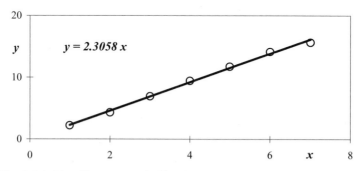

Fig. 2.6.1: Trendline automatically plots the computed curve through the data in Fig. 2.3.1 when these are presented graphically. Optionally it can also show the corresponding equation, but without useful imprecision estimates.

Even though we have so far already described four least squares routines, we will encounter yet another, Solver, which will be introduced in section 4.1. Therefore you can rest assured that, with Excel, you will not need to evaluate the sums in (2.2.2) through (2.2.4) anymore!

2.7 Fitting data to a straight line

Often we deal with a function that can be expected to fit a straight line, as in $y = a_0 + a_1 x$, with intercept a_0 with the vertical axis, and with slope a_1. In that case (2.2.2) must be replaced by

$$a_0 = \left(\sum_{i=1}^{N} x_i^2 \sum_{i=1}^{N} y_i - \sum_{i=1}^{N} x_i \sum_{i=1}^{N} x_i y_i \right) / D \qquad (2.7.1)$$

$$a_1 = \left(N \sum_{i=1}^{N} x_i y_i - \sum_{i=1}^{N} x_i \sum_{i=1}^{N} y_i \right) / D \qquad (2.7.2)$$

where

$$D = N \sum_{i=1}^{N} x_i^2 - \left(\sum_{i=1}^{N} x_i \right)^2 = N \sum_{i=1}^{N} (x_i - x_{av})^2 \qquad (2.7.3)$$

for the *intercept* and *slope* respectively. Likewise, instead of (2.2.3) and (2.2.4) we now should use

$$v_{ff} = s_f^2 = \frac{\sum_{i=1}^{N} \Delta_i^2}{N-2} = \frac{\sum_{i=1}^{N} (y_i - a_0 - a_1 x_i)^2}{N-2} \qquad (2.7.4)$$

$$v_{00} = s_0^2 = v_{ff} \sum_{i=1}^{N} x_i^2 / D \qquad (2.7.5)$$

$$v_{11} = s_1^2 = v_{ff} N / D \qquad (2.7.6)$$

for the variances v (or their square roots, the standard deviations s) of the fit, and of the two coefficients, a_0 and a_1. The doubling of the indices on the variances anticipates the introduction of covariances in section 2.9. As before, the residuals Δ_i are the differences between the observed quantities y_i and their assumed, 'theoretical' expressions, $a_0 + a_1 x_i$, i.e., $\delta_i = (y_i - a_0 - a_1 x_i)$. Equations (2.7.1) and (2.7.2) can then be derived by minimizing the quantity $\Sigma \delta_i^2 = \Sigma (y_i - a_0 - a_1 x_i)^2$ with respect to a_0 and a_1 respectively. Because Greek symbols, subscripts and superscripts are somewhat awkward to use in spreadsheets, we will often abbreviate the sum as S, the residual δ_i as R, its square δ_i^2 as RR, and the corresponding sum $\Sigma\delta^2_i$ as SRR or (in order to fit conventional statistical notation) SSR, where the first S signifies a *S*um, the second a *S*quare.

While we could use the spreadsheet to make the above sums, the expressions are now becoming so complicated that spreadsheet help is welcome – and we have already seen that it is readily available. In LinEst, all we need to do is to specify the third argument as True or 1, signifying the presence of an intercept. In Regression, we do not activate Constant is Zero. For the custom least squares macro we select LS1 rather than LS0, because the latter forces the fitted line through the origin. And in Trendline, we do not activate Set intercept = 0. You might want to try them with a data set such as shown in Fig. 2.3.1, after addition of a constant to the expression for *y*.

In general, when fitting data to a straight line, the slope and intercept will not be independent quantities. This does not affect their values, or those of the corresponding standard deviations, but may complicate using these values in subsequent computations. This occurs when one wants to estimate how the experimental imprecisions in the slope and intercept work their way (or 'propagate') through a calculation to affect the experimental uncertainty of any subsequently derived results. We will therefore briefly explore the propagation of experimental uncertainty, and the new parameter involved, the *covariance*, before returning to least squares data fitting per se.

2.8. Simple propagation of imprecision

The parameters produced by a least squares fitting of experimental data are seldom the final answers sought. Often they need to be combined with other numbers or otherwise manipulated to generate the numerical end results of the experiment. We will now consider how the standard deviations obtained in the least squares data fitting propagate through any subsequent computation to affect that final numerical result.

We will first consider the relatively 'simple' case in which the input data to such a calculation are mutually *in*dependent. On the other hand, when two or more data are derived from a single set of measurements, as is often the case with least squares analysis, the resulting parameter values are in general mutually *inter*dependent. The general treatment appropriate to that more general situation will be given in section 2.9.

We therefore consider a function *F* computed from one or more mutually independent experimental parameters x_j that have associated imprecision estimates (standard deviations, confidence limits, etc.), and ask what will be the resulting imprecision in the final result. For example, we might compute the volume V of a cylinder from its measured diameter d and height h as $\pi d^2 h/4$, then ask how the imprecision in V is obtained from the experimental imprecisions in the measurements of d and h. In a few special cases (addition & subtraction, multiplication & division, exponentiation & log taking) one can formulate simple rules, but in general it is easier to use the general formula

$$v_{FF} = s_F^2 = \sum_j \left(\frac{\partial F}{\partial x_j} \right)^2 s_{x_j}^2 = \sum_j \left(\frac{\partial F}{\partial x_j} \right)^2 v_{x_j x_j} \qquad (2.8.1)$$

which reduces to

$$s_F = \left| \frac{dF}{dx} \right| s_x \qquad (2.8.2)$$

when, for $j = 1$, y depends on a single parameter x. Excel does not provide a convenient tool to calculate the imprecision in y given the known imprecisions in x (or in several x_j's), but the macro Propagation in the MacroBundle does. Below we will illustrate its application. Exactly how Propagation achieves its magic will be explained in section 8.5.

Exercise 2.8.1:

(1) Say that we want to compute the value of $F = \ln(4X+3/Y) + YZ^2$, and compute the associated imprecision f given the imprecisions x, y, and z in X, Y, and Z respectively. We can use partial differentiation to find $\partial F/\partial X = 4/(4X+3/Y)$, $\partial F/\partial Y = (-3/Y^2)/(4X+3/Y)+Z^2$, and $\partial F/\partial Z = 2\,Y\,Z$, so that $f^2 = \{4x/(4X+3/Y)\}^2 + \{-3y/[Y^2(4X+3/Y)]+yZ^2\}^2 + \{2zYZ\}^2$, from which the sought imprecision f follows as its square root.

(2) When we use the spreadsheet, we will usually have numerical values for X, Y, and Z on that sheet, together with the values of their imprecision x, y, and z, e.g., in the form of their standard deviations. In cells A1, A2, and A3 enter the labels X=, Y=, and Z= respectively, and place numerical values for them in cells B1 through B3. In cells C1 through C3 deposit the labels x=, y=, and z=, and in D1 through D3 their values. In cells A5 and A6 place the labels F= and f= respectively, in cell B5 deposit the instruction =LN(4*B1+3/B2)+B2*(B3^2), and in cell B6 compute f using the formula given above, i.e., =SQRT(((4*D1/ (4*B1+3/B2))^2)+(3*D2/((B2^2)*(4*B1+3/B2))+D2*B3^2)^2+(2* D3*B2*B3)^2). The spreadsheet might now look like Fig. 2.8.1, except that you will of course have different values for the parameters X, Y, Z, x, y, and z, and therefore also different results for F and f.

(3) Call Propagation, and answer the input boxes. Specifically, for the example of Fig. 2.8.1, enter the location of the input parameters as B1:B3 (either by typing, or by pointing to that block with the mouse, followed by OK or Enter), that of the standard deviations as D1:D3, and that of the function as B5. Note that we left cell C5 free because that is where the macro will deposit its result. If C5 is used and cannot be overwritten, the answer will come as a message box, and you will need to write it down, busywork you can do without.

	A	B	C	D	E
1	X = 30		x = 4		
2	Y = 20		y = 2		
3	Z = 10		z = 0.5		
4					
5	F = 2004.79				
6	f = 282.84				

B5 =LN(4*B1+3/B2)+B2*(B3^2)
B6 =SQRT(((4*D1/(4*B1+3/B2))^2)+(3*D2/((B3^2)
     *(4*B1+3/B2))+D2*B3^2)^2+(2*D3*B2*B3)^2)

Fig. 2.8.1: The spreadsheet as it looks just before calling Propagation. The instructions shown below the screenshot merely serve as reminders of the formulas involved. Because the input data are organized column-wise, the answer from Propagate will automatically appear to the right of F, in cell C5, if empty.

(4) Verify that you get the same result in C5 as that computed in B6 (to well within 0.001%), but without having to derive the expression for f, and without having to use that expression to find its numerical value. Try other input parameters, and other formulas. Note that, like most macros, Propagation does not update automatically. Beyond that it does it all for you, automatically.

2.9 Interdependent parameters

Equation (2.8.1) applies only when the various parameters x_j are mutually independent, but that is often not the case. Say that we linearly extrapolate data, using the slope a_1 and intercept a_0 of a straight line determined by a least squares fit. Since a_0 and a_1 are obtained from the same data set in a single least squares minimization, a deviation in a_1 may be partially compensated by a corresponding change in a_0, in which case a_0 and a_1 will be mutually dependent.

When F is a function of two mutually *in*dependent parameters a_i and a_j, (2.8.1) reads

$$v_{FF} = \left(\frac{\partial F}{\partial a_i}\right)^2 v_{ii} + \left(\frac{\partial F}{\partial a_j}\right)^2 v_{jj} \qquad (2.9.1)$$

but when a_i and a_j are *correlated* parameters we must replace (2.9.1) by

$$v_{FF} = \left(\frac{\partial F}{\partial a_i}\right)^2 v_{ii} + 2\left(\frac{\partial F}{\partial a_i}\right)\left(\frac{\partial F}{\partial a_j}\right) v_{ij} + \left(\frac{\partial F}{\partial a_j}\right)^2 v_{jj} \qquad (2.9.2)$$

where the *covariance* v_{ij} between the parameters a_i and a_j is defined as

$$v_{ij} = v_{ji} = \frac{1}{N} \sum_{k=1}^{N} (a_{i,k} - a_{i,av})(a_{j,k} - a_{j,av}) \qquad (2.9.3)$$

The covariance has the dimension of a variance, but can be either positive or negative. The absolute value of the covariance is limited by

$$|v_{ij}| \leq \sqrt{v_{ii} v_{jj}} = s_i s_j \qquad (2.9.4)$$

so that (2.9.4) can have values between $\{(\partial F/\partial a_i) s_i - (\partial F/\partial a_j) s_j\}^2$ and $\{(\partial F/\partial a_i) s_i + (\partial F/\partial a_j) s_j\}^2$. When v_{ij} is zero, the two parameters a_i and a_j are not correlated, and the middle term on the right-hand side of (2.9.2) vanishes. We here treat the variance v_{ii} as a covariance v_{ij} with $i = j$.

For more than two input parameters the general relation for the variance v_{FF} of the function $F(x_1, x_2, \ldots x_i, \ldots x_N)$ is

$$v_{FF} = \sum_i \left(\frac{\partial F}{\partial x_i} \right)^2 v_{ii} + 2 \sum_i \sum_{j \neq i} \left(\frac{\partial F}{\partial x_i} \right) \left(\frac{\partial F}{\partial x_j} \right) v_{ij}$$

$$= \sum_i \sum_j \left(\frac{\partial F}{\partial x_i} \right) \left(\frac{\partial F}{\partial x_j} \right) v_{ij} \qquad (2.9.5)$$

The variances and covariances are most conveniently arranged in a *covariance matrix* (also known by the unnecessarily long term *variance-covariance matrix*). For a function with P adjustable parameters, such a matrix is a square array of $P \times P$ terms that contains all variances and covariances between these P parameters. For a straight line, with only two parameters, intercept a_0 and slope a_1, the covariance matrix is a 2×2 square containing four data, v_{00}, v_{01}, v_{11}, and $v_{10} = v_{01}$.

Often the covariances between the various parameters will not be known, because many standard software routines (including Excel's LinEst, Regression, and Trendline) do not provide them. Fortunately the macro LS does, and Propagation can use that information to compute the correct precision estimate for any derived function F. This was one of the major reasons to create a custom least squares macro.

How much difference will it make to neglect the covariances? As we will see shortly, it all depends on the computation used. To illustrate this we will use a century-old test data set from K. Pearson, *Phil. Mag. 2* (1901) 559 which, as we will see in section 4.18, was used by Pearson for a quite different purpose. In exercise 2.9.1 we will analyze this data set, shown in Fig. 2.9.1, in two different ways: first we will assume that y is the dependent variable, and x the independent one, and write $y = a_0 + a_1 x$. Then we will invert these roles, and instead write $x = b_0 + b_1 y$.

(1) Enter the data shown in the first two columns of Fig. 2.9.1 in a spreadsheet, highlight them, and call LS1.

(2) Copy the columns for y and x to a different location, and change their order, so that the column for x is not to the left of that for y. Again highlight the data block, and call LS1. The covariance matrix will show in color, with the label CM.

(3) Go to the results obtained under (2), and below them calculate the values of $-b_0/b_1$ and $1/b_1$ respectively.

(4) Now call Propagation, and in response to its queries highlight the values for b_0 and b_1, the covariance matrix, and the cell in which you have just computed $-b_0/b_1$. Propagation will calculate the standard deviation of $-b_0/b_1$, and place this immediately below its value. Do the same for $1/b_1$.

In the first case we obtain $y = 5.7_6 \pm 0.1_9 - (0.54_0 \pm 0.04_2) \, x$, in the other $x = 10.3_6 \pm 0.5_4 - (1.7_7 \pm 0.1_4) \, y$. How do these results compare? We rewrite the second set of results $x = b_0 + b_1 y$ as $y = -b_0/b_1 + x/b_1$. Combining within parentheses the coefficients with their imprecisions, in terms of their standard deviations, we can then compare a_0 ($5.7_6 \pm 0.1_9$) with $-b_0/b_1$ ($5.8_6 \pm 0.2_0$), and a_1 ($0.54_0 \pm 0.04_2$) with $1/b_1$ ($0.56_6 \pm 0.04_4$).

The agreement between the two slopes and intercepts is close, though not perfect. The small differences in the coefficients are due to the different assumptions made about the sources of the experimental uncertainties in the two analyses. The same applies to the corresponding standard deviations, computed here with the macro Propagation using the covariance matrix. However, if we use the standard deviations of b_0 and b_1 rather than the covariance matrix, we find a quite *different* standard deviation ($\pm 0.5_5$ instead of $\pm 0.2_0$) for $-b_0/b_1$, but the *same* answer for $1/b_1$. You have the data, and you can therefore verify this for yourself.

(5) Move the results just obtained one row lower (so as not to overwrite them), and again call Propagation. Repeat the procedure outlined in (4), except that, in response to the second input box, you now enter the standard deviations rather then the covariance matrix. Note that you find the same answer as under (4) for the standard deviation in $1/b_1$, but a quite different result for that in $-b_0/b_1$.

Why is this so? Because the calculation of the uncertainty in $1/b_1$ requires only one imprecision estimate, whereas that of b_0/b_1 involves the imprecisions in *both* b_0 and b_1. Since b_0 and b_1 are highly correlated quantities, their interdependence must be taken into account. The actual imprecision in $-b_0/b_1$ in this case is $2\frac{1}{2}$ times smaller than one would compute by neglecting their mutual dependence. Much more dramatic examples of such effects will be encountered in sections 2.15 and 2.16.

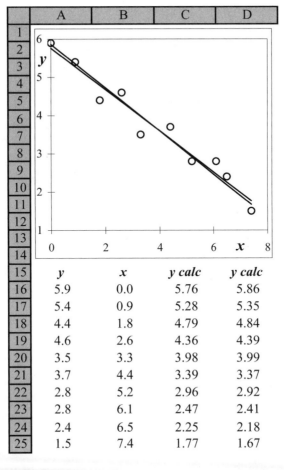

	y	x	y calc	y calc
16	5.9	0.0	5.76	5.86
17	5.4	0.9	5.28	5.35
18	4.4	1.8	4.79	4.84
19	4.6	2.6	4.36	4.39
20	3.5	3.3	3.98	3.99
21	3.7	4.4	3.39	3.37
22	2.8	5.2	2.96	2.92
23	2.8	6.1	2.47	2.41
24	2.4	6.5	2.25	2.18
25	1.5	7.4	1.77	1.67

cell:	*instruction:*	*copied to:*
	C16=5.7612-0.5396*B16	C17:C25
	D16=5.8617-0.5659*B16	D17:D25

Fig. 2.9.1: A data set from K. Pearson, *Phil. Mag.* 2 (1901) 559, analyzed either as *y* vs. *x* or as *x* vs. *y*.

2.10 Centering

When the covariances are not known, one often treats the input parameters as mutually independent ones, even though the resulting imprecision estimate will then be uncertain, and may sometimes be quite far off. There are, of course, other ways in Excel to deal with the propagation of imprecisions in derived results, though none of them as convenient as the combined use of LS and Propagation. For example, for the straight line $y = a_0 + a_1 x$ the covariance v_{01} between the intercept and slope can be calculated from the variances v_{00} and v_{11} as

$$v_{01} = v_{10} = -v_{00} \frac{\sum x}{\sum x^2} = -v_{11} \frac{\sum x}{N} \qquad (2.10.1)$$

Consequently we can make that covariance vanish by making $\sum x$ equal to zero, i.e., by *centering* the data set around its average x-value, $x_{av} = (1/N) \sum x$. For a linear relationship we can therefore avoid covariances by proper *design* of the experiment, before any experimental data are collected, by selecting the x-values at which data will be taken in such a way that x_{av} will be zero. This can always be done by redefining the zero of the x-scale. On the other hand, the more eccentric the x-values, the larger the resulting covariance.

Sometimes we are not so much interested in the absolute values of the covariances v_{ij} as in the corresponding *linear correlation coefficients* r_{ij}, which are defined as

$$r_{ij} = \frac{v_{ij}}{\sqrt{v_{ii} v_{jj}}} = \frac{v_{ij}}{s_i s_j} \qquad (2.10.2)$$

These show us immediately the relative strength of the linear correlation between the parameters a_i and a_j, i.e., $|r_{ij}| = 1$ signifies complete linear correlation between a_i and a_j, whereas $r_{ij} = 0$ indicates the absence of any linear correlation. From the linear correlation coefficients r_{ij} and the standard deviations s_i and s_j we can readily reconstruct the covariances as $v_{ij} = r_{ij} s_i s_j$. However, when mutually dependent data may be involved, use of the Propagation macro requires the covariance matrix rather than the linear correlation matrix plus the standard deviations. Incidentally, there is no need to check first whether the data are or are not mutually dependent, since we treat them in general as mutually dependent. If they are not, the covariance matrix will contain zeros in the appropriate places. And when the mutual dependence is minor, as when $r_{ij} < 0.9$, it usually is of little or no consequence.

*****

A short digression may be useful here. The term "(linear) correlation coefficient" can mean different things in different contexts, depending on which quantities are being correlated. In many least squares calculator and computer programs (including LinEst and Regression) a correlation coefficient r or R (or its square) is displayed for the correlation *between x and y*, answering the question *whether* there is a linear correlation between these two input parameters, x and y. That may be an issue when one needs to decide, e.g., whether using a cordless phone increases the likelihood of brain cancer (it doesn't), or whether unprotected sunbathing increases the chances for skin cancer (unfortunately it does), but is usually irrelevant when, as in the examples used in this book, we apply least squares analysis to problems with well-established causality. The linear correlation coefficient r_{xy} in LinEst or Regression is described by a formula just like (2.10.2), but its meaning is entirely different. This is also why r_{xy} should *not* be used as a measure of goodness-of-fit, which it isn't. Incidentally, when the relation between x and y is strictly causal but nonlinear, as with an exponential or power law, r_{xy} will not be unity.

On the other hand, the linear correlation r_{ab} deals with the correlation *between the coefficients a and b*, and provides information useful for subsequent propagation of imprecision when both a and b are involved, a topic that will be illustrated in the next five sections. The moral of this digression is, therefore: when you see or hear the term "correlation coefficient", ask yourself the question: correlation *between what and what*?

*****

When the result of a least squares fit to a straight line is plotted, one may want to indicate in the graph not only the original points and the best-fitting line through them, but also some imprecision estimate of that line. This is most readily done by drawing *imprecision contours* at, e.g., plus or minus one standard deviation. Such contours will enclose an *imprecision band*. Their construction is most readily appreciated when based on mutually independent parameters.

The procedure is as follows. First we find the average x_{av}, calculate a column of values $x - x_{av}$, and fit the data to the line $y = a_0 + a_1(x - x_{av})$. This will yield the mutually independent coefficients a_0 and a_1 plus the standard deviations s_0, s_1, and s_y. We use the coefficients a_0 and a_1 to plot the line $y = a_0 + a_1 (x - x_{av})$ together with the experimental data points. The vertical spacing between the line $y = a_0 + a_1 (x - x_{av})$ and the imprecision contours will then be given by

$$s = \sqrt{s_f^2 + s_0^2 + s_1^2 (x - x_{av})^2} \tag{2.10.3}$$

where s denotes the estimated standard deviation for the individual observations. This result is fully equivalent to (1.4.11) in N. R. Draper & H. Smith, *Applied Regression Analysis*, 2nd ed., Wiley 1981. Exercise 2.10.1 illustrates this for data taken from table 1.1 on p. 9 of that same book.

	A	B	C	D	E	F	G
1	Data from Draper & Smith, *Applied Regression Analysis* , Wiley 1981 p. 9.						
2			x_{av} = 52.6				
3							
4	*x*	*y*	*x - x av*	*y calc*	*s*	*y calc - s*	*y calc + s*
5							
6	28.1	11.88	-24.5	11.3798	0.9437	10.4361	12.3235
7	28.6	11.08	-24.0	11.3399	0.9422	10.3977	12.2821
8	28.9	12.19	-23.7	11.3159	0.9414	10.3745	12.2573
9	29.7	11.13	-22.9	11.2521	0.9392	10.3129	12.1913
10	30.8	12.51	-21.8	11.1643	0.9363	10.2280	12.1006
11	33.4	10.36	-19.2	10.9567	0.9300	10.0267	11.8867
12	35.3	10.98	-17.3	10.8050	0.9258	9.8792	11.7309
13	39.1	9.57	-13.5	10.5017	0.9188	9.5829	11.4205
14	44.6	8.86	-8.0	10.0626	0.9116	9.1510	10.9743
15	46.4	8.24	-6.2	9.9189	0.9101	9.0088	10.8290
16	46.8	10.94	-5.8	9.8870	0.9098	8.9772	10.7968
17	48.5	9.58	-4.1	9.7513	0.9088	8.8425	10.6601
18	57.5	9.14	4.9	9.0328	0.9092	8.1236	9.9421
19	58.1	8.47	5.5	8.9849	0.9096	8.0753	9.8945
20	58.8	8.40	6.2	8.9291	0.9101	8.0190	9.8392
21	59.3	10.09	6.7	8.8891	0.9105	7.9787	9.7996
22	61.4	9.27	8.8	8.7215	0.9125	7.8090	9.6340
23	70.0	8.11	17.4	8.0350	0.9260	7.1089	8.9610
24	70.0	6.83	17.4	8.0350	0.9260	7.1089	8.9610
25	70.7	7.82	18.1	7.9791	0.9275	7.0516	8.9066
26	71.3	8.73	18.7	7.9312	0.9288	7.0024	8.8600
27	72.1	7.68	19.5	7.8673	0.9307	6.9367	8.7980
28	74.4	6.36	21.8	7.6837	0.9363	6.7474	8.6200
29	74.5	8.88	21.9	7.6758	0.9366	6.7392	8.6123
30	76.7	8.50	24.1	7.5001	0.9425	6.5576	8.4426
31	*Coeff:*	*9.4240*	*-0.0798*				
32	*StDev:*	*0.1780*	*0.0105*	*CM:*	*0.0317*	*1.57E-19*	
33		*0.8901*			*1.57E-19*	*0.000111*	

Fig. 2.10.1: The data from table 1.1 in Draper &
Smith, analyzed as described in exercise 2.10.1.

Exercise 2.10.1:
   (1) The data are for *y* (pounds of steam used per month) as a function of *x*
(temperature in °F) but, for our purposes, they will be merely *y* vs. *x*. If you enter
them from the Draper & Smith book, or from the MacroSamples file, they will
not be ordered for increasing or decreasing values of *x*, but that is inconvenient
for making good graphs. Therefore first reorganize the data: move the column
with *x*-values to the left of the column for *y*, highlight the data block of both columns, and click on the sort ascending icon on the standard toolbar. Your data
should now look like those in columns A and B of Fig. 2.10.1.
   (2) Somewhere on the sheet calculate the average value of *x* (with the function
=AVERAGE) and use this to calculate in column C the corresponding values of $x-x_{av}$.

(3) Highlight the data in columns B and C, and call LS1. The covariance matrix should show (essentially) zero covariances.

(4) In column D calculate $y_{calc} = a_0 + a_1(x{-}x_{av})$ based on the just-computed values of a_0 and a_1.

(5) Plot the experimental data points and the computed line y_{calc} versus x (in column A).

(6) In column E calculate s using (2.10.3) as a function of $x{-}x_{av}$, and in columns F and G compute $y_{calc}{-}s$ and $y_{calc}{+}s$ respectively, then highlight the data in column F, copy them, and paste them into the figure. Do the same with the data in column G. Your plot should now resemble Fig. 2.10.2.

(7) Alternatively you could use the data in column E to plot error bars of length s on the line depicting y_{calc}. This has the advantages that you need not order the data as was done here under point (1), and need not calculate the data in columns F and G either, and the disadvantage that it doesn't look as good, at least to yours truly. But since tastes differ, try it, and judge for yourself.

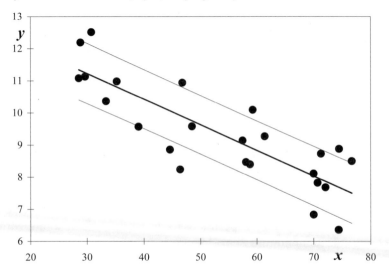

Fig. 2.10.2: The data from table 1.1 in Draper & Smith, analyzed as described in exercise 2.10.1.

Because of the term in $(x{-}x_{av})$ in the expression (2.10.3) for s, these contours are slightly curved, with a minimal vertical distance from the fitted line at $x = x_{av}$. Note that roughly 1 in 3 data points in Fig. 2.10.2 lie outside the contour lines, as one would expect for a single Gaussian distribution.

We can also draw these imprecision contours without centering, in which case the covariances are needed. Specifically, for the straight line $y = a_0 + a_1x$, instead of (2.10.3) we should then use

$$s = \sqrt{s_f^2 + v_{00} + 2v_{01}x + v_{11}x^2} \qquad (2.10.4)$$

The imprecision contours defined here pertain to the probability that a *single*, *individual* observation will fall within a given band around the least squares line. They therefore differ from those proposed by Working & Hotelling (*J. Am. Statist. Assoc.* 24 (1929) Suppl. p. 73), which pertain to the *mean* value, do not include the term s_y^2, and are therefore much more strongly curved.

If you prefer confidence contours and confidence bands instead, multiply s as defined in, e.g. (2.10.3) and (2.10.4), by $t(\alpha, N-P)$ or by $\sqrt{F(\alpha, 1, N-P)}$, where $1-\alpha$ is the confidence level, N the number of data points, and P the number of model parameters. The Student t function $t(\alpha, N-P)$ for, e.g., $\alpha = 0.05$ and $N-P = 12$ is obtained in Excel with =TINV(0.05, 12), and the corresponding Fisher function $F(\alpha, 1, N-P)$ with =FINV(0.05, 1, 12).

2.11 Extrapolating the ideal gas law

In this and the next four sections we will consider several rather common applications of fitting experimental data to a straight line, including extrapolation, calibration, standard addition, finding the intersection of two straight lines, and a standard undergraduate physico-chemical lab experiment.

Kim et al. (*J. Chem. Educ.* 78 (2001) 238) recently described an elegantly simple high school experiment to determine the absolute zero on the centigrade temperature scale. Since it involves various elements of linear least squares fitting, we will analyze those data here.

Kim et al. measured the volume V of air trapped in an inverted graduated cylinder immersed in water, as a function of temperature t, ranging between 0 and 75°C. The specific set of measurements we will consider is shown in table 2.11.

t	0.0	4.8	8.9	18.2	23.4	28.2	34.6	43.5	50.0	60.0	61.7	72.0
V	3.80	3.90	3.98	4.10	4.20	4.40	4.50	4.80	5.15	5.75	6.00	7.25

Table 2.11: The measured volumes V, in mL, as a function of temperature t, in °C.

Its analysis consists of two parts. First these air volumes V must be corrected for the volume occupied by water vapor. The corrected, dry air volumes V_d are found as $V_d = V (P_b - P_w) / P_b$ where P_w is the vapor pressure of water at temperature t, and P_b the barometric pressure. The resulting volumes V_d of dry air are a linear function of temperature t, as expected for an ideal gas, and can then be extrapolated to $V_d = 0$ to yield the absolute zero of the temperature scale.

First we must determine what type of least squares analysis to use, i.e., whether either V or t can be considered to be the dominant source of the experimental imprecisions. Analysis of the experimental data shows that the volume and temperature measurements have absolute imprecisions of about ±0.05 mL and ±0.1°C respectively. Since V and t have different dimensions, we can compare these numbers no better than we can compare apples and pears. After conversion into relative imprecisions, to about ±1% in volume and ±0.05% in absolute temperature T, it is clear that V is by far the more error-prone, and should be taken as the dependent variable. Note that the centigrade temperature scale t contains an arbitrary constant ($t = 0$ °C for $T = 273.16$ °K) that might be misleading in determining relative imprecisions. Since the data involve extrapolation to zero absolute temperature, the relative imprecision on the Kelvin scale is the one that counts here.

The vapor pressure P_w of water as a function of temperature t is a well-tabulated quantity that is readily parameterized, see section 3.20.2. These data are so much more precise than the reported volumes V that the correction does not add significantly to the experimental imprecision in V_d, even though, at 72 °C, the correction amounts to almost 35% of the measured gas volume! Figure 2.11.1 shows the raw and corrected volumes, V and V_d respectively, as a function of temperature t. The remaining question is one of linear extrapolation.

Exercise 2.11.1:

(1) Copy the data from Kim's paper or from Fig. 2.11.1. Copy the values of V_d as listed, or compute them from the values for V minus the volume occupied by water vapor as calculated in section 3.20.2. The results will be similar, though not identical, because the computation results in additional digits of V_d not shown in Fig. 2.11.1. From the point of view of the exercise, the difference is rather immaterial. Make sure that the column with V_d is directly to the left of that with t.

(2) Call LS1. In making Fig. 2.11.1, we have used the option to display the linear correlation coefficients, and have moved it and the covariance matrix to save some space.

(3) Calculate $t_0 = -a_0 / a_1$, which yields $t_0 = -278.1$ °C.

(4) Call Propagation to find the associated standard deviation. Using the covariance matrix in Propagation produces the (correct) standard deviation of 9.6 °C, so that the experiment yields $t_0 = -(278._1 \pm 9._6)$ °C. This can be compared with the accepted value of $-(273.1_6 \pm 0.0_1)$ °C. The main reasons for the large imprecision in the computed value for t_0 are the reading errors in using graduated cylinders for volume measurements, and the long extrapolation.

(5) Using the standard deviations a_0 and a_1 would have given the incorrect value of 8.7 °C for the standard deviation, incorrect because the linear correlation coefficients show that a_0 and a_1 are strongly correlated. In this particular case, that actually has only a minor effect on the resulting precision.

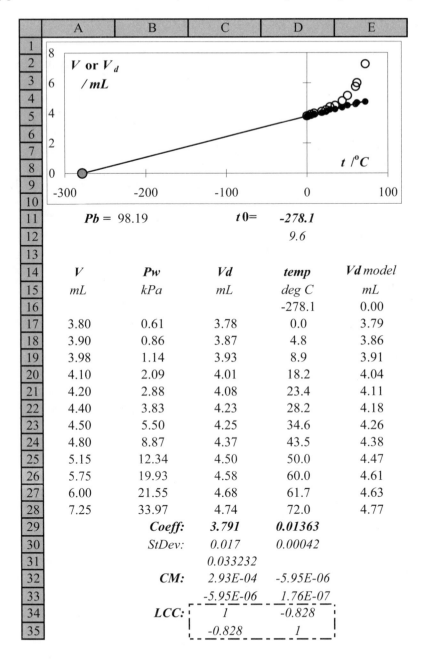

	A	B	C	D	E
11	*Pb* =	98.19		*t* 0=	*-278.1*
12					*9.6*
14	*V*	*Pw*	*Vd*	*temp*	*Vd model*
15	*mL*	*kPa*	*mL*	*deg C*	*mL*
16				-278.1	0.00
17	3.80	0.61	3.78	0.0	3.79
18	3.90	0.86	3.87	4.8	3.86
19	3.98	1.14	3.93	8.9	3.91
20	4.10	2.09	4.01	18.2	4.04
21	4.20	2.88	4.08	23.4	4.11
22	4.40	3.83	4.23	28.2	4.18
23	4.50	5.50	4.25	34.6	4.26
24	4.80	8.87	4.37	43.5	4.38
25	5.15	12.34	4.50	50.0	4.47
26	5.75	19.93	4.58	60.0	4.61
27	6.00	21.55	4.68	61.7	4.63
28	7.25	33.97	4.74	72.0	4.77
29		*Coeff:*	*3.791*	*0.01363*	
30		*StDev:*	*0.017*	*0.00042*	
31			*0.033232*		
32		*CM:*	*2.93E-04*	*-5.95E-06*	
33			*-5.95E-06*	*1.76E-07*	
34		*LCC:*	*1*	*-0.828*	
35			*-0.828*	*1*	

Fig. 2.11.1: Spreadsheet for the data of exercise 2.11.1, after use of the LS1 and Propagation macros. Open circles: V; solid circles: V_d. The sought parameter, t_0, was computed in cell E11 as = –C29/D29.

(6) Use column E to compute $V_{model} = a_0 + a_1 t$, e.g., in cell E17 use $= \$C\$29 + \$D\$29 * D17$. By adding the values for $t = t_0$ you can show the extrapolated point and curve.

(7) Verify that you get the same result by centering the temperatures (see section 2.10), in which case there is no need to consider the covariance.

(8) Using the opposite assumption, namely that the temperature is the more error-prone measurement and should be used as the dependent parameter, would have been incorrect, as shown by the data themselves. It also would have been rather impractical, because in that case correction for the water vapor pressure would have been much more complicated.

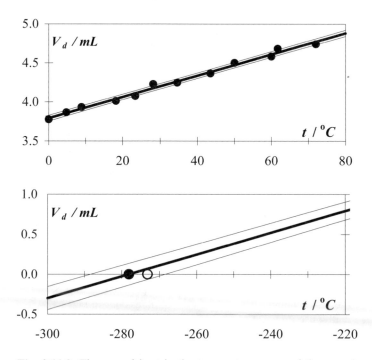

Fig. 2.11.2: The spreadsheet in the temperature range of the experimental data (top), and the same near the absolute zero on the temperature scale (bottom). Both figures are drawn to the same scale. In the bottom panel, the closed circle shows the extrapolated point, and the open circle the true value of the absolute zero temperature, –273.16°C.

(9) Finally, in order to illustrate generating imprecision contours, add three columns to the spreadsheet, one in which you compute s according to (2.10.4), one in which you calculate $V_{model} - s$, and a third in which you do the same for $V_{model} + s$. Plot these contours next to the line through the points, both in the temperature range of the observations and near absolute zero temperature. As is clear from Fig. 2.11.2, the curvature of these imprecision contours is barely noticeable, but away from $x = x_{av}$ they gradually move apart, thereby providing a good indication of the problems inherent in a long extrapolation.

2.12 Calibration curves

A standard measurement procedure is to make a calibration curve of parameter y versus x, using a set of well-characterized, known samples, and to use this to find the best estimate for the x-value x_u corresponding to a measured *un*known with observed response y_u. This is therefore a problem of *inverse interpolation*: given a set of measurements $y(x)$, find the most likely x_u for a given y_u. We will here consider the simplest calibration curves, namely those that consist of proportionalities or straight lines.

Typically, first determine the dependent variable y for a number of values of the independent variable x under well-controlled circumstances, plot these data, and determine the best proportionality $y = a_1 x$ or straight line $y = a_0 + a_1 x$ through those points. Then make a measurement of the y_u-value of an unknown, and use the calibration curve to compute the corresponding x-value, x_u. As our example we will use a synthetic data set from table 5.1 in D. Harvey, *Modern Analytical Chemistry*, McGraw-Hill 2000. As our calibration curve we will first use a proportionality, then a straight line.

Exercise 2.12.1:

(1) In a new spreadsheet enter the data shown in cells A3:B8 of Fig. 2.12.1.

(2) Use LS0 (or either LinEst or Regression) to find the slope a_1 and its standard deviation, s_1.

(3) Assume that we measure the response of an unknown three times, with the results shown in cells C3:C5. Enter those data, and in C9 and C10 compute the corresponding average and standard deviation respectively.

(4) In cell C12 compute the value of $x_u = y_u / a_1$, as done in Fig. 2.12.1.

(5) Finally, use Propagation to calculate the precision of this result, based on the input parameters (in Fig. 2.12.1 these are located in B9:C9), their standard deviations (in B10:C10), and the function (in C12).

(6) As shown in Fig. 2.12.1, we find $x_u = 0.241_8 \pm 0.001_0$.

Exercise 2.12.2:

(1) Use another part of the same spreadsheet, or open a new one, and copy the same data, see Fig. 2.12.2.

(2) With LS1 find the intercept a_0 and slope a_1, their standard deviations s_0 and s_1, and the corresponding covariance matrix.

(3) Again assume that we measure the response of an unknown three times, so that we can compute the average and standard deviation of y_u in cells D9 and D10 respectively.

(4) Compute the value of $x_u = (y_u - a_0) / a_1$, as = (D9−B9) /C9.

(5) Using the Propagation macro is now somewhat more complicated, because the precision information is now a mixed bag: for a_0 and a_1 we clearly need to use the covariance matrix (since they are correlated), whereas for y_u we only have the standard deviation. Propagation can handle either format, but not its mixture.

	A	B	C
1	*y*	*x*	*y u*
2			
3	0.00	0.0	29.32
4	12.36	0.1	29.16
5	24.83	0.2	29.51
6	35.91	0.3	
7	48.79	0.4	
8	60.42	0.5	
9	*Coeff.:*	*121.2745*	*29.33*
10	*St.Dev.:*	*0.517*	*0.18*
11	*0.383*		
12		*x u :*	*0.2418*
13			*0.0010*

C9 = AVERAGE(C3:C5)
C10 = STDEV(C3:C5)
C12 = C9/B9

Fig. 2.12.1: A spreadsheet for reading data from a calibration line through the origin, using the LS0 and Propagation macros.

(6) Without loss of information we cannot reduce the imprecision in a_0 and a_1 to just two standard deviations, but we can add the variance of y_u to the covariance matrix. Since the imprecision in y_u is clearly unrelated to that in a_0 and a_1 we simply add the corresponding variance in y_u to the *main diagonal* (from top left to bottom right) of the covariance matrix. We therefore deposit in cell D15 the square of the standard deviation stored in D10, see Fig. 2.12.2. The covariance terms in cells B15:C15 and D13:D14 are zero, and need not be entered. So here is the procedure.

(7) In cell D15 calculate the square of the standard deviation s_u of y_u (located in D10). Leave cells B15, C15, D13, and D14 blank, or fill them with zeroes.

(8) Call Propagation and, in reply to its queries, enter the locations of the input parameters (B9:D9), of the covariance matrix (B13:D15), and of the function (in C16). This will yield $x_u = 0.241_3 \pm 0.001_4$, not significantly different from the value $x_u = 0.241_8 \pm 0.001_0$ obtained earlier.

(9) Verify that, by ignoring the correlation between a_0 and a_1, and therefore entering in Propagation the standard deviations in B10:D10 instead of the covariance matrix in B13:D15, you would have found the significantly larger (but incorrect) value of 0.003_1 for the standard deviation in x_u.

Incidentally, the above result shows that there is no good reason to use a straight line rather than a proportionality in this case, because the absolute value of the intercept, $|a_0| = 0.209$ is smaller than its standard deviation $s_0 = 0.292$. The result obtained in exercise 2.12.1 is therefore preferable.

	A	B	C	D
1		*y*	*x*	*y u*
2				
3		0.00	0.0	29.32
4		12.36	0.1	29.16
5		24.83	0.2	29.51
6		35.91	0.3	
7		48.79	0.4	
8		60.42	0.5	
9	*Coeff.:*	*0.209*	*120.706*	*29.33*
10	*St.Dev.:*	*0.292*	*0.964*	*0.18*
11		*0.403*		
12	*CM:*	0.085	-0.232	
13		-0.232	0.929	
14				0.031
15				
16		*x u :*	*0.2413*	
17			*0.0014*	

D9 = AVERAGE(D3:D5)
D10 = STDEV(D3:D5)
D14 = D10^2
C16 = (D9−B9)/C9

Fig. 2.12.2: A spreadsheet for reading data from a straight-line calibration curve, using LS1 and Propagation. The box around B12:D14 shows the enlarged covariance matrix.

Alternatively, if we insist on using a straight-line calibration curve, we can center the calibration data to $y = a_0' + a_1 (x - x_{av})$ with $a_0' = a_0 + a_1 x_{av}$, and then compute any unknown x_u from $x_u = (y_u - a_0) / a_1 = (y_u - a_0' + a_1 x_{av}) / a_1$ where a_0' and a_1 are now mutually independent. This is illustrated in exercise 2.12.3 and Fig. 2.12.3, and of course yields the same result as that obtained in exercise 2.12.2. Or we can use nonlinear least squares to accomplish the same, as described in section 4.16. Again, there are several ways of doing it right – although, as usual, there are still more ways of getting it wrong, e.g., by applying standard formulas thoughtlessly.

Exercise 2.12.3:
(1) Fig. 2.12.3 illustrates a possible layout of the spreadsheet for a centered calibration line. In column C we plot $x - x_{av}$ where $x_{av} = \Sigma x / N = 0.25$.
(2) Compute the average value of y_u, then copy its *value* to cell D9. And in cell D12 calculate x_u as $x_u = (y_u - a_0' + a_1 x_{av}) / a_1$, i.e., with =(D9−B9+C9*0.25)/C9.

(3) The standard deviation in cell D13 is now obtained with Propagation using the standard deviations in B10:D10.

	A	B	C	D
1	*x*	*y*	*x - x* av	*y u*
2				
3	0.0	0.00	-0.25	29.32
4	0.1	12.36	-0.15	29.16
5	0.2	24.83	-0.05	29.51
6	0.3	35.91	0.05	
7	0.4	48.79	0.15	
8	0.5	60.42	0.25	
9	*Coeff.:*	*30.385*	*120.706*	*29.33*
10	*St.Dev.:*	*0.165*	*0.964*	*0.18*
11		*0.403*		
12			*x u :*	*0.2413*
13				*0.0014*

D9 = AVERAGE(D3:D5)
D10 = STDEV(D3:D5)
D12 = (D9-B9+C9*0.25)/C9

Fig. 2.12.3: A spreadsheet for reading data from a centered straight-line calibration curve, using LS1 and Propagation.

With only a single measurement of y_u we do not have a value for its standard deviation or variance. In that case the best we can do is to use the standard deviation s of a single y-measurement in the standard curve, as long as the methods used in making the standard curve and in determining the unknown are the same, as they should be anyway.

2.13 Standard addition

The standard addition method is sometimes used in, e.g., chemical analysis. This method presumes a proportionality between the concentration of the sample and the resulting, measured response, but does not presume a priori knowledge of that proportionality constant k. In its simplest form, a sample of known volume V_u and unknown concentration C_u yields a measured signal $y_u = k\,C_u$. One adds a known volume V_a of known concentration C_a to that sample, and measures the corresponding signal of that mixture, which should now be $y_a = k\,(C_aV_a+C_uV_u)/(V_a+V_u)$. Eliminating k then yields an explicit expression for the unknown concentration, $C_u = C_aV_ay_u/[(V_a+V_u)y_a-V_uy_u]$ in terms of measured quantities.

In a more sophisticated form, one prepares a series of solutions of

constant total volume V_t by using a fixed, known volume V_u of a sample
solution of unknown concentration C_u, adding to it known volumes V_i of
a standard solution of known concentration C_a, and adding solvent (e.g.,
water) to give all solutions to be measured the same total volume V_t. One
then measures the responses of these solutions which, for an added vol-
ume V_i, will be $y_i = k(C_u V_u + C_a V_i) / V_t$. Least squares fitting of y_i vs. V_i
then should yield a straight line of intercept $a_0 = kC_u V_u / V_t$ and slope $a_1 =
kC_a / V_t$ from which we obtain $C_u = a_0 C_a / a_1 V_u$. This calculation involves
the ratio a_0 / a_1, which are both derived from the same set of measurements and therefore, in general, are mutually dependent. By centering the
independent variable, we can make a_0 and a_1 mutually independent parameters, and thus avoid having to use the covariance.

As our experimental data we will use those reported by G. R. Bruce &
P. S. Gill, *J. Chem. Educ.* 76 (1999) 805, reproduced in table 2.13. These
data are for measurements on an aqueous sample containing an unknown
lead concentration. To a 25.0 mL sample was added 25.0 mL of an electrolyte solution (in order to give the sample sufficient conductivity for
the electrochemical experiment) and 1.0 mL of 10.0 mg/L cadmium as
an internal standard. The standard additive contained 10.0 mg/L lead,
and presumably the same electrolyte as the electrolyte solution, and apparently was added instead of an equal volume of electrolyte solution in
order to keep the final volumes of the solutions to be measured at 51 mL.
The ratio R of the peak currents due to lead and cadmium was then
measured by stripping voltammetry.

$V_i =$	0	0.5	1.0	1.5	2.0	2.5	mL
$R =$	0.86	1.11	1.44	1.74	2.04	2.33	

Table 2.13: The data of Bruce & Gill, *Anal. Chem.* 76 (1999) 805.

Exercise 2.13.1:
(1) Enter the data from table 2.13 in a spreadsheet, then calculate the average
value of V_i, and make a column for the centered volumes $V_c = V_i - V_{av}$.
(2) Treating R as the dependent variable, and V_c as the independent one, use
LS1 to compute the slope and intercept of a straight line through these points.
Display the covariance matrix, and note that the covariance terms are indeed
zero, see Fig. 2.13.1.
(3) Calculate the unknown concentration as $C_u = a_0' C_a / a_1 V_u = (a_0/a_1 - V_{av}) \times
(C_a/V_u)$ where $C_a = 10$ $\mu g/mL$ of lead, and $V_u = 51$ mL, so that C_u is in $\mu g/L$.

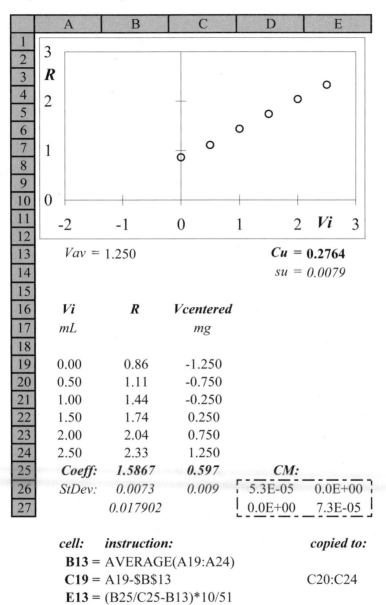

	Vi	R	Vcentered
	mL		mg
	0.00	0.86	-1.250
	0.50	1.11	-0.750
	1.00	1.44	-0.250
	1.50	1.74	0.250
	2.00	2.04	0.750
	2.50	2.33	1.250

Vav = 1.250   *Cu* = **0.2764**

su = *0.0079*

	Coeff:	*1.5867*	*0.597*	CM:	
	StDev:	*0.0073*	*0.009*	5.3E-05	0.0E+00
		0.017902		0.0E+00	7.3E-05

cell:	instruction:	copied to:
B13 = AVERAGE(A19:A24)		
C19 = A19-$B$13		C20:C24
E13 = (B25/C25-B13)*10/51		

Fig. 2.13.1: The spreadsheet analyzing the data of Bruce & Gill *by centering* them.

(4) Use Propagation (with input parameters in B25:C25, standard deviations in B26:C26, and the function in E13) to calculate the standard deviation in c_u.

(5) Copy the input data to a different location on the same spreadsheet, or start a new spreadsheet, and analyze the data from table 2.13 without centering.

(6) Note that, in this case, the covariance terms are not zero, and the covariance matrix must therefore be used as input to Propagation. Verify that, if this is not

done, a slightly different (and incorrect) answer (0.0059 instead of 0.0079) is found for s_u. Figure 2.13.2 shows the computational part of the new spreadsheet.

		R	*Vi*	*Cu* = **0.2764**	
16					
17			*mL*	*su* = *0.0079*	
18					
19		0.86	0.00		
20		1.11	0.50		
21		1.44	1.00		
22		1.74	1.50		
23		2.04	2.00		
24		2.33	2.50		
25	*Coeff:*	*0.8410*	*0.597*	*CM:*	
26	*StDev:*	*0.0130*	*0.009*	1.7E-04	-9.2E-05
27		*0.017902*		-9.2E-05	7.3E-05

cell: instruction:
D13 = (B25/C25)*10/51

Fig. 2.13.2: The spreadsheet directly analyzing the *uncentered* data of Bruce & Gill.

2.14 The intersection of two straight lines

Say that we need to determine the coordinates $x_\times$ and $y_\times$ of the inter-section $\times$ between two straight lines, $y = a_0 + a_1 x$ and $z = b_0 + b_1 x$. The value of $x_\times$ follows from setting $y_\times$ equal to $z_\times$ as $x_\times = (b_0 - a_0)/(a_1 - b_1)$, and that of $y_\times$ as $y_\times = a_0 + a_1 x_\times$.

For the imprecision in $x_\times$ we realize that the least squares fits to the two line segments are mutually independent. We can therefore generate their combined covariance matrix by merely adding the two along a shared diagonal, as shown below. Then we can use Propagate to compute the standard deviation in $x_\times$.

For the imprecision in $y_\times$ we cannot use $y_\times = a_0 + a_1 x_\times$ because the im-precision in $x_\times$ is not independent of those in a_0 and a_1. We circumvent this problem by expressing $y_\times$ explicitly in terms of the four coefficients a_0 through b_1 as $y_\times = a_0 + a_1 x_\times = (a_1 b_0 - a_0 b_1) / (a_1 - b_1)$, and then use Propagation to calculate the standard deviation in $y_\times$.

Exercise 2.14.1:
(1) Arrange a spreadsheet for the calculation of the intersection between the

two straight lines, $y = a_0 + a_1 x$ and $z = b_0 + b_1 x$, by entering labels and values for the coefficients a_0, a_1, b_0, b_1, and the noise 'amplitudes' s_{ny} and s_{nz}. Also make column headings for y, x, z, x, and for two columns of random noise, n_y and n_z. Then deposit values for x, and let the spreadsheet compute corresponding values for noisy straight lines y and z.

(2) Use LS1 to find approximate values for the coefficients a_0 and a_1 and the corresponding standard deviations and covariance matrix, then do the same for b_0, b_1, etc.

(3) Use these coefficients to let the spreadsheet compute values of $x_x = (b_0 - a_0)$ / $(a_1 - b_1)$ and $y_x = (a_1 b_0 - a_0 b_1) / (a_1 - b_1)$.

(4) If necessary, rearrange the coefficients so that a_0, a_1, b_0, and b_1 are aligned in a single, contiguous row. Arrange the two covariance matrices such that the right-bottom corner of one touches the left-top corner of the other, so that they will form a single 4×4 matrix with a shared main diagonal. Then call Propagation to find the standard deviations in x_x and y_x. Figure 2.14.1 illustrates what you might get.

In the example shown in Fig. 2.14.1 we have used a small angle between the two lines, and rather generous noise, to emphasize the difficulties one may face. We find $x_x = 8.2_9 \pm 0.6_8$ and $y_x = 8.1_2 \pm 0.7_0$ whereas, in the absence of noise (i.e., for $s_{ny} = s_{nz} = 0$), the intersection would be at the point $(10, 10)$. By using the standard deviations of a_0 through b_1 instead of the combined covariance matrix, we would have obtained a standard deviation in x_x of 1.6_8 instead of 0.6_8, and an (equally incorrect) standard deviation in y_x of 1.7_2 instead of 0.7_0.

Alternatively we can center the x-values to avoid having to deal with covariances. In this case we first compute the averages $x_{av,y}$ and $x_{av,z}$ of the two data sets $y(x)$ and $z(x)$, fit $y = a_0' + a_1 (x - x_{av,y})$ and $z = b_0' + b_1 (x - x_{av,z})$ where $a_0' = a_0 + a_1 x_{av,y}$ and $b_0' = b_0 + a_1 x_{av,z}$, and then calculate $x_x = (b_0 - a_0) / (a_1 - b_1) = (b_0' - b_1 x_{av,z} - a_0' + a_1 x_{av,y}) / (a_1 - b_1)$, and $y_x = (a_1 b_0 - a_0 b_1) / (a_1 - b_1) = [a_1 (b_0' - b_1 x_{av,z}) - (a_0' - a_1 x_{av,y}) b_1] / (a_1 - b_1)$.

The standard deviations in x_x and y_x are then calculated with Propagation, using the mutually independent standard deviations of a_0', a_1, b_0', and b_1. This alternative method is neither faster nor simpler, given the custom macros that generate and use covariance matrices. Nonetheless the exercise is useful, because it confirms the earlier result obtained with the covariance matrix.

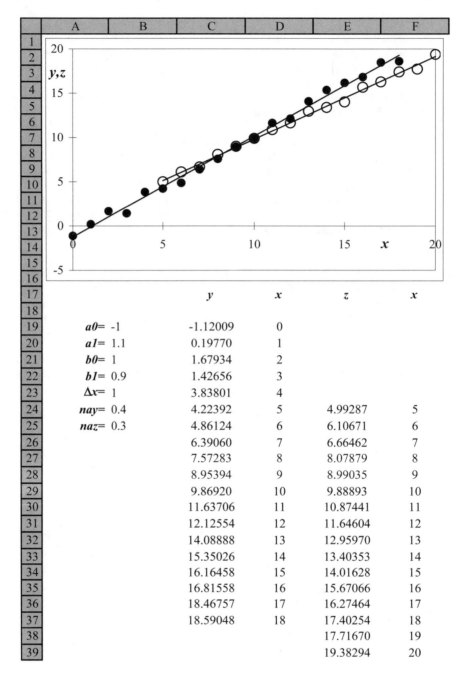

			y	x	z	x
	$a0$=	-1	-1.12009	0		
	$a1$=	1.1	0.19770	1		
	$b0$=	1	1.67934	2		
	$b1$=	0.9	1.42656	3		
	Δx=	1	3.83801	4		
	nay=	0.4	4.22392	5	4.99287	5
	naz=	0.3	4.86124	6	6.10671	6
			6.39060	7	6.66462	7
			7.57283	8	8.07879	8
			8.95394	9	8.99035	9
			9.86920	10	9.88893	10
			11.63706	11	10.87441	11
			12.12554	12	11.64604	12
			14.08888	13	12.95970	13
			15.35026	14	13.40353	14
			16.16458	15	14.01628	15
			16.81558	16	15.67066	16
			18.46757	17	16.27464	17
			18.59048	18	17.40254	18
					17.71670	19
					19.38294	20

Fig. 2.14.1: A spreadsheet to calculate the intersection between two straight lines.

	A	B	C	D	E	F
40		*Coeff:*	*-1.24887*	*1.13954*	*0.45729*	*0.93377*
41	x=	*StDev:*	*0.20945*	*0.01988*	*0.18706*	*0.01404*
42	8.2913035		*0.47462*		*0.25889*	
43	0.68269					
44		*CM:*	*4.39E-02*	*-3.56E-03*		
45	y=		*-3.56E-03*	*3.95E-04*		
46	8.1994208				*3.50E-02*	*-2.46E-03*
47	0.69553				*-2.46E-03*	*1.97E-04*

cell:	instruction:	copied to:
C19 = $B$19+$B$20*D19+$B$24*G19		C20:C37
D20 = D19+$B$23		D21:D37
E24 = $B$21+$B$22*F24+$B$25*H24		E25:E39
F25 = F24+$B$23		F26:F39
A42 = (E40-C40)/(D40-F40)		
A46 = (D40*E40-C40*F40)/(D40-F40)		
Gaussian noise in G19:H39		

Fig. 2.14.1 continued: A spreadsheet to calculate the intersection between two straight lines. The data in C40:F42 were obtained with LS1, and those in A43 and A47 with Propagation. The noise in columns G and H is shown in Fig. 2.14.2. The lines drawn through the points were calculated from the coefficients in C40:F40.

Finally we note that the computed coordinates are about three standard deviations away from their 'correct' values ($x_x = 10$, $y_x = 10$), again illustrating that standard deviations should not be considered as outer bounds, just as a first-order rate constant is not the time within which a first-order reaction runs to completion. Both are characteristic parameters, not delimiting ones.

Fig. 2.14.2 (next page): Continuation of the spreadsheet of Fig. 2.14.1 showing the centered calculation as well as the noise columns G and H. The output in H40:L42 has again been aligned for subsequent use of the Propagation macro. The covariance matrices show zeros for the covariances. The data in H40:L42 were obtained with LS1, those in G43 and G47 with Propagation.

	G	H	I	J	K	L
16			*x av,y* =	9	*x av,z* =	12.5
17	*ny*	*nz*	*y*	*x*	*z*	*x*
18						
19	-0.3002	-1.2777	-1.1201	-9		
20	0.2443	1.2765	0.1977	-8		
21	1.1984	1.7331	1.6793	-7		
22	-2.1836	-0.2342	1.4266	-6		
23	1.0950	-1.0867	3.8380	-5		
24	-0.6902	-1.6904	4.2239	-4	4.9929	-7.5
25	-1.8469	-0.9776	4.8612	-3	6.1067	-6.5
26	-0.7735	-2.1179	6.3906	-2	6.6646	-5.5
27	-0.5679	-0.4040	7.5728	-1	8.0788	-4.5
28	0.1349	-0.3655	8.9539	0	8.9904	-3.5
29	-0.3270	-0.3702	9.8692	1	9.8889	-2.5
30	1.3426	-0.0853	11.6371	2	10.8744	-1.5
31	-0.1862	-0.5132	12.1255	3	11.6460	-0.5
32	1.9722	0.8657	14.0889	4	12.9597	0.5
33	2.3757	-0.6549	15.3503	5	13.4035	1.5
34	1.6615	-1.6124	16.1646	6	14.0163	2.5
35	0.5389	0.9022	16.8156	7	15.6707	3.5
36	1.9189	-0.0845	18.4676	8	16.2746	4.5
37	-0.5238	0.6751	18.5905	9	17.4025	5.5
38	-0.3002	-1.2777			17.7167	6.5
39	0.2443	1.2765			19.3829	7.5
40			*9.0070*	*1.1395*	*12.1294*	*0.9338*
41	*x=*		*0.1089*	*0.0199*	*0.0647*	*0.0140*
42	*8.29130*		*0.4746*		*0.2589*	
43	*0.68269*					
44		*CM:*	*1.19E-02*	*0.00E+00*		
45	*y=*		*0.00E+00*	*3.95E-04*		
46	*8.199421*				*4.19E-03*	*0.00E+00*
47	*0.69553*				*0.00E+00*	*1.97E-04*

cell:	instruction:	copied to:
J16 = AVERAGE(J19:J39)		
L16 = AVERAGE(L24:L39)		
J19 = C19-$J$16		J20:J37
L24 = F24-$L$16		L25:L39
G42 = (K40-F40*L16-I40+C40*J16)/(J40-L40)		
G46 = (J40*(K40-E40*L16)-(I40-C40*J16)*L40)/(J40-L40)		

2.15 Computing the boiling point of water

A rather dramatic example of the need to consider the covariance was reported by Meyer (*J. Chem. Educ.* 74 (1997) 1339), who described the determination of the boiling point of water from measurements of its vapor pressure as a function of temperature.

	A	B	C	D
1				
2	7			
3				
4	**ln**			
5				
6	6			
7				
8				
9				
10	5			
11	0.0026		0.0028 **1/T**	0.0030
12				
13	*t*	*p*	*ln p*	*1/T*
14	$^\circ C$	*torr*		$^\circ K^{-1}$
15				
16	99.19	740.4	6.6072	0.00269
17	97.55	700.6	6.5519	0.00270
18	96.18	660.7	6.4933	0.00271
19	94.39	628.4	6.4432	0.00272
20	85.90	443.2	6.0940	0.00279
21	63.62	172.3	5.1492	0.00297
22	70.39	235.1	5.4600	0.00291
23	76.78	308.7	5.7324	0.00286
24	81.63	375.5	5.9283	0.00282
25	87.26	469.6	6.1519	0.00277
26	90.40	529.3	6.2716	0.00275
27	99.21	740.4	6.6072	0.00269
28		*Coeff:*	*20.3871*	*-5130.0*
29		*StDev:*	*0.0547*	*19.7*
30			*0.0061*	
31		*CM:*	0.0030	-1.0740
32			-1.0740	386.2979
33		*LCC:*	1	-0.9995
34			-0.9995	1

Fig. 2.15.1: The spreadsheet for fitting data to (2.15.1).

In this example the pressure p (in torr) was determined with a mercury manometer, and the temperature t (in °C) with a thermistor. A set of such data, kindly provided by Prof. Meyer, is shown in Fig. 2.15.1, which also shows its analysis. The latter consists of converting p into $\ln p$, and t into $1/T$, where $T = t + 273.16$ is the absolute temperature. The quantity $\ln p$ is used as the dependent parameter in fitting the data to the straight line

$$\ln p = a_0 + a_1/T \qquad (2.15.1)$$

From the resulting values for a_0 and a_1 the boiling point t_b of water is then computed as

$$t_b = -273.16 + a_1 / [\ln(760) - a_0] \qquad (2.15.2)$$

where we have substituted $p = 760$ torr. More complicated, for sure, than directly measuring the water or steam temperature at 760 torr, but standard fare in undergraduate physical chemistry labs because it demonstrates adherence to the Clausius-Clapeyron equation.

We use (2.15.2) to compute t_b, and estimate the corresponding precision with the custom macro Propagation, using the covariance matrix as input, and so obtain $t_b = 99.83 \pm 0.07$ °C, which is within 3 standard deviations of the accepted value of 100 °C. However, had we instead used the standard deviations s_0 and s_1 (shown in Fig. 2.15.1 in cells C29 and D29 respectively) for the computation of the standard deviation in t_b, the result would have been $t_b = 99.83 \pm 2.06$ °C, a considerably larger (and, more importantly, incorrect) imprecision estimate. In this example, the linear correlation coefficient between a_0 and a_1 is -0.9995.

The above computation would be improved by using weighting, see section 3.20.1. Introduction of the appropriate weighting factors $w = p^2$ indeed modifies the specific results to $a_0 = 20.37$, $a_1 = -5125$, and $t_b = 99.84 \pm 0.06$ °C. And if this were 'malculated' without the covariance, we would get $t_b = 99.84 \pm 3.43$ °C, more than 50 times too large, because the linear correlation coefficient between a_0 and a_1 is now -0.9998.

Clearly, weighting does not change our main conclusion regarding the need to use the covariance, but merely accentuates it.

2.16 Phantom relations

In using least squares it is tacitly assumed that the input data represent *independent* measurements. If that is not the case, quite misleading results may be obtained, as illustrated by the following problem (#9 on p.

383) of K. Connors, *Chemical Kinetics, the Study of Reaction Rates in Solution* (VCH 1990):

> "From the last four digits from the office telephone numbers of the faculty in your department, systematically construct pairs of "rate constants" as two-digit numbers times 10^{-5} s^{-1} at temperatures 300 K and 315 K (obviously the larger rate constant of each pair to be associated with the higher temperature). Make a two-point Arrhenius plot for each faculty member, evaluating $\Delta H^{\ddagger}$ and $\Delta S^{\ddagger}$. Examine the plot of $\Delta H^{\ddagger}$ against $\Delta S^{\ddagger}$ for evidence of an isokinetic relationship."

Essentially, the reader is asked to take two arbitrary two-digit y-values y_1 and y_2, assign them to pre-selected x-values x_1 and x_2 respectively, compute the resulting slope a_1 and intercept a_0, repeat this for a number of arbitrary input parameter pairs y (for the same x-values), and then plot the resulting a_1-values versus a_0, or vice versa. The actual procedure is somewhat less transparent, since it also involves sorting the input data, a logarithmic transformation, and giving the slopes and intercepts thermodynamic names, all steps that tend to obscure the true nature of the problem. Moreover, the above assignment uses only positive input numbers. Below we will simply take pairs of random two-digit integer values for y, associate them with two fixed x-values such as $x_1 = 300$ and $x_2 = 320$, compute the resulting slopes and intercepts, and then plot these against each other.

Exercise 2.16.1:

(1) In cells B2 and C2 place the labels y1 and y2 respectively. Do the same in cells E2:F2, and in cells H2:I2 deposit the labels a0 and a1 respectively.

(2) In cells B4 and C4 deposit the instruction =INT(200*(RAND()-0.5)), which will generate random two-digit integers between -100 and $+100$. Copy these instructions down to row 23.

(3) The numbers in B4:C23 will change every time you change something on the spreadsheet. In order to have a fixed set of random numbers, highlight B4:C23, copy it with Ctrl⌣c, highlight cell E4, and use Edit ⇒ Paste Special ⇒ Values to copy the *values* of y_1 and y_2 so obtained. After that, use the data in block E4:F23 as your random input data, while ignoring those in B4:C23 that keep changing while you work the spreadsheet.

(4) Based on the data in E4:F23, compute in column H the slope of each pair of data points (x_1, y_1), (x_2, y_2) as $(y_2-y_1)/(x_2-x_1)$, and in column I the corresponding intercepts as $(x_2 y_1 - x_1 y_2)/(x_2-x_1)$.

(5) Make a plot of a_0 (in column H) versus a_1 (in column I), or vice versa, see Fig. 2.16.1.

The data in Fig. 2.16.1 seem to fall on or near a straight line, for which Trendline yields the formula $y = -311.18\,x - 0.8877$, with $R^2 = 0.9983$. Is this what you would have expected for having used random input numbers for y? If not, what happened?

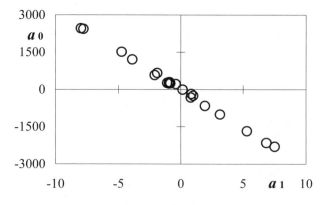

Fig. 2.16.1: An example of a phantom line
you might find with $x_1 = 300$ and $x_2 = 320$.

Because each pair of input numbers y of this graph is completely determined by the calculated slope and intercept for given input values of x,
the graph uses highly *correlated* pairs of input data. We already encountered the formula for that correlation, (2.10.1). The sign of (2.10.1) explains the negative correlation, and the effect is the more pronounced the
larger is Σx, i.e., the more eccentric are the x-values used. Plotting such
slopes and intercepts against each other will then lead to a convincingly
linear but physically meaningless near-linear relationship, approximating
the proportionality $y = -x_{av} x$. Instead, you are merely verifying the correlation between slope and intercept, see (2.10.1), as is perhaps more evi-
dent after we rewrite $y = -x_{av} x$ using more appropriate symbols as $a_0 = -$
$x_{av} a_1$.

This is the origin of the isokinetic relationship (J. E. Leffler, *J. Org.
Chem.* 20 (1955) 1202), and illustrates what the covariance can do for
you if you don't watch it. An extensive discussion of this problem, as
well as a suggested solution, was given by Krug et al., *J. Phys. Chem.* 80
(1976) 2335, 2341. For an interesting (and only seemingly alternative)
explanation of this phantom relationship see G. C. McBane, *J. Chem.
Educ.* 75 (1998) 919.

Exercise 2.16.1 (continued):
     (6) Use the same y-values collected in columns H and I, but now analyze them
for a pair of x-values *centered* around the average $x_{av} = 310$, so that $x_1 = -10$ and
$x_2 = +10$. Does this support the above explanation?

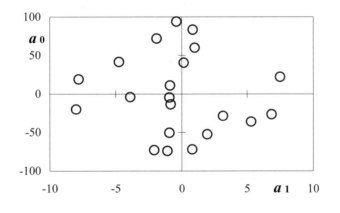

Fig. 2.16.2: The same *y*-values as in Fig. 2.16.1 analyzed with $x_1 = -10$ and $x_2 = +10$.

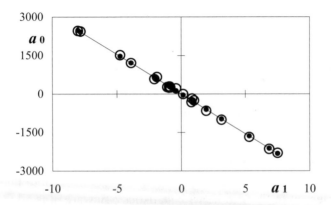

Fig. 2.16.3: The data from Fig. 2.16.1 (open circles) and, for comparison, those computed as $a_0 = -x_{av} a_1$ (filled circles connected by a thin line).

Given that the input data were random, which are the parameters that determine the 'line' in Fig. 2.16.1? There is no significant intercept, just a slope, and the latter is simply $-(\Sigma x)/N$, i.e., minus the average value of *x*. In the above example we have $-(\Sigma x)/N = -(300+320)/2 = -310$, so that we would expect $y = -310\,x$, which compares well with the result of Trendline, $y = -311.18\,x - 0.8877$, as illustrated in Fig. 2.16.3. Indeed, as already noticed by Leffler, in many instances the reported slopes of isokinetic plots were close (in absolute value) to the average temperatures of the data sets considered. In such cases, the isokinetic effect is nothing more than an artifact of incorrectly applied statistics.

2.17 Summary

Typical experimental data are occasional samples of some underlying continuous feature, corrupted by scatter. Linear least squares methods often allow the experimenter to recover the underlying trend from the sporadic, noisy data. Note that this underlying, noise-free trend can contain systematic errors, and that the standard deviations, variances and covariances generated by least squares methods only deal with precision, not with accuracy.

Because least squares methods have become so easy to apply, they have become ubiquitous in many fields of science and technology. Keep in mind, however, that the method and the results obtained with it presume that the noise is random and can be described adequately by a single Gaussian distribution. We seldom have (or take) the time to verify those assumptions, and therefore should take the results with the proverbial grain of salt.

In this chapter we have focused our attention on fitting data to a straight line, because this problem is so common in applied science. It is often assumed that the parameters obtained by least squares fitting to a straight line are mutually independent, but this is usually not the case. Consequently, quite misleading results may be obtained, as illustrated in section 2.16, where the culprit was the (easily overlooked) covariance of those input data. Working backwards, it shows how to convert perfectly random data from the 'scatter' plot of Fig. 2.16.2 into the convincingly linear relationship of Fig. 2.16.1 (with an R^2 factor of more than 0.998), an object lesson in 'how to lie with statistics'. Beware, it is all too easy to fool oneself! With appropriate software, getting the correct result is not particularly difficult, but attention must be paid.

Fitting data to a proportionality generates only one coefficient, the slope, and therefore seldom involves problems of covariance. Fitting a straight line yields two adjustable parameters, a_0 and a_1, which in general will be mutually dependent. The macro LS provides the corresponding covariance (and, as we will see in chapter 3, does the same for polynomial and multivariate fits as well) and the macro Propagation can subsequently take their covariance(s) into account. Centering will avoid this problem, because it leads to mutually independent coefficients a_0 and a_1, i.e., it renders their covariance zero. In section 3.11 we will encounter the equivalent of centering for polynomial and multivariate fits.

The problem of data analysis starts with data acquisition. Then, if one does not want to hold on to the original data, the covariance v_{01} should be recorded and preserved, or the data analyzed in their centered form, and the result stored together with the value(s) of x_{av}. If only the fitting parameters a_0 and a_1 are available, together with their standard deviations s_0 and s_1, one will in general *not* be able to compute the correct precision of subsequently derived results, because there is no way to determine, retroactively, the value of the covariance v_{01}. Unfortunately, such careless and misleading use of least squares occurs far more often than one would hope. Of course, one should not get carried away with this: imprecision estimates are just that: *estimates*. Still, if time and effort are spent on making those estimates, they might as well be done correctly.

In chapter 3 we will extend the least squares analysis to polynomials and multivariate functions. We will see that we can further broaden the application of least squares methods by transforming data that do not fit that mold into a polynomial form. That still leaves many functions out; for those, chapter 4 will describe nonlinear least squares.

2.18 For further reading

Excellent, highly readable starting points for linear least squares methods are *An Introduction to Error Analysis* by J. R. Taylor (University Science Books, 1982, 1997), and the classic *Data Reduction and Error Analysis for the Physical Sciences* by P. R. Bevington (McGraw-Hill 1969, 1992). These books (and many others) clearly explain the underlying assumptions, and show many examples of practical applications. For the lighter side, take a look at L. Gonick & L. Smith, *The Cartoon Guide to Statistics* (Harper Perennial, 1994), or its predecessor, D. Hill, *How to Lie with Statistics* (Norton 1982).

Chapter 3

Further linear least squares

In this chapter we apply least squares methods to polynomials in the independent parameter x, and to multi-parameter functions. We also describe weighted least squares, and show how least squares methods can be simplified when the x-values are spaced equidistantly.

3.1 Fitting data to a polynomial

Excel makes it easy to extend the procedures discussed in chapter 2 to fitting data to a power series of the general form $y = a_0 + a_1x + a_2x^2 + a_3x^3 + a_4x^4 + \ldots + a_mx^m = \Sigma\, a_j\, x^j$, where $j = 0$ (1) m, again assuming that y contains all the experimental uncertainties, and that these follow a single Gaussian distribution. For either LinEst, Regression, LS0, or LS1, we merely have to arrange m adjacent, contiguous columns, for $x, x^2, x^3, \ldots,$ x^m instead of one for x, so that they can be entered as a block. For LS0 or LS1, the first two columns should still contain the values of y_i and x_i, but the highlighted block should now include one or more adjacent columns for, say, x_i^2, x_i^3, etc. There is neither a requirement that consecutive orders of x be used (you need not include columns for powers you do not need), nor that they be in any particular order (although that is usually easier to work with). LS1 fits data to a general polynomial, while LS0 sets the value of a_0 equal to zero, thereby forcing the fitted curve to go through the origin. With LinEst(*y-range, x-range, type, statistics*) the equivalent choice is made by setting *type* to 0 or false in order to force a_0 to zero; with Regression the same is achieved by activating Constant is Zero in the dialog box.

With Trendline you do not need to make any new columns for higher orders of x, but merely select the power series and specify its order (between 2 and 6). In order to display its numerical results, click on the Options tab, then select Display equation on chart. Trendline yields the individual coefficients a_i, but neither the corresponding standard deviations s_i nor the standard deviation s_f of the fit. It can only provide the rather uninformative R^2, the square of the multiple correlation coefficient, with

Options, Display R-squared value on chart. A convenient Forecast feature of Trendline Options allows you to extrapolate the curve on the basis of the calculated parameters, but without any indications of the resulting uncertainties.

Sections 3.2 through 3.4 illustrate fitting data to a polynomial.

3.2 Fitting data to a parabola

Exercise 3.2.1:

(1) Start a new spreadsheet, make up a data set from a quadratic expression plus some noise, and fit it with each of the above methods. For LinEst, Regression, or LS use columns for y, x, and x^2 in this order. For Trendline the data placement doesn't matter, as long as the data are plotted in a graph.

(2) Figure 3.2.1 shows an example, in which we have used the instruction =LINEST(A15:A27,B15:C27,1,1) to find the coefficients a_i used in computing $y_{calc} = a_0 + a_0x + a_0x^2$ in column D, which is then plotted as a line through the points. (The second range is now a block, for both x and x^2. Since there are three coefficients to be calculated, use three columns for the result, and enter the array instruction with Ctrl⌣Shift⌣Enter.).

(3) The LinEst output is

-0.793484	9.0412407	-11.9781
0.051121	0.7355022	2.23884
0.974976	2.2873408	#N/A
194.8118	10	#N/A
2038.483	52.319277	#N/A

(4) These results in the top two lines, $a_0 = -12._0 \pm 2._2$, $a_1 = 9.0_4 \pm 0.7_4$, and $a_2 = -0.79_3 \pm 0.05_1$, can be compared with the values used in generating the synthetic data, $a_0 = -10$, $a_1 = 8$, and $a_2 = -0.7$. While the fitted quadratic is noise-free, the presence of noise in the parent data results in rather uncertain coefficients: the relative standard deviation $|s_0/a_0|$ is more than 18%.

(5) For a_1 and a_2 the correct results lie beyond one standard deviation. As we already saw in chapter 2, standard deviations should not be interpreted as indicating the likely range of deviations; for that purpose, confidence intervals (which depend on the standard deviation s, the number N of data points used, and a selected probability, such as 95% or 99%) are more appropriate.

(6) The coefficients a_j obtained from a single least squares operation are of course mutually dependent. If they are to be used in subsequent computations, you will need the corresponding covariance matrix, which can be displayed by the custom macros LS.

(7) Save the data for use in exercise 3.11.1.

For polynomials of second and higher order, centering no longer suffices, and orthogonal polynomials are needed to make the covariance(s) zero. We will discuss a particular set of such orthogonal polynomials in section 3.11, but (except for equidistant data) it is often easier to use LS0 or LS1 to find a straightforward polynomial fit and, if the results require further mathematical manipulation, to use the covariance matrix with Propagation to compute the precision of the resulting answers.

	A	B	C	D	E			N	
1									
2									
3									
4									
5									
6									
7									
8									
9									
10									
11	a0 = -10			a2 = -0.7					
12	a1 = 8			na = 2					
13									
14	*y*	*x*	*xx*	*ycalc*				*noise*	
15	-3.300	1	1	-3.7303				-0.3002	
16	0.645	2	4	2.93045				-1.2777	
17	8.189	3	9	8.00427				0.24426	
18	13.353	4	16	11.4911				1.27647	
19	14.897	5	25	13.391				1.19835	
20	16.266	6	36	13.7039				1.73313	
21	7.333	7	49	12.4299				-2.1836	
22	8.732	8	64	9.56888				-0.2342	
23	7.490	9	81	5.1209				1.09502	
24	-2.173	10	100	-0.914				-1.0867	
25	-8.080	11	121	-8.536				-0.6902	
26	-18.181	12	144	-17.745				-1.6904	
27	-27.994	13	169	-28.541				-1.8469	

Fig. 3.2.1: A spreadsheet to fit noisy data to a parabola. Cell A15 contains the instruction =$B$11+$B$12*B15+$D$11*C15+$D$12*N15, and is copied to A16:A27, while the instruction =B15^2 in cell C15 is copied to C16:C27. Cells N15:N27 contain Gaussian noise with zero mean and unit standard deviation.

3.3 The iodine vapor spectrum

As our next example we consider the visible absorption spectrum of iodine vapor, I_2, a homonuclear diatomic molecule. Because of its symmetry, I_2 has no dipole moment in any of its vibrational or rotational modes. It therefore does not absorb light in the infrared and microwave regions of the spectrum, where one usually observes vibrational and rotational transitions respectively. In the visible part of the spectrum, however, I_2 can be excited from its electronic ground state to an (at room temperature essentially unoccupied) electronically excited state.

In both the ground state (here indicated with °) and the electronically excited state (labeled with '), the molecules exist in discrete vibrational and rotational states, defined by the quantum numbers v and J respectively. The electronic transition is associated with a change in dipole moment, and can therefore lead to light absorption. There are no quantum-mechanical restrictions (selection rules) that govern the changes in vibrational levels during this electronic transition. When, as in the experiments used here, the vapor phase absorption spectrum is observed with relatively low resolution ($\Delta\lambda \approx 0.5$ nm), the rotational states are not resolved. One can observe several series of spectral absorption lines, each originating from a different vibrational level (such as $v° = 0, 1, 2$, etc.) in the electronic ground state, and leading to various vibrational levels (with their quantum numbers v') in the electronically excited state. The data we will analyze here reflect transitions between the vibrational and electronic ground state ($v° = 0$) and different vibrational states (with vibrational quantum numbers v') in the electronically excited state.

As our experimental data we will use a set of measurements discussed in C. J. Pursell & L. Doezema, *J. Chem. Educ.* 76 (1999) 839; the actual data used were kindly provided by Dr. Pursell and are listed in Fig. 3.3.1. This same data set has also been reproduced by Ogren, Davis & Guy, *J. Chem. Educ.* 78 (2001) 827, table 1.

In the simplest model, that of the harmonic oscillator, the energy $E(v)$ of a particular vibrational state can be described as $E(v)/hc = \overline{\omega_e}\,(v+\frac{1}{2})$, where h is Planck's constant, c the vacuum speed of light, and $\overline{\omega_e}$ the fundamental vibrational 'frequency' in units of wavenumbers (cm^{-1}), as indicated by the superscripted bar. The latter can be expressed in terms of the force constant k and the reduced mass μ (here half the atomic mass of iodine) as $\overline{\omega_e} = [1/(2\pi c)]\sqrt{k/\mu}$. A more realistic description includes a second-order term, as in

$$E(v)/hc = \overline{\omega_e}(v+1/2) - \overline{\omega_e x_e}(v+1/2)^2 \tag{3.3.1}$$

where $\overline{\omega_e x_e}$ is called the anharmonicity constant.

	A	B	C	D	E
1	vibrational	wave-	v+1/2	(v+1/2)^2	wave-
2	quantum	number			number
3	number	(obs)			(calc)
4					
5	18	17702	18.5	342.25	17703
6	19	17797	19.5	380.25	17797
7	20	17889	20.5	420.25	17888
8	21	17979	21.5	462.25	17978
9	22	18064	22.5	506.25	18065
10	23	18149	23.5	552.25	18150
11	24	18235	24.5	600.25	18234
12	25	18318	25.5	650.25	18315
13	26	18396	26.5	702.25	18394
14	27	18471	27.5	756.25	18471
15	28	18546	28.5	812.25	18546
16	29	18618	29.5	870.25	18619
17	30	18688	30.5	930.25	18691
18	31	18755	31.5	992.25	18759
19	32	18825	32.5	1056.25	18826
20	33	18889	33.5	1122.25	18891
21	34	18954	34.5	1190.25	18954
22	35	19019	35.5	1260.25	19015
23	36	19077	36.5	1332.25	19074
24	37	19131	37.5	1406.25	19130
25	38	19186	38.5	1482.25	19185
26	39	19238	39.5	1560.25	19238
27	40	19286	40.5	1640.25	19288
28	41	19339	41.5	1722.25	19337
29	42	19384	42.5	1806.25	19383
30	43	19429	43.5	1892.25	19428
31	44	19467	44.5	1980.25	19470
32	45	19512	45.5	2070.25	19510
33	46	19546	46.5	2162.25	19549
34	47	19585	47.5	2256.25	19585
35	Coeff.:	*15603.7*	*132.42*	*-1.0232*	
36	St.Dev.:	*6.0*	*0.38*	*0.0057*	
37		*2.092*			
38			35.740	-2.243	0.033
39		*CM:*	-2.243	0.144	-0.002
40			0.033	-0.002	0.000
41			1	-0.990	0.968
42		*LCC:*	-0.990	1	-0.993
43			0.968	-0.993	1

Fig. 3.3.1: The spectroscopic data for I_2 vapor from Pursell & Doezema.

The optically observable transition energy $\bar{v}$ from the vibrational and electronic ground state $v° = 0$ to the electronically excited state at various vibrational quantum states v' is then given by

$$\bar{v} = [E(v') - E(v°)]/hc = E_{el} + \overline{\omega_e}'(v'+1/2)$$
$$- \overline{\omega_e°}/2 - \overline{\omega_e'x_e'}(v'+1/2)^2 + \overline{\omega_e°x_e°}/4 \qquad (3.3.2)$$

which is a quadratic function of $(v'+1/2)$, as is more readily seen after rewriting it as

$$\bar{v} = \left(E_{el} - \overline{\omega_e°}/2 + \overline{\omega_e°x_e°}/4\right) + \overline{\omega_e}'(v'+1/2) - \overline{\omega_e'x_e'}(v'+1/2)^2 \qquad (3.3.3)$$

where E_{el} is the (theoretical) energy difference between the minima for the electronic ground state and excited state in the diagrams of potential energy vs. bond length.

Exercise 3.3.1:

(1) In a new spreadsheet, enter the vibrational quantum numbers v' and the corresponding wavenumbers in columns A and B respectively.

(2) In column C calculate $v'+\frac{1}{2}$, and in column D the quantity $(v'+\frac{1}{2})^2$.

(3) Highlight the data in columns B through D, call LS1, and find the corresponding values for $\left(E_{el} - \overline{\omega_e°}/2 + \overline{\omega_e°x_e°}/4\right)$, $\overline{\omega_e}'$, and $\overline{\omega_e'x_e'}$, and the associated uncertainty estimates. Figures 3.3.1 and 3.3.2 illustrate how well a quadratic fits these experimental data.

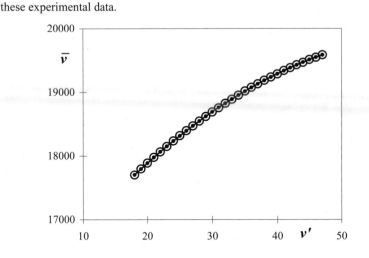

Fig. 3.3.2: A quadratic fit of the observed spectral lines, in wavenumbers, as a function of the assigned vibrational quantum numbers v' of the electronically excited state, for the iodine vapor spectral data of Pursell & Doezema, *J. Chem. Educ.* 76 (1999) 839. Open circles: experimental data; line and small solid points: fitted data.

(4) Compute the quantity $\overline{x_e}'$ from $\overline{\omega_e}'$ and $\overline{\omega_e'x_e}'$, using the covariance matrix and the Propagation macro. When the data are organized as in Fig. 3.3.1 and $\overline{x_e}'$ is computed in cell B41 as $\overline{\omega_e x_e}\,/\,\overline{\omega_e}$ or = –D35/C35, for Propagation specify the location of the input parameters as B35:D35, that of the covariance matrix as C38:E40, and the address of the function as B41. This will yield $\overline{x_e}'$ = 0.007727 ± 0.000021 cm^{-1}, whereas specifying the standard deviations in B36:D36 would have led to 0.007727 ± 0.000048 cm^{-1} instead, i.e., to a standard deviation more than twice as large. This should not be surprising, since $\overline{\omega_e}'$ and $\overline{\omega_e'x_e}'$ are clearly mutually dependent quantities. This is also clear from the linear correlation coefficients shown in Fig. 3.3.1, which are close to ±1.

(5) Apart from the calculation of the standard deviation of $\overline{x_e}'$ you could also have obtained the same results with LinEst or Regression. However, when such numbers are used for further calculations, as illustrated by Pursell & Doezema and also by, e.g., Long et al., *J. Chem. Educ.* 76 (1999) 841, the covariance matrix may again have to be taken into account.

3.4 The intersection of two parabolas

Say that we need to determine the coordinates of an intersection of two parabolas, or of curves that, in the neighborhood of their intersection, can be approximated as parabolas. We fit the first curve (or curve fragment) to $y = a_0 + a_1 x + a_2 x^2$, and the second to $z = b_0 + b_1 x + b_2 x^2$, in order to determine the coefficients a_i and b_i. We then compute the x-value at their intersection by setting y equal to z, so that $(a_2–b_2)\,x^2 + (a_1–b_1)\,x + (a_0–b_0) = 0$ or $x_x = \{-(a_1–b_1) \pm \sqrt{[(a_1–b_1)^2 - 4(a_0–b_0)\,(a_2–b_2)]}\}\,/\,\{2(a_2–b_2)\}$, where the choice of sign before the square root depends on the numerical values used. The corresponding values y_x and z_x then follow from substitution of x_x into $y = a_0 + a_1 x + a_2 x^2$ or $z = b_0 + b_1 x + b_2 x^2$.

Exercise 3.4.1:

(1) In cells A1:A3 of a new spreadsheet enter labels for a_0 through a_2, and in cells A4:A6 labels for b_0 through b_2. In cells B1:B6 deposit their numerical values.

(2) In cells A10:H10 place column headings for y_n, x, xx (or x^2), z_n, x, xx, n_y, and n_z respectively, in cells E7 and E8 place labels for the noise standard deviations S_{ny} and S_{nz}, and in cells F7 and F8 deposit their numerical values.

(3) In B12 and E12 start duplicate columns with x-values, and do the same in C12 and F12 for x^2.

(4) In columns G and H, starting from row 12 down, deposit Gaussian ('normal') noise of zero mean and unit standard deviation.

(5) In A12 compute y_n as =$B$1+$B$2*$B12+$B$3*$C12+$F$7*G12, and copy this down. Likewise, starting with cell D12, compute z_n as =$B$4+$B$5*$E12+$B$6*$F12+$F$8*H12. Extend all columns down to the same row as the x-values in columns B and E.

(6) Plot the resulting parabolas, and adjust the parameters in B1:B6 to yield intersecting curves.

(7) Call LS1 and fit the data in columns A, B, and C. Place the covariance matrix in E1:G3. Using Edit $\Rightarrow$ Paste Special $\Rightarrow$ Transpose, copy the resulting coefficients a_0 through a_2 to cells C1:C3, and their standard deviations to D1:D3.

(8) Now call LS1 for the data in columns D through F, and place the covariance matrix in (no, this is no misprint) H4:J6. Again using Edit $\Rightarrow$ Paste Special $\Rightarrow$ Transpose, copy the resulting coefficients b_0 through b_2 to C4:C6. Copy the corresponding standard deviations to D4:D6.

(9) For the coordinates of the intersection, compute the value of x_x in cell C7 from the formula given above, and in cell C9 calculate the associated value of y_x = z_x as $z_x = b_0 + b_1 x_x + b_2 x_x^2$.

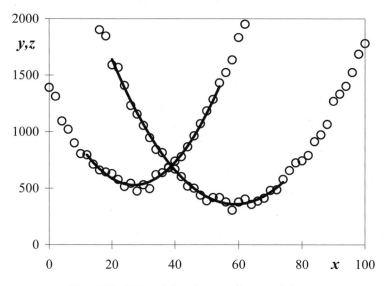

Fig. 3.4.1: Determining the coordinates of the intersection of two parabolas. The solid lines show the least squares parabolas used in the computation.

So far this is not much different from exercise 3.2.1. What is new here is the estimate of the resulting standard deviations in x_x and y_x. The value of x_x depends on six parameters, a_0 through a_2 and b_0 through b_2, of which the a_j are a mutually dependent set, as are the b_j. As long as the two parabolas are mutually independent, we can handle this by combining the covariance matrices of their fits, i.e., by placing the two matrices such that their main diagonal is joined, just as we did in exercise 2.14.1. This is why we put the second matrix in H4:J6, because the first was located in E1:G3. The resulting 6×6 matrix E1:J6, with the six variances on its main diagonal, can then serve as the input for the custom macro Propagation.

	A	B	C	D
1	*a0=*	1400	1397	*35*
2	*a1=*	-65	-64.5	*2.1*
3	*a2=*	1.2	1.195	*0.029*
4	*b0=*	3300	3332	*81*
5	*b1=*	-100	-102.4	*4.3*
6	*b2=*	0.85	0.883	*0.053*
7		*x inters =*	38.68	*0.21*
8		*z inters =*	691.49	*6.44*

Fig. 3.4.2: The left top corner of the spreadsheet of exercise 3.4.1.

	E	F	G	H	I	J
1	1228.2	-72.26	0.9326			
2	-72.26	4.586	-0.0617			
3	0.9326	-0.0617	0.00086			
4				6507.02	-339.8	4.08377
5				-339.8	18.311	-0.2248
6				4.08377	-0.2248	0.00281
7	*sn y =*	30				
8	*sn z =*	30				

Fig. 3.4.3: The section of the spreadsheet
showing the combined covariance matrix.

Exercise 3.4.1 (continued):

(10) Call Propagation to calculate the standard deviation in x_x. For input parameters use the data in C1:C6, for their uncertainties the combined covariance matrix in E1:J6, and for the function cell C7.

(11) If we use the values in D1:D6 instead of those in E1:J6 as the uncertainty estimates, we will obtain a quite different (but incorrect) result, just as we saw earlier in sections 2.12 and 2.14. For the data in Fig. 3.4.1 the resulting standard deviation in x_x is then found as 3.61, whereas the correct answer is only 0.21.

For the standard deviation of y_x the procedure is similar, except that we must first convert the expression for y_x explicitly in terms of the coefficients a_0 through a_2 and b_0 through b_2, e.g. as $y_x = a_0 + a_1 \{-(a_1-b_1) \pm \sqrt{[(a_1-b_1)^2 - 4(a_0-b_0)(a_2-b_2)]}\} / \{2(a_2-b_2)\} + a_2 \{-(a_1-b_1) \pm \sqrt{[(a_1-b_1)^2 - 4(a_0-b_0)(a_2-b_2)]}\} / \{2(a_2-b_2)\}^2$.

Exercise 3.4.1 (continued):

(12) In cell C8 calculate y_x as just indicated, then use Propagation to find its standard deviation.

(13) Again check the difference between using the covariance matrix or merely the individual standard deviations of the coefficients. In our numerical example we find $y_x = 691.5 \pm 6.4$ using the covariance matrix, and $y_x = 691.5 \pm 105.7$ when the covariances are ignored.

3.5 Multiparameter fitting

We can also use LinEst, Regression, and LS (but *not* Trendline) to fit data as a linear function of a variety of parameters, say x, x^3, $\sqrt{z}$ and log t, as long as the experimental uncertainties are all concentrated in y, and can be assumed to follow a single Gaussian distribution. Just make columns for the parameters to which y is to be fitted. The various parameters need not be independent; in fact, one can consider fitting to a polynomial as a special case of a multiparameter (or multivariate) fit. LinEst, Regression, and LS all will accept multiparameter fits in the same way as polynomial ones. Trendline cannot handle them since the graph has only one horizontal axis, and it therefore has no way to determine what the independent parameters might be. As in all applications of least squares methods, the number of adjustable parameters should preferably be much smaller than the number of data points. Sections 3.6 and 3.7 will illustrate such multiparameter data fitting.

3.6 The infrared spectrum of $H^{35}Cl$

As our first example we will fit a set of frequencies of the infrared absorption spectrum of $H^{35}Cl$ vapor between 2500 and 3100 cm^{-1} (for the fundamental) and between 5400 and about 5800 cm^{-1} (for the first harmonic or overtone) as published by R. W. Schwenz & W. F. Polik in *J. Chem. Educ.* 76 (1999) 1302. The actual spectrum of HCl vapor consists of a set of doublets, due to the presence of about 24.5% naturally occurring ^{37}Cl; the corresponding lines are easily recognized by their lower intensities. These data can be fitted at two levels: that of the usual first-order approximations of a rigid rotor and a harmonic oscillator, and that of a more complete theory. We will here use the second approach since there is no good reason to oversimplify the mathematics when the spreadsheet can just as easily apply the more complete theoretical model.

Rotational-vibrational transitions are usually observable in the infrared part of the spectrum. The corresponding frequencies $E(v,J)/hc$ of a heteronuclear diatomic molecule such as HCl, which has a permanent dipole moment, are given by

$$E(v,J)/hc = \overline{\omega}_e(v+1/2) + B_e J(J+1) - \overline{\omega_e x_e}(v+1/2)^2$$

$$-D_e J^2 (J+1)^2 - \alpha_e (v+1/2) J(J+1) \qquad (3.6.1)$$

where $E(v, J)$ is the energy, v is the vibrational quantum number, J the rotational quantum number, h is Planck's constant, and c the speed of light in vacuum. The harmonic vibrational frequency $\overline{\omega_e}$ can again be expressed in terms of the force constant k and the reduced mass $\mu = 1 \,/\, (1/m_1 + 1/m_2)$ as $\overline{\omega_e} = (1/2\pi c)\sqrt{k/\mu}$, and the rotational constant $\overline{B_e}$ as $\overline{B_e} = h/8\pi^2 c I_e$ where $I_e = \mu r^2$ is the moment of inertia, r the bond distance, and m_1 and m_2 are the atomic mass of H and ^{35}Cl respectively. Finally, $\overline{\omega_e x_e}$ is the anharmonicity constant, and $\overline{D_e}$ the centrifugal distortion constant, while $\overline{\alpha_e}$ describes rotational-vibrational interactions. As in section 3.3, the bar indicates that the quantities involved are energies expressed in wavenumbers, so that, e.g., $\overline{\omega_e}$ is not misinterpreted as an angular frequency.

The lines in the absorption spectrum correspond to transitions between these energy states, i.e., to differences between the energy levels given by (3.6.1). In this case the observation does not involve an electronic transition (as in the preceding example of iodine vapor), and light absorption is now restricted by the selection rule $\Delta J = \pm 1$ (except for diatomic molecules with an odd number of electrons, such as NO). Moreover, room temperature observations are mostly restricted to transitions from the vibrational ground state $v = 0$ either to $v = 1$ (producing the fundamental) or to $v = 2$ (yielding the overtone).

The experimentally observed frequencies are listed in table 1 of the paper by Schwenz & Polik, and can also be downloaded from their web site at http://www.chem.hope.edu/~polik/doc/hcl.xls. We will fit them to the expression

$$
\begin{aligned}
\overline{v} &= [E(v',J') - E(v^\circ, J^\circ)]/hc \\
&= \overline{\omega_e}\left[(v'+1/2) - (v^\circ+1/2)\right] + \overline{B_e}\left[J'(J'+1) - J^\circ(J^\circ+1)\right] \\
&\quad - \overline{\omega_e x_e}\left[(v'+1/2)^2 - (v^\circ+1/2)^2\right] - \overline{D_e}\left[J'^2(J'+1)^2 - J^{\circ 2}(J^\circ+1)^2\right] \\
&\quad - \overline{\alpha_e}\left[(v'+1/2)J'(J'+1) - (v^\circ+1/2)J^\circ(J^\circ+1)\right]
\end{aligned}
\qquad (3.6.2)
$$

where the zero and prime denote the lower-energy and higher-energy states of the particular transition respectively. Equation (3.6.2) can be rewritten in a compact form suitable for multiparameter least squares as

$$\overline{y} = \overline{\omega_e} z_1 + \overline{B_e} z_2 + \overline{\omega_e x_e} z_3 + \overline{D_e} z_4 + \overline{\alpha_e} z_5 \tag{3.6.3}$$

where

$$\overline{y} = [E(v',J') - E(v°,J°)]/hc \tag{3.6.4}$$

and

$$z_1 = (v'+1/2) - (v°+1/2) \tag{3.6.5}$$

$$z_2 = J'(J'+1) - J°(J°+1) \tag{3.6.6}$$

$$z_3 = -(v'+1/2)^2 + (v°+1/2)^2 \tag{3.6.7}$$

$$z_4 = -J'^2(J'+1)^2 + J°^2(J°+1)^2 \tag{3.6.8}$$

$$z_5 = -(v'+1/2)J'(J'+1) + (v°+1/2)J°(J°+1) \tag{3.6.9}$$

The experimental data for $\overline{y} = [E(v',J') - E(v°,J°)]/hc$ are given as a function of the (readily assigned) quantum numbers $v°, v', J°,$ and J', so that the functions z_i are all known. The problem therefore reduces to finding the five unknown parameters ω_e, B_e, $\omega_e x_e$, D_e, and α_e, a situation tailor-made for fitting with a multiparameter linear least squares routine. Note that we must treat the product $\omega_e x_e$ as an independent parameter, otherwise the problem is no longer linear in the fitting parameters.

Exercise 3.6.1:

(1) In a spreadsheet, enter the data as provided in the above-mentioned paper or web site, in five adjacent columns for $v°$, v', $J°$, J', and $(E'-E°)/hc$ respectively.

(2) Enter five more columns, for z_1 through z_5 respectively, in which you calculate these functions using the relations given in eqs.(3.6.5) through (3.6.9).

(3) Highlight the columns for $(E'-E°)/hc$ and z_1 through z_5, and call LS0. This will provide you with the values and standard deviations in ω_e, B_e, $\omega_e x_e$, D_e, and α_e. Also display the covariance matrix, which you will need in order to compute x_e as $\omega_e x_e / \omega_e$, which are of course strongly correlated (with, in this case, a linear correlation coefficient of 0.982).

(4) Your spreadsheet should resemble Figs. 3.6.1 and 3.6.2.

These results can of course be used to compute the bond distance $r = \sqrt{(h/8\pi^2 B_e c\mu)}$ and to fit a potential-energy surface. They can also be compared, e.g., with similar data (from the same source) for $D^{35}Cl$, as reported in table 1 of P. Ogren, B. Davis & N. Guy, *J. Chem. Educ.* 78 (2001) 827. By relegating the mechanics of curve fitting to the spreadsheet, the researcher can focus on the interpretation and further uses of the extracted information.

	A	B	C	D	E	F	G	H	I	J
1	v^o	v'	J^o	J'	nu	z1	z2	z3	z4	z5
2	0	1	0	1	2905.995	1	2	-2	-4	-3
3	0	1	1	2	2925.581	1	4	-2	-32	-8
4	0	1	2	3	2944.577	1	6	-2	-108	-15
5	0	1	3	4	2962.955	1	8	-2	-256	-24
6	0	1	4	5	2980.689	1	10	-2	-500	-35
7	0	1	5	6	2997.788	1	12	-2	-864	-48
8	0	1	6	7	3014.202	1	14	-2	-1372	-63
9	0	1	7	8	3029.941	1	16	-2	-2048	-80
10	0	1	8	9	3044.965	1	18	-2	-2916	-99
11	0	1	9	10	3059.234	1	20	-2	-4000	-120
12	0	1	10	11	3072.771	1	22	-2	-5324	-143
13	0	1	11	12	3085.600	1	24	-2	-6912	-168
14	0	1	12	13	3097.550	1	26	-2	-8788	-195
15	0	1	13	14	3108.914	1	28	-2	-10976	-224
16	0	1	14	15	3119.418	1	30	-2	-13500	-255
17	0	1	15	16	3129.099	1	32	-2	-16384	-288
18	0	1	1	0	2864.834	1	-2	-2	4	1
19	0	1	2	1	2843.315	1	-4	-2	32	0
20	0	1	3	2	2821.249	1	-6	-2	108	-3
21	0	1	4	3	2798.641	1	-8	-2	256	-8
22	0	1	5	4	2775.499	1	-10	-2	500	-15
23	0	1	6	5	2751.817	1	-12	-2	864	-24
24	0	1	7	6	2727.624	1	-14	-2	1372	-35
25	0	1	8	7	2702.907	1	-16	-2	2048	-48
26	0	1	9	8	2677.697	1	-18	-2	2916	-63
27	0	1	10	9	2651.932	1	-20	-2	4000	-80
28	0	1	11	10	2625.689	1	-22	-2	5324	-99
29	0	1	12	11	2598.979	1	-24	-2	6912	-120
30	0	1	13	12	2571.861	1	-26	-2	8788	-143
31	0	1	14	13	2544.220	1	-28	-2	10976	-168
32	0	1	15	14	2516.141	1	-30	-2	13500	-195
33	0	2	0	1	5687.494	2	2	-6	-4	-5
34	0	2	1	2	5705.926	2	4	-6	-32	-14
35	0	2	2	3	5723.158	2	6	-6	-108	-27
36	0	2	3	4	5739.109	2	8	-6	-256	-44
37	0	2	4	5	5753.793	2	10	-6	-500	-65
38	0	2	5	6	5767.262	2	12	-6	-864	-90

Fig. 3.6.1: The top part of a spreadsheet with the infrared spectral data on $H^{35}Cl$ vapor of Schwenz & Polik (columns A through E), containing the fundamental band. In order to display the calculation, some column widths have been adjusted.

39	0	2	6	7	5779.441	2	14	-6	-1372	-119
40	0	2	7	8	5790.312	2	16	-6	-2048	-152
41	0	2	8	9	5799.833	2	18	-6	-2916	-189
42	0	2	9	10	5808.141	2	20	-6	-4000	-230
43	0	2	1	0	5646.969	2	-2	-6	4	1
44	0	2	2	1	5624.896	2	-4	-6	32	-2
45	0	2	3	2	5601.612	2	-6	-6	108	-9
46	0	2	4	3	5577.185	2	-8	-6	256	-20
47	0	2	5	4	5551.571	2	-10	-6	500	-35
48	0	2	6	5	5524.865	2	-12	-6	864	-54
49	0	2	7	6	5496.971	2	-14	-6	1372	-77
50	0	2	8	7	5467.968	2	-16	-6	2048	-104
51	0	2	9	8	5437.895	2	-18	-6	2916	-135
52				*Coeff:*	*2989.281*	*10.58919*	*51.796*	*0.0005206*	*0.30167*
53				*StDev:*	*0.034*	*0.00089*	*0.012*	*0.0000029*	*0.00010*
54					*0.048*				
55				*CM:*	*0.0011548*	*2.975E-06*	*0.000384*	*9.23475E-10*	*1.83E-06*
56					*2.975E-06*	*7.871E-07*	*9.58E-07*	*2.21736E-09*	*7.84E-09*
57					*0.000384*	*9.578E-07*	*0.000132*	*7.74469E-10*	*4.96E-07*
58					*9.235E-10*	*2.217E-09*	*7.74E-10*	*8.3649E-12*	*-3.09E-11*
59					*1.827E-06*	*7.842E-09*	*4.96E-07*	*-3.0883E-11*	*9.63E-09*

Fig. 3.6.2: The bottom part of a spreadsheet with the infrared spectral data on $H^{35}Cl$ vapor of Schwenz & Polik (columns A through E), containing the overtone data as well as the results obtained with the macro LS0.

3.7 Spectral mixture analysis

Figure 3.7 illustrates the absorption spectra of four fantasy species, made of one or more Gaussian peaks, and of an imaginary mixture made of these species. Such peaks can be calculated as $a \exp[-(x-c)^2/(2b^2)]$; instead of the exponential part you can also use the instruction =NormDist(x,mean,stdev,false) to generate Gaussian curves $\left(1/\sigma\sqrt{2\pi}\right)\exp\left[-(x-\bar{x})^2/2\sigma^2\right]$ where $\bar{x}$ is the mean (locating the position of the peak center), σ the standard deviation (defining its width), and where 'false' specifies the Gaussian curve rather than its integral. In exercise 3.7.1 we simulate such spectra, compute the spectrum of a mixture of these components (assuming the applicability of Beer's law, and the absence of chemical interactions), add noise to all components, then use multivariate analysis to reconstruct the composition of that mixture.

Exercise 3.7.1:

(1) In column A deposit wavelengths, and in columns B through E calculate four fantasy spectra, each with one or more Gaussian peaks. Each Gaussian peak requires three constants: an amplitude a, a standard deviation b or σ, and a center frequency c or mean $\bar{x}$.

(2) In columns M through Q generate random Gaussian ('normal') noise, and in columns H through K make somewhat noisy single-component spectra by adding some noise from column N to the spectrum of column B, etc., in order to create more realistic single-species spectra.

(3) Near the top of the spreadsheet enter four concentrations, and use these in column G to make a synthetic 'mixture spectrum' of the four single-component spectra, each multiplied by its assigned concentration, plus added noise from column M. (You could do without columns B through E by adding noise directly to the data in columns B through E, and then subtracting that same noise from the mixture spectrum. Noise in the single-component spectra and in the spectrum of the simulated mixture should of course be independent.)

(4) Plot the spectra of columns G through K, which might now look like those in Fig. 3.7.1. Note that the resulting curve does not show distinct features easily identifiable with any of its constituent spectra. In this particular example we have used the data of table 3.7.1, together with noise standard deviations of 0.005 for all components as well as for the synthetic mixture. You should of course use your own data to convince yourself that this is no stacked deck.

(5) Highlight the data block in columns G through K, and call LS0 for a multivariate analysis of the mixture spectrum in terms of the spectra of its four com-

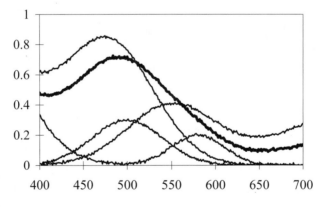

ponents.

Fig. 3.7.1: The simulated single-component spectra (thin lines) and the spectrum of their mixture (heavy line). The simulation parameters used, as well as the composition of the mixture and the results of its analysis, are listed in tables 3.7.1 and 3.7.2. Independent Gaussian noise (mean 0, st. dev. 0.005) has been added to all curves.

The results of that analysis are shown in table 3.7.2. Despite the added noise, the absence of stark features, and considerable overlap between the various single-component spectra, the composition of the mixture is recovered quite well.

	ampl:	*mean:*	*st.dev.:*		*ampl:*	*mean:*	*st.dev.:*
curve 1:	300	270	80	*curve 3*:	30	500	40
	100	480	50	*curve 4*:	200	300	60
curve 2:	50	550	50		15	580	30
	70	760	80				

Table 3.7.1: The constants for the Gaussian peaks used in generating Fig. 3.7.1 with the function `NormDist()`.

	curve 1	*curve 2*	*curve 3*	*curve 4*
mixture composition:	0.650	0.500	0.300	0.200
recovered:	0.648±0.003	0.496±0.003	0.305±0.011	0.207±0.007

Table 3.7.2: The assumed and recovered composition of the synthetic mixture.

The above method is simple and quite general, as long as spectra of all mixture constituents are available. In the analysis you can include spectra of species that do not participate in the mixture: for those species, the calculation will simply yield near-zero contributions. However, a missing constituent spectrum will cause the method to fail if its contribution to the mixture spectrum is significant.

A final note: the numbers obtained for the recovered composition are mutually dependent. Therefore the covariance matrix should be used in subsequent computations, rather than standard deviations.

3.8 How many adjustable parameters?

Now that it has become so easy to fit data to a polynomial, such as a power series in x, one might be tempted to throw in more terms, on the (mistaken) assumption that 'the more terms, the better the fit'. Ultimately this will defeat the noise-reducing purpose of least squares, since we can fit N data points *exactly* (including all noise) to a polynomial of order $N - 1$ (with its N coefficients a_0 through a_{N-1}). Moreover, we would then have replaced N experimental y-values with the same number N of fitting parameters, defeating the data-reduction purpose of least squares as well.

Long before we reach such an extreme situation, we may already include statistically meaningless terms. We therefore ask whether there is an optimal polynomial degree, and if so, how it can be determined. And because the least squares method is about data reduction while simultaneously filtering out as much noise as possible, the answer cannot be based solely on the exactitude of the fit. Ideally, theory should be our guide in selecting the model to which to fit the data. Often, however, we lack sufficient theoretical guidance, in which case decisions such as the optimal length of a power series must be made on the basis of statistical information inherent in the data. In sections 3.9 through 3.13 we will address that problem.

In many cases we do have theoretical models to guide us in deciding what function to use in fitting experimental data. We did just that with the vapor-phase spectra of I_2 (section 3.3) and $H^{35}Cl$ (section 3.6). However, even when a reliable theory is available, matters are not always that simple. For instance, Ohm's law requires that we use $V = I\,R$ without a constant, because (short of making a perpetual motion machine) we cannot have a current I without a driving force V. But the *measurement* might still show a non-zero intercept if the meter had not been zeroed properly, in which case we might indeed want to fit the data to the line $V = V_{offset} + I\,R$. Such possible sources of systematic error are best avoided at the time of measurement, through careful calibration, rather than corrected later, but that is of little help once the experiment has been performed.

Back to the main question of this section: what do we do when we have no theory to guide us? In that case we may want to use a polynomial such as the power series $y = a_0 + a_1x + a_2x^2 + a_3x^3 + \ldots + a_mx^m$ as a rather general-purpose fitting function, but then we will need some criterion to help us decide what the order m of that polynomial should be. (It is sometimes claimed that, with enough high-order terms, one could draw an elephant, but that is bull.) There are several such criteria, none infallible, of which we will here illustrate three. While such criteria can guide us, they do not always yield identical answers. Consequently, individual judgment is still called for.

Before we use a power series in x without theoretical guidance, we must first consider two caveats. (1) The over-all trend of the experimental data should be representable in terms of the model used. For many functions, such as sine waves, an expansion in terms of a power series in x would be rather inefficient; for others, e.g., for points that lie approximately on a circle, such a power series would be totally inadequate. (2) Absent theoretical guidance, the information on the optimal order of the polynomial must be extracted from the data themselves. Since random noise can be of no help in this respect, we can only hope for reasonable success when the signal-to-noise ratio is sufficiently large. When the signal-to-noise ratio is too small, such methods must fail. (There are methods available to pull a small signal from a large amount of noise, such as synchronous detection or boxcar amplification, but these require additional information, and typically must be built into the experiment, i.e., they cannot be used ex post facto.)

3.9 The standard deviation of the fit

The simplest approach we will illustrate here is based on the standard deviation of the fit, s_f, or its square, the variance v_{ff}, by selecting that polynomial for which s_f (or v_{ff}) is minimal. Because $v_{ff} = (\Sigma \delta^2)/(N-P)$, where the residual δ is given by $y - y_{model}$, and $P = m + 1$ denotes the number of parameters used to describe y_{model} by the polynomial, s_f and v_{ff} will decrease with increasing polynomial order P even if $\Sigma \delta^2$ remains constant. There usually is at least one minimum in a plot of s_f vs. polynomial order. One often stops at the first local minimum, in effect setting the termination requirement equal to $s_{f,m+1} / s_{f,m} > 1$ where the added index on s_f denotes the highest term in the polynomial used.

In order to find the minimal value of s_f we can use LinEst, Regression, LS0, or LS1 repeatedly, gradually increasing the order of the polynomial, and each time extracting the corresponding value of s_f. Collecting those values, we can then make our choice of polynomial if s_f indeed goes through a minimum. This would be a somewhat tedious process, but since we have a computer at our fingertips, and the above protocol is eminently suitable for automation, we will use a custom macro for that purpose. Depending on whether or not we want to force the polynomial through zero, we use the custom macro LSPoly0 or LSPoly1. Both macros yield s_f-values together with the individual fitting coefficients a_i and their standard deviations s_i. (They were not designed to stop automatically whenever s_f encounters a local minimum, but can easily be modified to do so, or even to display only that polynomial.) Exercise 3.12.1 illustrates the use of LSPoly0.

3.10 The F-test

A second, closely related approach is based on the F-test, named after one of its originators, R. A. Fisher. It likewise considers the variance v_{yy} of the entire fit. In the power series $y = a_0 + a_1 x + a_2 x^2 + a_3 x^3 + \ldots + a_p x^p$ the number of parameters used to define the polynomial is $p + 1$, because there are $p + 1$ terms, from $a_0 x^0$ through $a_p x^p$, so that the number of degrees of freedom is $N - p - 1$. (If we were to leave out the constant term a_0, we would instead have $N - p$ degrees of freedom.)

The F-test, which in Excel can be computed with the function =FINV (`criterion,df1,df2`), requires the user to select a *criterion* for the acceptable probability α (expressed as a decimal fraction, such as 0.05 for 5%), while $df1$ and $df2$ denote the degrees of freedom of the two fitting functions that are being compared. The most commonly used α-values are 0.05 (i.e., 5%) and 0.01 (1%).

An application of the F-test to evaluate the usefulness of extending a polynomial fit of N data points from order p to order q (with $q > p$) involves comparing the ratio

$$
F_{q,p} = \frac{(\Sigma \Delta_p^2 - \Sigma \Delta_q^2)/(q-p)}{\Sigma \Delta_q^2 /(N-q-1)}
$$

$$
= \frac{(N-p-1)\,(v_{pp}/v_{qq})-(N-q-1)}{(q-p)} \tag{3.10.1}
$$

where $v_{pp} = \Sigma \Delta_p^2 /(N-p-1)$ and $v_{qq} = \Sigma \Delta_q^2 /(N-q-1)$, with the F-test $F(\alpha, q\!-\!p, N\!-\!q\!-\!1)$ in

$$
FR\alpha = \frac{F_{q,p}}{F(\alpha, q-p, N-q-1)}
$$

$$
= \frac{(N-p-1)\,(\Sigma \Delta_p^2 / \Sigma \Delta_q^2 -1)}{(q-p)\,F(\alpha, q-p, N-q-1)}
$$

$$
= \frac{(N-p-1)\,(v_{pp}/v_{qq})-(N-q-1)}{(q-p)\,F(\alpha, q-p, N-q-1)} \tag{3.10.2}
$$

If $FR\alpha$ is substantially larger than one, the additional terms up to q can be considered to be statistically significant *at the chosen value of* α. Note that $q\!-\!p$ is the *difference* between the degrees of freedom of the two fits, and that this method can only be applied for $q < N-1$. We typically apply (3.10.1) with $q = p + 1$ although, especially when dealing with symmetrical functions, it may be useful to consider $q = p + 2$ as well. The above result applies to the general polynomial $y = a_0 + a_1 x + a_2 x^2 + a_3 x^3 + \ldots + a_p x^p$. For the polynomial $y = a_1 x + a_2 x^2 + a_3 x^3 + \ldots + a_p x^p$ through the origin we have instead

$$
FR\alpha = \frac{F_{q,p}}{F(\alpha, q-p, N-q)} = \frac{(N-p)\,(v_{pp}/v_{qq})-(N-q)}{(q-p)\,F(\alpha, q-p, N-q)} \tag{3.10.3}
$$

where $v_{pp} = \Sigma \Delta_p^2 /(N-p)$ and $v_{qq} = \Sigma \Delta_q^2 /(N-q)$.

The custom macro LSPoly1 displays both s_f and two values of $FR\alpha$ as defined in (3.10.2), for $q = p + 1$ with $\alpha = 0.05$ and 0.01 respectively.

Likewise, LSPoly0 incorporates s_f and two $FR\alpha$-values based on (3.10.3). For an added term to be included within a given probability (5% for $FR5$, 1% for $FR1$), its F-ratio should be larger than one, preferably by at least a factor of 3. If desired, $FR\alpha$-values for $q = p + 2$ can also be incorporated in those custom macros.

3.11 Orthogonal polynomials

In fitting data to a straight line, one can make the covariance disappear by fitting to $y = a_0' + a_1(x-x_{av})$ instead of to $y = a_0 + a_1x$, i.e., by using a function of x (in this case $x-x_{av}$) rather than x itself. This principle can be extended to least squares fitting to a power series such as $y = a_0 + a_1x + a_2x^2 + a_3x^3 + \dots + a_mx^m$, or to multiparameter fitting as in $y = a_0 + a_xx + a_zz + \dots$, and requires that we use *orthogonal polynomials*. Making the covariances zero makes the fitting coefficients mutually independent, so that they can be computed one at a time, and can then be evaluated individually for statistical significance. In principle this would seem to be the optimal way to determine at what term to terminate a power series. In practice there are several constraints.

(1) In general, finding orthogonal polynomials can be rather laborious, because such polynomials must be constructed anew for every data set, on the basis of its individual x-values. We already encountered this in centering: the quantity $(x-x_{av})$ indeed depends on all x-values in the data set. For equidistant data, i.e., data for which the increment Δx is constant, this complication is relatively minor, because the sought polynomials then are the readily computed *Gram polynomials*, which depend only on the number N of data points in the set, on the order j of the polynomial, and on the average x-value x_{av}. At any rate, being laborious is no valid excuse when we can use macros to take care of the busywork. Two custom macros, Ortho0 and Ortho1, are therefore provided to compute orthogonal polynomials for finite sets of x-values. Ortho0 should be used for curves that go through the origin, whereas the intercept of curves fitted by Ortho1 is not constrained. The x-values need not be equidistant.

(2) A particular set of orthogonal polynomials corresponds to a particular power series or other parametric expression, e.g., the orthogonal polynomials of order j considered below will be linear combinations of $x^0, x^1, x^2, x^3, \dots, x^j$. Note that the data fit obtained with orthogonal polynomials is no better than that obtained with the corresponding power series or parametric expression, and in fact is entirely equivalent. The ad-

vantage of using orthogonal polynomials is that they provide mutually independent fitting coefficients, which can be tested for statistical relevance. Since the coefficients are mutually independent, their covariances are zero, which may be convenient to simplify the propagation of experimental uncertainty through subsequent calculations.

(3) The method indeed works beautifully for noise-free data but, as with any other statistical method, can be overwhelmed by too much noise. This is, of course, nothing new: statistical data analysis always labors under the constraint that the validity of the analysis results is questionable when the quality of the input data is insufficient. This is summarized succinctly in the expression "garbage in, garbage out".

But enough provisos already. *Orthogonal* polynomials are defined as polynomials that have mutually independent (i.e., uncorrelated) coefficients. Specifically, a set of polynomials $P_j(x)$ is orthogonal if

$$\sum_i P_j(x_i)\, P_k(x_i) = 0 \quad \text{for } j \neq k \tag{3.11.1}$$

$$\sum_i P_j(x_i)\, P_k(x_i) \neq 0 \quad \text{for } j = k \tag{3.11.2}$$

Expressing an unknown function in terms of orthogonal polynomials $y = p_0 + p_1 P_1(x) + p_2 P_2(x) + p_3\, P_3(x) + \ldots + p_m P_m(x)$ instead of as a power series $y = a_0 + a_1 x + a_2 x^2 + a_3 x^3 + \ldots + a_m x^m$ involves the same number $m+1$ of terms, with the polynomial $P_j(x)$ containing terms in x up to and including x^j. As already indicated, an advantage of expressing y in terms of orthogonal polynomials $P_j(x)$ instead of as a direct power series in x is that the resulting coefficients p_j are mutually independent. In going from, say, a quadratic to a cubic, we need not recalculate the coefficients p_0 through p_2 because these remain the same, so that we only have to compute the added coefficient p_3. Moreover, we can test whether p_3 is statistically significant by comparing its absolute magnitude with, e.g., its standard deviation and/or the numerical uncertainty of the computation. If p_3 passes that test, we can increase the order of the polynomial by 1, repeat the procedure by testing p_4, etc. In other words, orthogonal polynomials allow us to approach data fitting as a problem of successive approximation, including a termination criterion. This method therefore satisfies the intuitive notion of testing each added term for its statistically significance.

Fitting a set of data to the function $y = p_0 + p_1 P_1(x) + p_2 P_2(x) + p_3 P_3(x) + \ldots + p_m P_m(x)$ yields the various coefficients p_j. Because these p_j are mutually independent, multiplying a given term $P_j(x)$ by a constant λ_j

will only affect the corresponding coefficient p_j, because $(p_j/\lambda_j) \times \lambda_j P_j(x)$ $= p_j P_j(x)$. Consequently, orthogonal polynomials can be defined with arbitrary scale factors λ_j. This has led to various normalizing schemes. The resulting multitude of equivalent expressions, differing only by order-dependent constants λ_j, can be quite confusing to the novice.

The custom macro Ortho works for all situations to which LS can be applied, since it does not rely on a fixed formula for the orthogonal polynomials but, instead, computes these for any data set by Gram-Schmidt orthogonalization.

In order to illustrate how orthogonal polynomials work we will here illustrate them for data that are equidistant in the independent parameter x, in which case the resulting *Gram polynomials* (J. P. Gram, *J. reine angew. Math.* 94 (1883) 21) take on a rather simple form. As our example we will consider fitting data to the power series $y = a_0 + a_1 x + a_2 x^2 + a_3 x^3 + \ldots + a_m x^m$, which can be represented by the corresponding set of Gram polynomials $G_j(x)$, i.e., $y = g_0 + g_1 G_1(x) + g_2 G_2(x) + g_3 G_3(x) + \ldots + g_m G_m(x)$ with coefficients g_j. The first two Gram polynomials are

$$G_0(x)/\lambda_0 = 1 \tag{3.11.3}$$

$$G_1(x)/\lambda_1 = \xi \tag{3.11.4}$$

with the compact notation $\xi = (x-x_{av})/d$, where $d = \Delta x$ is the distance between adjacent x-values, and λ_j is an arbitrary constant for the Gram polynomial G_j. Typically, both λ_0 and λ_1 are set equal to 1, but no dominant convention has yet emerged for $\lambda_{j>1}$. For a set of N data points, additional polynomials G_j can then be computed with the recursion formula

$$G_{j+1}(x) = \xi\, G_j(x) - \frac{j^2\,(N^2 - j^2)}{4\,(4j^2 - 1)}\, G_{j-1}(x) \tag{3.11.5}$$

so that (for $\lambda_0 = \lambda_1 = 1$) the next few terms are

$$G_2(x)/\lambda_2 = \xi^2 - \frac{(N^2 - 1)}{12} \tag{3.11.6}$$

$$G_3(x)/\lambda_3 = \xi^3 - \frac{(3N^2 - 7)}{20}\,\xi \tag{3.11.7}$$

$$G_4(x)/\lambda_4 = \xi^4 - \frac{(3N^2 - 13)}{14}\,\xi^2 + \frac{3\,(N^2 - 1)\,(N^2 - 9)}{560} \tag{3.11.8}$$

$$G_5(x)/\lambda_5 = \xi^5 - \frac{5\,(N^2-7)}{18}\,\xi^3 + \frac{(15N^4 - 230N^2 + 407)}{1008}\xi \qquad (3.11.9)$$

$$G_6(x)/\lambda_6 = \xi^6 - \frac{5\,(3N^2-31)}{44}\,\xi^4 + \frac{(5N^4 - 110N^2 - 329)}{176}\,\xi^2$$

$$-\frac{5\,(N^2-1)\,(N^2-9)\,(N^2-25)}{14784} \qquad (3.11.10)$$

We note that $G_1(x) = \xi = (x - x_{av,})/d$, so that centering is indeed equivalent to fitting data to a Gram polynomial of order 1. Since $G_0(x) = 1$, the above polynomials pertain to a power series with arbitrary intercept. For a curve through the origin a different set of Gram functions is obtained, as is readily verified with the custom macro Ortho0.

*****

In section 2.10 we saw how to draw imprecision contours around a straight line, providing the graph with some visual uncertainty estimates. With the tools now at hand we can extend this approach to power series of the type $y = a_0 + a_1x + a_2x^2 + a_3x^3 + \ldots + a_mx^m$. Upon their transformation into the orthogonal power series $y = p_0 + p_1P_1(x) + p_2P_2(x) + p_3\,P_3(x) + \ldots + p_mP_m(x)$ these can be fitted by least squares to find the coefficients p_j and the corresponding standard deviations s_j. We now generalize (2.10.3) to

$$s_y = \sqrt{s_f^2 + s_0^2 P_0^2 + s_1^2 P_1^2 + \ldots + s_m^2 P_m^2} = \sqrt{s_f^2 + \sum_{j=0}^{m} s_j^2 P_j^2} \qquad (3.11.11)$$

For a straight line, $j = 1$, $P_0 = 1$ and $P_1 = x - x_{av}$, so that (3.11.11) indeed reduces to (2.10.3). Since the custom macro Ortho1 provides both P_j and s_j, application of (3.11.11) is rather straightforward, as illustrated in exercise 3.11.1 for the data shown in Fig. 3.2.1. For curves through the origin, j in (3.11.11) should run from **1** to m.

Exercise 3.11.1:

(1) Return to exercise 3.2.1, or make a new data set along similar lines. The instructions below will assume the format of Fig. 3.2.1, and may need modification if you make your own data set.

(2) Highlight the data block A15:C27, and call Ortho1, which skips one column and will therefore leave the data in D15:D27 intact. Label the data in columns E through G with headings for y, P_1, and P_2 respectively.

(3) Because the increments in x are constant, the input data are equidistant, so that Ortho1 generates Gram polynomials. Verify that column F indeed shows $\xi = (x - x_{av})/d$ with $d = 1$ for the increment Δx, and that column G contains $\xi^2 - (N^2 - 1)/12$ where $N = 13$, the number of data points used, see (3.11.6).

(4) In column H, under a second label y_{calc}, verify that you obtain the very same answers as in column D when using the coefficients p_0, p_1, and p_2 shown in

E28:G28. In other words, the instruction `=$E$28+$F$28*F15+$G$28*G15` in cell H15 will reproduce the value in cell D15, etc.

(5) In column I calculate s according to (3.11.11), and in columns J and K compute $y_{calc} - s$ and $y_{calc} + s$ respectively. The value of s_f can be found in cell E31, those of s_0, s_1, and s_2 in cells E29 through G29 respectively.

(6) Plot the data in columns H, J, and K vs. those in column B, together with the individual data points, see Fig. 3.11.1.

(7) To keep matters in perspective (and keep you humble), also calculate and plot (in a different color) the function $y = -10 + 8x - 0.7x^2$ that was the starting point for the data in Fig. 3.2.1.

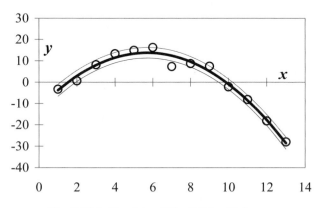

Fig. 3.11.1: The data of Fig. 3.2.1 with imprecision contours at ± one standard deviation.

We can also find the imprecision contours from the usual series expression for y, as long as we have access to the corresponding covariance matrix. In that case we must use

$$s_y = \sqrt{s_f^2 + \sum_{j=0}^{m} \sum_{k=0}^{m} v_{jk} x_i^j x_i^k} \tag{3.11.12}$$

instead of (3.11.11) or, for a multivariate analysis,

$$s_y = \sqrt{s_f^2 + \sum_{j=0}^{m} \sum_{k=0}^{m} v_{jk} x_{ji} x_{ki}} \tag{3.11.13}$$

where x_{ji} denotes the value of x_j for observation i. Again, for curves where $a_0 \equiv 0$, the indices j and k should start at 1.

Again, for confidence contours, multiply s in expressions such as (3.11.11) through (3.11.13) by $\sqrt{\{F(\alpha, 1, N-P)\}}$. For $N-P \geq 10$, $F(1/3, 1, N-P) \approx 1$, i.e., ± one standard deviation corresponds roughly with a confidence level $1 - \alpha$ of 2/3.

3.12 Gas-chromatographic analysis of ethanol

As our first example we will use a small data set provided by Leary & Messick, *Anal. Chem.* 57 (1985) 956, who reported the observations listed in table 3.12.1 for the peak area fraction in a gas chromatogram due to ethanol, as a function of the ethanol content (in volume %) of an injected ethanol-water mixture.

$x =$	10	20	30	40	50	60	70	80	90	*vol%*
$y =$	8.16	15.9	22.7	31.5	39.8	49.4	59.7	70.6	83.6	*area%*

Table 3.12.1: The relative peak area y due to ethanol, in area%, as a function of the volume fraction x of the injected sample, in volume%.

Theoretically these data should fit a straight line that, if extended, would pass through the points (0,0) and (100,100). (How to force the least squares program to do that will be illustrated in section 4.9.) Unfortunately, a plot of y vs. x will show that the data exhibit a clearly nonlinear trend. We do not know what causes this trend, nor do we know whether a power series would be an appropriate model. The following exercise is simply that: an exercise in finding the optimal fit of these data *assuming* that they can be represented meaningfully by a power series. We merely use this example because it contains equidistant data points, so that we can illustrate the application of orthogonal polynomials at its simplest level, with closed-form solutions of the type shown in section 3.11. We will use Gram polynomials to check the data for nonlinearity.

Exercise 3.12.1:

(1) In a spreadsheet deposit the values for x and y respectively from table 3.12.1. In column A deposit x, and in column B the corresponding values of y. In column C calculate $G_1 = \xi = (x-x_{av})/d$, i.e., –4 (1) 4 (= –4, –3, –2, –1, 0, 1, 2, 3, 4) because $x_{av} = 50$ and $d = 10$. Finally, in columns D through G calculate the polynomials G_2, G_3, G_4, and G_5 using (3.11.6) through (3.11.8), as in Fig. 3.12.1.

(2) Highlight the data in columns B and C, and call LS1, which will calculate the fit to a first-order Gram polynomial. Condense the output by overwriting the label st. dev.: with s_y, then save the results by moving them at least three rows down. Repeat LS1, each time including one more column to the right as input to LS1, and arrange the results in tabular form, as in Fig. 3.12.2.

(3) For each application of LS1, display the corresponding covariance matrix, and verify that it only contains significant values on its main diagonal; all off-diagonal terms should be zero except for computer round-off errors.

(4) The most significant aspect of Fig. 3.12.2 is that the coefficients g_j obtained at lower polynomial order are not changed when higher-order polynomials are included in the data analysis. For G_0 through G_3 the (absolute magnitudes of the) corresponding coefficients g_j clearly exceed the corresponding standard deviations s_i, i.e., they are statistically significant. However, this is not the case for the

next coefficients, 0.018 and 0.0029, and we can use this as a criterion for determining the optimal polynomial order. In terms of an integer power series in x, the data in table 3.12.1 are therefore best represented by a third-order polynomial.

(5) Because G_1 is simply the average value of x, the data in Fig. 3.12.2 do *not* indicate whether they are best represented with or without a term a_0. For this we now use LSPoly0 and LSPoly1, see Figs. 3.12.3 and 3.12.4. (Note that this requires interchanging the columns for x and y.)

	A	B	C	D	E	F	G
1							
2	*x*	*y*	*G1*	*G2*	*G3*	*G4*	*G5*
3							
4	10	8.16	-4	9.333	-16.800	24.000	-26.667
5	20	15.9	-3	2.333	8.400	-36.000	73.333
6	30	22.7	-2	-2.667	15.600	-18.857	-26.667
7	40	31.5	-1	-5.667	10.800	15.429	-60.000
8	50	39.8	0	-6.667	0.000	30.857	0.000
9	60	49.4	1	-5.667	-10.800	15.429	60.000
10	70	59.7	2	-2.667	-15.600	-18.857	26.667
11	80	70.6	3	2.333	-8.400	-36.000	-73.333
12	90	83.6	4	9.333	16.800	24.000	26.667

Fig. 3.12.1: The analysis of the data in table 3.12.1 in terms of Gram polynomials.

(6) We first note that the values for s_f in Figs. 3.12.2 and 3.12.4 are the same. These s_f values show a first minimum at order 3, as does LSPoly0 in Fig. 3.12.3. For LSPoly0, both F-ratios (FR5 and FR1, representing $\alpha = 0.05$ and 0.01 respectively) clearly exceed unity for the second and third orders, and drop to well below 1 at order 4. For LSPoly1, the result for the third order F-ratios is more ambiguous, and depends on the value of α, with FR5 > 1, FR1 < 1. Note that s_y, FR5, or FR1 are all non-monotonic functions of polynomial order.

	term 0	term 1	term 2	term 3	term 4	term 5
Coeff.:	42.37	9.296				
2.516	0.84	0.325				
Coeff.:	42.37	9.296	0.373			
0.509	0.17	0.066	0.029			
Coeff.:	42.37	9.296	0.373	0.0262		
0.339	0.11	0.044	0.019	0.0090		
Coeff.:	42.37	9.296	0.373	0.0262	0.0018	
0.372	0.12	0.048	0.021	0.0099	0.0049	
Coeff.:	42.37	9.296	0.373	0.0262	0.0018	0.0029
0.354	0.12	0.046	0.020	0.0094	0.0046	0.0025

Fig. 3.12.2: The results of applying LS1 to the data in Fig. 3.12.1. The numbers below the labels *Coeff.:* are the standard deviations of the fit, s_f.

(7) Where does all this lead us? The orthogonal polynomials suggest that we use terms up to and including x^3; at higher polynomial order, the standard deviations s_i are of the same order of magnitude as the corresponding coefficients a_i.

(8) Representing the data of table 3.12.1 as a cubic power series through the origin, $y = a_1x + a_2x^2 + a_3x^3$ with $a_1 = 0.79_9 \pm 0.02_2$, $a_2 = (-1.8_2 \pm 0.7_2) \times 10^{-3}$, and $a_3 = (3.6_1 \pm 0.5_6) \times 10^{-5}$, is clearly supported by all the above criteria, and leads to coefficients a_i that are all much larger than the corresponding uncertainties s_i.

Order 1	*term 1*				*Sf:* 3.088		
Coeff.:	8.648				*FR5:* N/A		
St.Dev.:	0.183				*FR1:* N/A		
Order 2	*term 1*	*term 2*			*Sf:* 0.936		
Coeff.:	6.712	0.272			*FR5:* 14.301		
St.Dev.:	0.223	0.030			*FR1:* 6.530		
Order 3	*term 1*	*term 2*	*term 3*		*Sf:* 0.362		
Coeff.:	7.994	-0.181	0.036		*FR5:* 6.833		
St.Dev.:	0.218	0.072	0.006		*FR1:* 2.976		
Order 4	*term 1*	*term 2*	*term 3*	*term 4*	*Sf:* 0.373		
Coeff.:	8.317	-0.389	0.075	-0.002	*FR5:* 0.100		
St.Dev.:	0.458	0.266	0.048	0.003	*FR1:* 0.041		
Order 5	*term 1*	*term 2*	*term 3*	*term 4*	*term 5*	*Sf:* 0.319	
Coeff.:	9.322	-1.394	0.399	-0.044	0.002	*FR5:* 0.366	
St.Dev.:	0.715	0.641	0.197	0.025	0.001	*FR1:* 0.133	

Fig. 3.12.3: Analysis of the data of table 3.12.1 with LSPoly0.

(9) On the other hand, a fit of the same data in terms of the general cubic expression $y = a_0 + a_1x + a_2x^2 + a_3x^3$ is much less successful, as is best seen when we consider the resulting coefficients, $a_0 = 0.9_9 \pm 0.7_3$, $a_1 = 0.72_3 \pm 0.06_0$, $a_2 = (-0.2_1 \pm 1.3_6) \times 10^{-3}$, and $a_3 = (2.6_2 \pm 0.9_0) \times 10^{-5}$, where a_0 is only marginally significant, and a_2 is not significant at all.

(10) Incidentally, this conclusion differs from that reached by L. M. Schwartz, *Anal. Chem.* 58 (1986) 246, who considered neither the ratios of the individual coefficients and their standard deviations, nor the possibility of a curve through the origin.

(11) For equidistant data, the orthogonal polynomials can be written in terms of simple integers. Verify that this is indeed the case in the spreadsheet of Fig. 3.12.1 by multiplying G_2 by 3, G_3 by 5 (or, if you want to make these integers as small as possible, by 5/6), G_4 by 7 (or 7/12), and G_5 by 3 (or 3/20). Another common way to standardize these polynomials is to divide all polynomials of given order j by the value of that polynomial at its last data point, at $i = N$. In that case all polynomials will alternately start (for $i = 1$) with either 1 (for even values of j) or -1 (for odd j).

(12) The above illustrates both the advantages and limitations of fitting data to a power series. The method does *not* tell us whether a power series expansion is appropriate, but if it is, we can use orthogonal polynomials to determine how many terms to include. Whether that power series should include a constant term a_0 is a separate question that we have here answered using LSPoly0 and LSPoly1.

Order 1	*term 0*	*term 1*					*Sf:* 2.52E+00	
Coeff.:	-4.107	0.930					*FR5:* N/A	
St.Dev.:	1.828	0.032					*FR1:* N/A	
Order 2	*term 0*	*term 1*	*term 2*				*Sf:* 5.09E-01	
Coeff.:	2.724	0.557	3.73E-03				*FR5:* 2.76E+01	
St.Dev.:	0.648	0.030	2.90E-04				*FR1:* 1.20E+01	
Order 3	*term 0*	*term 1*	*term 2*	*term 3*			*Sf:* 3.39E-01	
Coeff.:	0.993	0.723	-2.08E-04	2.62E-05			*FR5:* 1.29E+00	
St.Dev.:	0.733	0.060	1.36E-03	8.98E-06			*FR1:* 5.25E-01	
Order 4	*term 0*	*term 1*	*term 2*	*term 3*	*term 4*		*Sf:* 3.72E-01	
Coeff.:	1.439	0.662	2.22E-03	-1.01E-05	1.82E-07		*FR5:* 1.82E-02	
St.Dev.:	1.437	0.176	6.66E-03	9.76E-05	4.86E-07		*FR1:* 6.62E-03	
Order 5	*term 0*	*term 1*	*term 2*	*term 3*	*term 4*	*term 5*	*Sf:* 3.54E-01	
Coeff.:	-1.360	1.150	-2.54E-02	6.63E-04	-7.16E-06	2.94E-08	*FR5:* 1.41E-01	
St.Dev.:	2.708	0.441	2.39E-02	5.70E-04	6.15E-06	2.45E-08	*FR1:* 4.20E-02	

Fig. 3.12.4: Analysis of the data of table 3.12.1 with LSPoly1.

3.13 Raman spectrometric analysis of ethanol

In a recent paper, Sanford, Mantooth & Jones (*J. Chem. Educ.* 78 (2001) 1221) used laser spectrometry to determine the ethanol content of ethanol-water mixtures. They reduced random noise by integrating the signal in the area of the Raman peak, between -2825 and -3096 cm^{-1} over a one-minute period, and they applied a baseline correction using the average of the signals at -2815 and -3106 cm^{-1}. The resulting low-noise calibration data (kindly provided by Prof. Sanford) are listed in table 3.13.1 and illustrated in Fig. 3.13.1, where y is the integrated, baseline-corrected peak area, and x the ethanol percentage. These data were reported to fit the straight line $y = -181.82 + 101.40x$ with a squared linear correlation coefficient R^2 of 0.9978, i.e., $R = \pm 0.9989$. In section 2.10 we already commented on r_{xy}^2 or r_{xy}, feel-good parameters provided by many software packages, including LinEst and Regression in Excel.

x	0	1	2.5	5	7.5	10	15	20	25	30	35
y	0.0	100.7	194.8	420.7	667.2	874.6	1359.1	1764.9	2287.9	2769.2	3230.1

x	37.5	40	42.5	45	47.5	50	60	70	80	90	100
y	3532.1	3708.1	3998.2	4295.9	4526.1	4799.8	5763.9	6817.4	7974.0	9048.7	10352.6

Table 3.13.1: The measured Raman intensities y (in arbitrary units) as a function of the percentage of ethanol x in the ethanol-water mixtures.

However, visual inspection of Fig. 3.13.1 suggests some curvature: the reported points at the extremes of the curve tend to lie above the fitted straight line, those in the middle region lie below it. We therefore calculate and plot the residuals, as shown in Fig. 3.13.2. The magnitudes of those residuals are rather small, considering that the signal range is about 10000, i.e., these integrated data show relatively little random scatter. However, the residuals clearly exhibit a systematic trend.

Alerted by this residual plot, we use LSPoly0 and LSPoly1 to find whether a power series in x might improve the fit. Figs. 3.13.3 and 3.13.4 show the resulting outputs. We see that the value of s_f exhibits a big drop in going from 1st to 2nd order, and thereafter shows only minor changes. Likewise, the F ratios are much larger than 1 for first and second order, and just barely exceed 1 for fourth order.

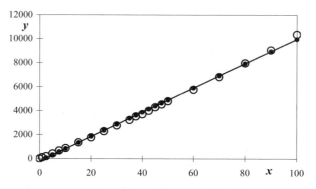

Fig. 3.13.1: The measured Raman intensities y as a function of the percentage of thanol x in the ethanol-water mixture (open circles). The line shows $y = -181.82 + 101.40\ x$, and the small solid points the resulting y-values at the x-values of the data.

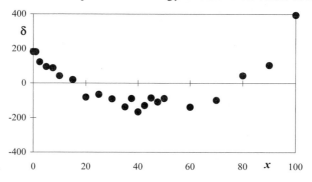

Fig. 3.13.2: The corresponding residuals clearly show a systematic trend.

Figures 3.13.5 and 3.13.6 show the results obtained with orthogonal polynomials. Because the data are not equidistant, we use the custom macros Ortho0 and Ortho1 to generate the appropriate orthogonal polynomials.

Order 1	term 1						Sf: 180.922
Coeff.:	98.325						FR5: N/A
St.Dev.:	0.824						FR1: N/A
Order 2	**term 1**	**term 2**					Sf: 35.842
Coeff.:	87.325	0.155					FR5: 106.539
St.Dev.:	0.511	0.007					FR1: 57.260
Order 3	**term 1**	**term 2**	**term 3**				Sf: 35.381
Coeff.:	88.848	0.102	3.98E-04				FR5: 0.311
St.Dev.:	1.333	0.043	3.22E-04				FR1: 0.167
Order 4	**term 1**	**term 2**	**term 3**	**term 4**			Sf: 28.520
Coeff.:	83.066	0.448	-5.68E-03	3.24E-05			FR5: 2.264
St.Dev.:	2.032	0.109	1.83E-03	9.66E-06			FR1: 1.206
Order 5	**term 1**	**term 2**	**term 3**	**term 4**	**term 5**		Sf: 28.747
Coeff.:	85.287	0.226	1.26E-03	-5.28E-05	3.58E-07		FR5: 0.142
St.Dev.:	3.329	0.284	8.40E-03	1.01E-04	4.23E-07		FR1: 0.075
Order 6	**term 1**	**term 2**	**term 3**	**term 4**	**term 5**	**term 6**	Sf: 29.632
Coeff.:	85.357	0.216	1.73E-03	-6.24E-05	4.47E-07	-3.09E-10	FR5: -1.53E-06
St.Dev.:	5.232	0.640	2.81E-02	5.57E-04	5.11E-06	1.76E-08	FR1: -8.06E-07

Fig. 3.13.3: The output of LSPoly0 for the first 6 orders.

Order 1	term 0	term 1						Sf: 143.942
Coeff.:	-181.823	101.396						FR5: N/A
St.Dev.:	50.090	1.071						FR1: N/A
Order 2	**term 0**	**term 1**	**term 2**					Sf: 36.699
Coeff.:	-4.553	87.514	0.154					FR5: 62.428
St.Dev.:	16.491	0.861	0.009					FR1: 33.413
Order 3	**term 0**	**term 1**	**term 2**	**term 3**				Sf: 35.203
Coeff.:	-20.231	90.503	0.067	6.11E-04				FR5: 0.567
St.Dev.:	18.520	2.014	0.054	3.75E-04				FR1: 0.302
Order 4	**term 0**	**term 1**	**term 2**	**term 3**	**term 4**			Sf: 29.243
Coeff.:	6.158	82.212	0.479	-6.11E-03	3.43E-05			FR5: 1.921
St.Dev.:	17.701	3.220	0.144	2.25E-03	1.14E-05			FR1: 1.018
Order 5	**term 0**	**term 1**	**term 2**	**term 3**	**term 4**	**term 5**		Sf: 29.632
Coeff.:	-0.114	85.310	0.225	1.29E-03	-5.31E-05	3.59E-07		FR5: 0.116
St.Dev.:	19.810	5.282	0.371	1.02E-02	1.18E-04	4.82E-07		FR1: 0.061
Order 6	**term 0**	**term 1**	**term 2**	**term 3**	**term 4**	**term 5**	**term 6**	Sf: 30.604
Coeff.:	-0.293	85.439	0.210	1.96E-03	-6.64E-05	4.80E-07	-4.10E-10	FR5: 4.14E-06
St.Dev.:	22.202	8.238	0.831	3.39E-02	6.49E-04	5.82E-06	1.97E-08	FR1: 2.16E-06

Fig. 3.13.4: The output of LSPoly1 for the first 6 orders.

Fits to LSPoly1 (see Fig. 3.13.4) yield rather large relative standard deviations for a_0. This is not surprising, because the data had already been baseline-corrected. Moreover, for all but the first order, the absolute magnitudes of the corresponding coefficients a_0 are either smaller than their standard deviations s_0, or only marginally larger, instilling little confidence in their statistical significance. The corresponding ratios from the orthogonal polynomials are above 20 for the linear and quadratic terms, and at or below 3 for terms of order 3 or higher, for both Ortho0 and Ortho1.

	term 1	term 2	term 3	term 4	term 5
Coeff.:	98.3250	0.15511	3.98E-04	3.24E-05	3.58E-07
st.dev.:	0.1310	0.00548	2.62E-04	9.73E-06	4.23E-07
ratio:	750.58	28.30	1.52	3.33	0.85

Fig. 3.13.5: The output of Ortho0 for the first five orders.

Exercise 3.13.1:
(1) Make a spreadsheet with the data from table 3.13.1, plot them, and calculate and plot their residuals.
(2) Apply LSPoly0 and LSPoly1 to those data, as well as Ortho0 and Ortho1. Verify that you indeed obtain the results shown here.

	term 0	term 1	term 2	term 3	term 4	term 5
Coeff.:	3567.55	101.396	0.1535	6.11E-04	3.43E-05	3.59E-07
st. dev.:	6.32	0.220	0.0073	3.16E-04	1.15E-05	4.82E-07
ratio:	564.69	460.05	21.04	1.93	2.97	0.75

Fig. 3.13.6: The output of Ortho1 for the first five orders.

Guided by the parsimony principle, we therefore opt for the simplest of the second-order fits, the function $y = a_1x + a_2x^2$, which has no more parameters than the linear function $y = a_0 + a_1x$ it replaces. This fit, and the corresponding residuals, are shown in Figs. 3.13.7 and 3.13.8 respectively. Note that the residuals now indicate only a very slight amplitude increase at larger x-values, which perhaps could be corrected by the inclusion of a fourth order term.

Exercise 3.13.1 (continued):
(3) Calculate and plot the data of table 3.13.1 to the equation $y = a_1x + a_2x^2$, and also compute and plot the corresponding residuals.
(4) Do the same using the equation $y = a_1x + a_2x^2 + a_4x^4$.

The above example illustrates the benefits of plotting residuals, and of subjecting the data to statistical tests that can indicate whether higher-order polynomials would yield a statistically better fit. The above tests do not reveal what specific form, if any, would best fit the data, nor do they clarify the reason for the nonlinearity in the above results. The latter may be an artifact from the integration procedure used, or reflect a more basic nonlinear feature in the data.

For the purpose of chemical analysis, the quadratic calibration curve should yield more accurate results than a straight line, assuming of course that all other experimental parameters are kept constant, including the integration procedure. We will now illustrate how to use such a quadratic calibration curve for that purpose. Say that we make three replicate measurements on an ethanol-water mixture of unknown composition that, on the same equipment and under the same experimental conditions, yield Raman intensities of 4000, 4050, and 3980. We now wish to determine the corresponding ethanol percentage x_u, and its uncertainty. With the expression $y = a_1 x + a_2 x^2$ we have $x_u = [-a_1 \pm \sqrt{(a_1^2 + 4a_2 y_u)}] / [2a_2]$ where y_u is the average Raman intensity of the unknown.

Exercise 3.13.1 (continued):

(5) Use LS0 to fit the data of table 3.13.1 to $y = a_1 x + a_2 x^2$. Display the covariance matrix.

(6) In another column, place the three observations of the Raman intensity of the sample of unknown composition (4000, 4050, and 3980) and compute its average y_u with =AVERAGE (), and its variance v_u with =VAR ().

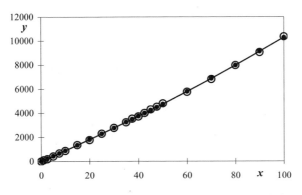

Fig. 3.13.7: The same data analyzed as a quadratic through the origin, $y = a_1 x + a_2 x^2$. The line is drawn with $a_1 = 87.325$, $a_2 = 0.155$.

(7) Use Copy $\Rightarrow$ Paste Special to copy the average y_u-value to be aligned with the values for a_1, a_2, so that they are on one contiguous row, or in one contiguous column. Likewise align the variance v_{uu} so that the covariance matrix and the standard deviation s_u in y_u share a diagonal, with the variances v_{11}, v_{22}, and v_{uu} in the same order as a_1, a_2, and y_u, cf. Fig. 3.13.9. Calculate x_u from the equation shown above.

(8) Call the custom macro Propagation and find the standard deviation s_u. For this example, the correct answer for the unknown ethanol concentration is $x_u = 42.6_8 \pm 0.3_7$ vol%, i.e., with a relative standard deviation of less than 1%, a quite respectable result.

(9) If you had used the standard deviations s_1, s_2, and s_u instead of the covariance matrix, the answer would have been $42.6_8 \pm 0.4_4$ vol%, quite close to the answer under (8). If you had used the straight-line fit $y = a_0 + a_1 x$ you would have found $x_u = 41.3_4 \pm 0.3_1$ with the covariance matrix (or with centering), or $x_u = 41.3_4 \pm 0.6_6$ without it. Unfortunately, there are many ways to get incorrect answers even from quite good data.

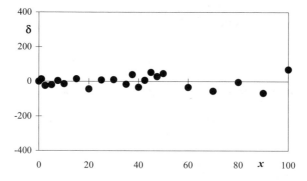

Fig. 3.13.8: The residuals of the quadratic fit in Fig. 3.13.7 exhibit only a slight trend towards larger-amplitude residuals at larger *x*-values. The scale is the same as that in Fig. 3.13.2.

4295.9	45	2025	
4526.1	47.5	2256.25	
4799.8	50	2500	4000
5763.9	60	3600	4050
6817.4	70	4900	3980
7974.0	80	6400	
9048.7	90	8100	*4010*
10352.6	100	10000	
Coeff:	*87.325*	*0.1551*	*4010*
StDev:	*0.511*	*0.0068*	36.06
	35.84173		

$$CM: \quad \begin{array}{|cc}
0.262 & -0.003312 \\
-0.003312 & 4.67\text{E-}05 \\
\end{array}$$

1300

xu=   *42.684*
su=   *0.374*

Fig. 3.13.9: Spreadsheet detail showing the bottom of the columns for the calculation of a_1, a_2, and y_u, and the subsequent computation of x_u. The variance $v_{uu} = s_u^2$ is entered in the covariance matrix.

We now ask a practical question: given these calibration data, is it worthwhile to make more repeat measurements of y_u to obtain a result with higher precision? For the answer we go to the part of the spreadsheet shown in Fig. 3.13.9, substitute 0 (instead of 1300) for the variance of the measurement, and use Propagation, which now yields a standard deviation of 0.11. In other words, the major part of the uncertainty in the answer indeed comes from the uncertainty in y_u. That is encouraging.

However, an uncertainty-free measurement is not a realistic goal, and we therefore ask what the result would be if we quadrupled the number of observations, from 3 to 12, assuming that the average would stay the same, and that their individual deviations would be similar. In that case $\Sigma\Delta^2$ would increase 4 times, $N-1$ would increase from $3-1=2$ to $12-1=11$, so that the variance v_{uu} would be reduced by a factor $4/(11/2) = 8/11$ to $8 \times 1300/11 = 945.45$. Substituting this into the covariance matrix and again using Propagation we find that the standard deviation in x_u would go down from 0.3_7 to 0.3_2, a rather minor improvement for four times as many measurements. Depending on the subsequent uses of the result of the analysis, it may or may not be worth your while to spend so much extra effort on a relatively minor improvement in the precision of the answer. Establishing why the calibration data do not quite fit a straight line might be a wiser use of your time.

We note that the method used here and illustrated in Fig. 3.13.9 is similar to that of section 3.4, except that we here deal with the intersection of a parabola and a horizontal line, $y = y_u$. If the curvature of the calibration curve is so severe that terms of higher than second order are required, the above method cannot be used, because it relies on having a closed-form solution for y_u. However, in that case it may still be possible to approximate the calibration curve in the region around x_u by a parabola.

3.14 Heat evolution during cement hardening

A much-studied example of a multiparameter fit can be found in the measurements of H. Woods, H. H. Steinour & H. R. Starke (Ind. Eng. Chem. 24 (1932) 1207) on the heat evolved during the first 180 days of hardening of Portland cement, studied as a function of the amounts (in weight percentage) of its dry ingredients: tricalcium aluminate, tricalcium silicate, tricalcium aluminoferrate, and β-dicalcium silicate. Because the sum of the four weight percentages must add to 100%, the four weight percentages are mutually dependent. We now consider the question: which parameters should we include in the analysis as significant, and which (if any) would better be left out? The experimental data are shown in Fig. 3.14.1.

In order to answer this question, we highlight block B3:F15 and call the macro Ortho1. The result is shown in Fig. 3.14.2, and speaks for itself: the parameters a_0, a_1, and a_2 are significant, a_3 is only marginally so, and a_4 is not at all.

	A	B	C	D	E	F
1		*y*	*x1*	*x2*	*x3*	*x4*
2						
3		78.5	7	26	6	60
4		74.2	1	29	15	52
5		104.3	11	56	8	20
6		87.6	11	31	8	47
7		95.9	7	52	6	33
8		109.2	11	55	9	22
9		102.7	3	71	17	6
10		72.5	1	31	22	44
11		93.1	2	54	18	22
12		115.9	21	47	4	26
13		83.8	1	40	23	34
14		113.3	11	66	9	12
15		109.4	10	68	8	12

Fig. 3.14.1: The experimental data of Woods, Steinour & Starke, *Ind. Eng. Chem.* 24 (1932) 1207, for the heat evolution *y* (in calories per gram of cement) as a function of the weight percentages *x* of the clinkers used in making the cement, where x_1 refers to the chemical composition $Al_2Ca_3O_6$, x_2 to Ca_3SiO_5, x_3 to $Al_2Ca_4Fe_2O_{10}$, and x_4 to β-Ca_2SiO_4.

Armed with this knowledge we now use LS1 on block B3:D15 in Fig. 3.14.1, and obtain the results shown in Fig. 3.14.3. These three figures are adjacent parts of a single, larger spreadsheet; the reader will have no difficulty seeing how they fit together.

The answer we obtain is $y = (52._5 \pm 2._3) + (1.4_7 \pm 0.1_2) x_1 + (0.66_3 \pm 0.04_6) x_2$. It agrees with the result obtained via a much more laborious route by N. R. Draper & H. Smith, *Applied Regression Analysis*, 2nd ed., Wiley 1981, who devote most of their chapter 6 to this problem. It had earlier been discussed in A. Hald, *Statistical Theory with Engineering Applications*, Wiley 1952 pp. 635-649.

Is this the only possible answer? No, we have yet to try Ortho0. Note that Ortho0 is not a special case of Ortho1, because the orthogonal polynomials for forcing a curve through the origin are quite different. This is most readily seen when we compare the orthogonal polynomials for equidistant data of *y* vs. *x*, in which case Ortho1 produces $P_0 = G_0 = 1$ and $P_1 = G_1 = x - x_{av}$, whereas Ortho0 uses $P_0 = G_0 = 0$ and $P_1 = G_1 = x$.

G	H	I	J	K	L
	y	*X1*	*X2*	*X3*	*X4*
	78.5	-0.461538	-21.87477	-5.716573	1.037882
	74.2	-6.461538	-15.24676	-2.242237	-0.683594
	104.3	3.538462	5.706558	-0.715707	-2.326357
	87.6	3.538462	-19.29344	-0.182183	-0.792525
	95.9	-0.461538	4.125232	-6.271438	0.522698
	109.2	3.538462	4.706558	0.305634	-0.31691
	102.7	-4.461538	25.54391	0.68199	0.165842
	72.5	-6.461538	-13.24676	4.715081	0.550354
	93.1	-5.461538	9.148574	1.134513	-1.128102
	115.9	13.53846	-9.340126	4.579097	0.443878
	83.8	-6.461538	-4.246758	5.523012	0.746268
	113.3	3.538462	15.70656	0.070883	0.888204
	109.4	2.538462	18.31123	-1.882072	0.892361
Coeff.:	*95.41538*	*1.870304*	*0.662804*	*0.251449*	*-0.13832*
St.Dev.:	*0.676303*	*0.119665*	*0.046467*	*0.194808*	*0.706859*
Ratio:	**141.0839**	**15.62947**	**14.2641**	**1.290753**	**0.195678**

Fig. 3.14.2: The results produced by Ortho1. The columns for X1 through X4 display the orthogonal polynomials for the data in C3:F15, while the three bottom lines show the corresponding coefficients a, their standard deviations s, and the ratios a/s.

16	*Coeff.:*	*52.53388*	*1.469527*	*0.662804*
17	*St.Dev.:*	*2.282175*	*0.121089*	*0.045774*
18		*2.402125*		
19				
20		5.208321	-0.048395	-0.091443
21	*CM:*	-0.048395	0.014662	-0.001267
22		-0.091443	-0.001267	0.002095
23				
24		1	-0.175126	-0.875347
25	*LCC:*	-0.175126	1	-0.228579
26		-0.875347	-0.228579	1

Fig. 3.14.3: The results produced with LS1 on the original data set, restricting the analysis to x_1 and x_2.

y	X1	X2	X3	X4
78.5	7	-4.249342	2.672732	37.93956
74.2	1	24.67867	6.201072	22.92501
104.3	11	8.46532	-2.213322	-2.223176
87.6	11	-16.53468	6.01623	10.89775
95.9	7	21.75066	-5.886002	25.37379
109.2	11	7.46532	-0.88414	-3.603877
102.7	3	58.036	-4.129871	-10.9925
72.5	1	26.67867	12.54271	-3.743438
93.1	2	45.35733	1.718872	-4.464174
115.9	21	-43.74802	4.222839	-17.83383
83.8	1	35.67867	10.58007	-11.57251
113.3	11	18.46532	-4.505143	-7.497086
109.4	10	24.78665	-6.910859	-0.769587
Coeff:	*8.807638*	*1.585151*	*2.131376*	*0.485647*
StDev:	*0.071371*	*0.022193*	*0.108016*	*0.041254*
Ratio:	*123.4056*	*71.42726*	*19.73201*	*11.77198*
	2.408722			

Fig. 3.14.4: The results produced by Ortho0. The orthogonal polynomials are quite different from those shown in Fig. 3.14.2.

	Coeff:	*2.194809*	*1.153154*	*0.759162*	*0.485647*
16					
17	*StDev:*	*0.184584*	*0.047764*	*0.158919*	*0.041254*
18		*2.408722*			
19	*CM:*	0.034071	-0.007636	0.022144	-0.004751
20		-0.007636	0.002281	-0.00651	0.000945
21		0.022144	-0.00651	0.025255	-0.004809
22		-0.004751	0.000945	-0.004809	0.001702
23					
24	*LCC:*	1	-0.866155	0.754908	-0.62393
25		-0.866155	1	-0.857707	0.479507
26		0.754908	-0.857707	1	-0.733495
27		-0.62393	0.479507	-0.733495	1

Fig. 3.14.5: The results produced with LS0 on the original data set.

Figure 3.14.4 shows what we find with Ortho0 instead of Ortho1: all four parameters are now statistically significant. Using LS0 we then find the coefficients a_1 through a_4 displayed in Fig. 3.14.5. We therefore have a choice; here the parsimony principle favors the three-parameter solution found in Fig. 3.13.3 over the four-parameter version of Fig. 3.14.5.

But wait a minute: what does a_0 mean in Fig. 3.14.3? Could there be heat evolution independent of any of the chemical constituents of cement? And could that be a significant part of the observed heat evolution? Given the care the authors have shown in obtaining their data, a_0 is unlikely to be due to calibration error, or to some unexpected offset. Consequently it is possible, even probable, that a_0 is an artifact of the data fitting, and our conclusion must therefore be a little more ambiguous. As long as we restrict our analysis to linear terms, as in the above example, fitting the heat data to $y = a_0 + a_1x_1 + a_2x_2$ provides the *most compact* description, and is therefore 'best' if data compression is the goal. But as far as an *interpretation* of these results is concerned, i.e., for a chemical understanding of the hardening of cement, a description as $y = a_1x_1 + a_2x_2 + a_3x_3 + a_4x_4$ in terms of the four constituents would seem to be more appropriate. What constitutes the 'best' description is here seen to depend on the intended purpose of the data analysis.

3.15 Least squares for equidistant data

Equidistant data sets are collections of data for which the *independent* variable is equidistant, i.e., for which all successive increments Δx in the independent variable x are equal. Such data sets are quite common in science, because many instruments produce data at constant increments in time, voltage, magnetic field, wavelength, wavenumber, etc. Least squares analysis can be simplified significantly when the data are equidistant, in which case they can be represented conveniently in terms of Gram polynomials. This has led to new applications of least squares methods, which are readily implemented on a spreadsheet. The use of Gram polynomials for moving polynomial fits was further developed by Gram, *Mitt. Ver. Schweiz. Versicherungsmath.* (1915) 3, by Sheppard, *Proc. London Math. Soc.* (2) 13 (1914) 97, and by Sherriff, *Proc. Roy. Soc. Edinburgh* 40 (1920) 112, who all provided tables of so-called convoluting integers. This approach was further popularized by Whittaker & Robinson in *The Calculus of Observations*, their well-known 1924 treatise on numerical analysis that was still reprinted in the 1960's, as well as in other textbooks, such as Milne's 1949 *Numerical Calculus* and Wylie's *Advanced Engineering Mathematics* (1951, 1960). In chemistry it is often associated with the names of Savitzky & Golay, *Anal. Chem.* 36 (1964) 1627, who reminded analytical chemists of this method when computers became more generally available. Unfortunately, the latter authors confused their readers with tables containing an unusually large number of errors, subsequently corrected by Steinier et al., *Anal. Chem.* 44 (1972) 1906.

Here we will explore how the moving polynomial method can be used with a relatively low-order polynomial to fit a small, contiguous sample section of the data to the 'moving polynomial', typically containing a small, odd number of data points. From this fit we compute and store the resulting, smoothed value at the midpoint of the sample. The polynomial is then moved up by one point along the data set (by dropping an extreme point on one side, and adding a new data point on the other side), where-upon the process is repeated. By doing this until the moving polynomial has slithered along the entire data set, we can compute a smoothed replica thereof, except near the ends of the data set, where a slightly modified algorithm is needed. An advantage of this method is that we need not know the precise mathematical description of the curve. As long as the data density is sufficiently large with respect to the shape-defining features of that curve, any small subset of the data can usually be fitted reasonably well to a low-order polynomial.

For an odd number of equidistant data points, the moving polynomial method is very easy to implement on a spreadsheet, because the least squares analysis can then be performed with a set of fixed, tabulated *convoluting integers*. The macro ELSfixed makes it even simpler, be-cause it computes those convoluting integers, and subsequently uses them in the analysis. You specify the data set, and the length and order of the moving polynomial. As illustrated in exercise 3.14.1, the length of the moving data sample should not exceed the characteristic width of the smallest features you want to be resolved without appreciable distortion. The order of the polynomial should be as low as possible for maximum smoothing, and as high as possible for minimal data distortion. This choice therefore depends on the signal-to-noise ratio. A variant, ELS-auto, automatically selects the order each time the polynomial is moved, using an F-test, so that the order varies throughout the curve. Since it uses Gram polynomials, it can readily be modified to use the ratio of the highest-order orthogonal coefficient and its standard deviation as an alternative criterion.

It is sometimes necessary to compute the first or higher derivative of a function represented by experimental data points. It is obviously impossible to determine the derivative of a set of individual data points, but that is not what is meant here. Instead, we desire the derivative of the *reconstructed, continuous* curve on which the individual, experimental data points are assumed to lie in the absence of noise. In this case, smoothing is usually necessary because differentiation is highly sensitive to noise. The moving polynomial method fits the bill, because it provides smoothing to an algebraic expression, which can then be differentiated. For example, when we smooth a data segment by fitting it to the quadratic expression $y = a_0 + a_1x + a_2x^2$, its first derivative is immediately available as $dy/dx = a_1 + 2a_2x$. ELS can therefore be used on equidistant data to determine not only the smoothed values of the sample, but also the corresponding first and second derivatives. Again, you can modify ELS to provide higher derivatives.

Exercise 3.15.1:

(1) As test set we will use a set of four Lorentzian peaks, such as occur in, e.g., nuclear magnetic resonance spectra. In order to illustrate the effects of distortion, we will use peaks of unit height but of gradually diminishing half-widths. In A4:A1403 deposit 1 (1) 1400, in cell B4 the instruction `=10/(0.001*(A4-550)^2+10)+10/(0.01*(A4-900)^2+10)+10/(0.1*(A4-1100)^2+10)+10/((A4-1200)^2+10)`, and copy this instruction down (e.g., by clicking on its handle). Plot these data; you should see a graph such as Fig. 3.15.1, which will represent our idealized (i.e., noise-free) data set.

(2) First we will do the analysis manually, to get an idea of how it works. We use a sliding 5-point parabola, $y = a_0 + a_1 x + a_2 x^2$, for which the convoluting integers are -3, 12, 17, 12, and -3, with as common divisor their algebraic sum, 35.

(3) In cell G6 place the instruction `=(-3*B4+12*B5+17*B6+12*B7-3*B8)/35` and copy this instruction down through cell G1401. Column G will now contain the smoothed values, except for the first and last two points. There are ways to fill in those missing ends, but we will not worry about such details.

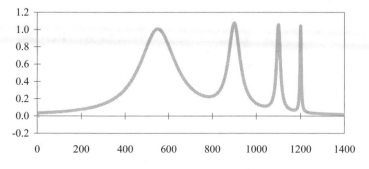

Fig. 3.15.1: A set of four Lorentzian peaks of diminishing widths.

(4) Having to look up the convoluting integers for a given polynomial length and order can be a bother. The custom macro ELSfixed will compute these integers, and then apply them to the data. Call <u>T</u>ools ⇒ <u>M</u>acro ⇒ <u>M</u>acros, select ELSfixed, and click on <u>R</u>un or Enter. In the input boxes enter the location of the data set (B4:B1403), the length of the polynomial (say, 35), its order (e.g., 3), and the order of the derivative (0 for smoothing). You should get a result such as in

Fig. 3.14.2, where the moving cubic is too long to represent the sharpest peaks in the graph. To quantify the distortion, compute $\Sigma\Delta^2$ with =SUMXMY2(B4:B1403, C4:C1403), and place the resulting value in the graph. Verify that you find less distortion with a shorter moving polynomial of, e.g., only 7 data points.

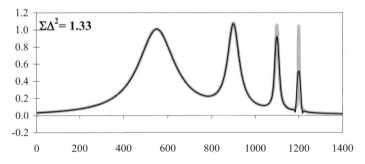

Fig. 3.15.2: The noise-free data set of Fig. 3.14.1 after smoothing with a 35-point cubic.

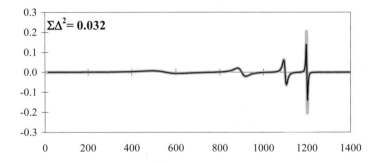

Fig. 3.15.3: The first derivative of the data of Fig. 3.15.1, obtained with a 7-point moving quadratic (thin line) and, for comparison, the separately computed true first derivative of the function. The few data points around the fourth peak contribute virtually all of $\Sigma\Delta^2$.

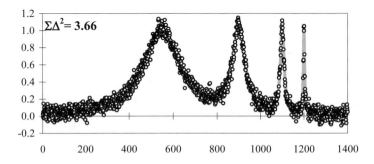

Fig. 3.15.4: The data of Fig. 3.15.1 with added Gaussian noise, $s_n = 0.05$. The signal amplitude is 1, so that the resulting signal-to-noise ratio is $1 / 0.05 = 20$.

(5) Now make the data set more realistic by adding Gaussian noise, see Fig. 3.15.4, and repeat these analyses. Figures 3.15.5 and 3.15.6 illustrate what you might obtain with ELSfixed, while Fig. 3.15.7 shows results obtained with ELS-optimized.

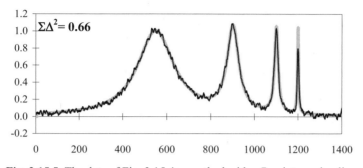

Fig. 3.15.5: The data of Fig. 3.15.4 smoothed with a 7-point moving line.

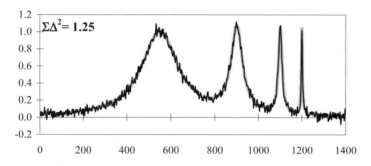

Fig. 3.15.6: The data of Fig. 3.15.4 smoothed with a 7-point moving quadratic.

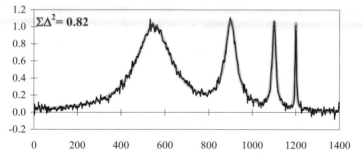

Fig. 3.15.7: The data of Fig. 3.15.4 smoothed with a 7-point moving polynomial of variable order, between 1 and 5.

The above examples demonstrate several points.

(1) When the sample length exceeds the characteristic width of the smallest feature you want to resolve, distortion will result, even in the absence of any noise.

(2) Comparison of, e.g., Figs. 3.15.5 and 3.15.6 illustrates that the lower the order of the smoothing polynomial, the more noise is removed, but the more the signal is distorted (see the line at $x = 1200$). The self-optimizing ELSauto can negotiate a useful compromise between these two, as illustrated in Fig. 3.15.7, but you still must tell it what polynomial length to use. As can be seen in Fig. 3.15.8, you can also use ELSauto (or ELSfixed) for differentiation.

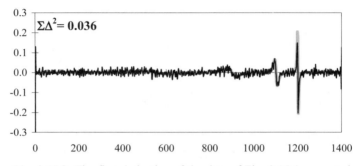

Fig. 3.15.8: The first derivative of the data of Fig. 3.15.4 computed with a 7-point moving polynomial of variable order, between 1 and 5.

3.16 Weighted least squares

Sometimes we know that an instrument is noisier in one region of its range than in another. In that case we can put more weight on some of the data than on data obtained in a different region. This is not unlike listening to witnesses in a court of law, and giving more credence to those that appear to be more trustworthy. The difference is, of course, that courts supposedly deal with accuracy, but least squares with precision, i.e., measurement repeatability.

Assigning weights to data requires that we know how much (relative) weight to allot to each measurement, and how to handle such individual weights or weighting factors w_i in an analysis. If we have sufficient replicates of each observation, we might, e.g., assign each measurement its proper *individual* weight, equal to the reciprocal of its variance, $w_i = 1/v_{ii}$ $= 1/s_i^2$. Unfortunately, such information is seldom available.

A second need for weighting arises when we use a *transformation* to make experimental data suitable for least squares analysis. For instance, data involving radioactive decay, first-order chemical kinetics, or the electrical current following a stepwise voltage change in a resistor-capacitor circuit, all follow an exponential decay of the type $y = a \, e^{-bt}$ where t denotes time. It is usual to 'rectify' such an expression by taking (natural) logarithms, so that $\ln y = \ln a - bt$, which is the expression for a straight line of $\ln y$ vs. t. If we then fit the transformed data using least squares, we minimize the sum of the residuals in $\ln y$ rather than those in y. In some cases that may well be correct, namely when the errors in y are *relative* ones, proportional to the magnitude of the signal y. But when the experimental errors are *absolute*, the resulting fit will overemphasize the tail end of the data set. In this particular example, the transformation runs into additional trouble when the signal decays to the baseline, because the experimental noise will then make a number of observations negative, in which case Excel will not know how to take the corresponding logarithms.

The first of these problems can be avoided by using weighting, which in this case simply follows from

$$\frac{\Delta \ln y}{\Delta y} \approx \frac{d \ln y}{dy} \tag{3.16.1}$$

which is valid when Δy is sufficiently small, because by definition

$$\frac{d \ln y}{dy} \equiv \lim_{\Delta y \to 0} \frac{\ln(y + \Delta y) - \ln y}{\Delta y} = \lim_{\Delta y \to 0} \frac{\Delta \ln y}{\Delta y} \tag{3.16.2}$$

Consequently we can assign each point of the transformed data set a *global* weight

$$w_i = \frac{1}{(d \ln y / dy)^2} = \frac{1}{(1/y)^2} = y^2 \tag{3.16.3}$$

or, in general, upon transforming the dependent parameter y into Y,

$$w_i = \frac{1}{(dY/dy)^2} \tag{3.16.4}$$

so that the total weight will be the product of the individual and global weights, i.e.,

$$w_i = \frac{1}{s_i^2 \, (dY/dy)^2} \tag{3.16.5}$$

There may be additional problems with a transformation. For example, when an exponential decays to zero, the experimental data will be scattered around zero, so that some of them may be negative. Because the spreadsheet cannot take the logarithms of negative numbers, the data set must be truncated before the data become negative. We would *bias* the result if we merely left out the logarithms of the negative data.

Excel has no explicit, built-in facility to handle weighted least squares. We therefore provide a weighted least squares macro, WLS, that is similar to LS but has an additional column (between the columns for the dependent and independent parameters) for the weights w_i. By leaving the second column empty (or filling it with ones), WLS can also be used for unweighted least squares.

equation	Y	X	a_0	a_1	w	comments
$y = a + b/x$	y	$1/x$	a	b	1	$x \neq 0$
$y = a + bx^p$	y	x^p	a	b	1	$x > 0$ for non-integer p
$y = a + b \ln x$	y	$\ln x$	a	b	1	$x > 0$
$y = ax^p + bx^q$	yx^{-p}	x^{q-p}	a	b	x^{2p}	$x > 0$ for non-integer p, q
$y = ab^x$	$\ln y$	x	$\ln a$	$\ln b$	y^2	$y > 0$
$y = ab^{1/x}$	$\ln y$	$1/x$	$\ln a$	$\ln b$	y^2	$x > 0, y > 0$
$y = ae^{bx}$	$\ln y$	x	$\ln a$	b	y^2	$y > 0$
$y = ae^{b/x}$	$\ln y$	$1/x$	$\ln a$	b	y^2	$x \neq 0, y > 0$
$y = ax^b$	$\ln y$	$\ln x$	$\ln a$	b	y^2	$x > 0, y > 0$
$y = ax^{bx}$	$\ln y$	$x \ln x$	$\ln a$	b	y^2	$x > 0, y > 0$
$y = ax^{b/x}$	$\ln y$	$(\ln x)/x$	$\ln a$	b	y^2	$x > 0, y > 0$
$y = e^{b/(x+a)}$	$1/\ln y$	x	a/b	$1/b$	$y^2(\ln y)^4$	$x \neq a, y > 0$
$y = \dfrac{1}{a + bx}$	$1/y$	x	a	b	y^4	$y \neq 0$
$y = \dfrac{x}{ax + b}$	$1/y$	$1/x$	a	b	y^4	$x \neq 0, y \neq 0$

Table 3.16.1: Some equations that can be transformed into the linear form $Y = a_0 + a_1 X$, with the associated global weights w as given by (3.16.4). The values of a and b are unknown, but those of p and q must be known.

equation	Y	X	a_0	a_1	a_2	w	comments
$y = a + b/x + cx$	xy	x	b	a	c	x^{-2}	van Deemter eqn., $x \neq 0$
$y = ae^{(x-b)^2/c}$	$\ln y$	x	$\ln a + b^2/c$	$-2b/c$	$1/c$	y^2	Gauss distribution
$y = ae^{(\ln x - b)^2/c}$	$\ln y$	$\ln x$	$\ln a + b^2/c$	$-2b/c$	$1/c$	y^2	lognormal distribution, $x > 0, y > 0$
$y = \dfrac{a}{(x - b)^2 + c}$	$1/y$	x	$(b^2 + c)/a$	$-2b/a$	$1/a$	y^4	Lorentz distribution, $y > 0$
$y = \dfrac{a}{(x + b)^2 + c}$	$1/y$	x	$(b^2 + c)/a$	$2b/a$	$1/a$	y^4	Cauchy distribution, $y > 0$

Table 3.16.2. Some equations that can be transformed into the quadratic form $Y = a_0 + a_1 X + a_2 X^2$.

As with LS, WLS comes in two flavors, WLS0 for curves that should go through the origin, and WLS1 for curves that need not do so. WLS provides the best-fitting coefficients a_0 through a_m, the associated sample standard deviations, as well as the corresponding covariance matrix. Tables 3.16.1 and 3.16.2 list several functions that can be transformed into linear or quadratic form respectively, and the associated global weights.

Exercise 3.16.1:

(1) As a first illustration of a weighted least squares analysis we again use the data set from D. Harvey, see exercise 2.12.1, with the added standard deviations s_i shown in column D of Fig. 3.16.1. Enter the y-values in column A, the x-values in column C (leaving the B column free for the weights w), and the standard deviations s_i of the individual y_i-values in column D.

(2) In column B calculate the weights $1/s_i^2$ according to (3.16.15) without a global transformation, i.e., with $Y = y$ so that $dY/dy = 1$.

(3) Highlight the data in columns A through C and call WLS0. Then copy your data and now call WLS1. The results are shown in Fig. 3.16.1.

	A	B	C	D
1	*y*	*w*	*x*	*s(y)*
2				
3	0	2500	0	0.02
4	12.36	2500	0.1	0.02
5	24.83	204.0816	0.2	0.07
6	35.91	59.1716	0.3	0.13
7	48.79	20.66116	0.4	0.22
8	60.42	9.182736	0.5	0.33
9		*Coeff:*	*122.9652*	
10		*StDev:*	*0.645729*	
11			*0.144358*	

	A	B	C	D
1	*y*	*w*	*x*	*s(y)*
2				
3	0	2500	0	0.02
4	12.36	2500	0.1	0.02
5	24.83	204.0816	0.2	0.07
6	35.91	59.1716	0.3	0.13
7	48.79	20.66116	0.4	0.22
8	60.42	9.182736	0.5	0.33
9	*Coeff:*	*0.044459*	*122.6411*	
10	*StDev:*	*0.085417*	*0.935897*	
11		*0.156195*		
12	*CM:*	*0.007296*	*-0.05319*	
13		*-0.05319*	*0.875904*	

Fig. 3.16.1: Fitting a set of data with standard deviations s_i of the individual y_i-values to a proportionality with WLS0 (top panel) or to a straight line with WLS1 (bottom panel).

(4) As in exercise 2.12.1, and absent any contra-indication, these data are best fitted to a proportionality rather than to a general line, because in the latter case the standard deviation in the intercept is larger than the absolute value of the intercept.

Sections 3.17 through 3.19 will illustrate the application of WLS to (1) an exponential decay of the form $y = a\,e^{-bx}$; (2) fitting enzyme kinetic data; and (3) fitting data to a Lorentzian curve.

3.17 An exponential decay

Exercise 3.17.1:

(1) Start by making a test set. Deposit 'normal' (i.e., Gaussian) noise in column N, using Tools $\Rightarrow$ Data Analysis $\Rightarrow$ Random Number Generation. In column D deposit some x-values, and in column A compute $y = a_0 \exp[-a_1 x]$ + noise, using noise from column N multiplied by some noise 'amplitude' s_n. In column B calculate the transformed quantity $Y = \ln y$, and in column C the weights y^2, see the entry for $y = b\,e^{ax}$ in table 3.16.1. Include a plot of your data. Your spreadsheet might now resemble Fig. 3.17.1. As the exponential function $y = a_0 \exp[-a_1 x]$ approaches zero, the added noise can bring the signal below zero, and interfere with taking logarithms, as can be seen in Fig. 3.17.1 in cells B21 and B25.

(2) Highlight the data in columns B through D, range B12:D25 in Fig. 3.17.1, and call the weighted least squares macro WLS1. If the dependent variable, $\ln y$, contains error messages, the macro will tell you so, and sign off. Try again, in the above example by highlighting range B12:D20 instead. The custom macro will now provide values for both $\ln a_0$ and a_1, with their standard deviations, either by overwriting cells B21:D22, or with message boxes that need to be acknowledged by pressing OK or Enter.

(3) Compare the values of $a_0 = \exp[\ln a_0]$ and a_1 obtained with those used in the calculation of y. For our example we find $\ln a_0 = 2.250975 \pm 0.031581$ and $a_1 = 0.415494 \pm 0.023354$, i.e., $a_0 = 9.5_0 \pm 0.3_0$ and $a_1 = 0.41_5 \pm 0.02_3$, which can be compared with the assumed values of 10 and 0.5 respectively. No resounding success, but what can you expect from only 7 data points in the presence of considerable noise?

(4) By changing the standard deviation s_n of the noise, verify that the difference indeed vanishes in the absence of noise. Save the spreadsheet for later use.

The Excel function LogEst (for *log*arithmic *est*imator) is the logarithmic analog of LinEst. It automatically takes the logarithm of y, and can therefore be used to fit an exponential. However, LogEst does not include any weighting.

3.18 Enzyme kinetics

The simplest kinetic relation in enzyme kinetics, first derived by Henri, *Compt. Rend.* 135 (1902) 916, but usually associated with the names of Michaelis and Menten, *Biochem. Z.* 49 (1913) 333, is

$$v = \frac{s \, v_m}{K + s} \qquad (3.18.1)$$

where v is the initial rate of the enzymatic conversion of the substrate S with concentration s, v_m is the maximum rate, and K is a constant.

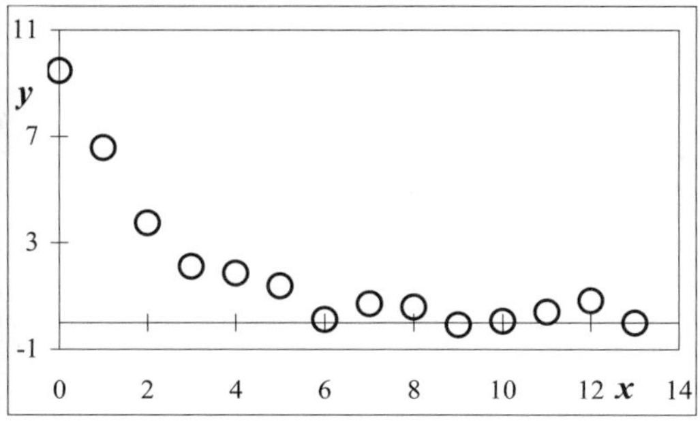

	A	B	C	D	E	F		N
1								
2								
3								
4								
5								
6								
7								
8								
9								
10								
11	*y*	*Y*	*w*	*x*				*noise*
12	9.470	2.248	89.678	0	a0 = 10			-1.325
13	6.585	1.885	43.363	1	a1 = 0.5			1.299
14	3.739	1.319	13.981	2				0.151
15	2.107	0.745	4.439	3	sn = 0.4			-0.311
16	1.856	0.618	3.444	4				1.256
17	1.373	0.317	1.885	5				1.381
18	0.118	-2.137	0.014	6				-0.950
19	0.707	-0.347	0.499	7				1.012
20	0.584	-0.538	0.341	8				1.002
21	-0.087	#NUM!	0.008	9				-0.495
22	0.055	-2.908	0.003	10				-0.032
23	0.392	-0.936	0.154	11				0.878
24	0.827	-0.190	0.683	12				2.005
25	-0.008	#NUM!	0.000	13				-0.057

The chart (rows 1–10) plots *y* vs *x*, showing a decaying curve from about 9 at $x=0$ toward near zero.

cell:	instruction:	copied to:
A12	=$F$12*EXP(-$F$13*D12)+$F$15*N12	A13:A25
B12	=LN(A12)	B13:B25
C12	=A12^2	C13:C25

Fig. 3.17.1: Fitting a synthetic exponential decay with Gaussian noise using weighted least squares. The text below the screenshot shows some of the instructions used. Cells N14:N27 contain Gaussian ('normal') noise with zero mean and unit standard deviation.

Traditionally, experimental data have been fitted to this equation after linearizing it. Hanes, *Biochem. J.* 26 (1932) 1406, rewrote (3.18.1) as

$$\frac{s}{v} = \frac{K}{v_m} + \frac{s}{v_m} \qquad\qquad\qquad (3.18.2)$$

which suggests a linear plot of s/v vs. s, with slope $1/v_m$ and intercept K/v_m. In a similar vein, Lineweaver & Burk, *J. Am. Chem. Soc.* 56 (1934) 658, inverted (3.18.1) to

$$\frac{1}{v} = \frac{K}{s\,v_m} + \frac{1}{v_m} \qquad\qquad\qquad (3.18.3)$$

so that a plot of $1/v$ vs. $1/s$ would be linear, with slope K/v_m and intercept $1/v_m$. The usual experimental uncertainties are such that the initial reaction velocity v should be the dependent variable. The two methods therefore yield somewhat *different* results for the very same experimental input data, because the transformations from v to either s/v or $1/v$ introduce a different bias to the residuals. We will use the data in table 3.18.1 to illustrate this in exercise 3.18.1.

One final comment before we are ready for this exercise. Both (3.18.2) and (3.18.3) will yield $1/v_m$ and K/v_m, so that K must subsequently be computed as $K = (K/v_m)\,/\,(1/v_m)$. Since $1/v_m$ and K/v_m are obtained from the same data analysis, they will be correlated, and we will therefore need the covariance matrices to estimate the resulting precision of K. These are included in Fig. 3.18.1.

Here, then, are the experimental data:

s / mM	0.138	0.220	0.291	0.560	0.766	1.460
v *	0.148	0.171	0.234	0.324	0.390	0.493

Table 3.18.1: The initial rate v (*: in μM / 3 min / mg enzyme) of formation of nicotinamide adenine dinucleotide at pH = 4.95 as a function of the concentration s of the corresponding mononucleotide. Data from Atkinson et al., *Biochem. J.* 80 (1961) 318, as reported by Wilkinson, *Biochem. J.* 80 (1961) 324.

Exercise 3.18.1:

(1) Open a new spreadsheet, with columns for s, v, s/v, and s, and enter the data from table 3.18.1 in the first two columns. Use LS1 to analyze these data according to (3.18.2), and determine both K/v_m (the intercept, a_0) and $1/v_m$ (the slope, a_1) with their respective standard deviations and the corresponding covariance matrix.

(2) Extend the spreadsheet by adding columns for $1/v$ and $1/s$, then use this to analyze the data according to (3.18.3). Again compute K/v_m and $1/v_m$ (which are now slope and intercept respectively) with their imprecision estimates.

(3) For the weighted least squares analysis, use a column between the dependent and the independent parameter for the weights w. Enter their appropriate values; for the Lineweaver-Burk method, which uses $1/v$ as its dependent variable,

$d(1/v)/dv = -1/v^2$, so that (3.16.4) leads to $w = v^4$. Call WLS1 to do the analysis, and thereafter repeat for the Hanes method, where we have instead $w = v^4/s^2$.

(4) Compute v_m as $1/(1/v_m)$, and K as $(K/v_m)/(1/v_m)$, then call Propagation to calculate the corresponding precisions using the covariance matrix. You should get the results shown in row 39 of Fig. 3.18.1.

	A	B	C	D	E	F	G	G
1	**unweighted:**			**Hanes**			**Lineweaver-Burk**	
2	*s*	*v*		*s/v*	*s*		*1/v*	*1/s*
3								
4	0.138	0.148		0.93243	0.138		6.75676	7.24638
5	0.220	0.171		1.28655	0.220		5.84795	4.54545
6	0.291	0.234		1.24359	0.291		4.27350	3.43643
7	0.560	0.324		1.72840	0.560		3.08642	1.78571
8	0.766	0.390		1.96410	0.766		2.56410	1.30548
9	1.460	0.493		2.96146	1.460		2.02840	0.68493
10			*Coeff:*	*0.85005*	*1.46034*	*Coeff:*	*1.70846*	*0.75279*
11			*StDev:*	*0.05958*	*0.081784*	*StDev:*	*0.30327*	*0.07815*
12			*Sf:*	*0.09024*		*Sf:*	*0.42912*	
13			*CM:*	*0.00355*	*-0.00383*	*CM:*	*0.09197*	*-0.01935*
14				*-0.00383*	*0.006689*		*-0.01935*	*0.00611*
15			*LCC:*	1	-0.78589	*LCC:*	1	-0.81627
16				-0.78589	1		-0.81627	1
17				*v max*	*K*		*v max*	*K*
18				**0.68477**	**0.58209**		**0.58532**	**0.44063**
19				*0.03835*	*0.06941*		*0.10390*	*0.11854*
20								
21		**weighted:**		**Hanes**			**Lineweaver-Burk**	
22	*s*	*v*	*s/v*	*w*	*s*	*1/v*	*w*	*1/s*
23								
24	0.138	0.148	0.932432	0.02519	0.138	6.756757	0.00048	7.24638
25	0.220	0.171	1.286550	0.01767	0.220	5.847953	0.00086	4.54545
26	0.291	0.234	1.243590	0.03541	0.291	4.273504	0.00300	3.43643
27	0.560	0.324	1.728395	0.03514	0.560	3.08642	0.01102	1.78571
28	0.766	0.390	1.964103	0.03943	0.766	2.564103	0.02313	1.30548
29	1.460	0.493	2.961460	0.02771	1.460	2.028398	0.05907	0.68493
30			*Coeff:*	*0.83984*	*1.47089*	*Coeff:*	*1.47089*	*0.83984*
31			*StDev:*	*0.05590*	*0.07605*	*StDev:*	*0.076052*	*0.05590*
32				*0.07958*			*0.108258*	
33			*CM:*	*0.00313*	*-0.00346*	*CM:*	*0.005784*	*-0.00346*
34				*-0.00346*	*0.00578*		*-0.00346*	*0.00313*
35			*LCC:*	1	-0.81381	*LCC:*	1	-0.81381
36				-0.81381	1		-0.81381	1
37				*v max*	*K*		*v max*	*K*
38				**0.67986**	**0.57097**		**0.67986**	**0.57097**
39				*0.03515*	*0.06436*		*0.03515*	*0.06436*

Fig. 3.18.1: The spreadsheet analyzing the enzyme kinetic data of Atkinson et al., *Biochem. J.* 80 (1961) 318 with unweighted and weighted linear least squares.

(5) For comparison, also use Propagation incorrectly, just using the standard deviations. Verify that it makes no difference for the precision estimate of v_m, which depends on only one coefficient, but does affect the standard deviation of K, which depends on both intercept and slope.

(6) Save the spreadsheet, because we will return to it in section 4.14.

In this particular example, the unweighted Lineweaver-Burk analysis is significantly off, as can be seen in Fig. 3.18.1: $K = 0.4_4 \pm 0.1_2$ (for the unweighted Lineweaver-Burk analysis) vs. $0.58_2 \pm 0.06_9$ (for unweighted Hanes analysis) or $0.57_1 \pm 0.06_4$ (for properly weighted Lineweaver-Burk and Hanes analysis), and the corresponding values $v_m = 0.58_5 \pm 0.10_4$ vs. $0.68_0 \pm 0.03_5$. But the failure of the unweighted Lineweaver-Burk analysis is not their fault: Lineweaver, Burk & Deming in *J. Am. Chem. Soc.* 56 (1934) 225 strongly emphasized the need for proper weighting. With such weighting, the two methods give identical results for identical input data, as well they should. But then, who reads the original papers any more?

In the above discussion we have not considered two other well-known linearizations of (3.18.1), viz. those of Eadie-Hofstee, $v = v_m - Kv/s$, and of Scatchard, $v/s = v_m/K - v/K$, because they contain the independent variable v on both sides of the equal sign, and are therefore unsuitable for linear least squares analysis.

3.19 Fitting data to a Lorentzian

The inherent shape of many optical absorption peaks is Lorentzian, i.e., it is described by an equation of the form

$$y = \frac{a}{(x-b)^2 + c} \qquad (3.19.1)$$

with a maximum at $x = b$. For the same peak height, half-width, and area, a Lorentzian peak is much broader at its base than a Gaussian. As a three-parameter curve, it cannot be linearized, but (3.19.1) can be converted into a quadratic with the transformation $Y = 1/y = x^2/a - 2bx/a + (c+b^2/a)$. According to (3.16.4) this transformation must be given the weight $w = y^4$, cf. table 3.16.2.

Exercise 3.19.1:

(1) Open a new spreadsheet, with space at the top for a graph and for four constants, a, b, c, and s_n. Below those, enter column labels for Y, w, x, x^2, and y in A through E respectively. Also place a label for noise at the same row in column N.

(2) Enter numerical constants for a, b, and c next to their labels. The value for b should be well within the range of x-values you will use. For s_n enter the numerical value 0.

(3) In column N enter Gaussian ('normal') noise of unit amplitude and zero mean.

(4) Enter x-values in column C, then calculate the corresponding y-values in column E using (3.19.1) plus noise, and the numerical constants for a, b, c, and s_n. For noise use s_n times the value in column N.

(5) Now complete the columns: calculate $Y = 1/y$ in column A, $w = y^4$ in column B, and x^2 in column D.

(6) In column F compute the resulting, fitted curve for $y_{reconstructed}$ as $1/(a_0 + a_1x + a_2x^2)$ with the coefficients a_0, a_1, and a_2 computed by WLS1.

(7) Plot y and $y_{reconstructed}$ as a function of x, and compare with Fig. 3.19.1.

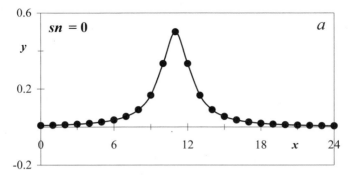

Fig. 3.19.1: Points calculated for a noise-free Lorentzian (filled circles) with $a = 1$, $b = 11$, and $c = 2$, and the curve fitted through them using the coefficients computed by using the macro WLS with appropriate weights.

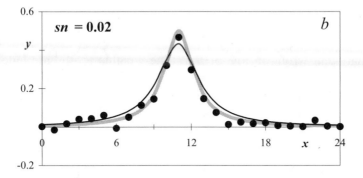

Fig. 3.19.2: Points calculated for the same Lorentzian as in Fig. 3.19.1 (gray background band) plus Gaussian noise (filled circles), and the curve fitted through them using the coefficients computed with the least squares macro WLS.

(8) Now change the value of s_n from 0 to a more realistic value (but still much smaller than 1), highlight the data block in columns A through D, and call WLS1 again (because macros do not update automatically). You might now get something like Fig. 3.19.2. When in column B you use unit weights instead, equivalent

to an unweighted fit, you would have found a correct answer in the absence of noise, but nonsense even with a relatively low amount such as shown in Fig. 3.19.2. This is because y is maximal near the peak center, for $x \approx b$, where the signal/noise ratio is maximal, whereas the transform $Y = 1/y$ is maximal *away* from the peak center, where the signal is much smaller than the noise.

(9) Keep pushing the envelope, by increasing the standard deviation s_n of the noise. Figure 3.19.3 illustrates what will eventually happen: the fitted function $y_{reconstructed}$ will broaden and no longer serve any useful purpose, as in Fig. 3.19.3.

(10) Save your spreadsheet.

The above illustrates the usefulness of testing realistic (i.e., noisy) data. The transform looks fine on paper, but a small amount of added noise disrupts it unless we use the proper weighting. That helps for weak noise, see Fig. 3.19.2, but is still not very robust, as illustrated in Fig. 3.19.3.

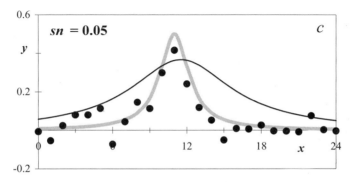

Fig. 3.19.3: The same as in Fig. 3.19.2 but with a larger noise amplitude. The fitted curve no longer provides a useful representation of the data.

What went wrong in Fig. 3.19.3? The weights $w = y^4$ are indeed appropriate for the Lorentzian curve, but are wholly *in*appropriate for noise, which they emphasize by converting noise that averages to zero into an always positive contribution. Here, then, we clearly see the limit of usefulness of weighted least squares, because we cannot find weights that would be appropriate for *both* signal *and* noise. This is why, in Fig. 3.19.3, the analysis becomes overwhelmed by noise. But don't give up, and hold on to the spreadsheet: a more noise-resistant solution to this problem will be described in section 4.15.

3.20 Miscellany

After so many worked-out examples here are a few that are just mentioned, without much handholding. By now you will know your way around the spreadsheet in order to solve them.

3.20.1 The boiling point of water

In section 2.15 we indicated that a proper analysis of the data shown in Fig. 2.15.1 requires weighting, since the measured quantity is pressure p while the fitted quantity is its natural logarithm, ln p. Use weighted least squares to analyze these data, and compare your results with those listed at the end of section 2.15.

3.20.2 The vapor pressure of water

In section 2.11 we used an algebraic expression for the temperature-dependence of the vapor pressure P_w of water between 0 to 75°C. Use tabulated values for P_w as a function of temperature t from the 1984 *NBS/NRC Steam Tables*, as reproduced in, e.g., the *CRC Handbook of Chemistry and Physics*, 81st edition, D. R. Lide, ed., Chemical Rubber Co. 2000/2001, p. 6-10. These already smoothed data clearly don't fit a straight line, but are readily represented in terms of a power series in t. Use LSPoly1 to find the optimal order of such a series, determine its co-efficients, and plot the resulting residuals.

Since ln P_w is a more linear function of temperature t, the vapor pressure of water can also be represented as a lower-order polynomial of the type $P_w = \exp[a_0 + a_1 t + a_2 t^2 + \ldots]$. Compute ln P_w and express it as a power series in t, then calculate $P_w = \exp[\ln P_w]$ and display the resulting residuals.

3.20.3 Fitting data to a higher-order polynomial

The foregoing examples all involved successful applications of least squares methods, with the notable exception of Fig. 3.19.3, to which we will return in section 4.15. Here is another unsuccessful case: fitting a data set with relatively little structure to a high-order polynomial. Especially with polynomials of order 6 or higher, truncation errors in the numerical manipulations can sometimes hijack the computation, and yield nonsensical results. *It is therefore always prudent to check the answer.*

As our specific example we will use a file from the Statistical Reference Dataset, specifically Filip.dat, which is accessible at www.itl.nist. gov/div898/strd/lls/data/LINKS/DATA/Filip.dat. This file contains 82 x,y data pairs, to be fitted to a tenth-order polynomial in x. Go to the web at the above address, highlight the page, copy it, save it as a Notepad, then import the Notepad file into Excel. Fig. 3.20.1 shows the results for this data set with Trendline, which goes only up to sixth order.

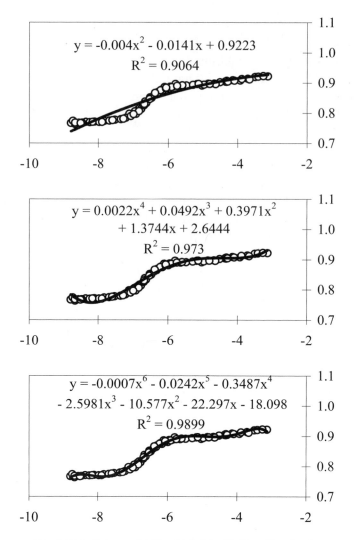

Fig. 3.20.1: Polynomial fits obtained with Trendline for the
Filip data set for polynomial order 2, 4, or 6 respectively.

Highlight the data set and call LSPoly1. As the order increases, the value of s_f goes through a fairly deep minimum: from $s_f = 0.0059$ for a sixth order polynomial to a 50 times larger value for a tenth order polynomial. That is far more than can be understood by the change in $\sqrt{(N-P)}$ from $\sqrt{(82-6)} = 8.72$ to $\sqrt{(82-10)} = 8.49$, and indicates that the sum of squares of the residuals increases as the polynomial order becomes higher. That can only be the result of computational errors. And while the parameters of the sixth-order polynomial yield a somewhat crude approximation to the data, see Fig. 3.20.1, the coefficients of the tenth order polynomial trace a curve that does not even come close, as shown in Fig. 3.20.2. You might suspect a custom macro such as LSPoly, but the Excel-provided least squares routines yield equivalent answers, possibly reflecting similar matrix inversion problems in those algorithms.

Of the least squares routines we have encountered so far, only Ortho uses a significantly different algorithm, specifically one that keeps truncation errors to a minimum by avoiding matrix inversions. The results obtained with Ortho1 suggest that none of the coefficients is statistically significant above 7th order, i.e., that the tenth-order model used is really no good. Still, if a tenth-order polynomial is prescribed, Ortho comes closest to fitting the data satisfactorily, as illustrated in Fig. 3.20.2, which also shows how poorly the traditional least squares routine does in this case. Yet, NIST lists a set of 11 coefficients, a_0 through a_{10}, that are all about 5 times their standard deviations, and that indeed can be used to fit the data set quite well, with $s_f = 0.0033$. Such results, however, require a computation with much more than double precision.

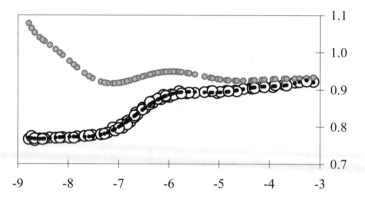

Fig. 3.20.2: Tenth-order polynomial fits of the Filip data set (large open circles) as obtained with LSPoly1 (gray filled circles) and with Ortho1 (small black solid circles, $s_f = 0.0039$). But a tenth-order polynomial is clearly overkill, and LSPoly1 indicates that lower-order polynomials can provide quite reasonable fits, such as a sixth-order fit with $s_f = 0.0059$.

The take-home lesson: always check whether the model used and the resulting answers make sense. The model may be inefficient or unsuitable, the algorithm may be mathematically correct yet may introduce enough numerical errors to invalidate the results. The more complicated the calculation, the more such errors can accumulate. Since Ortho uses a different, simpler least squares algorithm, it can serve in this case as a useful first verification tool for critical results.

3.21 Summary

In this chapter we have applied linear least squares methods to functions far beyond a proportionality or a straight line. Because the computer takes care of the mathematical manipulations, the least squares method has become very easy to apply, and has therefore become ubiquitous in many fields of science and technology. It provides a convenient way to fit data to a polynomial or a multivariate function, or to any other function that can be transformed into one of these. Weighting may then be required to correct for the bias introduced by the transformation.

The least squares method furnishes estimates of the precision of its results, based on the (usually tacit) assumptions that the noise is random and can be described adequately by a single Gaussian distribution. The latter is a useful working assumption, which often can only be verified or falsified with large data sets. For that same reason, the likely errors resulting from incorrectly assuming a single Gaussian distribution for small data sets will usually be rather inconsequential. It is therefore customary to assume a single Gaussian distribution of errors, unless there is evidence to the contrary. Such evidence may be in the form of 'outliers' that may, e.g., indicate the presence of more than one distribution.

An example is the weight of US pennies, which typically have a mass of about 2.5 g. But if our sample includes pennies from before 1982, when they were still made of copper rather than of zinc with a copper coating, we will encounter two distinct Gaussian distributions, around 3 g for the older, solid copper pennies, and around 2.5 g for the zinc ones. If our measurements include only one old penny, it might easily be considered an outlier, and disregarded. But in doing so we merely create a semblance of orderliness where none exists. Outliers are often the canaries in the coal mine, warning us of potential problems.

*****

The least squares algorithm can be simplified greatly when applied to equidistant data, thereby making them practical for use in 'sliding' polynomials for smoothing, interpolation, and differentiation, even if the data set has no known theoretical description and, in its entirety, does not fit a polynomial at all. Of course, the convenience of least squares methods should not lead to carelessness. The example of enzyme kinetics summarized in Fig. 3.18.1 illustrates but one of the many ways in which incorrect answers can be obtained by thoughtless application of least squares. And they are often not quite as obvious as those described by Darrell Hill in his delightful book on *How to Lie with Statistics* (Norton, 1982).

When theoretical guidance is absent, there are ways to determine whether higher-order terms are statistically significant. Even though we have not illustrated this here, you can readily prove to yourself (by trying it out on a spreadsheet) that use of terms higher than necessary can lead to problems, such as oscillations between the points used for determining the parameters. The probability of such oscillatory behavior between data points increases with higher polynomial order and with larger data spacing, and they can be particularly troublesome for interpolation or differentiation. This, as well as maximal noise reduction, are good reasons to favor the lowest possible polynomial order in fitting experimental data. On the other hand, low-order polynomials can introduce systematic distortion if the underlying signal has sharp features. The optimal solution to this dilemma is to collect a sufficiently large number of closely spaced data, and to analyze them with a relatively short, low-order moving polynomial. In this case the working assumption is that, in the limit of infinitesimally small spacing, everything is linear, and that, for slightly larger spacing, a quadratic or cubic fit will do.

*****

In this and the previous chapter we encountered the covariance and its companion, the linear correlation coefficient, which specify the interrelatedness of specific parameters obtained by least squares, such as the slope and intercept of a straight line. There is another, more prevalent but often incorrect application of the linear correlation coefficient, in which r_{xy} is used as a measure of goodness of a least squares fit. We already commented on this in section 2.10, but the point bears repeating.

In the usual application of the linear correlation coefficient as a measure of goodness of fit for, say, a straight line, that correlation is between a straight line $y = a_0 + a_1x$ and a straight line $x = b_0 + b_1y$, and therefore answers the question whether there is a linear correlation between x and y. This assumes that we are not yet concerned with any details of the specific numerical relation between x and y, but ask the more basic question whether x and y are (linearly) correlated at all. That can be a valid question when one needs to answer whether cigarette smoking can cause lung cancer (as it clearly does), or whether living close to power lines can cause leukemia (it apparently does not). However, in the type of data analysis we emphasize in this book, the existence of a causal relationship can be assumed, and we seek to answer a different question: not *whether* a linear relation exists, but specifically *what* that relationship is. For such applications, the linear correlation coefficient r_{xy} or its square are poor (and inappropriate) gauges.

*****

It is sometimes assumed that least squares methods are inherently objective. This is true insofar as their number-crunching aspects are concerned (apart from such numerical errors as encountered in section 3.20.3), but not in terms of the underlying assumptions about the nature of the experimental fluctuations (random or biased, following a single or multiple distribution, assumed to be either Gaussian or other) or in terms of the various choices made by the experimenter (which variable to take as the dependent one, or what equation, polynomial order, and/or weighting factors to use in fitting the data). Least squares analysis can be misapplied just as easily as any other method. Remember that all that glitters isn't necessarily gold, and that fool's gold (FeS_2) is far more abundant than the more precious commodity it resembles (Au).

For the many functions that cannot be fitted to a polynomial or be transformed into one, a nonlinear least squares analysis is possible as long as we have an analytical expression (or find an approximate one) to which the experimental data can be fitted. Nonlinear least squares may even be preferable in cases where one has a choice between linear and nonlinear least squares. Nonlinear least squares will be described in the next chapter.

3.22 For further reading

There are many books on linear least squares methods and on multivariate analysis, although not that many that bridge the gap between the introductory texts and the specialist books written for statisticians. A very good text, more advanced than the ones already listed in section 2.18, is *Applied Regression Analysis* by N. R. Draper & H. Smith, (Wiley, 1966, 1981, 1998). It uses the powerful (but initially perhaps somewhat forbidding) matrix formalism now standard among statisticians, and used in most computer-based least squares computer routines, including those provided by Excel, and in all the custom least squares macros of the MacroBundle.

Chapter 4

Nonlinear least squares

In the previous chapters we have encountered the *linear* least squares method, so called because it fits data to equations that are linear functions of their adjustable *coefficients* a_i. Note that the equations themselves can be highly nonlinear in the dependent and independent *parameters*, as in $y^3 = a_0 + a_1 x^2 + a_2 \log(x) + a_3 \exp(z^5)$, as long as they are linear *in the coefficients* a_i, as in this example. This is readily seen by substituting $Y = y^3$, $X_1 = x^2$, $X_2 = \log(x)$, and $X_3 = \exp(z^5)$, which converts the above expression into the standard form of multiparameter linear least squares, $Y = a_0 + a_1 X_1 + a_2 X_2 + a_3 X_3$. Linear least squares methods use algorithms that lead to singular, usually well-defined results.

Unfortunately, there are many problems to which linear least squares analysis cannot be applied, e.g., when the term $a_3 \exp(z^5)$ in the above expression for y^3 is replaced by $\exp(a_3 z^5)$. The only least squares methods then applicable are *nonlinear* ones, which will be discussed in the present chapter. We will also encounter a few examples (e.g., in section 4.15) in which it may be preferable to use nonlinear least squares analysis even though a linear least squares analysis is feasible.

In a nonlinear least squares method, one compares a given data set (which we will here call the experimental one, even though in some of our exercises we will again simulate it, for lack of real experimental data) with a model expression that depends on one or more numerical parameters. We compute the sum of squares of the residuals, SSR, or some other appropriate single parameter, then minimize that parameter by adjusting the numerical coefficients used in the model. If the model is appropriate, and the noise is not overwhelmingly large, we can usually find a set of coefficients to provide a reasonably close fit to the experimental data. Unlike the case of linear least squares, there is no guarantee that we will necessarily find the 'best' fit for the model assumptions made. Where a direct comparison with linear least squares is possible, we usually end up with a similar answer, as long as the initial (guessed) values of the coefficients are fairly close to their final values. Again, one of the best checks on the reasonableness of our fit is to plot the residuals, because that graph can often reveal the presence of systematic deviations.

The sophistication of a nonlinear least squares method lies in how efficiently it adjusts the model parameters. In Excel, nonlinear least squares methods use Solver, a powerful and convenient add-in based on the algorithm proposed by K. Levenberg, *Q. Appl. Math.* 2 (1944) 164 and implemented by D. W. Marquardt, *J. SIAM* 11 (1963) 431, and further refined by Leon Lasdon, Allan Waren, John Watson, and Dan Fylstra. It can be found in the Tools submenu, and apart from its basic function it has several useful Options, such as Use Automatic Scaling and Show Iteration Results. These options are explained in the Excel Help files, and some of them are illustrated in exercise 4.21.5.

Solver is provided with Excel, both in its stand-alone version and as part of the Microsoft Office bundle, but its code is provided by Frontline Systems (www.frontsys.com), and it may still have to be installed in case a minimal version of the software was installed originally.

As provided by Excel, Solver has one major deficiency: it yields results without any associated uncertainty estimates. This can be remedied by subsequently running a custom macro, SolverAid, which will reconstruct the standard deviations based on (2.8.1), (2.9.1), or (2.9.2), and deposit them next to the parameters found by Solver if that space is available. SolverAid can also furnish the covariance matrix or its scaled version, the linear correlation coefficient matrix. The way SolverAid does all this is detailed in section 9.9.

The first group of examples, in sections 4.1 through 4.6, will illustrate the power of Solver to fit data to expressions for which there are no easy or known ways to transform them into a polynomial with integer powers, the usual circumstance for using a nonlinear least squares analysis. In section 4.1 we will analyze data from the cosmic microwave background radiation detector aboard the COBE (*Co*smic *B*ackground *Ex*plorer) satellite. This satellite measured the so-called black body radiation in interstellar space, radiation believed to be a relic of the big bang. Black body radiation is described by the Planck equation, famous because its derivation heralded the birth of quantum theory. There is no known transformation of the Planck equation to allow a linear least squares analysis of these data, but fortunately that is no requirement for nonlinear least squares. Our next, more down-to-earth examples will involve fitting a molecular potential energy-distance profile, acid-base titrations, and phosphorescence decay. Sections 4.5 and 4.6 will deal with curves that contain several peaks, as occur in, e.g., spectra and chromatograms.

As an introduction to using Solver we will first use it in a simple example of reverse-engineering a complex mathematical operation. Imagine that you know how to multiply, and therefore how to compute $b = a^3 = a \times a \times a$, but that you do not know how to perform its reverse operation, taking the cube root $\sqrt[3]{b}$ to find a. Several approaches come to mind: (1) learn about cube roots and how to calculate them, (2) get a machine or algorithm that will do the trick, or (3) use a trial-and-error method based on Solver. Here is how you might do that: take b and some (preferably fairly close) estimate of a, calculate a^3, then let Solver adjust the value of a in order to minimize the difference between b and a^3.

Exercise 4.0.1:

(1) In a new spreadsheet, deposit in cells A1:A4 the labels b=, a=, aaa=, and SR= where SR stands for Square of the Residual, i.e., $(b-a^3)^2$.

(2) In cell B1 deposit the number 3, in cell B2 the number 1, in cell B3 the instruction =B2*B2*B2, and in cell B4 the instruction = (B1-B3) * (B1-B3).

(3) Call Solver, Set Target Cell to B4, Equal To Min, By Changing Cells B2, and press OK. Bingo: the cube root of 3 will appear in cell B2, correct to 8 significant digits. As you can see, it works indeed, although we hardly advocate this as your method of choice for cube-rooting.

(4) This gives us a convenient chance to look into the Options of Solver. Max Time and Iterations are self-explanatory and, anyway, inconsequential because, for serious computations with Solver, you should always try Solver again to make sure it gave you its best, final answer. Change the value of b to the cube of an integer number, say, 8, so that you can more readily see how good the answer is. Then play with Precision to establish that it defines how tightly your condition must be met. You should of course reset the value of a every time, otherwise Solver may just nod and leave well enough alone.

(5) Tolerance only works when you use integer constraints. It might better be called 'Integer tolerance'.

(6) Convergence determines the amount of relative change in the last five iterations; if that is less than the set amount, Solver will stop and consider its job done. Try various values to see how it works.

(7) Assume Linear Model is seldom useful, but Assume Non-Negative can be, as already illustrated in sections 4.9 and 4.11. See what happens when you start with $b = 9$, $a = -3.1$ and in cell B3 the modified instruction =B2*B2, with or without Assume Non-Negative. Then try it with $a = 3.1$. It may remind you of the need to have good initial estimates.

(8) Use Automatic Scaling is useful when the adjustable parameters are of different orders of magnitude. This is equivalent to taking their logarithms, as will be done in sections 4.3 and 4.4.

(9) Show Iteration Results can be instructive, because it shows snapshots of what happens during the iterations.

(10) Estimates, Derivatives, and Search are best left alone.

4.1   Cosmic microwave background radiation

We will use the spectral data given by S. Bluestone, *J. Chem. Educ.*
78 (2001) 215, as reproduced in table 4.1, then fit these data to Planck's
expression for black body radiation,

$$B = \frac{2h\nu^3}{c^2(e^{h\nu/kT} - 1)} \tag{4.1.1}$$

where B denotes the optical brightness, h is Planck's constant, ν is the
frequency of the light, c is the speed of light in vacuum, and T is the absolute temperature. In terms of fitting experimental brightness data B as a
function of wavenumber $\bar{\nu} = \nu/c$ we can rewrite (4.1.1) as

$$B = \frac{a\bar{\nu}^3}{e^{b\bar{\nu}} - 1} \tag{4.1.2}$$

where a and b are adjustable parameters.

Exercise 4.1.1:

(1) Open a spreadsheet, leave room at its top for a graph, and enter the wavenumber $\bar{\nu}$ and experimental brightness B_{exp} in columns A and B, e.g., starting in
row 18.

(2) In column C compute B_{model} according to (4.1.2), using assumed values for
a and b located in. e.g., cells G3 and G4 respectively.

(3) Plot both B_{exp} and B_{model} vs. $\bar{\nu}$, and adjust the values of a and b so that both
curves are visible in the same plot, such as $a = 1$ and $b = 1$.

(4) In cell G5 compute the sum of the squares of the residuals $R = \Delta = (B_{exp} -$
$B_{model})$, i.e., SSR (for the *S*um of *S*quares of the *R*esiduals) $= \Sigma \Delta^2 = \Sigma (B_{exp} -$
$B_{model})^2$. This is most readily done with the command =SUMXMY2 (), where the
argument contains the address ranges for B_{exp} and B_{model} respectively.

(5) Call Solver with <u>T</u>ools $\Rightarrow$ Sol<u>v</u>er. In the window to Set target cell enter the
address of SSR, specify Equal to Mi<u>n</u>, and in the window <u>B</u>y changing cells enter
the addresses of the parameters a and b, then press Solve or Enter. Accept the answer by checking the <u>K</u>eep Solver solution and press OK. Look at the fit in the
graph. If it is poor, repeat Solver with the new values for a and b. If that doesn't
work, use different starting values for a and b to get Solver past what may be a
'false' (i.e., local rather than global) minimum.

(6) Now call the macro SolverAid to get estimates of the precision of your results. In the example of Fig. 4.1.1, the parameters determined by Solver are located in G3:G4, the sum of squares of the residuals in G5, and the column containing Y_{calc} is C18:C60. Do request to see the covariance matrix, and specify its
space as G6:H7.

$\bar{v}$ /cm^{-1}	B_{exp} /10^{-18}	w_{rel} /10^{-3}	$\bar{v}$ /cm^{-1}	B_{exp} /10^{-18}	w_{rel} /10^{-3}	$\bar{v}$ /cm^{-1}	B_{exp} /10^{-18}	w_{rel} /10^{-3}
2.27	2.0110	5.10	8.62	2.7281	8.26	15.43	0.4265	2.77
2.72	2.5003	2.77	9.08	2.4957	6.94	15.88	0.3669	2.27
3.18	2.9369	1.60	9.53	2.2721	5.10	16.34	0.3136	1.89
3.63	3.2858	1.89	9.98	2.0552	3.91	16.79	0.2684	1.48
4.08	3.5503	2.07	10.44	1.8438	3.09	17.24	0.2287	1.28
4.54	3.7316	2.27	10.89	1.6488	2.07	17.70	0.1945	1.11
4.99	3.8269	3.09	11.34	1.4672	2.07	18.15	0.1657	0.98
5.45	3.8477	3.09	11.80	1.2973	1.89	18.61	0.1396	0.92
5.90	3.8027	3.91	12.25	1.1438	1.89	19.06	0.1185	0.82
6.35	3.7025	5.10	12.71	1.0019	1.89	19.51	0.1003	0.59
6.81	3.5551	5.92	13.16	0.8771	2.07	19.97	0.0846	0.33
7.26	3.3773	6.94	13.61	0.7648	2.27	20.42	0.0717	0.13
7.71	3.1752	8.26	14.07	0.6631	2.50	20.87	0.0587	0.04
8.17	2.9535	10.00	14.52	0.5749	2.77	21.33	0.0459	0.01
			14.97	0.4965	2.77			

Table 4.1.1: The cosmic background radiation data from COBE as summarized by S. Bluestone in *J. Chem. Educ.* 78 (2001) 215.

(7) Your spreadsheet may now look like that shown in Fig. 4.1.1. Notice that SolverAid places the standard deviations in a and b to the right of these parameters, and the standard deviation of the over-all fit to the right of the sum of squares of the residuals, here labeled SSR.

(8) The covariance matrix in G6:H7 contains the variances v_{aa} and v_{bb} on its (top-left to bottom-right) diagonal, and the covariances $v_{ab} = v_{ba}$ in the off-diagonal locations. Verify that, indeed, $v_{aa} = s_a^2$ (v_a is found in cell G6, s_a in cell H3) and, likewise, $v_{bb} = s_b^2$, but that v_{ab} (in cell G7) is not given by (2.10.1), which applies specifically to a straight line.

(9) Also verify that v_{ab}^2 has almost the same value as the product $v_{aa}v_{bb}$, indicating that a and b are highly correlated, see (2.9.4). What this means is readily illustrated by setting a to a different value, and then using Solver to adjust only b, showing that an error in a causes a corresponding error in b, and vice versa.

In this initial attempt to fit these data we have only considered the first two columns in table 4.1.1, but the information in the third column should not be neglected. This column lists the relative weights w_i that should be assigned to each individual brightness B_i. We now modify the spreadsheet in order to accommodate these weights.

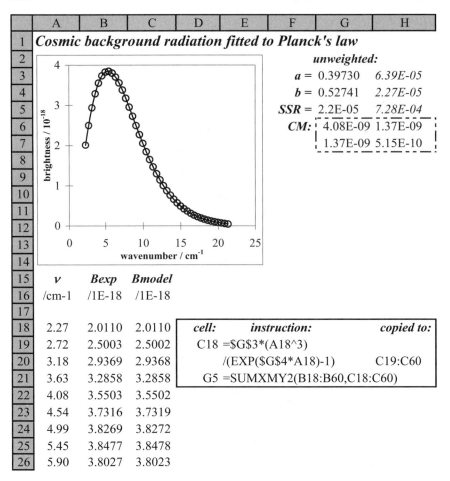

Fig. 4.1.1: The top of the spreadsheet of exercise 4.1.1 after using Solver and SolverAid for an unweighted nonlinear least squares analysis of the COBE data. Note that v should read $\bar{v}$, which Excel cannot display.

The appropriate criterion to be minimized is now $\Sigma w(B_{exp}-B_{model})^2$. Because Excel does not have a conveniently compact function (analogous to SUMXMY2 (*range1, range2*)) to compute such a weighted sum of squares of residuals, we use an additional column to compute it. Moreover, for the sake of comparing the results obtained with unweighted and weighted nonlinear least squares, we will normalize the relative weights used in $\Sigma w\Delta^2$ (denoted on the spreadsheet by *SwSR*) through division by the normalizing factor $(\Sigma w)/N$, which is here displayed separately on the spreadsheet, but could have been included directly in the formula used for *SwSR*.

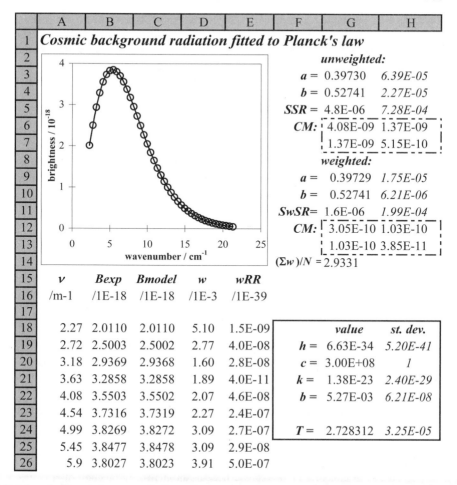

	A	B	C	D	E	F	G	H
1	**Cosmic background radiation fitted to Planck's law**							

unweighted:

a = 0.39730   6.39E-05
b = 0.52741   2.27E-05
SSR = 4.8E-06   7.28E-04
CM: 4.08E-09 1.37E-09
      1.37E-09 5.15E-10

weighted:

a = 0.39729   1.75E-05
b = 0.52741   6.21E-06
$SwSR$ = 1.6E-06   1.99E-04
CM: 3.05E-10 1.03E-10
      1.03E-10 3.85E-11

$(\Sigma w)/N$ = 2.9331

	v	$Bexp$	$Bmodel$	w	wRR
15	/m-1	/1E-18	/1E-18	/1E-3	/1E-39
18	2.27	2.0110	2.0110	5.10	1.5E-09
19	2.72	2.5003	2.5002	2.77	4.0E-08
20	3.18	2.9369	2.9368	1.60	2.8E-08
21	3.63	3.2858	3.2858	1.89	4.0E-11
22	4.08	3.5503	3.5502	2.07	4.6E-08
23	4.54	3.7316	3.7319	2.27	2.4E-07
24	4.99	3.8269	3.8272	3.09	2.7E-07
25	5.45	3.8477	3.8478	3.09	2.9E-08
26	5.9	3.8027	3.8023	3.91	5.0E-07

	value	*st. dev.*
h =	6.63E-34	5.20E-41
c =	3.00E+08	1
k =	1.38E-23	2.40E-29
b =	5.27E-03	6.21E-08
T =	2.728312	3.25E-05

Fig. 4.1.2: The top of the final form of the spreadsheet of exercise 4.1.1, after using Solver and SolverAid for a weighted nonlinear least squares analysis of the COBE data. Again please read $\bar{v}$ for the column heading v.

***Exercise 4.1.1 (continued)*:**

(10) Enter the relative weights w listed in table 4.1.1 in column D, and in column E calculate w times the square of the residuals, i.e., $w \Delta^2 = w (B_{exp} - B_{model})^2$, or wSR for short. In cell G14 calculate $(\Sigma w)/N$, and in cell G11 compute the weighted sum of squares of the residuals, $SwSR$, as $N \Sigma w(B_{exp} - B_{model})^2 / \Sigma w$, so that cells G14 and G11 will contain the instructions =AVERAGE(D18:D60) and =SUM(E18: E60)/G14 respectively.

(11) Let the expressions now refer to a and b in cells G9 and G10 respectively. Engage Solver again (now using G11 as the target cell, and G9:G10 as the adjustable parameters), and recalculate the values for a and b. In this particular case, where the data clearly fit the model very well and are virtually noise-free, weighting makes only a relatively minor improvement, mostly on the uncertainty.

(12) Comparison of equations (4.1.1) and (4.1.2) shows that $b = hc/kT$. You can use this to calculate the background temperature T of the universe! With the numerical values $h = (6.6260687_6 \pm 0.0000005_2) \times 10^{-34}$ J · s, $c = 2.99792458 \times 10^8$ m · s^{-1}, and $k = (1.380650_3 \pm 0.000002_4) \times 10^{-23}$ J · °K^{-1} we find $T = (2.72831_2 \pm 0.00003_2)$ °K for the temperature of interstellar space. Here we have used the Propagation macro to estimate the propagated imprecision in $T = hc/kb$, after division of b by 100 to convert it from measuring centimeters (i.e., inverse wave numbers) to meters. Note that this computation only requires b, so that there is no need to use the covariance matrix.

Because these measurements allow determinations of the temperature of interstellar space with a precision of the order of 10^{-4} °K, the fine structure of the cosmic background radiation can now be observed. This will be done by the Microwave Anisotropy Probe that was launched by NASA in 2001.

4.2   The I_2 potential energy vs. distance profile

Spectroscopic measurements such as those described in sections 3.3 and 3.6 can be used to determine the potential energy – distance profile (often called the potential energy curve) of a diatomic molecule. This can then be used to test various model expressions for such a profile, and to estimate the equilibrium distance r_e and the dissociation energy D_e. As our example we will use a set of data reported by R. D. Verma in *J. Chem. Phys.* 32 (1960) 738, table VII, for the ground state of iodine, I_2. We reproduce these data in Fig. 4.2.1, and analyze them in exercise 4.2.1.

Exercise 4.2.1:

(1) Enter the data of table VII of R. D. Verma, *J. Chem. Phys.* 32 (1960) 738 (reproduced in table 4.2.1) in a spreadsheet, as an increasing function of r. Use three columns: one for the vibrational quantum number v, one for the energy $U(r)$, and one for the distance r. Note that the values for v, $U(r)$, and r will appear twice, once for r_{min} and once for r_{max}. Plot the data as $U(r)$ vs. r.

(2) Enter labels and initial guess values for fitting $U(r)$ to the Morse function $U(r) = a\{1-\exp[-b(r-r_e)]\}^2$, add a column in which you compute U_{Morse} on the basis of these data, and plot the resulting curve. Adjust the guessed values to achieve a crude fit with the experimental data. Such visually adjusted initial guess values might be $a = 12000$, $b = 0.02$, and $r_e = 250$ when (as in Fig. 4.2.1) r has been entered in picometers. For r in Ångstrom units, use $r_e = 2.5$ instead.

(3) Compute SSR using the function SUMXMY2(), then call Solver to adjust the values of a, b, and r_e, and call SolverAid to compute the precision.

(4) Another often used fitting function is that of Lennard-Jones, which has the form $U(r) = a+4a\{(b/r)^{12}-(b/r)^6\}$. Enter the labels and guess values for a and b, compute $U(r)$ according to the Lennard-Jones formula in the next column, add these data to the plot, and calculate the corresponding sum of squares of the residuals. Then call Solver to optimize the fit, and SolverAid for uncertainty estimates. Your spreadsheet might now look like Fig. 4.2.1.

	A	B	C	D	E	F
1	Data from R.D.Verma, JPC 32 (1960) 738.					
2						
3	*Morse:*			*Lennard-Jones:*		
4	*a =*	12666.6	*67.7*	*a =* 12385		*150*
5	*b =*	0.019899	*0.000162*	*b =* 229.14		*0.157*
6	*r eq =*	236.342	*0.237*	*r eq =* 257.2		*0.176*
7	*SSR =*	4.14E+06	*252.4*	*SSR =* 3.34E+07		*771.6*
8						
9	*v*	*U(r)*	*r*	*U(M)*	*U(LJ)*	
10		*/cm*	*pm*	*pm*	*pm*	
11						
12	112	12547.52	228.8	12375.58	12826.54	
13	107	12532.22	228.8	12375.58	12826.54	
14	105	12522.32	228.8	12375.58	12826.54	
15	103	12509.82	228.8	12375.58	12826.54	
16	101	12495.02	228.8	12375.58	12826.54	
17	99	12476.92	228.8	12375.58	12826.54	
18	97	12454.62	228.9	12276.80	12693.71	
19	95	12427.12	228.9	12276.80	12693.71	
20	93	12393.42	228.9	12276.80	12693.71	
21	91	12352.32	229.0	12178.61	12561.98	
22	89	12302.32	229.0	12178.61	12561.98	
23	85	12170.52	229.1	12081.00	12431.33	
24	82	12039.72	229.2	11983.98	12301.77	
25	78	11824.50	229.4	11791.69	12045.83	
26	74	11562.11	229.6	11601.71	11794.13	
27	70	11251.24	229.8	11414.02	11546.58	
28	66	10893.54	230.1	11136.72	11182.94	
29	62	10490.72	230.5	10774.81	10712.12	
30	58	10045.19	230.9	10421.67	10256.93	
31	54	9559.11	231.5	9908.06	9602.49	
32	50	9034.45	232.1	9413.30	8980.82	
33	46	8474.73	232.8	8859.19	8295.11	
34	42	7882.80	233.6	8255.42	7561.13	
35	38	7260.45	234.6	7543.24	6713.89	
36	34	6608.93	235.8	6748.11	5793.17	
37	30	5930.54	237.1	5955.98	4904.44	

Fig. 4.2.1a: The top of the spreadsheet of exercise 4.2.1, with the distances *r* in pm, and the results of Solver and SolverAid. Also shown is the value of the equilibrium distance calculated for the Lennard-Jones model as $r_{eq} = b \sqrt[6]{2}$, and the associated precision computed with Propagation.

38	26	5226.63	238.6	5125.97	4006.76
39	22	4498.49	240.3	4286.43	3138.03
40	18	3747.28	242.3	3425.21	2294.54
41	14	2973.82	244.6	2587.99	1531.05
42	10	2179.06	247.4	1765.36	852.58
43	6	1363.60	251.0	981.65	307.46
44	2	527.44	256.4	277.98	4.37
45	0	102.08	262.1	7.94	142.16
46	0	102.08	271.7	297.35	974.25
47	2	527.44	279.0	907.76	1848.12
48	6	1363.60	287.4	1833.15	2929.52
49	10	2179.06	294.0	2641.68	3770.59
50	14	2973.82	300.1	3409.03	4514.22
51	18	3747.28	305.6	4096.19	5146.75
52	22	4498.49	311.1	4765.69	5738.77
53	26	5226.63	316.4	5385.98	6269.43
54	30	5930.54	321.7	5976.61	6761.07
55	34	6608.93	327.3	6564.94	7239.36
56	38	7260.45	332.9	7114.63	7677.34
57	42	7882.80	338.9	7660.05	8104.65
58	46	8474.73	345.1	8176.90	8504.03
59	50	9034.45	351.7	8676.66	8886.13
60	54	9559.11	359.1	9178.51	9267.03
61	58	10045.19	367.1	9656.67	9628.65
62	62	10490.72	376.0	10117.48	9977.58
63	66	10893.54	386.1	10560.30	10315.26
64	70	11251.24	397.3	10965.80	10629.02
65	74	11562.11	410.8	11355.44	10938.05
66	78	11824.50	426.3	11696.45	11219.20
67	82	12039.72	444.8	11991.12	11476.48
68	85	12170.52	462.8	12192.54	11666.03
69	89	12302.32	494.2	12411.70	11897.73
70	91	12352.32	513.3	12492.03	11996.09
71	93	12393.42	535.4	12554.02	12082.46
72	95	12427.12	556.3	12592.28	12144.26
73	97	12454.62	577.8	12618.13	12193.06
74	99	12476.92	601.0	12636.06	12233.31
75	101	12495.02	626.3	12648.15	12266.47
76	103	12509.82	652.2	12655.59	12292.01
77	105	12522.32	682.3	12660.57	12314.03
78	107	12532.22	723.6	12663.97	12335.09
79	112	12547.52	881.4	12666.52	12369.70

Fig. 4.2.1b: The remainder of that spreadsheet.

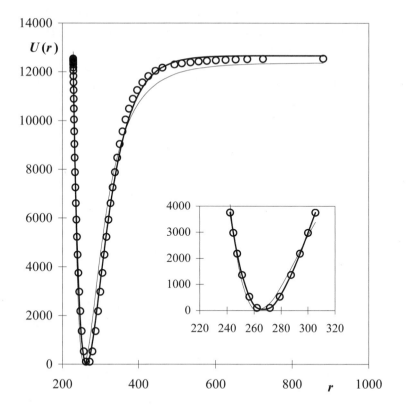

Fig. 4.2.2: The data of Verma (open circles) and two fitting functions: a Morse curve (thick line) and a Lennard-Jones curve (thin line). The inset shows the 12 data around the minimum, fitted (as sets of 12) to these two model functions.

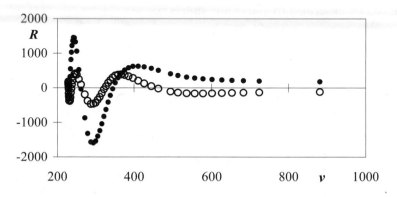

Fig. 4.2.3: The residuals of fitting Verma's data to the Morse equation (open circles) are about three times smaller than those for the Lennard-Jones formula (solid circles), though both clearly show similar, systematic trends.

(5) For both the Morse equation and the Lennard-Jones expression, the parameter a denotes the dissociation energy $\overline{D_e}$ in units of wavenumbers. The Morse curve fits the data better in Fig. 4.2.2 than the Lennard-Jones curve, although the residuals in Fig. 4.2.3 show considerable systematic deviations for both. The two analyses yield different results for both the dissociation energy and the equilibrium distance r_e, a difference that persists if we only analyze, say, the 12 data points surrounding the curve minimum, as shown in the inset in Fig. 4.2.2.

(6) Fitting the Morse function to all data yields $r_e = 263.3_4 \pm 0.2_4$ pm, while fitting the 12 points nearest to the curve minimum curve leads to $r_e = 266.74_7 \pm 0.04_4$ pm. Even within a given model, the result can depend strongly on the number of data points used.

(7) The uncertainty in the dissociation energy is even larger, and clearly depends on the model used. It should be realized in this context that r_e and $\overline{D_e}$ are only model parameters, because they both refer to a physically non-realizable, vibrationless "basement" state below the ground state at $v = 0$.

(8) One can also use linear least squares to fit the data to a Lennard-Jones function, with $U(r) = a_0 + a_1 r^{-6} + a_2 (r^{-6})^2$. So analyzed, the data yield $U(r) = (1.23_7 \pm 0.01_6) \times 10^4 - (7.1_0 \pm 0.1_6) \times 10^{18} r^{-6} + (1.02_8 \pm 0.02_3) \times 10^{33} r^{-12}$, from which one finds $a = a_0 = (1.23_7 \pm 0.01_6) \times 10^4$, $b = (-a_2/a_1)^{1/6} = 229.1_4 \pm 1._2$, and $r_{eq} = 2^{1/6} b = 257.2_0 \pm 0.1_8$ pm, in full agreement with the results obtained with Solver and SolverAid. By erroneously using the standard deviations s_1 and s_2 rather than the covariance matrix, one would instead find $b = 229._1 \pm 1._2$ and $r_{eq} = 257._2 \pm 1._4$ pm.

4.3   Titrating an acid with a strong base

As our next examples we will use Solver to find the concentrations and equilibrium constants in the titration of a single weak acid, e.g., acetic or citric acid, with a single strong monoprotic base, e.g., sodium hydroxide, NaOH. For a monoprotic acid HA such as acetic acid this titration can be described by the expression

$$V_b = V_a \frac{C_a \alpha_0 - [H^+] + K_w / [H^+]}{C_b + [H^+] - K_w / [H^+]} \tag{4.3.1}$$

$$\alpha_0 = \frac{K_a}{([H^+] + K_a)} \tag{4.3.2}$$

where V_a is the (known) volume of acid placed in the test cell (typically a beaker or Erlenmeyer flask), V_b is the (measured) volume of titrant added at any given time, C_a is the (unknown) concentration of the acid, α_0 is the concentration fraction of the acid anions, $K_a = [H^+] [A^-] / [HA]$ is the dissociation constant of the acid, $K_w = [H^+] [OH^-]$ is the ion product of water, C_b is the (known) concentration of the strong base used as titrant, and $[H^+]$ is the concentration of hydrogen ions at that same time, to be computed from the (measured) pH.

The value of [H^+] is taken as the independent parameter, and the titrant volume V_b as the dependent parameter. The values of K_a and K_w are known in principle, but are best considered as adjustable parameters since they vary with temperature, an experimental variable seldom controlled during practical acid-base titrations. The equilibrium constants also vary somewhat with ionic strength; if needed, the corresponding activity corrections can also be made on the spreadsheet, but this will not be done here, since it is a detail that has little to do with Solver. However, for those interested, it is fully described in, e.g., section 4.10 of my book *Excel in Analytical Chemistry*, Cambridge University Press, 2001, or in my *Aqueous Acid-Base Equilibria and Titrations*, Oxford University Press, 1999. Both books also provide the general theory of acid-base titrations which, in its most compact form, can be found in R. de Levie, *Chem. Educator* 6 (2001) 272.

Below we will use Solver to find the unknowns C_a, K_a, and K_w. As experimental data we will simulate a titration curve with added Gaussian noise on both the volume and pH axes. In practice the pH noise is not quite so uniform, because it is smaller in the buffer regions than near the equivalence point, but you will get the general idea. If you have actual titration data, please substitute these for the make-believe set.

Exercise 4.3.1:

(1) Open a spreadsheet, leave space at its top for a graph, and immediately below it provide spaces and labels for the known parameters V_a, C_b, two values s_n (for pH and V_b) for the standard deviation of the noise, two sets of the adjustable parameters C_a, K_a, and K_w, and one set of associated pK-values. Also deposit numerical values for the constants. Figure 4.3.1 shows such a layout.

(2) Make columns for pH, pH$_{noisy}$, [H^+]$_{noisy}$, $V_{b,exp}$, $V_{b,calc}$, the squares of the residuals R, and two columns of noise (only one of which is shown in Figs. 4.3.1 and 4.3.2).

(3) For pH use the values 2 (0.2) 12. (To make the set more realistic, a wider pH spacing can be used in the range between pH 6 to pH 10. Only a small section is shown in Figs. 4.3.1 and 4.3.2.) Compute pH$_{noisy}$ as pH + $s_{n,pH}$ times noise from one of the noise columns, and [H^+]$_{noisy}$ as 10^(−pH$_{noisy}$).

(4) In the next column calculate $V_{b,exp}$ using eqs. (4.3.1) and (4.3.2) with an added noise term, $s_{n,Vb}$ times noise from the second noise column. For [H^+] in this calculation use [H^+]$_{noisy}$; for the constants K_a, K_w, and C_a use the first set of these.

(5) Plot the progress curve $V_{b,exp}$ vs. pH or, if you are more comfortable with a titration curve, pH vs. $V_{b,exp}$, as shown in the figures.

(6) For $V_{b,calc}$ again use eqs. (4.3.1) and (4.3.2), but now with [H^+] from the noise-free columns, and K_a, K_w, and C_a from the second set, with slightly different parameter values. Compute K_a from pK_a as =10^(−pK_a), and do the same for K_w. This is helpful because especially K_w is too small to be adjusted by Solver's steps; taking logarithms levels the playing field. Add the calculated curve to the plot.

(7) The computation of the squares of the residuals $R^2 = (V_{b,exp} - V_{b,calc})^2$ in the next column is somewhat more complicated. A general equation such as (4.3.1) applies regardless of the parameter values, but does not incorporate any physical constraints. Obviously, we cannot generate a pH lower than that of the acid sample, or higher than that of the base solution used to titrate it, and we therefore use IF statements to excise those physically unrealizable values (such as negative volumes or concentrations), because they should not affect the fitting. If we left them in, they might be like the tail that wags the dog.

An If statement in Excel has the syntax =IF (*condition, action when condition is true, action when condition is false*). Consequently, when we want to compute the square of the residuals only when $V_{b,exp}$ is positive, we would write =IF (D21<0,0,(D21-E21)^2), which can be read as "if $V_{b,exp}$ is negative, make the cell output zero, otherwise make it equal to R^2."

In the present case we want to compute $(V_{b,exp} - V_{b,calc})^2$ for $0 < V_{b,exp} < 50$, and we therefore use a *nested* IF. Here, then, is the instruction to go in cell F21 of Fig. 4.3.1: =IF(D21<0,0,IF(D21>50,0,(D21-E21)^2)).

(8) Calculate SSR as the sum of all the terms in the column for SR. Note that the only contributions counted will be for $0 < V_{b,exp} < 50$. The spreadsheet might now resemble Fig. 4.3.1.

(9) Call Solver, and let it minimize the sum of squares of the selected residuals by adjusting the values of pK_a, pK_w, and C_a. Then call SolverAid to get the associated standard deviations, and the covariance matrix.

Figure 4.3.2 illustrates what you might obtain. The relevant parameters are obtained *directly*, i.e., without the usual two-step approach of first determining the equivalence volume, from which the unknown concentration C_a is then calculated. Note that, in this example, the uncertainty estimate for C_a does not include any experimental uncertainties in V_a and C_b, but that these can be included (if they are known) in the same way an additional variance was included in the calibration curve in Fig. 2.12.2. The covariance matrix indicates that C_a and K_w are only weakly correlated (with a linear correlation coefficient r of 0.79), and K_a and K_w hardly at all ($r = 0.15$).

While (4.3.1) for a single weak monoprotic acid can be linearized (L. M. Schwartz, *J. Chem. Educ.* 64 (1987) 947) by considering K_w as a known parameter, that is certainly no longer the case for a triprotic acid such as citric or phosphoric acid, here abbreviated as H_3A. Especially when the K_a-values for such a polyprotic acid are of similar orders of magnitude, as is the case for citric acid, we have little choice but to use a nonlinear least squares fit, unless we want to rely on approximations of rather questionable reliability.

The formal description of the titration of a triprotic acid with NaOH is similar to that of acetic acid, but involves three acid dissociation constants, K_{a1} through K_{a3}. Instead of (4.3.1) and (4.3.2) we must now use

$$\frac{V_b}{V_a} = \frac{C_a(\alpha_2 + 2\alpha_1 + 3\alpha_0) - [H^+] + K_w/[H^+]}{C_b + [H^+] - K_w/[H^+]}$$ (4.3.3)

with

$$\alpha_2 + 2\alpha_1 + 3\alpha_0$$

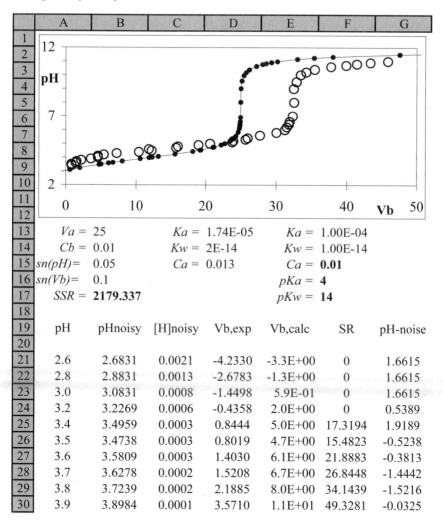

	A	B	C	D	E	F	G
13	*Va* = 25		*Ka* =	1.74E-05	*Ka* =	1.00E-04	
14	*Cb* = 0.01		*Kw* =	2E-14	*Kw* =	1.00E-14	
15	sn(pH)=	0.05	*Ca* =	0.013	*Ca* =	**0.01**	
16	sn(Vb)=	0.1			pKa =	**4**	
17	SSR =	**2179.337**			pKw =	**14**	
18							
19	pH	pHnoisy	[H]noisy	Vb,exp	Vb,calc	SR	pH-noise
20							
21	2.6	2.6831	0.0021	-4.2330	-3.3E+00	0	1.6615
22	2.8	2.8831	0.0013	-2.6783	-1.3E+00	0	1.6615
23	3.0	3.0831	0.0008	-1.4498	5.9E-01	0	1.6615
24	3.2	3.2269	0.0006	-0.4358	2.0E+00	0	0.5389
25	3.4	3.4959	0.0003	0.8444	5.0E+00	17.3194	1.9189
26	3.5	3.4738	0.0003	0.8019	4.7E+00	15.4823	-0.5238
27	3.6	3.5809	0.0003	1.4030	6.1E+00	21.8883	-0.3813
28	3.7	3.6278	0.0002	1.5208	6.7E+00	26.8448	-1.4442
29	3.8	3.7239	0.0002	2.1885	8.0E+00	34.1439	-1.5216
30	3.9	3.8984	0.0001	3.5710	1.1E+01	49.3281	-0.0325

Fig. 4.3.1: Part of the spreadsheet just before the actual data adjustment. Open circles denote the 'experimental' data, which include noise on both the pH and volume axis (a second column of noise data, labeled Vb-noise, is present as column H but not shown here), while the drawn line represents the calculated curve for the assumed parameter values (in cells F13:F17). The guess values for the acid concentration C_a and the various pK_a-values are shown in bold, as is the as yet unadjusted sum of the squares of the residuals.

$$= \frac{[H^+]^2 K_{a1} + 2[H^+]K_{a1}K_{a2} + 3K_{a1}K_{a2}K_{a3}}{[H^+]^3 + [H^+]^2 K_{a1} + [H^+]K_{a1}K_{a2} + K_{a1}K_{a2}K_{a3}} \qquad (4.3.4)$$

where α_i denotes the concentration fraction of the species H_iA^{i-3}. In all other aspects the approach is the same.

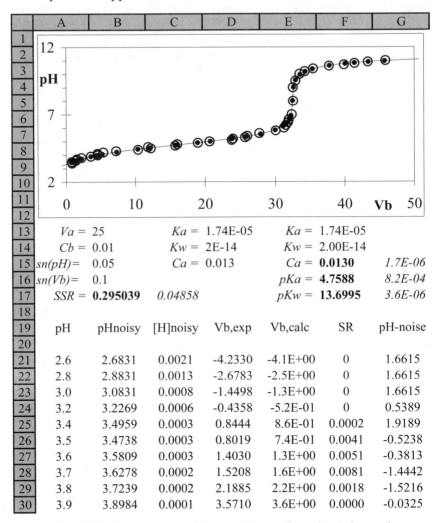

	pH	pHnoisy	[H]noisy	Vb,exp	Vb,calc	SR	pH-noise

_Va_ = 25, _Ka_ = 1.74E-05, _Ka_ = 1.74E-05
_Cb_ = 0.01, _Kw_ = 2E-14, _Kw_ = 2.00E-14
sn(pH)= 0.05, _Ca_ = 0.013, _Ca_ = **0.0130**, _1.7E-06_
sn(Vb)= 0.1, pKa = **4.7588**, _8.2E-04_
SSR = **0.295039**, _0.04858_, pKw = **13.6995**, _3.6E-06_

pH	pHnoisy	[H]noisy	Vb,exp	Vb,calc	SR	pH-noise
2.6	2.6831	0.0021	-4.2330	-4.1E+00	0	1.6615
2.8	2.8831	0.0013	-2.6783	-2.5E+00	0	1.6615
3.0	3.0831	0.0008	-1.4498	-1.3E+00	0	1.6615
3.2	3.2269	0.0006	-0.4358	-5.2E-01	0	0.5389
3.4	3.4959	0.0003	0.8444	8.6E-01	0.0002	1.9189
3.5	3.4738	0.0003	0.8019	7.4E-01	0.0041	-0.5238
3.6	3.5809	0.0003	1.4030	1.3E+00	0.0051	-0.3813
3.7	3.6278	0.0002	1.5208	1.6E+00	0.0081	-1.4442
3.8	3.7239	0.0002	2.1885	2.2E+00	0.0018	-1.5216
3.9	3.8984	0.0001	3.5710	3.6E+00	0.0000	-0.0325

Fig. 4.3.2: The same part of the spreadsheet after using Solver and SolverAid. Note that the calculated line fits the data quite well, as do the individual data points. The standard deviation of the fit is shown in italics to the right of SSR, and the standard deviations of the adjusted parameters are likewise shown in italics to the right of their numerical values. The guess values for the acid concentration C_a, the various pK_a-values, and the unadjusted sum of the squares of the residuals SSR, are shown in bold. The covariance matrix is not shown.

Exercise 4.3.2:

(1) Open a spreadsheet like that used in exercise 4.3.1, but now with three K_a-values, K_{a1} through K_{a3}, instead of one. Likewise, the formulas used for $V_{b,exp}$ and $V_{b,calc}$ should now be based on (4.3.3) and (4.3.4). Figure 4.3.3 shows such a spreadsheet with some initial guess values appropriate for citric acid, and Fig. 4.3.4 its final form after Solver and SolverAid have been used. Note that, in this case, there is only one clear step in the curve, because the three pK_a-values are too close together to yield resolved equivalence points.

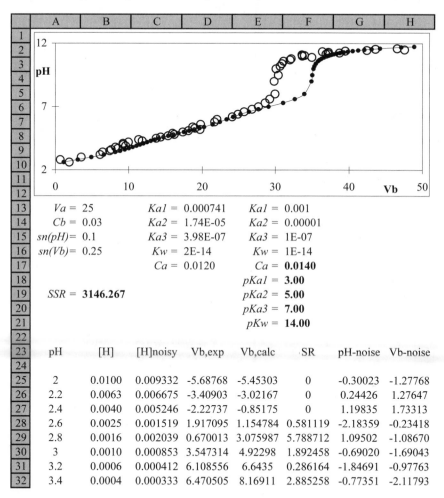

	A	B	C	D	E	F	G	H
13		*Va* = 25		*Ka1* = 0.000741		*Ka1* = 0.001		
14		*Cb* = 0.03		*Ka2* = 1.74E-05		*Ka2* = 0.00001		
15	*sn(pH)*= 0.1			*Ka3* = 3.98E-07		*Ka3* = 1E-07		
16	*sn(Vb)*= 0.25			*Kw* = 2E-14		*Kw* = 1E-14		
17				*Ca* = 0.0120		*Ca* = **0.0140**		
18						*pKa1* = **3.00**		
19		*SSR* = 3146.267				*pKa2* = **5.00**		
20						*pKa3* = **7.00**		
21						*pKw* = **14.00**		
22								
23	pH	[H]	[H]noisy	Vb,exp	Vb,calc	SR	pH-noise	Vb-noise
24								
25	2	0.0100	0.009332	-5.68768	-5.45303	0	-0.30023	-1.27768
26	2.2	0.0063	0.006675	-3.40903	-3.02167	0	0.24426	1.27647
27	2.4	0.0040	0.005246	-2.22737	-0.85175	0	1.19835	1.73313
28	2.6	0.0025	0.001519	1.917095	1.154784	0.581119	-2.18359	-0.23418
29	2.8	0.0016	0.002039	0.670013	3.075987	5.788712	1.09502	-1.08670
30	3	0.0010	0.000853	3.547314	4.92298	1.892458	-0.69020	-1.69043
31	3.2	0.0006	0.000412	6.108556	6.6435	0.286164	-1.84691	-0.97763
32	3.4	0.0004	0.000333	6.470505	8.16911	2.885258	-0.77351	-2.11793

Fig. 4.3.3: The top part of a spreadsheet for the titration of a triprotic acid. Gaussian noise has been added to the simulated 'experimental' data. The guess values for the acid concentration C_a, the various pK_a-values, and the unadjusted value of SSR are all shown in bold.

(2) Try the same spreadsheet for other triprotic acids, such as benzene-1,2,3-tricarboxylic acid (hemimellitic acid) with pK_a-values of about 2.9, 4.8, and 7.1, or phosphoric acid with pK_a-values of about 2.2, 7.2, and 12.2, and observe how the shape of the titration curve changes, including the number of steps in that curve. In the case of hemimellitic acid, only two clear steps are observed because pK_{a1} and pK_{a2} are too similar in value. With phosphoric acid, the three pK_a-values are quite distinct, yet only two clear steps in the titration curve are observed, because the third pK_a is too close to that of water, i.e., HPO_4^{-2} is too weak an acid. A hypothetical triprotic acid with pK_a-values of about 1, 5, and 9 would yield a titration curve with three clearly distinct steps.

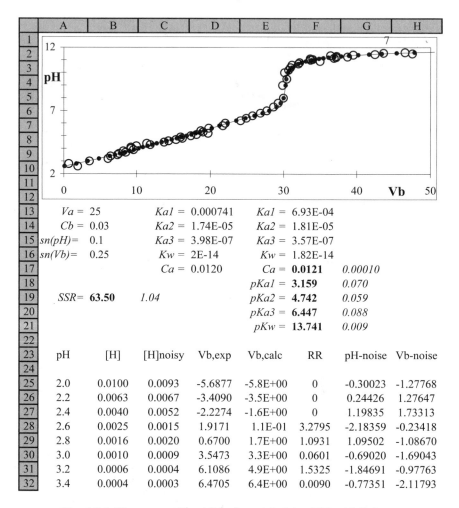

	pH	[H]	[H]noisy	Vb,exp	Vb,calc	RR	pH-noise	Vb-noise
	2.0	0.0100	0.0093	-5.6877	-5.8E+00	0	-0.30023	-1.27768
	2.2	0.0063	0.0067	-3.4090	-3.5E+00	0	0.24426	1.27647
	2.4	0.0040	0.0052	-2.2274	-1.6E+00	0	1.19835	1.73313
	2.6	0.0025	0.0015	1.9171	1.1E-01	3.2795	-2.18359	-0.23418
	2.8	0.0016	0.0020	0.6700	1.7E+00	1.0931	1.09502	-1.08670
	3.0	0.0010	0.0009	3.5473	3.3E+00	0.0601	-0.69020	-1.69043
	3.2	0.0006	0.0004	6.1086	4.9E+00	1.5325	-1.84691	-0.97763
	3.4	0.0004	0.0003	6.4705	6.4E+00	0.0090	-0.77351	-2.11793

Values in the upper panel:

$Va =$ 25, $Cb =$ 0.03, $sn(pH)=$ 0.1, $sn(Vb)=$ 0.25, $SSR=$ **63.50**, 1.04

$Ka1 =$ 0.000741, $Ka2 =$ 1.74E-05, $Ka3 =$ 3.98E-07, $Kw =$ 2E-14, $Ca =$ 0.0120

$Ka1 =$ 6.93E-04, $Ka2 =$ 1.81E-05, $Ka3 =$ 3.57E-07, $Kw =$ 1.82E-14

$Ca =$ **0.0121**, 0.00010
$pKa1 =$ **3.159**, 0.070
$pKa2 =$ **4.742**, 0.059
$pKa3 =$ **6.447**, 0.088
$pKw =$ **13.741**, 0.009

Fig. 4.3.4: The same as Fig. 4.3.3 after minimizing SSR with Solver, and estimating the resulting parameter uncertainties with SolverAid.

Ca	1	0.10067	0.329113	0.507069	0.731018
pKa1	0.10067	1	-0.267	0.107261	0.073587
pKa2	0.329113	-0.267	1	-0.020597	0.240601
pKa3	0.507069	0.107261	-0.020597	1	0.370622
pKw	0.731018	0.073587	0.240601	0.370622	1

Fig. 4.3.5: The linear correlation coefficients generated by SolverAid for the data in Fig. 4.3.4 show no strong correlations between any of the computed parameters.

In the case of acid-base titrations, it is not always clear whether V_b or pH carries the larger experimental errors, i.e., which of these (if any) should be taken as *the* independent parameter. (In an undergraduate laboratory, there is seldom any question that the volume read from a buret is the more error-prone observation, unless the pH meter is far below par or poorly calibrated.) Here we therefore take a rather pragmatic approach: nonlinear least squares fitting requires that we have a closed-form expression for the curve, which is available when we fit V_b as a function of pH, but not the other way around. An example of applying this method to a practical (and rather complicated) sample can be found in section 4.11 of my *Excel in Analytical Chemistry*, Cambridge University Press, 2001.

4.4 Conductometric titration of an acid mixture

L. M. Schwartz & R. I. Gelb (*Anal. Chem.* 56 (1984) 1487) reported data for a conductometric titration of a mixture of a strong (perchloric) acid of concentration C_{a1} plus a weak (acetic) acid of concentration C_{a2} with the strong base, KOH. Such a titration works because, in water, the molar conductances g of H^+ and OH^- are several times larger than those of any other ions present. Therefore, as one neutralizes acid with base, the total conductance $G = \Sigma G_i$ of the solution will first decrease as a result of the neutralization of the protons of the perchloric acid via H^+ + $OH^- \rightarrow H_2O$, which effectively replaces H^+ with K^+. The conductance then slowly rises while K^+ is added and, simultaneously, HA is converted into Ac^- in the reaction $HA + OH^- \rightarrow Ac^- + H_2O$, and subsequently increases faster, as excess base introduces both K^+ and OH^-. These three near-linear regions can be seen in the data from Schwartz & Gelb listed in table 4.4.1 and shown as open circles in Fig. 4.4.1.

The traditional analysis of such data is to re-plot them after correction for dilution, to fit the approximately straight regions in the resulting curve (excluding points in the transition regions) to three straight-line segments, and to compute the intersections between these extrapolated line segments to find the equivalence points, from which one can then calculate the sought concentrations of the two acids. This is a rather laborious procedure, well illustrated by Schwartz & Gelb, but with several problems. (1) There are no clear criteria for including or excluding points in the "linear" sections. (2) Finding the intersections between such straight-line segments can be rather imprecise if the covariances are not taken into account (cf. section 2.14). (3) The computation of intermediary quantities, the equivalence points, complicates the procedure, and can further reduce the precision of the results unless the covariances are used. None of these difficulties are insurmountable, but they can be avoided by fitting the entire titration curve as one single curve, fitting all adjustable constants directly with Solver, as was done in section 4.3 with a potentiometric titration.

V_b	4	6	8	10	12	14	15	16	17	18	19	20	22	*mL*
G	6.975	6.305	5.638	5.020	4.432	3.865	3.610	3.415	3.328	3.330	3.370	3.420	3.522	*mS*

V_b	24	26	28	30	32	33	34	35	36	38	40	42	44	*mL*
G	3.633	3.742	3.840	3.946	4.052	4.097	4.145	4.280	4.445	4.772	5.080	5.380	5.680	*mS*

Table 4.4.1: The titrant volumes V_b, in mL, and the corresponding cell conductances G, in mS, as reported by L. M. Schwartz & R. I. Gelb in *Anal. Chem.* 56 (1988) 1487.

There are two ways to approach this problem with Solver. One is to find an explicit mathematical expression for the conductance as a function of either $[H^+]$ or V_b. In this case, such expressions will be relatively messy. The other approach is to make the calculation on the spreadsheet as if the constants involved were all known, but without using an overarching closed-form mathematical solution. Below we will illustrate the latter approach, which (when such an algebraic solution is not already available) is often faster and simpler, and leads to the same answers. It not only avoids the derivation step if the theoretical expression is not known to the user, but also makes it easy to display the individual components of the measured conductance.

Since this is an acid-base titration we start with the corresponding relation between the titrant volume V_b and the proton concentration $[H^+]$,

$$V_b = V_a \frac{C_{a1} + C_{a2}K_a/([H^+]+K_a) - [H^+] + K_w/[H^+]}{C_b + [H^+] - K_w/[H^+]} \qquad (4.4.1)$$

The corresponding ionic contributions to the solution conductance G are then given by

$$G_{H^+} = [H^+] g_{H^+} \qquad (4.4.2)$$

$$G_{K^+} = \frac{C_b V_b}{V_a + V_b} g_{K^+} \qquad (4.4.3)$$

$$G_{\text{ClO}_4} = \frac{C_{a1} V_a}{V_a + V_b} g_{\text{ClO}_4^-} \tag{4.4.4}$$

$$G_{\text{Ac}^-} = \frac{C_{a2} K_a}{([\text{H}^+] + K_a)} \frac{V_a}{(V_a + V_b)} g_{\text{Ac}^-} \tag{4.4.5}$$

$$G_{\text{OH}^-} = \frac{K_w}{[\text{H}^+]} g_{\text{OH}^-} \tag{4.4.6}$$

where the g_i are the molar conductances of the species i, and the solution conductance G is given by

$$G = G_{\text{H}^+} + G_{\text{K}^+} + G_{\text{ClO}_4^-} + G_{\text{Ac}^-} + G_{\text{OH}^-} \tag{4.4.7}$$

Exercise 4.4.1:

(1) In cells A13:A16 of a new spreadsheet place the labels Ca1=, Ca2=, pKa=, and pKw=. In cells D13:D17 deposit gH=, gK=, gClO4=, gAc=, and gOH= respectively. And in cells G13:G17 write Va=, Cb=, Ka=, Kw=, and SSR= .

(2) Deposit guessed values in B13:B16, such as 0.02 for C_{a1} and C_{a2}, 4.76 for pK_a, and 14 for pK_w.

(3) For the ionic conductances use crude literature data, such as $gH = 300$, $gK = 50$, $gClO4 = 50$, $gAc = 50$, and $gOH = 150$.

(4) In cell H13 place the value 100 (since the sample volume used was 100 mL), in cell H14 the value 0.1 since $C_b = 0.1$ M, in cell H15 the instruction =10^-B15 for K_a, and in cell H16 the command =10^-B16 for K_w.

(5) In cells A19:K19 write the column headings [H+], Vb, G(H), G(K), G(ClO4), G(Ac), G(OH), G, Gintpol, Vb,exp, and Gexp.

(6) In cell A21 place the value 0.1, in cell A22 the instruction =A21/sqrt(sqrt(10)), then copy this instruction down to row 61, which gives you four points per pH unit, enough for the rather smooth conductometric titration curve.

(7) Use (4.4.1) to compute V_b in column B, starting in cell B21, (4.4.2) for $G(\text{H}^+)$ in column C, (4.4.3) for $G(\text{K}^+)$ in column D, etc.

(8) Leave column I blank, and in columns J and K copy the experimental values for G and V_b from table 4.4.1.

(9) In A1:E12 and F1:J12, plot G vs. V_b in separate graphs for columns H vs. B and J vs. K respectively. Verify that they have similar shapes.

Now we face a problem: we have two sets of data for G as a function of V_b, or the other way around. However, since the two scales are different, we cannot compute the residuals, i.e., the differences $y_{exp} - y_{calc}$ for common values of x. The solution is to interpolate the calculated curve to yield x-values that coincide with those of the experimental data set. We will here use the conventional choice, by identifying V_b with the independent variable x. (The same method applies if we make the opposite choice, with G as the independent parameter, which in this case might be more rational because the authors wrote that they "did not actually take care to add exactly 1.00 mL at a time. Rather we added approximately this amount.") For the interpolation we will use the quadratic Lagrange interpolation function described in section 1.11.

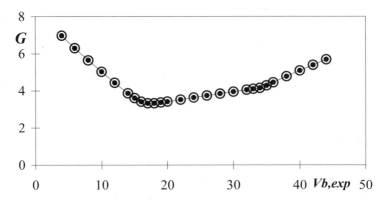

Fig. 4.4.1: Open circles: the data of Schwartz & Gelb, plotted as cell conductance G (in mS) vs. titrant volume $V_{b,exp}$ (in mL). Closed circles and connecting line: data calculated with exercise 4.4.1, with the values found: $g_H \approx 349$, $g_K \approx 59$, $g_{ClO4} \approx 167$, $g_{Ac} \approx 48$, and $g_{OH} \approx 208$. Other combinations of g-values can be found that yield an equally satisfying fit to the data.

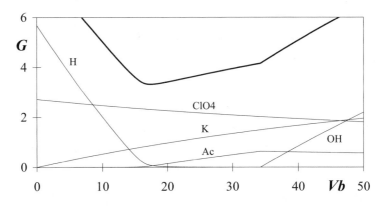

Fig. 4.4.2: The components of the cell conductance as a function of the base volume added. Perchlorate is merely diluted by the addition of KOH, while the contribution of potassium gradually increases. The added OH^- ions first neutralize the protons from the perchloric acid, forming water, then react with those from acetic acid, generating both water and Ac^-. The contribution of OH^- soars after both $HClO_4$ and HAc have been neutralized.

Exercise 4.4.1 (continued):

(10) In cells I21 deposit the instruction =Lagrange($B$21:$B$60,$H$21:
$H$60,J21,2) and copy this down to row 46, i.e., to the end of columns J and
K. Make sure that the Lagrange function is defined in an open VBA module, otherwise enter it.

(11) Copy the data from column I into the graph of G_{exp} vs. $V_{b,exp}$.

(12) In cell J17 deposit the instruction =SUMXMY2(I21:I46,K21:K46).

(13) Call Solver, and let it minimize SSR in cell J17 by first adjusting the val-
ues of C_{a1} and C_{a2}, then of C_{a1}, C_{a2}, $g(H)$, $g(K)$, $g(ClO4)$, $g(Ac)$, and $g(OH)$.

(14) Copy the results obtained in I21:I46 to the graph in A1:E12, cf. Fig. 4.4.1.

(15) In the second plot, in F1:J12, display the values of the individual ionic
conductances $G()$ that make up the total value of G, compare Fig. 4.4.2.

One can raise several objections to the above procedure: the ratios of
the equivalent conductances, especially those involving perchloric anions, do not fit those of the published values very well (absolute values
are meaningless here since Schwartz & Gelb did not mention their cell
constant), the equilibrium constants K_a and K_w might need to be corrected for activity effects, and the dependence of the molar conductances
g on ionic strength might likewise have to be incorporated. Such corrections, which may vary during the titration, can indeed be made, but are
not illustrated here. For that to be meaningful one should start with much
more careful measurements.

The above exercise, then, is neither a detailed examination of conduc-
tometry nor advocacy of its use for acid-base titrations, for which purpose potentiometry is usually far superior, because it is specific for the
reactant, H^+. Our point is merely to illustrate how even such a rather
complicated data analysis problem can be addressed adroitly with Solver,
and leads to quite acceptable results: Schwartz & Gelb list $C_{a1} = 0.01637$
mM, $C_{a2} = 0.01789$ mM, whereas we find $C_{a1} = 0.01631$ mM and $C_{a2} =$
0.01795 mM respectively, for different combinations of g-values.

4.5 Fitting a luminescence decay

Glow-in-the-dark toys based on copper-doped zinc sulfide can be excited with visible light, and then placed in a light-tight box with a
photodetector. Prof. Carl Salter of Moravian College lets his students in
physical chemistry lab do this experiment, and has kindly provided a set
of such data. Copy them from here, or download them from the web site.

Often, kinetic processes are of first order, i.e., they follow an equation
of the form $I = I_0 e^{-k_1 t}$ where t is time, I_0 is the amplitude of the signal I

at $t = 0$, and k_1 is the first-order rate constant. A plot of the experimental data suggests that there may be a significant background signal, see Fig. 4.5.2a. The box may not have been light-tight after all, or perhaps it had not been closed properly. We therefore fit the data to $I = I_0 e^{-k_1 t} + I_b$, where I_b is a constant representing an unspecified, constant background signal.

t	I_{exp}	t	I_{exp}	t	I_{exp}	t	I_{exp}	t	I_{exp}
0	0.2006	18	0.0904	36	0.0773	54	0.0713	72	0.0670	90	0.0644
1	0.1798	19	0.0916	37	0.0765	55	0.0709	73	0.0665	91	0.0646
2	0.1550	20	0.0898	38	0.0767	56	0.0695	74	0.0667	92	0.0646
3	0.1504	21	0.0908	39	0.0750	57	0.0703	75	0.0660	93	0.0641
4	0.1431	22	0.0852	40	0.0752	58	0.0714	76	0.0668	94	0.0641
5	0.1325	23	0.0843	41	0.0743	59	0.0696	77	0.0661	95	0.0645
6	0.1234	24	0.0857	42	0.0739	60	0.0695	78	0.0668	96	0.0638
7	0.1174	25	0.0834	43	0.0740	61	0.0675	79	0.0669	97	0.0634
8	0.1171	26	0.0865	44	0.0739	62	0.0670	80	0.0664	98	0.0638
9	0.1126	27	0.0871	45	0.0726	63	0.0694	81	0.0660	99	0.0605
10	0.1079	28	0.0836	46	0.0730	64	0.0771	82	0.0653	100	0.0619
11	0.1056	29	0.0825	47	0.0727	65	0.0677	83	0.0663	101	0.0632
12	0.1048	30	0.0762	48	0.0741	66	0.0665	84	0.0583	102	0.0635
13	0.1024	31	0.0794	49	0.0727	67	0.0678	85	0.0662	103	0.0626
14	0.0857	32	0.0823	50	0.0715	68	0.0640	86	0.0659	104	0.0635
15	0.0959	33	0.0766	51	0.0715	69	0.0675	87	0.0638		
16	0.0964	34	0.0785	52	0.0709	70	0.0672	88	0.0635		
17	0.0897	35	0.0776	53	0.0705	71	0.0673	89	0.0649		

Table 4.5.1: The luminescence decay data used in Figs. 4.5.1 through 4.5.3.

The resulting fit is fair, but the systematic trends in the residuals plotted in Fig. 4.5.2b suggest that the model used is still inadequate. Since the photo excitation generates equal numbers of electrons and ions (electron 'holes'), which subsequently recombine to cause the observed luminescence, we actually should expect second-order kinetics in this case. We therefore fit the data to the corresponding rate expression $I = I_0/(1 + I_0 k_2 t) + I_b$, where k_2 is a second-order rate constant. Figure 4.5.3 shows both the resulting fit and the corresponding residuals, and Fig. 4.5.1 the top of the corresponding spreadsheet. It is clear from Fig. 4.5.3b that this simple second-order model satisfactorily represents the data, without obvious systematic bias.

	A	B	C	D	E	F
1		*I*o=	0.1121	*0.0027*	0.1418	*0.0017*
2		*k=*	0.0904	*0.0038*	1.2128	*0.0356*
3		*Ib=*	0.0679	*0.0006*	0.0565	*0.0005*
4		*SSR=*	0.0018	*0.0049*	0.0004	*0.0024*
5						
6	*t*	*I exp*	*I calc*	*R*	*I calc*	*R*
7			*1st order*		*2nd order*	
8	0	0.2006	0.1801	0.0205	0.1983	0.0023
9	1	0.1798	0.1704	0.0094	0.1775	0.0023
10	2	0.1550	0.1615	-0.0065	0.1620	-0.0070
11	3	0.1504	0.1534	-0.0030	0.1500	0.0004
12	4	0.1431	0.1461	-0.0030	0.1405	0.0026
13	5	0.1325	0.1393	-0.0068	0.1327	-0.0002

Fig. 4.5.1: The top of the spreadsheet used for the data in table 4.5. The results of Solver are shown in C1:C3 and E1:E3 for the first-order and second-order fits, while D1:D3 and F1:F3 contain the corresponding results of SolverAid.

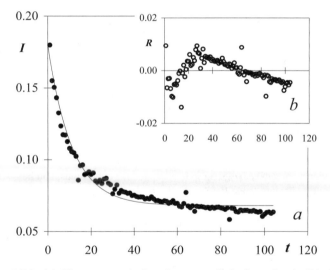

Fig. 4.5.2: (*a*) The measured phosphorescent light intensity (solid circles), in arbitrary units, vs. time *t* in seconds, and its analysis (drawn line) in terms of a *first*-order decay with offset, and (*b*) the resulting residuals.

4.6 Fitting a curve with multiple peaks

Our next example of Solver as a rather general curve-fitting tool will illustrate the principle of a spectrum analyzer, sometimes used to decompose spectra or chromatograms into their presumed substituent components. For the purpose of our illustration we will assume that all peaks conform to a given general shape, which we will here take to be Gaussian. We will first generate a noisy 'experimental' curve, then analyze this curve in terms of a number of Gaussian peaks of the general form $y = a \exp[-(x-b)^2/c^2]$. The method is primarily visual, in that it displays the guessed values, as well as the adjustments. Often, peaks with considerable overlap can be resolved, provided the assumed peak shapes are correct.

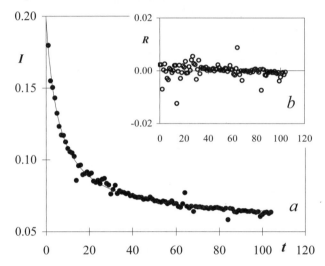

Fig. 4.5.3: (*a*) The measured phosphorescent light intensity (solid circles), in arbitrary units, vs. time *t* in seconds, and its analysis (drawn line) in terms of a *second*-order decay with offset, and (*b*) the resulting residuals.

Exercise 4.6.1:

(1) Open a spreadsheet, at its top leave space for two graphs, and below that for labels and constants, specifically for the peak amplitudes, center positions, and widths in the experimental and calculated function. Also enter labels for the standard deviation s_n of the noise, and for the sum of the squares SSR of the residuals.

(2) Below these parameter labels, enter a row of column labels for X, noise, Y_{exp}, Y_{calc}, and R.

(3) The values for X can be arbitrary: they represent sample number, wavelength or wavenumber, elution time, magnetic field shift, or whatever appropriate independent variable. In the example of Fig. 4.6.1 we use $X = 1$ (1) 1000, a sufficiently large data array to ensure that random noise will average out. One cannot expect to get similar results with small data sets.

(4) Fill the noise column with Gaussian noise of unit standard deviation and zero average.

(5) For Y_{exp} assume the sum of, say, three Gaussians, plus added noise. The instruction in cell C21 of Fig. 4.6.1 might then read =$A$15*EXP(-1*((A21-$B$15)/$C$15)^2)+$A$16*EXP(-1*((A21-$B$16)/$C$16)^2)+$A$17*EXP(-1*((A21-$B$17)/$C$17)^2)+$H$15*B21. We use -1* instead of - in view of Excel's precedence of negation over exponentiation, see section 1.16.

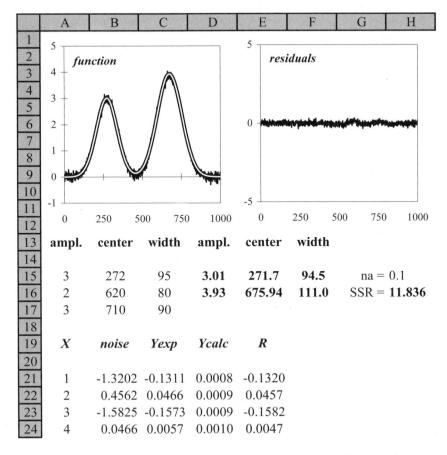

	A	B	C	D	E	F	G	H
13	**ampl.**	**center**	**width**	**ampl.**	**center**	**width**		
14								
15	3	272	95	**3.01**	**271.7**	**94.5**	na = 0.1	
16	2	620	80	**3.93**	**675.94**	**111.0**	SSR = **11.836**	
17	3	710	90					
18								
19	*X*	*noise*	*Yexp*	*Ycalc*	*R*			
20								
21	1	-1.3202	-0.1311	0.0008	-0.1320			
22	2	0.4562	0.0466	0.0009	0.0457			
23	3	-1.5825	-0.1573	0.0009	-0.1582			
24	4	0.0466	0.0057	0.0010	0.0047			

Fig. 4.6.1: The top of the spreadsheet, showing the noisy combination of three Gaussian peaks, and their analysis in terms of two Gaussians (double black line).

(6) For Y_{calc} we will first assume two peaks, so that the instruction in cell D22 might then read `=$D$15*EXP(-1*((A21-$E$15)/$F$15)^2)+$D$16*EXP(-1*((A21-$E$16)/$F$16)^2)`.

(7) The residual R is simply the difference between Y_{exp} and Y_{calc}.

(8) Plot Y_{exp} and Y_{calc} vs. *X* and, in a separate graph, *R* vs. *X*.

(9) Try some parameter values for a fit. By playing with the parameters in block D16:F17 you will quickly home in on a visually reasonable fit, such as peak centers at about 270 and 675 nm, amplitudes of about 3 and 3.8, and base widths of about 100 and 115.

(10) Calculate SSR as `=SUMSQ(E21:E1020)`, then optimize the parameters in D16:F17 with Solver. Figure 4.6.1 shows an example.

(11) Comparison with the initially assumed values is quite good for the peak centered around *X* = 270, but only fair for the second peak. In fact, the residuals give a (very slight) hint of a systematic deviation. We therefore test whether this peak can be resolved into two parts, by extending the expression for V_{calc} in column D with a third Gaussian, and introducing the corresponding parameters in

D18:F18, as in Fig. 4.6.2. Run Solver again; you can save computer time by only adjusting D17:F18, i.e., by keeping the first peak as is, leaving good enough alone. Figure 4.6.3 shows what you may obtain.

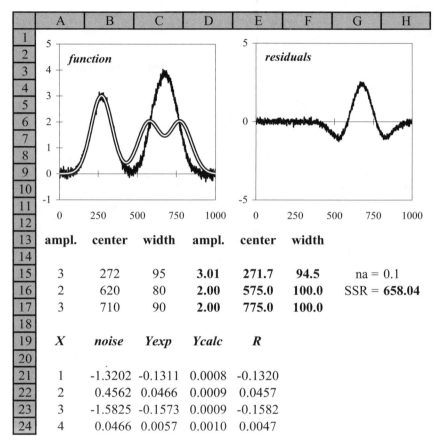

	A	B	C	D	E	F	G	H
13	ampl.	center	width	ampl.	center	width		
14								
15	3	272	95	**3.01**	**271.7**	**94.5**	na = 0.1	
16	2	620	80	**2.00**	**575.0**	**100.0**	SSR = **658.04**	
17	3	710	90	**2.00**	**775.0**	**100.0**		
18								
19	*X*	*noise*	*Yexp*	*Ycalc*	*R*			
20								
21	1	-1.3202	-0.1311	0.0008	-0.1320			
22	2	0.4562	0.0466	0.0009	0.0457			
23	3	-1.5825	-0.1573	0.0009	-0.1582			
24	4	0.0466	0.0057	0.0010	0.0047			

Fig. 4.6.2: The top of the spreadsheet just before
adjusting the curve with Solver to three Gaussians.

How do we know whether the extra peak is significant? In general this question cannot be answered: the peak in the experimental set might be a Lorentzian or have another shape sufficiently different from a Gaussian to require more than one Gaussian to represent it. Only if we *know* that the peaks are all Gaussian, as is the case here, can we use the F-test described in section 3.10 to estimate the likelihood that the third Gaussian is statistically significant.

In this case the variance ratio is 11.836 / (1000 − 6) divided by 9.8788 / (1000 − 9) or 1.1945, where 11.836 and 9.8788 are the values of SSR,

$N = 1000$ is the number of data points, and $P = 6$ or 9 is the number of variables used to describe them in Figs. 4.6.1 and 4.6.3 respectively. Some playing with the Excel function =FINV(*criterion, df1, df2*) will show that this variance ratio is approximately equal to FINV(0.003, 994, 991), i.e., it corresponds with a probability of 0.00258 or less than 0.3% of being a coincidence. By this criterion, the third peak is surely significant, even though the positions, heights, and widths of the second and third peak are rather inaccurate.

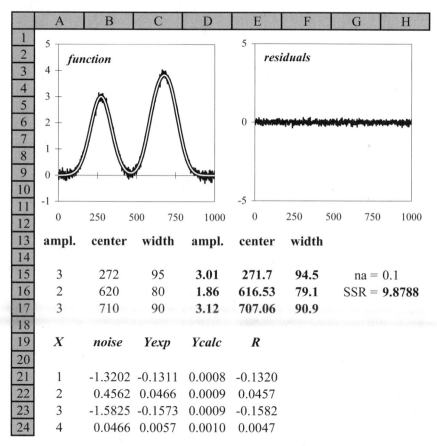

	A	B	C	D	E	F	G	H
13	ampl.	center	width	ampl.	center	width		
15	3	272	95	**3.01**	**271.7**	**94.5**	na = 0.1	
16	2	620	80	**1.86**	**616.53**	**79.1**	SSR = **9.8788**	
17	3	710	90	**3.12**	**707.06**	**90.9**		
19	X	noise	Yexp	Ycalc	R			
21	1	-1.3202	-0.1311	0.0008	-0.1320			
22	2	0.4562	0.0466	0.0009	0.0457			
23	3	-1.5825	-0.1573	0.0009	-0.1582			
24	4	0.0466	0.0057	0.0010	0.0047			

Fig. 4.6.3: The top of the spreadsheet after adjusting the curve with Solver to three Gaussians.

It cannot be emphasized enough that the usefulness of the above fitting procedure depends on the appropriateness of the model: one may instead need to use Lorentzians, asymmetric peak shapes, or any mixture thereof. The above procedure can easily be automated in a custom macro. The point to be made here lies not in any specific peak shape used, but in the flexibility of Solver as a general curve-fitting tool. Choosing the specific model to be used for fitting is the responsibility of the user, who knows the source of the data and the purpose of the curve fitting. Note also that significant noise reduction is achieved when the number of fitting parameters used, P, is much smaller than the number of experimental data points N. On the other hand, fitting to an incorrect model may lead to significant distortion of the underlying curve.

4.7 Fitting a multi-component spectrum with wavenumber-shifted constituents

In section 3.7 we saw how to use linear least squares to resolve the composite spectrum of a mixture when the (additive) constituent spectra are known. Spectra in a mixture can usually be considered as mutually independent, in which case that approach is all that is required. However, matters might be more complicated because the component spectra were taken in a different medium, in which case they may be subject to shifts to longer or shorter wavelengths due to the interaction with the solvent. In that case the simple method illustrated in section 3.7 does not work, and we will need to parameterize the spectra so that they can be shifted smoothly. For the sake of the exercise we will assume here that the spectra merely shift along the energy (rather than wavelength) axis but otherwise retain their shape, a somewhat idealized situation but often the best we can do without much more specific information. We then have a two-dimensional problem with adjustable parameters for both x (wavenumber shifts) and y (amplitudes).

As our specific example we will use a preliminary analysis of the spectrum of CP29, a light-harvesting pigment-protein complex, in terms of its dominant constituent pigments: chlorophyll a, chlorophyll b, and xanthophyll (lutein). The data for this exercise were kindly provided by Prof. Harry Frank of the University of Connecticut. The spectra of the three main constituents shown in Fig. 4.7.1 are sufficiently broad that they can each be represented quite satisfactorily with six Gaussians. Once that is done, we construct a linear combination of the spectra of these three components, and adjust the resulting six parameters (three for amplitude, three for wavenumber shift) in order to minimize the sum of the squares of the difference between this combination and the spectrum of CP29. Although it is not strictly necessary, we will use a custom spectral function S to give the problem a more compact notation.

Exercise 4.7.1:

(1) Download the spectra from the web site www.oup-usa.org/advancedexcel, where they can be found under SampleData, and should be entered into a spreadsheet. Plot the individual spectra, as illustrated in Fig. 4.7.1. Then convert the wavelength scale into one of wavenumbers since the spectral shifts are in terms of energy (1 nm = 10^{-7} cm so that v in cm^{-1} = $10^7 / \lambda$ where λ is in nm).

(2) Use the keystroke combination Alt∪F11 (Mac: Opt∪F11), or Tools ⇒ Macro ⇒ Visual Basic Editor, then (in the Visual Basic Editor menu bar) select Insert ⇒ Module. This will give you a blank sheet in which you type the instructions for the function.

(3) In that module, type or copy (from SampleMacros) the text shown below. You need not enter the spaces between the symbols, as the Visual Basic editor will insert them. The spacer lines and indents are used for easy readability.

```
Function S(x, amplitude, shift, a1, b1, c1, a2, b2, c2, _
    a3, b3, c3, a4, b4, c4, a5, b5, c5, a6, b6, c6)

Dim T1 As Double, T2 As Double, T3 As Double
Dim T4 As Double, T5 As Double, T6 As Double

T1 = a1 / Exp(((x - c1 - shift) / b1) ^ 2)
T2 = a2 / Exp(((x - c2 - shift) / b2) ^ 2)
T3 = a3 / Exp(((x - c3 - shift) / b3) ^ 2)
T4 = a4 / Exp(((x - c4 - shift) / b4) ^ 2)
T5 = a5 / Exp(((x - c5 - shift) / b5) ^ 2)
T6 = a6 / Exp(((x - c6 - shift) / b6) ^ 2)

S = amplitude * (T1 + T2 + T3 + T4 + T5 + T6)

End Function
```

(4) The first long line (wrapped around for better visibility on the monitor screen, by typing a space followed by an underscore) specifies the name of the function (here called S) and its 21 input parameters (within parentheses). The last line specifies the end of the function.

(5) Then there are two lines that specify the parameters T1 through T6 as having double precision. All other parameters come from the spreadsheet, and are therefore already in double precision. This may seem (and is) strange, but Visual Basic was developed independently and, unlike Excel, does not automatically use double precision. So we must insist on it, with those dimension statements.

(6) The lines of code specifying T1 through T6, and that specifying S, are the heart of S, because they instruct the function what to do: to calculate S as the sum of Gaussians. We can use more elaborate expressions for Gaussians, or even use the Excel-provided function NORMDIST, but these are not as convenient because their amplitudes vary with their standard deviations, whereas no such interactions between the parameters occur in the simple-minded definitions of T used here.

(7) Go back to the spreadsheet with Alt∪F11 (Mac: Opt∪F11) which acts as a toggle switch between the module and the spreadsheet, and deposit labels and values for the 18 constants a_1, b_1, c_1, a_2, b_2, etc.

(8) Make a column for the calculated spectrum of, say, Chlorophyll a, and in its top row deposit the instruction =S($B27,1,0,P$4,P$5,P$6,P$7,P$8, P$9,P$10,P$11,P$12,P$13,P$14,P$15,P$16,P$17,P$18,P$19, P$20,P$21) if you have, say, placed the wavelengths λ (typically in nm = 10^{-9}

m) in A27:A227, the corresponding wavenumbers ν (in cm^{-1} = 10^2 m^{-1}, so that ν = $10^7/\lambda$) in B27:B227 and the constants a_1 through c_6 in, e.g., P4:P21. Copy this instruction down 200 rows, i.e., the same length as the spectrum. Here $B27 refers to the top of the column with the wavenumber scale, 1 sets the amplitude to one, 0 makes the shift zero, and the rest refer to the locations of the 18 fitting parameters. The optional dollar signs following the column identifier (P) facilitates copying this expression to another row for the next component.

(9) The function only changes the contents of the cell in which it resides, just as standard instructions such as sqrt() or exp() would. Each cell in the column must therefore contain the function statement.

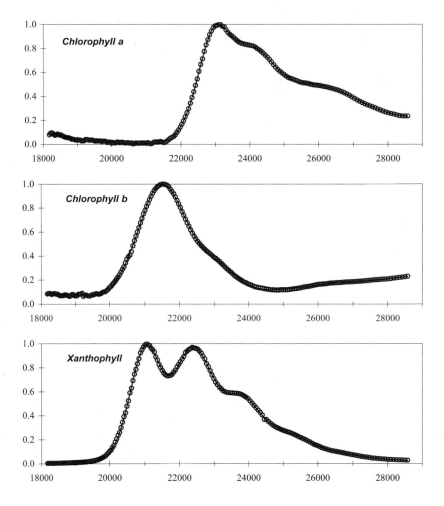

Fig. 4.7.1: The experimental spectra of chlorophyll a, chlorophyll b, and xanthophyll (open circles) and their parameterizations in terms of six Gaussian peaks (solid curve, almost entirely hidden by the points). Horizontal scale: energy in wavenumbers; vertical scale: arbitrary absorbance units.

(10) Highlight the column containing the calculated data, copy it, and paste it into the graph for chlorophyll a. Select wave numbers at the centers of visible peaks, such as at 23,000, 24,000 and 26,000 cm^{-1} and corresponding amplitudes, such as 0.8, 0.7, and 0.4 respectively, and play with the corresponding values of b to get the peak widths approximately right. Then add minor peaks at different wave numbers to fit the extremes of the curve. Play with these parameters (since they are independent, this is easier than it sounds) to get as tight a visual fit to the experimental data as you can.

(11) Enter a label and formula for the sum of squares of the residuals. Then call Solver, and let it minimize SSR by adjusting, say, the three parameters defining the major peak near 23,000 cm^{-1}. Then do the same for a, b, and c for the peak at 24,000 cm^{-1}, and repeat for each of the six peaks.

(12) Now increase your range and fit, say, the six parameters describing the peaks at both 23,000 and 24,000 cm^{-1}. Gradually widen your net, until you finally fit all 18 parameters simultaneously. You may have to reduce Solver parameters such as Precision, Tolerance, and Convergence, that you will find under Options, by adding zeros behind their decimal points.

(13) You may encounter trouble with the computed values, showing the error #NUM!. This most likely reflects a numerical *underflow*, in which a number becomes too small for Excel to represent, while it is too dumb to replace it by 0. That can easily happen with an expression such as $1/exp[x^2]$ which for $x = 27$ is already smaller than about 10^{-306}, the approximate numerical limit for Excel. To prevent this from happening we change the instructions for function S, as illustrated below, where we merely repeat the coding with, in bold, the changes to be made to guard against underflow.

```
Function S(x, amplitude, shift, a1, b1, c1, a2, b2, c2, _
    a3, b3, c3, a4, b4, c4, a5, b5, c5, a6, b6, c6)

Dim T1 As Double, T2 As Double, T3 As Double
Dim T4 As Double, T5 As Double, T6 As Double
If ((x - c1 - aa) / b1) < 25 Then _
    T1 = a1 / Exp(((x - c1 - aa) / b1) ^ 2) Else T1 = 0
If ((x - c2 - aa) / b2) < 25 Then _
    T2 = a2 / Exp(((x - c2 - aa) / b2) ^ 2) Else T2 = 0
If ((x - c3 - aa) / b3) < 25 Then _
    T3 = a3 / Exp(((x - c3 - aa) / b3) ^ 2) Else T3 = 0
If ((x - c4 - aa) / b4) < 25 Then _
    T4 = a4 / Exp(((x - c4 - aa) / b4) ^ 2) Else T4 = 0
If ((x - c5 - aa) / b5) < 25 Then _
    T5 = a5 / Exp(((x - c5 - aa) / b5) ^ 2) Else T5 = 0
If ((x - c6 - aa) / b6) < 25 Then _
    T6 = a6 / Exp(((x - c6 - aa) / b6) ^ 2) Else T6 = 0

S = amplitude * (T1 + T2 + T3 + T4 + T5 + T6)

End Function
```

(14) By now you should have a well-fitting curve through the experimental data for chlorophyll a. Repeat the same procedure for the two other pigments, chlorophyll b and xanthophyll.

(15) With the three constituent spectra parameterized, you are ready for the final fitting of these spectra to the data for CP29. In order to keep the equations relatively simple, we make three additional rows, one for each constituent, in

which we compute the spectrum with two additional adjustable parameters, amplitude and shift. For example, when these two parameters are stored in cells P2 and P3 respectively, we would use in the new column for Chlorophyll a the command =S($B27,**P$2,P$3**,P$4,P$5,P$6,P$7,P$8,P$9,P$10,P$11, P$12,P$13,P$14,P$15,P$16,P$17,P$18,P$19,P$20,P$21), where the differences are bold-faced. (Don't worry: the Visual Basic Editor will not recognize boldfacing even if you try.) Do the same for the other two species.

(16) Make a column where you calculate the algebraic sum of the three last-made columns, and display this in the graph for CP29.

(17) Now play with the three amplitudes and the three shifts, without altering any of the other parameters. First try to fit the dominant peak by adjusting the amplitude and shift for chlorophyll a, then do the same for chlorophyll b, and finally for xanthophyll. After you get as close by manual adjustment as you can, call Solver and repeat the same approach, first fitting single components, then fitting all six parameters together. You are now refining the last 6 of a system with a total of $6 + 3 \times 18 = 60$ adjustable parameters!

(18) The result, displayed in Fig. 4.7.2, shows an imperfect fit, with systematic deviations around 24000 and 26000 cm^{-1}.

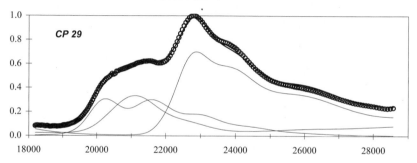

Fig. 4.7.2: The observed spectrum of CP29 (open circles) and that for the combination of its three major pigments, scaled and shifted in order to obtain an optimal fit (solid line). Also shown (as thin lines) are the three individual components of this synthesis, each properly scaled and shifted.

Yet, like the cup that is either half empty or half full, depending on what you want to see, the fit is quite good, considering the limitations inherent in the underlying model. There are two additional known pigments in CP29, violaxanthine and neoxanthine, with spectra that resemble shifted spectra of xanthophyll. Furthermore, CP29 contains multiple copies of these pigment molecules, which may find themselves in different molecular surroundings. Since these surroundings cause the spectral shifts, it is unrealistic to assume, as done here, that all pigments will exhibit the same wavenumber shifts. Moreover, the original assumption that the spectra merely shift is only a first approximation. That we nonetheless obtain a reasonable fit with such simplifying assumptions is, in a way, quite encouraging, and clearly illustrates what can be achieved with parameterization.

4.8 Constraints

Constraining the parameter space searched by Solver may be needed when it would otherwise, e.g., find a negative answer for a quantity that, for physical reasons, cannot be negative. Solver has provisions for limiting its search of particular parameter values (in the Solver Parameter dialog box under S̲ubject to the Constraints:) or, in this particular example, as a general constraint (in Solver Options with Assume Non-Negative). Here we will not explore these in detail, although they will occasionally come up in particular examples. Instead we will focus on constraints that involve the functions rather than their specific parameters.

When data are to be fitted to several related curves, Solver may be used to maintain one or more mutual relations between them, thereby constraining the fit. Several types of constraints will be illustrated in this and the next five sections. Below we will fit data to two separate but parallel lines; in section 4.9 to a curve through two fixed points; and in section 4.10 to three lines with a common intersection. In section 4.11 we will illustrate how to fit results for chemical kinetics at various temperatures, in section 4.12 we will fit data to a discontinuous curve, while section 4.13 will demonstrate a piecewise fit. Clearly, the possibilities are endless, and we can merely give a sense for what can be done.

Say that we want to fit two sets of data to straight lines, the first set to $y_p = a_{p0} + a_{p1}x$, the second to $y_q = a_{q0} + a_{q1}x$. This is readily accomplished by separately fitting the two data sets with linear least squares. In that case, the slopes a_{p1} and a_{q1} as well as the intercepts a_{p0} and a_{q0} will in general be different. If there are theoretical or other good reasons to expect the slopes to be the same, then the two sets should be fitted simultaneously, with a common value for a_1, i.e., the first to $y_p = a_{p0} + a_1x$, the second to $y_q = a_{q0} + a_1x$. Below we illustrate how to do this.

Exercise 4.8.1:

(1) Open a spreadsheet, and enter two small sets of linear functions of x with different intercepts but identical slopes, such as (in the example given in Fig. 4.8.1) $y_p = 2 + 1.5\,x$ and $y_q = 13.5 + 1.5\,x$. Then add a generous amount of noise.

(2) Using a linear least squares routine, fit the first and second data sets individually, and plot the corresponding lines through these data.

(3) Then deposit guess values for a_{p0}, a_{q0}, and a_1, fit the first data set to $y_p = a_{p0} + a_1x$, the second to $y_q = a_{q0} + a_1x$, compute the sum of the squares of the residuals for *both*, and use Solver to minimize this sum by adjusting a_{p0}, a_{q0}, and a_1, and plot the results, as in Fig. 4.8.1. You can of course add uncertainty estimates for the coefficients found.

	A	B	C	D	E	F

a0p = -0.4481		a0q = 14.1337		ap = 2.751122
a1p = 2.0322		a1q = 1.2379		aq = 13.01747
				a1 = 1.450532
				SSR 12.18893

X	Y	Y+noise	Yp, Yq	Ypq	noise
3	6.5	6.200	5.649	7.103	-0.300
4	8	6.722	7.681	8.553	-1.278
5	9.5	9.744	9.713	10.004	0.244
6	11	12.276	11.745	11.454	1.276
7	12.5	13.698	13.777	12.905	1.198
8	14	15.733	15.810	14.355	1.733
1	15	14.766	15.372	14.468	-0.234
3	18	19.095	17.847	17.369	1.095
4	19.5	18.413	19.085	18.820	-1.087
6.5	23.25	22.560	22.180	22.446	-0.690
8	25.5	23.810	24.037	24.622	-1.690
9	27	25.153	25.275	26.072	-1.847

cell:	instruction:	copied to:
B19	= 2+1.5*A19	B20:B24
B26	= 13.5+1.5*A26	B27:B31
C19	= B19+F19	C20:C24, C26:C31
D19	= $B$13+$B$14*A19	D20:D24
D26	= $D$13+$D$14*A26	D27:D31
E19	= $F$13+$F$15*A19	E20:E24
E26	= $F$14+$F$15*A26	E27:E31
F16	= SUMXMY2(C19:C31,E19:E31)	

Fig. 4.8.1: The spreadsheet for exercise 4.8.1.

4.9 Fitting a curve through fixed points

We now consider the data of Leary & Messick, *Anal. Chem.* 57 (1985) 956, displayed in table 3.12.1. Since *in theory* the detector response at 0 and 100% ethanol should be 0 and 100% of the measured area, they fixed these values. This assumes the absence of any offset or baseline drift, or any other unanticipated phenomenon. By similar reasoning one might then anticipate a strictly linear rather than a quadratic relationship, but Leary & Messick instead elected to fit their data to a quadratic.

Let us first focus on the mechanics of fitting the data of table 3.12 to $y = a_0 + a_1x + a_2x^2$ while this expression is forced to go through the points (0,0) and (100,100). The requirement that $y = 0$ for $x = 0$ leads directly to $a_0 = 0$, while $y = 100$ for $x = 100$ then yields the relation $100 = 100 \, a_1 + 10000 \, a_2$ or $a_2 = (1-a_1)/100$. We therefore use Solver to fit the data of table 3.12.1 to $y = a_1x + (1-a_1) \, x^2/100$, as illustrated in Fig. 4.9.1, which also shows how these constraints skew the fit. Note that this approach can include as many constraints as the fitting equation allows.

Now that the mechanics of fitting these data are out of the way (i.e., relegated to the computer), it is interesting to take a second look at these data, because they illustrate some of the real difficulties involved in data fitting: what fitting function should we use, and what constraints.

The question is only answerable within a given context: do we use the experiment (1) to extract model coefficients, (2) to verify or falsify a particular model, or (3) to find a representation of the experimental data for subsequent use in, e.g., a calibration? Leary & Messick did not specify any specific model, but they must have had one in mind in order to justify their constrained quadratic fit. What if we consider these data for calibration purposes only?

If we let the data speak for themselves, without any theoretical guidance, we conclude that, by all three of the criteria (minimal s_y, FR5 > 1 and FR1 > 1, or all ratios a_i/s_i > 1) these data are best represented by an unconstrained quadratic, see section 3.12.1. But if, for some reason, one wants to constrain the curve, the above illustrates how this can be done, and the thick curve in Fig. 4.9.1 shows the result.

4.10 Fitting lines through a common point

This is a simple variation on the same theme. When we require the line $y = a_0 + a_1x$ to pass through a particular point (X,Y), we have $Y = a_0 + a_1X$ or $a_0 = Y - a_1X$, so that the expression for the line becomes $y = Y + a_1 (x - X)$. Fitting several sets of data to lines all intersecting at point (X,Y) therefore requires that the first set be fitted to $y_1 = Y + a_1 (x - X)$, the second to $y_2 = Y + a_2 (x - X)$, etc. Again, the constraint that all lines go through the point (X,Y) is readily handled by Solver.

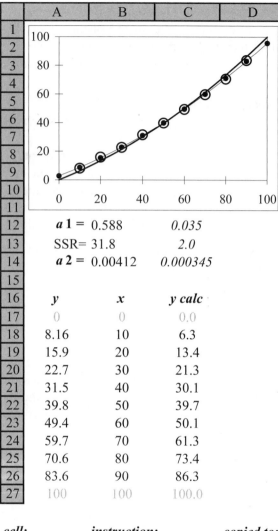

y	x	y calc
0	0	0.0
8.16	10	6.3
15.9	20	13.4
22.7	30	21.3
31.5	40	30.1
39.8	50	39.7
49.4	60	50.1
59.7	70	61.3
70.6	80	73.4
83.6	90	86.3
100	100	100.0

Within the figure:

$a1 =$ 0.588   *0.035*
SSR= 31.8   *2.0*
$a2 =$ 0.00412   *0.000345*

cell:	instruction:	copied to:
C18 =	$B$12*B18+(1-$B$12)	
	*B18*B18/100	C19:C26
B13 =	SUMXMY2(A18:A26,C18:C26)	
B14 =	(1-B12)/100	

Fig. 4.9.1: A spreadsheet using Solver to find a quadratic (thick line) through the points (0,0) and (100,100) and closely fitting the data (open circles) of table 3.12.1. SolverAid was used to find the standard deviation in a_1, and Propagation to calculate the resulting standard deviation in a_2. The small closed circles (including those for $x = 0$ and $x = 100$) connected by a thin line show the unconstrained quadratic $y = 2.7 + 0.56\,x + 0.0037\,x^2$.

Exercise 4.10.1:

(1) Open a spreadsheet, provide space for graphs and labels, then make columns for x, y, n, and $y+n$, where n represents noise. In the column for n deposit Gaussian noise using the Random Noise Generator.

(2) Split the columns in three parts by inserting two empty rows, as in Fig. 4.10.1. Assume values for the coordinates X and Y of the point of intersection of the three lines. Then take some values for x, and compute corresponding values for y as $y = Y + a_i (x - X)$, where a_i assumes different values for the three segments.

(3) Calculate the corresponding values of $y+n$, then use linear least squares to compute separate, straight lines through the three noisy data sets, and plot these as well as the noisy data.

(4) Somewhere near the top of the spreadsheet, insert spaces for three slopes a_1 through a_3, as well as for the coordinates X and Y, and enter guess values for all of these. As guess values for a_1 through a_3 you can use the slopes obtained under (3) by linear least squares.

(5) Make a column in which you calculate $y = Y + a_i (x - X)$, using the guess values and, in each segment, the appropriate value of the slope a_i.

(6) Compute the sum of squares of the residuals by comparing the data in the just-made column with those in the column for $y+n$.

(7) Call Solver to minimize that sum of squares of the residuals, by letting it adjust the three slopes and the two coordinates of the intersection point.

(8) Plot the resulting lines. Compare your spreadsheet with that in Fig. 4.10.1.

In Fig. 4.10.1 we have used few points and rather generous noise in order to illustrate the effect of the constraint. The individual straight line segments start out intersecting at the point X,Y before noise is added to them. After noise has been added, they no longer pass through a common point. Because of the paucity of data and the large noise amplitudes used, the lines drawn are of course quite uncertain, as can best be seen from their standard deviations, which have been collected in table 4.10.

Incidentally, in order to draw the lines across the entire width of the graph, points for $x = 0$ and $x = 10$ were added, though of course not included in the analysis. These have been printed in gray italics in Fig. 4.10.1; one could make them disappear from a printout by coloring them white. Forcing the three data sets through a common point makes the resulting parameter values interdependent, so that their covariances may have to be considered in subsequent computations.

Alternatively, if the coordinates of the point of intersection are fixed at $x = X$ and $y = Y$, say at $X = 2$ and $Y = 10$, one can use Solver to adjust the values of a, b, and c, either separately or simultaneously. In this case, separate linear least squares fits of $y-Y = a_1(x-X)$ will also work.

	intercept	slope		slope
a	9.02	-0.47	a	-0.68
b	11.79	0.12	b	0.59
c	3.41	2.34	c	2.19
			X	2.08
			Y	9.11
			SSR	10.6

X	Y	noise	Y+noise	Ya, Yb, Yc	Yabc
0	12			9.0197	10.5263
4	8	-0.3002	7.6998	7.1485	7.8135
5	7	-1.2777	5.7223	6.6807	7.1353
6	6	0.2443	6.2443	6.2129	6.4571
7	5	1.2765	6.2765	5.7452	5.7789
8	4	1.1984	5.1984	5.2774	5.1007
9	3	1.7331	4.7331	4.8096	4.4225
10	2			4.3418	3.7443
0.0	8.80			11.7887	7.8839
5.2	11.92	-0.2342	11.6858	12.3946	10.9532
6.0	12.40	1.0950	13.4950	12.4878	11.4255
7.6	13.36	-1.0867	12.2733	12.6742	12.3699
8.0	13.60	-0.6902	12.9098	12.7208	12.6060
9.5	14.50	-1.6904	12.8096	12.8955	13.4914
10.0	14.80	-1.8469	12.9531	12.9538	13.7865
0.0	5.80			3.4067	4.5493
4.0	14.20	-0.7735	13.4265	12.7482	13.3134
5.5	17.35	-2.1179	15.2321	16.2512	16.5999
7.0	20.50	-0.5679	19.9321	19.7543	19.8864
8.5	23.65	-0.4040	23.2460	23.2573	23.1729
10.0	26.80	0.1349	26.9349	26.7604	26.4594

Fig. 4.10.1: A spreadsheet for exercise 4.10.1, showing three sets of straight lines intersecting in the common point (2,10) in column B, and the same with Gaussian noise of zero mean and unit standard deviation in column D, (a) analyzed separately, and (b) forced to go through one common point. The data printed in gray italics are used for the graph but not in the analysis.

	Assumed:	Found for three separate lines:	Found for three lines through a common point:
intercept 1	12	$a_0 = 9.0_2 \pm 0.9_9$	
slope 1	-1	$a_1 = -0.4_7 \pm 0.1_5$	$-0.6_7 \pm 0.1_0$
intercept 2	8.8	$b_0 = 11._8 \pm 1._2$	
slope 2	0.6	$b_1 = 0.1_2 \pm 0.1_5$	$0.59_0 \pm 0.06_7$
intercept 3	5.8	$c_0 = 3._4 \pm 1._1$	
slope 3	2.1	$c_1 = 2.3_4 \pm 0.1_5$	$2.19_1 \pm 0.09_3$
X	2		$2.0_8 \pm 0.2_3$
Y	10		$9.1_1 \pm 0.3_2$

Table 4.10.1: The results obtained in Fig. 4.10.1, analyzed as three independent straight lines, or as three straight lines through a common point.

Whenever two or more curves must be fitted with mutually dependent parameters, Solver is a convenient tool to use; the corresponding uncertainties can then be obtained from SolverAid. The above approach is quite general, as will be illustrated in the next example.

4.11 Fitting a set of curves

We now consider a set of data representing the progress of a first-order chemical reaction at various temperatures and times, taken from page 124 of Y. Bard, *Nonlinear Parameter Estimation* (Academic Press 1974). The dependent variable f is the fraction of the initial reagent remaining after a reaction time t at an absolute temperature T. The assignment is to analyze these numbers in terms of the rate expression $f = \exp(-kt)$ where the rate constant k has the temperature dependence $k = a \exp(-b/T)$, so that $f = \exp[-at \exp(-b/T)]$. Figure 4.11.1 illustrates such an analysis using Solver and SolverAid.

Exercise 4.11.1:

(1) Again open a spreadsheet as usual, and enter the labels, parameter values, column headings, and data. For subsequent plotting of the calculated curves, it is convenient to keep empty rows between the data for different temperatures, so that the graph will show the solution as three unconnected line segments. (And leave more rows free if you want to extend the calculated curves from $t = 0$ to $t = 0.5$ hrs.) Plot the data.

(2) Compute f as $f = \exp[-at \exp(-b/T)]$ based on initial guess values for a and b, and show the resulting curve. Also calculate SSR, the sum of the squares of the residuals.

(3) Use Solver and SolverAid to find a solution. Figure 4.11.1 shows what you will get when you start with, e.g., $a = b = 1$, and then ask SolverAid to display the correlation coefficients.

The data used in Fig. 4.11.1 are clearly hypothetical, made up by a non-experimentalist: the data at $100°K$ show virtually no reaction, and there are only two data points at $300°K$ that are significantly different from zero. Moreover, with more realistic data the noise in the data should also be smaller, and hence the standard deviations for a and b shown in cells C13 and C14 respectively. Yet, even with such poor data, Solver finds a plausible solution. As can be seen from the correlation coefficient r_{12} of about 0.98, the values for a and b are quite interdependent.

Note, however, that we were lucky that $a = 1$ and $b = 1$ led to a plausible answer. It does not always work that way: $a = 8000$ and $b = 8000$ might not get you anywhere, even though your initial guess values are now within a factor of 10 of their 'best' values. In this case the calculated values of y are all very close to 1, so that SSR, the sum of the squares of the residuals, doesn't change perceptibly, making it impossible for Solver to minimize it. This trouble is easy to spot by the fact that the initial guess values are not changed.

If you had started with $a = -100$ and $b = -100$ you would have run into the same problem but for a different reason: now some of the y-values are so large that they essentially mask any changes in SSR, and again get Solver stuck. In this case, you can find the correct answer by using Solver with Options $\Rightarrow$ Assume Non-Negative, which prevents Solver from accepting negative values for any of the adjustable parameters for which you have not specified any particular constraints.

A more interesting case occurs with, e.g., $a = -10$ and $b = -10$, which leads to a local minimum that is not the global one. In this case, simply engaging Solver once more will get you to the correct answer: apparently, the initial iteration step differs from subsequent ones. This trick sometimes works: if you don't trust the answer Solver provides, accept that result, then use it as the starting point for a second try with Solver and see whether it gets Solver unstuck. In this particular example, Options $\Rightarrow$ Assume Non-Negative would again have avoided the problem.

This illustrates, again, that Solver may not always work when the initial guess values are far off. This typically occurs when you know little or nothing about the context of the data, something that should not happen, but occasionally does. Even so, in such a case one might try Solver once or twice with wild guess values, on the chance that these just might work. If not, use a fraction of the data for which the analysis is simpler, assemble estimates for most or all of the parameters that way, then use these as guess values in the final nonlinear fit of the entire data set.

For instance, if you have no clue what to use for plausible starting guesses for the data of Fig. 4.11.1, you might start with separate parts of the data set, say with those for 200 °K and 300°K. You fit each of these to $f = \exp(-kt)$, either with Solver or with any of the linear least squares programs in Excel. You will find k-values of about 6.7 and 33 hr^{-1}. Now fit these two values to the temperature dependence $k = a \exp(-b/T)$, and you find $a = 810$ and $b = 960$. With these as guess values you are virtually guaranteed to home in on the final answer when you subsequently analyze the complete data set, especially since the data at 100°K don't contribute much information.

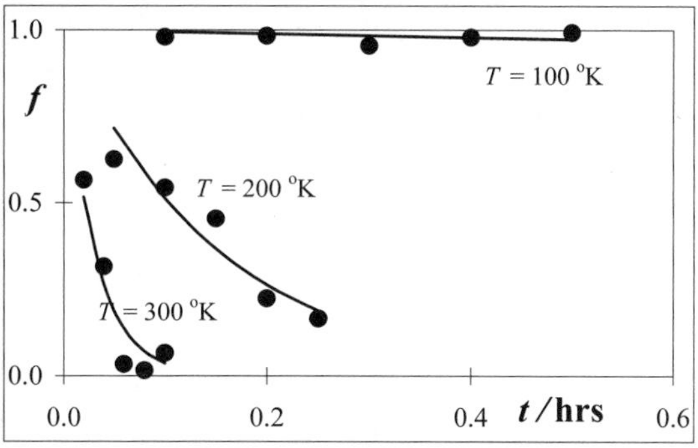

	A	B	C	D	E

13	**a** = 8.14E+02	*246.2385*	**LCC:**		
14	**b** = 9.61E+02	*68.53395*		1	0.981216
15	**SSR**= 0.039806	*0.055335*	0.981216	1
16					
17	*T / oK*	*t / hrs*	*y exp*	*y calc*	
18					
19	100	0.10	0.980	0.994557	
20	100	0.20	0.983	0.989145	
21	100	0.30	0.955	0.983761	
22	100	0.40	0.979	0.978407	
23	100	0.50	0.993	0.973082	
24					
25	200	0.05	0.626	0.716608	
26	200	0.10	0.544	0.513527	
27	200	0.15	0.455	0.367998	
28	200	0.20	0.225	0.26371	
29	200	0.25	0.167	0.188977	
30					
31	300	0.02	0.566	0.516184	
32	300	0.04	0.317	0.266446	
33	300	0.06	0.034	0.137535	
34	300	0.08	0.016	0.070993	
35	300	0.10	0.066	0.036646	

Fig. 4.11.1: The remaining concentration fraction f of a species undergoing a first-order chemical reaction, as a function of time t, at different temperatures T. Lines calculated with Solver-determined parameters.

How will you know whether you have hit the jackpot? Look at the resulting fit of the calculated model curve to the data points. Plot the residuals and see whether they show a trend, although in the present example there are too few data points to make this a meaningful criterion. Check whether a subsequent application of Solver modifies the result: sometimes a second application of Solver does change its results, and it is good practice to repeat Solver at least once to see whether it has reached a steady answer. And, most of all, remain skeptical: nonlinear least squares do not come with any guarantees, a problem which we will take up again in sections 4.17 and 4.21.5. Fortunately, you will typically know what order of magnitude to expect for your data, and you should preferably have more and better data points than in Fig. 4.11.1, in which case Solver usually works well.

4.12 Fitting a discontinuous curve

One sometimes encounters experimental data sets that exhibit a discontinuity, as may occur, e.g., with phase transitions. We can treat its constituent parts as separate segments, but often the coordinates of the transition are also subject to experimental uncertainty, in which case it may be preferable to fit the entire data set. As always, the best description starts with the appropriate model describing the phenomenon. Here we will merely illustrate the method for a simulated, discontinuous data set.

Say that we have a set of data that can be described by $y = a_0 + a_1x$ for $x \leq c$, and by $y = b_0 + b_1x + b_2x^2$ for $x > c$. We now express that behavior in a single equation with six unknowns, a_0, a_1, b_0, b_1, b_2, and c, and then use Solver to find their optimum values. The single equation will contain an IF statement. If the curve contains a knee rather than a break, one of the unknowns can be eliminated since continuity at $x = c$ requires that $a_0 + a_1c = b_0 + b_1c + b_2c^2$.

Exercise 4.12.1:
(1) Set up a spreadsheet similar to that shown in Fig. 4.12.1, with (at the top of the spreadsheet) the model and adjustable parameters, and below it the corresponding columns for x, y, and y_{calc}. Include a column of random noise, and add s_n times this noise to the data for y. Also compute the sum of the squares of the residuals.
(2) Plot both y and y_{calc} vs. x, and adjust the parameters in C1:C6 so that the calculated line roughly fits the (in this case simulated) experimental data. Such a first-order fit is shown in Fig. 4.12.2.
(3) Call Solver and let it minimize SSR by adjusting the parameters in C1:C6.
(4) Call SolverAid and let it determine the corresponding uncertainties. Note that SolverAid *cannot* find the uncertainty in c (which is $\pm\Delta x/2$), which it therefore indicates (while displaying an appropriate warning message) as 0.

	A	B	C
1	*a0* =	3	2
2	*a1* =	1	1.5
3	*b0* =	25	30
4	*b1* =	-1	-0.9
5	*b2* =	-0.2	-0.3
6	*c* =	5	4.5
7	*sn*=	0.5	
8	*SSR*=	924.15	
9			
10	*x*	*y*	*y calc*
11			
12	0	2.849884	2
13	0.1	2.461158	2.15
14	0.2	3.322129	2.3

Fig. 4.12.1: The top of the spreadsheet of exercise 4.12.1. Cell B12 contains the instruction =IF(A12<$B$6,$B$1+$B$2*A12,$B$3+$B$4*A12 +$B$5*A12*A12)+$B$7*N12, while cell C12 contains =IF(A12< $C$6,$C$1+$C$2*A12,$C$3+$C$4*A12+$C$5*A12*A12).

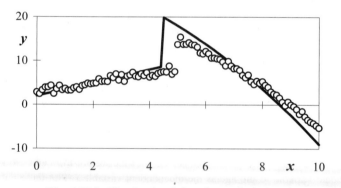

Fig. 4.12.2: The simulated data (open circles) and an unadjusted, crudely fitted curve through them.

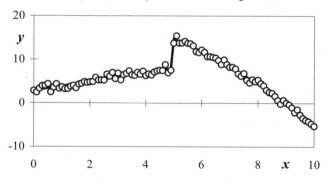

Fig. 4.12.3: The simulated data (open circles) and the adjusted curve through them.

(5) Figure 4.12.3 illustrates the resulting graph. Perhaps more telling is the co-variance matrix obtained with SolverAid, which shows a_0 and a_1 to be independent of b_0, b_1, and b_2, as they should be, as well as the (incorrect) zeros for the uncertainty in c.

4.13 Piecewise fitting a continuous curve

Sometimes it may be desirable to represent data by a smooth-looking curve, perhaps even in the absence of a theoretical justification for such a piecemeal approach. A smooth appearance usually requires that the segments and their first derivatives are continuous. This can readily be achieved with splines (e.g., with the Smoothed line option in Excel XY graphs) but will here be illustrated with least squares.

A study of E. S. Eppright et al. published in *World Rev. Nutr. Dietet.* 14 (1972) 269 reported the weight/height ratios (weights in pounds, heights in inches) of preschool boys in the North-Central region of the USA as a function of their age (in months). These data were subsequently analyzed by A. R. Gallant et al. (*J. Am. Stat. Assoc.* 68 (1973) 144; 72 (1977) 523) in terms of two connected sections. For the sake of the exercise we will do the same here, first fitting them to two straight-line sections with a knee, and subsequently fitting them with the smooth combination of a parabola and a straight line. The experimental observations can also be found in G. A. Seber & C. J. Wild, *Nonlinear Regression*, Wiley 1989 p. 461.

Exercise 4.13.1:

(1) Copy the data into your spreadsheet, with the weight-to-height ratio as the dependent variable y, and age as the independent variable x. Plot these data; neither the beginning nor the end fits a line or higher-order power series in x through the origin, and we will therefore use straight lines with arbitrary intercepts. Continuity of a fit with $y = a_0 + a_1 x$ for $x < c$, and $y = b_0 + b_1 x$ for $x > c$, requires that $a_0 + a_1 c = b_0 + b_1 c$ so that $b_0 = a_0 + (a_1 - b_1) c$.

(2) Enter labels and values for a_0, a_1, b_1, and c, then compute y_{calc} with an instruction containing an IF statement, as $a_0 + a_1 x$ for $x < c$, and $y = a_0 + (a_1 - b_1) c + b_1 x$ for $x > c$. Plot the resulting curve for y_{calc} in the above graph, and adjust the values of a_0, a_1, b_1, and c to provide an approximate fit with the experimental data.

(3) Compute SSR using the SUMXMY2 function, call Solver to minimize SSR, then call SolverAid to find the associated uncertainties. Keep in mind that the uncertainty estimate of c derives exclusively from its role in defining the slope of the longer straight-line segment. The resulting curve is shown in Fig. 4.13.1.

(4) There is no known reason to assume that something suddenly happens at $x = c$ to render the slope dy/dx discontinuous at that age. As long as we are merely looking for a smooth-looking mathematical description of these data in terms of

relatively few parameters, a curve without a knee would seem preferable. We therefore fit these same data to $y = a_0 + a_1x + a_2x^2$ for $x < c$, and $y = b_0 + b_1x$ for $x > c$, with the constraints that both y and dy/dx are continuous at $x = c$.

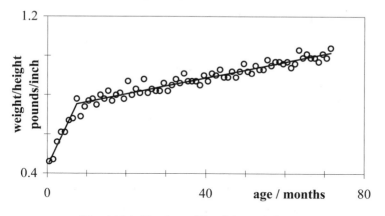

Fig. 4.13.1: The data of Eppright et al. fitted
with two connected straight-line segments.

(5) Calculate $b_0 = a_0 + (a_1 - b_1)c$.

(6) Since this exercise already provided reasonable guess values for $b_0 = a_0 + (a_1 - b_1)c$ and b_1, we now express a_0 and a_1 in terms of b_0 and b_1, i.e., $a_1 = b_1 - 2a_2c$ and $a_0 = b_0 + (b_1 - a_1)c - a_2c^2 = b_0 + a_2c^2$. We therefore calculate y_{calc} in an IF statement as $(b_0 + a_2c^2) + (b_1 - 2a_2c)x + a_2x^2$ for $x < c$, otherwise $b_0 + b_1x$.

(7) Using the graph displaying y and y_{calc} as a guide, set a_2 and c to some plausible guess values, such as -0.001 and 20, compute SSR, and call Solver to adjust a_2, b_1, b_2, and c. (In case you encounter trouble, do this in steps, first adjusting only a_2 and c.) Finally, find the corresponding uncertainty estimates with SolverAid. Figure 4.13.2 shows the result.

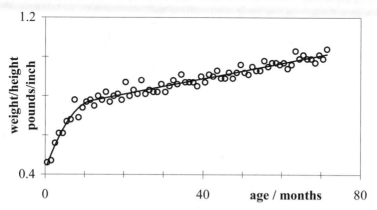

Fig. 4.13.2: The data of Eppright et al. fitted with a parabola plus a straight line, with both the function and its slope continuous at the joint.

4.14 Enzyme kinetics, once more

Nonlinear least squares can be used for convenience in order to avoid the complications of weighting and/or error propagation. We will illustrate how Solver can bypass the need for weighted linear least squares, by revisiting enzyme kinetics. In a second example, in section 4.15, we will see how Solver can sometimes be used when weighted least squares yield unsatisfactory results. In section 4.16 we will then reconsider linear extrapolation.

In section 3.17 we encountered a set of data on enzyme kinetics that, after some rearrangement, could be analyzed with linear least squares as Hanes or Lineweaver-Burk plots. Using unweighted least squares we found answers that depended on the rearrangement used, whereas properly weighted linear least squares gave consistent results. Still, the procedure was rather laborious: it required us to determine the appropriate weights, then to apply a weighted least squares, and finally to perform an analysis of the propagation of uncertainty. Below we will show that similar results can be obtained more simply by using Solver, without the need for weights or special error propagation.

Exercise 4.14.1:

(1) Extend the spreadsheet of exercise 3.17.1 or enter the data of table 3.17 into a new spreadsheet, as in Fig. 4.14.1. Also enter labels and initial values for the two parameters to be determined, K and v_m, and use these to compute v as a function of s according to (3.17.1).

(2) Compute SSR, then call Solver to adjust the values of K and v_m.

(3) Call SolverAid to calculate the associated uncertainties, and to provide the covariance matrix in case subsequent computations will use both K and v_m. Figure 4.14.1 shows it all.

	A	B	C	D	E	F	G
1	s	v exp	v model		*Solver + SolverAid*		
2	/mM	/μM	/μM			K	v m
3					*Value:*	0.597	0.690
4	0.138	0.148	0.130		*St.Dev.:*	*0.068*	*0.037*
5	0.220	0.171	0.186				
6	0.291	0.234	0.226		*SSR:*	0.0007	*0.014*
7	0.560	0.324	0.334				
8	0.766	0.390	0.388		*CM:*	0.0047	0.0024
9	1.460	0.493	0.490			0.0024	0.0014

C4 = A4*$G$3/($F$3+A4)   copied to C5:C9

Fig. 4.14.1: A spreadsheet for analyzing enzyme kinetics with Solver plus SolverAid.

Comparison of the above results ($K = 0.059_7 \pm 0.06_8$, $v_m = 0.69_0 \pm 0.03_7$) with those of the weighted least squares method ($K = 0.0571 \pm 0.064$, $v_m = 0.68_0 \pm 0.035$) show them to be similar but not identical. And when the values for K and v_{max} found earlier with weighted least squares in section 3.17 are substituted into cells F3 and G3 of the spreadsheet of Fig. 4.14.1, a slightly higher value for SSR results. What went wrong here?

The answer lies in the approximation (3.15.1) used to determine the appropriate weights, which is only valid when the relative deviations $\Delta y/y$ are much smaller than 1. This is not quite the case in the present example, thereby making Solver not only more convenient (because it homes in directly on the quantities of interest) but also slightly superior in terms of its numerical results.

4.15 The Lorentzian revisited

In section 3.19 we used a weighted least squares routine to fit data to a Lorentzian. There was no problem as long as the signal did not contain much noise, but the method failed miserably when the signal-to-noise ratio was too small, see Fig. 4.15.1. Here we will revisit this problem with Solver.

Exercise 4.15.1:
   (1) Extend the spreadsheet of exercise 3.19.1, by entering labels and initial values for the parameters a, b, and c of (3.19.1). Use these to compute y as a function of x according to (3.19.1) for the data used in Fig. 3.19.3.
   (2) Calculate SSR, and let Solver minimize SSR by changing the parameters a, b, and c. Figure 4.15.2 shows the result.

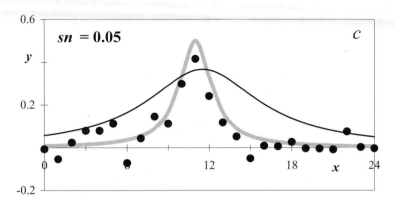
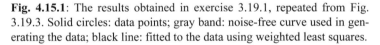

Fig. 4.15.1: The results obtained in exercise 3.19.1, repeated from Fig. 3.19.3. Solid circles: data points; gray band: noise-free curve used in generating the data; black line: fitted to the data using weighted least squares.

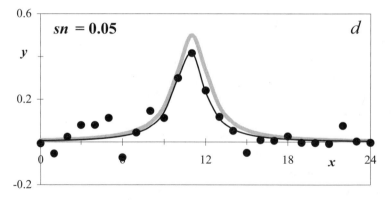

Fig. 4.15.2: The results of exercise 4.15.1. Solid circles: data points; gray band: noise-free curve used in generating the data; black line: fitted line.

In this example, Solver is clearly much more impervious to noise than a weighted least squares analysis. Indeed, Solver is often more robust than weighted least squares. Eventually, though, the Lorentzian (or any other signal) can be overwhelmed by noise no matter what algorithm is used. In that case, different experimental methods, such as signal averaging or synchronous detection must be used, but these must be designed into the experiment, and cannot be used after the fact.

4.16 Linear extrapolation

We also briefly revisit the problem of linear extrapolation addressed in section 2.11. Here, Solver will allow us to home in directly on the parameter of interest. In the experimental determination of absolute zero temperature, one wants to know the intercept t_0 of a straight line $V = a_0 + a_1t$ with the horizontal axis, where $V_0 = 0$ so that $a_0 = -a_1t_0$. We reformulate the problem as $V_{model} = V - V_0 = a_1(t-t_0)$, use Solver to find the best-fitting values for a_1 and t_0, and SolverAid to determine the corresponding uncertainties. In Fig. 2.11.1 we displayed the linear correlation coefficients showing a slope and intercept that were highly correlated, thus requiring the use of the covariance matrix. By using Solver plus SolverAid, we bypass this complication.

Exercise 4.16.1:

(1) Extend the spreadsheet of exercise 2.11.1, where V is assumed to have the dominant experimental uncertainties, see Fig. 2.11.1. Enter labels and initial values for the parameters a_1 and t_0, and use these to compute V as a function of t according to $V = a_1 (t-t_0)$.

(2) Calculate SSR, call Solver, and let it minimize SSR by changing $a1$ and $t0$, then call SolverAid to get the associated uncertainties. Figure 4.16.1 shows what

such a spreadsheet computation might look like. The results are substantially the same as those of Fig. 2.11.1, and again will depend on whether you start from the data in Table 2.11 or from the rounded V_d values shown in Fig. 4.16.1.

11	**Pb** = 98.19			**t₀** = **-278.0**		*9.6*
12	**SSR**= 0.011		*0.033*	**a₁** = 0.01364		*0.00042*
13						
14	*V*	*Pw*	*Vd*	*temp*	*Vmodel*	
15	*mL*	*kPa*	*mL*	*deg C*	*mL*	
16				-278.0	0.00	
17	3.80	0.61	3.78	0.0	3.79	
18	3.90	0.86	3.87	4.8	3.86	
19	3.98	1.14	3.93	8.9	3.91	
20	4.10	2.09	4.01	18.2	4.04	
21	4.20	2.88	4.08	23.4	4.11	
22	4.40	3.83	4.23	28.2	4.18	
23	4.50	5.50	4.25	34.6	4.26	
24	4.80	8.87	4.37	43.5	4.38	
25	5.15	12.34	4.50	50.0	4.47	
26	5.75	19.93	4.58	60.0	4.61	
27	6.00	21.55	4.68	61.7	4.63	
28	7.25	33.97	4.74	72.0	4.77	

Fig. 4.16.1: The spreadsheet computation of Fig. 2.11.1 as modified for use with Solver and SolverAid.

4.17 Guarding against false minima

The convenience of Solver must be balanced against the possibility that it produces an incorrect answer. This is the consequence of the method by which the Levenberg-Marquardt algorithm finds its way to the lowest value of the minimization criterion. That method is analogous to the flow of rainwater that, after haven fallen on land, usually finds its way to the ocean, which we will here take as its lowest level. But sometimes the rainwater flows into a mountain lake high above sea level, with no outlet, and can go no lower. As with any analogy, the above image is only partially applicable, because water can also run into a lake below sea level, such as the Dead Sea. But even that observation reinforces the message: finding a minimum does not guarantee that it is the lowest possible one. How can we guard against getting stuck in a *local* minimum rather than in the *global* minimum?

There is no foolproof way to find the global minimum, or even a local minimum. Just imagine a golf ball rolling on a golf course; its chances of finding a hole by itself, just under the influence of gravity, are minuscule. Fortunately, most minima are not so restrictive, and we can often reduce our chances of ending in a local minimum by starting Solver from different initial values that cover most of the likely parameter space, i.e., the range of parameter values within which we expect the global minimum to occur.

The following exercise illustrates the problem. Say that we have a curve with two well-separated peaks, one Gaussian, the other Lorentzian, that we want to fit with Solver. In order to simplify the problem, we select the same height and width parameters for both curves, so that they differ only in their peak positions. We must now assign two initial values to Solver, one each for the guessed peak positions of the Gaussian and the Lorentzian. We will call the initial guess value for the peak center of the Gaussian G, and that for the Lorentzian L, and will try Solver for various values of G and L. Thus we will probe a two-dimensional parameter space, varying both G and L.

Figure 4.17.1 illustrates what we find when Solver starts with peak positions that are reasonably close to their final values: the fit is as good as can be expected in the presence of noise, and the residuals look perfectly random. Indeed, when we set the noise parameter s_n equal to zero we find almost perfect agreement, with SSR less than 10^{-7}.

Figure 4.17.2 illustrates what happens when, in assigning the initial guess values of the peak positions for Solver, we sneakily interchange the positions of the Gaussian and Lorenzian. In that case we clearly obtain a *false minimum* in SSR. And it is not due to the added noise: when we set s_n to zero, we still get a similar result, with a value for SSR of about 48. The added noise for $s_n = 0.1$ only adds about 10 to the SSR values.

In Fig. 4.17.2 we have generated a false minimum in order to ask the question: how close need we be to get the correct answer, and how attractive is a false minimum? There is, of course, no simple general answer to such a question, but we can at least use the spreadsheet to give us some idea, by trying out where various initial values lead us. It is impractical to perform such a search manually, but we can automate the process. This is done by the macro SolverScan, modeled after a recent paper by P. Nikitas & A. Pappa-Louisi in *Chromatographia* 52 (2000) 477, which applies Solver for various values of G and L. There are several ways to conduct such a search. The simplest is to use a regular grid, where the initial guess values for the two peak positions are each given one of, say, 10 equidistant values. That will force the macro to apply Solver $10 \times 10 = 100$ times. Even if Solver takes only 5 seconds on your computer, 100×5 s will consume more than 8 minutes. If we insist on an n times higher resolution, we need to apply Solver n^2 times as often. Except for a very simple calculation performed on a very fast computer, this will quickly become a time-consuming proposition.

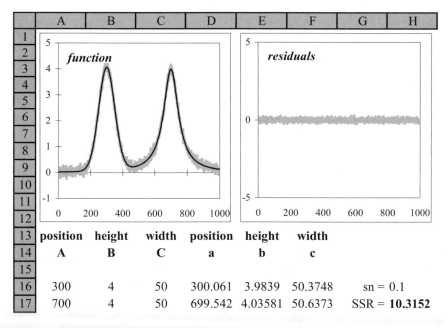

	position	height	width	position	height	width	
	A	**B**	**C**	**a**	**b**	**c**	
	300	4	50	300.061	3.9839	50.3748	sn = 0.1
	700	4	50	699.542	4.03581	50.6373	SSR = **10.3152**

Fig. 4.17.1: The top of a spreadsheet containing 1000 data points, showing a Gaussian peak $B \exp[-(x-A)^2/2C^2]$ centered at $A = 300$ plus a Lorentzian peak $3000B / [(x-A)^2 + 60C]$ at $A = 700$ plus Gaussian noise of zero mean and amplitude $s_n = 0.1$. The lowercase symbols represent the corresponding parameters as found by Solver.

Instead of using regular steps we can randomize the initially assumed values for the peak positions in such a way that they cover the same parameter space. However, such a scheme often produces a rather uneven coverage of that parameter space for practical (i.e., fairly small) numbers of trials. An intermediate solution is to use a regular grid to divide the parameter space in equal-sized cells, and then to assign the initial parameter values inside each of those cells with random numbers. This leads to a so-called pseudorandom search, which is somewhat less likely to cluster. Figure 4.17.3 illustrates these three options.

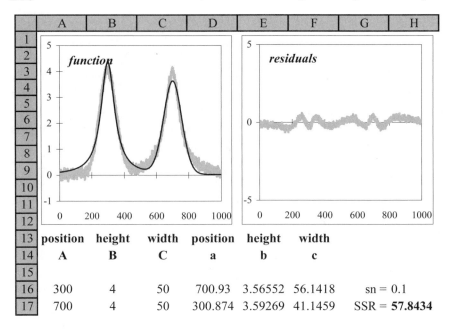

position	height	width	position	height	width	
A	B	C	a	b	c	
300	4	50	700.93	3.56552	56.1418	sn = 0.1
700	4	50	300.874	3.59269	41.1459	SSR = **57.8434**

Fig. 4.17.2: The same as Fig. 4.17.1, but obtained with Solver upon assuming the Lorentzian to be centered at $x = 300$, and the Gaussian at $x = 700$.

Unfortunately, results obtained with the second and third option are more difficult to plot, because Excel can only handle 3-D plots of equidistant data, and the same restriction applies to the macro Mapper. Moreover, the result is probably substantially the same: if the minimum is very narrow, it will be a hit-or-miss proposition no matter how we distribute the points. Therefore, SolverScan is set up to use a regular grid.

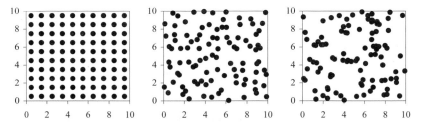

Fig. 4.17.3: Three different grids for searching an area. Leftmost panel: a regular grid, here with points at $G = i + 0.5$, $L = j + 0.5$, where $i = 0$ (1) 9 and $j = 0$ (1) 9. Central panel: a pseudorandom grid, with $G = i + $ RAND(), $L = j + $ RAND(), where RAND() yields a random number between 0 and 1. Rightmost panel: $G = 10*$RAND(), $L = 10*$RAND().

Before you use SolverScan please make sure that the Excel version on your computer has access to the Solver object library, because otherwise

SolverScan cannot call Solver (or, rather, SolverScan can call all it wants, but Solver won't come). To see whether this is the case, use Alt◡ F11 (Mac: Opt◡F11) to switch to the Visual Basic Editor. On the Visual Basic Editor menu bar, click on Tools ⇒ References. The computer will now display the References – VBAProject dialog box. Check whether SOLVER.xls is listed and has been check-marked; if so, you are OK. If not, use the procedure described in section 1.7.2 to add Solver to the object library. Fortunately you need to do this only once, i.e., until the next time you update your software.

Figure 4.17.4 shows the results for such an exercise using 11 initial positions, 0 (100) 1000, for both G and L, for a total of 121 combinations. Of these, we find 27 combinations that lead to the correct minimum, 32 combinations that reverse the peak positions as in Fig. 4.16.2, and 62 initial guesses that yield other, *completely false* results (that do not even appear to represent local minima) with much higher SSR-values. In other words, *more than half* of the initial guesses lead to completely unacceptable 'solutions', and less than a quarter find the correct answer. And Gaussian noise is not the main culprit here: when we repeat the analysis with $s_n = 0$, the values obtained for SSR are all about ten units smaller, but the overall pattern remains the same. In a tricky situation such as considered here, we clearly cannot start with just any parameter estimates and expect Solver to do the rest! That is also why a graphical display of the fit, before and after Solver, is important.

1000	356	**58**	**58**	**58**	**58**	1235	694	694	694	694	1255
900	1270	**58**	**58**	**58**	**58**	694	694	1233	694	1255	1281
800	**58**	1220	**58**	**58**	**58**	**58**	694	694	694	1412	**58**
700	**58**	**58**	**58**	**58**	**58**	**58**	694	694	**58**	**58**	**58**
600	1003	**58**	**58**	**58**	**58**	**58**	**58**	475	694	1270	**58**
500	1220	**58**	475	**58**	475	475	475	475	475	**10**	1272
400	893	1220	469	475	475	**10**	**10**	**10**	**10**	**10**	**10**
300	891	**10**	**10**	469	**10**	**10**	**10**	**10**	**10**	**10**	**10**
200	893	**10**	469	469	469	1157	**10**	**10**	**10**	**10**	**10**
100	1590	1149	469	469	469	**10**	**10**	**10**	**10**	**10**	1281
0	1149	469	469	469	469	1157	1412	1412	1412	1412	1275
	0	*100*	*200*	*300*	*400*	*500*	*600*	*700*	*800*	*900*	*1000*

Fig. 4.17.4: The values for the sum of the squares of the residuals, SSR, for Solver solutions starting from various initial values for the peak centers x_1 and x_2 respectively. The correct result, SSR = 10, and the incorrect, interchanged result, SSR = 58, are both displayed in bold, and the axes in bold italics.

It may be possible to improve the odds slightly, by applying some constraints, such as that the fitted parameters must be positive. Still, the message is clear: nonlinear least squares need reasonably close initial estimates to work reliably, and the resulting fit and its residuals should always be displayed and inspected before the answer is accepted.

4.18 Inverse interpolation with Solver

We now revisit the problem of section 1.12, inverse interpolation, as another example of using a macro to control Solver. Lagrange interpolation assumes that the function to be interpolated can be approximated as a polynomial, and the result will therefore depend on the assumed polynomial order. When the function has a closed-form analytical description, as in the spreadsheet of exercise 1.12.1, Solver can be used instead, without the need to make any such assumptions.

Say that, in the titration of a V_a mL sample of C_{a1} M HCl + C_{a2} M HAc with C_b M NaOH, one needs to determine the pH as a function of the volume V_b of base added. The theory readily provides V_b as a function of $[H^+]$ or pH, and one can therefore use Solver to determine the pH for an individual titrant volume V_b, as illustrated below.

Exercise 4.18.1:

(1) In cells A13:A15 enter labels for C_{a1}, C_{a2}, and C_b, and in C13:C15 those for V_a, K_a, and K_w. In B13:B15 place some corresponding values, such as 0.1, 0.1, and 0.1, and in D13:D15 the values 10, $10^{-4.76}$, and 10^{-14}. The latter must be coded with equal signs, as =10^–4.76 and =10^–14.

(2) In cell A19 of a spreadsheet enter a pH value, such as 5. In cell B19 calculate the corresponding value of $[H^+] = 10^{-pH}$. In cell then C19 compute $V_b = V_a(C_{a1} + C_{a2}K_a/([H^+]+K_a) - [H^+] + K_w/[H^+]) / (C_b + [H^+] - K_w/[H^+])$, which should yield a V_b-value of 16.34.

(3) Say that one needs to compute the pH for $V_b = 13.27$. Call Solver, Set Target Cell C19 to the Value of 13.27 By Changing Cells A19, which will yield pH = 4.448.

The above works well for a single point, but becomes tedious when a whole set of data is needed in order to generate a curve. It is here that the macro ColumnSolver can be helpful.

Exercise 4.18.1 (continued):

(4) In cells A17:D17 place column labels for pH, $[H^+]$, V_b, and V_b.

(5) If one wants, say, data for $V_b = 0$ (1) 30, place the values 0 (1) 30 in cells D19:D49. Then copy cells A19:C19 down to row 49.

(6) Make sure that Excel has access to the Solver object library, as described in section 4.17, otherwise ColumnSolver will not run.

(7) Call ColumnSolver, and select ColumnSolver_Value. Specify the target cells as C19:C49, the wanted target values as D19:D49, and the adjustable parameters as located in A19:A49.

(8) Plot the result in A1:D12, which will show that, indeed, the titration curve is now computed for the titrant volumes specified.

(9) Note that this method would not work in exercise 4.4.1, because ColumnSolver is a macro, and therefore doesn't update automatically.

4.19 General least squares fit to a straight line

So far we have assumed that we can assign one variable to be *the* dependent one. Often that is indeed possible, in which case it greatly simplifies the analysis. However, there are situations where it makes no physical sense to assign all the uncertainty to only one variable. Treating both x and y as equivalent parameters will in general require a special macro. Here we will merely illustrate the approach for the relatively simple case of a straight line, for which the spreadsheet solution using Solver and SolverAid is fairly straightforward, so that no special macro is needed. In section 4.20 we will do the same for a semicircle.

In chapter 2 we fitted data to the line $y = a_0 + a_1x$ by minimizing the sum of squares of the deviation Δy. If we want to minimize instead the sum of squares of the distance d_i between the points x_i, y_i and the line $y = a_0 + a_1x$ we use a simple trigonometric argument illustrated in Fig. 4.19.1, i.e., $d_i = \Delta y_i \cos\alpha$ and $\tan\alpha = dy/dx = a_1$, which can be combined with the trigonometric relation $\cos\alpha = 1/\sqrt{(1+\tan^2\alpha)} = 1/\sqrt{(1+a_1^2)}$ to $d_i^2 = \Delta y_i^2/(1+a_1^2)$. Consequently we minimize $\Sigma d_i^2 = \Sigma\Delta y_i^2/(1+a_1^2)$ instead of $\Sigma\Delta y_i^2$. (Even though we here fit data to a line, this approach is not suitable for a linear least squares algorithm, since the term $(1+a_1^2)$ makes the expressions nonlinear in the coefficients a_i.) Similarly, we can fit data to a plane $y = a + bx + cz$ by minimizing $\Sigma d_i^2 = \Sigma\Delta y_i^2/(1+b^2+c^2)$, etc.

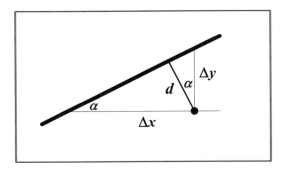

Fig. 4.19.1: The shortest distance d between the point (x,y) (solid circle) and the line $y = a_0 + a_1x$.

The above expression $d_i^2 = \Delta y_i^2/(1+a_1^2)$ can be converted into $d_i^2 = \Delta y_i^2/(1+\Delta y_i^2/\Delta x_i^2) = \Delta y_i^2 \, \Delta x_i^2/(\Delta x_i^2 + \Delta y_i^2)$ or $1/d_i^2 = 1/\Delta x_i^2 + 1/\Delta y_i^2$, an expression symmetrical in x and y that is convenient for the introduction of individual weights. Likewise, $\Sigma d_i^2 = \Sigma \Delta y_i^2 / (1 + b^2 + c^2)$ can be rewritten as $1/d_i^2 = 1/\Delta x_i^2 + 1/\Delta y_i^2 + 1/\Delta z_i^2$.

Exercise 4.19.1:

(1) Use the data set from Fig. 2.9.1. Make labels and cells for the (initially assumed) parameter values a_0 and a_1, and a column in which you calculate the squares of the residuals, $1/\{1/[(y_i - a_0 - a_1 x_i)^2] + 1/[(x_i + a_0/a_1 - y_i/a_1)^2]\}$ for each row. Compute the sum of these squares of residuals, minimize it by using Solver, compute the properly scaled value of SSR, i.e., SSR $\times$ $(1+a_1^2)$ since $d^2 = \Delta y^2/(1+a_1^2)$, and finally use the latter to find the associated uncertainties with SolverAid.

(2) You will obtain the correct values for a_0 and a_1 regardless of whether the sum of the squares of the residuals is properly scaled, but in order to get correct uncertainty estimates with SolverAid, that sum should be scaled through multiplication by $(1+a_1^2)$. This is why the spreadsheet in Fig. 4.19.2 contains SSR (to be used for Solver) and its scaled version, sSSR (to be used subsequently with SolverAid). You will obtain $y = 5.7_8 \pm 0.1_9 - (0.54_6 \pm 0.04_2) x$, the same result as obtained by Pearson.

In section 3.15 we introduced weights w_i as multipliers of Δy_i^2 in the least squares minimization procedure, and we can do likewise in the present context. If certain data points must be emphasized more than others, we can minimize $\Sigma w_i d_i^2 = \Sigma w_i \Delta y_i^2/(1+a_1^2) = \Sigma 1/[1/(w_i \Delta x_i^2) + 1/(w_i \Delta y_i^2)]$; if the x_i- and y_i-values of individual points should be assigned separate weights, we instead minimize $\Sigma 1/[1/(w_{xi} \Delta x_i^2) + 1/(w_{yi} \Delta y_i^2)]$. We will illustrate this more general situation below.

Exercise 4.19.1 (continued):

(3) Insert two new columns, one each for w_x and w_y. Modify the column label from SR to wSR, and the corresponding instructions to $1/\{1/[w_{yi} (y_i - a_0 - a_1 x_i)^2)]$ $+1/[w_{xi} (x_i + a_0/a_1 - y_i/a_1)^2]\}$. Also make a column for the weights $1/(1/w_{yi} + a_1^2/w_{xi})$. And for SolverAid again use the scaled sum sSwSR, which is equal to SwSR divided by the average value of the terms $1/(1/w_{yi} + a_1^2/w_{xi})$.

(4) First verify that you obtain the same result as under (1) and (2) by setting all w_x and w_y equal to 1. Then make all w_x equal to 1000000, in which case you will recover the result for y as the dependent parameter, $a_0 = 5.7612 \pm 0.1895$, $a_1 = -0.5396 \pm 0.0421$. Also check that for, say, all $w_y = 1000$ and all $w_x = 0.001$, you get the result for x as the dependent parameter, $a_0 = 5.8617 \pm 0.1941$, $a_1 = -0.5659 \pm 0.0431$.

(5) Now try some arbitrary individual weights. Often the resulting differences will be small, although you can find examples where weighting really makes a difference, e.g., by emphasizing a small subset of the data. This is illustrated in Fig. 4.19.3, where the lowest points of the graph dominate the fit through a rather extreme choice of individual weights.

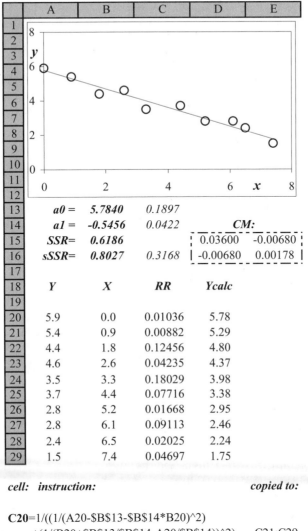

	A	B	C	D	E
13	a0 =	**5.7840**	*0.1897*		
14	a1 =	**-0.5456**	*0.0422*	*CM:*	
15	SSR=	**0.6186**		0.03600	-0.00680
16	sSSR=	**0.8027**	*0.3168*	-0.00680	0.00178
17					
18	*Y*	*X*	*RR*	*Ycalc*	
19					
20	5.9	0.0	0.01036	5.78	
21	5.4	0.9	0.00882	5.29	
22	4.4	1.8	0.12456	4.80	
23	4.6	2.6	0.04235	4.37	
24	3.5	3.3	0.18029	3.98	
25	3.7	4.4	0.07716	3.38	
26	2.8	5.2	0.01668	2.95	
27	2.8	6.1	0.09113	2.46	
28	2.4	6.5	0.02025	2.24	
29	1.5	7.4	0.04697	1.75	

cell:	*instruction:*		*copied to:*

C20=1/((1/(A20-$B$13-$B$14*B20)^2)
    +(1/(B20+$B$13/$B$14-A20/$B$14))^2)   C21:C29
D20=$B$13+$B$14*B20   D21:D29
B15=SUM(C20:C29)
B16=B15*(1+$B$14^2)

Fig. 4.19.2: A spreadsheet for general unweighted data fitting to a straight line.

The above approach is readily extendable to those cases for which $y = F(x)$ can be inverted to an algebraic solution $x = G(y)$, such as the proportionality $y = a_1 x$ and the quadratic $y = a_0 + a_1 x + a_2 x^2$, so that Δx can be evaluated for a given Δy.

	A	B	C	D	E	F	G
1							
2							
3							
4							
5							
6							
7							
8							
9							
10							
11							
12							
13	*a 0 =*	*8.7429*	*0.0187*				
14	*a 1 =*	*-0.9786*	*0.0042*		*CM:*	3.5E-04	-6.6E-05
15	*SSR=*	*6.5857542*				-6.6E-05	1.7E-05
16	*SwSR=*	*0.0078193*	*0.0313*				
17							
18	*Y*	*X*	*Wy*	*Wx*	*wSR*	*w*	*Ycalc*
19							
20	5.9	0.0	0.00001	0.00003	6.126E-05	7.58E-06	8.74
21	5.4	0.9	0.0001	0.0003	0.00046	7.58E-05	7.86
22	4.4	1.8	0.001	0.003	0.00505	0.00076	6.98
23	4.6	2.6	0.01	0.03	0.01937	0.00758	6.20
24	3.5	3.3	0.1	0.3	0.30730	0.07580	5.51
25	3.7	4.4	1	3	0.41171	0.75802	4.44
26	2.8	5.2	10	30	5.52947	7.58017	3.65
27	2.8	6.1	100	300	0.05391	75.801744	2.77
28	2.4	6.5	1000	3000	0.24877	758.01744	2.38
29	1.5	7.4	10000	30000	0.00965	7580.1744	1.50

cell:	instruction:		copied to:

E20=1/((1/(C20*(A20-$B$13-$B$14*B20)^2))
      +(1/(D20*(B20+$B$13/$B$14-A20/$B$14))^2))   E21:E29
F20=1/((1/C20)+(($B$14^2)/D20))   F21:F29
G20=$B$13+$B$14*B20   G21:G29
B15=SUM(E20:E29)
B16=B15/AVERAGE(F20:F29)

Fig. 4.19.3: The spreadsheet for a general weighted least squares fit to a straight line for an arbitrarily chosen set of weights $w_{x,i}$ and $w_{y,i}$ that greatly emphasize the lowest points.

Clearly, the spreadsheet presents no problem to a weighted general least squares fit to a straight line. The difficulty of such use does not lie in its mechanics, but rather in the assignment of appropriate weights. If the standard deviations s_x and s_y are known, weights $w_x = s_x^{-2}$ and $w_y = s_y^{-2}$ may be appropriate for individual data points, unless transformations add global weights. A more detailed discussion of this topic lies beyond our current, necessarily limited purview.

4.20 General least squares fit to a complex quantity

Consider an impedance plot, in which we make a graph of the imaginary component $-Z''$ of the impedance versus its real component Z'. Both of these quantities are typically measured at the same time, using the same instrument, as a function of frequency. When we plot the magnitude $\sqrt{\{(Z')^2+(Z'')^2\}}$ and the phase angle $\arctan(Z'/Z'')$ as a function of frequency, we can consider the frequency (especially when derived from a quartz oscillator) as the independent variable. However, in a typical impedance plot of $-Z''$ vs. Z' the frequency is *implicit*, and both Z' and $-Z''$ are subject to similar experimental uncertainties, so that it will not do to assign all experimental uncertainty to either the real or the imaginary component of the measured impedance. Below we will use as our model the electrical circuit formed by resistance R_s in series with the parallel combination of a resistance R_p and a capacitance C, which yields a semicircular impedance plot. Similar graphs occur, e.g., in Cole plots of the dielectric constant. Note that the method is generally applicable, regardless of the complexity of the equivalent circuit used, as long as the coordinates of both the real and imaginary component are given.

The impedance of the above-mentioned circuit is given by

$$Z = R_s + \frac{1}{j\omega C + 1/R_p} = R_s + \frac{R_p(1 - j\omega R_p C)}{1 + (\omega R_p C)^2} \tag{4.20.1}$$

with the in-phase (real) and quadrature (imaginary) components

$$Z' = R_s + \frac{R_p}{1 + (\omega R_p C)^2}, \qquad Z'' = \frac{-\omega R_p^2 C}{1 + (\omega R_p C)^2} \tag{4.20.2}$$

We simply minimize the square of the distance d between the experimental and calculated points, where $d^2 = (Z'_{exp} - Z'_{calc})^2 + (Z''_{exp} - Z''_{calc})^2$.

Exercise 4.20.1:

(1) In a new spreadsheet, in block A15:B18, deposit the labels and values of the constants R_s, R_p, C, and s_n, and in block C15:D18 for the constants R_s, R_p, C, and SSR. Below these make column labels for ω, $-Z''$, Z', $-Z''_{calc}$, Z'_{calc}, and SR.

(2) As the first cell in column A deposit, say, 0.01, and in the next a number that is a factor of $10^{0.1}$ larger. Do this for, say, a total of 41 points, ending at a value of 100. (The same could of course be achieved with two columns, one for log ω and the other for ω, where log $\omega = -2$ (0.1) 2, while the second column calculates its antilog.) In columns M and N deposit Gaussian noise of zero mean and unit standard deviation.

(3) In columns B and C compute $-Z''$ and Z' respectively, based on (4.20.2) with added noise, using the constants in B15:B18 plus the values of ω in column A. These will serve as our stand-in for experimental data. In columns D and E again calculate $-Z''$ and Z' respectively, again based on (4.20.2) but without noise, and now using the guessed constants listed in D15:D17 instead.

(4) In column F compute the squares of the residuals, $SR = (Z' - Z'_{calc})^2 + (Z'' - Z''_{calc})^2$, and in cell D18 place the instruction =SUM ( ) to calculate SSR.

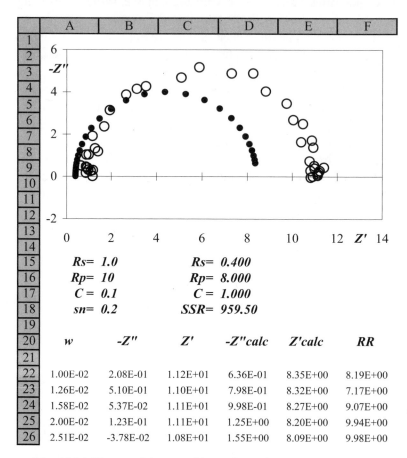

	A	B	C	D	E	F
15	Rs= 1.0		Rs= 0.400			
16	Rp= 10		Rp= 8.000			
17	C = 0.1		C = 1.000			
18	sn= 0.2		SSR= 959.50			
19						
20	w	-Z"	Z'	-Z"calc	Z'calc	RR
21						
22	1.00E-02	2.08E-01	1.12E+01	6.36E-01	8.35E+00	8.19E+00
23	1.26E-02	5.10E-01	1.10E+01	7.98E-01	8.32E+00	7.17E+00
24	1.58E-02	5.37E-02	1.11E+01	9.98E-01	8.27E+00	9.07E+00
25	2.00E-02	1.23E-01	1.11E+01	1.25E+00	8.20E+00	9.94E+00
26	2.51E-02	-3.78E-02	1.08E+01	1.55E+00	8.09E+00	9.98E+00

Fig. 4.20.1: The top of the spreadsheet of exercise 4.20.1, before using Solver. Open circles: simulated noisy ("experimental") data; closed circles: calculated using the rough estimates for R_s, R_p, and C shown.

(5) Call Solver and let it minimize D18 by adjusting D15:D17, which will yield the required values for R_p, R_s, and C. Then call SolverAid for estimates of the precision of the found parameters. Figures 4.20.1 and 4.20.2 illustrate this approach for a rather noisy data set; by varying the value of s_n you can see how the parameters found depend on the noise level. For $s_n = 0$ you will of course recover the parameter values in B15:B17 exactly.

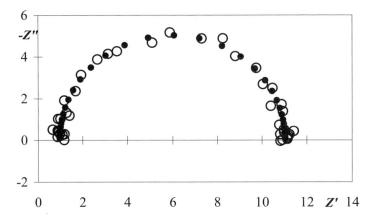

Fig. 4.20.2: The result after Solver has adjusted the parameter values, and SolverAid has determined the associated uncertainties. For the data shown in Fig. 4.20.1 this results in $R_s = 0.96_5 \pm 0.04_6$, $R_p = 10.0_7 \pm 0.06_2$, and $C = 0.098_1 \pm 0.001_6$, with SSR = 3.077 and a standard deviation of the fit of 0.197. Note that SolverAid cannot accommodate two adjacent columns for Y_{calc}, so that E22:E62 must first be cut and pasted to D63:D103 before SolverAid can be used.

This example shows the flexibility of the above approach. The model can be much more elaborate, with many adjustable parameters, as long as both its real and imaginary component are measurable. It allows for the introduction of individual weights, by including them in column F. In this way, quite complicated equivalent circuits can be accommodated.

4.21. Miscellany

In this section are collected a few additional examples of using Solver for data analysis. You, my reader, will have enough experience and self-confidence by now to tackle these problems without step-by-step instructions. The primary purpose of this section is to illustrate the wide range of problems that can be addressed efficiently by nonlinear least squares, and to provide some exercises for your self-testing.

4.21.1 Viscosity vs. temperature and pressure

As an example of fitting a set of high-quality experimental data to an equation with several adjustable parameters, use measurements from T. Witt, Ph.D. thesis, Technological University Eindhoven 1974, on the pressure dependence of the kinematic viscosity of a lubricant at four different temperatures, as listed by D. M. Bates & D. G. Watts, *Nonlinear Regression Analysis and its Applications*, Wiley 1988, table A1.8, p. 275.

Here the dependent variable, y, is the natural logarithm of the measured kinematic viscosity v_{kin} (in Stokes), and is to be fitted to the empirical expression

$$y = \frac{a_1}{a_2 + t} + a_3 p + a_4 p^2 + a_5 p^3 + (a_6 + a_7 p^2)\, p \, \exp\left[\frac{-t}{a_8 + a_9 p^2}\right]$$

(4.21.1)

where t is temperature, in °C, and p is pressure, in kAtm.

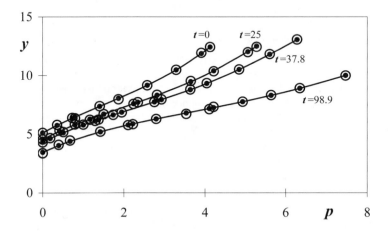

Fig. 4.21.1: Comparison of the experimental data (open circles) and those calculated with Solver (line plus small solid points) by fitting the data to (4.21.1).

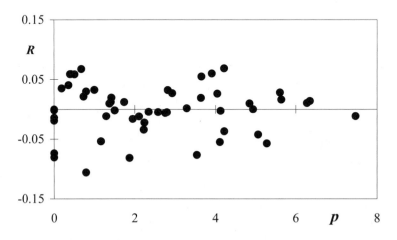

Fig. 4.21.2: The residuals of the fit shown in Fig. 4.21.1.

Use Solver, with the initial values $a_1 = a_2 = \ldots = a_9 = 1$, then SolverAid, compare your results with those listed on p. 89 of Bates & Watts, and find the significant typo in one of their listed constants. Plot your results and the corresponding residuals, and compare with Figs. 4.21.1 and 4.21.2.

4.21.2 Potentiometric titration of a diprotic base

In *Technometrics* 18 (1975) 161, W. H. Sachs reported data for a potentiometric titration of N,N-dimethylaminoethylamine with HCl, see table 4.21.1, and its analysis assuming that the volume of titrant added was the independent variable, and pH the dependent one. In this case it is not clear which parameter carries more experimental uncertainty, and no arguments are offered one way or the other. Because the analysis is much more straightforward when it is assumed that the titrant volume is the dependent variable instead, we will take that approach here.

Va	pH	Va	pH	Va	pH	Va	pH
1.695	10.002	6.790	8.830	10.410	6.889	15.221	5.837
2.402	9.820	7.090	8.731	10.840	6.777	15.720	5.686
2.743	9.739	7.294	8.660	11.280	6.675	16.220	5.489
3.195	9.643	7.660	8.497	11.730	6.578	16.634	5.249
3.599	9.559	8.097	8.230	12.230	6.474	16.859	5.045
4.104	9.457	8.386	7.991	12.725	6.378	17.000	4.852
4.678	9.339	8.671	7.735	13.229	6.280	17.101	4.656
4.990	9.276	9.070	7.430	13.726	6.184	17.140	4.552
5.589	9.145	9.531	7.194	14.225	6.078	17.170	4.453
6.190	8.994	9.980	7.026	14.727	5.959	17.228	4.220

Table 4.21.1: The titration data from W. H. Sachs, *Technometrics* 18 (1975) 161.

Analyze these data in terms of the expression for the titration of a diprotic base with a strong monoprotic acid, using K_{a1}, K_{a2}, K_w, and V_b as adjustable parameters, by making columns for V_a, pH, $[H^+]$, and $V_{a,calc}$, and calculating SSR from the differences between the entries for V_a and $V_{a,calc}$. The sample concentration is listed by Sachs as $C_b = 0.04305$ M, its volume as $V_b = 20.000$ mL, and the concentration C_a of the titrant, HCl, as $C_a = 0.09975$ M. For $V_{a,calc}$ use the theoretical expression

$$V_a = \frac{\dfrac{2[H^+]^2 + [H^+]K_{a1}}{[H^+]^2 + [H^+]K_{a1} + K_{a1}K_{a2}}C_b + [H^+] - K_w/[H^+]}{C_a - [H^+] + K_w/[H^+]} \qquad (4.21.2)$$

Assume that $pK_{a1} = 6$ and $pK_{a2} = 10$, set pK_w to 14, and from these calculate $K_{a1} = 10^{(-pK_{a1})}$ and $K_{a2} = 10^{(-pK_{a2})}$. It is these pK_a values (rather than the far smaller K_a-values themselves) that Solver should optimize. You should get a result similar to that shown in Fig. 4.21.3. Plot the residuals $R = V_a - V_{a,calc}$, which will show that systematic rather than random deviations control the standard deviation, see Fig. 4.21.4. Similar systematic deviations are apparent in Fig. 1 of the Sachs paper.

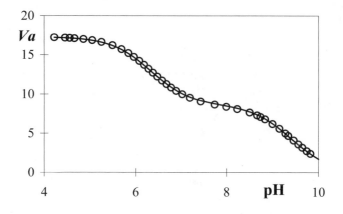

Fig. 4.21.3: Open circles: experimental data; line: the theoretical progress curve for the titration calculated by Solver with pK_{a1} = 6.33 and pK_{a1} = 9.40.

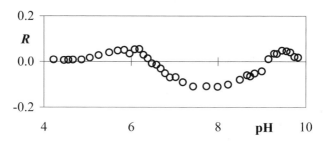

Fig. 4.21.4: The corresponding residuals.

The above fit neglects activity corrections that, though approximate in principle, usually lead to results believed to be more realistic. They require that we calculate an auxiliary concentration parameter $I = \frac{1}{2} \Sigma z^2 c$, the ionic strength, where c is the concentration of any ionic species in solution, and z its valency. We then estimate the activity corrections with the approximation $f = 10^\wedge\{-0.5 \ [(\sqrt{I}) / (1 + \sqrt{I}) - 0.3I]\}$ due to C. W. Davies (*Ion Association*, Butterworth 1962) and $K^t_{a1} = K_{a1} / f^2$, $K^t_{a2} = K_{a1}$, and $K^t_w = f^2 K_w$, where the superscript t denotes 'thermodynamic' or (most likely closer to) 'truly constant'. The ionic strength (buffered by the presence of 0.09658 M NaCl incorporated in the sample) is given by

$$I = 0.5 \left([H^+] + [OH^-] + 4[H_2B^{2+}] + [HB^+] + [Na^+] + [Cl^-] \right)$$

$$= 0.5 \left([H^+] + \frac{K_w}{[H^+]} \right)$$

$$+ \frac{V_b}{V_a + V_b} \left(\frac{(2[H^+]^2 + 0.5[H^+]K_{a1})C_b}{[H^+]^2 + [H^+]K_{a1} + K_{a1}K_{a2}} + 0.09658 \right)$$

$$+ \left(\frac{0.5 C_a V_a}{V_a + V_b} \right) \tag{4.21.3}$$

Such corrections can be incorporated directly in the Solver procedure, but here we will make the correction separately, using a simpler, iterative procedure described in chapter 6 of my *Aqueous Acid-Base Equilibria and Titrations*, Oxford University Press 1999. Add three new columns. In the first, compute the ionic strength I using (4.21.3). In the second calculate $f^2 = 10^{\wedge}[0.3\, I - (\sqrt{I})/(1+\sqrt{I})]$, and in the third compute $V_{a,calc}$ by again using (4.21.2) in which K_{a1} is now replaced by K_{a1}/f^2, and K_w by $f^2 K_w$. Then use Solver again. You will find $pK'_{a1} = 6.55$ and $pK'_{a2} = 9.40$, changes that hardly justify the additional effort.

Strictly speaking, we should now repeat this procedure by using the new pK_a estimates to recalculate I, then f, and again $V_{a,calc}$, until the results no longer change, but such iterations are obviously not necessary here since they will not lead to substantial further changes. Because of the presence of added NaCl in the sample, the ionic strength does not change much during the titration, so that the result is only marginally different from that obtained without activity correction. Plotting the residuals R will show that the systematic deviations illustrated in Fig. 4.21.4 likewise persist after activity correction, so that the absence of an activity correction did not cause the systematic deviations in R; they seldom do.

Finally we note that we do not obtain results identical to those of Sachs, $pK'_{a1} = 5.97$ (rather than 6.55) and $pK'_{a2} = 9.28$ (instead of 9.40), nor would we expect to, because we have interchanged the dependent and independent parameters. Since insufficient information is available about the titration (such as the chemical purity of the sample used), the origin(s) of the systematic deviations in the fit cannot be ascertained.

4.21.3 Analyzing light from a variable star

In their book *The Calculus of Observations* (Blackie & Sons, 4th ed. 1944, pp. 349-352), E. Whittaker & G. Robinson list the brightness of a variable star supposedly recorded during 600 successive midnights, and rounded to integer values. These data can also be downloaded from http://www.york.ac.uk/depts/maths/data/ts/ts.26.dat, and are shown as open circles in Fig. 4.21.5. They exhibit an interference pattern implying at least two sinusoids, plus a constant offset. Counting maxima one quickly finds that the period of one of these sinusoids must be approximately $24\frac{1}{2}/600 \approx 0.041$ day^{-1}, while the beat pattern indicates that the other must differ from it by about 6 day^{-1}. Therefore use Solver fit these data to an equation of the form $y = a_0 + a_1 \sin(2\pi f_1 + b_1) + a_2 \sin(2\pi f_2 + b_2)$ with initial guess values for f_1 and f_2 of 0.03 and 0.05 respectively.

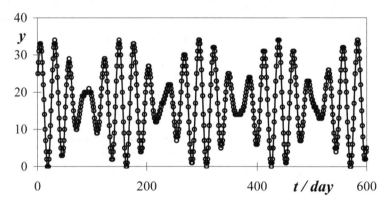

Fig. 4.21.5: The intensities of the variable star (open circles) observed on 600 successive midnights, and their analysis (line) in terms of a constant plus two sinusoids.

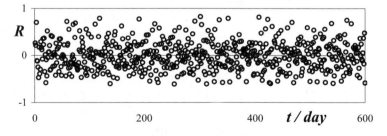

Fig. 4.21.6: The residuals for the fit of Fig. 4.21.5 show no discernable trend, just a standard deviation of 0.302. This is roughly what one would expect on the basis of merely rounding the data to integer values, suggesting that this was a made-up data set.

Using these data, you should find $a_0 = 17.08_6 \pm 0.01_2$, $a_1 = 10.03_1 \pm 0.01_8$, $f_1 = 0.0344824 \pm 0.0000017$, $b_1 = 0.6504 \pm 0.0036$, $a_2 = 7.084 \pm 0.018$, $f_2 = 0.0416665 \pm 0.0000023$, and $b_2 = -0.2616 \pm 0.0050$. Figures 4.21.5 and 4.21.6 indicate how close a fit you can obtain. The analysis used here is both much faster and more precise that that discussed by Whittaker & Robinson (before nonlinear least squares were readily available), which yielded $a_0 = 17$, $a_1 = 10$, $f_1 = 1/29 \approx 0.0345$, $b_1 = 6\pi/29 \approx 0.6500$, $a_2 = 7$, $f_2 = 1/24 \approx 0.0417$, and $b_2 = -2\pi/24 \approx -0.6218$. By standing on their shoulders, we can now see much further than the giants of the past.

The above data lack any indication of a possible experimental source, and their noise is certainly compatible with a made-up set rounded to integer values. You may therefore want to add some random noise, and delete some data points (to represent missing observations on overcast nights) in order to make the analysis more realistic.

Incidentally, the above-mentioned web site contains 74 interesting time series, listed in http://www.york.ac.uk/depts/maths/data/ts/welcome.

4.21.4 The growth of a bacterial colony

In his book on *Elements of Mathematical Biology*, Williams & Wilkins 1924, Dover 1956, A. J. Lotka listed data by Thornton on the area A occupied by a growing colony of Bacillus dendroides in a growth medium containing 0.2% KNO_3, and reproduced here in table 4.21.2. Fit these data to the equation $A = a / (b + e^{-ct})$ where a, b, and c are adjustable parameters, and t is age, in days. Give the best-fitting values for a, b, and c, together with their uncertainty estimates, and plot your results.

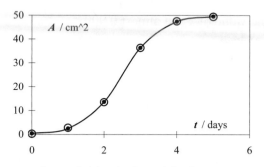

Fig. 4.21.7: The area A occupied by the bacterial colony at age t, as described by Solver and SolverAid with $a = 0.37_0 \pm 0.02_5$, $b = 0.0074_2 \pm 0.0005_0$, $c = 1.96_2 \pm 0.02_8$.

time t, in days:	0	1	2	3	4	5
area A, in cm^2:	0.24	2.78	13.53	36.3	47.5	49.4

Table 4.21.2: The area A occupied by the bacterial colony at age t, in days. For experimental details see H. G. Thornton, *Ann. Appl. Biol.* 9 (1922) 265.

Incidentally, the fit shown in Fig. 4.21.7 has a ten times lower value for SSR than that given by Lotka. However, one should consider both sets of numerical results with skepticism, because all three adjustable parameters are strongly correlated, especially a and b, which in our solution exhibit a linear correlation coefficient of 0.9987.

4.21.5 Using NIST data sets

The National Institute for Science and Technology (NIST, the former National Bureau of Standards or NBS) makes available standard data sets that can be used to test statistical software. Relevant to the present chapter are the data sets for nonlinear least squares, accessible at www.itl.nist. gov/div898/strd/nls/nls_info.shtml, which contains 27 test data sets of varying difficulty. Here we will sample a few.

The first data set, Misra 1a, is illustrated in Fig. 4.21.8. The function to be fitted is $y = a\,[1 - \exp(-bx)]$ with the initial values $a = 500$ and $b = $ 1E–4. The results in block D20:F24 of Fig. 4.21.8 illustrate what you find when using Solver unthinkingly. Because a and b have such dissimilar magnitudes, it is crucial to use its autoscaling (Options $\Rightarrow$ Use Automatic Scaling $\Rightarrow$ OK), which leads to the results displayed in block D26:F30 and shown in the graph. Within their standard deviations, the latter results, $a = 240._2 \pm 2._5$ and $b = (5.47_0 \pm 0.06_6) \times 10^{-4}$, are fully compatible with the certified values given by NIST, $a = 238._9 \pm 2._7$ and $b = (5.50_2 \pm 0.07_3) \times 10^{-4}$. The difficulty in this problem lies in the fact that $b/a \approx 2 \times 10^{-6}$, so that we either must use autoscaling or, equivalently, adjust the logarithms of the constants, as we did with the acid-base problems in section 4.3. Also note the strong correlation between a and b, as evidenced by the value of r_{ab} of almost 0.999.

	found:	*NIST-certified values:*
Misra 1a	$a = 240._2 \pm 2._5$	$a = 238._9 \pm 2._7$
	$b = (5.47_0 \pm 0.06_6) \times 10^{-4}$	$b = (5.50_2 \pm 0.07_3) \times 10^{-4}$
Misra 1b	$a = 339._9 \pm 2._9$	$a = 338._0 \pm 3._2$
	$b = (3.87_9 \pm 0.03_8) \times 10^{-4}$	$b = (3.90_4 \pm 0.04_3) \times 10^{-4}$
Misra 1c	$a = 640.3 \pm 4._3$	$a = 636.4 \pm 4._7$
	$b = (2.06_7 \pm 0.01_6) \times 10^{-4}$	$b = (2.08_1 \pm 0.01_8) \times 10^{-4}$
Misra 1d	$a = 439._9 \pm 3._3$	$a = 437._4 \pm 3._6$
	$b = (3.00_3 \pm 0.03_6) \times 10^{-4}$	$b = (3.02_3 \pm 0.02_9) \times 10^{-4}$

Table 4.21.3: Results obtained with Solver (using Automatic Scaling) and SolverAid for four NIST data sets.

This is an interesting data set because it can be used, with the same initial values, to fit a variety of test functions: $y = a\,[1 - \exp(-bx)]$ in Misra 1a, $y = a\,\{1-[1/(1+bx/2)^2]\}$ in Misra 1b, $y = a\,\{1-[1/(1+2bx)^{1/2}]\}$

in Misra 1c, and $y = abx/(1+bx)$ in Misra 1d. Table 4.21.3 shows the results of these four tests, using Solver with Autoscaling, then SolverAid.

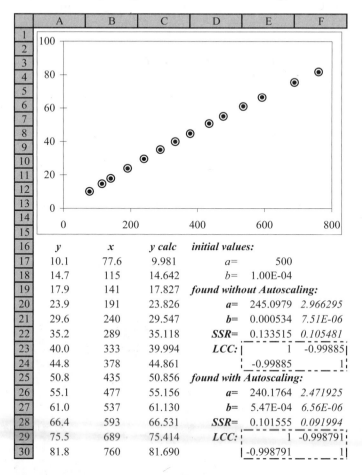

	y	x	y calc	initial values:		
	10.1	77.6	9.981	a=	500	
	14.7	115	14.642	b=	1.00E-04	
	17.9	141	17.827	*found without Autoscaling:*		
	23.9	191	23.826	a=	245.0979	*2.966295*
	29.6	240	29.547	b=	0.000534	*7.51E-06*
	35.2	289	35.118	SSR=	0.133515	*0.105481*
	40.0	333	39.994	LCC:	1	-0.99885
	44.8	378	44.861		-0.99885	1
	50.8	435	50.856	*found with Autoscaling:*		
	55.1	477	55.156	a=	240.1764	*2.471925*
	61.0	537	61.130	b=	5.47E-04	*6.56E-06*
	66.4	593	66.531	SSR=	0.101555	*0.091994*
	75.5	689	75.414	LCC:	1	-0.998791
	81.8	760	81.690		-0.998791	1

Fig. 4.21.8: The NIST data set Misra 1a and its analysis. Open circles: test data; solid points: data as calculated with Solver plus SolverAid.

4.22 Summary

Solver is designed for use with nonlinear least squares, but it is equally applicable to problems normally solved with linear least squares. After Solver has done its thing, SolverAid can provide both the standard deviations and the covariances, which can be used to calculate the propagation of imprecision, or to draw imprecision contours using equation (3.11.12) or (3.11.13). Figure 4.22.1 compares the various least squares methods discussed in this book, and their relative advantages and disadvantages.

As with linear least squares, there are two complementary questions: how appropriate is the model used, and how good is the fit between the data and that model? Again, there are no absolute answers, although looking for systematic trends in a plot of residuals can usually smoke out some inappropriate or incomplete models, while the standard deviation of the fit can give some indication of the quality of fit between model and data.

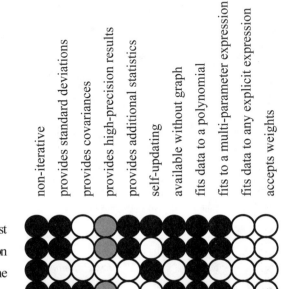

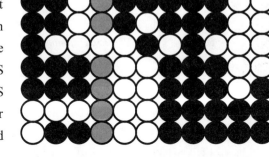

Fig. 4.22.1. Comparison of the various least squares methods available in Excel. Closed circles show availability of listed option, open circles show lack thereof. Gray circles denote approximately single precision: even though the results can be displayed to fifteen figures, usually no more than the first six or seven of these are significant. The methods labeled with an asterisk use the special custom macros provided with this book.

Solver is not tied to the least squares criterion, but can also be used, e.g., with more robust algorithms, where in this context 'robust' usually means less sensitive to the effects of outliers. (We can consider outlier rejection an extreme, binary case of weighting, using all-or-none weights of 1 or 0 only.) Solver can also be incorporated into custom functions and macros since they can call it, as illustrated by SolverScan. Consequently Solver can be used to solve nonlinear problems as they might occur in, e.g., implicit numerical simulations. However, Solver is a complex and rather time-consuming program that may cause noticeable delays when used repeatedly.

*****

In this chapter we have not used Goal Seek, because it is limited to just one variable, and often yields poor precision. You can improve the latter by decreasing the numerical value in Tools ⇒ Options, Calculations tab, Maximum change:, but that doesn't always help, and may even destabilize it. Since the Newton-Raphson method in Goal Seek doesn't appear to be as carefully crafted as the Levenberg-Marquardt method in Solver, and has no obvious advantages either, my advice is to stay away from it.

*****

For many users, Solver may well be the most useful single routine in Excel. Often, it can provide a quick and hassle-free fit of a set of experimental data to an appropriate model expression. If you are uncertain whether a false minimum may have been obtained, try several different initial guess values; if the problem is serious, use SolverScan for a more systematic search of the likely parameter space. Finally, use SolverAid to provide the uncertainties in the calculated parameters.

This is not to suggest that Solver is the answer to all least squares problems; it clearly is not, and it can sometimes lead us astray (i.e., to a false minimum). However, if yours truly could take only one least squares program with him to the proverbial uninhabited island (assuming that, mysteriously, it would have an electric outlet for his desktop computer, or fresh batteries for his laptop), it certainly would be Solver.

4.23 For further reading

An extensive treatment of nonlinear least squares is provided by D. M. Bates & D. G. Watts, *Nonlinear Regression Analysis and its Applications*, Wiley 1988. It contains many fine examples of nonlinear curve fitting in the physical sciences, including their original data, and therefore provides excellent practice material for the present chapter. Additional applications are described in J. F. Russling & T. F. Kumosinski, *Nonlinear Computer Modeling of Chemical and Biochemical Data*, Academic Press 1996.

Chapter 5

Fourier transformation

5.1 Sines and cosines

This chapter deals with the application of Fourier transformation in numerical data analysis rather than in instrumentation, where it is often built in. We are all familiar with manipulating functions of a number, or of a single variable representing such a number, as in $\sqrt{3}$, $\log x$, or $\sin \alpha$. In a Fourier transform we operate instead on a whole *set* of numbers, such as a spectrum or a transient. The methods for dealing with entire data sets are somewhat more involved, but are perfectly suited to spreadsheets.

Fourier transformation is a method designed to determine the *frequency* content of a *time*-dependent signal. Since it is a mathematical operation, 'frequency' f (in Hz) and 'time' t (in s) are symbols that can just as easily represent another pair of physical variables whose product is dimensionless, such as wavelength or distance (in cm) and wavenumber (in cm^{-1}). The Fourier transformation $G(f)$ of a continuous, time-dependent function $g(t)$ can be defined as

$$G(f) = \int_{-\infty}^{+\infty} g(t)\, e^{-2\pi j f t}\, dt = \int_{-\infty}^{+\infty} g(t)\, e^{-j\omega t}\, dt$$

$$= \int_{-\infty}^{+\infty} g(t)\cos(2\pi f t)\, dt - j \int_{-\infty}^{+\infty} g(t)\sin(2\pi f t)\, dt$$

$$= \int_{-\infty}^{+\infty} g(t)\cos(\omega t)\, dt - j \int_{-\infty}^{+\infty} g(t)\sin(\omega t)\, dt \qquad (5.1.1)$$

where we have used Euler's rule, $e^{\pm jx} = \cos(x) \pm j\sin(x)$, with $j = \sqrt{-1}$ and $\omega = 2\pi f$, in radians per second (rad s^{-1}). If we count time t in seconds, f should be counted in Hertz; for t measured in days, f has the dimension day^{-1}, i.e., 'per day'. Likewise, if t represents wavelength, f stands for wavenumber; if t is voltage, f has the dimension of V^{-1}, etc. (Because the symbols F and f are commonly used for function and frequency respectively, we here use the symbols G and g.) The corresponding inverse Fourier transformation is then

$$g(t) = \int_{-\infty}^{+\infty} G(f)\, e^{+2\pi j f t}\, df \qquad (5.1.2)$$

In experimental science we often deal with a *sampled* function, i.e., with a *finite* number of *discrete, equidistant* data points, in which case the definition corresponding to (5.1.1) is

$$G(f) = \sum_{k=1}^{N} g(t) \cos(2\pi k / N) - j \sum_{k=1}^{N} g(t) \sin(2\pi k / N) \qquad (5.1.3)$$

where N denotes the number of data points, and $k = 1, 2, \ldots, N$. Efficient, fast-executing methods exist for computing (5.1.3) and its inverse, especially when N is an integer power of 2, i.e., $N = 2, 4, 8, 16, 32, 64, 128,$ 256, 512, 1024, etc. The application of such *fast* Fourier transform algorithms to discrete, equidistant data is the central subject of this chapter.

Excel provides a tool for Fourier transformation in its Data Analysis Toolpak. Unfortunately it has a rather awkward input and output format, in the form of labels. In this chapter we will therefore use two custom macros, ForwardFT and InverseFT respectively, which are much easier to apply. They require that the input data be organized in three contiguous columns of 2^n data, where n is a positive (non-zero) integer.

For forward Fourier transformation the first (leftmost) column should contain time t, in equidistant intervals, while the next two columns should hold the real and imaginary components of the function $g(t)$ respectively. The data for time t should either start at $t = 0$ or, preferably, be 'centered' around $t = 0$, with 2^{n-1} data at $t < 0$, one point at $t = 0$, and the remaining $2^{n-1} - 1$ data at $t > 0$. When $g(t)$ is a real function, the third column can either be left blank or be filled with zeros. Similarly, if $g(t)$ is imaginary, the second column should be left blank or be filled with zeros.

In order to initiate the transformation, highlight the data in the three columns (including the third column, even if it only contains blanks) and call the custom macro ForwardFT. Its output, i.e., the result of the forward Fourier transformation, will be written in the three columns immediately to the right of the block of input data, displaying from left to right the frequency, the real (in-phase) component, and the imaginary (quadrature, or 90° out-of-phase) component of the transformed data $G(f)$.

The macro InverseFT converts the transformed data back from the frequency domain to the time domain. It uses the same three-column format for input and output, with the positions of the time and frequency columns interchanged. Its frequency scale must be centered around $f = 0$, with 2^{n-1} data at $f < 0$, and the remaining 2^{n-1} data at $f \geq 0$. (In case you wonder what might be the physical meaning of a negative frequency, just consider it a mathematical consequence of the Nyquist theorem, to be described in section 5.3.) The format of ForwardFT and InverseFT is such that you can easily transform data sets back and forth. Exercise 5.1.1 will familiarize you with the operation of these custom macros.

Exercise 5.1.1:

(1) Open a spreadsheet, and enter column headings such as time, Re, Im, freq, Re, and Im, or (if you prefer to denote real and imaginary components with ' and " respectively) t, g', g", f, G', and G".

(2) In its first column enter the numbers –8 (1) 7.

(3) In its second column compute a cosine wave such as $a \cos (2\pi b \, t / N)$.

(4) Fill the third column with zeros, so that the graph will show them.

(5) Highlight the data in these three columns, and call ForwardFT. (Use FT ⇒ ForwardFT on the MacroBundle toolbar or the CustomMacros menu, otherwise Alt⌣F8 or Tools ⇒ Macro ⇒ Macros to get the Macro dialog box.)

(6) Plot the resulting transform, see Fig. 5.1.1, and verify that it shows two non-zero points of amplitude $a/2$ at $f = \pm b/N$.

(7) Replace the cosine wave in column A by a sine wave of, say, double the frequency, and repeat the process. Note that the Fourier transform of a sine wave has only imaginary components, one positive, the other negative, see Fig. 5.1.2.

(8) Replace the signal in column A by the sum of a sine wave and a cosine wave, of different amplitudes so that you can more readily identify their transforms. Then add another sine or cosine wave, and identify the transforms of each. In order to see the effect of a larger number of input signals, you may have to extend the range from 16 to, e.g., 32, 64, or 128 data points.

The discrete Fourier transform operates on a limited data set, but tacitly assumes that this is *one repeat unit* of an infinitely long, self-repeating signal. Section 5.4 will discuss what happens when this is not the case.

The Fourier transform accepts complex input data, i.e., with real and/or imaginary components, and likewise produces complex output. However, experimental data are often real, and we will therefore focus briefly on real functions. The cosine function has the property that $\cos(-x) = \cos(x)$, and is therefore called an *even* function. On the other hand, the sine is an *odd* function, because $\sin(-x) = -\sin(x)$. Figure 5.1.1 illustrates that the Fourier transform of a real, even function is real, whereas

Fig. 5.1.2 suggests that the Fourier transform of a real, odd function is imaginary. This turns out to be true in general for any real function $g(t)$.

	A	B	C	D	E	F
1–8						
9		$a = 2$			$b = 1$	
10						
11	*time*	*Re*	*Im*	*freq*	*Re*	*Im*
12						
13	-8	-2.000	0	-0.5000	0.000	0.000
14	-7	-1.848	0	-0.4375	0.000	0.000
15	-6	-1.414	0	-0.3750	0.000	0.000
16	-5	-0.765	0	-0.3125	0.000	0.000
17	-4	0.000	0	-0.2500	0.000	0.000
18	-3	0.765	0	-0.1875	0.000	0.000
19	-2	1.414	0	-0.1250	0.000	0.000
20	-1	1.848	0	-0.0625	**1.000**	0.000
21	0	2.000	0	0.0000	0.000	0.000
22	1	1.848	0	0.0625	**1.000**	0.000
23	2	1.414	0	0.1250	0.000	0.000
24	3	0.765	0	0.1875	0.000	0.000
25	4	0.000	0	0.2500	0.000	0.000
26	5	-0.765	0	0.3125	0.000	0.000
27	6	-1.414	0	0.3750	0.000	0.000
28	7	-1.848	0	0.4375	0.000	0.000

cell:	*instruction:*	*copied to:*
B13 =	$B$9*COS(PI()*$D$9*A13/8)	B14:B28
FFT:	highlight A13:C28, then call custom macro ForwardFT	

Fig. 5.1.1: The spreadsheet showing a *cosine* wave and its Fourier transform. Solid circles: real components; open circles: imaginary components. In column E the two non-zero points in the transform are shown boldface for emphasis.

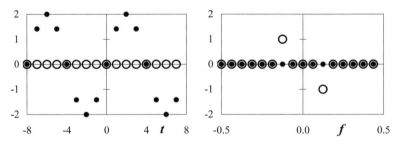

Fig. 5.1.2: The spreadsheet showing a *sine* wave and its Fourier transform. Solid circles: real components; open circles: imaginary components.

We can always write a real function as the sum of an even and an odd real function:

$$g_{real}(t) = g_{even}(t) + g_{odd}(t) \tag{5.1.4}$$

Likewise we can write (5.1.1) in compact notation as

$$G(f) = G'(f) - j\,G''(f) \tag{5.1.5}$$

where the superscripts $'$ and $''$ denote the real and imaginary components of $G(f)$. Since multiplying an even and an odd function produces an odd function which yields zero when integrated from $-\infty$ to $+\infty$, we have

$$G(f) = \int_{-\infty}^{+\infty} g_{real}(t)\,e^{-2\pi jft}dt = \int_{-\infty}^{+\infty} [g_{even}(t) + g_{odd}(t)]\,e^{-2\pi jft}dt$$

$$= \int_{-\infty}^{+\infty} [g_{even}(t) + g_{odd}(t)][\cos(2\pi ft) - j\sin(2\pi ft)]\,dt \tag{5.1.6}$$

$$= \int_{-\infty}^{+\infty} g_{even}(t)\cos(2\pi ft)\,dt - j\int_{-\infty}^{+\infty} g_{odd}(t)\sin(2\pi ft)\,dt$$

so that

$$G'(f) = \int_{-\infty}^{+\infty} g_{even}(t)\cos(2\pi ft)dt \tag{5.1.7}$$

$$G''(f) = -\int_{-\infty}^{+\infty} g_{odd}(t)\sin(2\pi ft)dt \tag{5.1.8}$$

Equivalent rules apply to the discrete (rather than continuous) Fourier transform.

5.2 Square waves and pulses

We will now use a square wave, which can be considered as an infinite set of cosines,

$$sqw(\omega t) = \frac{4}{\pi} \sum_{n=1}^{\infty} \frac{(-1)^n \cos\left[(2n+1)\omega t\right]}{2n+1} \qquad (5.2.1)$$

$$= \frac{4}{\pi} \left\{ \cos(\omega t) - \frac{1}{3}\cos(3\omega t) + \frac{1}{5}\cos(5\omega t) - \frac{1}{7}\cos(7\omega t) + \cdots \right\}$$

In a discrete Fourier transformation, with only a limited number of input data and an equally limited number of frequencies, the square wave is represented by a truncated series, which therefore has somewhat different coefficients. When we follow the Fourier transform by its inverse, we recover the original input data. However, if we were to use the coefficients of the forward Fourier transform to reconstruct the input data, we find a curve that indeed passes through all input data, but is a caricature of a square wave. But then, we did not enter a square wave, but only the discrete data points. Whatever curve we want to see in those discrete data is our prerogative, like seeing images in groupings of unrelated stars and calling them constellations.

Exercise 5.2.1:

(1) Modify the spreadsheet by replacing the input signal by that of a square wave, as in Fig. 5.2.1. Note that the zero-crossings of the square wave must be entered explicitly, as the *average* of the function values just before and after the change.

(2) Transform these, and immediately follow this by an inverse transform. In this 16-point analysis you will find only four components of the series (5.1.3), with coefficients slightly different from $4/\pi$, $-4/3\pi$, $4/5\pi$, and $-4/7\pi$, i.e., 1.273, -0.424, 0.255, and -0.182 instead of the found values of 1.257, -0.374, 0.167, and -0.050 respectively. Note that the inverse transform only approximates the presumed underlying square wave, but will reconstruct the discrete input data exactly.

(3) This is more readily seen by computing values of equation (5.2.1) at intermediate values of t (e.g., at intervals of 0.1) and by plotting the resulting curve in the same thumbnail sketch.

(4) For this, extend the second time scale, starting e.g. in cell G30 with $t = -8$, and proceeding downwards with increments of 0.1 till cell G180. In cell J30 then deposit the instruction =E\$21+2*(E\$22*COS(2*PI()*D\$22*G30)+E\$23* COS(2*PI()*D\$23*G30)+...+E\$28*COS(2*PI()*D\$28*G30)), and copy this all the way to cell J180. You can speed up the computation by calculating the term 2*PI() in a separate cell and referring to that numerical value rather than repeating the calculation of 2π in every cell.

	A	B	C	D	E	F	G	H	I
1									
2									
3									
4									
5									
6									
7									
8									

$a = 2$ $b = 8$

	time	Re	Im	freq	Re	Im	time	Re	Im
13	-8	-2	0	-0.5000	0.000	0.000	-8	-2.0	0.0
14	-7	-2	0	-0.4375	**-0.050**	0.000	-7	-2.0	0.0
15	-6	-2	0	-0.3750	0.000	0.000	-6	-2.0	0.0
16	-5	-2	0	-0.3125	**0.167**	0.000	-5	-2.0	0.0
17	-4	0	0	-0.2500	0.000	0.000	-4	0.0	0.0
18	-3	2	0	-0.1875	**-0.374**	0.000	-3	2.0	0.0
19	-2	2	0	-0.1250	0.000	0.000	-2	2.0	0.0
20	-1	2	0	-0.0625	**1.257**	0.000	-1	2.0	0.0
21	0	2	0	0.0000	0.000	0.000	0	2.0	0.0
22	1	2	0	0.0625	**1.257**	0.000	1	2.0	0.0
23	2	2	0	0.1250	0.000	0.000	2	2.0	0.0
24	3	2	0	0.1875	**-0.374**	0.000	3	2.0	0.0
25	4	0	0	0.2500	0.000	0.000	4	0.0	0.0
26	5	-2	0	0.3125	**0.167**	0.000	5	-2.0	0.0
27	6	-2	0	0.3750	0.000	0.000	6	-2.0	0.0
28	7	-2	0	0.4375	**-0.050**	0.000	7	-2.0	0.0

Fig. 5.2.1: The spreadsheet of a square wave and its Fourier transform. Solid circles: real components; open circles: imaginary components. The drawn line in the leftmost panel, computed also for intermediate, non-integer values of t, illustrates that the (bold-faced) coefficients define a curve through all input data but do *not* trace a square wave.

(5) Highlight the real data set in the third thumbnail sketch, and in the formula box extend its time scale from G13:G28 to G13:G180, and its function reach from H13:H28 to H13:H180.

(6) Highlight the column J13:J180, copy it to the clipboard (with Ctrl∪c), highlight the plot area of the third thumbnail sketch, and paste the data in with Ctrl∪v.

(7) Do the same for the input function. If necessary, sharpen its corners by changing, e.g., $t = -4.1$ and -3.9 to $t = -4.001$ and -3.999 respectively. For better visibility, offset this new curve by adding 0.5 to its y-values.

Exercise 5.2.2:

(1) Modify the spreadsheet by replacing the input signal by that of a narrow pulse, as in Fig. 5.2.2. Again, the zero-crossings of the pulse should be entered explicitly as the average of the values before and after the change.

(2) Transform these, apply the inverse transformation, and display the results.

(3) Again use the coefficients in the output of the forward FFT to construct the function at intermediate values of t.

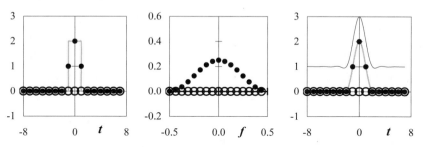

Fig. 5.2.2: A rectangular pulse, its FFT, and the inverse FFT of the latter. The thin line represents the reconstructed curve shifted up by 1 for better visibility, and clearly shows the oscillatory nature of that reconstruction.

Exercise 5.2.3:

(1) Move the pulse in time so that it is no longer symmetrical with respect to $t = 0$, see Fig. 5.2.3. Again, the zero-crossings of the pulse should be entered explicitly as the average of the values before and after the change.

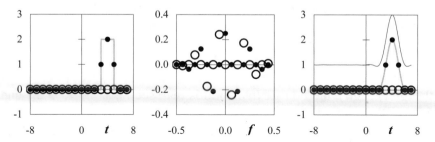

Fig. 5.2.3: The same for a rectangular pulse shifted in time. The recovered function is also shown as a thin line offset by 1.

Exercise 5.2.4:

(1) Use an exponential function, such as $y = 0$ for $t < 0$, and $y = ae^{-bt}$ for $t > 0$, as in Fig. 5.2.4. Again, the zero-crossings of the pulse should be entered explicitly as the average of the values before and after the change: $y = a/2$ for $t = 0$.

Exercise 5.2.5:

(1) Shift the exponential function in time to, e.g., $y = 0$ for $t < -6$, $y = 3/2$ for $t = -6$, and $y = 3e^{-0.8(t+6)}$ for $t > -6$, as in Fig. 5.2.5.

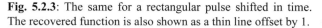

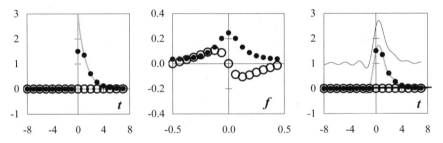

Fig. 5.2.4: The exponential $y = 0$ for $t < 0$, $y = 3e^{-0.8t}$ for $t > 0$, its FFT, and the inverse FFT of the latter. The recovered function is also shown offset by +1.

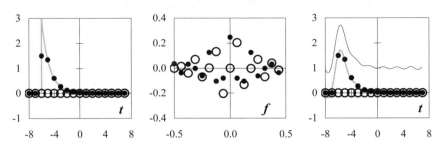

Fig. 5.2.5: The same for the function $y = 0$ for $t < -6$, $y = 3e^{-0.8(t+6)}$ for $t > -6$.

The above examples demonstrate that the input signal is by no means restricted to sines and cosines; we merely started with these because they yield the simplest and most satisfactory transforms. Moreover, these examples illustrate the following aspects of Fourier transformation:

(1) For an input signal that is symmetrical with respect to $t = 0$, so that $g(-t) = g(t)$, the Fourier transform is real, see Figs. 5.1.1, 5.2.1 and 5.2.2. When we write $g(t)$ and $G(f)$ explicitly in terms of their real and imaginary components as $g(t) = g'(t) + j\,g''(t)$ and $G(f) = G'(f) + j\,G''(f)$ respectively, a so-called *even* input function $g(-t) = g(t)$ yields a real Fourier transform, i.e., $G''(f) = 0$.

(2) When the input signal has mirror symmetry with respect to $t = 0$, so that $g(-t) = -g(t)$, it is called *odd*, as for the sine wave in Fig. 5.1.2. In that case its Fourier transform is imaginary, hence $G'(f) = 0$.

(3) If the input signal lacks either of the above symmetries, its Fourier transform will be complex, i.e., it will have both real and imaginary components, as illustrated in Figs. 5.2.3 through 5.2.5.

(4) All the above examples have a real input, i.e., $g''(t) = 0$, and consequently their Fourier transforms all have an even real part, i.e., $G'(-f) = G'(f)$, and an odd imaginary part, $G''(-f) = -G''(f)$. Likewise, when $g(t)$ is

imaginary, $G'(f)$ is odd and $G''(-f)$ is even. Because the Fourier transform of a sum $g(t) = g'(t) + j\, g''(t)$ is the sum of the Fourier transforms of its components, the entire information content of any Fourier transform can in principle be repackaged in terms of non-negative frequencies f, although this is not customary. However, it does imply that the Fourier transform of N input data contains information on only $(\tfrac{1}{2}N + 1)$ frequencies, a conclusion that is related to the sampling theorem of section 5.3. The one 'extra' frequency beyond $\tfrac{1}{2}N$ is the zero frequency, $f = 0$, which represents the average value of the function.

(5) Forward Fourier transformation followed by inverse Fourier transformation recovers the original data points exactly (within the round-off errors of the computation, i.e., in Excel usually well within 1 in 10^{15}). While we may have *meant* the input data to represent a particular, underlying function, such as a square pulse in Figs. 5.2.1 through 5.2.3, or a single exponential in Figs. 5.2.4 and 5.2.5, in a discrete Fourier transform algorithm there is no way to specify such a function other than through the discrete input points used. We cannot expect the algorithm to guess what we mean; it can only respond to the specific input data provided. Therefore, especially when we furnish relatively few points of a continuous function, its discrete Fourier transformation will only *approximate* the continuous Fourier transform of that function at *intermediate* times or frequencies. This can be seen clearly in the continuous curves calculated in Figs. 5.2.1 through 5.2.5. Because the input function is only specified *at* those N points, it cannot be reconstructed reliably *between* them, just as one cannot count on getting a reliable interpolation from a Lagrange polynomial for an arbitrary input function unless the underlying function is a polynomial of the same order.

5.3 Aliasing and sampling

One of the most amazing aspects of the continuous Fourier transform, and the one that delayed its initial publication for many years at the hand of some of Fourier's great French contemporaries, is that it can even express a *discontinuous* function in terms of an infinite series of *continuous* sines and cosines, as in (5.2.1). That is clearly not possible with a *finite* set of sines and cosines, and consequently this property does not carry over to the discrete Fourier transform, which only uses a finite sample of the function, and likewise has only a finite number of frequencies with which to represent it.

In the present section we will consider aliasing and the related sampling theorem, while section 5.4 will discuss leakage. Both are artifacts of the *discrete* Fourier transformation, and are without counterparts in the continuous transform. Finally, in section 5.5, we will encounter an uncertainty relationship similar to that of Heisenberg, although in a strictly classical context.

Aliasing results when the signal frequencies fall *outside* the frequency range covered, while leakage occurs with signal frequencies that lie *inside* that range but fall *in between* the limited set of frequencies provided by the discrete Fourier transformation. Aliasing is easily understood with a series of examples, such as those of exercise 5.3.1.

Exercise 5.3.1:

(1) Return to (or recreate) the spreadsheet shown in Fig. 5.1.1.

(2) Leaving row 29 empty, extend column A with cells A30:A190 containing the times –8 (0.1) 8, and in cells G30:G190 enter the corresponding values of the cosine wave. Show these data in the graph as a thin line.

(3) Change the value of b from 1 to 2, and Fourier transform the data, which will now exhibit contributions at $f = \pm 0.125$ instead of $f = \pm 0.0625$.

(4) Increment the value of b by 1 to $b = 3$, and Fourier transform A13:C28. Observe that the non-zero points in the transform hop over to the next-higher (absolute) frequency.

(5) Continue this for the next few integer values of b. It works fine up to and including $b = 8$, but at $b = 9$ you have obviously run out of the frequency scale. What happens then is shown in Fig. 5.3.1: the Fourier transformation yields the same result as for $b = 7$.

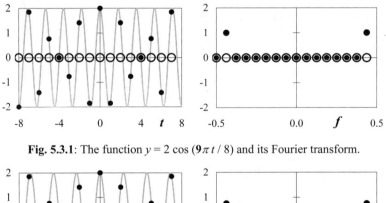

Fig. 5.3.1: The function $y = 2 \cos (9\pi t / 8)$ and its Fourier transform.

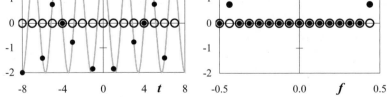

Fig. 5.3.2: The function $y = 2 \cos (7\pi t / 8)$ and its Fourier transform.

(6) Comparison with the earlier result, for $b = 7$, shows why: the input data for both cases are identical, as illustrated in Fig. 5.3.2. No wonder we get the same transform when the input *data* are the same. The only difference between the two left panels is in the *line drawn through them*. The Fourier transform merely sees the input data, whereas the line indicates what we *intend* the data to represent. The Fourier transform only finds the lowest possible frequency that fit these data. The same Fourier transform would be obtained with 16 equally spaced data calculated with $y = 2 \cos (b \pi t / 8)$ for $b = 23, 25, 39, 41$, etc.

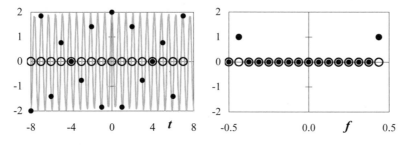

Fig. 5.3.3: The function $y = 2 \cos (\mathbf{23} \pi t / 8)$ and its Fourier transform.

(7) What we see here is called aliasing, as if these higher frequencies masquerade under an alias. But it really is a problem of sampling, because we give the Fourier transformation insufficient information. That this is so is perhaps even more clearly seen when we select $b = 15$ or $b = 17$, as illustrated in Figs. 5.3.4 and 5.3.5, which should be compared with Fig. 5.1.1.

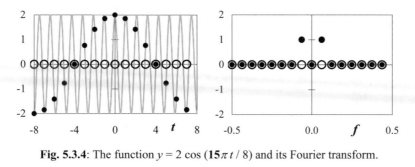

Fig. 5.3.4: The function $y = 2 \cos (\mathbf{15} \pi t / 8)$ and its Fourier transform.

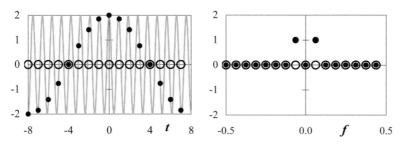

Fig. 5.3.5: The function $y = 2 \cos (\mathbf{17} \, \pi t / 8)$ and its Fourier transform.

The above examples suggest that we can put an infinity of cosine waves through 16 points. The Fourier transform yields the lowest possible of these, i.e., it uses the *parsimony principle*. Clearly, the problem lies with the input data rather than with the Fourier transformation. This is where the *Nyquist* or *sampling theorem* comes in. It states that, in order to define a periodic signal *unambiguously*, we must sample it more than twice per period. The assumed infinite periodicity of the sampled signal fragment then fills in the rest. Aliasing results when the signal is undersampled, as it was in Figs. 5.3.1 through 5.3.5.

5.4 Leakage

Another problem specific to the discrete Fourier transform is leakage. Again, it is most readily demonstrated with a sine or cosine wave. It occurs when the signal is amply sampled according to the Nyquist criterion, but contains frequencies in between those used in the Fourier transformation. This is illustrated in exercise 5.4.1, where we consider a sine wave with frequency 2.1. The transform shows the dominant frequency as 2, but it needs contributions from the other frequencies to make the fit, because it cannot represent the frequency 2.1 directly, just as integers cannot represent numbers such as e or π. It is, therefore, as if the frequency 'leaks out' into the adjacent frequencies. Another way of looking at it is that, when the signal is repeated (as is implied in Fourier transformation), it exhibits discontinuities that can only be represented with higher frequencies.

Exercise 5.4.1:
(1) On the same spreadsheet, now use $b = 2.1$. Figure 5.4.1 shows the result.

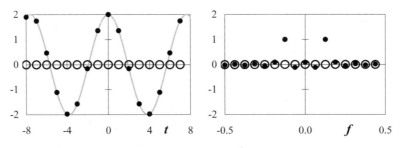

Fig. 5.4.1: The function $y = 2 \cos (\mathbf{2.1} \, \pi t / 8)$ and its Fourier transform.

Leakage often occurs when data are acquired at rates that are not exact (sub)multiples of the power line frequency (60 Hz in the US, 50 Hz elsewhere) because many signals are contaminated by that ubiquitous signal. In such cases the problem is readily avoided by synchronizing the data acquisition rate to that of the power line frequency. Once that is done, and the noise contribution is isolated at those specific frequencies, it can be filtered out after Fourier transformation by removing the contribution at that specific frequency, e.g., by setting it to zero or, better yet, by using its nearest neighbors to interpolate the removed value. The same may have to be done also for its prominent harmonics.

5.5 Uncertainty

When we hear a sustained note we can recognize its pitch and, if we have perfect pitch, identify its name and therefore (at least in principle) its frequency. If that same note is sounded only very briefly, we cannot do this; apparently we need several complete cycles of the sinusoid involved in order to define its pitch.

A continuous sine wave supposedly lasts indefinitely, and is specified by a precise frequency f, i.e., within an infinitely narrow spread. In this case the product of the time interval (∞) and the corresponding frequency spread (0), is $\infty \times 0$, which is ill defined. But as soon as we restrict the sine wave to a finite interval τ, its frequency is no longer so precisely defined, as can be seen by Fourier transformation when we select one or a small number of cycles of that sine wave, setting its remainder to zero.

> **Exercise 5.5.1:**
> (1) Generate a sine wave and its Fourier transform, as in Fig. 5.5.1a.
> (2) Delete most of the sine wave, leaving first three, then only one of its central cycles. Avoid generating a break (which would generate spurious high frequencies) by setting the signal to zero up to a point where the sine wave itself is zero.
> (3) Apply the Fourier transform. Figures 5.5.1b and 5.5.1c illustrate what you may get: a broadened set of frequencies centered *around* the frequency value of the left panel in Fig. 5.5.1a. This is the trick used in nuclear magnetic resonance spectroscopy to generate a narrow *range* of frequencies to encompass any chemical shifts.

In this example the time period is well defined, but the range of frequencies is not. However, when we just take the width of the frequency peak at its base as a crude measure, we find that it is 5×0.0078125 wide in Fig. 5.5.2, and 15×0.0078125 wide in Fig. 5.5.3, i.e., it is inversely proportional to the length of the signal burst. The number 0.0078125 is the unit of f, equal to 1/128 for a 128-point signal. This suggests a constant product of the time interval and the associated frequency spread.

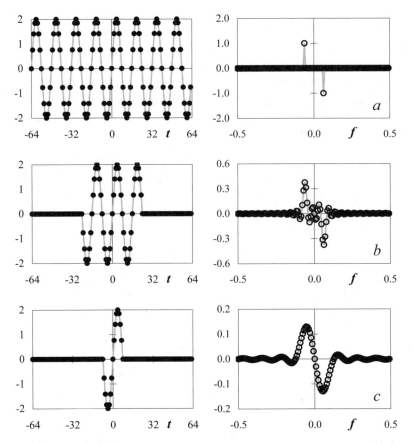

Fig. 5.5.1: The transform of a continuous sine wave (*a*, top panels) and of two bursts of the same, lasting only three cycles (*b*) and one cycle (*c*) respectively. For the sake of clarity only the imaginary part of the transform is shown. In all these cases the signal is odd so that the real part of the transform is zero. Note the changing vertical scales of the right-hand panels.

Thus, even though we used a pure sine wave, its brevity converted its single frequency into a frequency *distribution*. It is not a deficiency of our ears that we cannot identify the pitch of a very brief note played on a double bass; it simply does not *have* a well-defined pitch. (Note that this property is exploited in pulsed nuclear magnetic resonance spectrometry to excite a narrow *range* of frequencies of interest by gating a short section of a pure sinusoidal signal.) In other words: the shorter the signal lasts, the fuzzier its frequency gets.

For features for which the characteristic widths in time and frequency can be defined in terms of standard deviations, the above can be formulated mathematically by stating that the product $s_\tau s_f$ of the standard deviation s_τ of the time interval τ over which the signal is observed, times the standard deviation s_f of its frequency f, cannot be determined to better than $1/(2\pi)$. Or, even simpler: the product of the standard deviation in time t and that in angular frequency $\omega = 2\pi f$ is at least 1. Below we will illustrate this uncertainty principle with a Gaussian curve, because (a) its width is expressed in terms of its standard deviation, and (b) the Fourier transform of a Gaussian is again a Gaussian.

> ***Exercise 5.5.2:***
>
> (1) Make a spreadsheet in which you compute $2N$ points of a Gaussian, such as for $t = -64$ (1) 63, the function $g(t) = (s\sqrt{2\pi})^{-1} \exp[-t^2/(2s^2)]$ where you refer to the value of s as stored in a separate location, such as cell B9 in Fig. 5.5.2. Start with, say, $s = 10$. Plot the Gaussian input curve.
>
> (2) Apply the Fourier transform, and again plot the resulting Gaussian peak.
>
> (3) In a seventh column calculate a Gaussian in terms of frequency f, $H'(f) = A \exp[-f^2/(2S^2)]$, using externally stored values for A and S.
>
> (4) Now use Solver to match this Gaussian, $H'(f)$, with the result of the Fourier transformation, $G'(f)$. This will verify that, indeed, the Fourier transform $G'(f)$ fits a Gaussian, and will yield a numerical value for its standard deviation S.
>
> (5) Compute the product of $2\pi s$ and the just-found value of S. If indeed s times S is $1/(2\pi)$, this product should be close to 1.
>
> (6) Change the value of s from 10 to, say, 5 or 3, and repeat steps (2), (4), and (5). Qualitatively, the more the signal extends in the time domain, the more tightly it is restricted in the frequency domain, and vice versa. Quantitatively, you should find close adherence of the product of the standard deviations s and S to the value of $1/(2\pi)$. The above is illustrated in Fig. 5.5.2.

5.6 Filtering

So far we have dealt with mathematical functions rather than with experimental data, i.e., we have not yet considered the effects of random noise on the input signal. In this and the next few sections we will include noise, and we will transform noisy data into the frequency domain, manipulate them there, and return the modified data to the time domain. Below we will consider filtering, while sections 5.7 through 5.9 will deal with differentiation, interpolation, and data compression respectively.

We can distinguish two types of filtering, equivalent to their analog equivalents: tuned and general. A *tuned filter* either enhances or rejects signals in an extremely narrow frequency band. Fourier transformation allows for the ideal tuned filter, because it can be as narrow as one single frequency. If we want to filter out a particular frequency from a signal, we Fourier-transform the signal, set the real and imaginary contributions at that frequency to zero, and inverse transform the resulting data set. If we want to remove all frequencies other than a particular one, we Fourier transform, set the contributions at all other frequencies to zero, and transform back. Of course, the narrower the tuned filter, the smaller the margin of error in matching that frequency with the desired signal frequency we want to single out for enhancement or rejection, otherwise we will encounter leakage.

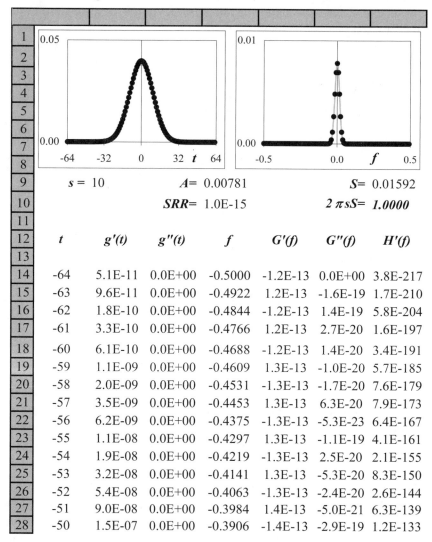

t	$g'(t)$	$g''(t)$	f	$G'(f)$	$G''(f)$	$H'(f)$
-64	5.1E-11	0.0E+00	-0.5000	-1.2E-13	0.0E+00	3.8E-217
-63	9.6E-11	0.0E+00	-0.4922	1.2E-13	-1.6E-19	1.7E-210
-62	1.8E-10	0.0E+00	-0.4844	-1.2E-13	1.4E-19	5.8E-204
-61	3.3E-10	0.0E+00	-0.4766	1.2E-13	2.7E-20	1.6E-197
-60	6.1E-10	0.0E+00	-0.4688	-1.2E-13	1.4E-20	3.4E-191
-59	1.1E-09	0.0E+00	-0.4609	1.3E-13	-1.0E-20	5.7E-185
-58	2.0E-09	0.0E+00	-0.4531	-1.3E-13	-1.7E-20	7.6E-179
-57	3.5E-09	0.0E+00	-0.4453	1.3E-13	6.3E-20	7.9E-173
-56	6.2E-09	0.0E+00	-0.4375	-1.3E-13	-5.3E-23	6.4E-167
-55	1.1E-08	0.0E+00	-0.4297	1.3E-13	-1.1E-19	4.1E-161
-54	1.9E-08	0.0E+00	-0.4219	-1.3E-13	2.5E-20	2.1E-155
-53	3.2E-08	0.0E+00	-0.4141	1.3E-13	-5.3E-20	8.3E-150
-52	5.4E-08	0.0E+00	-0.4063	-1.3E-13	-2.4E-20	2.6E-144
-51	9.0E-08	0.0E+00	-0.3984	1.4E-13	-5.0E-21	6.3E-139
-50	1.5E-07	0.0E+00	-0.3906	-1.4E-13	-2.9E-19	1.2E-133

Fig. 5.5.2: The top of the spreadsheet for exercise 5.5.2 illustrating the uncertainty principle.

A more complicated problem is that of general filtering, with has a less clearly defined purpose, and often a correspondingly more tentative solution. General filtering is essentially a statistical process, and we will therefore assume that a sufficiently large number of data points has been collected. Much noise will then occur at frequencies higher than those of the signal. A crude approach to removing high-frequency noise is to Fourier transform the data, to set a number of highest-frequency contributions to zero, and to transform the result back into the time domain. However, the sharp transition between the frequencies that are included and those that are excluded can lead to oscillations in the filtered output.

A way to avoid such artificial oscillations is to use a more gradual filter, typically again applied in the frequency domain (i.e., after Fourier transformation) to reduce the highest-frequency contributions to zero, while leaving intact most of the frequencies carrying the signal.

Many different *window functions* have been proposed for that purpose, often based on either trigonometric functions or exponentials. For an extensive listing see F. J. Harris, *Proc. IEEE* 66 (1978) 51, or chapter 6 in D. F. Elliott & K. R. Rao, *Fast Transforms: Algorithms, Analyses, Applications*, Academic Press 1982.

In our context perhaps the most generally useful window is the cosine window apparently first proposed by Julius von Hann (and sometimes called the Hanning window, a confusing name since a different window function was proposed by R. W. Hamming and is therefore called the Hamming window). In its simplest form, the von Hann window function is

$$W(n) = \cos^2\left(\frac{\pi n}{N}\right) = 0.5 + 0.5 \cos\left(\frac{2\pi n}{N}\right) \tag{5.6.1}$$

where N is the total number of data points used in a centered data set (i.e., $n = -N/2, -N/2+1, -N/2+2, \dots, -1, 0, 1, \dots, N/2-2, N/2-1$), and $n = t$ when the windowing is applied in the time domain, or $n = f$ when used in the frequency domain. At its extremes (i.e., at $n = -N/2$ and $n = +N/2$), $\cos^2(\pi n/N) = \cos^2(\pm\pi/2) = 0$, as are all its derivatives $d^p \cos^2(\pi n/N)/dn^p$.

For more variable filtering we can extend the von Hann filter with a single adjustable parameter s (for *s*tenosis, Greek for narrowness) where $0 \le s \le \infty$,

$$W(n) = \cos^{2s}\left(\frac{\pi n}{N}\right) = \left[0.5 + 0.5 \cos\left(\frac{2\pi n}{N}\right)\right]^s \tag{5.6.2}$$

and $-N/2 \leq n \leq N/2 - 1$. Exercise 5.6.1 and Fig. 5.6.1 illustrate the adjustable von Hann window.

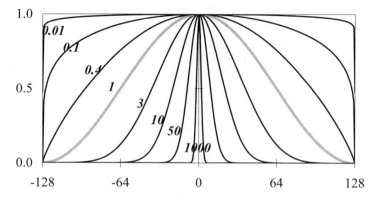

Fig. 5.6.1: The adjustable von Hann window for various values of s as indicated with the curves. The gray curve for $s = 1$ is the original von Hann filter.

An alternative window function introduced by Tukey uses the two halves of the von Hann filter to remove some of the abruptness of an otherwise sharp cutoff filter. This filter has two adjustable parameters, a and b, where $0 \leq a \leq b \leq 1$, and is described (again, for a centered set with $n = -N/2, -N/2+1, -N/2+2, \dots, -1, 0, 1, \dots, N/2-2, N/2-1$) by

$$W(n) = 1 \qquad \text{for } 0 \leq 2|n|/N \leq a$$

$$W(n) = \cos^2\left[\frac{\pi}{b-a}\left(\frac{|n|}{N} - \frac{a}{2}\right)\right] = 0.5 + 0.5\cos\left[\frac{2\pi}{b-a}\left(\frac{|n|}{N} - \frac{a}{2}\right)\right]$$

$$\text{for } a \leq 2|n|/N \leq b \qquad (5.6.3)$$

$$W(n) = 0 \qquad \text{for } b \leq 2|n|/N \leq 1$$

The Tukey window compresses the gradual cosine function within the region between a and b; it is identical to the von Hann window (5.6.1) for $a = 0$ and $b = 1$, whereas it becomes a rectangular window for $a = b$. A combination of the von Hann filter for $s \geq 1$ and a Tukey filter with $a = 1 - s$ and $b = 0$ for $s < 1$ is illustrated in Fig. 5.6.2 for various values of s.

When a von Hann or Tukey window is used to filter (by multiplication) a *time* sequence, it can gradually reduce the value of the function and of its derivatives near the extremes of its range. In the *frequency* domain, such a window predominantly attenuates the highest frequencies, which usually contain mostly noise. In Fourier transform instruments so-called *apodizing* window functions are often used that somewhat resemble a raised von Hann filter of the form $W(n) \approx a + (1-a)\cos(2\pi n/N)$

where $0.5 \leq a \leq 1$, see R. N. Norton & R. Beer, *J. Opt. Soc. Am.* 60 (1976) 259, 67 (1977) 418.

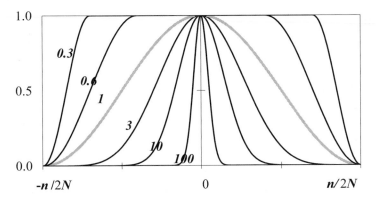

Fig. 5.6.2: A combined von Hann-Tukey window for various values of *s* as indicated with the curves.

Exercise 5.6.1:

(1) For $N = 256$ and $n = -128$ (1) 127, compute and plot (5.6.2) for various values of *s*, and compare your results with Fig. 5.6.1.

(2) For $N = 256$ and $n = -128$ (1) 127, compute and plot (5.6.3) for various values of *a* and *b*, and compare your results with Fig. 5.6.1. Note that this requires two nested IF statements, as in (symbolically) `=IF(ABS(n)<a*128, 1,IF(ABS(n)>b*128,0,0.5+0.5*COS(2*`π`*(ABS(n)/256-a/2)/ (b-a))))`. Compare with Fig. 5.6.2.

Both the von Hann and Tukey windows allow for a more gradual filtering action than the simple high-frequency cutoff method, and are usually preferable to a sharp cutoff. Still, as long as they do not take into account any specific information of the data set used, they are at best shots in the dark. Fortunately, we can let the data themselves guide us in the choice of filter.

The simplest way to do this is to Fourier-transform the data, and to display the corresponding *power spectrum*. This is a logarithmic plot of the magnitude M (i.e., the square root of the sum of its real and imaginary components) of the transformed data as a function of frequency f. For a real input signal, the power spectrum has mirror symmetry along $f = 0$, i.e., $M(-f) = M(f)$. Therefore the power spectrum is often plotted only for $f \geq 0$, although it may be helpful to display the entire (positive and negative) frequency range as a reminder of that symmetry, i.e., of the need to use the absolute values $|f|$ of all odd powers of f. For our present purpose it is actually easier to plot $\log M^2 = 2 \log M$.

Since the power spectrum omits all phase information, it has a simpler appearance than the frequency spectrum: as a real (rather than a complex) function it is easier to visualize and to plot. The wider a feature is in the time domain, the narrower it will be in the frequency domain, and hence in the power spectrum. The position of a single feature in the time domain is represented in the frequency domain by a phase shift, and is therefore lost in the power spectrum.

As an example, Fig. 5.6.3 shows a collection of Gaussian curves with added random noise, and Fig. 5.6.4 illustrates the corresponding power spectrum. Note that we have extended the data set with zeros to the nearest integer power of 2 in order to facilitate its Fourier transformation. We can readily distinguish the contributions of signal and noise by their different frequency dependences. In this simple example the noise is 'white', i.e., it is essentially independent of frequency, and therefore shows in the power spectrum as a horizontal band. It can also have a frequency-dependent power, as in, e.g., so-called $1/f$ noise.

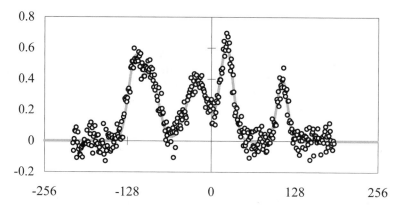

Fig. 5.6.3a: A test function composed of five Gaussian peaks $a \exp[-(x-c)^2/(2b^2)]$ (thick gray curve) and the same plus Gaussian noise of zero mean and standard deviation 0.05 (open circles). The constants used for the Gaussian peaks were a = 0.5, 0.4, 0.4, 0.6, 0.4, b = 10, 12, 15, 10, 8, and c = –117, –92, –22, 23, 108 respectively. The original data set of 401 points was extended to 512 to facilitate Fourier transformation.

Exercise 5.6.2:

(1) First generate a sample data set. The data shown in Fig. 5.6.3 were created with five Gaussians plus Gaussian noise, but you are of course welcome to use other functions.

(2) If the curves are all properly contained within the original data set, extend that data set with zeros at both ends; otherwise, extrapolate the data to taper off smoothly to zero in the added 'wings'.

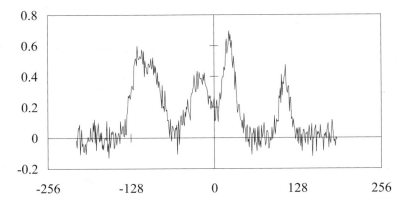

Fig. 5.6.3*b*: Another representation of the same noisy data (the points in Fig. 5.6.3*a*), here drawn as a 'continuous' curve.

(3) Fourier-transform the extended set.

(4) Calculate and plot log M or 2 log M, where M is the sum of the squares of the real and imaginary components of the Fourier-transformed data. Such a plot is shown in Fig. 5.6.4, and often exhibits two distinct regions: one (typically at lower values of $|f|$) in which the signal dominates, the other (at the high-frequency end) in which noise is the determining factor.

At its simplest we can use the power spectrum (see Fig. 5.6.4) to conclude that, in this example, the signal predominates at $|f|$-values smaller than about 0.055, while noise is the most important factor at higher frequencies. We can then filter the data by zeroing all frequency components above 0.055 before inverse transformation. Figure 5.6.5 illustrates such smoothing. A Tukey filter with a narrow transition range (e.g., $a = 3/32$, $b = 1/8$) yields an essentially similar result.

Exercise 5.6.2 (continued):

(5) Estimate by eye at what frequency f_0 the two regions intersect. Then copy the Fourier transform obtained under (3), and in that copy replace all values of the transform by zero whenever $|f| > f_0$.

(6) Inverse Fourier transform these data back into the time domain, and plot the result. Also compute and plot the residuals, and calculate the sum of the squares of these residuals. Figure 5.6.5 illustrates such results.

Wiener showed that one can use the power spectrum to obtain *optimal* least squares filtering, by considering the signal and noise components of $M^2(f)$ as the algebraic sum of two smooth functions, $S^2(f)$ and $N^2(f)$, where $S^2(f)$ approximates the contribution of the *s*ignal to $M^2(f)$, and $N^2(f)$ that of the *n*oise. We can usually estimate $S^2(f)$ and $N^2(f)$ only in those regions of the frequency spectrum where they dominate. However, in the absence of better information, we will typically extrapolate them to the other regions of the spectrum. The resulting *Wiener filter* then is $S^2(f)$ / $[S^2(f) + N^2(f)]$, and attenuates the data more strongly the smaller is the value of $S^2(f)$ / $N^2(f)$, the square of the *signal-to-noise ratio*. As long as the noise is not overwhelming the signal, Wiener filtering tends to affect the peak signal amplitudes only weakly because, at the frequencies describing those peaks, $S^2(f) \gg N^2(f)$, so that $S^2(f)$ / $[S^2(f) + N^2(f)] \approx 1$. On the other hand, contributions from frequency regions where noise predominates are much more strongly attenuated, because there $S^2(f)$ / $[S^2(f) + N^2(f)] \ll 1$.

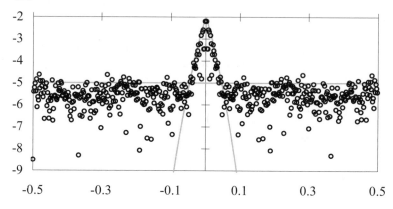

Fig. 5.6.4: A plot of 2 log $M(f)$ as a function of frequency f for the data of Fig. 5.6.3. The lines drawn are 2 log $M(f) = -2 - 50 \, |f| - 300 \, f^2$ and 2 log $M(f) = -5$ respectively.

Exercise 5.6.2 (continued):

(7) Fit simple polynomials to the two parts of the plot of 2 log $M(f)$ vs. f. Do not use unweighted least squares, since the top points should carry more weight than the lower points. For a visual estimate use a curve near the top of the data, but disregarding a few high points which are most likely due to noise. The parameters for the two lines shown in Fig. 5.6.4 were guessed in this way.

(8) Multiply the Fourier transform obtained under (3) with the Wiener function $S^2(f)/[S^2(f)+N^2(f)]$, then call the inverse transform to convert the data back to the time domain. Plot the resulting, filtered data, and compare with Fig. 5.6.6. Also compute and plot the residuals, calculate the sum of the squares of these residuals, and compare this with SSR obtained under (6).

Because the Wiener method requires only a crude approximation of the signal and noise components in the data set, we can fit the data in the logarithmic plot (of log $M^2(f)$ vs. f) to obtain, e.g., low-order polynomial expressions for log $S^2(f)$ and log $N^2(f)$, then exponentiate these to obtain $S^2(f)$ and $N^2(f)$, see the legend of Fig. 5.6.6. Wiener showed that use of his filter yields the smallest value of SSR, the sum of squares of the residuals, which makes it 'optimal' in a least squares sense. Table 5.6.1 lists a few simple expressions for Wiener filters.

function	approximation for $\log S^2(f)$	
Lorentzian	$a_0 + a_1 \,\|f\|$	
Gaussian	$a_0 + a_1 \,\|f\| + a_2 \, f^2$	
exponential	$a_0 + a_1 \log \left[(\|f\|+a_2)/(f_{max}+a_2-\|f\|) \right]$	$0 < a_2 \ll 1$

Table 5.6.1: Useful approximations for $\log S^2(f)$ for some prototypical signals $s(t)$.

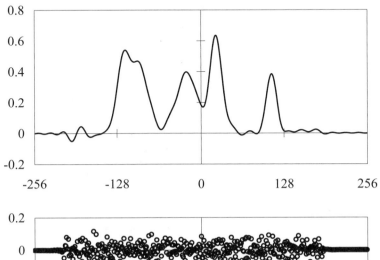

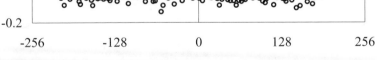

Fig. 5.6.5: The result of filtering the data of Fig. 5.6.3 with a simple cutoff filter at $|f/f_{max}| = 0.11$ in the frequency domain. Top: the filtered curve; bottom: the residuals, i.e., the differences between the original, noisy data set and the filtered one. The sum of the squares of the 401 residuals is 0.918.

The noise reduction achieved by the Wiener filter is perhaps best illustrated by Fig. 5.6.7, where we plot the random noise originally added to the Gaussian peaks of Fig. 5.6.3, and the noise remaining after filtering. Note the absence of perceptible bias.

If we knew the functional form of S, we could fit the data to that form directly, e.g., with Solver, and obtain a completely smooth result. While the Wiener method removes only part of the noise, it is rather general, requires no a priori information on the nature of the signal, and derives its information directly from the data set to be filtered. It does assume that the contributions of signal and noise can be identified separately, and can be extrapolated validly. Provided that the noise can be described as following a single Gaussian distribution and is additive to the signal, Wiener filtering is optimal in a least squares sense.

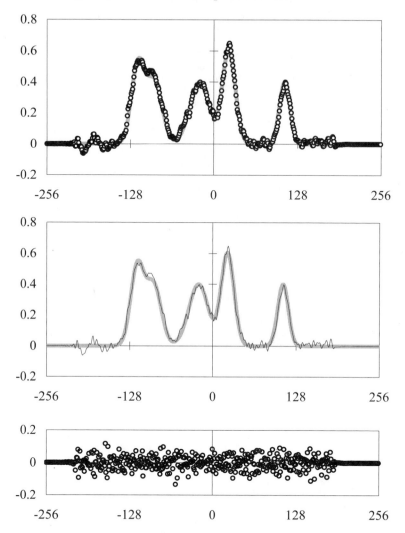

Fig. 5.6.6: The result of filtering the data of Fig. 5.6.3 with the Wiener filter $10^{\wedge}(-2 -50|f| -300f^2)/[10^{\wedge}(-2 -50|f| -300f^2) +10^{\wedge}(-5)]$. Top and middle panels: the filtered data (open circles and thin black line respectively) and the initially assumed, noise-free data (gray curve); bottom panel: the residuals between the unfiltered noisy data, and the filtered curve. The sum of the squares of the 401 residuals is 0.688.

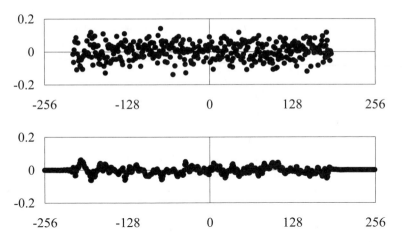

Fig. 5.6.7: The noise originally added to the Gaussian peaks in the model signal used (top panel), and the remaining noise after Wiener filtering (bottom panel). The standard deviations are 0.051 (top panel) and 0.022 (bottom panel) respectively.

5.7 Differentiation

In principle, differentiation is readily performed using Fourier transformation because differentiation with respect to time t in the time domain is equivalent to multiplication by $j\omega = 2\pi jf$ in the frequency domain, where $j = \sqrt{-1}$. One can therefore differentiate a function by transforming it into the frequency domain, multiplying it by $j\omega$, and transforming the resulting product back to the time domain. Since the Fourier transform is in general a complex quantity, say $a + jb$, multiplication by $j\omega$ yields $j\omega(a + jb) = -b\omega + j\omega a$. Below we illustrate the procedure with three examples. (Double differentiation can be obtained in a single operation through multiplication in the frequency domain by $(j\omega)^2 = -\omega^2$, triple differentiation through multiplication by $(j\omega)^3 = -j\omega^3$, etc., though noise enhancement often makes the one-step approach unadvisable.)

Exercise 5.7.1:

(1) In column A of a new spreadsheet enter $x = -16$ (1) 15 and, separated by one empty row, $x = -16$ (0.0625) 15.9375. In column B calculate, for $x = -16$ (1) 15, the corresponding values for $y = 0.7 \exp[-0.3(x+0.4)^2]$. In column C compute the same y for $x = -16$ (0.0625) 15.9375. Plot both series, with markers and with a line respectively, as in Fig. 5.7.1.

(2) Highlight the data for $x = -16$ (1) 15 in column A, the corresponding y-values in column B, and the associated empty spaces in column C, and call FFT to generate the transform in columns D through F.

(3) In column G copy the data from column D. In column H calculate -2π times the corresponding frequency (in column G) times the corresponding imagi-

nary component (in column F). It is most efficient to pre-calculate the value of 2π and then refer to its address, rather than have the spreadsheet compute PI() each time. Likewise, in column I, calculate 2π times f (from column G) times the real component (from column E).

(4) Highlight the data in columns G:I, call IFT, and plot the resulting real component of column K in Fig. 5.7.1.

(5) For $x = -16$ (0.0625) 15.9375 calculate the derivative $dy/dx = -0.6$ $(x + 0.4)$ y, and plot these results in Fig. 5.7.1 as well.

The result of this differentiation is very satisfactory: the fit in Fig. 5.7.1 between the derivative computed by Fourier transformation (solid circles) and those calculated algebraically for the Gaussian peak (line) is very good, with errors smaller than $\pm 0.1\%$.

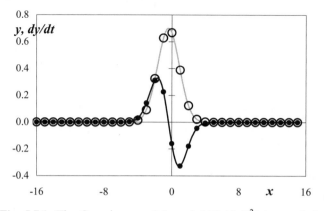

Fig. 5.7.1: The Gaussian $y = 0.7 \exp[-0.3(x+0.4)^2]$ (open circles and gray line through them) and its derivative as calculated by Fourier transformation (closed circles) and by calculation (black line).

Now that we have established the principle of differentiation by Fourier transformation, we examine how it holds up under strain, such as caused either by noise or by discontinuities.

***Exercise 5.7.1 (continued)*:**

(6) Since it is more instructive (and more fun) to illustrate what works than what does not, we will here use the second data set, for $x = -16$ (0.0625) 15.9375.

(7) Add a column of Gaussian noise of zero mean and unit standard deviation, a label for a noise amplitude *na*, and a place for its numerical value.

(8) Add s_n times noise from the column made under (7) to your Gaussian curve in order to make it noisy.

(9) Fourier transform the noisy Gaussian, then (to the right of that transform) insert three columns. In the first of these, calculate the logarithm of the sum of the squares of the real and imaginary components of the transform. Plot these data for positive frequencies, in order to make a Wiener filter.

(10) Use the two remaining, empty columns to generate simple functions (such as a parabola and a horizontal line) to approximate the contributions of signal and

noise, log $S^2(f)$ and log $N^2(f)$ respectively. The resulting plot of log $M^2(f)$ vs. f might now look like Fig. 5.7.2.

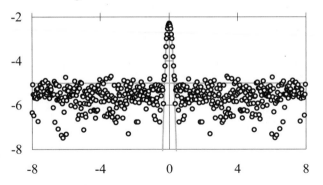

Fig. 5.7.2: Plot of log $M^2(f)$ vs. f for a simulated, noisy Gaussian curve. The gray lines are drawn with log $S^2(f) = -2.2 + |f| - 40 f^2$ and log $N^2(f) = -5$.

(11) Now perform the cross-multiplication as under (3) but, in addition, incorporate in all terms the Wiener filter $S^2(f) / [S^2(f)+N^2(f)]$. Then inverse Fourier transform to get the derivative, and plot your result, as in Fig. 5.7.3. The fit is not perfect, but differentiation of noisy data does not get any better than this.

(12) Now that you know what filter to use, you can actually mimic it with a Tukey filter in the frequency domain. Use Solver to adjust a and b of the Tukey filter, (5.6.3) with $n = f$ and $N = 2f_{max}$, to match the Wiener filter. You can indeed approximate the Wiener filter in this case by a Tukey filter with $a \approx 0.023$ and $b \approx 0.043$, which indicates how 'narrow' this Wiener filter is.

(13) Follow the same procedure with the smaller data set for $x = -16$ (1) 15. Even if you use the Wiener filter you found earlier (which is cheating, but it is difficult to define $S^2(f)$ and $N^2(f)$ with only a few noisy data points) the result is unsatisfactory: you simply have too few data points to pull it off.

Noise requires filtering before differentiation, and efficient filtering requires a sufficient number of data points so that noise can be averaged out. The moral: if you want to differentiate a set of data for which you have no good model, get as many data points as possible to define the curve. This applies to differentiation by Fourier transformation, just as much as it does to differentiation with least squares, e.g., with equidistant least squares (ELS, see section 3.15).

You can get away with differentiating relatively few data points when you know the precise mathematical formula to which the data can be fitted, in which case you find the fitting parameters with Solver, then use these parameters to calculate the derivative algebraically. However, if you need to differentiate data without an a priori model, make sure you have enough of them, because you will then have to rely on statistical methods, which do not work well for small data sets.

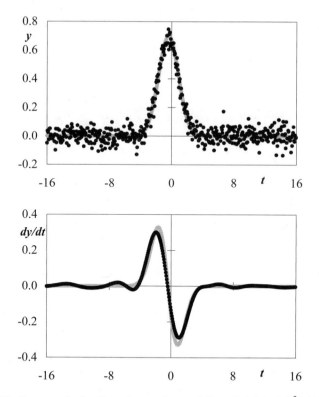

Fig. 5.7.3: Top panel: the Gaussian peak $y = 0.7 \exp[-0.3(t+0.4)^2]$ (thick gray line) and the same with Gaussian noise with zero mean and standard deviation 0.05 (filled black circles). Bottom panel: the first derivative of the noise-free curve (thick gray line) and that of the experimental data (dots) after Wiener filtering.

Noise is not the only source of trouble: differentiation can also run into difficulties when the data include one or more discontinuities, because there the derivative would be infinite, beyond the reach of digital representation. Below we will study this first with a square wave, then with an exponential.

Exercise 5.7.2:

(1) Generate one cycle of a square wave as follows. Generate the numbers $x = -16$ (1) 15 in cells A16:A47. In cells B16 and B32 place a zero, in cells B17:B31 a minus one (−1), and in cells B33 through B47 a one (1). Leave C16:C47 blank.

(2) Fourier transform A16:C47, and use the result in D16:F47 to generate, in G16:I47, the same quantity multiplied by $j\omega$, as already done in exercise 5.7.1.

(3) Inverse Fourier transform G16:I47, then plot the result, I16:I47 vs. G16:G47, see Fig. 5.7.4a.

(4) Repeat the same, but now for $x = -16$ (0.0625) 15.9375. For y now use one zero, followed by 255 terms −1, another 0, and the remaining 255 terms 1. Use Fourier transformation to generate its derivative, and plot it, as in Fig. 5.7.4b.

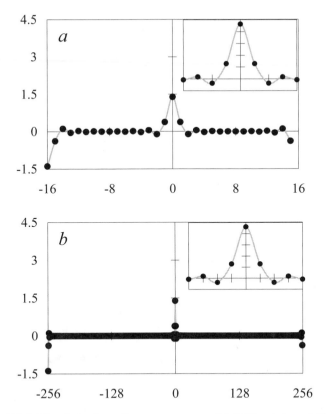

Fig. 5.7.4: The derivative of a square wave of (*a*) 32 points and (*b*) 512 points. The inserts show the central regions of both plots, with (in both cases) a horizontal range from –4 to +4, and a vertical range from –0.2 to +1.5.

In Fig. 5.7.4*a* a relatively large number of points is affected by the discontinuities in the middle and at the edges of the range, whereas this is much less apparent in Fig. 5.7.4*b*. However, as the inserts show, the derivatives at the discontinuities are the same, and affect the same number of adjacent points. In the larger data set there are just many more unaffected numbers!

Because the input consists of discrete, evenly-spaced points, we cannot really represent a truly sudden parameter change; at best we can make a change over one interval Δx. In fact, so far we have made that change over *two* intervals Δx. The next exercise illustrates the effect of making the transition less abrupt. (Even the continuous Fourier transform has a problem, known as the Gibbs phenomenon, with a step function.)

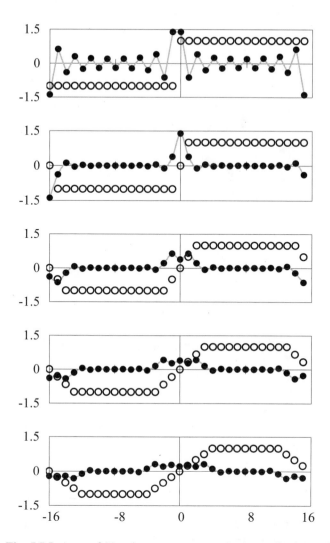

Fig. 5.7.5: A set of 32-point square waves of unit amplitudes, and slopes $\Delta y/\Delta x$ = 1, 1/2, 1/3, etc. (open circles), and their Fourier-transform derivatives (solid circles connected by straight-line segments) illustrating that the severity of the oscillations in the computed derivative decreases as the transition is made more gradual.

Exercise 5.7.3:

(1) Use the block A19:L47 of the previous exercise, or make a similar new one.

(2) Modify the input sequence from 0, −1 (fifteen times), 0, 1 (fifteen times), to sixteen terms −1 followed by sixteen terms 1, and repeat the analysis.

(3) Now make changes in the other direction, by performing the differentiation on the following input sequences: 0, −0.5, −1 (×13), −0.5, 0, 0.5, 1 (×13), 0.5, then 0, −1/3, −2/3, −1 (×11), −2/3, −1/3, 0, 1/3, 2/3, 1 (×11), 2/3, 1/3, and finally

0, –0.25, –0.5, –0.75, –1 (×9), –0.75, –0.5, –0.25, 0, 0.25, 0.5, 0.75, 1 (×9), 0.75, 0.5, 0.25.

(4) Figure 5.7.5 illustrates the results. Clearly, the more sudden the transition, the more oscillations we get. And the shorter the data array, the less space there is for these oscillations to die down.

Figure 5.7.5 illustrates that the differentiation of sharp transitions by Fourier transformation can cause oscillations, and is therefore only practical when the data set is sufficiently large so that the oscillations can taper off long before the signal has done so.

The message is clear: in order to use Fourier transformation to differentiate a function with one or more discontinuities, you need many data points in order to restrict the inevitable oscillations to a relatively narrow range. If you can describe the function in terms of an appropriate model, especially if that model describes sections of the data set that do not contain discontinuities, fit that model piecemeal, and use Fourier transformation to differentiate its parts. If you absolutely must use Fourier transformation to differentiate a small set of data without an appropriate model but with discontinuities and including much noise, consult your almanac or palm reader.

5.8 Interpolation

Often, data sets need to be interpolated. If the shape of the function is known, say as a Gaussian or Lorentzian peak, nonlinear least squares can of course be used to fit the data to that function. If the data cannot be described mathematically but can be represented reasonably well in terms of polynomials, Lagrange interpolation may be indicated. Likewise, if the data can be fitted in terms of sines and cosines, Fourier transformation might be considered, especially when, inside the measuring instrument, the data are already available in Fourier-transformed format. Below we will examine how Fourier transformation can be used for data interpolation.

In interpolation we use the existing data to construct intermediate values for which no direct evidence is available. This can only be done by assuming that no significant features of the signal are missing, despite the limited data set. In the present context this means that we assume the absence of signals at frequencies higher than those sampled. The procedure therefore is as follows: take the existing data points, Fourier transform them, extend the frequency range with contributions of zero amplitude at the added higher frequencies, then transform the data back. Such *zero filling* results in a larger data set without added information, i.e., in a smooth interpolation. If still higher resolution is necessary, the few data near the maximum can then be fitted to a low-order polynomial in order to find the precise peak maximum.

For example, in mass spectrometry it is common to acquire the fragmentation pattern as equidistant points on an m/z scale, where m denotes mass and z valency. The chemical identity of a fragment can usually be identified unambiguously when the peak maximum can be specified to within 10^{-4} mass units, but it may be impractical to acquire data at such a high resolution, in terms of either acquisition rate or storage requirements. The question therefore arises: can one reconstruct the position of the peak maximum from a small number of measurements in the peak region?

Exercise 5.8.1:

(1) In a new spreadsheet, make up a signal by, e.g., computing a Gaussian peak of which only few data points have been sampled, such as that shown in Fig. 5.8.1, where 32 data points were taken for $x = -16$ (1) 15 with $y = 0.7$ exp[-0.3 $(x+0.4)^2$], and where this function is plotted for $x = -16$ (0.0625) 15.

(2) Taking the Fourier transform of the 32 data yields a transform for $f = -0.5$ (0.03125) 0.46875.

(3) Make a table with $f = -8$ (0.03125) 7.96875, i.e., 16 times as long. For the real and imaginary components enter zeros, then copy the data for $f = -0.5$ (0.03125) 0.46875 in the appropriate place in that data set. Repeat the y-value for $x = -0.5$ at $x = +0.5$.

(4) Upon inverse transformation you will obtain 16 times more data, i.e., 15 data points will have been interpolated between every two original points. Plot these together with the original data, as in Fig. 5.8.2 where we have focused on the peak region.

(5) Estimate the position of the maximum by fitting the points around the peak maximum to a low-order polynomial, such as a quadratic. Use the fitted parameters to calculate the sought x-value, see the inset to Fig. 5.8.2.

Using least squares, say from $t = -0.6875$ to -0.125, to fit the top ten interpolated data to a parabola $y = a_0 + a_1x + a_2x^2$, then yields the maximum as $x_{max} = -a_1/(2a_2) = -0.3998 \pm 0.0001$ and $y_{max} = 0.69991 \pm 0.00001$, quite close to the correct values of $x_{max} = -0.4$ and $y_{max} = 0.7$.

However, when the function is asymmetric, the above method can lead to systematic distortion. For the function $y = 1/\{\exp[-0.5(x+0.1)]$ $+\exp[4(x+0.1)]\}$ we find $x_{max} = -0.843 \pm 0.001$ and $y_{max} = 0.6346 \pm 0.0002$, whereas the correct values are $x_{max} \approx -0.5621$ and $y_{max} \approx 0.70551$, see Figs. 5.8.3 and 5.8.4. The interpolated function goes through the data points, but doesn't fit the function. Note that, in this case, the differences in x_{max} and y_{max} far exceed their standard deviations, illustrating the danger of interpreting the standard deviation as a measure of accuracy.

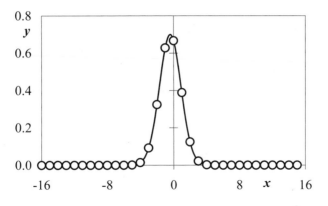

Fig. 5.8.1: The test function $y = 0.7 \exp[-0.3\,(x+0.4)^2]$ plotted for just 32 points (open circles) and with 16 times smaller increments, i.e., 512 points (drawn curve).

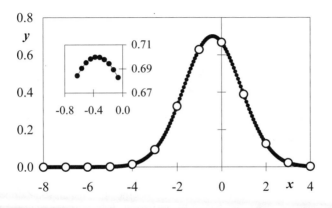

Fig. 5.8.2: The result of Fourier transform interpolation of the test function of Fig. 5.8.1 (small solid circles) in the region of the peak. Inset: the top ten points of the interpolated data with a linear least squares parabola fitted through them.

Exercise 5.8.1 (continued):

(6) Replace the Gaussian test function by the asymmetrical function $y = 1/\{\exp[-0.5(x+0.1)] + \exp[4(x+0.1)]\}$, while otherwise treating the data in the same way as before. Figure 5.8.3 shows the function, and Fig. 5.8.4 its interpolation. Now the distortion is obvious, and no least squares fitting to a parabola is needed to bring it out.

It is clear from Fig. 5.8.4 that Fourier transform interpolation, like any other interpolation, introduces distortion when the *tacitly implied basis set* (here sinusoids; with Lagrange interpolation it would be a polynomial) poorly fits the interpolated shape. The paucity of data only makes the distortion worse.

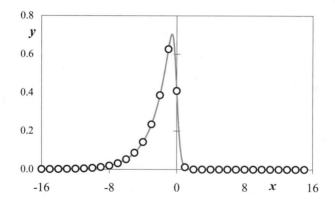

Fig. 5.8.3: The test function $y = 1/\{\exp[-0.5(x+0.1)] + \exp[4(x+0.1)]\}$ plotted for just 32 points (open circles) and with 16 times smaller increments (gray drawn curve).

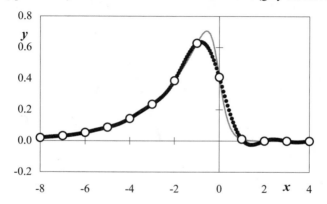

Fig. 5.8.4: The result of Fourier transform interpolation (small solid circles) of 32 samples (large open circles) of the test function $y = 1/\{\exp[-0.5(x+0.1)] + \exp[4(x+0.1)]\}$ (gray drawn line) of Fig. 5.8.3 in the region of the peak.

Another problem with interpolation is its extreme sensitivity to noise when only few data points are available, because the interpolated curve will tend to go as closely as possible through those points, even if they contain noise.

In general, interpolation is a poor substitute for making more closely spaced measurements, and the spreadsheet is a convenient tool to visualize its consequences. If the functionality involved is known, it is preferable to fit sparse data to that function using nonlinear least squares, because this can avoid the above-illustrated systematic distortion. You can readily verify that, given the functional forms (though not the particular parameter values) of the equations used, Solver can recover the peak position and height exactly (i.e., to within its numerical precision of about

$\pm 10^{-14}$) from the above, sparse but noise-free data sets. Solver is also much less sensitive to noise, because it does not try to fit all data points exactly.

However, when we don't know the correct functionality, the Fourier transform may well provide as good a guess as other convenient methods. And in some applications, where we look specifically for periodic phenomena, and where finer detail is largely illusory anyway, as in scanning tunneling microscopy, Fourier transform smoothing is clearly the preferred method.

5.9 Data compression

Least squares can be used to extract the essential data from, say, a noisy but otherwise linear calibration curve. Likewise we can use Fourier transformation to extract some essential features from an arbitrary signal. For example, a common chromatographic detector uses ultraviolet light to illuminate the effluent, and monitors the resulting fluorescence. This can give both qualitative and quantitative information on the eluted sample components. We will here focus on the qualitative aspect, i.e., on how to use the spectral information to identify the chemical identity of the eluting sample, assuming that we have a computer 'library' of reference spectra that can be consulted.

A fluorescence spectrum can cover a fairly wide spectral range, but often contains only a relatively small number of identifiable features. A library search can therefore be simplified considerably by compressing the data, even if such compression leads to some distortion. Fourier transform filtering can often serve this purpose, as described, e.g., by Yim et al. in *Anal. Chem.* 49 (1977) 2069. We will illustrate the method here with spectral data available on the web from the Oregon Medical Laser Center of the Oregon Graduate Institute at omlc.ogi.edu/spectra/PhotochemCAD/html/index.html.

Exercise 5.9.1:

(1) Go to the above web site, and select a compound. At the bottom of its page, below its fluorescence spectrum (assuming it has one), click on Original Data, then highlight and copy those data. Below we will use tryptophan as an example; feel free to select instead any other fluorescence spectrum, from this or any other source. Some of these fluorescence spectra exhibit less fine-structure, some have more. Obviously, the more details one can measure and compare, the more reliable the identification can be.

(2) Leave the web page, open Notepad, and paste the spectral data there; Notepad is a convenient intermediary between external data and Excel. Save the file.

(3) Open a spreadsheet, select File $\Rightarrow$ Open, and in the resulting Open dialog box specify where to look for the data file, the file name, and the file type (in this

case: Text Files). In the Text Import Wizard specify Delimited, and the spectral data will appear in your spreadsheet.

(4) Graph both the fluorescent intensity FI and its logarithm. The logarithmic representation will be used here because it shows more characteristic features.

(5) Since these data were not intended for use with Fourier transformation, the number of data points, 441, is not an integer power of 2. We now have two options: reducing the data set to the nearest smaller suitable number, 256, or 'padding' the data to 512, the next-higher integer power of 2. Here we illustrate how to accomplish the latter.

(6) Perusal of the graph of log(FI) vs. wavelength shows that, at long wavelengths λ, it exhibits an essentially linear dependence on λ. We therefore extrapolate this linear relationship to $\lambda = 535.5$ nm by fitting the data to a line from, e.g., 380 to 400 nm, and by then using the computed intercept and slope to calculate values for $400 < \lambda < 540$ nm. Plot these to make sure that the extrapolated data are indeed continuous with the measured ones.

(7) Fourier transform this extended data set, and plot the result. Most of the signal will be concentrated in the few lowest frequencies, see Fig. 5.9.1.

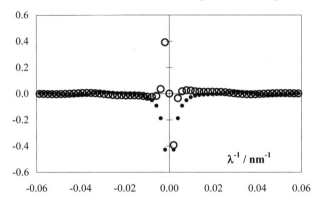

Fig. 5.9.1: The 61 low-frequency components of the Fourier transform of the tryptophan fluorescence spectrum (for excitation at 270 nm) after its extrapolation to 512 data points. The zero-frequency point is far off-scale in this plot.

(8) In a copy, set the higher-frequency contributions to zero, inverse transform the data, and again plot the result. By repeating this while retaining, say, the 10, 20, 30, and 40 lowest frequencies, you will get a sense of how few low-frequency data are needed to represent the overall shape of the curve, and how many more must be kept to show the minor shoulder near 300 nm.

(9) Figure 5.9.1 shows that retaining only 30 of the 256 frequencies is sufficient to exhibit the general shape of the fluorescence peak, without noticeable loss of information. On the other hand, the main fluorescence peak can be represented with fewer than 10 (positive and negative) frequencies.

(10) The small 'hook' at the lowest wavelengths is an artifact resulting from the requirement that the Fourier-transformed signal be a repeatable unit. In this example we were lucky; had the signal levels at the two extremes of the wavelength scale been very different, the consequent change would have led to undesirable oscillations, which can only be avoided with additional effort.

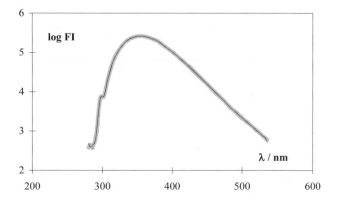

Fig. 5.9.2: The original data set extrapolated to 535.5 nm (thin black line) and its representation in terms of only 30 frequencies (broad gray band).

By Fourier transformation, a fluorescence spectrum can be represented by a relatively small number of frequency terms, thereby greatly facilitating library search routines for computer-based identification. In the present example, 61 data (the real and imaginary components at the lowest 30 frequencies plus the zero-frequency term) can be used to replace the original 441 data points. A further reduction to 31 points can be achieved through symmetry, because the data at negative frequencies can be reconstituted from those at the corresponding positive frequencies: since the input function $g(t)$ is real, $G(-f)$ must be the complex conjugate of $G(f)$.

In section 4.6 we already encountered examples of spectral fitting, and we therefore ask here how the Fourier transform and least squares methods compare. In principle, nonlinear least squares methods are more flexible, since they are not limited to a basis set of sines and cosines. Relatively simple spectra can often be described to the same accuracy with far fewer parameters than required for Fourier transformation. But this strongly depends on the number of features to be represented: with more peaks the balance shifts in favor of the Fourier transform method, as it does with typical nuclear magnetic resonance, infrared, and mass spectra.

Then there are practical constraints: fitting by nonlinear least squares may require personal judgment, and may therefore be more difficult to automate than Fourier transformation. On the other hand, Fourier transformation may need some help if the spectrum does not tend to zero at its extremes. The choice may also depend on whether the spectral information already exists in Fourier-transformed format inside a measuring instrument. For cataloguing and data searching, the Fourier transform method may be the more convenient, because it expresses all data sets in terms of the same, limited set of fixed frequencies, which greatly facilitates their intercomparison.

5.10 Analysis of the tides

Below we will analyze a particular data set to illustrate how one can often combine Fourier transformation and least squares analysis for efficient data fitting of periodic phenomena. Each method has its own strengths and weaknesses: Fourier transformation can show us many simultaneous frequency components, but has limited frequency resolution, which may lead to leakage. Least squares fitting is more flexible in what it can fit, but needs extensive guidance. Because the two methods complement each other in many ways, their combined use can make a very powerful data analysis tool.

The tides have been understood quantitatively through the work of such scientific giants as Newton, Euler, Daniel Bernouilli, Laplace, and Kelvin as due to the combined effects of lunar and solar attraction on the earth and its surface water. What we experience as tides is the differential effect of the attractive forces on the solid earth and on the more mobile surface water, modulated by the shape (area and depth profile) of the particular body of water and by the cohesive forces that produce drag to water movement, and further modified by wind, barometric pressure, and local currents (as where rivers meet oceans). We need not look here into its detailed mathematical description, but merely consider the tidal record as a signal that should have as its principal frequency components the lunar and solar half-days, and take it from there. Fortunately, tidal records are readily available on the Web from NOS, the National Ocean Service of NOAA, the National Oceanic and Atmospheric Administration, and we will use one such record. You are of course welcome to select a record from another location, and/or pick a different time period. Since arbitrarily chosen data sets seldom contain precisely $2n$ data points, we will deliberately take a record that does not fit that restriction, and then select a subset of it whenever we need to use Fourier transformation.

Exercise 5.10.1:

(1) Go to the web site co-ops.nos.noaa.gov/, and under Observations select Verified/Historical Water Level Data: U.S. and Global Coastal Stations.

(2) Select a station; in the example given below we will use 8410140 Eastport, Passamaquoddy Bay, ME, but you can of course pick another.

(3) Specify a time interval (we have used W2, hourly heights), a Begin Data (here: 20010601 for June 1, 2001) and an End Data (here: 20010831, for August 31, yielding a 2208-hour period).

(4) Take a preview of the data in ViewPlot.

(5) Select the data with View Data, highlight them all with Edit ⇒ Select All, and copy them to the clipboard with Ctrl‿c. Minimize or close the web site.

(6) Start Word, then click Open, Look in: Windows, select Notepad.exe, and paste the file into it with Ctrl‿v. Save the file as a Notepad file using any name that suits your fancy. As you will see in the next few steps, Notepad triggers Excel to open its Text Import Wizard, which is useful to format the data properly.

(7) Open Excel, Select Open, then specify Files of type: as All Files (*.*) so that you will see the just-saved Notepad.txt file, and select it.

(8) You will now see Step 1 of the Text Import Wizard, in which you specify that the data are of Fixed width, i.e., they are tab-delimited. Preview the file to see where the file header (containing all the explanatory text) ends, and then specify the row at which to start importing the data. (In our example, that would be at row 23.) Move to the next Step.

(9) In the Data preview of Step 2 of the Text Import Wizard, enter lines to define the columns you want (in our example, at lines 8, 12, 13, 15, 16, 19, 21, 27, 32, 35, and 40. You can use fewer columns, but then you will have more cleanup to do. Click Finish.

(10) You will now have all the data in your spreadsheet, in columns, starting in cell A1. In the first column replace the station number (8410140) by a row counter: 0 in the top row, 1 in the next row, etc. Delete all peripheral columns, such as the one containing the year (2001), a slant (/), minutes (:00).

(11) You can also delete the rightmost columns, except the column between 35 and 40 that had been labeled Sigma, which you may want to save for the end of the exercise. Regardless of whether or not you save this column, first place the instruction =STDEV(F3:F2210) (or whatever appropriate range) at its top to compute the standard deviation of the fit between the observations and the predicted data. In our example it is only 0.006 m, or 6 mm, out of an average tidal swing of several meters!

(12) Insert two rows at the top, and use the higher one of these to enter the labels time, month, data, hour, and Height (after having made sure that these labels are indeed appropriate). Also label the next two columns Hcalc and residuals. These labels and data will occupy columns A through G.

(13) Plot the water heights versus time *t*, in hours.

Figure 5.10.1 illustrates the 2208 data points so imported, as a function of time. It clearly shows a periodic oscillation, with a variable amplitude that is slightly more pronounced and alternating at its tops than at its bottom values. For our Fourier analysis we will take the last 2048 data points, thereby leaving some space near the top of the spreadsheet and avoiding two missing points. After their Fourier transformation we calculate and plot the magnitude of the response as a function of frequency.

Exercise 5.10.1 (continued):

(14) In row 163 (or wherever you find *t* = 160) copy the water level in, say, column J, and in column I enter the shifted time *t* − 160. Copy both down to the end of the data file. You should now have 2048 data in columns I and J. Highlight these, extend the highlighted area to include column K, and call the forward Fourier transform macro.

(15) In column O calculate the square root of the sum of the squares of the real and imaginary components so obtained, and plot these versus the frequency (in column L).

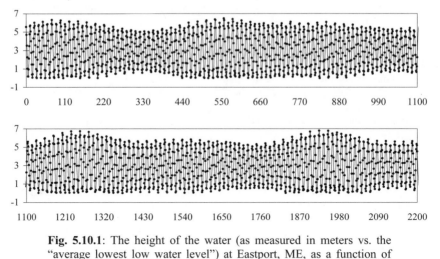

Fig. 5.10.1: The height of the water (as measured in meters vs. the "average lowest low water level") at Eastport, ME, as a function of time (in hours) during the period from June 1 through August 3, 2001.

The result is illustrated in Fig. 5.10.2 at three different vertical scales. The top panel shows a large contribution, of value 2.991, at zero frequency. This component merely reflects the average value of the signal, which is measured versus a "mean lowest low level" in order to make most data values positive quantities. Indeed, by using the function =AVERAGE(*range*) to calculate the average we likewise obtain 2.991.

The largest peak at a non-zero frequency is found at $f = 0.0806$ h^{-1}, a value that roughly corresponds with half a moon day of 24 h 50 min 28.32 s or $1/12.4206$ h$^{-1} = 0.0805114$ h^{-1}. This peak has a rather wide base, suggesting that it may be broadened by multiple components and/or leakage. In addition, there are low-frequency components clustered near zero frequency, and two series of minor peaks, one at integer multiples of 0.08 h^{-1}, i.e., at 0.16, 0.32, 0.40, and 0.48 h^{-1}, the other at half-integer multiples of the same value, at 0.04, 0.12, 0.20, 0.28, 0.36, and 0.44 h^{-1}. Neither series has quite died out at $f = 0.5$, and one can therefore assume that there will be still higher-order terms as well.

We can either fit these data on a purely empirical basis, or try to identify signals with known astronomical time constants, as we did in the above paragraph. The latter approach, which introduces independently obtainable information into the data analysis, is usually the more powerful, and will be pursued here. We therefore fit the data to an adjustable constant a_0 plus a sine wave of adjustable amplitude a_1 and phase shift p_1 but with a fixed frequency f_1 of 0.0805114 h^{-1}, i.e., to $h = a_0 + a_1$ $\sin(2\pi f_1 t + p_1)$ where t is time in hours, starting with 0 at the first data point. We then calculate the residuals, and Fourier transform them in order to find the next-largest term(s), etc.

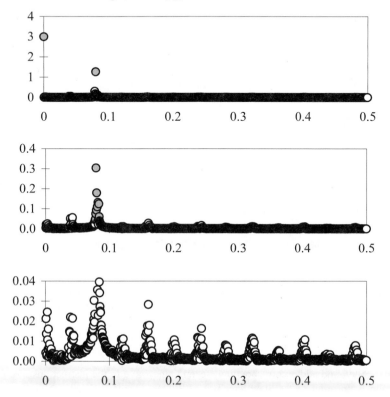

Fig. 5.10.2: Results of the Fourier analysis of 2048 data from Fig. 5.10.1, shown here as the magnitudes of the resulting frequency components at three different vertical scales, in m. Note that the gray-filled circles, if still present, would have fallen beyond the scales of the lower panels. The horizontal scale shows the frequency, in h^{-1}. For a more compact representation of these data see Fig. 1.2.6.

Exercise 5.10.1 (continued):

(16) Arrange labels and values for the adjustable parameters a_0, a_1, and p_1, in one column, and in another (leaving at least one space in-between) the fixed parameter f_1. Specify a_0, a_1, and p_1 as zero, and f_1 as 0.0805114.

(17) In column F compute the water height h_{calc} using the assumed parameters a_0, a_1, and p_1, and in column G calculate the difference between the measured and calculated water heights.

(18) Also deposit a label and cell for the computation of SSR as =SUMXMY2 (E3:E2210,F3:F2210) or for whatever the appropriate ranges are.

(19) Call Solver to minimize SSR by changing the values of a_0, a_1, and p_1.

(20) In cell R163 repeat the count of $t - 160$ that you already used in cell I163, and in cell S163 copy the residual from G163. Copy these down to row 2210. Highlight R163:T2210, apply the forward Fourier transformation, in row X calculate the corresponding magnitude (i.e., the square root of the sum of squares of the real and imaginary components of the Fourier transform, and plot these.

The next most-important term, clearly visible in Fig. 5.10.3, is at 0.079 h^{-1}, and is due to the ellipticity of the lunar orbit, which has a period of 27.55 days. As the moon travels from its perigee (at the shortest moon-earth distance) to its apogee (furthest away) and back, the gravitational attraction changes, and in our linear analysis this shows as a difference frequency. Indeed, the corresponding first-order correction term has a frequency of 0.0805114 $-$ 1 / (24 $\times$ 27.55) = 0.0805114 $-$ 0.0015124 = 0.078999 h^{-1}.

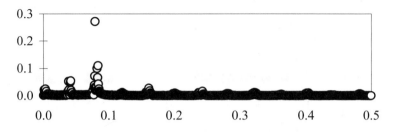
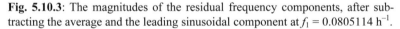

Fig. 5.10.3: The magnitudes of the residual frequency components, after subtracting the average and the leading sinusoidal component at $f_1 = 0.0805114$ h^{-1}.

Exercise 5.10.1 (continued):

(21) Extend the parameter lists to accommodate a_2, and p_2 as well as $f_2 = 0.078999$, and add a corresponding, second sine wave to the instructions in column F. In order to facilitate later use of SolverAid, place all adjustable coefficients (i.e., the amplitudes and phase shifts) in a single, contiguous column, one below the other.

(22) Rerun Solver, now simultaneously adjusting the five coefficients a_0, a_1, p_1, a_2, and p_2.

(23) Rerun the Fourier transform of the residuals, and look at the updated plot of these residuals.

(24) The next-highest peak in the residual plot is at 0.083 h^{-1}, close to the frequency of 2/24 = 0.083333 h^{-1} associated with half the solar day.

(25) After you include this frequency and repeat the protocol sketched in points (18) through (20) you will find that there is yet another frequency near 0.08 h^{-1}, viz. at about 0.082 h^{-1}, which can be identified with the *sum* frequency 0.0805114 + 1 / (24 $\times$ 27.55) = 0.0805114 + 0.0015124 = 0.082024 h^{-1}.

(26) Also incorporate this frequency, and call Solver to adjust the nine resulting coefficients a_0 through a_4 and p_1 through p_4, Fourier transform the residuals, and plot them.

(27) Extend the parameter lists to accommodate four new frequencies, amplitudes, and phase angles, and include them in the instruction for the calculated heights in column F.

(28) Set the frequencies at $f_1/2$, $f_2/2$, $f_3/2$, and $f_4/2$, and subsequently let Solver adjust the amplitudes a_0 through a_8 and p_1 through p_8.

(29) After you have done this, run SolverAid (which requires that a_0 through a_8 and p_1 through p_8 form one contiguous column) to calculate the standard deviations of the coefficients.

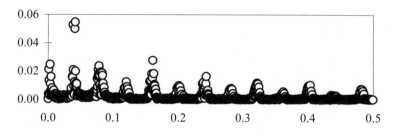

Fig. 5.10.4: The magnitudes of the residual frequency components, after accounting for the average and four sinusoidal components near $0.08\ \text{h}^{-1}$.

The resulting Fig. 5.10.4 shows that we finally have accounted for the *four* major frequency components near $0.08\ \text{h}^{-1}$. Even though the Fourier analysis showed only one peak around $0.08\ \text{h}^{-1}$, we used astronomical information to resolve this into four different signals, exploiting least squares analysis to find their amplitudes and phase angles. This *combination* of different methods is more powerful than each method by itself.

The next-largest contributions are around $0.04\ \text{h}^{-1}$. We therefore extend the analysis with four more frequencies, each one-half of the corresponding values near $0.08\ \text{h}^{-1}$, and subsequently use Solver to adjust the coefficients, which now number 17. As can be seen in Fig. 5.10.5, with the four frequencies we have found so far we can indeed represent the general envelope of the tidal curve, but not its alternating amplitudes or other details.

frequency	*amplitude*	*frequency*	*amplitude*
0	2.993 ± 0.004	standard deviation of the fit: 0.19	
0.03950	0.023 ± 0.006	0.078999	0.568 ± 0.006
0.040256	0.034 ± 0.006	0.080511	2.620 ± 0.006
0.041012	0.006 ± 0.006	0.082024	0.215 ± 0.006
0.041667	0.158 ± 0.006	0.083333	0.286 ± 0.006

Table 5.10.1: The amplitudes found, with their standard deviations as provided by SolverAid, for the nine frequencies considered so far.

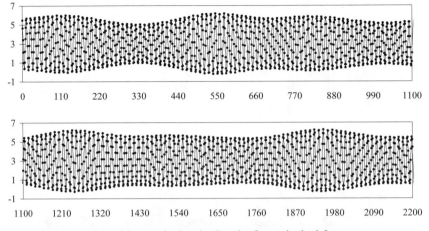

Fig. 5.10.5: The tides recalculated using the four principal frequency components near 0.08 h^{-1}. Comparison with Fig. 5.10.1 shows that this indeed represents the dominant longer-term features of the experimental data.

Table 5.10.1 lists the results so obtained for the (absolute values of the) various amplitudes; the phase angles are needed for the analysis but have no physical meaning because they are tied to the particular starting time chosen. We see that we can represent most of the signal in terms of predictable periodic functions, so that tide tables can indeed anticipate the tides. Such tables are, of course, based on much longer data sets (so as to include the length of the moon's node, a period of about 18.6 years) and on using more frequencies.

We see that only one of the four half-frequency components is important, and that (using 3 times the standard deviation as our criterion) one of them is not even statistically significant. However, the Fourier transform shows that not all frequency components around 0.04 h^{-1} have been accounted for, since there is a remaining signal at about 0.0386 h^{-1}, which we can tentatively associate with the difference frequency $0.0805114 / 2 - 0.0015128 = 0.038743$ h^{-1}. Indeed, if we replace the non-significant frequency 0.041012 by 0.038743, run Solver again, and then Fourier transform the residuals, we find that that all remaining components have amplitudes smaller than 0.03 m, see Fig. 5.10.6.

By comparing the data in Tables 5.10.1 and 5.10.2 we see that changing one frequency can alter the amplitudes of the neighboring frequencies, and we therefore look into the mutual dependence of these results. SolverAid can provide the corresponding array of linear correlation coefficients, in this case an array of 17 by 17 = 289 numbers. Below we show how we can quickly screen them for significant correlations.

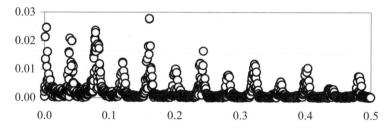

Fig. 5.10.6: The magnitudes of the residual frequency components, after accounting for the average and eight sinusoidal components near 0.08 and 0.04 h^{-1}.

frequency	*amplitude*	*frequency*	*amplitude*
0	2.994 ± 0.004	standard deviation of the fit: 0.17	
0.03950	0.007 ± 0.005	0.078999	0.568 ± 0.005
0.040256	0.020 ± 0.005	0.080511	2.620 ± 0.005
0.038743	0.114 ± 0.005	0.082024	0.216 ± 0.005
0.041667	0.156 ± 0.005	0.083333	0.286 ± 0.005

Table 5.10.2: The same results after one frequency near 0.04 h^{-1} has been redefined.

Exercise 5.10.1 (continued):

(30) Run SolverAid (again) and let it provide the matrix of linear correlation coefficients. Say that you have placed it in AA1:AQ17. Deposit in cell AS1 the instruction =IF(ABS(AA1)>0.9,ABS(AA1)," "), and copy this instruction to the entire block AS1:BI17. Any linear correlation coefficient with an absolute value larger than 0.9 will show, whereas all other cells will remain empty because they will contain the 'empty' string between the two quotation marks in the IF statement. You can of course set the bar lower, at 0.8 or wherever, since in this particular case none of the 17 adjusted parameters has a very pronounced dependence on any other. In fact, the largest linear correlation coefficients (apart from the 1's on the main diagonal) are smaller than 0.2!

(31) To get an idea of how well you can represent the observed tidal data with just eight frequencies, plot the original and calculated curves in one graph, using different symbols and/or colors, as in Fig. 5.10.7. If you want to see how far you still would have to go, plot the residuals, as in Fig. 5.10.8. And if you want to see what is possible by harmonic analysis (using a longer data base and many more harmonic terms), plot the data in the 'Sigma' column you may have set aside under point (11). This plot is shown in Fig. 5.10.9, and indicates that there is very little noise on this signal. Such noise may still be deterministic, when caused by, e.g., effects of earthquakes or storms, but could only be recognized as such in retrospect, by comparison with geological and meteorological records, and certainly would not be predictable.

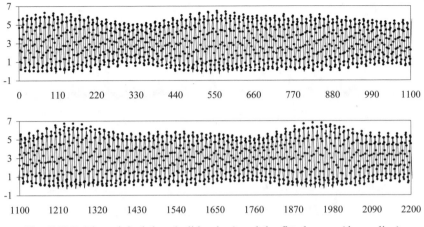

Fig. 5.10.7: The original data (solid points) and the fitted curve (drawn line) based on the average and eight sinusoidal components near 0.08 and 0.04 h^{-1}.

It is clear that we can continue this process and, by including more and more frequencies, make the fit better and better. This is indeed how tidal tables are made. Remember that the standard deviation between the observed and the predicted heights listed in the NOS-NOAA table was a mere 6 mm, see under point (11) in the exercise. The corresponding value for our fit so far is 174 mm, about 30 times larger. Still, you get the idea; in this case, with a large signal and apparently relatively little 'noise' from earthquakes, storms etc., the prediction can be extremely reliable, and the more so the longer is the experimental record on which it is based.

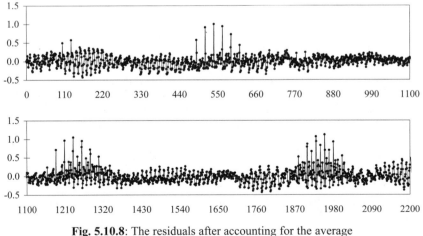

Fig. 5.10.8: The residuals after accounting for the average and eight sinusoidal components near 0.08 and 0.04 h^{-1}.

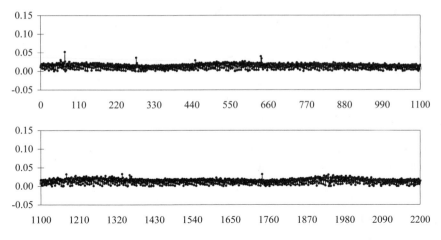

Fig. 5.10.9: The residuals in the NOS/NOAA harmonic analysis of the same data set. Note the ten times enlarged vertical scale.

5.11 Summary

For determining the frequency content of a signal, or a circuit, Fourier transformation is often the method of choice. It can also be used to manipulate data, as in filtering, differentiation, and interpolation. In all those areas, it tends to compete with least squares analysis. With Wiener filtering, the transform method can be combined with least squares curve fitting to get the best of the two, an optimal least squares filter. As we have also seen in the example of tidal analysis, the combined use of Fourier transformation and least squares methods can sometimes exploit the best features of both approaches.

Because Fourier transformation uses trigonometric functions as its basis set rather than polynomials, equivalent operations of the two approaches on the same data will yield somewhat different results. As in instrumentation, the advantages of Fourier transformation are most pronounced with large, information-rich data sets. Fourier transformation of a data set and rejection of its high-frequency components can yield a compact set of descriptors of the main (low-frequency) components of that signal, which can then be used for cataloguing and searching.

A minor nuisance in using Fourier transforms is the confusion between different conventions used in the literature: which transform to call forward, and what to use as normalizing factor. Here we have used the mathematical/physical sign convention, and we have shifted the burden of the normalization factor $1/(2\pi)$ entirely on the inverse transform in order to have a simple relation between the amplitude of a sine or cosine wave and that of its Fourier transform. This makes the frequency f (in Hz or cps) rather than the angular frequency $\omega = 2\pi f$ (in rad s^{-1}) the primary frequency parameter. This convention was advocated, among others, by R. B. Blackman & J. W. Tukey, *The Measurement of Power Spectra*, Dover 1958, and by R. N. Bracewell, *The Fourier Transform and its Applications*, McGraw-Hill 1965, because it makes Fourier and Laplace transforms compatible, i.e., in both cases we use the negative exponent for the forward transform. Alternative arguments can be advanced for a more equitable distribution of normalization factors $\sqrt{(1/2\pi)}$, which do for a square wave what the definition used here does for a sine and cosine. There is also the factor $1/N$, which is here bundled with the inverse transform but can also be shared more equitably by both forward and inverse transforms.

Ultimately, some consensus will be reached, just as it will be for keeping either right or left in traffic, a similar problem that has no inherently good or bad solution but would benefit from a globally accepted choice. But forging such a consensus may take a long time, and occasionally there may still be relapses, as when log is used in VBA where ln is meant, see section 1.16. But then, this is the price we pay for using the same concepts in different disciplines, with different purposes and different traditions. (As an analytical chemist I have often marveled at how my own professional tribe has been able to stick with liters, a volume measure that fits neither the cm/g/s nor the m/kg/s system. It has even managed to get the symbol changed to a capital L, presumably in honor of a mythical Dr. Liter (first name Milli?), even though its real etymological root, the Greek litra, denoted a rather ordinary *weight*.)

This short chapter is a mere teaser as far as Fourier transformation is concerned; for more complete coverage the reader should consult entire books devoted to this single topic. We have not even mentioned here the possibility of performing a fully equivalent frequency analysis without imaginary terms, as demonstrated by Hartley in 1942, or the existence of the Hadamard transform, the digital equivalent to Fourier transformation. In short, this chapter should be considered an appetizer rather than a main dish.

Fourier transformation can be used to predict the distortion (convolution) of experimental information by measuring instruments and/or complicating physical phenomena. Conversely, it can contribute to the correction of such distortion (deconvolution). It can also be applied to analyze the frequency components of time-dependent phenomena. Several such applications will be discussed in the next chapter.

5.12 For further reading

An excellent introduction to the discrete Fourier transform is E. O. Brigham's book on *The Fast Fourier Transform*, Prentice Hall 1974, 1997. A classic reference for the (closely related) continuous Fourier transformation is R. N. Bracewell, *The Fourier Transform and its Applications*, McGraw-Hill 1978. For the Hartley transform the reader is referred to Hartley's paper in *Proc. IRE* 30 (1942) 144, or to Bracewell's book *The Hartley Transform*, Oxford University Press, 1986.

Chapter 6

Convolution, deconvolution, and time-frequency analysis

In this chapter we will consider time-dependent signals. In principle these are different from stationary data sets, such as spectra, because *evolving* time has an inherent directionality, at least until the entire signal has been recorded and has thereby become just another set of numbers. We will see the consequences of this in convolution and its undo operation, deconvolution. These techniques will be discussed first as independent methods. Subsequently we will illustrate how they can sometimes be performed more efficiently with the help of Fourier transformation. Finally, we will examine time-frequency analysis or Gabor transformation, a direct application of Fourier transformation.

6.1 Time-dependent filtering

We first consider the well-known example of a so-called RC-filter, the combination of a series resistor and capacitor that has a characteristic rate constant $k = 1/RC$, where R is the resistance of the resistor, typically in Ω (the symbol for Ohms), and C is the capacitance of the capacitor, in F (for Farads). When we pass a stepwise signal change through such a filter, it will respond by exponentially approaching the new steady state. A characteristic property of such a filter is its memory, through the charge stored in its capacitor, which only slowly leaks out through its resistor. Below we will illustrate how we can use a spreadsheet to simulate the behavior of such a filter and, eventually, of much more complicated filters and other signal distortions.

> *Exercise 6.1.1:*
> (1) Start a new spreadsheet, leaving the top 12 rows for graphs, and with column headings for time, input, filter, and output in, say, A15:D15.
> (2) Start time at negative values, e.g., at $t = -20$ in cell A17, then extend the column down to as far in the positive domain as desired, say to $t = 100$ with increments Δt of 1.

(3) Place a signal in the input column, e.g., a unit step starting at $t = 30$ and returning to zero at $t = 65$. Don't worry about such a bland signal: you can soon make it as fancy as your heart desires.

(4) Place a time constant k somewhere at the top of the spreadsheet, say in cell B13, with its label in A13. A value for k between about 0.2 and 0.5 is convenient for the scale and unit step-size used here: if k is too large, there are only a few points that significantly differ from 0; if k is too small, the exponential hardly approaches 0 at $t = -20$.

(5) In the filter column, for non-positive values of time t only (i.e., in C17:C37), calculate the exponential e^{kt}. Fill the rest of the column with zeros.

(6) Place the label norm= in cell C13, and the instruction =SUM(C17:C37) in cell D13.

(7) In cell D37 place the instruction = (B37*$C$37+B36*$C$36+ ... + B18*$C$18+B17*$C$17)/$D$13, where the dots indicate 17 terms of similar form. Copy this instruction down to row 137.

(8) Make another column in which you compute the functions $1-e^{-k(t-\tau_1)}$ and $e^{-k(t-\tau_2)}$, where τ_1 and τ_2 are the times at which the signal jumps from 0 to 1 and from 1 to 0 respectively. In other words, in cell E66 deposit the instruction =1- EXP(-$B$13*(A66-$A$66)) and copy this down to cell E101, where you replace it with =EXP(-$B$13*(A101-$A$101)), and copy that down to row 137.

(9) Plot both the signal (in column B), its filtered form (in column D), and its calculated form (in column E) as a function of time (in column A), and compare with Fig. 6.1.1. The thin vertical lines shown there were drawn separately, and with Smoothed line turned off, in order to avoid the trapezoidal look you get by just connecting successive points, or the rounded corners and overshoot from using interpolating cubic splines.

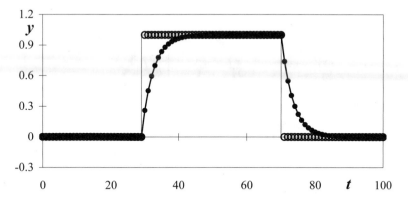

Fig. 6.1.1: The test function (open circles and, idealized, the thin line) and the same after filtering with a single time constant $k = 0.3$ (solid circles). The heavy line shows $1 - e^{-k(t-\tau_1)}$ and $e^{-k(t-\tau_2)}$, where τ_1 and τ_2 are the times at which the signal jumps from 0 to 1 and from 1 to 0 respectively.

(10) Either copy A13:D137 to, say, G13 for a new signal, or just modify the signal in column B. Now you can give your imagination free reign; an example of such a signal and its filtered response is illustrated in Fig. 6.1.2.

(11) Figure 6.1.3 illustrates the response of such a filter to a sinusoidal signal. You will recognize the reduced amplitude as well as the phase shift of the filtered output, the short initial transient before a steady-state harmonic response is reached, and the transient when the signal is terminated abruptly. Play with it.

(12) Also try a test function with added Gaussian noise, as in Fig. 6.1.4. The filter greatly reduces the noise but also distorts the signal, the usual trade-off.

(13) Save the spreadsheet for subsequent use.

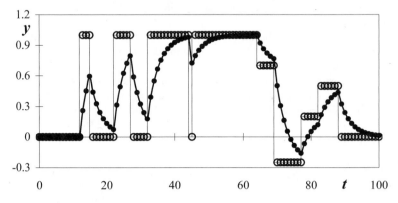

Fig. 6.1.2: A fantasy test function (open circles connected by a thin line) and the same after filtering with the same time constant $k = 0.3$ (solid circles connected by a heavier line).

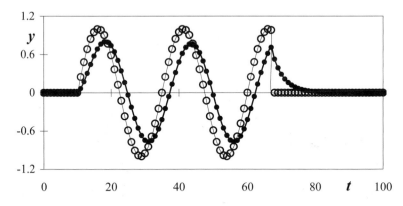

Fig. 6.1.3: A test function with a sinusoid (open circles connected by a thin line) and the same after filtering with the same time constant $k = 0.3$ (solid circles connected by a heavier line).

This simple spreadsheet program indeed mimics the effect of an RC filter. Regardless of the input signal to which it is applied, the RC filter is characterized by its rate constant $k = 1/RC$ or characteristic time RC. Its exponential response to a sudden input change of unit amplitude is called its *transfer function*. An interesting aspect of this simulation is that the filter function as it were looks backwards. The instruction under point (7) of exercise 6.1.1 multiplies the most recently observed signal value by $C$37 (which in this example has the value 1), the previously measured signal value by $C$36 (here 0.74), the point measured before that by $C$35 (only 0.55), and so on. In this manner the filter incorporates the past, but with factors that decrease as the information gets older, i.e., the past is included, but gradually forgotten. The smaller is k, the shorter is the memory, the faster the filter will respond to changes in the input signals, but (as trade-off) the less effective it will be in rejecting noise.

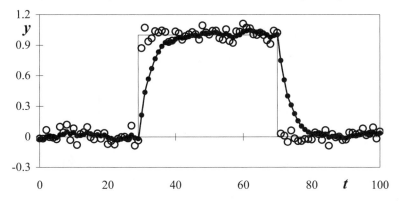

Fig. 6.1.4: A test function (thin line) with added noise (open circles), and the same after filtering with the same time constant $k = 0.3$ (solid circles connected by a heavier line).

This is no accident: an RC filter has a (short) memory, i.e., it stores the applied voltage as a charge, which then slowly leaks out. The asymmetry comes from the directionality (the 'arrow') of time: the past is knowable, whereas the future is not. Just ask your stockbroker: it is easy enough to spot, retrospectively, when the Dow Jones closing index last went through a maximum, but it is another matter entirely to predict correctly when next time it will crest. The filter therefore acts *asymmetrically*, in contrast to, e.g., the least squares smoothing method we encountered in section 3.15.

You can convolve the convolving data, and thereby achieve multiple filtering, just as you would with two successive, independent RC filters, as illustrated in Fig. 6.1.5, although it is usually more efficient to achieve the same in one single operation, by using a higher-order filter.

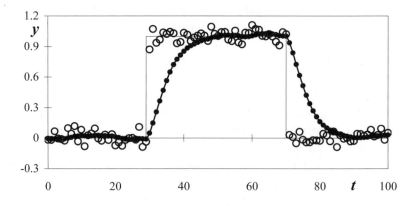

Fig. 6.1.5: The same test function (thin line) with added noise (open circles), filtered by convolution (see Fig. 6.1.4), and filtering that output again by convolution, in both cases with the same time constant $k = 0.3$ (solid circles connected by a heavier line).

If you want to use this method for symmetrical filtering, take the output of the filter (after it has been recorded in its entirety), copy it together with the associated time sequence using Edit ⇒ Paste Special ⇒ Values, invert it with Sort Descending, and run it again through the convolution protocol. This will indeed yield a symmetrically filtered result, with twice the filtering action, see Fig. 6.1.6. Obviously, you can do this only *after* the output has been completed, at which point it has become a fixed sequence of numbers rather than a signal evolving in time.

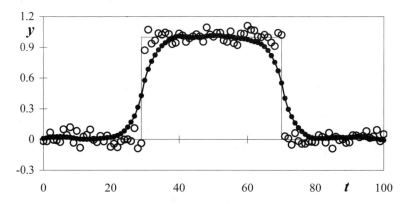

Fig. 6.1.6: The same test function (thin line) with added noise (open circles), after filtering, signal inversion, and filtering again with the same time constant $k = 0.3$ (solid circles connected by a heavier line). Signal inversion is possible only *after* the entire output of the first filter has been observed.

6.2 Convolution of large data sets

The above-described time-dependent filtering, in which we multiply a function term by term by the time-reverse of another function, is called convolution. When the data sets become large, the instructions required for direct spreadsheet convolution can become impracticably large: just imagine typing in 100, 1000, or 10000 product terms. By now you will not be surprised that we can deal with this complication with either a custom function or a custom macro. The macro Convolve simply automates what we have done manually in section 6.1.

Convolution is not only used for filters, but is also a very useful concept in describing how, e.g., an instrument can distort a phenomenon under observation. It is a mixed pleasure to listen on a tinny radio to a superb musical performance, because only distorted music reaches our ears, from which it may be difficult to reconstruct the original sound. When we use low-resolution equipment to observe a spectral feature, the output will reflect the original spectrum as well as the distorting effect of the instrument used. With a low-power microscope, we cannot expect to see fine details in the sample; those details exist, but they are lost to us in the limited resolution or chromatic aberration of our tool. In all the above examples we obtain a filtered, distorted signal; we get the image as if looking into a laughing mirror, as the Hubble telescope actually did before it got its eye glasses. Convolution describes mathematically how the effect of the measurement instrument distorts the input signal to produce the observed output. When we use a filter we distort intentionally, typically in order to reduce noise, whereas in a measurement instrument we usually do not mean to distort, but the effect is nonetheless the same.

The macro Convolve operates exactly as exercise 6.1.1, i.e., it approximates the continuous integral

$$x(t) \otimes y(t) = \int_{-\infty}^{+\infty} x(\tau) \ y(t-\tau) \ d\tau \tag{6.2.1}$$

by its discrete equivalent

$$x(t) \otimes y(t) = \frac{1}{N} \sum_{\tau=1}^{N} x(\tau) \ y(t-\tau) \tag{6.2.2}$$

where x and y are both functions of t, while τ is a 'dummy' variable that does not figure in the final result. Convolution is a sufficiently common operation that it is denoted here by a special symbol, $\otimes$. (In much of the literature the asterisk * is used for that purpose, but we will not do so here because * is easily confused with the multiplication symbol in computer code, including that of Excel and VBA.) The order of convolution makes no difference, i.e., convolution is commutative:

$$x(t) \otimes y(t) = y(t) \otimes x(t) \tag{6.2.3}$$

The macro requires three adjacent input columns, one each for time t, for $x(t)$, and for $y(t)$, and then produces the convolution $x(t) \otimes y(t)$ in the fourth column. The macro includes the inversion of $y(t)$ necessary to compute $y(\tau-t)$, so that both $x(t)$ and $y(t)$ should be listed as starting at $t = 0$ or 1, or at whatever starting number we want to assign. In fact, the macro does not use the time column, which is included here only for the sake of consistency with another macro, ConvolveFT, which we will encounter in section 6.4. If there are no time values, or even if that space is used for some other purpose, highlight it anyway; data or formulas in the first column will neither be used nor erased. The only requirements are that the time increments in the two data sets $x(t)$ and $y(t)$ are constant, and that the two signals $x(t)$ and $y(t)$ are defined at the same values of t.

Our first example will use the data already encountered in Figures 6.1.1 through 6.1.4.

Exercise 6.2.1:
    (1) In a new spreadsheet, reserve the top 12 rows for graphs, and place column headings for time, input, filter, and output in, say, A15:D15.
    (2) In cells A17:A216 deposit $t = 1$ (1) 200.
    (3) In B17:B216 enter a simple test function such as used in exercise 6.1.1.
    (4) In cell A13 write the label k=, and in cell B13 place a numerical value.
    (5) In cell C17 place the instruction =exp(–$B$13*A17), and copy this instruction down to row 216.
    (6) Highlight the area A17:C216, call Convolve, and plot your results.
    (7) Plot the input signal B17:B216 and its convolution D17:D216 vs. A17:A216.

Figure 6.2.1 clearly shows the trade-off involved in filtering. We reduce the effects of high-frequency noise, but at the expense of a sluggish response to signal changes, because the filter also reduces the high-frequency components in the signal that describe its sudden jump. The distinction between 'signal' and 'noise' is usually a subjective one.

Exercise 6.2.1 (continued):
    (8) Replace the input signal by a more fanciful one, perhaps resembling that in Fig. 6.1.2 or 6.1.3, highlight A17:C216, set the noise amplitude to zero, and call Convolve. You may have to reduce the filter time constant k in order to preserve some semblance of fidelity.
    (9) Reset the noise amplitude, and again call the macro. Save the spreadsheet. Fig. 6.2.2 illustrates what you may obtain.

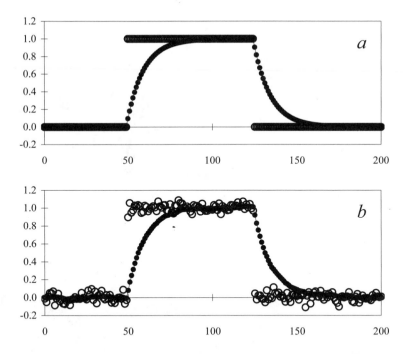

Fig. 6.2.1: The result of convolving a step function $x(t)$ with an exponential decay $y(t) = \exp[-kt]$ using the macro Convolve. The input function $x(t)$ is shown as open circles, and $x(t) \otimes \exp[-kt]$ as smaller solid points connected by line segments. In these examples $k = 0.1$. In panel (b) we use the same input as in panel (a) plus some Gaussian noise of standard deviation 0.04.

Again the trade-off is obvious: if k is too small, the signal is distorted beyond recognition; if k is chosen too large, the filter is inefficient in reducing noise. The best (proactive rather than after-the-fact) solution is to reduce the noise at its source, and to shield all noise-sensitive parts of the signal path. Filtering is only the next-best option; in that case collect data as closely spaced as possible for maximum noise rejection at small k.

Exercise 6.2.2 illustrates using this macro for a transient such as might be encountered in the study of short-lived fluorescence. We will assume that a laser pulse with a reproducible and known intensity-time profile is used to excite molecules to excited states, from which they decay soon thereafter by fluorescence. For the time course of laser light emission we take a skewed Gaussian (a rather arbitrary function picked here merely because it starts rather quickly and decays slowly), and we describe the fluorescent decay by a first-order rate process with rate constant k. Whereas with an RC filter the distortion is usually intentional (in order to remove noise), here it is the undesirable consequence of the unavoidably finite rise and fall times of the laser pulse, and its non-zero width.

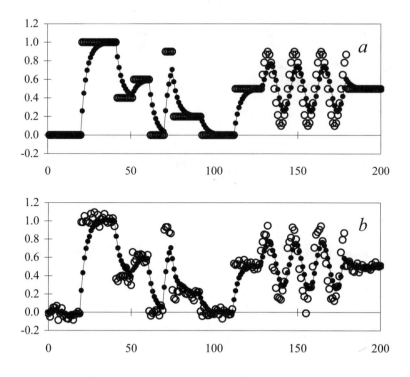

Fig. 6.2.2: Some results of convolving a function $x(t)$ with an exponential decay $y(t) = \exp[-kt]$ using the macro Convolve, with $k = 0.5$. In (*a*) the input function is a fanciful set of steps followed by a sinewave, and in (*b*) the same with added Gaussian noise with a standard deviation of 0.04. The input function $x(t)$ is shown as open circles, and $x(t) \otimes \exp[-kt]$ as smaller solid points connected by line segments.

Exercise 6.2.2:

(1) In a new spreadsheet, reserve the top 12 rows for graphs, and place column headings for time, input, filter, and output in, say, A15:D15.

(2) Start time at $t = 0$ in cell A17, then extend the column down to as far in the positive domain as desired, say to $t = 300$ with increments Δt of 1.

(3) Fill a top section of column B, say B17:B46, with zeros. In B47 then place a formula for the undistorted decay, such as =EXP(-$B$13*(A47-$A$47)), where B13 contains a value for the rate constant k, e.g., 0.03. Copy this instruction all the way down the column.

(4) In cell C17 deposit =IF(1+(A17-$D$13)/$D$14>0,EXP(-1*(LN(1+(A17-$D$13)/$D$14))^2),0), where D13 and D14 contain values for the filter parameters t_f and a_f of $y = \exp(-\{\ln[1+(t-t_f)/a_f]\}^2)$ for $1+(t-t_f)/a_f > 0$, and otherwise $y = 0$. In the example of Fig. 6.2.3 we have used $t_f = 10$ and $a_f = 7$.

(5) Call Convolve, then plot the functions in columns B, C, and D vs. time *t* in column A. Save your result, and compare it with Fig. 6.2.3.

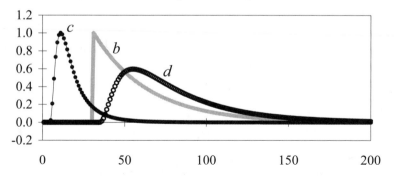

Fig. 6.2.3: The exponential decay of simulated fluorescence, defined by a first-order rate constant $k = 0.03$, as convolved by an excitation light pulse with finite rise and decay times. Wide gray curve (labeled *b* since it displays the contents of column B): the theoretical, exponential decay for a delta-function as excitation source, shown here with a delay for visual clarity. Small solid circles connected by thin curve (labeled *c*): an assumed profile of the light pulse, with finite rise and fall times. Open circles (labeled *d*): the emission signal that would result for this combination of fluorescence and excitation.

Note that the macro simply uses the resulting numbers, and will work equally well if one uses different fluorescent decay kinetics and an arbitrary shape for the laser pulse profile, such as one actually measured for a particular light source.

As our third example we will use the convolution macro to illustrate the effect of, say, limited optical resolution on spectral peaks, or of instrumental peak broadening on a chromatogram. For the sake of simplicity we will again assume simple forms, in this case Gaussians for both the undistorted peaks and for the broadening effect. The macro does not use the generating equations, only the resulting numbers, and arbitrary peak shapes and broadening functions will therefore work equally well.

Exercise 6.2.3:

(1) In yet another spreadsheet, again reserve the area A1:E16 for graphs, place the labels as1=, bs1=, cs1=, as2=, bs2=, cs2=, as3=, bs3=, cs3=, as4=, bs4=, cs4=, at=, bt=, ct= in cells F2:F16. Also place column headings for time, *s*, *t*, and *r* in, say, cells A20:D20.

(2) Start time at $t = 1$ in cell A22, then with increments Δt of 1 extend the column as far down as desired, say to A321 where $t = 300$.

(3) In column B generate a fantasy spectrum or chromatogram consisting of four Gaussian peaks, of different widths, and possibly overlapping or nearly so, using instructions such as, in cell B22, `=$G$2*EXP(-0.5*((A22-$G$4)/$G$3)^2)+ ... +$G$11*EXP(-0.5*((A22-$G$13)/$G$12)^2)`.

(4) Likewise, in column C, deposit the instruction for a single Gaussian representing the signal-distorting transfer function t with the parameters b_t and c_t, such as =$G$14*EXP(-0.5*((A22-$G$16)/$G$15)^2) in cell C22.

(5) Convolve the four-Gaussian signal s with the single-Gaussian function t, and use the area A1:F16 to plot the results, which might resemble Fig. 6.2.4. Save the spreadsheet. Unless you remove this feature from its code, the custom macro Convolve will ignore a_t and will, instead, normalize t to unit average value.

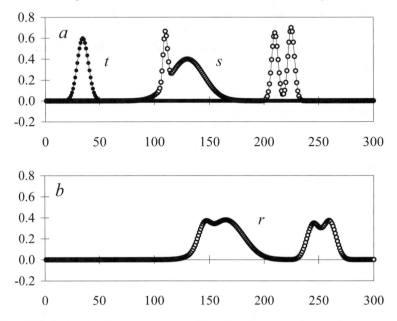

Fig. 6.2.4: A simulated spectrum s containing four Gaussians (connected open circles in panel a) calculated with the coefficients $a_{s1} = 0.5$, $b_{s1} = 2$, $c_{s1} = 110$, $a_{s2} = 0.4$, $b_{s2} = 15$, $c_{s2} = 130$, $a_{s3} = 0.65$, $b_{s3} = 3$, $c_{s3} = 210$, $a_{s4} = 0.7$, $b_{s4} = 3$, and $c_{s4} = 225$. The transfer function t (connected small solid circles in the same panel) with $a_t = 0.6$, $b_t = 5$, $c_t = 35$ is also displayed in panel a. The convolution r of s and t is shown in panel b, in which the peaks are shifted by the amount of c_t, as well as rounded.

We see that the convolved spectral peaks are broader (as is most noticeable with the narrower peaks) and less tall (because the convolution does not change their integrated areas), so that adjacent peaks tend to coalesce. The convolved spectrum is shifted with respect to the original spectrum by the amount of c_t. Therefore, make sure that there is enough space at the end of the signal to accommodate such a shift, otherwise just add zeros to the signal to provide that space. You can add any number of dummy data points: Convolve needs equidistant signals $x(t)$ and $y(t)$ (because these two functions will be sliding past each other), but requires neither symmetry, periodicity, nor a specific number of data points.

6.3 *Unfiltering*

Say that we have filtered a signal with an RC filter, and want to undo that operation. Just as we can exponentiate to counteract taking a (natural) logarithm, or integrate to undo differentiation, we can use the spreadsheet to *un*filter the data, as illustrated in exercise 6.3.1. The technical term for the undo operation of convolution is *deconvolution*. Beware: this term is sometimes misused to mean *decomposition* or *resolution*, i.e., the resolution of (often simply additive) constituent components, a much more trivial problem discussed in, e.g., section 4.6.

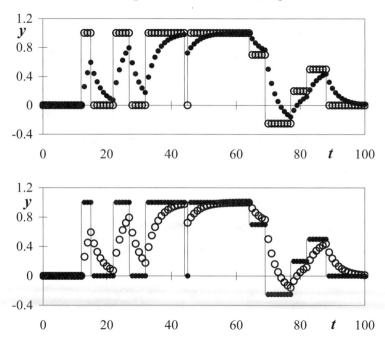

Fig. 6.3.1: Top: the original input signal, before filtering, (open circles) and its filtered output (solid circles), as reproduced from Fig. 6.1.2. Bottom: using the filtered signal as input (open circles), the unfilter operation now recovers the original signal (solid circles).

Exercise 6.3.1:

(1) Start a new spreadsheet, or add on to the spreadsheet of exercise 6.1.1.

(2) Make the following new columns (which, for ease of specifying the instructions, we will here assume to be columns H through L), leaving the top 12 rows for graphs, and with column headings for time, input, filter, output1, and output2.

(3) Also place the labels k= and norm= in cells H13 and J13 respectively, and repeat the earlier-used *k*-value, 0.3, in cell I13.

(4) For the time column, copy the earlier values: *t* = –20 (1) 100. For input, copy the data from column D to column I with, e.g., =D17 in cell I17.

(5) In cell J17 place the instruction =EXP($I$13*H17), and copy this filter function down to row 37.

(6) In cell K13 enter =SUM(J17:J37).

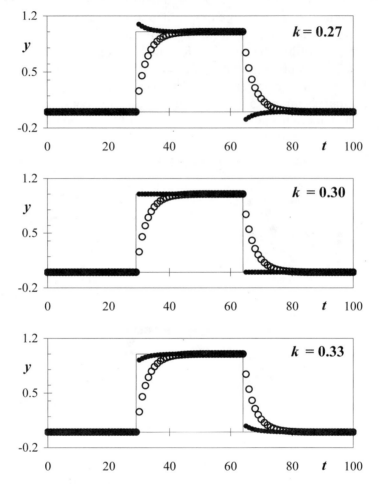

Fig. 6.3.2: Middle panel: when the filter rate constant in unfiltering is the same as that in filtering ($k = 0.30$ in this example), the original signal is recovered. Top and bottom: when a different k-value is used for filtering and unfiltering, distortion occurs, as shown here in the form of overshoot or undershoot.

(7) The expression for the deconvolution is slightly different from that for convolution. In cell K37 (to take a place equivalent to that of cell D37 in exercise 6.1.1) deposit the instruction =I37-(K36*$J$36+K35*$J$35+K34*$J$34+K33*$J$33+K32*$J$32+K31*$J$31+K30*$J$30+K29*$J$29+K28*$J$28+K27*$J$27+K26*$J$26+K25*$J$25+K24*$J$24+K23*$J$23+K22*$J$22+K21*$J$21+K20*$J$20+K19*$J$19+K18*$J$18+K17*$J$17), and in cell L37 place =K37*$K$13. Copy these instructions all the way down to row 137.

(8) Plot L17:L137 vs. H17:H137. You have now unfiltered the original signal, as illustrated in Fig. 6.1.1.

(9) Check the residuals, the differences between corresponding values in columns K and B.

(10) Try the same spreadsheet for other input functions, by changing the data in column B to signals such as used in Figs. 6.1.2 and 6.1.3.

(11) If we use a different k-value in the unfiltering operation from the one used for filtering, we will not recover the original input signal. This is illustrated in Fig. 6.3.2 for the simple square pulse of Fig. 6.1.1. Try it for yourself.

Again we can use a custom macro, Deconvolve, to ease our work.

The few examples given so far suggest that we can always undo the effects of filtering or distortion, but that is, unfortunately, too good to be true. The following exercises illustrate some of the limits involved.

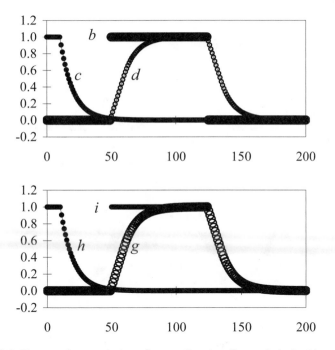

Fig. 6.3.3: Top panel: convolution of a step function (large circles) with an exponential filter function preceded by a constant level (connected small solid circles). Bottom panel: deconvolution of the same recovers the original step function (small circles) without problems. The labels refer to the spreadsheet columns used.

Exercise 6.3.2:

(1) Take the spreadsheet used in exercise 6.1.1, with a single step function as its signal in column B, and advance the function representing the RC filter in column C to start at $t = 10$ rather than at the very beginning of the data set, at $t = 1$, with the filter function set at 0 for $t < 10$.

(2) Set up columns F, G, and H to copy the data in columns A, D, and C respectively, so that convolution of the data in columns A through C can readily be followed by deconvolution of the data in columns F through H.

(3) Apply Convolve to the data in block A17:C217, then Deconvolve those in block F17:H217. You will find that the result of the deconvolution yields a wildly oscillating signal that bears little resemblance to the original.

(4) In order to see more clearly what happens, set the filter function for $t < 10$ to 1, and repeat the convolution and deconvolution. As you can see in Fig. 6.3.3, there is no problem here.

(5) Now give the filter function a slightly positive slope over the first few points, e.g., by giving it the values 0.50 (0.05) 1.00 for $t = 1$ (1) 10. Figure 6.3.4 illustrates the result, which shows the onset of instability in the form of a damped oscillation. If we increase the initial slope, the problem worsens, and is fully out of control (i.e., the oscillation is no longer damped) with initial values for the filter function of, e.g., 0 (0.1) 1 for $t = 1$ (1) 10. As you already saw, it is even worse if one steps suddenly from 0 to 1 at $t = 10$.

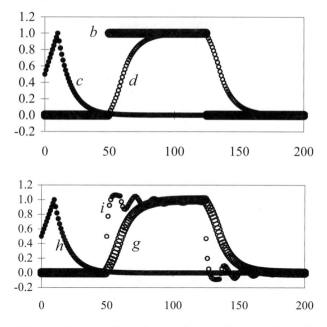

Fig. 6.3.4: Top panel: convolution of a step function (large circles) with an exponential filter function preceded by an initial rise (connected small solid circles). Bottom panel: deconvolution of the same recovers the original step function with a (damped) oscillation (small circles). The labels refer to the spreadsheet columns.

Apparently the deconvolution works reliably only when the transfer function has nowhere a positive time derivative, a requirement that often cannot be met, see e.g., Figs. 6.2.3 and 6.2.4. We therefore look for alternative methods to perform the deconvolution in those (many) cases in which direct deconvolution does not work.

6.4 Convolution by Fourier transformation

A different route to convolution and deconvolution can be based on Fourier transformation. One reason to consider such an alternative approach is algorithmic efficiency. For two 1000-point functions the direct method requires 1000^2 or 10^6 multiplications, whereas a Fourier transformation uses a number of operations of the order of $N \log_2 N$ rather than N^2. Since $2^{10} = 1024$, or $\log_2 1000 \approx \log_2 1024 = 10$, $1000 \log_2 1000$ is approximately 10^4. Even though convolution or deconvolution requires three Fourier transformations plus a complex multiplication or division, this still works out as much faster for sufficiently large data sets.

Parenthetically, when computers were slow, efficiency used to be an important problem. Now that the beast on your bench may work at or above 1 GHz, it may even get away with a rather inefficient method during the time it takes you to blink an eye. Computational efficiency still matters with large data sets, especially those in multidimensional arrays, which we will not consider here, as in general their handling should not be attempted on a spreadsheet. Because of their transparency, spreadsheets are great for learning and exploring the principles of the various methods, and for their applications to relatively small data sets, but they are often sub-optimal for collections of, say, more than a few thousand data points.

A second reason to consider Fourier transformation is that we already saw that direct deconvolution can lead to unstable results, and can not be used for curves such as those of Figs. 6.2.3 and 6.2.4. Finally, as we will see in section 6.6, use of Fourier transformation can make sophisticated noise-rejection methods readily available.

A basic theorem states that the Fourier transform of the convolution of two continuous functions $x(t)$ and $y(t)$ is equal to the product of the Fourier transforms of those functions. In other words, when

$$z(t) = x(t) \otimes y(t) = \int_{-\infty}^{+\infty} x(\tau)\ y(t-\tau)\ d\tau \qquad (6.4.1)$$

where t is time, wavelength, or whatever the relevant parameter is, and τ is a 'dummy variable', then

$$Z(f) = X(f) \times Y(f) \qquad (6.4.2)$$

where $X(f)$, $Y(f)$, and $Z(f)$ are the Fourier transforms of $x(t)$, $y(t)$, and $z(t)$ respectively, and f is the reciprocal of t. Applied to instrumental distortion, we can symbolically express the observed *result* *r* in terms of the original input signal *s* and the *transfer function* *t* (here printed in bold to avoid confusion of, e.g., *s* with standard deviation *s*, *t* with time *t*) as

$$r = s \otimes t \qquad (6.4.3)$$

where *r*, *s*, and *t* are functions. Upon Fourier transformation this yields

$$R = S \times T \qquad (6.4.4)$$

so that we can compute *r* by Fourier transformation of *s* to *S*, and *t* to *T*, multiply *S* and *T* to form *R*, whereupon inverse Fourier transformation of *R* yields *r*. Apart from the fact that we are dealing here with functions rather than with single numbers, the procedure is analogous to computing $a = b^c$ by taking logarithms to obtain $\ln a = c \times \ln b$, performing the multiplication, and taking the antilog of $\ln a$ to find *a*. In both cases, a transformation (Fourier transformation or taking logarithms) allows us to reduce a more complicated mathematical operation (convolution or exponentiation) to a multiplication.

A note on nomenclature: it is difficult to find a set of symbols that is convenient across many different disciplines. For example, in electronics, the 'true' signal might be called the *i*nput signal *i*, and the filtered result the *o*utput *o*. In optics, the reverse might make sense: to consider the *o*bject *o* the true signal, the *i*mage *i* its distorted response.

In exercises 6.4.1 and 6.4.2 we will use Fourier transformation to calculate the convolution already encountered in exercise 6.2.3.

Exercise 6.4.1:

(1) Use the spreadsheet of exercise 6.2.2. Extend the times in column A to 255, similarly extend the computations in columns B and C, then recalculate the data in column D, all in order to facilitate Fourier transformation.

(2) In new columns copy the data from columns A (for time) and B (for input), highlight them plus a third blank column (for the complex input, to be left blank), and call the macro ForwardFT. Label the resulting columns (containing the Fourier-transformed input) freq, a, and b.

(3) In a separate cell compute the average of the filter data, for which you can use the convenient function =AVERAGE().

(4) Again copy the column for time (from column A), and next to it calculate the filter value (from column C) divided by its just-computed average. Highlight these two new columns, together with an adjacent blank column, and again call ForwardFT. Label the resulting columns (with the Fourier-transformed filter) freq, c, and d respectively.

(5) For the multiplication of the Fourier transforms use $(a+jb) \times (c+jd) = (ac-bd) + j(bc+ad)$. In yet another column copy the frequency (from one of the earlier columns labeled freq), and in the next columns calculate $(ac-bd)$ and $(bc+ad)$ respectively, using values from the columns labeled a, b, c, and d. This yields the complex multiplication.

(6) Highlight the just-made three columns, call InverseFT, and plot your result. It should be (within round-off errors) the same as obtained with Convolve, see curve *d* in Fig. 6.2.3.

The above illustrates the principle of the method, but uses quite some time, effort, and spreadsheet space. It is far simpler to use the custom macro ConvolveFT, which incorporates the forward and inverse Fourier transformations, scales the filter (by dividing it by its average value), and performs the complex multiplications. Moreover, by limiting the input to real functions, it has an even smaller spreadsheet 'footprint' than a single Fourier transformation macro. Below we will illustrate its use by applying it to the same problem.

Exercise 6.4.1 (continued):
(7) Select another three columns in which you copy the data from columns A (time), B (input), and C (filter).
(8) Highlight these three columns, call ConvolveFT, and bingo, you again find the convolved result.

Now that we have reduced the process to invoking a single macro, it is easy to verify that convolution is indeed commutative, see (6.2.3):

Exercise 6.4.1 (continued):
(9) Move the output column to keep it for subsequent comparison. You can either cut and paste it into the adjacent column, or just insert a blank column between it and the copied filter function.
(10) Reverse the order of the columns in which you copied data from columns B (input) and C (filter).
(11) Highlight the three last columns, call ConvolveFT, and compare your latest result with the earlier one you just moved. There should be no significant differences, because convolution is indeed commutative.

Here is another application.

Exercise 6.4.2:
(1) Starting with cell A3 of column A in a new spreadsheet, enter 1 (1) 2048.
(2) In row M2:T2 enter the amplitudes 0.7, in row M3:T3 the standard deviations 100, 50, 30, 20, 10, 5, 3, 2, and 1, and in row M4:T4 the center values 500, 1050, 1370, 1590, 1740, 1840, 1910, 1970, and 2010.
(3) In cell B3 enter the instruction $=\$M\$2*EXP(-0.5*((A56-\$M\$4)/\$M\$3)^2)+$, copy the part beyond the equal sign, paste it back eight times in the instruction, and remove the final plus sign. Then change the M in $\$M\$3$, $\$M\$4$, and $\$M\$5$ in the second exponential into an N to make $\$N\$3$, $\$N\$4$, and $\$N\$5$, in the third into an O to get $\$O\$3$, $\$O\$4$, and $\$O\$5$, etc.
(4) Click on the cell handle to copy this instruction all the way down to row 2048. Then plot B3:B2050 vs. A3:A2050. There is nothing special about this set, other than that it has nine essentially baseline-separated Gaussian peaks of varying widths. You can of course make your own signal instead, or use the data from Fig. 3.15.1, which contains four Lorentzians.

(5) In cell D1 place the value 0.1, and in cell C3 deposit the instruction `=EXP(-0.5*((A3)/$D$1)^2)+EXP(-0.5*((A3-2048)/$D$1)^2)`. Copy this instruction down to row 2048 as well. This is a *single* Gaussian peak centered at zero, and will represent our transfer function. Again, feel free to use another function instead.

(6) Highlight A3:C2050, and call the custom macro Convolve. Plot the result, which has appeared in D3:D2050, vs. A3:A2050. It should resemble Fig. 6.4.2*a*.

(7) Repeat this with different values in D1, such as 0.01, 0.001, and 0.0001, and plot the resulting curves, as in Fig. 6.4.2*b,c,d*.

(8) Save this spreadsheet for use in exercise 6.5.2.

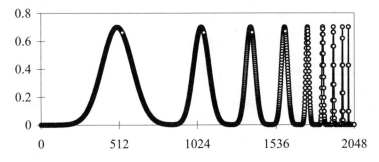

Fig. 6.4.1: The test function used in exercise 6.4.2. The open circles show the individual data points, the lines merely connect adjacent points.

Figure 6.4.2 illustrates how measurement instruments or other sources of broadening can distort a signal. Here we have assumed a Gaussian transfer function, but its precise form is less important than its characteristic width. We see that convolution can even wash out some of its qualitative features. In Fig. 6.4.2*c* the rightmost peak has almost disappeared, while Fig. 6.4.2*d* distorts all peaks and hides the narrower ones in a single broad shoulder.

Such broadening is not restricted to instruments. For example, an atomic absorption line has an inherent width governed by the Heisenberg uncertainty, because the product of the energy difference ΔE between the two states, and the sum of the reciprocals of their life times Δt, cannot be smaller than $h/2\pi$, where h is the Planck constant. This yields a Lorentzian line shape rather than the infinitely narrow line one might otherwise expect for a quantum transition.

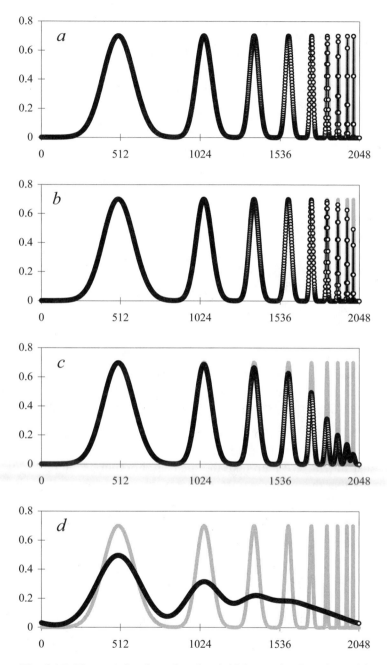

Fig. 6.4.2: The convoluted test function (which contains Gaussians with standard deviations ranging from 100 to 1) for (from *a* to *d*) increasingly broad transfer functions, with standard deviations of 0.1, 1, 10, and 100 respectively. The gray line in each panel repeats the test function.

However, the thermal motion of gaseous atoms with respect to the 'laboratory frame' (containing the light source and the detector) causes line broadening, mathematically described as the convolution of the Lorentzian line with a Gaussian distribution due to diffusional motion (W. Voigt, *Ann. Phys.* 311 (1901) 459). High gas pressure may result in further, so-called collisional broadening.

The same applies to molecular spectra, which typically show rotational fine structure in the gas phase. In condensed phases such rotational fine structure is often blurred as the result of interactions with neighboring molecules. The effects of such interactions must, again, be described in terms of convolutions.

6.5 Deconvolution by Fourier transformation

While convolution is useful in understanding instrumental distortion and in instrument design, instrument *users* are often more interested in correcting for such distortion. They may want to compensate for a finite laser pulse width in order to determine the rate constant k of a fast fluorescence decay (i.e., recover curve b from the measured curve d in Fig. 6.2.3), or reconstruct an actual spectrum by correcting it for the distortion of the nonzero slit width of their instrument (as in going from curve r to curve s in Fig. 6.2.4). Assuming that the *t*ransfer function t is both reproducible and known, deconvolution *in principle* allows reconstruction of the original, distortion-free signal s from its corrupted *r*esponse r.

Deconvolution based on Fourier transformation works as follows. Using an appropriate input signal, we first determine the transfer function t of the instrument. We then take the measured output of interest, r, which (assuming that the instrumental parameters have not changed) is given by $r = s \otimes t$, see (6.2.2), where s is the sought, undistorted signal. Now that we know both r and t, we want to find s. Fourier transformation of $r = s \otimes t$ yields $R = S \times T$, from which we obtain

$$S = R / T \tag{6.5.1}$$

or, in the time domain,

$$s = r \oslash t \tag{6.5.2}$$

where $\oslash$ denotes deconvolution, the inverse operation of convolution $\otimes$. The symbol $\oslash$ suggests the corresponding Fourier-domain division ($/$) just as $\otimes$ implies multiplication ($\times$) of the Fourier transforms. Consequently we transform r to R, and t to T, then calculate $S = R / T$, and inverse transform the latter to find s. In exercises 6.5.1 and 6.5.2 we will illustrate this alternative method of deconvolution.

Finally we note that convolution, like multiplication, is always commutative: $a \times b = b \times a$ and $a \otimes b = b \otimes a$, but that deconvolution, like division, is not: $a \diagup b \neq b \diagup a$ and, likewise, $a \oslash b \neq b \oslash a$.

Exercise 6.5.1:

(1) Modify, or copy and then modify, spreadsheet exercise 6.4.1 as follows.

(2) Instead of column B, as instructed under exercise 6.4.1 under point (2), copy the data in column D (for output), then proceed as before by highlighting them plus a third blank column, and by calling ForwardFT. Label the resulting columns (containing the Fourier-transformed output) freq, a, and b.

(3) Instead of multiplying the Fourier-transformed input and filter signal, we now divide the Fourier-transformed output and filter signal. Because they are both complex quantities, we have $(a+jb)/(c+jd) = (a+jb)(c-jd)/(c^2+d^2) = (ac+bd) /(c^2+d^2)+j(bc-ad)/(c^2+d^2)$.

(4) Therefore, in the columns where, according to the instructions in exercise 6.4.1 under point (5), you had earlier calculated $(ac-bd)$, now compute $(ac+bd)/ (c^2+d^2)$. Likewise, in the next column, instead of $(bc+ad)$, now compute $(bc-ad)/ (c^2+d^2)$.

(5) Proceed as before by highlighting these three columns (one for frequency, and two containing the real and imaginary parts of the quotient), call InverseFT, and compare your result with the original signal in column B.

(6) Instead of the instructions under point (7) of exercise 4.5.1, use copies of the data from columns A (time), D (output), and C (filter), i.e., replace the input from column B by the output from column D. Then highlight them, and call DeconvolveFT. (You will encounter two input boxes, one offering to apply an adjustable von Hann/Tuckey window and, if you decline that, a second to zero out high frequencies. Deny both by approving the default 0, i.e., by clicking on OK or pressing Enter.) DeconvolveFT condenses all this into a single macro operation.

Exercise 6.5.2:

(1) Use the spreadsheet of exercise 6.2.2. Extend the times in column A to 255, similarly extend the computations in columns B and C, then recalculate the data in column D, all in order to facilitate Fourier transformation.

(2) In new columns copy the data from columns A (for time) and D (for output), highlight them plus a third blank column, and call ForwardFT. Label the resulting columns (containing the Fourier-transformed output) freq, a, and b.

(3) Calculate the average of the filter function with =AVERAGE().

(4) Again copy the column for time (from column A), and next to it calculate the filter value (from column C) divided by the just-computed average.

(5) Highlight these two new columns, together with a blank column, and again call ForwardFT. Label the resulting columns (with the Fourier-transformed filter) freq, c, and d respectively.

(6) Now that you have Fourier-transformed both the distorted output signal and the filter, we need to divide the two. Since they are both complex quantities, we have $(a+jb)/(c+jd) = (a+jb)(c-jd)/(c^2+d^2) = (ac+bd)/(c^2+d^2)+j(bc-ad)/(c^2+d^2)$.

(7) In yet another column copy the frequency (from one of the columns labeled freq), in the next columns calculate the complex division $(ac+bd)/(c^2+d^2)$ and $(bc-ad)/(c^2+d^2)$ respectively, using values from the columns labeled a through d.

(8) All that still remains to be done is the inverse Fourier transformation. Highlight the just-made three columns, call InverseFT, and plot your result. You should recover the original exponential with very little distortion as the real result, together with a negligible imaginary result.

Exercise 6.5.3:

(1) We continue with the spreadsheet of exercise 6.4.2. In column E copy column A (i.e., in E3 place the instruction =A3 and copy this down to row 2050), and in columns F and G copy columns D and C respectively.

(2) Highlight E3:G2050, call the custom macro DeconvolveFT, and plot the result, i.e., H3:H2050 vs. either E3:E2050 or A3:A2050. Do this for the various transfer functions used in exercise 6.4.1. If there you obtained data resembling Fig. 6.4.2, you will now find results similar to those in Fig. 6.5.1.

Comparison of Fig. 6.5.1 with Figs. 6.4.1 and 6.4.2 shows that deconvolution has almost completely restored the original test function in panel *b*, and recovered sizable parts of the narrower peaks in panel *c*. However, in Fig. 6.5.1*d* all peaks but the first remain strongly distorted. It looks as if deconvolution, even in the complete absence of noise, cannot recover the information blurred by the earlier convolution when the characteristic width (expressed, e.g., as its standard deviation) of the convolving and deconvolving function is larger by about an order of magnitude than that of the feature involved.

Admittedly, it is a tall order to want to recover peaks with a standard deviation of 1 when they were first convolved with a 100 times broader peak, as in the case of Fig. 6.5.1*d*. Still, since exercise 6.5.3 deals with noise-free, *synthetic* data, there must be a reason why recovery of the original signal is so poor. Exercise 6.5.4 indicates where the shoe pinches.

Exercise 6.5.4:

(1) It is easiest to add to the spreadsheet of exercise 6.4.2. Repeat columns for #, signal, and transfer function, and in them deposit instructions that copy the data in columns A through C, for a transfer function with a standard deviation of 100. The only difference is that, in the third column, instead of an instruction such as =B10 in the tenth row you now use =(Int(16*B10)/16. This will make the transfer function exactly expressible in terms of binary numbers. (There is nothing special about the number 16. Other integer powers of 2 work equally well, as does the simple rectangular transfer function.)

(2) Call ConvolveFT, and plot your result. The curve you get is not very much different from what you found in Fig. 6.4.2*d*.

(3) Now use three more columns, one to copy time or #, the next to copy the result you just found, the third to copy the binarized transfer function.

(4) Call DeconvolveFT, and enter the result in the graph made under point (2). Now your result is quite different from that in Fig. 6.5.1*d*, compare Fig. 6.5.2. Apparently, the distortion is primarily associated with truncation errors in the transfer function *t*. Note that deconvolution does not commutate, but treats *r* and *t* differently.

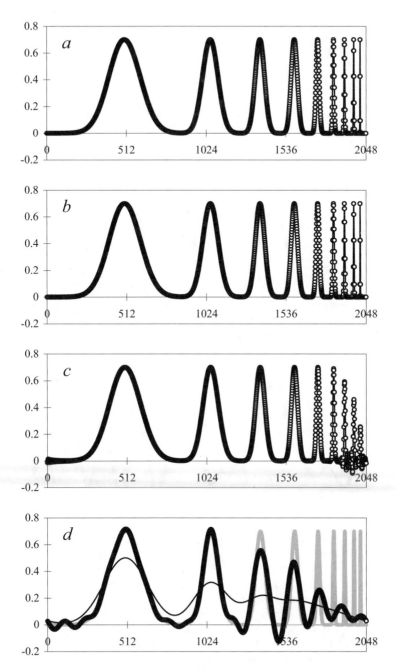

Fig. 6.5.1: The deconvolved test function for (from *a* to *d*) increasingly broad transfer functions, with standard deviations of (*a*) 0.1, (*b*) 1, (*c*) 10, and (*d*) 100. The thick gray line in panel *d* repeats the test function; the thin black line in *d* is a reminder of how convolution had distorted it.

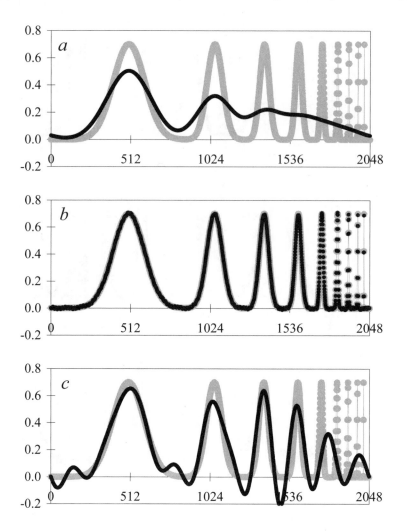

Fig. 6.5.2: Using a binarized transfer function allows total recovery, even when the transfer function has a standard deviation of 100. (*a*) The original function (gray), and its convolution (thin black curve) with a binarized transfer function (as shown here) is no different from that obtained with a non-binarized one, as shown in Fig. 6.4.2*d* for otherwise identical conditions. (*b*) Deconvolution with the same (binarized) transfer function (black points) recovers the original data (gray). (c) Normal convolution followed by deconvolution with the binarized transfer function (shown here as black points) yields results that (because of the mismatch in *t*) are slightly worse than those shown in Fig. 6.5.1*d*. (The original data are again shown in gray.) The same applies when binarization is used only in the convolution step, or when different binarizations are used. Clearly, identical binarization must be used for both convolution and deconvolution.

While one could exploit what we have just found in Fig. 6.5.2 for cryptographic encoding and decoding, we cannot use it in experimental science because, unlike the situation in a synthetic example, in data analysis we seldom have sufficient control over the distorting process. Moreover, experimental data contain irreproducible noise far in excess of truncation noise.

For all practical purposes we therefore have to live with the rather unsatisfactory results of Fig. 6.5.1. These are summarized in table 6.5.1, which lists the standard deviations s_s of the nine Gaussian peaks in Fig. 6.4.1, and the corresponding s_t values of the four Gaussians used to represent the transfer function in the convolutions and subsequent deconvolutions in Fig. 6.5.1a-d. Practical signal recovery by Fourier transform deconvolution of noise-free signals is possible only for signals with characteristic widths not much smaller than that of the distorting transfer function t.

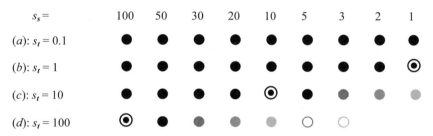

$s_s =$	100	50	30	20	10	5	3	2	1
(a): $s_t = 0.1$	●	●	●	●	●	●	●	●	●
(b): $s_t = 1$	●	●	●	●	●	●	●	●	◉
(c): $s_t = 10$	●	●	●	●	◉	●	●	●	●
(d): $s_t = 100$	◉	●	●	●	●	○	○		

Table 6.5.1: A semi-graphical display of signal recovery after Fourier transform convolution and deconvolution, as a function of the standard deviations s_s of the Gaussian signal peaks and s_t of the equally Gaussian transfer function. Quality of recovery is indicated crudely in the style of *Consumer Reports*, with solid black circles indicating excellent recovery. Encircled solid circles ◉ identify where $s_t = s_s$.

Now for the bad news. Convolution is an integration and, as such, attenuates noise: smoothing blurs many details. On the other hand its inverse operation, deconvolution, is akin to a differentiation, and tends to accentuate noise. We already saw the extreme sensitivity of the method to truncation errors in t, and below we will illustrate the effect of Gaussian noise added to r. Similar effects are observed by truncating or rounding the data for r to a limited number of digits, similar to what happens when analog signals are digitized. Truncation and rounding follow a triangular rather than a Gaussian distribution, with well-defined limits, but that detail is of minor importance here.

For noisy signals, deconvolution usually trades lower signal distortion for much enhanced noise. That may not be a problem if the enhanced noise can be removed subsequently, e.g., by fitting the data to a mathematical model expression, as was done by Hüfner & Wertheim, *Phys. Revs.* B11 (1975) 678. Otherwise we may have to use filtering to reduce the noise, as illustrated in exercise 6.5.5.

Exercise 6.5.5:

(1) This will be a fairly wide spreadsheet, which (including a few empty 'spacer' columns) will take up more than a full alphabet. It is therefore best to start with a fresh sheet. In column A, under the heading #, deposit the numbers 0 (1) 2047.

(2) In column B, labeled s, generate the function *s*, or copy it from another worksheet. Reminder: to copy a value from, say, cell B2 of Sheet1 to cell C3 of Sheet2 in the same workbook, place in cell C3 of Sheet2 the instruction =Sheet1!B2. To copy from Book1 Sheet1 cell B2 to Book2 Sheet2 cell C3 use =' [Book1]Sheet1' !B2 in the receiving cell.

(3) In column C generate or copy a transfer function *t*.

(4) Highlight the data in these three columns, and call ConvolveFT. This will yield *r* in column D.

(5) In column F generate Gaussian (or other) noise, e.g., with T̲ools ⇒ D̲ata Analysis ⇒ Random Number Generation.

(6) In column H copy the numbers from column A. In column I copy *r* from column D, and add to it a ('noise amplitude') multiplier times noise from column F. Figure 6.5.3*a* illustrates what you would get if you used for input the same data as shown in Fig. 6.4.2*c*. plus noise with a standard deviation ('noise amplitude') of 0.1. We now have set up the problem.

(7) Highlight the data in columns H through J (the latter being empty) and call ForwardFT. This will deposit the corresponding frequencies in column K, and the real and imaginary components *R'* and *R''* in columns L and M respectively.

(8) In column O calculate log $M^2 = \log[(R')^2 + (R'')^2]$, and plot it versus frequency (in column K).

(9) Find approximate functions for the signal (in column P) and the noise (in column Q). For the data shown in Fig. 6.5.3*b* we have used (and shown) log $S^2 = -2 -125\,|f|$ and log $N^2 = -4.6$. In column R then compute the Wiener filter as

$$10^{\log(S^2)} / \left(10^{\log(S^2)} + 10^{\log(N^2)}\right) = 10^{-2-125|f|} / \left(10^{-2-125|f|} + 10^{-4.6}\right).$$

(10) In column T copy the frequency from column K, in column U calculate the product of *R'* (from column L) and the Wiener filter (from column R), and in column V place the corresponding product of *R''* (from column M) and the Wiener filter.

(11) Highlight the data in columns T through V, and call InverseFT. This will produce the numbers 0 through 2047 in column W, and the filtered real and imaginary components of *r* in columns X and Y respectively. The data in column X are shown in Fig. 6.5.3*c*; those in column Y reflect computational imperfections and should therefore be quite small.

(12) In column AA copy the numbers 0 (1) 2047, in column AB the data from column X, and in column AC the transfer function *t* from column C.

(13) Highlight the data in columns AA through AC, and call DeconvolveFT. Column AD will now contain the deconvolved data, see Fig. 6.5.3*d*.

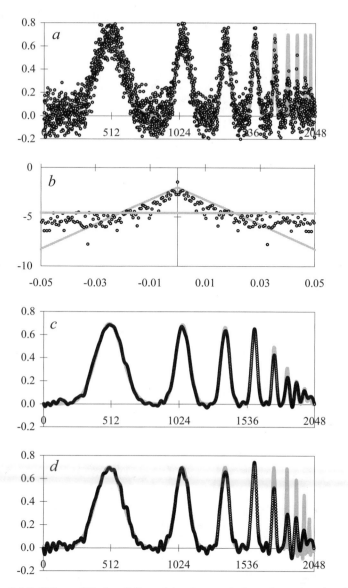

Fig. 6.5.3: Wiener filtering followed by deconvolution of a noisy signal. (*a*) The undistorted signal *s* (gray) and its convolution *r* with a Gaussian of standard deviation 10 (displayed in Fig. 6.4.2*c*), to which was added Gaussian noise, of zero mean and standard deviation 0.1 (black circles). (*b*) The central part of the power spectrum of the noisy *r*. This plot is used for the visual estimates of the parameters of the Wiener filter. (*c*) The resulting, smoothed *r* (black curve) with the corresponding noise-free curve (gray). (*d*) Upon deconvolving the smoothed data we obtain the final result (black curve) with the corresponding noise-free curve shown in gray.

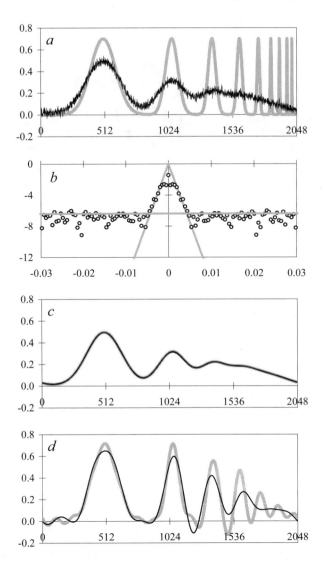

Fig. 6.5.4: Wiener filtering followed by deconvolution of a noisy signal. All data are as in Fig. 6.5.3, except that the original convoluting function had a standard deviation of 100 (see Fig. 6.4.2*d*), and the noise amplitude (the standard deviation of the added Gaussian noise) was only 0.02.

The above procedure is rather laborious. Its tedium could be reduced somewhat by constructing a custom macro, which in this case would require two parts, one to generate the power spectrum, log $[(R')^2 + (R'')^2]$, the second (after operator intervention to distinguish between signal and noise, and to approximate both components in terms of mathematical functions) to finish the process. We will leave this as an exercise to the interested reader.

What is worse than its tedium is that even the small amount of noise left after Wiener filtering interferes with the deconvolution which, after all this effort, often produces only a relatively minor correction for the original distortion.

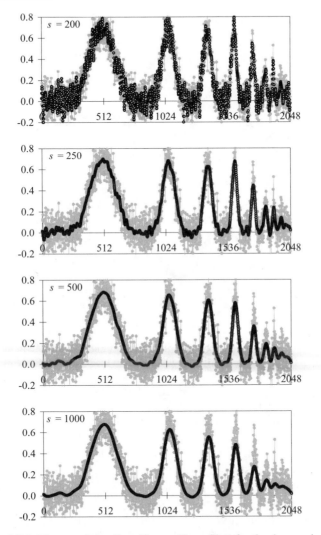

Fig. 6.5.5: The use of an adjustable von Hann filter for the deconvolution of the noisy trace illustrated in Fig. 6.5.3*a*. The input signal *r* is shown in gray, its devolution in black. The convolving and deconvolving *t* is a Gaussian curve of standard deviation 10; the signal has added Gaussian noise of standard deviation 0.1. The *s*-value used is noted in each panel.

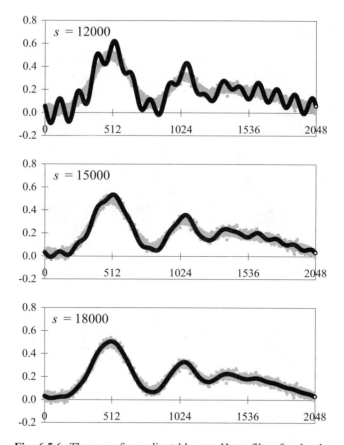

Fig. 6.5.6: The use of an adjustable von Hann filter for the de-convolution of the noisy trace illustrated in Fig. 6.5.4*a*. The input signal *r* is shown in gray, its devolution in black. The convolving and deconvolving *t* is a Gaussian of standard deviation 100; the signal has added Gaussian noise of standard deviation 0.02. The *s*-value used is noted in each panel. When *s* is too small, the re-sult oscillates; when it is too large, there is no deconvolution.

This is illustrated in Fig. 6.5.4, where we have used the same spread-sheet for the more strongly distorted case of Fig. 6.4.2*d*. Once the spreadsheet is set up and properly labeled (it helps to color code the data blocks to be highlighted for macro use), repeated operation is fairly easy, even though it still involves four macros (ConvolveFT, ForwardFT, In-verseFT, and DeconvolveFT) and making the necessary adjustments in the parameter estimates S^2 and/or N^2 of the Wiener filter. Nonetheless, despite Wiener filtering, the method often tolerates very little noise, lest it yields wildly oscillating results.

When the effort involved in Wiener filtering is not warranted, some nonspecific, 'general' filtering can be had with two filters included in the custom macro DeconvolveFT: an adjustable von Hann filter or, when this is rejected, a sharp frequency cutoff filter. The application of the von Hann filter is illustrated in exercise 6.5.6 and in Figs. 6.5.5 and 6.5.6. By increasing the value of the filter parameter s one can make the von Hann filter arbitrarily narrow, in which case it approaches a delta function. The deconvolution macro then merely reproduces its input. Similar results can be obtained with the sharper frequency cutoff filter, but its abruptness tends to enhance oscillations in the result.

Exercise 6.5.6:
(1) This will be a short continuation of exercise 6.5.5. In column AF copy the numbers from column A, in column AG copy the noisy test function $r+n$ from column I, and in column AH copy the transfer function t from column C.

(2) Highlight the data in columns AF through AH, and call DeconvolveFT. Select an appropriate filter parameter s; some filter curves are displayed in Fig. 5.6.1. You will find your answer in column AH. Figure 6.5.6 shows that, when the noise is too large, this approach does not work, but merely causes the result to oscillate around the input curve.

6.6 Iterative van Cittert deconvolution

An alternative, relatively robust approach to deconvolution that, for single data sets, is often easier to implement than deconvolution via Fourier transformation, can be based on the rather general principle of 'operating in reverse'. In exercise 4.0.1 we illustrated this for a *number*, by computing a cube root iteratively when only knowing how to calculate a cube. In the present case we try to find the unknown *function* that, when subjected to convolution, will yield the observed result. This approach was first applied to deconvolution by van Cittert et al. (*Z. Phys.* 65 (1930) 547, 69 (1931) 298, 79 (1932) 722, 81 (1933) 428 and, with modern computers, has become much more practical.

The idea is as follows. Say that we have a measured spectrum r, and the transfer function t with which is was convolved, and for which operation we want to correct r. In other words, we seek the undistorted spectrum $s = r \oslash t$ given the experimentally measured functions r and t. To this end we consider r the zeroth-order approximation s_0 to s, and convolve it with t to form $q_1 = s_0 \otimes t = r \otimes t$. This obviously goes the wrong way: q_1 is even more distorted than r. But we now assume that we can get a better approximation to s by adding to s_0 the difference between r and q_1, i.e., that $s_1 = s_0 + (r - q_1) = 2r - q_1$ will be a closer approximation to s than s_0.

Repeating this process, we compute $q_2 = s_1 \otimes t$, then add the difference $(r - q_2)$ to s_1 and obtain $s_2 = s_1 + (r - q_2) = 3r - q_1 - q_2$, etc. In general, after n such steps, we will have $s_n = (n+1) r - \sum_1^n q_i$. Van Cittert et al. already studied the convergence behavior of this method, but it is a fairly complicated matter, for which you may want to consult P. B. Crilly's chapter 5 in *Deconvolution of Images and Spectra*, P. A. Jansson ed., Academic Press 1997 and the references therein for recent results. Exercise 6.6.1 illustrates this approach.

Exercise 6.6.1:

(1) In a new spreadsheet, enter in row 1 the following column headings: #, s, t, r, leave a column blank, then #, r, t, q1, blank column, #, s1, t, q2, blank, #, s2, t, q3, blank, etc.

(2) In the column under #, say A3:A18, deposit the number sequence 0 (1) 15.

(3) In cell B3 then use the instruction =0.9*EXP(-0.5*(A3-8)^2) to calculate a signal, for which we here use a simple Gaussian with amplitude 0.9, standard deviation 1, centered at 8. Copy this instruction down to row 18.

(4) Place =EXP(-0.25*(A3)^2)+EXP(-0.25*(16-A3)^2) in cell C3. This instruction again uses wraparound to avoid a phase shift, by exploiting the fact that the Fourier transform assumes a cyclic repeat of the signal. (Incidentally, this only works for a *symmetrical* transfer function.) The amplitude of the transfer signal is immaterial, since ConvolveFT will normalize it anyway.

(5) Highlight A3:C18, and call ConvolveFT to compute r in column D.

(6) Copy #, r, and t into the next columns, e.g., with the instructions =A3, =D3, and =C3 in cells F3 through H3, to be copied down to row 18.

(7) Highlight F3:H18, call ConvolveFT, and thus calculate q_1 in column I.

(8) Copy # to column K, and t to M, and in L calculate s_1 as $s_1 = 2r - q_1$.

(9) Convolve s_1 with t to obtain q_2 in column N.

(10) Repeat the process: copy # and t into columns P and R, and in column Q calculate $s_2 = s_2 + r - q_2$. Then convolve to find q_3, and so on.

Figure 6.6.1 illustrates that s_1 is indeed a better approximation to s than is r, s_2 is better than s_1, etc. For noise-free curves the method usually converges onto s, albeit slowly, even though convergence cannot be taken for granted for arbitrary transfer functions. The first few iterations are usually the most effective, and are easily performed on the spreadsheet. We illustrate this here with 28 synthetic Gaussian peaks that crudely mimic those of Fig. 9 in chapter 7 by P. B. Crilly, W. E. Blass & G. W. Halsey in *Deconvolution of Images and Spectra*, P. A. Jansson, ed., Academic Press 1997. In order to make the exercise more realistic, we will add some noise to r.

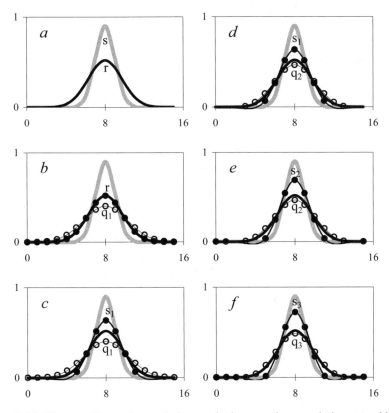

Fig. 6.6.1: The van Cittert *de*convolution method uses only *con*volutions to achieve its goal by working backwards, iteratively. (*a*) An assumed Gaussian signal *s* (gray) is convoluted by a Gaussian transfer function *t* (not shown here) to yield a measured result *r* (heavy black curve), which will be our starting function. (*b*) Convolution of *r* with *t* produces an even more broadened curve, q_1, shown as a thin line with open circles. (*c*) The difference between q_1 and *r* is then used to generate a better approximation s_1 of *s*, shown as a slightly thicker line with solid circles. The process is then repeated (*d*). Three cycles of this iterative procedure are shown, with panel (*e*) showing q_2 and s_2, and (*f*) illustrating q_3 and s_3. The latter is certainly much closer to *s* than *r* (shown as a thick black curve). For numerical details see exercise 6.6.1.

Exercise 6.6.2:

(1) In column A of a new spreadsheet place the numbers (0 (1) 511, and in column B generate a synthetic signal *s* using a number of Gaussian peaks of the form $a \exp[-b(x-c)^2]$. In the examples shown in Figs. 6.6.2 through 6.6.7 we have used $b = 0.1$ throughout (i.e., a standard deviation $s = 1/\sqrt{(2b)} = \sqrt{5} \approx 2.2$), and the parameters *a* and *c* as listed in table 6.6.1.

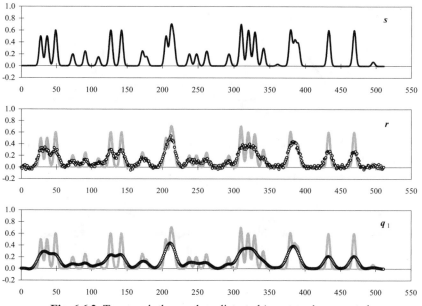

Fig. 6.6.2: Top panel: the mock undistorted 'spectrum' *s*, repeated in gray in the other panels. Middle panel: the convolution of *s* with a single Gaussian *t*, plus noise, simulating a measured spectrum. Bottom panel: q_1 as obtained by convolution of *r* with *t*.

$a=$	0.5	0.5	0.6	0.2	0.25	0.15	0.6	0.6	0.25	0.15	0.5	0.6	0.4	0.2
$c=$	28	37	49	73	91	110	127	142	172	178	205	212	216	238

$a=$	0.2	0.25	0.2	0.7	0.6	0.57	0.3	0.03	0.6	0.4	0.35	0.6	0.6	0.07
$c=$	248	262	293	310	320	329	341	361	379	385	390	433	469	496

Table 6.6.1: The parameters used in exercise 6.6.2 for the synthetic 'spectrum'.

(2) Column C for the transfer function *t* should again contain a simple Gaussian, split so that it has its maximum at the beginning of the data set, and its other half at the end of that set. In other words, for the 512-point data set used, the formula to be used is $\exp[-b_t t^2)] + \exp[-b_t(t-512)^2]$ if *t* runs from 0 to 511. In our example we have used $b_t = 0.03125$, for a standard deviation of 4.

(3) Highlight the data in columns A:C, identify them (e.g., by giving them a light background color), and call ConvolveFT. This will place the function $r = s \otimes t$ in column D.

(4) In the next column, E, deposit Gaussian noise of zero mean and unit standard deviation.

(5) In column F repeat the order numbers from column A, in column G copy *r* plus a fraction of the noise from column E (in our example we have used 0.02) to make the noisy measured signal r_n, and in column H repeat *t*. The data for r_n in column G will be our points of departure.

(6) Highlight (and provide background color to) the data in columns F:H, and call ConvolveFT to compute $q_1 = r_n \otimes t$, which will appear in column I.

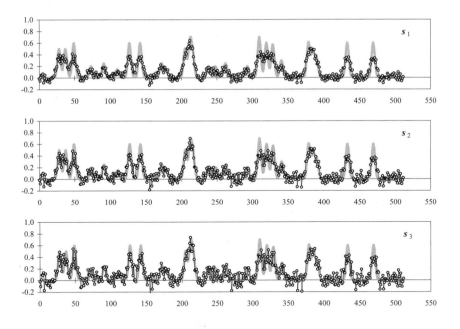

Fig. 6.6.3: Successive estimates of *s* by iterative deconvolution of the noisy simulated spectrum *r* shown in the middle panel of Fig. 6.6.2.

(7) In column J again copy the numbers from column A, in column K calculate $s_1 = 2r_n - q_1$, and in column L copy *t* from column C.

(8) Highlight (and color) the data in columns J:L, and call ConvolveFT to compute (in column M) the function $q_2 = s_1 \otimes t$.

(9) In column N copy the numbers from column A, in column O calculate $s_2 = s_1 + (r_n - q_2)$, and in column P copy *t* from column C.

(10) Repeat the instruction in (8) and (9) to calculate first $q_3 = s_2 \otimes t$, then $s_3 = s_2 + (r_n - q_3)$, etc.

(11) Plot your results. If you have used the numerical values listed, your results should resemble those in Figs. 6.6.2 and 6.6.3.

(12) Now if you want to modify the signal *s* and/or the transfer function *t*, just change them in column B and/or C, then highlight the color-coded areas one-by-one, going from left to right, and call ConvolveFT. In the same way you can change the noise level in column G and then call ConvolveFT starting with columns F:H.

Figure 6.6.3 illustrates the usual problem with deconvolution: noise. While the signal 'grows into' the peaks with each successive iteration, the noise also grows, but faster. To understand why this happens, consider that $s_1 = r_n + (r_n - q_1)$, and that q_1 is much smoother than r_n, see Fig. 6.6.2. We now write $r_n = r_0 + n$, where r_0 represents *r* in the absence of noise, and *n* is the noise. Let the convolution reduce the noise *n* in r_n to αn in q_1, where $|\alpha| \ll 1$. Then $s_1 = 2r_n - q_1 = (2r_0 - q_1) + (2n - \alpha) n$, which has almost twice as much noise as r since $|\alpha| \ll 1$. The same argument applies to subsequent iteration stages, so that the noise increases almost linearly with the number of iterations while s_i creeps up on s at the steadily decreasing rate of an asymptotic approach. But when the noise grows faster than the signal, the iteration cannot converge, and the process ultimately becomes oscillatory, completely obliterating the signal.

Exercise 6.6.2 (continued):

(13) In any iterative process we need to have a termination criterion, otherwise the process can go on indefinitely. Since our starting function is r_n, and the procedure is based on trying to match r_n with q_i, calculate the sum of squares of the residuals between the data in columns G and I, G and M, G and Q, etc., using the instruction =SUMXMY2 (*function1 , function2*) . These numbers duly decrease upon successive iterations. This suggests that you might be able to use this SSR to determine when to stop the iteration: whenever it becomes smaller than a given value, or starts to go up.

(14) But now try to use the same instruction to determine the sum of squares of the residuals between s (in column B) and successive versions of s_i (in columns K, O, etc.). This is not realistic, because we normally have no access to s which, after all, is the function we *seek*. Still, in this simulation, it is instructive to take a look: in the presence of sufficient noise, as in our numerical example, this SSR *in*creases with successive iterations. Therefore, using the sum of squares of the differences between r_n and q_i as suggested under point (13) can be misleading, yet in practice, we have no other option when using this method.

A possible way to get around noise is to incorporate smoothing at every iteration step, as was done, e.g., by Herget et al., *J. Opt. Soc. Am.* 52 (1962) 1113. Now the spreadsheet becomes much more complicated, and we therefore use a custom macro to take care of the busywork. DeconvolveIt performs the convolutions interspersed with smoothing steps, using a moving least squares parabola of variable length to keep the noise in check. Since the data must be equidistant for the Fourier transform convolution, we can use the method of section 3.15.

Exercise 6.6.2 (continued):

(15) In the next three columns copy the data from columns A (the numbers representing the independent variable), G (for r_n), and C (for t), then highlight the data in these three new columns, and call DeconvolveIt0. Accept the default no-filter value 0, and let the macro run. You can follow its progress by observing its intermediate results, displayed in the left-hand corner of the bar below the spreadsheet. After your patience has grown thin, interrupt the program with the Escape key (Esc), terminate it, and plot. You will find that the result oscillates wildly, and shows no inclination to converge.

(16) Again highlight the data in those three columns, and call DeconvolveIt0, but now use different lengths of the parabolic filter. If the noise level is not too

high, you should be able to find a filter length that will generate a useful decon-volution, such as in the top panel of Fig. 6.6.4.

(17) For comparison, also try DeconvolveFT. Again, without filter it will not converge (if you have noise comparable to that in Fig. 6.6.2r), but you should be able to find a workable result with the built-in, adjustable von Hann filter, see the bottom panel of Fig. 6.6.4.

Neither method would yield a convergent result without filtering. By using different filter parameters, both methods have some flexibility, and the nature of the filters is obviously quite different. Still, for comparable noise, the iterative method clearly outperforms direct deconvolution in this example.

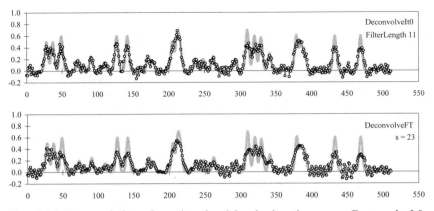

Fig. 6.6.4: Deconvolution of a noisy signal by the iterative macro DeconvolveIt0, which required 28 iterations (top panel) and, for comparison (bottom panel) the results of deconvolving with DeconvolveFT, using the adjustable von Hann filter with $s = 23$.

Instead of relying on the smoothing filters that are built into these macros, one can use Wiener filtering followed by filter-free deconvolu-tion. That gives a fairer comparison of the two methods, and is illustrated below and in Fig. 6.6.6. Again, the iterative method takes more time but comes out ahead of the direct one in terms of signal recovery.

Exercise 6.6.2 (continued):

(18) In the next two columns again copy the numbers from column A and from column G (for r_n), and C (for t), then highlight the data in these two new columns plus the one to its right (which should be empty), and call ForwardFT. This will create three now columns, one for frequency, one for R', and one for R''.

(19) In the next column compute $\log M^2 = \log [(R')^2 + (R'')^2]$, and plot it versus frequency.

(20) Fit simple curves to $\log (S^2)$ and $\log (N^2)$, see Fig. 6.6.5, and in the next column compute the Wiener filter $10^{\log(S^2)} \big/ (10^{\log(S^2)} + 10^{\log(N^2)})$ which, in our example, translates into $10^{-1.8-40|f|} \big/ (10^{-1.8-40|f|} + 10^{-5.5})$.

(21) In the next column again copy the numbers from column A, and in the next two calculate the product of R' and R'' respectively with the data in the Wiener filter column.

(22) Call InverseFT. The second of these contains the filtered r, while the third contains only junk data that should all be zero. Replace the latter by copies of t, then highlight these three columns and call DeconvolveIt0. You may have to interrupt it fairly early; if you let it run, it can consume considerable time but most likely make a worse fit. Plot your result. In the example shown in Fig. 6.6.6, the iteration was cut short at 100.

(23) For comparison also run DeconvolveFT. The two results are compared in Fig. 6.6.6.

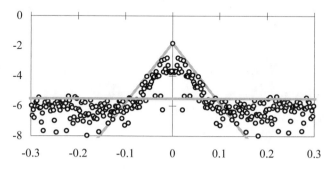

Fig. 6.6.5: The power spectrum of the noisy input data can be fitted to the simple, approximate expressions $\log(S^2) = -1.8 - 40|f|$ and $\log(N^2) = -5.5$, as shown.

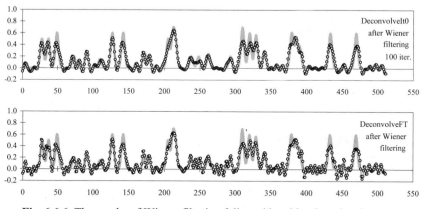

Fig. 6.6.6: The results of Wiener filtering followed by either iterative deconvolution (top panel) or straight Fourier transform deconvolution (bottom panel).

In this example, the iterative deconvolution again holds its own against direct deconvolution. We note that both methods produce negative values, mostly in regions where the signal is small. When these simulated data represent an actual optical spectrum, such negative values would be physically meaningless, and can of course be lopped off if that makes you feel better. DeconvolveIt1 removes the negative values during each iteration. The systematic bias introduced by doing so is believed to be small, because the correction occurs only in regions of weak signals. Results so obtained with DeconvolveIt1 are shown in Fig. 6.6.7.

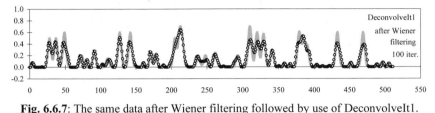

Fig. 6.6.7: The same data after Wiener filtering followed by use of DeconvolveIt1.

At this point it may be useful to look back, in order to compare Fig. 6.6.7 with Fig. 6.6.2*r* and the data of table 6.6.1. Starting from the left, the two peaks at 28 and 37 are clearly resolved by deconvolution, and the peak at 49 is almost baseline-separated. On the other hand, deconvolution has introduced peaks centered at 5, 82, and 104 that do not occur in the original. Likewise, the two overlapping peaks at 172 and 178 are replaced by two that are more clearly resolved than the original ones, plus two satellite peaks, at 162 and 190. And so it goes for the rest of the spectrum: the shapes of existing peaks are often improved, but additional, fabricated peaks appear as well. It would seem that the Fourier transformation, by looking for sinusoidal components, is the primary source of these extra peaks, and that cutting off their negative portions makes them more convincingly look like peaks rather than processing noise.

One can combine a weighting function that discriminates against negative points with one that removes data above a given limit, say 1. Such a modification was introduced by P. A. Jansson et al., *J. Opt. Soc. Am.* 58 (1968) 1665, 60 (1970) 184, and is implemented in DeconvolveIt2. If the latter macro is used, the data should be scaled to fit appropriately in the range from 0 to 1.

More efficient iterative deconvolution can often be achieved by introducing a relaxation factor. We will not do so here, as it would carry us too far from our simple goal of illustrating what deconvolution is and does. Instead, in section 6.7 we will explore an alternative approach that can give superior results in those cases to which it is applicable.

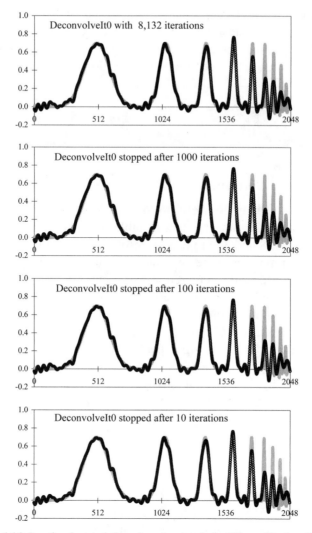

ig. 6.6.8: Iterative deconvolution of a noisy signal after Wiener filtering, illustrating that the built-in termination criterion may be gross overkill. Shorter runs were obtained by changing the iteration limit in the DeconvolveIt macro.

The above example involves a fairly typical, relatively easy deconvolution, because the original signal s did not contain any details that were lost completely in the original distortion. In this respect, iterative deconvolution has limitations similar to those of direct deconvolution, as illustrated in Fig. 6.6.8, where we use the noisy test data set illustrated in Fig. 6.5.3 after Wiener filtering, and merely replaced the final deconvolution step by DeconvolveIt0. The results are not significantly different from those of Fig. 6.5.3d.

We note that the iteration stopped after 8,132 steps, using as its termination criterion that SSR (for the difference between the input function **r** and that calculated during each iteration) decreases, but that there is relatively little gain (and much time to lose) in going beyond the first few iterations. It is amusing to look at those SSR values: SSR $= 4.8 \times 10^{-25}$ for 8,132 steps, 1.4×10^{-20} for 1,000 steps, 2.7×10^{-14} for 100 steps, and only 9.1×10^{-6} for 10 steps, yet the resulting deconvolutions are rather similar.

The above examples suggest that the iterative method can yield marginally better results. Whether this holds true in general cannot be answered in the abstract, because it will depend on the nature of the signal, on the kind of blurring for which correction is sought (such as amplifier distortion, optical aberration, camera motion, tip profile in scanning probe microscopy), and on the type of noise. The above comparisons all involved triply Gaussian data (based on Gaussian curves, with Gaussian blurring, plus added Gaussian noise), and may therefore be most appropriate for classical (near-ultraviolet to infrared) optical spectroscopy and chromatography. Other methods may well yield other outcomes.

Sometimes the signal itself may suggest how best to approach it. If we see a spectrum that exhibits characteristic sinc-like sidelobes, we can estimate the width of the pulse that most likely caused it, and use that information for deconvolution. The same approach, in two dimensions, may be applicable to astronomical data that show the equivalent rings around inherently point-like object such as stars.

A successful early application of the van Cittert approach was reported by S. Hüfner & G. K. Wertheim in *Phys. Revs.* B11 (1975) 678. They deconvolved x-ray photo-emission spectra of a number of metals in order to correct for the broadening effect of the spectrometer. The resulting (considerably narrower and higher but also much noisier) curves were then fitted by nonlinear least squares to their theoretical line shapes, thereby removing the noise introduced by the deconvolution.

6.7 Iterative deconvolution using Solver

The van Cittert deconvolution method is general but quite sensitive to noise. An alternative approach introduced by Grinvald & Steinberg, *Anal. Biochem.* 59 (1974) 583 is much less sensitive to noise. It also uses reverse engineering but requires an analytical (and therefore noise-free) model for the undistorted signal s_m, which will be assumed to be describable in terms of one or more model parameters a_i, i.e., $s_m = f(a_i)$. We convolve the model signal s_m with the experimental transfer function t to obtain $r_m = s_m \otimes t$, and then use Solver to adjust the model parameters a_i

by minimizing the sum of squares of the residuals between r_m and the experimental (or simulated) r_{exp}. The requirement that s_m be describable as an explicit analytical function makes this method less widely applicable than the van Cittert approach, but it also makes it much more immune to noise.

Because macros do not self-update, Solver cannot respond automatically to the effect of parameter changes that involve macros. This means that, for a non-manual program, we can either rewrite Solver so that it can accommodate macros, or (much simpler) perform the convolution using a function rather than a macro. The latter approach is illustrated in exercise 6.7.1.

Exercise 6.7.1:

(1) Our example will be modeled after exercise 6.2.2 and fig. 6.2.3, i.e., based on a single exponential decay. In cells A1:D1 deposit the column labels #, **s**, **t**, and **r** for the rank number # (which can represent time, wavelength, etc), original (undistorted) signal **s**, filter or transfer function **t**, and result **r**.

(2) In A3 place the value –100, in A4 the instruction =A3+1, and copy this down to cell A303.

(3) Go down to row 103, and in cell B103 insert the instruction =$D$97*EXP(-$D$98*A103) for the transfer function *t*, and copy this down to row 303. In cell D97 enter an amplitude value (such as 1) and in cell D98 a value for a rate constant (e.g., 0.03), with accompanying labels in column C.

(4) In cell D100 deposit a value for t_f, such as 10, and in D101 a value for a_f, e.g., 7, as in exercise 6.2.2 and Fig. 6.2.3. Place corresponding labels in column C.

(5) For the transfer function *t*, in cell C103 place the instruction =EXP(-1* (LN(1+(A103+4-$D$100)/$D$101))^2) and copy this down to row 303. The value $4 = 1 + t_f - a_f$ is used here in order to avoid a non-negative argument in the logarithm for the specific values of t_f and a_f suggested in (4).

(6) Highlight A103:C303 and call the macro Convolve, which will write the convolution *r* in D103:D303.

(7) Deposit Gaussian ('normal') noise (with mean 0 and standard deviation 1) in N103:O303, and supply corresponding scale values, such as 0.02 in cell N100 and 0.03 in cell O100, on purpose rather large to show the effect of noise.

(8) In cell E103 place the instruction =C103+$N$100*N103 to simulate a noisy transfer function t_{exp}. In cell F103 use =D103+$O$100*O103 for a noisy response signal r_{exp}. Copy both instructions down to row 303. In row 1 place appropriate labels. You now have a set of simulated, noisy data to try the deconvolution. In a real application these simulated values should of course to be replaced by experimental data, as anticipated by their labels.

(9) In G103 place a model function, such as =$I$97*EXP(-$I$98*A103). Copy it down to row 303, and label it in G1 as **s** model. Place a guess value for the amplitude in I97, such as 1.2, and an initial estimate for the rate constant in I98, e.g., 0.02, with accompanying labels in column H. Do not place any numbers or text in G3:G102, but instead fill it with, e.g., bright yellow, to remind yourself to keep it clear.

(10) In cell H103 deposit the function =Convol(G103:G202,$E$103:$E$202,$I$101,100) and copy it all the way to row 303. In cell H1 label the column as **r** model.

(11) In cell H101 place the label Denom=, and in cell I101 the instruction =SUM(E103:E202). This summation normalizes the convolution, based on the average value of *t*. If that is not desired, replace the instruction in I101 by the value of *N* or by =COUNT(E103:E202).

(12) Go to the VBA module and enter the following code for this function.

```
Function Convol(Array1, Array2, Denom, N)

Dim i As Integer
Dim Sum As Double
Dim Array3 As Variant
ReDim Array3(1 To 2 * N)

For i = 1 To N
  Array3(i) = Array2(N + 1 - i)
Next i

Sum = 0
For i = 1 To N
  Sum = Sum + Array1(i - N + 1) * Array3(i)
Next i

Convol = Sum / Denom

End Function
```

(13) In cell I100 deposit the function =SUMXMY2(F103:F303,H103:H303) and place a corresponding label such as SSR= in H100.

(14) Call Solver, and Set Target Cell to I100, Equal to Min, By Changing Cells I97:I98. Then engage SolverAid to find the corresponding uncertainties.

(15) Compare your results with those in fig. 6.7.1, which shows them before and after using Solver.

This exercise demonstrates the principle of the method. We started with amplitude $a = 1$ and rate constant $k = 0.03$, used as initial guess values $a_m = 1.2$ and $k_m = 0.02$ (unrealistically far off, as can be seen in fig. 6.7.1, but selected here for clarity of illustration), and then found $a_m = 1.01_5 \pm 0.01_4$ and $k_m = 0.0302_1 \pm 0.0005_3$, with a standard deviation $s_y = 0.03_1$ of the fit in **r**, and a correlation coefficient r_{ak} between a_m and k_m of 0.79.

In practice, try to keep the convolving custom function as simple as possible, and especially avoid IF statements which tend to slow Solver down. We have used a barebones custom function Convol() to keep it simple, even though it is rather wasteful of spreadsheet real estate. Use of a model function s_m keeps noise down, and yields non-oscillatory results.

This method is not restricted to single exponentials, and can also handle multi-exponential fits. One should of course be alert to the possibility that different models may yield experimentally indistinguishable results; Grinvald & Steinberg gave as examples $y_0 = 0.75\ e^{-t/5.5} + 0.25\ e^{-t/8}$ and $y_1 = 0.25\ e^{-t/4.5} + 0.75\ e^{-t/6.7}$ that never differ by more than 0.0025, or $y_2 = (1/2)\ e^{-t/2.26} + (1/2)\ e^{-t/5.46}$ and $y_3 = (1/3)\ e^{-t/2} + (1/3)\ e^{-t/3.5} + (1/3)\ e^{-t/6}$ for which the maximal difference is always less than 0.0034 even though y_2 and y_3 use quite different models. Especially in the latter case, the residuals may be dominated by experimental noise, and one might also want to compute and plot the autocorrelation function of the residuals as an aid to discriminate between various model assumptions.

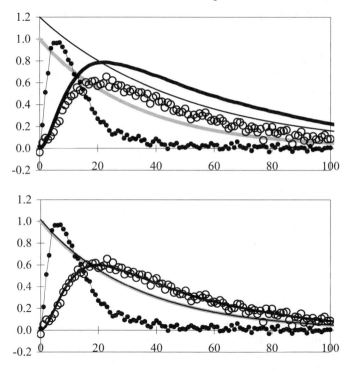

Fig. 6.7.1: The assumed signal s (gray band), the noisy transfer function t_{exp} (line with small solid points), the result r_{exp} obtained by convolving s with the (noise-free) transfer function and then adding noise (large open circles), the assumed model function s_m (line) and the resulting function r_m after convolving s_m with t_{exp} (heavy line). The top panel shows the situation just before calling Solver, the bottom panel that after Solver has been used.

Grinvald & Steinberg emphasized the use of properly weighted least squares based, e.g., on Poissonian counting statistics when the spectrum is obtained by single photon counting.

6.8 *Deconvolution by parameterization*

Many approaches to deconvolution are quite sensitive to noise, and may therefore require filtering, which (when not carefully compensated in the deconvolution routine) can again lead to distortion and loss of detail. The method described in section 6.7 avoids this problem by fitting the undistorted signal *s* to a noise-free analytical function. Below we will see how this approach can be carried to its logical conclusion by using a noise-free transfer function *t* as well, and by then performing the deconvolution algebraically. Even though it has an even more limited applicability, this approach may still work when earlier-described methods fail.

To illustrate the basic idea, we will here consider only a relatively simple case in which a measured *result* *r* of the convolution, say a spectrum or a chromatogram, can be described as a sum of Gaussian curves, *r* = Σ*g_r*, while the *transfer* function *t* is given by a single Gaussian, *t* = *g_t*. We have already seen in chapter 4 how we can use Solver to fit complicated functions in terms of sums of Gaussians, and we will now apply this to deconvolution. Again we use bold lowercase symbols to indicate time-dependent functions rather than constants.

The approach we will take here substitutes deconvolving *r* with *t* by instead deconvolving Σ*g_r* with *g_t*. Because *g_r* and *g_t* are fitted, noise-free analytical functions, this greatly reduces the effect of noise on the deconvolution. Noise only affects the result insofar as it limits the proper assignment of the Gaussians *g_r* and *g_t*. The actual calculation is straightforward, the most critical part of the procedure being the initial fitting of Gaussians to the experimental functions *r* and *t*.

We will first deconvolve two single *N*-point Gaussians, *g_r* and *g_t* that are both functions of a common parameter *t* which can represent elution time, wavelength, wavenumber, etc. We therefore start with the mathematical functions

$$g_r = a_r \exp\{-\tfrac{1}{2}\,[(t-c_r)/b_r]^2\} \tag{6.8.1}$$

and

$$g_t = a_t \exp\{-\tfrac{1}{2}\,[(t-c_t)/b_t]^2\} \tag{6.8.2}$$

which, upon analytical Fourier transformation, yield

$$G_r = [(2\pi)^{\frac{1}{2}}\,a_r\,b_r/N]\,\exp[-2\pi j f c_r]\,\exp[-2(\pi b_r f)^2] \tag{6.8.3}$$

$$= [(2\pi)^{\frac{1}{2}}\,a_r\,b_r/N]\,\exp[-2(\pi b_r f)^2]\,[\cos(2\pi f c_r) - j\sin(2\pi f c_r)]$$

and

$$G_t = [(2\pi)^{\frac{1}{2}}\,a_t\,b_t/N]\,\exp[-2\pi j f c_t]\,\exp[-2(\pi b_t f)^2] \tag{6.8.4}$$

$$= [(2\pi)^{\frac{1}{2}} a_t b_t /N]\, \exp[-2(\pi b_t f)^2]\, [\cos(2\pi f c_t) - j\sin(2\pi f ct_r)]$$

respectively, where we have used Euler's relation $e^{-jx} = \cos(x) - j\sin(x)$. From these we obtain by division

$$\mathbf{G}_s = \mathbf{G}_r / \mathbf{G}_t \tag{6.8.5}$$
$$= [a_r b_r / a_t b_t]\, \exp[-2\pi j f(c_r - c_t)]\, \exp[-2\pi^2 (b_r^2 - b_t^2) f^2]$$

so that the original, undistorted signal is given by

$$\mathbf{g}_s = \mathbf{g}_r \oslash \mathbf{g}_t = \frac{a_r b_r N}{a_t b_t \sqrt{2\pi(b_r^2 - b_t^2)}}\, \exp \frac{-(t - c_r + c_t)^2}{2(b_r^2 - b_t^2)^2}$$

$$= a_s \exp\{-\tfrac{1}{2}[(t - c_s)/b_s]^2\} \tag{6.8.6}$$

where

$$a_s = \frac{a_r b_r N}{a_t b_t \sqrt{2\pi(b_r^2 - b_t^2)}} = \frac{a_r b_r N}{a_t b_t b_s \sqrt{2\pi}} \tag{6.8.7}$$

$$b_s = (b_r^2 - b_t^2)^{\frac{1}{2}} \tag{6.8.8}$$

and

$$c_s = c_r - c_t \tag{6.8.9}$$

In other words, once we have characterized the two Gaussian functionss $\mathbf{g}_r$ and $\mathbf{g}_t$ in terms of the constants a_r, b_r, c_r and a_t, b_t, and c_t respectively, we can simply *calculate* the deconvoluted Gaussian $\mathbf{g}_s$.

Note that the constants b in (6.8.1) and (6.8.2) are simply standard deviations. Equation (6.8.8) shows that their squares, the corresponding variances, are additive in convolution, $b_r^2 = b_t^2 + b_t^2$, and subtractive in deconvolution, $b_s^2 = b_r^2 - b_t^2$. With Gaussian peaks it is therefore easy to predict how much convolution will broaden them and, conversely, how much deconvolution can possibly sharpen them.

Typically the experimental response r to be corrected by deconvolution is calibrated, in which case we will want to maintain that calibration by deconvolving with a function that has been scaled to have unit average. In the case of a Gaussian $\mathbf{g}_t$ that implies that we should use

$$a_t = \frac{N}{b_t \sqrt{2\pi}} \tag{6.8.10}$$

so that (6.8.7) reduces to

$$a_s = a_r b_r (b_r^2 - b_t^2)^{-\frac{1}{2}} = a_r b_r / b_s \tag{6.8.11}$$

Moreover, the value of c_t is usually arbitrary. If we simply set it to zero, (6.8.9) becomes

$$c_s = c_r \tag{6.8.12}$$

When r must be expressed as a *sum* of Gaussians, $r = \Sigma g_r$, the same approach can be used, because then $R = \Sigma G_r$ and $T = G_t$ so that

$$S = \frac{R}{T} = \frac{\sum_{i=1}^{r} G_{ri}}{G_t} = \sum_{i=1}^{r} \frac{G_{ri}}{G_t} = \sum_{i=1}^{r} S_i \tag{6.8.13}$$

Exercise 6.8.1 illustrates this procedure for the deconvolution of the data shown in Fig. 6.2.4.

Exercise 6.8.1:

(1) Retrieve the spreadsheet used in exercise 6.2.3, or repeat that exercise.

(2) In cells E20:H20 deposit column headings for t_{exp}, r_{exp}, t_{model}, r_{model}, and the recovered value s_{recov}, and in N20 and O20 place headings for noise n.

(3) Generate Gaussian noise of zero mean and unit standard deviation in N22:O321.

(4) Place appropriate noise amplitudes for t and r in cells C19 and D19 respectively, in E22:E321 compute the function t with added noise (with, e.g., the instruction =C22+$C$19*N22 in cell E22). Similarly compute a noisy version of r in column F, using noise from column O. Plot these noisy versions of t and s, as in Fig. 6.8.1c.

(5) In H2:H16 place the labels ar1=, br1=, cr1=, ar2=, br2=, cr2=, ar3=, br3=, cr3=, ar4=, br4=, cr4=, at=, bt=, and ct=. Alternatively you can copy them from F2:F16, then modify them.

(6) In cell G22 deposit =$I$14*EXP(-0.5*((A22-$I$16)/$I$15)^2), and copy this instruction down to row 321. Enter this curve in the just-made plot.

(7) Place numerical values in I14:I16 so that the resulting curve approximately fits curve t_{exp}. (You may first want to color the data in G2:G16 white, so that you will not be tempted to look at the data originally taken for the simulation of s. When you are done fitting the data, change their color back to black or whatever.)

(8) In cell F19 calculate *SSR* for t as =SUMXMY2(E22:E321,G22:G321).

(9) Call Solver, and let it minimize *SSR* in F19 by adjusting the guessed parameter values in I14:I16.

(10) Likewise, in cell H22 place the instruction =$I$2*EXP(-0.5*((A22-$I$4)/$I$3)^2)+ ... +$I$11*EXP(-0.5*((A22-$I$13)/$I$12)^2), copy this down to row 321, and enter this curve in the graph.

(11) Compute SSR for r as =SUMXMY2(F22:F321,H22:H321).

(12) Use the curve made under point (9) to guess numerical values for a_{r1} through c_{r4} in I2:I13 so that the resulting curve approximately fits the data r_{exp}.

(13) Call Solver to refine these values by minimizing SSR in cell H19. Do this adjustment group-wise: first let Solver adjust I2:I3, then call it again to adjust I5:I7, then I2:I7, then I8:I10, I11:I13, I8:I13, and finally I2:I13. The graph might now resemble Fig. 6.8.1d.

(14) In K2:K13 copy the labels as1=, bs1=, ... , cs4= from F2:F13.

(15) In L4 calculate $c_{s1} = c_{r1} - c_t$, i.e., as =H3-$H$15.

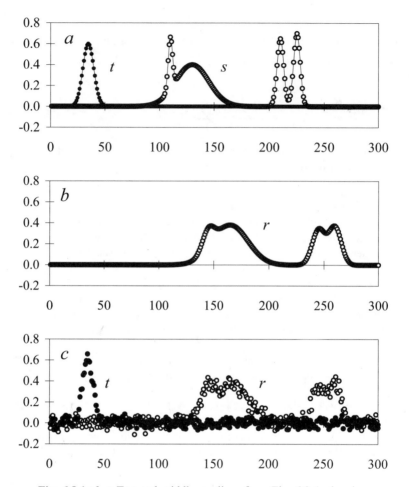

Fig. 6.8.1a,b,c: Top and middle: replicas from Fig. 6.2.4, showing in panel *a* the original simulated spectrum *s* and the distorting transfer function *t*, and in panel *b* its convolution leading to the result *r*. Bottom panel: the same as in panel *b* after adding random noise.

(16) In L3 compute $b_{s1} = \sqrt{(b_{r1}^2 - b_t^2)}$, or =SQRT(H2^2-$H$14^2).

(17) In L2 calculate $a_{s1} = a_{r1} b_{r1} / b_{s1}$, with =H1*H2/J2.

(18) Copy the block L2:L4 to L5, L8, and L11.

(19) In cell H22 compute the reconstituted signal s_{recov} with the instruction =$L$2*EXP(-0.5*((A22-$L$4)/$L$3)^2)+ ... +$L$11*EXP(-0.5*((A22-$L$13)/$L$12)^2), and copy this down to row 321.

(20) Plot this curve, and compare it with Fig. 6.8.1*f*.

(21) In this graph also display the function *s* used as the starting point of this simulation from B22:B321, a repeat from Fig. 6.8.1*a*.

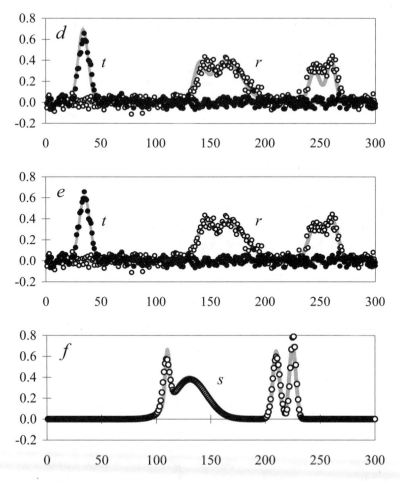

Fig. 6.8.1*d,e,f*: The manually adjusted curves (with the parameters selected 'by eye') through the noisy data (gray curves in panel *d*), the same after Solver has refined the parameter estimates (panel *e*), and the resulting deconvoluted signal *s* (open circles in panel *f*). Panel *f* also displays, as a thick gray line, the original curve of the simulated function *s* repeated from panel *a*.

This method can indeed reconstitute most features of the original curve, at least in a favorable case such as shown Fig. 6.8.1*f*, where all peaks are Gaussian, and can be identified as such in *r* despite the noise.

Exercise 6.8.1 continued:

(22) Call SolverAid, enter the Solver-determined parameters in I2:I13, the location of SSR for *r* (H19), and the column (H22:H321) in which *r* was calculated. Let SolverAid display the covariance matrix in N2:Y13. It will also deposit the standard deviations of the individual parameters in J2:J13.

(23) Once more call SolverAid, this time to find the uncertainty estimates for *t*. Therefore enter the location (I14:I16) of the Solver-determined parameters, the

location (F19) of SSR for t, and that (G22:G321) of the column where t was computed. Place the covariance matrix in Z14:AB16, so that it shares its main diagonal with that in N2:Y13.

(24) Call Propagation, and give it I2:I16 as input parameters, N2:AB16 as covariance matrix, and L2 as function. It will then place the corresponding standard deviation in M2. Repeat this for the other 11 results in column L. Sorry, Propagation handles only one parameter at a time.

The data in table 6.8.1 illustrate the results obtained, including the precision estimates generated by SolverAid and Propagation. These indicate satisfactory agreement between the parameters used to simulate s and those recovered after convolution, noise addition, and deconvolution: for all 12 coefficients of s_{found} the recovered value of s is within two standard deviations of that used in the simulation of Fig. 7.8.1. The standard deviations depend, of course, on the amount of noise added to the test functions, or present in the experimental data.

s_{taken}	$r_{guessed}$	r_{found}	$r_{st.dev.}$	s_{found}	$s_{st.dev.}$
$a_{s1}=0.5$	$a_{r1}=0.3$	0.23_1	0.03_0	$a_{s1}=0.44_4$	0.1_4
$b_{s1}=2$	$b_{r1}=5$	5.6_9	0.7_5	$b_{s1}=3._0$	$1._5$
$c_{s1}=110$	$c_{r1}=140$	144.3_0	0.4_9	$c_{s1}=109.1_1$	0.5_1
$a_{s2}=0.4$	$a_{r2}=0.4$	0.36_4	0.01_0	$a_{s2}=0.38_2$	0.01_1
$b_{s2}=15$	$b_{r2}=14$	15.9_5	0.9_6	$b_{s2}=15._2$	$1._0$
$c_{s2}=130$	$c_{r2}=165$	$166._3$	$1._2$	$c_{s2}=131._1$	$1._2$
$a_{s3}=0.65$	$a_{r3}=0.3$	0.34_5	0.01_7	$a_{s3}=0.6_0$	0.1_3
$b_{s3}=3$	$b_{r3}=5$	5.9_5	0.6_0	$b_{s3}=3._4$	$1._0$
$c_{s3}=210$	$c_{r3}=245$	245.3_6	0.7_1	$c_{s3}=210.1_9$	0.7_2
$a_{s4}=0.7$	$a_{r4}=0.4$	0.37_7	0.01_9	$a_{s4}=0.8_0$	0.2_6
$b_{s4}=3$	$b_{r4}=4$	5.5_0	0.5_0	$b_{s4}=2._6$	$1._1$
$c_{s4}=225$	$c_{r4}=260$	260.7_5	0.6_1	$c_{s4}=225.5_7$	0.6_2

t_{taken}	$t_{guessed}$	t_{found}	$t_{st.dev.}$
$a_t=0.6$	0.7	0.61_5	0.01_3
$b_t=5$	4.5	4.8_5	0.1_2
$c_t=35$	34	35.1_8	0.1_2

Table 6.8.1: Some numerical results from exercise 6.8.1. The column labeled s_{taken} lists the values used for simulating the data in fig. 6.8.1a. The columns $r_{guessed}$ and $t_{guessed}$ contain the initial guess values shown in fig. 6.8.1c, and the next two columns the values obtained by Solver for the parameters, and those obtained by SolverAid for their standard deviations. Finally, column s_{found} displays the deconvolved signal s as computed from r_{found} and t_{found}, and column $s_{st.dev.}$ the corresponding uncertainty estimates. The added noise was Gaussian with zero mean and standard deviations of 0.04 and 0.03 for r and t respectively.

This approach works, even with quite noisy signals, and does not lead to oscillatory instabilities. However, its applicability depends critically on how well one can represent both the measured result R and the transfer function T in terms of functions with relatively simple Fourier transforms, so that the inverse transform Fourier of their quotient R/T can be expressed in analytical form. All baseline-separated peaks and peak aggregates can be treated individually. This method, like that of section 6.7, can yield estimates of the standard deviations of the deconvolved signal s.

6.9 Time-frequency analysis

Fourier transformation presumes a steady state, because it considers the data set as one unit of an infinitely repeating sequence of identical units. Yet, there are many phenomena with frequency content that are not stationary, such as speech and music. In fact, music is an interesting example because its common form of notation, musical script, is really a graph of frequency (notes) as a function of time, complete with grid lines for both time (vertical lines identifying the various measures) and frequency (the horizontal lines of the staff). It even has explicit time notation (for the lengths of notes and rests) and the corresponding scale factors (tempo indicators and/or metronome settings). Musical script is, of course, a set of instructions for the performer. We here address how, other than by ear, can we analyze and visualize sound (or any equivalent, non-auditory signal) as a function of time *and* frequency.

Time-frequency or Gabor transformation (D. Gabor, *J. Inst. Elect. Engin.* 93 (1946) 429) is an analysis in which a sliding time window moves along the data, and in each window a Fourier transformation is applied to obtain its frequency content. It is an inherently imprecise approach because the product of the resolutions in time and frequency is subject to the uncertainty relationship discussed in section 5.5. (That uncertainty is intrinsic to the problem, and independent of the use of Fourier transformation or any other specific analysis method.) The uncertainty can be minimized with a Gaussian window function, which we will therefore use. As a practical matter, we will exploit the fast Fourier transformation algorithm, and therefore require that the data are equidistant in time, as they usually are when a time-dependent signal is sampled.

The Gabor transform macro uses a Gaussian window function of N contiguous data points (with $N = 2^n$ where n is a positive integer) on a data set containing M data, where $M > N$. It starts with the first N data points in the set, multiplies these by the window function, and then performs a Fourier transformation on that product. It then moves the window function over by one point, and repeats this process *M–N*+1 times until it has reached the end of the data set. The results are returned to the spreadsheet as a function of time and frequency, and can then be plotted as either a 3-D plot or a map of the absolute magnitude of the sound as a function of time and frequency. Such a plot or map is called a *sonogram*.

When the data set is so large that it would result in more than 250 columns (and therefore might exceed the 256-column width of the Excel spreadsheet), the macro will automatically move the window function each time by several data points, and the user can further restrict the size of the output file. If the 250-column limit presents a problem, modify the macro so that it stores rather than displays the data, or uses rows instead of columns, since the spreadsheet contains many more rows than columns.

Exercise 6.9.1:

(1) Start a new spreadsheet. Leave the top 10 rows for graphs, and the next 4 rows for constants and column headings.

(2) Starting in cell A15 of column A deposit time *t* in constant increments Δ*t*, such as *t* = 0 (1) 1000.

(3) In column B deposit a trial function, e.g., in cell B15 with the instruction `=(SIN($B$11*A15))/(EXP(-0.1*(A15-200))+EXP(0.003*(A15-200)))`, which has as frequency the value specified in B11 divided by 2π. Its amplitude, given by $1/\{\exp[-0.1(t-200)] + \exp[0.003(t-200)]\}$, quickly rises just before *t* = 200, and then slowly decays, somewhat like a note played on a piano. Copy this instruction down.

(4) Plot the trial function, which should resemble Fig. 6.9.1.

(5) Call the macro Gabor, and in its successive input boxes enter the time increments (here: 1), the location of the input data (here: B15:B1015), and the (optional) integer to restrict the number of samples to be analyzed (which you can leave at its default value of 5).

(6) The macro will now generate a data array, listing the frequency in its first column, and the rank number of the first data point used in each window in its top row. Inclusion of these parameters makes it easy to generate a labeled 3-D plot as well as a surface map.

(7) Make a 3-D plot of the result, and also a surface map with Mapper.

(8) Obviously, for such a simple trial function, you need not go through all this trouble. You may notice that the 3-D map for a sizable array is slow to rotate, and that its presence slows down the operation of the spreadsheet whenever it must be redrawn on the screen.

(9) Now add some harmonics, as in a chord. Extend the instruction in cells B15:B1015 to include three additional terms, identical to the first one except that their frequencies are specified by cells C11, D11, and E11 respectively.

(10) In C11 deposit the instruction `=B11*2^(3/12)`, in D11 the instruction `=C11*2^(4/12)`, and in E11 the instruction `=D11*2^(5/12)`, for the harmonics of a major chord, such as C-E-G-C. On the Western, 'well-tempered' musical scale, all half-notes differ in frequency by a factor of $2^{\wedge}(1/12)$.

(11) The resulting signal is not so transparent any more, see Fig. 6.9.2.

(12) Repeat the process of Gabor transformation and mapping. The map should now look similar to that of Fig. 6.9.3*b*.

(13) The surface map reveals very clearly the four different notes, starting at the same time but at different frequencies. The notes appear to start at about $t = 100$, whereas they really start only around $t = 200$. This time distortion results from the use of a Gaussian filter in the Gabor transformation macro.

(14) Modify the instruction in cells B15:B1015 to correspond with a broken chord, in which the various notes start one after the other, say at $t = 200$, 300, 400, and 500 respectively. Figure 6.9.4 illustrates such a signal, and Fig. 6.9.5 its Gabor transform.

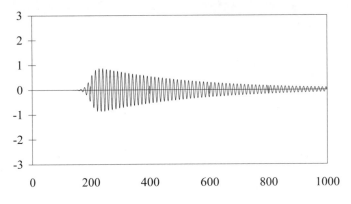

Fig. 6.9.1: The test function used, with the value 0.5 in cell B11.

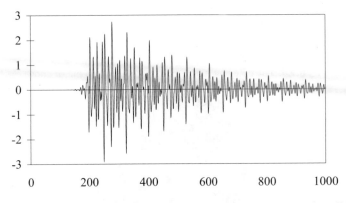

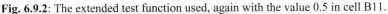

Fig. 6.9.2: The extended test function used, again with the value 0.5 in cell B11.

With such complicated signals we can readily appreciate the advantages of the Gabor transform and its representation as a 3-D graph or surface map. The different signal frequencies, and their time courses, are clearly displayed. This will become even more obvious when we consider more realistic musical signals, which may include short (staccato)

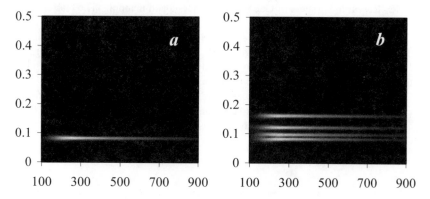

Fig. 6.9.3. Sonograms (i.e., surface maps of the Gabor transforms) of the functions shown in (a) Fig. 6.9.1 and (b) Fig. 6.9.2.

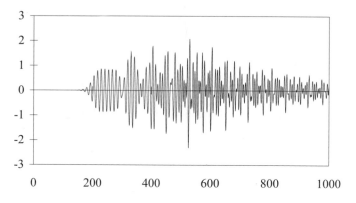

Fig. 6.9.4: The extended test function for a broken major chord.

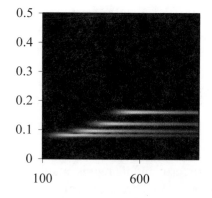

Fig. 6.9.5. The sonogram of the broken chord shown in Fig. 6.9.4.

and drawn-out (legato) notes, will have harmonics (characteristic for the musical instrument used), and may also exhibit gradually varying frequencies, as in a glissando. The sonogram exhibits the three basic attributes of sound: time, frequency (pitch, tone-height), and amplitude (intensity, loudness, volume). In some respects it mimics musical notation, in that it uses the horizontal axis for time (indicating the duration of the various notes), while the vertical axis shows their pitch. In addition it displays their harmonics. In musical notation, amplitude (loudness) must be indicated separately, whereas the sonogram displays it in 3-D or as a color or gray-scale map. We will analyze a real signal in the next section.

6.10 The echolocation pulse of a bat

Bats orient themselves at night by sending out short sound bursts of varying amplitude and frequency, and by analyzing the reflected sound. The echolocation pulses are short, so that they do not overlap with the reflected signals. A digitized echolocation pulse of a large brown bat (*Eptesicus fuscus*) can be downloaded from www.dsp.rice.edu/software/TFA/RGK/BAT/batsig.sig, and can also be obtained by e-mail from, e.g., richb@rice.edu. The recorded pulse, courtesy of Curtis Condon, Ken White, and Al Feng of the Beckman Center at the University of Illinois, contains 400 equidistant data points taken at 7 μs intervals, and therefore covers a total time of less than 3 ms duration.

> **Exercise 6.10.1:**
> (1) Start a new spreadsheet, leaving the top rows for graphs. Import the bat data, and plot them.
> (2) Apply the Gabor transform, and then map the results. The gray-scale of Fig. 6.10.1 and the two-color background of the back cover of this book illustrates what you might obtain; the front cover is left-right reversed. More subtle details can be discerned by using a full color palette, as with Mapper1 through Mapper3.

The signal in Fig. 6.10.1 starts out at about 30 kHz, descends to about 20 kHz, and after about 50 ms is joined by a second descending signal at its double frequency. The signal also contains weak higher harmonics at the triple and quadruple frequencies. The Gabor transform and its visualization make this much more transparent than the original data set.

The uncertainty relation causes some vagueness, most noticeable in the rather fuzzy onset of the pulse in Fig. 6.10.1. This can be reduced, at the cost of a correspondingly larger uncertainty in the frequency scale, by using a shorter data set for the Fourier transform analysis.

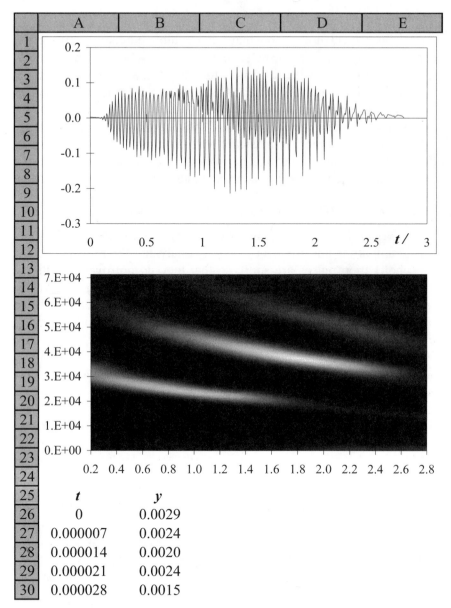

	A	B	C	D	E
25	*t*		*y*		
26	0		0.0029		
27	0.000007		0.0024		
28	0.000014		0.0020		
29	0.000021		0.0024		
30	0.000028		0.0015		

Fig. 6.10.1: The top of a spreadsheet for Gabor analysis of a bat chirp. Top graph: the echolocation signal as a function of time, in ms. Bottom graph: the corresponding sonogram: frequency (in Hz) vs. time (in start-of-sequence number). A two-color (red & black) version of this sonogram can be found on the cover.

6.11 Summary

This chapter illustrates several applications of Fourier transformation: convolution, deconvolution, and time-frequency analysis. We have belabored deconvolution because it is the counterpart of least squares analysis. Where the latter tries to minimize the effects of *random* fluctuations, deconvolution addresses a particular (but equally ubiquitous) type of *systematic* distortion inherent in all physical measurements.

Because of the practical importance of deconvolution (even though it is often underplayed in discussions of scientific data analysis, perhaps because it is considered too difficult) it has here been given rather extensive coverage, and several tools have been provided to make it more readily accessible and user-friendly. When direct or Fourier-transform deconvolution are not practicable, iterative approaches based on using convolution in reverse are often still possible, see sections 6.6 and 6.7. In favorable cases, more robust (i.e., noise-resistant) methods can be based on using theoretical models, as in section 6.7, or on combining non-linear least squares with Fourier transformation, as described in section 6.8. Incidentally, you may have noticed that least squares and Fourier transformation can often make a very powerful combination, as demonstrated earlier in the analysis of the tides in section 5.10 and, in the present chapter, in sections 6.6 and 6.8.

Some convolutions, such as those illustrated in section 6.1 and in Fig. 6.2.3, exhibit a clear sense of directionality, and a consequent, asymmetric action, while this is not the case in other examples, such as those in sections 6.4 through 6.8 and in Fig. 6.2.4. The distinction is due to the form of the transfer function used: asymmetrical transfer functions affect the signal asymmetrically, symmetrical transfer functions affect it symmetrically.

Analogous to cryptography, the transfer function is the key to the distortion, and to efforts to correct for it. Without knowledge of the transfer function, or of some calibration feature in the data set (cf. Fig. 6.3.2), deconvolution is usually not possible. An essential part of knowing your instrument is, therefore, knowing its transfer function. Still, deconvolution is an imperfect tool: whatever is lost to distortion to below the level of random noise is seldom retrievable. The prudent approach is, therefore, to design experiments with minimal noise and minimal distortion, and then to use deconvolution to reduce the effects of any remaining distortion.

*****

Visual information is primarily steady state: lighting conditions usually change slowly, and most objects around us are stationary. Even moving objects can often be represented as a sequence of stationary states, as in a movie or on television. It is therefore not surprising that spectroscopy is predominantly a steady-state method, and that the fast Fourier transform is its principal transformation tool.

On the other hand, sound is experienced primarily as a time-dependent phenomenon: we hear steps, voices, music, and tend to ignore constant background noises: the leaves rustling in the wind, the humming of fluorescent lamps, the sound of a refrigerator or of a fan moving air, the constant drone of car traffic near a highway. To analyze time-dependent phenomena we use time-frequency analysis, as described in sections 6.9 and 6.10. Note that a sonogram can be made continuously as the sound evolves, lagging only slightly because of the need to perform a single Fourier transformation.

6.12 For further reading

Many additional applications to electrical engineering and signal processing of the direct spreadsheet methods used in sections 6.1 and 6.3 are described by S. C. Bloch in his book *SSP, the Spreadsheet Signal Processor*, Prentice Hall 1992. The deconvolution of large data sets with the van Cittert algorithm is discussed in W. E. Blass and G. W. Halsey, *Deconvolution of Absorption Spectra*, Academic Press 1981, and in *Deconvolution of Images and Spectra*, edited by P. A. Jansson, Academic Press 1984, 1997.

Chapter 7

Numerical integration of ordinary differential equations

It is almost always easier to describe a complex physical system in terms of a set of differential equations than it is to solve them. Unfortunately, only relatively few of the differential equations encountered in science and technology have known solutions; many of these pertain to idealized geometries, such as that of the proverbial spherical cow. If airplane design had depended on closed-form solutions of aerodynamic equations, pigs might have evolved wings before humans would have flown in craft heavier than air.

If a closed-form solution does not exist, one can either simplify the problem while hoping to retain its most essential features, or use numerical integration. In principle, numerical integration can provide a solution to any desired accuracy for any properly specified set of differential equations. In practice, this is a large field of expertise, which often requires specialized hardware for complex problems such as the design of automobiles, camera lenses, or computer chips. However, for more mundane scientific tasks a spreadsheet may well fit the bill, which is why we will now illustrate how numerical integration can be performed in Excel. While a short chapter cannot begin to do justice to this topic, it may at least give you an idea of what is possible.

Ordinary differential equations only contain derivatives with respect to a single variable, such as time or distance, while partial differential equations have derivatives with respect to several such parameters, and are therefore more complicated. In this chapter we will illustrate the numerical integration of ordinary differential equations, with constant coefficients, that have initial or boundary conditions that are fully specified at one point in time or space. In that case, their solution can proceed in stepwise fashion from that starting moment or boundary. We will further restrict the discussion by illustrating only so-called one-point methods, and even there we will use only a few relatively simple ones.

We will use custom functions, written in VBA, the acronym for Visual BASIC for Applications. Readers unfamiliar with computer code may first want to read the introductory four sections of chapter 8 before delving into the present subject.

7.1   The explicit Euler method

When an ordinary differential equation is fully specified by initial conditions at one point in time or space, it is possible to start from that point, and to work systematically from there, repeatedly using the same *single step method*. For instance, when the differential equation is of first order, it describes the slope of the function $F(t)$, such as $dF(t)/dt$. Starting from the initial value F_0 at $t = t_0$ and its slope $(dF(t)/dt)_{t=t_0}$, we can compute $F(t_0+\Delta t)$ as long as the interval Δt is small enough so that we may consider the slope $dF(t)/dt$ as essentially constant over that interval. We then repeat this process by considering the value of $F(t_0+\Delta t)$ and the corresponding slope $(dF(t)/dt)_{t=t_0+\Delta t}$ to advance to $t = t_0 + 2\,\Delta t$, and so on. In its simplest form, the interval Δt is kept constant, but instead it might depend on some other criterion, such as the absolute magnitude of the slope at each point. In a spreadsheet, the time intervals are shown explicitly, and need not be constant throughout the calculation.

Below we will first consider two sequential first-order rate processes in series, such as occur in a two-step (mother/daughter) radioactive decay, or in two successive first-order chemical reactions. Since a closed-form solution is available, we can determine the errors involved in the simulation by comparison with the exact solution. We will use that exact solution, plus Gaussian noise, to simulate an 'experimental' data set. We will then use Solver to adjust the parameters of the numerical integration to fit the experimental data, and we will compare the thus found rate parameters with their correct values.

In this chapter we primarily consider a particular type of errors, viz. the *algorithmic* deviations caused by replacing a differential equation by an approximation thereof. These can lead to systematic bias, i.e., to inaccuracies that are by far the dominant errors in the context of this chapter. Other computational errors are seldom significant. Just for the record, among the errors not considered here are those caused by the finite representation of numbers in a computer, especially when taking differences between almost identical numbers. Those latter errors typically lead to imprecision, but the double precision of the spreadsheet usually keeps them at bay. Starting with section 8.3 we will use *custom functions*, and we will use dimensioning to make sure that double precision remains in force, so that we need not worry about truncation and round-off errors.

Below we first consider the conceptually simplest method, published by Euler as early as 1768, while the next section will describe a very useful yet still rather simple modification. We will then consider how to use custom functions to make the calculation more efficient, and how to accommodate extreme parameter values. In sections 7.5 and 7.6 we will use the more sophisticated Runge-Kutta method, while section 7.7 illustrates the application of these techniques to a somewhat more complex system of equations that can lead to oscillatory behavior; for this case no analytical solutions are known. There are many other, worthwhile methods, but this chapter cannot replace entire tomes written on this topic, and will merely indicate how to use a few of the many useful algorithms.

Here, and in the next four sections, we will consider two sequential, irreversible, first-order reactions, schematically represented by

$$A \rightarrow B \rightarrow C \tag{7.1.1}$$

which we will assume to be described by the differential equations

$$\frac{da}{dt} = -k_1 a \tag{7.1.2}$$

$$\frac{db}{dt} = k_1 a - k_2 b \tag{7.1.3}$$

$$\frac{dc}{dt} = k_2 b \tag{7.1.4}$$

where the concentrations of species A, B, and C are denoted by a, b, and c respectively, and the rate constants by k_1 and k_2. We will simulate this reaction sequence for the initial conditions

$$a_{t=0} = a_0, \qquad b_{t=0} = 0, \qquad c_{t=0} = 0 \tag{7.1.5}$$

The simplest (and crudest) approach to simulating such a set of equations is merely to replace the *differential* quotients by the corresponding *difference* quotients,

$$\frac{\Delta a}{\Delta t} \approx \frac{da}{dt} = -k_1 a \tag{7.1.6}$$

$$\frac{\Delta b}{\Delta t} \approx \frac{db}{dt} = k_1 a - k_2 b \tag{7.1.7}$$

$$\frac{\Delta c}{\Delta t} \approx \frac{dc}{dt} = k_2 b \tag{7.1.8}$$

and to compute successive changes Δa, Δb, and Δc from the resulting, approximate relations. That is precisely what is done in the *explicit Euler method*. In the present example, we start from the initial conditions at time t, and then calculate the concentrations of a, b, and c at time $t + \Delta t$ as

$$\Delta a \approx - k_1 \, a \,\, \Delta t \tag{7.1.9}$$

or

$$a_{t+\Delta t} = a_t + \Delta a \approx a_t - k_1 \, a_t \,\, \Delta t = a_t \, (1 - k_1 \, \Delta t) \tag{7.1.10}$$

and, likewise,

$$\Delta b \approx (k_1 \, a - k_2 b) \,\, \Delta t \tag{7.1.11}$$

or

$$b_{t+\Delta t} = b_t + \Delta b \approx b_t + a_t \, k_1 \,\, \Delta t - b_t \, k_2 \,\, \Delta t$$
$$= a_t \, k_1 \,\, \Delta t + b_t \, (1 - k_2 \,\, \Delta t) \tag{7.1.12}$$

and

$$\Delta c \approx k_2 \, b \,\, \Delta t \tag{7.1.13}$$

so that

$$c_{t+\Delta t} = c_t + \Delta c \approx c_t + b_t \, k_2 \,\, \Delta t \tag{7.1.14}$$

by moving a distance Δt in the direction given by the slopes defined by the right-hand sides of (7.1.6) through (7.1.8) respectively. Once we have found the concentrations at $t + \Delta t$, we use that solution to compute the value at $t + 2\Delta t$, and so on, just the way we walk, one step at a time. Typically we start the process at $t = 0$, and (except in some *chaotic* systems) we will ultimately reach a time when, for all practical purposes, either equilibrium or a cyclically repeating state is obtained, at which point the calculation can be stopped. Note that we have arbitrarily called zero the starting time of the simulation (or of the corresponding experiment), just as we might do when resetting a timer or stopwatch.

Exercise 7.1.1:

(1) Start a new spreadsheet. At its top deposit labels and numerical values for the initial conditions $a_{t=0} = a_0$, $b_{t=0} = b_0$, and $c_{t=0} = c_0$, e.g., in cells A1:B3. Do the same for the rate constants k_1 and k_2, and for the interval Δt, in C1:D3. Below those, we will use column A for time, columns B through D for the exact solutions, and columns F through H for our simulation. Since we have the benefit of an exact solution, we will use columns I:K to display the differences between our simulated solution and the exact one.

(2) In column A start at $t = 0$, and then use constant increments Δt. In columns B through D compute a through c, using their exact solutions

$$a = a_0 e^{-k_1 t} \tag{7.1.15}$$

$$b = a_0 k_1 \left(e^{-k_2 t} - e^{-k_1 t}\right) / \left(k_1 - k_2\right) \qquad (7.1.16)$$

$$c = (a_0 + b_0 + c_0) - (a + b) \qquad (7.1.17)$$

so that the instructions in, e.g., cell B8 might read =$B$1*EXP(-$D$1*$A8).

(3) In the row for $t = 0$, also deposit the initial values for a_0, b_0, and c_0 in columns F, G, and H respectively. In lower rows of those same columns, compute subsequent concentrations from their immediate predecessors using (7.1.10), (7.1.12), and (7.1.14) respectively.

(4) In column J show the differences between the simulated and exact results for a, and do the same in columns K and L for those in b and c. We use columns E and I merely as spacers.

(5) Plot your results. Your spreadsheet may now look like that in Figs. 7.1.1 and 7.1.3, and the graphs like those in Figs. 7.1.2 and 7.1.4.

The comparison of the simulated and exact curves in Fig. 7.1.2 shows that the simulation indeed yields the correct overall behavior, while focusing on their differences in Fig. 7.1.4 indicates that the agreement is only semi-quantitative. If maximum deviations of the order of a few percent are acceptable, stop right here; if not, read on.

In order to simulate a somewhat realistic data analysis, we create a make-believe data set from the exact theory with added Gaussian noise (to be replaced by experimental data if available), then use the numerical simulation to approximate the theory, and finally use Solver to adjust the latter to find the best-fitting concentration and rate parameters.

Exercise 7.1.1 (continued):

(6) Use <u>T</u>ools ⇒ <u>D</u>ata Analysis ⇒ Random Number Generation to add three columns of Gaussian ('normal') noise of zero mean and unit amplitude in some out-of-sight columns, as in N8:P108.

(7) Insert four new columns: highlight the column labels E:H, right-click, and in the resulting menu click on <u>I</u>nsert. In cell F8 place the instruction =B8+$G$1*N8, and copy this to the entire block F8:H108. Add the corresponding noise amplitude s_n in G1, with a label in F1.

(8) Temporarily set the value of s_n in G1 equal to zero. In block J1:K3 place another set of labels and numerical values for k_1, k_2, and a_0, and then make the necessary adjustments in the instructions in columns J through L so that these will now refer to the constants in K1:K3. Verify that this leaves the results in Fig. 7.1.1 unaffected. Then put a nonzero value of s_n (typically between 0.001 and 0.1) back in G1.

(9) Introduce the 'experimental' data of columns F:H into the concentration-time plot. Make the numbers in cells K1:K3 somewhat different from those in D1, D2, and B1. Now the plot will show show both the added noise and any misfit caused by changing the values in K1:K3.

(10) In order to provide Solver with criteria to gauge its progress towards a best-fitting solution, in cell N1 place the instruction =SUMXMY2(F8:F108,J8: J108), then copy this instruction to cells O1 and P1.

	A	B	C	D	
1	a0 = 1		k1 = 1		
2	b0 = 0		k2 = 0.5		
3	c0 = 0		Δt = 0.1		
4					
5			*exact solution*		
6	*t*	*a*	*b*	*c*	
7					
8	0.0	1.000	0.000	0.000	
9	0.1	0.905	0.093	0.002	
10	0.2	0.819	0.172	0.009	
11	0.3	0.741	0.240	0.019	
12	0.4	0.670	0.297	0.033	
13	0.5	0.607	0.345	0.049	
14	0.6	0.549	0.384	0.067	
15	0.7	0.497	0.416	0.087	
16	0.8	0.449	0.442	0.109	
17	0.9	0.407	0.462	0.131	
18	1.0	0.368	0.477	0.155	
19	1.1	0.333	0.488	0.179	

Fig. 7.1.1: The top left-hand corner of the spreadsheet of exercise 7.1.1.

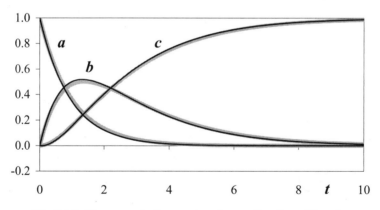

Fig. 7.1.2: The concentrations *a*, *b*, and *c* as a function of time *t*. Broad gray curves: exact solution; solid black curves: simulation.

(11) When we can monitor all three concentrations as a function of time *t*, a proper criterion for optimizing the adjustable parameters in K1:K3 with Solver might be the sum of the quantities computed in N1:P1. Therefore, calculate the sums of squares of all the residuals in O2 as =N1+O1+P1.

F	G	H	I	J	K	L

explicit Euler integration			errors		
a	*b*	*c*	*in a*	*in b*	*in c*
1.0000	0.0000	0.000	0.0000	0.0000	0.0000
0.9000	0.1000	0.000	-0.0048	0.0072	-0.0024
0.8100	0.1850	0.005	-0.0087	0.0128	-0.0041
0.7290	0.2568	0.014	-0.0118	0.0170	-0.0052
0.6561	0.3168	0.027	-0.0142	0.0200	-0.0058
0.5905	0.3666	0.043	-0.0160	0.0220	-0.0060
0.5314	0.4073	0.061	-0.0174	0.0233	-0.0059
0.4783	0.4401	0.082	-0.0183	0.0239	-0.0056
0.4305	0.4659	0.104	-0.0189	0.0239	-0.0051
0.3874	0.4857	0.127	-0.0191	0.0235	-0.0044
0.3487	0.5001	0.151	-0.0192	0.0228	-0.0036
0.3138	0.5100	0.176	-0.0191	0.0218	-0.0028

Fig. 7.1.3: Columns F through L of the spreadsheet of exercise 7.1.1.

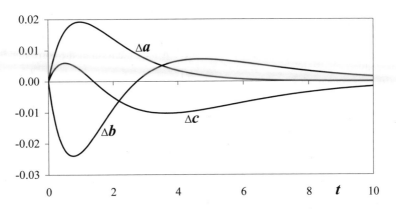

Fig. 7.1.4: The differences ε between the results from numerical integration and the exact solution, emphasized by using a greatly enlarged vertical scale.

(12) Call Solver, and instruct it to minimize O2 while adjusting K1:K3. As your finishing touch, call SolverAid and find the associated uncertainties. Figure 7.1.5 illustrates what you might get in the presence of a fair amount of noise.

(13) For smaller values of s_n the recovered parameters will be closer to those assumed in B1, D1, and D2, and the standard deviations will be smaller; for larger values of *na*, the opposite will be true.

(14) Save the spreadsheet for later use.

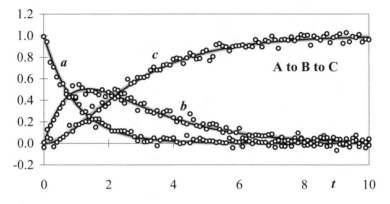

Fig. 7.1.5: Fitting simulated noisy data (open circles) to the model. The gray bands are the theoretical curves in the absence of noise; the found best-fitting curves are shown as thin black lines. Assumed data: $a_0 = 1$, $k_1 = 1$, $k_2 = 0.5$, $s_n = 0.03$.

(15) Using the explicit Euler method and Solver yields $a_0 = 0.9995$, $k_1 = 0.9411$, $k_2 = 0.5044$, while SolverAid yields the corresponding standard deviations $s_0 = 0.0111$, $s_1 = 0.1678$, $s_2 = 0.0665$, so that the results are best described as $a_0 = 0.99_9 \pm 0.01_1$, $k_1 = 0.9_4 \pm 0.1_7$, $k_2 = 0.50_4 \pm 0.06_7$, fairly close to the assumed values of $a_0 = 1$, $k_1 = 1$, and $k_2 = 0.5$.

(16) Keep in mind that the parameters you find will be correlated rather than independent, i.e., changes in one may affect the values of the others. If such parameters are to be used in subsequent calculations, the covariances between a_0, k_1, and k_2 should also be obtained from SolverAid, in the form of the corresponding covariance matrix.

(17) If you could only monitor the concentration *b* of species B as a function of time *t*, the proper criterion for optimizing Solver would instead be the sum of squares of residuals as calculated in O1. In that case you would obtain slightly different results; in the above example, you would find $a_0 = 0.97_3 \pm 0.07_0$, $k_1 = 0.9_8 \pm 0.1_0$, $k_2 = 0.49_7 \pm 0.04_2$. If you had only measurements on *c*, you would instead use the sum of the squares of the residuals in P1, and find $a_0 = 1.00_3 \pm 0.01_2$, $k_1 = 1.10 \pm 0.1_9$, $k_2 = 0.49_0 \pm 0.05_5$. A different simulation would also yield slightly different results, because (simulated or real) noise is never quite the same. Therefore, don't over-specify the found parameters: they are only estimates. Here they are given with one extra, subscripted guard digit that is *not* significant, but merely guards against systematic round-off errors in possible uses of these numbers in subsequent computations.

(18) Incidentally, measurements of *a* alone would not be as useful: since *a* does not depend on k_2, such measurements can only yield a_0 and k_1. If you tried, you would see that Solver in that case wouldn't change the value of k_2 from its initial

guess, and that SolverAid would therefore, somewhat misleadingly, assign it a standard deviation of zero.

(19) Save the spreadsheet.

7.2 The semi-implicit Euler method

The procedure illustrated above uses the *initial* concentrations to compute the behavior during the interval Δt. We do not know how those concentrations are going to change, but instead of assuming a to remain constant we will now approximate the change in a as linear over a sufficiently small interval Δt. This leads to the *semi-implicit Euler method*, in which we replace, say, the concentration a_n during the interval from t_n to t_{n+1} by its average value $(a_n + a_{n+1})/2 = a_n + (a_{n+1} - a_n)/2 = a_n + \Delta a/2$. Upon replacing the concentrations a, b, and c in (7.1.6) through (7.1.8) by their initial values plus half their anticipated changes we have

$$\frac{\Delta a}{\Delta t} \approx -k_1(a + \Delta a/2) \tag{7.2.1}$$

$$\frac{\Delta b}{\Delta t} \approx k_1(a + \Delta a/2) - k_2(b + \Delta b/2) \tag{7.2.2}$$

$$\frac{\Delta c}{\Delta t} \approx k_2(b + \Delta b/2) \tag{7.2.3}$$

from which we obtain

$$\Delta a \approx \frac{-a k_1 \Delta t}{1 + k_1 \Delta t/2} \tag{7.2.4}$$

$$a_{t+\Delta t} = a_t + \Delta a \approx \frac{1 - k_1 \Delta t/2}{1 + k_1 \Delta t/2} a_t \tag{7.2.5}$$

$$\Delta b \approx \frac{a k_1 \Delta t}{(1 + k_1 \Delta t/2)(1 + k_2 \Delta t/2)} - \frac{b k_2 \Delta t}{(1 + k_2 \Delta t/2)} \tag{7.2.6}$$

$$b_{t+\Delta t} = b_t + \Delta b$$

$$\approx \frac{a_t k_1 \Delta t}{(1 + k_1 \Delta t/2)(1 + k_2 \Delta t/2)} + \frac{(1 - k_2 \Delta t/2) b_t}{(1 + k_2 \Delta t/2)} \tag{7.2.7}$$

We need not compute c, because it follows directly from the mass balance (7.1.17). Still, for the sake of completeness, it is listed here as

$$\Delta c \approx (b + \Delta b/2) k_2 \Delta t \tag{7.2.8}$$

$$c_{t+\Delta t} \approx c_t + (b_t + b_{t+\Delta t}) \, k_2 \Delta t / 2 \qquad (7.2.9)$$

We see that equations such as (7.2.1), (7.2.2), and (7.2.3) cannot be used directly, but must first be solved for the concentration changes Δa, Δb, and Δc. This accounts for the *implicit* in the semi-implicit Euler method. It is only *semi*-implicit because $(a_n + a_{n+1})/2 = a_n + \Delta a/2$ combines half of the known term a_n with half of the next one, a_{n+1}. For linear systems, this is the best one can do and still retain an absolutely stable solution.

Exercise 7.2.1:

(1) Copy the spreadsheet of exercise 7.1.1 to a new page of the same workbook. In columns J and K of this copy, change the instructions to incorporate (7.2.5) and (7.2.7) instead of (7.1.10) and (7.1.12) respectively. In column L you can use either (7.1.17) or (7.2.9).

(2) Click on the curves in your equivalent of Fig. 7.1.4 to the new page, then redirect their definitions in the formula box to the current worksheet. In doing so, be careful not to alter the general format of the argument: (*,sheetname!* *Xn:Xm,sheetname!Yn:Ym,p*), where *Xn:Xm* and *Yn:Ym* specify the ranges, and *p* defines the relative precedence of the curves, with the highest number being shown on top of the other curves. All you need to change in the argument is the *sheetname*, which you find on the tab at the bottom of the spreadsheet. Incidentally, the equivalent of Fig. 7.1.2 is immaterial, because any differences are too small to be visible on this scale.

(3) The improvement in Fig. 7.2.1 over the results shown in Fig. 7.1.4 is immediate and dramatic: for the same step size ($\Delta t = 0.1$) the errors are now more than an order of magnitude smaller.

(4) Repeat the analysis of the simulated data set with added Gaussian noise. For the same noisy data as used in Fig. 7.1.4 we now find $a_0 = 0.992_1 \pm 0.009_6$, $k_1 = 0.995_4 \pm 0.007_0$, $k_2 = 0.496 \pm 0.01_4$, a much better overall fit to the assumed values of $a_0 = 1$, $k_1 = 1$, and $k_2 = 0.5$ than obtained earlier.

(5) As suggested by comparing Figs. 7.1.4 and 7.2.1, the improvement is more obvious for data that contain less noise. For example, for $\Delta t = 0.1$ and the same Gaussian noise but now with $s_n = 0.01$ the results of the explicit and semi-implicit Euler methods would be $a_0 = 0.998_3 \pm 0.003_8$, $k_1 = 0.944 \pm 0.05_8$, $k_2 = 0.50_3 \pm 0.02_3$ and $a_0 = 0.997_3 \pm 0.003_2$, $k_1 = 0.998_5 \pm 0.002_3$, $k_2 = 0.498_7 \pm 0.004_7$ respectively. Here the explicit method clearly shows its bias.

You may wonder what constitutes a *fully implicit* Euler method. Instead of the average value of the slope (as in the semi-implicit method), or its initial value (as in the explicit method), it uses the final value of the slope to evaluate the new value of $F(t)$. Since that is just as lopsided as using the initial value, the implicit Euler method has an inaccuracy proportional to Δt, i.e., comparable to that of the explicit Euler method, and inferior to the inaccuracy $\propto (\Delta t)^2$ of the semi-implicit method.

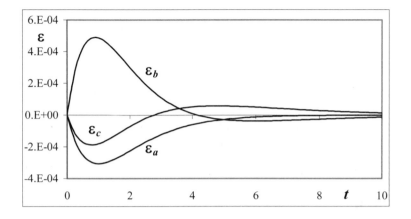

Fig. 7.2.1: The differences between the numerically integrated and exact solutions for the semi-implicit Euler method with $\Delta t = 0.1$.

In our example, the implicit Euler method would read

$$\frac{\Delta a}{\Delta t} \approx -k_1(a + \Delta a) \tag{7.2.10}$$

$$\frac{\Delta b}{\Delta t} \approx k_1(a + \Delta a) - k_2(b + \Delta b) \tag{7.2.11}$$

from which we would obtain

$$\Delta a \approx \frac{-a\,k_1\Delta t}{1 + k_1\Delta t} \tag{7.2.12}$$

$$a_{t+\Delta t} = a_t + \Delta a \approx \frac{a_t}{1 + k_1\Delta t} \tag{7.2.13}$$

$$\Delta b \approx \frac{a\,k_1\Delta t}{(1 + k_1\Delta t)\,(1 + k_2\Delta t)} - \frac{b\,k_2\Delta t}{(1 + k_2\Delta t)} \tag{7.2.14}$$

$$b_{t+\Delta t} = b_t + \Delta b \approx \frac{a_t\,k_1\Delta t}{(1 + k_1\Delta t)\,(1 + k_2\Delta t)} + \frac{b_t}{(1 + k_2\Delta t)}$$

$$= \frac{a_{t+\Delta t}\,k_1\Delta t + b_t}{(1 + k_2\Delta t)} \tag{7.2.15}$$

Upon comparing, e.g., (7.2.1) with (7.1.6) and (7.2.10), we verify that the semi-implicit method is indeed the average of the explicit and implicit Euler methods. It combines the absolute stability of the implicit method with an accuracy that is higher than that of either the explicit or implicit Euler method, and is therefore often the method of choice for solving simple problems involving ordinary differential equations.

7.3 Using custom functions

As indicated in the previous paragraph, the successful fitting of simulated, noisy data can be somewhat misleading, since a generous amount of noise may mask many inadequacies of the model. For fitting data with a high signal-to-noise ratio we may therefore need to improve the algorithm, as we will do in section 7.5. However, we can go a long way with the Euler methods by using the spreadsheet more intelligently.

Equations (7.1.6) through (7.1.8) clearly show that the simulation is based on replacing the differential quotients dy/dt by difference quotients $\Delta y/\Delta t$, a substitution that should become increasingly accurate as Δt becomes smaller. You can readily verify that the simulation errors shown in Figs. 7.1.4 and 7.2.1 indeed stem from the step size Δt. For example, upon reducing Δt by a factor of ten, the concentration differences Δc in Fig. 7.1.4 also become smaller by an order of magnitude, and those in Fig. 7.2.1 by two orders of magnitude.

However, in order to cover the same total time (in the above example: from $t = 0$ to $t = 10$), we would have to lengthen the columns ten-fold, to 1000 rows. Further reductions in Δt would make the columns even longer. This will quickly lead to impracticably long columns. Moreover, it may be undesirable to lengthen the columns, e.g., because we may only have experimental data at given intervals Δt. Below we will indicate how we can improve the accuracy of our simulation *without* increasing the column length.

Exercise 7.3.1:

(1) Return to the spreadsheet of exercise 7.2.1, and set the values in K1:K3 back to the corresponding values in B1:B3.

(2) For the concentration a an elegant solution exists that does not require an increased column length. We saw in (7.2.5) that $a_{t+\Delta t} \approx a_t (1 - k_1\Delta t/2) / (1 + k_1 \Delta t/2)$. Upon applying this n times with an n times smaller interval Δt we find $a_{t+n\Delta t} \approx a_t \{[1 - k_1\Delta t/(2n)]/ [1 - k_1\Delta t/(2n)]\}^n$, so that we can replace the instruction in cell J9 for a by, say, =J8*((1-$K$1*$D$3/20)/(1+$K$1* $D$3/20))^10 for $n = 10$. Copy this down through row 108. This will improve the precision of the simulated a-values another two orders of magnitude *without* lengthening the columns. Try it. Then change the value of n in these instructions from 10 to, say, 1000, and observe its effect.

Unfortunately, this trick does not work for the other concentrations, because (7.2.7) and (7.2.9) do not have such a simple recursivity. For those more general cases we will need to use some spreadsheet magic. Excel allows us to incorporate so-called *user-defined* or *custom* functions. These have much in common with small macros (to be discussed at length in chapter 8), except that they apply only to a *numerical value* in a *single* spreadsheet cell. On the other hand, custom functions update automatically, which in the present context is a significant advantage. Below we will use custom functions to compute the concentrations *a*, *b*, and *c* to higher accuracies by reducing the step size while keeping constant the number of spreadsheet cells used in the simulation. If writing computer code is new to you, you may first want to read sections 8.1 through 8.4 of the next chapter before continuing here.

Exercise 7.3.1 (continued):

(3) Return to the spreadsheet, and press Alt⌣F11 (on the Mac: Opt⌣F11). You will see a Microsoft Visual Basic screen appear, with its own menu bar. On *that* bar, select Insert ⇒ Module if the display does not show a white writing area to the right of the Project column; otherwise, if a page already exists, just move to the end of any text on it. Then enter (type, or copy from SampleMacros) the following instructions:

```
'semi-implicit Euler method for A
Function siEulerA(k1, oldT1, oldT2, n, oldA) As Double

Dim A As Double, f As Double, step As Double
Dim i As Integer

n = CInt(n)
A = oldA
step = (oldT2 - oldT1) / n
f = (1 - k1 * step / 2) / (1 + k1 * step / 2)

For i = 1 To n
  A = A * f
Next i
siEulerA = A

End Function
```

(4) A short explanation is in order. The top line, starting with an apostrophe, contains a *comment* that will be ignored by the spreadsheet but reminds the user of the purpose of the function. The next line specifies the name by which we can call this function, the parameters it will use (in exactly the same order as used here in the function *argument*, i.e., within the brackets following the function name), and (optionally) its precision; the last line identifies its end.

(5) The next three lines define the types of constants used in the function; do *not* specify the dimensions of parameters (such as k1, oldT1, etc.) that are imported through the function argument. In general these lines are optional though very useful; they are mandatory if you use Option Explicit, an option that, when used, is listed at the very top of your module.

(6) The sixth line (optional as well) makes sure that the method will work even if a non-integer value for *n* is used by mistake, by converting it to an integer *n* with the instruction CInt (for *c*onvert to *int*eger). This line will be executed from right to left, i.e., the computer takes the value of *n*, converts it to an integer (if it isn't already one), and then assigns that value to the variable to the left of the equal sign. We insert this line here merely to illustrate how you can make a function somewhat less error-prone by anticipating possible mistakes. This does not imply that the function is now immune to entry errors: using zero for *n* would certainly trip up the function when it tries to divide by 0 in the next line of code, and using a negative number, or a letter, would also give problems.

(8) Line 7 sets the concentration parameter A equal to the value of oldA imported through the function argument. The calculation starts in earnest on line 8 by defining the new step size, step. By letting oldT1 and oldT2 refer to relative addresses of cells containing *t* in successive rows of the spreadsheet, the time intervals in the spreadsheet need not be equidistant. Alternatively we can make the step size constant throughout the calculation by referring to absolute addresses for oldT1 and oldT2 respectively.

(9) Lines 10 through 12 contain the action part of the function, by *n* times repeating the computation of A for a time interval step that is *n* times smaller than the data spacing oldT2 − oldT1.

(10) Again, the equal sign here functions as an *assignment*. In other words, the line A = A * f should be read as if it were written as A ⇐ A * f, i.e., as "replace A by A * f."

(11) We calculate the value of f separately on line 9, rather than use, e.g., A= A*(1−k1*step/2)/(1+k1*step/2) directly in line 11, because line 9 is executed only once, whereas in line 11 the same calculation would be repeated *n* times. It is in such loops that we should be most careful to avoid busy work, because it can noticeably slow down the computation. Note that the line specifying f must follow the definition of step, because it uses its value which, otherwise, would not be defined.

(12) Finally, the output of the function is defined in its penultimate line. Incidentally, you will have noticed that a number of words you have entered (Function, As Double, Dim, As Integer, etc.) are displayed in blue after you have entered the line on which they appear. These are terms the Visual Basic editor recognizes as instruction keywords, and seeing them in color therefore assures you that your instructions are being read.

(13) Now enter the corresponding instructions for siEulerB, or copy the instructions for siEulerA and then correct and amend that copy. For your convenience, the changes between the two sets of instructions are shown below in boldface.

```
'semi-implicit Euler method for B
Function siEulerB _
  (k1, k2, oldT1, oldT2, n, oldA, oldB) As Double

Dim A As Double, B As Double, step As Double
Dim f As Double, fA As Double, fB As Double
Dim i As Integer

n = CInt(n)
A = oldA
B = oldB
```

```
step = (oldT2 - oldT1) / n
f = (1 - k1 * step / 2) / (1 + k1 * step / 2)
fA = k1 * step / ((1 + k1 * step / 2) _
  * (1 + k2 * step / 2))
fB = (1 - k2 * step / 2) / (1 + k2 * step / 2)
For i = 1 To n
  B = A * fA + B * fB
  A = A * f
Next i
siEulerB = B

End Function
```

(14) Note the use of a space followed by an underscore at the end of line 1, in order to indicate a *line continuation*. This allows us to break up a long instruction so that it will be visible on the monitor screen (or the printed page) while being interpreted by the computer as a single line. There can be no text on that line beyond the continuation sign.

(15) In order to use the functions you have just entered, exit the editor with Alt∪F11 (Mac: Opt∪F11), which toggles you back to the spreadsheet. On the spreadsheet, in cell F2 place the label n=, and in G2 its value, which should be a positive integer larger than 0.

(16) Replace the instruction in J9 by `siEulerA($K$1,$A8,$A9,$G$2, J8)`, and copy this instruction down to row 108. Likewise replace the instruction in K9 by `siEulerB($K$1,$K$2,$A8,$A9,$G$2,J8,K8)`, and see what happens with the concentration differences in columns N through P.

(17) Convert the instructions in columns N through P to the corresponding logarithms, so that you need not change the scale of the graph every time you change the value of *n*.

(18) Run the spreadsheet with $\Delta t = 0.1$ and various values for *n*, such as 1, 10, and 100. With $n = 100$, the plot of the concentration errors should look like Fig. 7.3.1. By using one-hundred times smaller steps, the error in the semi-implicit Euler method has been reduced ten-thousand-fold.

(19) Try $\Delta t = 0.1$ with $n = 1000$. Depending on the speed of your computer, the computation may now take its sweet time (after all, in each of the 100 cells you make the For ... Next loop do 1000 complete calculations), but you get rewarded with absolute errors that are all smaller than 5×10^{-10}! That will be good enough for almost any experiment.

(20) Reset the values in K1:K3 to new guess values, and rerun Solver and SolverAid. For almost any realistic noise the accuracy of your results will now be limited by that noise, rather than by inadequacies in the model. And that is precisely where you want to be: the computation should not add any inaccuracies to your experimental results.

(21) Go back to exercise 7.1.1 and write the corresponding functions eEulerA and eEulerB for the *explicit* case. Then try them out, see how they run. For the same $\Delta t = 0.1$, what value of *n* do you need in order to get the errors down to the same order of magnitude as those shown in Fig. 7.3.1?

(22) Save the spreadsheet for further use in section 7.5.

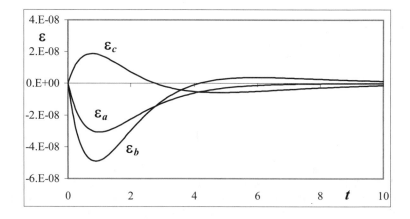

Fig. 7.3: The differences between the numerically integrated and exact solutions for the semi-implicit Euler method with $\Delta t = 0.1$ and $n = 100$ for an actual step size of 0.001.

7.4 Extreme parameter values

The reaction scheme we have adopted here has two rate constants, k_1 and k_2. In our examples we have so far assumed that k_1 and k_2 are of a similar order of magnitude, but that is not necessarily the case. For purely mathematical solutions, such as (7.1.15) through (7.1.17), the particular values of the rate constants make no difference. (There is a trivial exception to this statement, because setting k_2 equal to k_1 makes (7.1.16) equal to 0/0. This complication can readily be avoided by making the difference between k_2 and k_1 negligibly small rather than zero.) By contrast, in a numerical simulation the specific values of the rate constants often do matter. For instance, when $k_2 \gg k_1$, the simulation may fail, because it is based on $k_1\Delta t \ll 1$, whereas $k_2\Delta t$ might then be much greater than 1. And when this is accommodated by taking more steps, the computation may become far too slow to be practicable. Below we will consider what to do in such a situation.

We split the case into two parts. When k_2 is not much larger than k_1, we make sure that the step Δt size is appropriately decreased. However, with $k_2 \gg k_1$ this would lead to quite lengthy computations. On the other hand, in such an extreme case there is often a good approximation that can be used instead. Specifically, when the decay of B to C is very much faster than its generation from A, the concentration b will be small and, to a good approximation, will be given by the steady state approximation $db/dt \approx 0$, which upon substitution into (7.1.3) yields $b \approx k_1a/k_2$. We can set the switchover point such that the answers provided by the two methods coincide to within the desired accuracy. The following modified function will compute *b* for any value of k_2.

Exercise 7.4.1:

(1) Return to the spreadsheet of exercise 7.3.1, and test how far you can increase the value of k_2 (while keeping k_1 constant at, say, $k_1 = 1$) before the program starts to fail. Such failure is most readily seen in the plot of log ε vs. *t*, where ε is the inaccuracy obtained by comparison with the exact solution.

(2) Add the function iEulerBB listed below to the VBA module. The changes with respect to iEulerB are shown in bold.

```
'semi-implicit Euler method for B, modified so that
'it will switch automatically to the steady state
'approximation when k2/k1 becomes larger than a
'given value, here called crit (for criterium).
Function siEulerBB _
    (k1, k2, oldT1, oldT2, n, crit, oldA, oldB) As Double

Dim A As Double, B As Double, step As Double
Dim f As Double, fA As Double, fB As Double
Dim i As Long, m As Long

n = CLng(n)
A = oldA
B = oldB
step = (oldT2 - oldT1) / n
f = (1 - k1 * step / 2) / (1 + k1 * step / 2)
If k2 / k1 > crit Then
  For i = 1 To n
    A = A * f
  Next i
  B = k1 * A / k2                ' The steady state approximation
End If
If (k2 / k1 > 1 And k2 / k1 <= crit) Then
  m = CLng(Sqr(k2 / k1))
  n = m * n
  step = step / m
  f = (1 - k1 * step / 2) / (1 + k1 * step / 2)
End If
If k2 / k1 <= crit Then
  fA = k1 * step / ((1 + k1 * step / 2) _
    * (1 + k2 * step / 2))
  fB = (1 - k2 * step / 2) / (1 + k2 * step / 2)
  For i = 1 To n
    B = A * fA + B * fB
    A = A * f
  Next i
End If
siEulerBB = B

End Function
```

(3) The change from Integer to Long in the dimension statements reflects the fact that single precision integers can only count up to $2^{15} - 1 = 32\,767$, which may not suffice for the product of *n* times *crit*.

(4) For extremely large k_2-values the function uses the steady-state approxima-tion $b = k_1 a / k_2$. Otherwise, the calculation is as before, except that the step size is enlarged for $k_2 > k_1$.

(5) The first If ... Then statement singles out the case $k_2 / k_1 > crit$, calculates a in the usual way, then finds b with the steady state approximation. The second If ... Then statement increases the value of n when $1 \le k_2 / k_1 \le crit$. The final If ... Then condition contains code similar to that in siEulerB, except that the value of n will now depend on whether the second If ... Then condition was met.

(6) Enter a label and value for $crit$. You might try an initial value for $crit$ of 1000.

(7) Replace siEulerB by siEulerBB (including the added variable $crit$ in its ar-gument), and make sure that it yields the same results as before for values of k_2 not exceeding the product of k_1 and $crit$. Store a value for $crit$ in G3. For ease of testing, again set the values in K1:K3 back to those in B1:D3.

(8) Now test whether the function yields satisfactory results for $k_2 > crit \times k_1$. This is most readily done by examining the plot of log ε vs. t just before and after k_2 crosses the value of $crit \times k_2$. You must of course change the values of k_2 in both D2 and K2.

(9) Implement and test an equivalent extension to include large k_2-values for the explicit Euler method, by creating the corresponding function eEulerBB.

(10) Save the spreadsheet.

When $k_2 \ll k_1$, for the same initial conditions (7.1.5), we essentially have two *decoupled* reactions: first A decays to B which, in turn, though at a much more leisurely pace, reacts to form C. Staying with constant time intervals Δt then becomes very inefficient, because the time scale of the simulation was chosen such that $k_1 \Delta t \ll 1$, a time scale that is far more detailed than needed for the decay of B into C. Here, then, it is practical to change the data spacing after the concentration of A has decayed to near-zero. This is why it is convenient to let the function calculate the step size in every cell, depending on the local change in t between suc-cessive rows. It allows you to go slowly where needed, and fast where possible, just the way you would drive your car: slow near pedestrian crossings or in bad weather, fast on the open highway on a clear day with little traffic.

7.5   The explicit Runge-Kutta method

The combination of the semi-implicit Euler method with the increased efficiency (within a given column length) of custom functions can inte-grate virtually every ordinary differential equation to any desired accu-racy. It will serve to solve almost any problem simple enough to be done on a spreadsheet, and almost always will produce model curves more than adequate for comparison with experimental data.

Still, while the Euler methods are *conceptually* simple, they are *computationally* relatively inefficient. In the present section we explore another approach that leads to algorithms that use the computer more efficiently, although they tend to take more time to implement. How to balance personal time versus computer time depends, of course, on the speed of your computer, on the anticipated amount of use of the computation, and on the value and availability of your time.

In the explicit Euler method, we solve equations of the type of (7.1.6) through (7.1.8) by making small steps from t to $t + \Delta t$ with the slopes specified by the differential equations at time t. The Runge-Kutta approach instead uses slopes appropriately *averaged* over the interval Δt. This yields a method that needs fewer steps for a given accuracy, reaches higher accuracies for the same number of steps, or some combination of these.

We will here illustrate the most popular, fourth-order explicit Runge-Kutta method. Even for a given order, there are several possible Runge-Kutta formalisms, but the resulting differences in performance are too inconsequential to concern us here.

When applied to a single ordinary first-order differential equation

$$\frac{dy}{dt} = F(y) \tag{7.5.1}$$

such as encountered in (7.1.2), the explicit fourth-order Runge-Kutta method uses the relations

$$y_{n+1} = y_n + \frac{1}{6}\left(K_1 + 2K_2 + 2K_3 + K_4\right) \tag{7.5.2}$$

where

$$K_1 = \Delta t\, F(y_n) \tag{7.5.3}$$
$$K_2 = \Delta t\, F(y_n + K_1/2) \tag{7.5.4}$$
$$K_3 = \Delta t\, F(y_n + K_2/2) \tag{7.5.5}$$
$$K_4 = \Delta t\, F(y_n + K_3) \tag{7.5.6}$$

Exercise 7.5.1:
(1) Extend the spreadsheet used in exercise 7.1.1 to accommodate additional columns: three for a through c, and three for the corresponding errors ε.
(2) Switch to the module of the Visual Basic Editor, and enter the following function:

```
'explicit fourth-order Runge-Kutta method for A
Function e4RKA(k1, oldT1, oldT2, n, oldA) As Double

Dim A As Double, step As Double
```

```
Dim KA1 As Double, KA2 As Double
Dim KA3 As Double, KA4 As Double
Dim i As Integer

n = CInt(n)
A = oldA
step = (oldT2 - oldT1) / n
For i = 1 To n
  KA1 = step * -k1 * A
  KA2 = step * -k1 * (A + KA1 / 2)
  KA3 = step * -k1 * (A + KA2 / 2)
  KA4 = step * -k1 * (A + KA3)
  A = A + (KA1 + 2 * KA2 + 2 * KA3 + KA4) / 6
Next i
e4RKA = A

End Function
```

(3) In the definition of KA1 you will recognize the *function F(y)* of (7.5.1) as − k1*A, while the *variable y* is there specified as A. Therefore, the expression $K_2 = \Delta t \times F(y_n + K_1/2)$ in (7.5.4) is coded in the function statement as KA2=step*−k1*(A+KA1/2), i.e., with A replaced by (A+KA1/2).

For *b* the situation is more complicated, because the expression for *db/dt* depends not only on *b* but also on *a*. For an ordinary first-order differential equation of the form

$$\frac{dy}{dt} = F(y,z) \tag{7.5.7}$$

the corresponding relations for the explicit fourth-order Runge-Kutta method are

$$y_{n+1} = y_n + \frac{1}{6}\left(K_{y1} + 2K_{y2} + 2K_{y3} + K_{y4}\right) \tag{7.5.8}$$

$$z_{n+1} = z_n + \frac{1}{6}\left(K_{z1} + 2K_{z2} + 2K_{z3} + K_{z4}\right) \tag{7.5.9}$$

where

$$K_{y1} = \Delta t\, F(y_n,\ z_n) \tag{7.5.10}$$

$$K_{y2} = \Delta t\, F(y_n + K_{y1}/2,\ z_n + K_{z1}/2) \tag{7.5.11}$$

$$K_{y3} = \Delta t\, F(y_n + K_{y2}/2,\ z_n + K_{z2}/2) \tag{7.5.12}$$

$$K_{y4} = \Delta t\, F(y_n + K_{y3},\ z_n + K_{z3}) \tag{7.5.13}$$

$$K_{z1} = \Delta t\, G(y_n,\ z_n) \tag{7.5.14}$$

$$K_{z2} = \Delta t\, G(y_n + K_{y1}/2,\ z_n + K_{z1}/2) \tag{7.5.15}$$

$$K_{z3} = \Delta t\, G(y_n + K_{y2}/2,\ z_n + K_{z2}/2) \tag{7.5.16}$$

$$K_{z4} = \Delta t\, G(y_n + K_{y3},\ z_n + K_{z3}) \tag{7.5.17}$$

which relations are used in the spreadsheet function e4RKB.

When the ordinary first-order differential equation has the form

$$\frac{dy}{dt} = F(t, y, z) \tag{7.5.18}$$

the corresponding relations for the explicit fourth-order Runge-Kutta method are

$$y_{n+1} = y_n + \frac{1}{6}\left(K_{y1} + 2K_{y2} + 2K_{y3} + K_{y4}\right) \tag{7.5.19}$$

$$z_{n+1} = z_n + \frac{1}{6}\left(K_{z1} + 2K_{z2} + 2K_{z3} + K_{z4}\right) \tag{7.5.20}$$

where

$$K_{y1} = \Delta t\, F(t_n,\ y_n,\ z_n) \tag{7.5.21}$$

$$K_{y2} = \Delta t\, F(t_n + \Delta t/2,\ y_n + K_{y1}/2,\ z_n + K_{z1}/2) \tag{7.5.22}$$

$$K_{y3} = \Delta t\, F(t_n + \Delta t/2,\ y_n + K_{y2}/2,\ z_n + K_{z2}/2) \tag{7.5.23}$$

$$K_{y4} = \Delta t\, F(t_n + \Delta t,\ y_n + K_{y3},\ z_n + K_{z3}) \tag{7.5.24}$$

$$K_{z1} = \Delta t\, G(t_n,\ y_n,\ z_n) \tag{7.5.25}$$

$$K_{z2} = \Delta t\, G(t_n + \Delta t/2,\ y_n + K_{y1}/2,\ z_n + K_{z1}/2) \tag{7.5.26}$$

$$K_{z3} = \Delta t\, G(t_n + \Delta t/2,\ y_n + K_{y2}/2,\ z_n + K_{z2}/2) \tag{7.5.27}$$

$$K_{z4} = \Delta t\, G(t_n + \Delta t,\ y_n + K_{y3},\ z_n + K_{z3}) \tag{7.5.28}$$

Exercise 7.5.1 (continued):
(4) Add the code for the function e4RKB; as before, those regions that are different from e4RKA are shown in boldface.

```
'explicit fourth-order Runge-Kutta method for B
Function e4RKB (k1, k2, oldT1, oldT2, n, oldA, oldB) _
  As Double

Dim A As Double, B As Double, step As Double
Dim KA1 As Double, KA2 As Double
Dim KA3 As Double, KA4 As Double
Dim KB1 As Double, KB2 As Double
Dim KB3 As Double, KB4 As Double
Dim i As Integer

n = CInt(n)
A = oldA
B = oldB
step = (oldT2 - oldT1) / n
For i = 1 To n
  KA1 = step * -k1 * A
  KA2 = step * -k1 * (A + KA1 / 2)
  KA3 = step * -k1 * (A + KA2 / 2)
  KA4 = step * -k1 * (A + KA3)
  KB1 = step * (k1 * A - k2 * B)
  KB2 = step * (k1 * (A + KA1 / 2) - k2 * (B + KB1 / 2))
```

```
      KB3 = step * (k1 * (A + KA2 / 2) - k2 * (B + KB2 / 2))
      KB4 = step * (k1 * (A + KA3) - k2 * (B + KB3))
      B = B + (KB1 + 2 * KB2 + 2 * KB3 + KB4) / 6
      A = A + (KA1 + 2 * KA2 + 2 * KA3 + KA4) / 6
  Next i
  e4RKB = B

End Function
```

(5) Return to the spreadsheet with Alt⌣F11 (Mac: Opt⌣F11).

(6) Refer to the numerical values of a_0, b_0, and c_0 in the top cells of the first three new columns.

(7) In the second row in the new column for a place the instruction =e4RKA(), where the addresses within the brackets refer to the parameters listed in the function argument.

(8) Similarly, in the cell to its immediate right, deposit the instruction =e4RKB() with the appropriate arguments. Copy both instructions down.

(9) In the third added column calculate c by difference, based on (7.1.17), as done earlier. And in the next three columns compute the algorithmic errors by comparing the results of the explicit fourth-order Runge-Kutta expressions for a, b, and c with their exact solutions.

(10) You should now find results similar to those shown in Fig. 7.5.1. The algorithmic errors are now already quite small for $n = 1$, i.e., for steps of $\Delta t = 0.1$, so that there is hardly a need for using multiple iterations per cell.

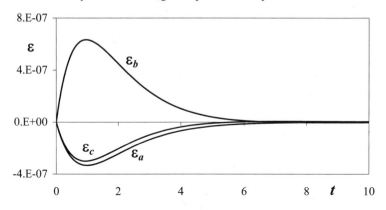

Fig. 7.5.1: The differences ε between the numerically integrated and exact solutions for the explicit fourth-order Runge-Kutta method with $\Delta t = 0.1$ and $n = 1$, i.e., for a step size of 0.1.

In this example, the much greater accuracy of the Runge-Kutta method makes it possible to use rather large steps and still have quite acceptable accuracy. Multiple steps per cell may still be needed to accommodate values of k_2 much larger than k_1, see section 7.4. Starting from the custom functions given here, the time and effort needed in order to apply the Runge-Kutta method to another set of differential equations are relatively small, since you only need to change the specific formulas in the definitions for the various K-values.

7.6 The Lotka oscillator 1

We will now apply the above methods to the Lotka model of two coupled autocatalytic reactions that, for certain combinations of concentrations and rate parameters, can give rise to steady-state oscillations. In a catalytic reaction, the catalyst speeds up (or retards) a reaction without being consumed itself. Formally, such a reaction can be depicted as $A \xrightarrow{C} B$ where C denotes the catalyst.

Of course, in order to affect the reaction rate, C cannot be a mere spectator, but must be involved in the reaction, e.g., as $A + C \rightarrow B + C$. The efficiency of many technologically important chemical processes, such as the production of gasoline or of nitrogen-based fertilizer, depend on catalytic processes. Similarly, many biochemical processes depend on nature's catalysts, the enzymes.

In an *auto*catalytic reaction, the reaction product itself serves as a catalyst. The simplest example of such a process is the reaction $A + B \rightarrow 2B$, which can be written alternatively as $A \xrightarrow{B} B$. One typically excludes from such chemical reaction schemes the (often catalytic) effects of macroscopic bodies, such as solid surfaces or water droplets.

There are many known examples of autocatalytic reactions, e.g., the Landolt clock reaction (Landolt, *Ber. Deut. Chem. Ges.* 19 (1886) 1317), or the MnO_2-catalyzed reduction of permanganate. The Lotka oscillator (A. J. Lotka, *J. Am. Chem. Soc.* 42 (1920) 1595; *Proc. Nat'l. Acad. Sci. USA* 6 (1920) 410) is based on the reaction scheme

$$A + B \xrightarrow{k_1} 2B \tag{7.6.1}$$

$$B + C \xrightarrow{k_2} 2C \tag{7.6.2}$$

$$C \xrightarrow{k_3} \text{products} \tag{7.6.3}$$

In order to obtain stationary oscillations, we will assume that the concentration a of A is kept constant, so that $da/dt = 0$, and that the concentrations of the reactants and products are homogeneous throughout the reaction vessel, e.g., by using a so-called continuously stirred reactor. The corresponding rate expressions for b and c then read

$$\frac{db}{dt} = k_1\, ab - k_2\, bc \tag{7.6.4}$$

$$\frac{dc}{dt} = k_2\, bc - k_3\, c \tag{7.6.5}$$

Below we will use the explicit Euler method, in section 7.7 we will solve the same problem with the semi-implicit Euler method, and in section 7.8 we will use the explicit fourth-order Runge-Kutta approach. For the explicit Euler method we approximate (7.6.4) and (7.6.5) as

$$\frac{\Delta b}{\Delta t} = k_1\, ab - k_2\, bc \tag{7.6.6}$$

$$\frac{\Delta c}{\Delta t} = k_2\, bc - k_3\, c \tag{7.6.7}$$

so that

$$b_n = b_{n-1} + \Delta b = b_{n-1} + (k_1\, a\, b_{n-1} - k_2\, b_{n-1}\, c_{n-1})\Delta t \tag{7.6.8}$$
$$c_n = c_{n-1} + \Delta c = c_{n-1} + (k_2\, b_{n-1}\, c_{n-1} - k_3\, c_{n-1})\Delta t \tag{7.6.9}$$

Exercise 7.6.1:

(1) Start a new spreadsheet. Leave space at its top for a row of figures. Below these place labels for a, k_1, k_2, k_3, and Δt, and their values, such as 1, 2, 2, 5, and 0.01.

(2) Name the cells containing these parameters as a, kk1, kk2, kk3, and dt. Note that k1 cannot be used as a name because it is a valid cell address; kk1 is fine since Excel has only 256 columns, i.e., the highest column label is IV.

(3) Deposit column headings for time t and for the concentrations b and c.

(4) Fill the column for t with 0 (dt) 10.

(5) For $t = 0$ deposit the initial values $b = 1$ and $c = 2$.

(6) For $t = 0.01$ deposit the instructions =B21+(kk1*a*B21-kk2*B21* C21)*dt and =C21+(kk2*B21*C21-kk3*C21)*dt for b and c, assuming that B21 and C21 refer to b_0 and c_0 respectively.

(7) Copy these instructions all the way down to $t = 10$.

(8) Plot your results; they should look similar to those shown in Fig. 7.6.1.

Even though the value of Δt used, 0.01, is considerably smaller than $1/k$ for the largest k-value used ($1/k_3 = 0.2$), these results are clearly unsatisfactory, because they do not lead to the *steady-state* oscillations one should expect when the concentration a is kept constant. In a cyclic process, a small but systematic error can accumulate in successive cycles, thereby quickly leading to quite significant deviations. By reducing Δt we can verify that it was indeed too large, and thereby caused the runaway behavior shown in Fig. 7.6.1. Because the column is already fairly long, we use custom functions. Note that the concentrations b and c are mutually dependent, so that both must be computed inside the For ... Next loop. And because we here have an open system (in which we must continually supply A to keep its concentration a constant) there is no convenient mass balance equation to eliminate either b or c. The following custom functions will work.

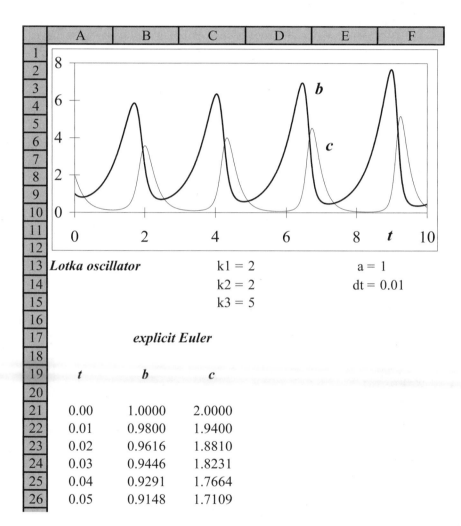

	A	B	C	D	E	F
13	*Lotka oscillator*		k1 = 2		a = 1	
14			k2 = 2		dt = 0.01	
15			k3 = 5			
16						
17		*explicit Euler*				
18						
19	*t*	*b*	*c*			
20						
21	0.00	1.0000	2.0000			
22	0.01	0.9800	1.9400			
23	0.02	0.9616	1.8810			
24	0.03	0.9446	1.8231			
25	0.04	0.9291	1.7664			
26	0.05	0.9148	1.7109			

Fig. 7.6.1: The top of the spreadsheet for exercise 7.6.1.

Exercise 7.6.1 (continued):
    (9) Replace the cell instructions for b and c by the custom functions shown below, and verify that they indeed work more efficiently.

```
Function eEb(a, oldb, oldc, kk1, kk2, kk3, dt, n) _
  As Double

Dim b As Double, c As Double
Dim i As Integer

b = oldb
c = oldc
For i = 1 To n
  b = b + (kk1 * a * b - kk2 * b * c) * dt / n
  c = c + (kk2 * b * c - kk3 * c) * dt / n
Next i
eEb = b

End Function

Function eEc(a, oldb, oldc, kk1, kk2, kk3, dt, n) _
  As Double

Dim b As Double, c As Double
Dim i As Integer

b = oldb
c = oldc
For i = 1 To n
  b = b + (kk1 * a * b - kk2 * b * c) * dt / n
  c = c + (kk2 * b * c - kk3 * c) * dt / n
Next i
eEc = c

End Function
```

For $n = 10$ this yields a stationary oscillation, see Fig. 7.6.2.

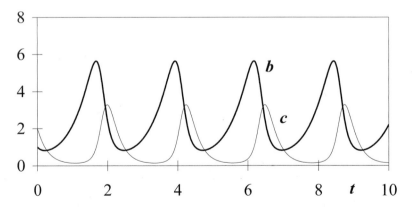

Fig. 7.6.2: The results for an explicit Euler simulation of the Lotka oscillator with $\Delta t = 0.01$ and $n = 10$ for effective time increments of 0.001.

How will you know whether this n-value is sufficient? Copy the numerical values (with Ctrl⌣c, Edit ⇒ Paste Special, Values) to another spot on the spreadsheet, then run the simulation with, say, $n = 20$, and compare the results. Keep increasing n by, say, factors of 2 until you are satisfied with the consistency of the result.

You can readily see whether you have reached a steady state from a phase diagram in which you plot c as a function of b, as illustrated in Fig. 7.6.2. In the steady state it shows a closed loop, a *limit cycle*.

Exercise 7.6.1 continued:
(10) Make a phase diagram by plotting c as a function of b. In such a diagram, the time t is an implicit parameter. Compare your result with Fig. 7.6.2.

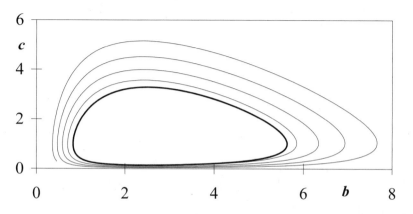

Fig. 7.6.2: The phase diagram, displaying c as a function of b. Thin line: results from explicit Euler method with $\Delta t = 0.01$, $n = 1$. Thick line: same with $\Delta t = 0.01$, $n = 10$ for an effective Δt of 0.001.

7.7 The Lotka oscillator 2

In a semi-implicit simulation we use

$$\frac{\Delta b}{\Delta t} = k_1 \, a\,(b + \Delta b/2) - k_2\,(b + \Delta b/2)(c + \Delta c/2) \qquad (7.7.1)$$

$$\frac{\Delta c}{\Delta t} = k_2\,(b + \Delta b/2)(c + \Delta c/2) - k_3\,(c + \Delta c/2) \qquad (7.7.2)$$

Upon neglecting terms containing the product $\Delta b\,\Delta c$ this yields

$$\left(\frac{1}{\Delta t} - k_1\,a/2 + k_2 c/2\right)\Delta b + \left(k_2\,b/2\right)\Delta c = k_1\,ab - k_2\,bc \qquad (7.7.3)$$

$$\left(-k_2\,c/2\right)\Delta b+\left(\frac{1}{\Delta t}-k_2\,b/2+k_3/2\right)\Delta c = k_2\,b\,c-k_3\,c \qquad (7.7.4)$$

Thus we have two equations, (7.7.3) and (7.7.4), and two unknowns, Δb and Δc, which are most readily obtained by matrix algebra as

$$\Delta b = \frac{\begin{vmatrix} k_1ab-k_2bc & k_2\,bc/2 \\ k_2bc-k_3c & 1/\Delta t-k_2\,b/2+k_3/2 \end{vmatrix}}{\begin{vmatrix} 1/\Delta t-k_1\,a/2+k_2\,c/2 & k_2\,b/2 \\ -k_2\,c/2 & 1/\Delta t-k_2\,b/2+k_3/2 \end{vmatrix}} \qquad (7.7.5)$$

$$= \frac{(k_1ab-k_2bc)\,(1/\Delta t-k_2\,b/2+k_3/2)-(k_2\,b/2)\,(k_2bc-k_3c)}{(1/\Delta t-k_1\,a/2+k_2\,c/2)\,(1/\Delta t-k_2\,b/2+k_3/2)-(k_2\,b/2)\,(-k_2\,c/2)}$$

and

$$\Delta c = \frac{\begin{vmatrix} 1/\Delta t-k_1\,a/2+k_2\,c/2 & k_1ab-k_2bc \\ -k_2\,c/2 & k_2bc-k_3c \end{vmatrix}}{\begin{vmatrix} 1/\Delta t-k_1\,a/2+k_2\,c/2 & k_2\,b/2 \\ -k_2\,c/2 & 1/\Delta t-k_2\,b/2+k_3/2 \end{vmatrix}} \qquad (7.7.6)$$

$$= \frac{(1/\Delta t-k_1\,a/2+k_2\,c/2)\,(k_2bc-k_3c)-(k_1ab-k_2bc)\,(-k_2\,c/2)}{(1/\Delta t-k_1\,a/2+k_2\,c/2)\,(1/\Delta t-k_2\,b/2+k_3/2)-(k_2\,b/2)\,(-k_2\,c/2)}$$

from which we can compute b_n as $b_{n-1}+\Delta b$ and c_n as $c_{n-1}+\Delta c$. Such results, for a column of 1001 rows, with $\Delta t = 0.01$, are visually indistinguishable from those obtained with the explicit method supplemented with functions to reduce their effective Δt to 0.001. If desired, we can further improve the numerical accuracy of these results with custom functions that subdivide the interval Δt into smaller steps.

Exercise 7.7.1:
(1) Implement the semi-implicit Euler method on your spreadsheet, using custom functions based on (7.7.5) and (7.7.6) for b and c respectively.

7.8   The Lotka oscillator 3

For applying the fourth-order Runge-Kutta method we combine (7.5.7) through (7.5.17) with (7.6.4) and (7.6.5), so that $F = k_1ab - k_2bc$, $G = k_2bc - k_3c$, and a is a constant. Therefore we replace the custom function e4RKB of section 7.5 by

```
Function eRKb(a, kk1, kk2, kk3, oldb, oldc, dt, n) _
   As Double

Dim b As Double, c As Double, step As Double
Dim KB1 As Double, KB2 As Double
Dim KB3 As Double, KB4 As Double
Dim KC1 As Double, KC2 As Double
Dim KC3 As Double, KC4 As Double
Dim i As Integer

step = dt / n
b = oldb
c = oldc
For i = 1 To n
  KB1 = step * (kk1 * a * b - kk2 * b * c)
  KB2 = step * (kk1 * a * (b + KB1 / 2) _
    - kk2 * (b + KB1 / 2) * (c + KC1 / 2))
  KB3 = step * (kk1 * a * (b + KB2 / 2) _
    - kk2 * (b + KB2 / 2) * (c + KC2 / 2))
  KB4 = step * (kk1 * a * (b + KB3) _
    - kk2 * (b + KB3) * (c + KC3))
  KC1 = step * (kk2 * b * c - kk3 * c)
  KC2 = step * (kk2 * (b + KB1 / 2) * (c + KC1 / 2) _
    - kk3 * (c + KC1 / 2))
  KC3 = step * (kk2 * (b + KB2 / 2) * (c + KC2 / 2) _
    - kk3 * (c + KC2 / 2))
  KC4 = step * (kk2 * (b + KB3) * (c + KC3) _
    - kk3 * (c + KC3))
  b = b + (KB1 + 2 * KB2 + 2 * KB3 + KB4) / 6
  c = c + (KC1 + 2 * KC2 + 2 * KC3 + KC4) / 6
Next i
eRKb = b

End Function
```

and

```
Function eRKc(a, kk1, kk2, kk3, oldb, oldc, dt, n) _
   As Double

Dim b As Double, c As Double, step As Double
Dim KB1 As Double, KB2 As Double
Dim KB3 As Double, KB4 As Double
Dim KC1 As Double, KC2 As Double
Dim KC3 As Double, KC4 As Double
Dim i As Integer

step = dt / n
b = oldb
c = oldc
For i = 1 To n
  KB1 = step * (kk1 * a * b - kk2 * b * c)
  KB2 = step * (kk1 * a * (b + KB1 / 2) _
    - kk2 * (b + KB1 / 2) * (c + KC1 / 2))
  KB3 = step * (kk1 * a * (b + KB2 / 2) _
    - kk2 * (b + KB2 / 2) * (c + KC2 / 2))
  KB4 = step * (kk1 * a * (b + KB3) _
    - kk2 * (b + KB3) * (c + KC3))
  KC1 = step * (kk2 * b * c - kk3 * c)
```

```
    KC2 = step * (kk2 * (b + KB1 / 2) * (c + KC1 / 2) _
       - kk3 * (c + KC1 / 2))
    KC3 = step * (kk2 * (b + KB2 / 2) * (c + KC2 / 2) _
       - kk3 * (c + KC2 / 2))
    KC4 = step * (kk2 * (b + KB3) * (c + KC3) _
       - kk3 * (c + KC3))
    b = b + (KB1 + 2 * KB2 + 2 * KB3 + KB4) / 6
    c = c + (KC1 + 2 * KC2 + 2 * KC3 + KC4) / 6
Next i
eRKc = c

End Function
```

Exercise 7.8.1:
   (1) Implement the explicit fourth-order Runge-Kutta method on your spreadsheet, using the above custom functions.

   In this example, judging by the constancy of the various repeat cycles, the Runge-Kutta method is almost as satisfactory as the semi-implicit Euler method under otherwise identical conditions.

   It is the interplay between the two autocatalytic reactions that causes the oscillatory behavior. The conversion of A into B in reaction (7.6.1) is catalyzed by the reaction product B, while the conversion of B into C is catalyzed by C. When the concentration of C increases, it will speed up the decomposition of B, so that the corresponding concentration b will decrease. This is clearly visible in Fig. 7.6.2. However, the decrease in b will lead to a decrease in the rate of production both of B, through reaction (7.6.1), and of C, through reaction (7.6.2). Depending on the numerical values of the rate constants involved, b may recover while, initially, c remains low, in which case the process may become cyclic. In that case, the concentrations b and c will reach their maximum values at different times: while both are cyclic, they are out of phase with each other, see Fig. 7.6.2. Another way to display this behavior is to plot, e.g., c versus b, as in the phase diagram of Fig. 7.7.1, which shows a limit cycle. Figures 7.6.2 and 7.7.1 represent the same information in different formats, viz. in the time and frequency domains respectively. Such alternative representations are of course readily made on the spreadsheet, with its convenient, built-in graphing capabilities.

7.9 Stability

   While the fourth-order Runge-Kutta method leads to higher accuracy, the semi-implicit method can be more stable. We will illustrate this by numerically integrating the differential equation

$$\frac{dy}{dx} = y^2 + 1 \qquad\qquad (7.9.1)$$

with $y_{x=0} \equiv y_0 = 0$. For the semi-implicit Euler method we rewrite (7.9.1) as

$$\frac{\Delta y}{\Delta x} = (y + \Delta y / 2)^2 + 1 = y^2 + y\Delta y + (\Delta y)^2 / 4 + 1$$

$$\approx y^2 + y\Delta y + 1 \tag{7.9.2}$$

so that

$$\Delta y \approx \frac{y^2 + 1}{1 / \Delta x - y} \tag{7.9.3}$$

where we have again linearized y^2 by neglecting the term $(\Delta y)^2/4$.

Exercise 7.9.1:

(1) Start a new spreadsheet, with space for values of n at the top, and below this a column for x, and four columns for y. Fill the x-column with the numbers 0 (0.01) 3, and the top cells in the y-columns with zeroes for y_0.

(2) In the first y-column, implement the semi-implicit Euler method with the command (say in cell B6, assuming that the value of y_0 is placed in cell B5) =B5+(B5^2+1)/(1/(A6-A5)-B5).

(3) In the next y-column use a custom function to compute y with smaller time increments, such as

```
'semi-implicit Euler method for exercise 7.9.1
Function siEulerY(oldX1, oldX2, n, oldY) As Double

Dim Y As Double, step As Double
Dim i As Integer

n = CInt(n)
Y = oldY
step = (oldX2 - oldX1) / n
For i = 1 To n
   Y = Y + (Y * Y + 1) / ((1 / step) - Y)
Next i
siEulerY = Y

End Function
```

(4) Place a corresponding value of n in cell C1, and the instruction =siEulerY(A5,A6,$C$1,C5) in cell C7.

(5) In the next y-column compute y with the explicit fourth-order Runge-Kutta method, using a custom function such as

```
'explicit 4th order Runge-Kutta for exercise 7.9.1
Function e4RKY(oldX1, oldX2, n, oldY)

Dim X As Double, Y As Double, step As Double
Dim k1 As Double, k2 As Double
Dim k3 As Double, k4 As Double
Dim i As Integer

X = oldX1
```

```
Y = oldY
n = CInt(n)
step = (oldX2 - oldX1) / n
For i = 1 To n
  k1 = step * (Y ^ 2 + 1)
  k2 = step * (((Y + k1 / 2) ^ 2) + 1)
  k3 = step * (((Y + k2 / 2) ^ 2) + 1)
  k4 = step * (((Y + k3) ^ 2) + 1)
  Y = Y + (k1 + 2 * k2 + 2 * k3 + k4) / 6
  X = X + step
Next i
e4RKY = Y

End Function
```

(6) Place the value $n = 1$ in cell D1, and in cell D6 the instruction =e4RKY(A5,A6,$D$1,D5).

(7) Use the same custom function in the last y-column, but this time with $n = 10$ (in cell E1).

(8) Plot the results for y as a function of x obtained with these two methods.

Figure 7.9.1 illustrates what you will find. The semi-implicit Euler method has no problem with the integration, either for a simple one-line instruction and $\Delta t = 0.01$, or with a custom function and an effective Δt of $0.01/1000 = 0.00001$. The Runge-Kutta method starts out fine, but stops at $x = 1.57$, regardless of whether we use $\Delta t = 0.01$ or multiple steps (as with $n = 10$).

By now you may have recognized the function we have just integrated: it is $y = \tan(x)$ which, as you can readily verify, is indeed the solution to (7.9.1) with $y_0 = 0$. The Runge-Kutta method apparently cannot get past the discontinuity in y at $x = \pi/2 \approx 1.5708$, while this same hurdle doesn't faze the semi-implicit Euler method. We merely illustrate this here for a particular differential equation, but it reflects a rather general property: implicit methods, and even semi-implicit ones, are more *stable* than explicit methods.

Having the exact solution allows us to compute and plot the errors. The results so obtained are shown in Figs. 7.9.2 and 7.9.3, and show that the Runge-Kutta method has far smaller algorithmic errors when it works, but fails completely when it doesn't. When a custom function is used to reduce the effective step size, the semi-implicit Euler method can combine accuracy and reliability, as illustrated in Fig. 7.9.3.

It is sometimes suggested that the Runge-Kutta method is all you need for the numerical integration of ordinary differential equations with one-point boundary conditions. But in Fig. 7.9.2 the one-line semi-implicit Euler instruction eventually outperforms the Runge-Kutta method, and the use of smaller effective step sizes $\Delta t/n$ makes the corresponding inaccuracies quite acceptable, see Fig. 7.9.3. Because of its greater stability, the semi-implicit Euler method is often a better bet, except when you already *know* the function to be well behaved over the entire range of interest.

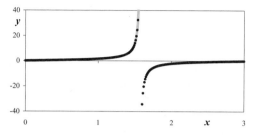

Fig. 7.9.1: The function y found by numerical integration of (7.9.1) with $y_0 = 0$. Solid dots: results from the semi-implicit Euler method for $\Delta t = 0.01$. Broad gray band: results from the explicit fourth-order Runge-Kutta method for $\Delta t = 0.01$. Note that the latter fails for $x > 1.57$.

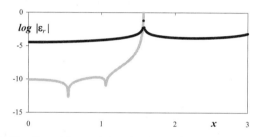

Fig. 7.9.2: The (logarithms of the absolute values of the) relative errors ε_r in the numerical simulation. Solid dots: results from the semi-implicit Euler method for $\Delta t = 0.01$. Broad gray band: results from the explicit fourth-order Runge-Kutta method for $\Delta t = 0.01$, which fails for $x > \pi/2$. The cusps in the latter curve correspond to sign changes in $\varepsilon_r(x)$.

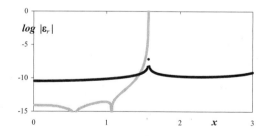

Fig. 7.9.3: The (logarithms of the absolute values of the) relative errors ε_r in the numerical simulation. Solid dots: results from the semi-implicit Euler method for $\Delta t = 0.01$ with $n = 1000$, yielding relative errors smaller than 10^{-7}. Broad gray band: results from the explicit fourth-order Runge-Kutta method for $\Delta t = 0.01$ with $n = 10$.

7.10 Chaos

Apart from problems caused by the method used for numerical integration, difficulties can be caused by the differential equation itself. This can occur, e.g., when the solution is highly dependent on the precise value of the initial condition. Since in science and technology (as distinct from mathematics) such an initial value is never known *exactly*, the solution can become uncertain. A prototypical example of this phenomenon is the weather forecast, which depends on equations that, when integrated over long periods to yield a prediction, turn out to depend critically on the precision of the (often imprecisely known) initial conditions. This is why the predictive power of the farmer's almanac is not much worse than the long-term weather forecast.

A clear example, taken from section 9.1B of J. R. Rice, *Numerical Methods, Software, and Analysis* (McGraw-Hill 1983), is the differential equation

$$\frac{dy}{dx} = 5y - 6e^{-x} \tag{7.10.1}$$

which has the general solution

$$y = e^{-x} + Ae^{5x} \tag{7.10.2}$$

For the initial condition $y_{x=0} = 1$ we find $A = 0$, so that the solution is $y = e^{-x}$. However, for $y_0 = 1 \pm \varepsilon$ equation (7.10.2) yields $A = \pm\varepsilon$, with the solution $y = e^{-x} + \varepsilon\,e^{5x}$. As x increases, the term in e^{5x} will eventually dominate the solution no matter how small $|\varepsilon|$, as long as it is not *exactly* zero. This is illustrated in Fig. 7.10.1, and somewhat resembles a needle balancing on its point, a situation that is unstable to any perturbation, no matter how small.

No numerical process handles data with complete precision. Consequently, pathological equations such as (7.10.1) will eventually give problems when integrated numerically with the simple methods described here. Figure 7.10.2 illustrates how the semi-implicit Euler and the explicit fourth-order Runge-Kutta methods fare with this equation.

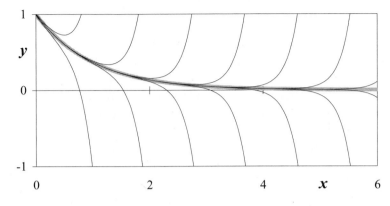

Fig. 7.10.1: The solutions for $dy/dx = 5y - 6e^{-x}$ for various values of the initial condition $y_0 = 1 + \varepsilon$. Broad gray curve: $\varepsilon = 0$, where $y = e^{-x}$. Thin black curves above the line $y = e^{-x}$, from left to right, for $\varepsilon = 10^{-2}$, 10^{-4}, 10^{-6}, 10^{-8}, 10^{-10}, 10^{-12}, and 10^{-14} respectively. Likewise, the thin black curves below the line $y = e^{-x}$, from left to right, for $\varepsilon = -10^{-2}$, -10^{-4}, -10^{-6}, -10^{-8}, -10^{-10}, -10^{-12}, and -10^{-14} respectively.

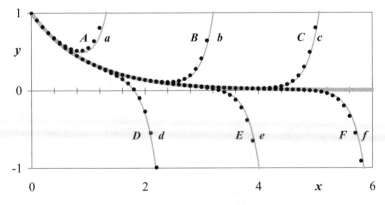

Fig. 7.10.2: Numerical integration of $dy/dx = 5y - 6e^{-x}$ with the semi-implicit Euler method (A through C) and the explicit fourth-order Runge-Kutta method (curves D through F) for $\Delta t = 0.1$. Curves B and C used custom functions with $n = 100$ and $n = 10^4$, effectively making Δt equal to 0.001 and 0.00001, while curves D through F used $n = 1$, $n = 10$, and $n = 100$ (or $\Delta t = 0.1$, 0.01, and 0.001) respectively. All these results are displayed as individual data points. For comparison, the curve $y = e^{-x} + \varepsilon e^{5x}$ for $\varepsilon = 0$ is shown as a thick gray line, with thin gray lines for $\varepsilon = 10^{-3}$ (*a*), 10^{-7} (*b*), 10^{-11} (*c*), -2×10^{-5} (*d*), -2×10^{-9} (*e*), and -2×10^{-13} (*f*).

7.11 Summary

In this chapter we have looked in some detail at a few simple methods for the numerical integration of ordinary differential equations with one-point boundary conditions. We have encountered three methods: the explicit and semi-implicit Euler methods, and the most popular of the explicit Runge-Kutta methods. The explicit Euler method is the simplest, both conceptually and in terms of its practical implementation, but it yields rather crude results. The explicit fourth-order Runge-Kutta method is much more efficient, and is readily implemented in Excel with custom functions. Implicit methods are inherently more stable. The semi-implicit Euler method combines relative simplicity with often quite acceptable stability and accuracy, especially when we again use custom functions to reduce the step size. For higher stability, fully implicit methods may be needed (implicit Runge-Kutta methods are described in, e.g., M. K. Jain, *Numerical Solutions to Differential Equations*, Wiley 1979, 1984) but they do not appear to have significant advantages in linear systems, and they become quite complicated in nonlinear cases.

Since step size is such an important parameter in achieving accuracy, *adaptive* (i.e., self-correcting) methods have been developed to automatically adjust the step size in order to keep the inaccuracy within prescribed limits. These may well be desirable for fully automated software systems, but are usually unnecessary on spreadsheets, where the intermediate results are directly visible, so that the step size can be adjusted manually, such as when a function changes rapidly. If needed, there is no problem incorporating adaptive step size control along the lines described in, e.g., chapter 15 of the *Numerical Recipes*.

There are, of course, many other methods we have not encountered here. These are described in standard textbooks on numerical integration of ordinary differential equations, and if desired can readily be incorporated into the spreadsheet. The present chapter is merely meant to illustrate how to approach such problems on a spreadsheet. For more complicated systems or routine uses a spreadsheet may well be too slow and/or too limiting, in which case the user should explore the capabilities of more specialized software. But even then, the transparency and ease of visualizing intermediate results may well make the spreadsheet a useful first stage for exploring the underlying algorithms.

An additional advantage of the spreadsheet over dedicated software is that you, my reader, already have it at your fingertips, and that you have direct access to its code and therefore complete control over its operation. A disadvantage is that you must know what you are doing, usually in more detail than necessary with prepackaged software, and that you may have to spend some time coding and trouble-shooting.

In order to demonstrate the properties of the few methods illustrated here they have first been introduced for differential equations with known solutions. Obviously, that is not where one would use numerical integration, and the example in sections 7.6 through 7.8 illustrates an application where no closed-form solution is available.

We have encountered some limitations of explicit methods, which may not be able to get past discontinuities, as in the example of section 7.9. Semi-implicit methods do better there, as they often do with so-called *stiff* systems of differential equations, which contain parameters of quite different orders of magnitude. Such stiff systems are often encountered in, e.g., chemical kinetics.

In section 7.10 we briefly encountered chaos, in which the differential equations are so sensitive to their boundary conditions that numerical integration becomes extremely difficult. Chaotic systems differ, at least in principle, from stochastics, where the phenomena are inherently subject to random effects, although the results may look quite similar. Fortunately, most differential equations of practical importance in the physical sciences are well behaved within the range of their practical application.

Why is it that numerical methods can integrate differential equations that have no known algebraic solutions? A main reason is that the most general analytical methods, such as Laplace transformation, are effectively restricted to linear differential equations. This is not a requirement for numerical integration, which can either linearize the nonlinearities, as illustrated, e.g., in sections 7.8 and 7.9, or can incorporate nonlinear methods such as Solver.

A well-known disadvantage of numerical integration is that it yields an answer valid only for the particular parameter values chosen. However, as illustrated in exercise 7.1.1, this disadvantage vanishes when one uses Solver to vary those parameters by optimizing the fit between the simulation and experimental data. Because the simulation is inherently noise-free, this approach at the same time rejects random noise. Incidentally, the automatically self-updating functions are much easier to use in combination with Solver than macros would be.

7.12 For further reading

Virtually any college or university library will have books on numerical methods that provide more details than can possibly be provided here, as well as different perspectives. Many useful formulas for numerical integration are listed by P. J. Davis & I. Polonsky in chapter 25 of M. Abramowitz & I. Stegun, *Handbook of Mathematical Functions*, NBS 1964, Dover 1965, an extremely useful yet inexpensive book that every scientist should have on his or her desk. The *Numerical Recipes* by Press et al., Cambridge University Press 1986, another highly recommended book, devotes three full chapters to the numerical integration of differential equations. And a quite extensive collection of methods can be found in M. K. Jain, *Numerical Solution of Differential Equations*, Wiley 1979, 1984.

Chapter 8

Write your own macros

Macros make it possible to extend the already quite considerable range of capabilities of Excel, in order to suit *your* personal computing needs. Moreover, you can import preexisting higher-language programs into Excel, so that you need not re-invent the wheel. This chapter will demonstrate how to copy spreadsheet data into a macro, manipulate them, and return the result to the spreadsheet. Subsequently it will illustrate writing a few nontrivial macros. Earlier exposure to some computer language (Basic, Fortran, C, etc.) is helpful though not absolutely required.

Macros are written in VBA, which stands for Visual Basic for Applications. VBA contains a subset of Visual Basic, plus instructions specifically designed for interacting with its host application, here Excel. Visual Basic is a higher-level language developed (via Borland's TurboBasic and Microsoft's QuickBasic) from the original Dartmouth Basic (for Beginner's All-purpose Symbolic Instruction Code). It has lost its original line numbers, and now is a competent higher-level language, resembling earlier versions of Fortran such as Fortran77. It can be compiled, but as used here is interpreted line by line.

The computer code of a custom macro resides in a *module*, as already mentioned in section 1.11. In early versions of Excel, modules were like spreadsheets without row and column lines, but starting with Excel 97 the modules are hidden in a Visual Basic Editor, reachable with Alt‿F11 (Mac: Opt‿F11), or with Tools ⇒ Macro ⇒ Visual Basic Editor. In order to open a new module, use Alt‿F11 (Mac: Opt‿F11), followed by (on the Visual Basic Toolbar) Insert ⇒ Module. Thereafter, toggle back and forth between spreadsheet and module with Alt‿F11 (Mac: Opt‿F11) or, easier yet, use a split screen to place the module next to or below the spreadsheet, so that you can switch between them merely by moving and clicking the mouse.

If `Option Explicit` appears at the top of your macro module, disable it by placing an apostrophe in front of it ('commenting it out'), at least until you have read most of this chapter. Then reactivate it, so that you can benefit from its typo-catching feature. In that case you must dimension every parameter used, at least by name, i.e., by statements such as Dim A, B, C, and preferably (because that makes the computer run more efficiently) as Dim A As Integer, B As Double, C As Variant. Dimension statements must occur *before* the dimensioned parameter is used; for substantial macros it is best to place all dimension statements at the top of the macro, sorted by type and, within type, in some logical (or, otherwise, alphabetical) order. Unfortunately, VBA does not allow you to use generic dimension statements, or even to bundle dimension statements on a single line with a single declaration. Instead, each parameter must be dimensioned individually: Dim A, B As Double specifies B as double-precision but dimensions A by name only.

8.1 Reading the contents of a cell

Start by letting a macro read a number, then make it display that number to make sure it got it right. Open a spreadsheet, open a module, and type the following code:

```
Sub Read()
'Read the cell value

cellValue = Selection.Value
MsgBox "The cell value is " & cellValue

End Sub
```

Notes:

(1) The first line defines the start of the macro and its name, here Read. The *empty* brackets following the name are necessary, and identify the subroutine as a *macro*. A function also has brackets, but these are seldom empty.

(2) The editor recognizes the term Sub (for *sub*routine) and shows it in blue, as a reserved word. Reserved words cannot be used as names of variables, but variations on them, such as sub1 or mySub, can be.

(3) The second line starts with an apostrophe, which defines it as a *comment* line. A comment is meant for the convenience of the user, and is ignored by the computer. The computer screen will show it in green (assuming you use the default colors which, like almost everything else in Excel, you can change to suit your own taste), thereby identifying it as a comment, and letting the user know that the editor is working. Comments need not occupy an entire line: any text to the right of an apostrophe is considered a comment. Comments can be placed anywhere inside a macro, or even before or after them, except following a line continuation.

(3) The third line does all the work. Despite the (symmetrical) equal sign, the editor reads it as an *assignment*, to be interpreted *from right to left*, and to mean: take the value of the highlighted selection, and then assign it to the parameter named cellValue. Instead of cellValue you could have used any other pa-

rameter name, such as y or unknown or ThisIsIt, but not a word the editor recognizes as an instruction, such as value. (Capitals or lower case makes no difference here. Except for literal quotes, VBA is not case sensitive, i.e., it ignores the difference between capitals and lower case letters.) By adding the prefix cell we avoid this problem; any other prefix, suffix, or other name modification such as myValue, thisValue, or Value3 would also do the trick. Parameter names cannot contain any empty spaces, but we can improve their readability by using capitals, as in cellValue or ThisIsIt, or by using underscores.

(4) The fourth line is our check that the macro indeed reads the highlighted value. Upon execution of the macro a message box will appear in the spreadsheet, with the message The cell value is exactly as it appears within the quotation marks in the instruction, followed by its read value. The empty space at the end of the quoted text string separates that text from the subsequent parameter value. The ampersand, &, both separates and ties together (concatenates) the two dissimilar parts of the line: text and contents displayed. The text is helpful as a reminder of what is displayed, but is optional: MsgBox cellValue would also work.

(5) The last line specifies the end of the macro, and will be shown in blue. Recent versions of Excel write this line for you automatically as soon as you enter a line defining a macro name, so you may not even have to type this line.

In order to run this macro, exit the Visual Basic Editor with Alt⌣F11 (Mac: Opt⌣F11), place a number somewhere on the spreadsheet, and enter it. Select <u>T</u>ools ⇒ <u>M</u>acro ⇒ <u>M</u>acros, and double-click on Read. You should now see a message box that shows the value just entered in the spreadsheet. Change this number, and check that the macro indeed reads it correctly. Verify that it only reads the contents of the active cell, the one identified by a thick border.

Now go back to the Visual Basic Editor with Alt⌣F11 (Mac: Opt⌣F11), make the changes indicated below in bold, then run the macro. (The editor does not recognize bold characters, which are only meant for you, to identify the changes.)

```
Sub Read()
'Read & change the cell value

cellValue = Selection.Value
MsgBox "The cell value is " & cellValue
cellValue = cellValue * 7
Selection.Value = cellValue

End Sub
```

Notes (continued):

(6) The fifth line is, again, an assignment, to be interpreted as: take the old value of cellValue, multiply it by 7, and make that the new value of cellValue. Again the equal sign acts like an arrow pointing from right to left, as in cellValue ⇐ cellValue * 7.

(7) The sixth line is again an assignment: it takes the new value of cellValue, and writes it in the highlighted cell of the spreadsheet. This is therefore a *writing* instruction, to be compared with the *reading* instruction cellValue = Selection.Value. In both cases, the directionality of execution is from right to left.

Try the macro, and verify that it indeed keeps multiplying the value in the highlighted cell by 7. Play with it by, e.g., changing the instruction in the fifth line to cellValue = -cellValue + 2, or whatever suits your fancy.

It is usually undesirable to overwrite spreadsheet data. Therefore, modify the macro as indicated below so that it will write its output *below* its input, then run this macro.

```
Sub Read()
'Read & change the cell value

cellValue = Selection.Value
'MsgBox "The cell value is " & cellValue
cellValue = cellValue * 7
Selection.Offset(1,0).Select
Selection.Value = cellValue

End Sub
```

Notes (continued):

(8) Verify that you can write the output *next to* the input cell with Offset(0,1) instead of Offset(1,0), and that you can place it anywhere else on the spreadsheet (as long as you stay within its borders) with Offset(n,m) where n and m are integers. A negative n moves the output up, a negative m moves it to the right.

(9) You can now delete the line specifying the message box because, by displaying the answer, the spreadsheet shows the macro to work. Instead of deleting the line containing the message box, you can also *comment it out* by placing an apostrophe in front of the line, so that the editor will ignore it. That was done here. In this way you can easily reactivate the message box in case you need it during troubleshooting. But don't forget to remove such auxiliary lines in the final, finished version of the macro: the finished painting need not show the underlying sketch.

There is more to a cell than the value it displays: there may be a formula that generates this value, and you may also want to read the cell address. In order to extract all these pieces of information from the spreadsheet, modify the macro as follows:

```
Sub Read()
'Read the cell address, formula, and value

cellAddress = Selection.Address
MsgBox "The cell address is " & cellAddress
```

```
cellFormula = Selection.Formula
MsgBox "The cell formula is " & cellFormula
cellValue = Selection.Value
'MsgBox "The cell value is " & cellValue
cellValue = cellValue * 7
Selection.Offset(1,0).Select
Selection.Value = cellValue

End Sub
```

Notes (continued):

(10) Again, address and formula are reserved terms recognized by the Visual Basic Editor, and therefore cannot be used without modification as parameter names.

8.2 Reading & manipulating a cell block

Reading the contents of a highlighted cell *block* or *array* (terms we will here use interchangeably) is as easy as reading that of a single cell, but using a message box to verify that the array was read correctly may be somewhat more tedious. Open a spreadsheet, open a module, and type the following code:

```
Sub ReadArray1()

arrayAddress = Selection.Address
MsgBox "The array range is " & arrayAddress
arrayValue = Selection.Value
MsgBox "The value of cell (1,1) is " & arrayValue(1,1)
MsgBox "The value of cell (5,2) is " & arrayValue(5,2)
arrayFormula = Selection.Formula
MsgBox "The formula in cell (1,1) is " & arrayFormula(1,1)
MsgBox "The formula in cell (5,2) is " & arrayFormula(5,2)

End Sub
```

Note:

(1) The array elements are always specified as row first, then column. As a mnemonic, use the *RC* time of an electrical circuit: *R*(ow) followed by *C*(olumn). This conforms to the standard way indices are assigned in matrices, as in

$$\begin{vmatrix} a_{11} & a_{12} \\ a_{21} & a_{22} \end{vmatrix}$$

Test the above macro as follows. Return to the spreadsheet with Alt⌣F11 (Mac: Opt⌣F11), and deposit, say, 1, 2, 3, 4, and 5 respectively in cells A1:A5, and 6, 7, 8, 9, and 10 in B1:B5. In cell D1 deposit the instruction =sqr(A1), and copy this instruction to D1:E3. Then highlight D1:E5, and call the macro.

Notes (continued):

(2) In Excel, the instruction for taking the square root of x is sqrt(x), but in VBA it is sqr(x). There are more of such incongruencies between the two, because they started off independently, and were subsequently joined. We have listed several of these differences in section 1.16, and occasionally will alert you to them as we encounter them.

Now that we know how to read the data in an array, we will use the macro to modify them. Enter and run the macro shown below:

```
Sub Cube1()
'Cube all array elements

For Each cell In Selection.Cells
  cell.Value = cell.Value ^ 3
Next cell

End Sub
```

Notes (continued):

(3) Here you encounter a For ... Next loop, which performs an operation repeatedly until all the cells have been acted on. Note the indentation used to make it easier for the user to identify the instructions inside the loop. The editor will ignore such indentations.

(4) Cell is not a term the Visual Basic Editor knows, but cells is. See what happens when you replace cell by cells in the above macro.

Also enter and run the following macro:

```
Sub Cube2()
'Cube all array elements

Dim Array2 As Variant
Dim r As Integer, c As Integer
Array2 = Selection.Value
For r = 1 To 5
  For c = 1 To 2
    Array2(r, c) = Array2(r, c) ^ 3
  Next c
Next r
Selection.Value = Array2

End Sub
```

Notes (continued):

(5) Array is a recognized term, and therefore cannot be used as a parameter name, hence Array2 or some otherwise modified name.

(6) The dimensioning in the two lines following Sub Cube2() is not strictly necessary (as long as Option Explicit is not used), but it is good to start the habit of dimensioning early.

(7) Here we use two *nested* loops: for the first value of c the inner loop is executed until all values of r have been used, then the process is repeated for subsequent values of c.

(8) You can let the Visual Basic Editor find the lower and upper bounds of the ranges with For r = LBound(Array2, 1) To UBound(Array2, 1) and For c = LBound(Array2, 2) To UBound(Array2, 2), in which case you need not specify these bounds when you change the array size.

(9) Another way to leave the array size flexible is to let the macro determine it explicitly, as in

```
Sub Cube3()
'Cube all array elements

Dim Array3 As Variant
Dim c As Integer, cMax As Integer
Dim r As Integer, rMax As Integer

Array3 = Selection.Value
cMax = Selection.Columns.Count
rMax = Selection.Rows.Count
For r = 1 To rMax
  For c = 1 To cMax
    Array3(r, c) = Array3(r, c) ^ 3
  Next c
Next r
Selection.Value = Array3

End Sub
```

Test Cube1 versus either Cube2 or Cube3, as follows. Return to the spreadsheet. In cells A1 through A10 as well as in cells B1:B10 deposit the numbers 1 through 10. In cells C1 and D1 deposit the number 1, in cell C2 the instruction =C1+1, and copy this instruction to C2:D10. Highlight A1:A10 and call Cube2 or Cube3, then highlight C1:C10 and apply Cube2 or Cube3 again. Thereafter, highlight B1:B10 and call Cube1, then do the same with D1:D10. The results obtained in columns A through C should be identical, but those in column D will be way off. In fact, the program will almost certainly crash. (When the overflow error message appears, just press End.) What has happened here?

When the contents of cell D2 are cubed to the value $2^3 = 8$, the contents of cell D3 are changed to $8 + 1 = 9$, and when that is cubed we obtain $9^3 = 729$. Then D4 is changed to $729 + 1 = 730$, and subsequently cubed to $730^3 = 389,017,000$, whereupon D5 is modified to $389,017,001$, which is again cubed, and so on. By the time we have reached cell D7 we have exceeded the numerical capacity of the spreadsheet, and the program overflows! The problem with Cube1 is that it does not give us any control over the *order* in which it operates. In the present example, that order is not what we had intended.

Obviously, Cube1 has the appeal of a more compact code. However, the more cumbersome code of Cube2 or Cube3 is more reliable, because it first *internalizes* all input the values *before* it computes any results. Rather pedestrian code may sometimes be preferable over its more 'clever' counterpart!

8.3 Conditional statements

Conditional statements make it possible for a program to make decisions. The spreadsheet already contains an `If` function, which has a precise VBA counterpart in the `IIf` function. More convenient is the `If ... Then` line statement (which must be a one-liner) such as

```
If b ^ 2 - 4 * a * c < 0 Then MsgBox "The roots are imaginary"
```

When more than one consequence of the If decision must be spelled out, readability is enhanced by using an `If ... Then` block structure, in which case the end of the If statement must be specified, as in

```
If b ^ 2 - 4 * a * c > 0 Then
  Root1 = (-b + Sqr(b ^ 2 - 4 * a * c)) / (2 * a)
  Root2 = (-b - Sqr(b ^ 2 - 4 * a * c)) / (2 * a)
End If
```

The latter format can be expanded to include multiple options, as in

```
Discr = b ^ 2 - 4 * a * c
If Discr > 0 Then
  RealRoot1 = (-b + Sqr(Discr)) / (2 * a)
  ImagRoot1 = 0
  RealRoot2 = (-b - Sqr(Discr)) / (2 * a)
  ImagRoot2 = 0
ElseIf Discr = 0 Then
  RealRoot1 = -b / (2 * a)
  ImagRoot1 = 0
  RealRoot2 = RealRoot1
  ImagRoot2 = 0
Else
  RealRoot1 = -b / (2 * a)
  ImagRoot1 = Sqr(-Discr) / (2 * a)
  RealRoot2 = RealRoot1
  ImagRoot2 = -ImagRoot1
End If
```

with as many `ElseIf`'s as necessary. The final, optional `Else` can take care of any unforeseen situations. Note that `End If` has a space before the `If`, but `ElseIf` does not, and the VBA editor is not helpful in this respect. Indentation is used to enhance program readability. One can jump out of an `If ... Then` loop with `If ... Then Exit If` or `If ... Then GoTo ...` and, of course, with a macro-terminating `End`. The macros in the MacroBundle are full of examples of `If ... Then` loops.

8.4 Control loops

For repeat calculations, including iterations, VBA has several types of control loops. The `For … Next` loop has a fixed number of repeats, whereas the number of repeat operations in a `Do … Loop` is conditional. In section 8.2 we already encountered a `For … Next` loop in the macro Cube1( ), and two nested `For … Next` loops in Cube2( ) and Cube3( ). The counter is often an integer, and its default increment (or step size) is +1, but neither is needed: `For c = 0.7 To -1.300001 Step -0.4` will assign the sequence $c = 0.7, 0.3, -0.1, -0.5, -0.9, -1.3$. The limit 1.300001 protects against possible digital rounding: because 0.4 has no exact binary representation, subtracting it five times from 0.7 might not be exactly -1.3. To exit a `For … Next` loop, use `If … Then Exit For` or `If … Then GoTo …`.

The `For Each … Next` loop is similar to the `For … Next` loop, and can be a convenient alternative involving an entire group of objects, such as all cells in an array, without the need to describe them more precisely. However, this convenience has its price, because the instruction doesn't provide any control over the order in which it is executed, and therefore should be used only when that order is immaterial, as illustrated in Cube1( ) in section 8.2.

The most useful `Do` loops are `Do While … Loop, Do … Loop While, Do Until … Loop`, and `Do … Loop Until`. They differ only in whether the condition is permissive (`While`) or prohibitive (`Until`), and in whether it is applied at the beginning or the end of the loop. To interrupt execution of a `For … Next` or `Do` loop, use Esc or Ctrl‿Break. To exit a `Do … Loop` loop, use `If … Then Exit Do` or `If … Then GoTo …`.

The `GoTo` statement requires a label, that is repeated as a single line followed by a colon, as in, e.g., `GoTo Output` followed at the appropriate place by the line `Output:`.

In older code, the `GoTo` statement was often used as the main device for controlling the information flow in computer programs. This could lead to programs that were difficult to follow and, therefore, to maintain or modify, especially since they referred to a line number rather than an more easily recognized name. As a result, use of the `GoTo` statement now tends to be frowned upon. It is indeed good practice to avoid `GoTo` statements whenever possible, but there is no harm in using them sparingly when this simplifies the code and does not lead to confusion.

Interestingly, VBA also contains a modern version of the `GoTo` statement, called `Select Case`, as illustrated in, e.g., the Propagation macro. Its structure is helpful when there are many statements following each choice, so that a later reader of that code (most likely you, its author!) might otherwise lose sight of the particular case considered.

8.5 *Numerical precision*

In the module, make a copy of Cube3, then modify this copy as follows:

```
Sub Root3()
'Take the cube root of all array elements

Dim Array3 As Variant
Dim c As Integer, cMax As Integer
Dim r As Integer, rMax As Integer

Array3 = Selection.Value
cMax = Selection.Columns.Count
rMax = Selection.Rows.Count
For r = 1 To rMax
  For c = 1 To cMax
    Array3(r, c) = Array3(r, c) ^ (1 / 3)
  Next c
Next r
Selection.Value = Array3

End Sub
```

Return to the spreadsheet in order to test this macro. Make two test arrays containing some simple numbers, such as 1, 2, 3, 4, 5 in A1:A5, and 6, 7, 8, 9, 10 in B1:B5, then copy these data to A7:B11. In D4 enter the instruction =A1-A7, and copy this instruction to D4:E8. Call Cube3 and apply it, three times in succession, to the data in A1:B5. Then call Root3 and apply it, again three times, to the resulting data in that same block. You should of course end up with the original data. Is that what you see in D4:E8? What is going on now?

The answer to the above riddle is that Excel always, automatically, uses double precision, but VBA does *not*, unless it is specifically told to do so. Therefore, force it to do so, as in

```
Sub Root3()
'Take the cube root of all array elements

Dim Array3 As Variant
Dim c As Integer, cMax As Integer
Dim r As Integer, rMax As Integer
Dim p As Double

p = 1 / 3
```

```
Array3 = Selection.Value
cMax = Selection.Columns.Count
rMax = Selection.Rows.Count
For r = 1 To rMax
  For c = 1 To cMax
    Array3(r, c) = Array3(r, c) ^ p
  Next c
Next r
Selection.Value = Array3

End Sub
```

Verify that you can now repeatedly cube a function, and subsequently undo it by taking the cube root, without accumulating unacceptably large errors.

8.6 Communication boxes

VBA uses three types of dialog boxes to facilitate communication between the macro and the user: message boxes, input boxes, and user-defined dialog boxes. We will describe message and input boxes, which are easy to use, and can do anything you need to write your own macros. Dialog boxes are more versatile and professional-looking, and can be more user-friendly. However, they are also considerably more complex to set up (although the latest versions of Excel have reduced that complexity), and for that reason they are not discussed here. For commercial software, however, dialog boxes are clearly the way to go, because they provide the programmer maximal control over data input and output, and the user an overview of all choices made before the macro takes off.

8.6.1 Message boxes

Message boxes can carry a simple message,

```
MsgBox a
```

where a represents a value calculated by the macro, or

```
MsgBox "Well-done!"
```

or they can combine a message with specific information, as in

```
MsgBox "Excellent! The answer was " & a
```

In the latter example, note the use of an ampersand, &, to concatenate the two parts, i.e., to *separate* the textual message (within quotation marks) from the output value as well as to *link* them in one instruction. Message boxes can also be used for (limited) information flow from the user to the macro, as in

```
Sub QandA1()
```

```
              ' < Space for questions
Response = MsgBox("No, the answer was " & 3 & _
  Chr(13) & "Do you want to try again? ", vbYesNo)
If Response = vbNo Then End
              ' < Continue with questions
End Sub
```

> *Notes*:
>   (1) Chr(13) continues on a new line, and is therefore equivalent to a type-writer 'carriage return'. Alternatively you can use the somewhat shorter vbCr. Other often used characters and/or their alternative abbreviations are

Chr(9)	or	vbTab	for tab
Chr(10)	or	vbLf	for linefeed
Chr(11)	or	vbVerticalTab	for tab
Chr(12)	or	vbFormFeed	for page break
		vbCrLf	for carriage return plus linefeed
Chr(149)			for bullet
Chr(150)			for en dash (–)
Chr(151)			for em dash (—)

>   (2) The line continuation symbol is a space followed by an underscore. It cannot be followed by any text, including comments.
>   (3) In the above example, the message box will display two buttons, labeled Yes and No respectively, instead of the usual OK button.
>   (4) The instruction starting with If Response = is a one-line If statement, and therefore does not require an End If. An alternative, more explicit form is

```
Sub QandA2()
              ' < Space for questions >
Msg = "No, the answer was 3. Try again?"
Style = vbYesNo
Title = "Quizz"
Response = MsgBox(Msg, Style, Title)
If Response = vbNo Then MsgBox "Sorry, this question netted" _
  & Chr(13) & "you no additional points."
              ' < Continue with questions >
End Sub
```

>   (5) In this case, End If is still not needed because the compiler considers the continued line starting with If Response = as one.

8.6.2 Input boxes

Input boxes can transfer numerical information to the macro:

```
Sub DataInput1()

yourChoice = InputBox("Enter a number", "Number")
MsgBox "The number is " & yourChoice

End Sub
```

> *Notes*:
>   (1) Again we use a message box to verify that the input box works.

(2) If you want to use a longer message, and therefore want to break and continue the line starting with `yourChoice = `, the quotation marks must be closed and reopened, and the ampersand must be used to concatenate (separate and link) the two parts of the text message, as in

```
yourChoice = InputBox("After you have finished this," _
  & "enter a number", "Number")
```

or you can make it into a narrower, taller box with

```
yourChoice = InputBox("After you have finished this," _
  & Chr(13) & "enter a number", "Number")
```

Input boxes can have default values, and can be followed by extensive verification schemes such as

```
Sub DataInput2()

Message = "Enter an integer between 1 and 100:"
Title = "Integer"
Default = "25"
inputValue = InputBox(Message, Title, Default)
If inputValue < 1 Then
  MsgBox "The selected number is too small."
  End
End If
If inputValue > 100 Then
  MsgBox "The selected number is larger than 100."
  End
End If
If inputValue - Int(inputValue) <> 0 Then
  MsgBox "The selected number is not an integer."
  End
End If
MsgBox "You entered the number " & inputValue

End Sub
```

The above macro is rather unforgiving of data entry mistakes, because any entry error forces the user to start anew. A friendlier approach gives the user a number of chances to get it right, as in

```
Sub InputANumber()

Tries = 0
MaxTries = 5
Message = "Enter an integer" & _
  Chr(13) & "between 1 and 100:"
Title = "Integer"
Default = "25"

Do
  myValue = InputBox(Message, Title, Default)
  Tries = Tries + 1
  If Tries > MaxTries Then End
```

```
  If myValue < 1 Then MsgBox _
    "The selected number is too small."
  If myValue > 100 Then MsgBox _
    "The selected number is larger than 100."
  If myValue - Int(myValue) <> 0 Then MsgBox _
    "The selected number is not an integer."
Loop Until (myValue >= 0 And myValue <= 100 _
  And myValue - Int(myValue) = 0)
MsgBox "You chose the number " & myValue

End Sub
```

Notes (continued):

(3) This method allows the user to correct faulty entries without aborting the macro. The maximum number MaxTries of tries must be specified beforehand.

(4) Comparison with our simple starting macro, Read(), indicates the large part of a macro that may have to be devoted to data input controls. This often happens, regardless of whether the input is defined by highlighting, or by using an input box. The amount of code devoted to data input is even larger when using a dialog box as the input stage.

(5) The editor will again interpret the above If statements as one-liners, which do not require End If statements. Note that such an End If statement must be written as two words, whereas ElseIf should be written as one word.

Convenient data entry of arrays often involves the highlight & click method, in which we read a range, as in

```
Sub InputARange()

Dim myRange As Range
Set myRange = Application.InputBox _
  (Prompt:="The range is:", Type:=8)
myRange.Select

End Sub
```

where Type:=8 indicates what input information should be expected. Type:=8 denotes a range, i.e., a cell or block reference rather than, say, a formula (Type:=0), a number (Type:=1), a text string (Type:=2), a logical value (i.e., True or False, Type:=4), an error value (such as #N/A, Type:=16), or an array (Type:=64). For more than one possible type of input, add the various numbers: Type:=9 would accept either a number or a range.

In order to verify that we have indeed read the range correctly, we might add the temporary test code

```
Dim c As Integer, cMax As Integer
Dim r As Integer, rMax As Integer
Dim myValue As Variant

cMax = myRange.Columns.Count
rMax = myRange.Rows.Count
```

```
MsgBox "The range is " & myRange.Item(1, 1) _
   .Address & ":" & myRange.Item(rMax, cMax).Address
myValue = Selection.Value
For c = 1 To cMax
   For r = 1 To rMax
      MsgBox "Address number " & r & "," & c & _
         " is " & Selection.Item(r, c).Address & _
         " and contains the value " & myValue(r, c)
   Next r
Next c
```

> *Notes (continued):*
>
> (6) The nested `For … Next` loops will display all cell addresses and their corresponding numerical values, one at a time, because the OK button on the message box must be pressed after each display.
>
> (7) The output first lists the contents of the first column, from top to bottom, then that of the second column, etc. If you want the output to read the rows first, just interchange the lines `For c = 1 To cMax` and `For r = 1 To rMax`, and similarly `Next c` and `Next r`. *You* are in complete control.

Another way to test for proper reading is to copy the input values to another array, to be printed out elsewhere on the spreadsheet. This method makes comparison of the original and its copy somewhat easier. Here is the resulting macro:

```
Sub InputARange()

Dim c As Integer, cMax As Integer
Dim r As Integer, rMax As Integer
Dim myValue As Variant, myRange As Range

Set myRange = Application.InputBox _
   (Prompt:="The range is:", Type:=8)
myRange.Select

cMax = myRange.Columns.Count
rMax = myRange.Rows.Count

ReDim myValue(1 To rMax, 1 To cMax)
For c = 1 To cMax
   For r = 1 To rMax
      myValue(r, c) = myRange.Value(r, c)
   Next r
Next c

Selection.Offset(0, cMax + 1).Select
Selection.Value = myValue
Selection.Offset(0, -cMax - 1).Select

End Sub
```

Test the above macros by placing a small block of arbitrary numbers somewhere on the spreadsheet. Highlight it, then use the macro to read the range addresses and their cell values.

8.7 Case study 1: the propagation of imprecision

So-called 'error' propagation deals with the transmission of experimental imprecision through a calculation. Say that we have a function $F(x)$ which is computed from a single parameter x. We then want to calculate the imprecision $\pm\Delta F$ in F resulting from the (assumedly known) imprecision $\pm\Delta x$ in the parameter x. For the usual assumption $\Delta x \ll x$ we have

$$\frac{\Delta F}{\Delta x} \approx \frac{dF}{dx} \tag{8.7.1}$$

so that the magnitude of ΔF is given by

$$\Delta F \approx \left|\frac{dF}{dx}\right| \Delta x \tag{8.7.2}$$

or, in terms of standard deviations,

$$\sigma_F = \left|\frac{dF}{dx}\right| \sigma_x \tag{8.7.3}$$

Spreadsheets cannot compute the *algebraic formula* for the derivative dF/dx (as, e.g., Mathematica or Maple can), but they can find its *numerical value*, which is all we need. We do this by going back to the definition of the differential quotient as

$$\frac{dF}{dx} \equiv \lim_{\Delta x \to 0} \frac{\Delta F}{\Delta x} = \lim_{\Delta x \to 0} \frac{F(x+\Delta x)-F(x)}{\Delta x} \tag{8.7.4}$$

Therefore we calculate dF/dx by computing the function F twice, once with the original parameter x, and subsequently with that parameter slightly changed from x to $x + \Delta x$, using the Excel function `Replace`. We then divide their difference by the magnitude of that change, Δx. When Δx is sufficiently small (but not so small that Δx itself becomes imprecise), (8.7.4) will calculate the value of dF/dx without requiring any formal differentiation! A value for $\Delta x/x$ between 10^{-6} and 10^{-8} satisfies the requirements that $\Delta x \ll x$ while Δx is still much larger than the truncation errors of the program, which in Excel are of the order of 10^{-14}.

We will write the macro in two parts: first the data input stage, then the actual calculation. Here we go:

```
Sub Propagation()

' Read the x-value
```

```
Dim XRange As Range
Set XRange = Application.InputBox _
  (Prompt:="The value of x is:", Type:=8)
XRange.Select
XValue = Selection.Value

' Read the corresponding standard deviation s

Set SValue = Application.InputBox _
  (Prompt:="The standard deviation s is:", Type:=8)

' Read the formula F and its value

Dim FRange As Range
Set FRange = Application.InputBox _
  ("The formula F is:", Type:=8)
FRange.Select
FFormula = Selection.Formula
FValue = Selection.Value

' Verify that x, s, and F are read correctly

MsgBox "The value of x is " & XValue
MsgBox "The standard deviation in x is " & SValue
MsgBox "The formula has the value " & FValue
MsgBox "The formula reads " & FFormula

End Sub
```

Note:
(1) Set XRange and Set SValue could use a simpler input box.

Test this section. When the input part of the program works correctly, comment out the verification section, and insert the following code on the lines just above End Sub.

```
' Change x

XRange.Select
NewXValue = XValue * 1.000001
Selection.Replace XValue, NewXValue
MsgBox "The new value for x is " & NewXValue

' Read the resulting change in F

FRange.Select
NewFValue = Selection.Value
MsgBox "The new value for F is " & NewFValue

' Compute the standard deviation SF in F

SFValue = Abs((NewFValue - FValue) _
  * SValue / (XValue * 0.000001))
MsgBox "The standard deviation in F is " & SFValue

' Reset x

XRange.Select
Selection.Replace NewXValue, XValue
```

Again, test the program, now with some numbers and equations for which you know how the uncertainty propagates, such as $F(x) = x^3$ or $\sqrt{x}$, for which $dF / dx = 3x^2$ or $1 / (2\sqrt{x})$ respectively. (The test will of course use numbers rather than symbols. Avoid numbers such as 0 or 1 that often yield non-informative answers.) When everything works well, delete all message boxes except for the last one. Congratulations, you have now written a useful, nontrivial scientific macro!

The macro Propagation in the MacroBundle is essentially the same as the one you have just written, except that it can also handle functions of multiple parameters, can use either standard deviations or the covariance matrix as input, and will write its results onto the spreadsheet unless that action would risk overwriting valuable data. Those 'extras' make the macro somewhat more complicated, and much longer, but the principle of the method is the same. The macro is shown in section 9.10, and retains some semblance of readability by being broken up into smaller sections, each with their own comment headings, just as you would break up a long chapter into paragraphs with subtitles. See whether you can now follow its logic.

8.8 Case study 2: bisection

Often we need to find the root of a complicated expression $y(x)$ within a well-defined interval of x-values. An example might be to compute the pH of a complicated mixture, such as a 'universal' buffer mixture. The pH of any acid-base mixture can be formulated in general terms, see, e.g., R. de Levie, *Chem. Educ.* 6 (2001) 272. While such a general expression is conceptually and formally quite simple, its explicit form in terms of the proton concentration $[H^+]$ will be quite complicated when applied to a multi-component mixture of monoprotic and polyprotic acids and bases, reflecting the complexity of the chemical equilibria involved.

In such cases we can use Solver (or GoalSeek) to find the root, but that often requires some manual guidance. A bisection method, though in principle somewhat less efficient, can often be a preferred alternative because, as long as there is only one real root in the specified interval, bisection will always find it, reliably and without external assistance.

We start with a set of data $y(x)$ as a function of a monotonically changing variable x in an interval within which $y(x)$ crosses zero once. We will label the first value of $y(x)$ as y_{first}, and its last value as y_{last}, where y_{first} and y_{last} have different signs so that the product $y_{first} \times y_{last}$

must be negative. We then compute y_{new} for $x_{new} = (x_{first} + x_{last})/2$. If the product $y_{first} \times y_{new}$ is negative, the root lies in the interval between x_{first} and x_{new}, and we replace x_{last} by x_{new}; on the other hand, if $y_{first} \times y_{new}$ is positive, x_{new} will replace x_{first}. Thus we reduce the size of the interval $x_{last} - x_{first}$, and this process can be repeated until the interval is sufficiently small, at which point x_{new} can be taken as the sought answer.

The macro shown below performs just one step, so that you can see the progress of successive bisections by calling it repeatedly. Since the computer only needs the input data, there is no need for input boxes, and the input process has been reduced to highlighting the data array and calling the macro, in that order. The downside of this approach is that the input block must be organized in a set way so that the macro can interpret the data unambiguously. If you prefer to use input boxes, or a single multi-input dialog box, by all means change the macro to suit your taste.

In the present example the input block should contain two columns, of which the leftmost must contain the function $y(x)$, and the rightmost column the independent variable x. That assignment was chosen here to be consistent with the data arrangements in the custom least squares macros of the MacroBundle, even though it is somewhat less convenient for making graphs. But then, you can readily modify the macro, and arrange its input format to suit your own taste.

The macro writes new x-values into the spreadsheet, which subsequently computes the corresponding y-values that are then read back into the macro. Consequently the macro need not 'know' the equation used for y as a function of x, and therefore can be directly applicable to any data set that includes one zero crossing.

```
Sub RootFinder()

Dim i As Integer, nc As Integer, nr As Integer

Dim Ffirst As Double, Flast As Double
Dim Fnew As Double, Xdif As Double
Dim Xfirst As Double, Xlast As Double, Xnew As Double

Dim FormulaArray As Variant, ValueArray As Variant

nc = Selection.Columns.Count
nr = Selection.Rows.Count

' Read the input from the highlighted block

FormulaArray = Selection.Formula

ValueArray = Selection.Value
```

```
' Bisection

Ffirst = ValueArray(1, 1)
Flast = ValueArray(nr, 1)
Xfirst = ValueArray(1, 2)
Xlast = ValueArray(nr, 2)
Xdif = Xlast - Xfirst
Xnew = (Xfirst + Xlast) / 2
FormulaArray(2, 2) = Xnew
Selection.Formula = FormulaArray
ValueArray = Selection.Value
Fnew = ValueArray(2, 1)

If Ffirst * Fnew > 0 Then
  For i = 1 To nr
    FormulaArray(i, 2) = Xnew + _
      (Xlast - Xnew) * (i - 1) / (nr - 1)
  Next i
  Selection.Formula = FormulaArray
End If

If Ffirst * Fnew < 0 Then
  For i = 1 To nr
    FormulaArray(i, 2) = Xfirst + _
      (Xnew - Xfirst) * (i - 1) / (nr - 1)
  Next i
  Selection.Formula = FormulaArray
End If

' Display result

MsgBox "Xroot = " & Xnew

End Sub
```

Note that RootFinder requires a zero *crossing*, i.e., with both positive and negative values for $y(x)$ bracketing the root at $y = 0$. Therefore it will not find the root of functions that merely touch the abscissa, such as $y = |x - a|^2$, for which $y \geq 0$ with a root at $x = a$. When a function exhibits two or more distinct zero crossings, make the x-increments sufficiently small to separate the roots, and then apply RootFinder separately to x-intervals that each contain only one root. In order to facilitate such applications to parts of a data set, the output is provided in a message box.

The version incorporated in the MacroBundle makes a few initial checks, uses a DO loop to automate the process, saves the original data, holds the screen image constant during the calculation, and restores the original data before the screen is finally updated to display the root. The point of exit of the DO loop depends on the resolution criterion F_{res}, which for optimal results with a particular problem may have to be changed in value or made absolute rather than relative.

8.9 Case study 3: Fourier transformation

The next example will illustrate a somewhat different approach to writing macros. You will take the core code from the literature. Left for you to write are, then, the VBA code to read the data into the macro and to return the results to the spreadsheet, plus any error checks to prevent the most common operator mistakes. If you leave out the latter, you may be dismayed later to fall into a trap of your own making.

Excel already provides a Fourier transformation routine, under <u>T</u>ools $\Rightarrow$ <u>D</u>ata Analysis $\Rightarrow$ Fourier Analysis, so why re-invent the wheel? The reason is that, in this case, the wheel is rather wobbly, and not very serviceable: the Excel routine is not properly scaled (transformation followed by inverse transformation does not return the original) and, more importantly, its output is coded as labels, from which the data need to be extracted with =IMREAL() and =IMAGINARY(). You therefore would have to work hard merely to get the output in a form useful for, e.g., subsequent calculations or a graph. While such defects can be corrected or circumvented, it is sometimes easier to avoid them altogether by starting afresh. That is what we will illustrate here.

Fourier transformation is in principle a simple matter: once the input data have been provided, the computer needs no further information. Consequently there is no need for input boxes, and the input process can be reduced to highlighting the data array and then calling the macro, as already illustrated in section 8.8.

The so-called fast Fourier transformation is most efficient when applied to a number of data points that is an integer power of 2, and most software packages, including this one, are therefore restricted to 2^N data where N is a positive integer.

8.9.1 A starter macro

We start by putting together a rudimentary yet working Fourier transform macro by providing a simple input statement, a routine taken from the literature, and an output statement. Such a macro might just contain `dataArray = Selection.Value` as input statement, `Selection.Value = dataArray` as output instruction, and have the Fourier transform routine in the middle, together with whatever that routine requires.

There are many places in the literature where a Fourier transform subroutine can be found. Here we will use a particularly convenient source, the *Numerical Recipes* by W. H. Press, B. P. Flannery, S. A. Teukolsky, and W. T. Vetterling, published in several versions (such as Fortran, Pascal, or C^{++}) by Cambridge University Press. This book not only gives many useful routines, but also presents a very lucid explanation of their uses and limitations. Moreover, in an accompanying booklet complete with diskette, J. C. Sprott has provided these routines in Basic, i.e., in a format that you can use *as is* because it is fully compatible with VBA. Therefore, get hold of the diskette of Sprott's *Numerical Recipes: Routines and Examples in BASIC*, Cambridge University Press 1991, and copy it onto your computer. And, at the same time, also get yourself a copy of the *Numerical Recipes* (preferably the Fortran77 version that was the source for Sprott's Basic programs) for useful (and sometimes, as we will shortly see, quite essential) background information.

You will find that Press et al. describe a subroutine called FOUR1, which requires that the input data are arranged as alternating real and imaginary terms, and returns the answer in the same format. Since such a sequence is unsuitable for graphs, we will start with two input columns, one each for the real and imaginary signal components respectively. Likewise we will use two output columns. We will then use the macro to rearrange the data from two columns to one, as input for the subroutine, and afterwards to decode its single-column output into two columns for the spreadsheet. Open a new spreadsheet, and type:

```
Sub Fourier()

' Determine the array length

Dim r As Integer, rMax As Integer
rMax = Selection.Rows.Count

' Read the input

Dim dataArray As Variant
dataArray = Selection.Value

' Rearrange the input

ReDim Term(1 To 2 * rMax) As Double
For r = 1 To rMax
  Term(2 * r - 1) = dataArray(r, 1)
  Term(2 * r) = dataArray(r, 2)
Next r

' Call the subroutine

Dim iSign As Integer
iSign = 1
'Call Four1(Term, 2 * rMax, iSign)

' Rearrange the output

For r = 1 To rMax
  dataArray(r, 1) = Term(2 * r - 1)
  dataArray(r, 2) = Term(2 * r)
```

```
Next r

' Write the output data

Selection.Offset(0, 2).Select
Selection.Value = dataArray

End Sub
```

Notes:

(1) `Selection.Rows.Count` is a convenient instruction to find the length of the input columns.

(2) The macro reads the entire input array with the simple instruction `dataArray = Selection.Value`.

(3) The next few lines put the input data in the required format: Re_1, Im_1, Re_2, Im_2, etc., where Re_n and Im_n are the real and imaginary parts of the nth data point.

(4) An Array has two dimensions, one each for rows and columns. Therefore, `dataArray(r, 1)` refers to the cell at row number `r` and column 1 of the array, i.e., its leftmost one.

(5) Specify any as yet undefined parameters that `Four1()` may need (here: `iSign`), and call the subroutine. By initially commenting out the subroutine call, as done here, this part can be checked out first, separately.

(6) Unscramble the output by taking the alternating real and imaginary components from their single file, and putting them back into separate columns.

(7) Offset the highlighted array with `Selection.Offset(0, 2). Select` in order not to overwrite the input data, and return the result to the spreadsheet with `Selection.Value = dataArray`. We already encountered this type of code at the end of section 2.5.2.

(8) If you have followed the above, you will have dimensioned all variables. You need not do so (as long as you do not use Option Explicit), but in general it is a good practice, which from now on we will follow in all our examples. For one thing, it can make the computer run more efficiently. For another, it can alert you to some typos, because Option Explicit will catch most misspelled variable names.

(9) The typo alert works whenever you use variable names that contain at least one capital, provided that you type them everywhere in lower case, except in the dimension statement. The ever-alert Visual Basic Editor will then convert any lower case letters to the corresponding capitals in accordance with the dimension statement. When you see the computer-inserted capitals pop up on your screen you will know that the Visual Basic Editor has recognized the name. Most typos will be caught this way, unless your typo specifies another parameter name you have also dimensioned. Although it is good programming practice to use the dimension statement to specify the data type (e.g., `As Integer` or `As Variant`), you do *not* need do so to get this advantage. When in doubt about its proper data type, at least dimension the variable by name.

Now place the subroutine FOUR1 after the macro, or use its slightly modified form as shown below.

```
Sub Four1(Term, nn, iSign)

Dim tr As Double, ti As Double, theta As Double
Dim wtemp As Double, wi As Double, wr As Double
Dim wpi As Double, wpr As Double
Dim i As Integer, istep As Integer, j As Integer
Dim m As Integer, mmax As Integer
j = 1

For i = 1 To nn Step 2
  If j > i Then
    tr = Term(j)
    ti = Term(j + 1)
    Term(j) = Term(i)
    Term(j + 1) = Term(i + 1)
    Term(i) = tr
    Term(i + 1) = ti
  End If
  m = Int(nn / 2)
  While m >= 2 And j > m
    j = j - m
    m = Int(m / 2)
  Wend
  j = j + m
Next i

mmax = 2
While nn > mmax
  istep = 2 * mmax
  theta = 2 * [Pi()] / (-iSign * mmax)
  wpr = -2 * SIN(0.5 * theta) ^ 2
  wpi = SIN(theta)
  wr = 1
  wi = 0
  For m = 1 To mmax Step 2
    For i = m To nn Step istep
      j = i + mmax
      tr = wr * Term(j) - wi * Term(j + 1)
      ti = wr * Term(j + 1) + wi * Term(j)
      Term(j) = Term(i) - tr
      Term(j + 1) = Term(i + 1) - ti
      Term(i) = Term(i) + tr
      Term(i + 1) = Term(i + 1) + ti
    Next i
    wtemp = wr
    wr = wr * wpr - wi * wpi + wr
    wi = wi * wpr + wtemp * wpi + wi
  Next m
  mmax = istep
Wend

End Sub
```

Notes (continued):

(10) The first (and major) modification here is the dimensioning, especially the use of double precision. As already emphasized in section 8.5, VBA uses *single* precision unless specifically instructed otherwise.

(11) Instead of spelling out the numerical value of π, we merely invoke the spreadsheet function `Pi()` by placing it between straight brackets. A more general way to do this is to precede the function by 0, as in `theta = 2* Application.Pi()/(-iSign*mmax)`. This convenient trick works for all built-in Excel spreadsheet functions we may want to use in VBA.

(12) On the same line you may notice a sign change, because the *Numerical Recipes* use an engineering sign convention for Fourier transformation that is the opposite of the common scientific one used here, see section 5.11.

Remove the apostrophe in front of the `Call` statement, and test the entire macro. (The word `Call` in the line calling the subroutine is optional, but is highly recommended, because it makes the macro easier to read.) As test data you might first use $y_{Re} = \cos(\pi x/8)$ and $y_{Im} = 0$ for $x = 0$ (1) 15. Then try $y_{Re} = \sin(\pi x/8)$ and $y_{Im} = 0$ for the same x values. The cosine is symmetrical around $x = 0$, while the sine is not. Keep in mind that any numbers smaller than about 10^{-14} are likely to be zeros corrupted by computational (truncation and round-off) errors.

8.9.2 Comments & embellishments

a. Scaling: The Fourier transform of $y = \cos(\pi x/8)$ for $x = 0$ (1) 15 should yield two nonzero points, each of magnitude $0.5j$ (where $j = \sqrt{-1}$) at $f = +1/8$ and $-1/8$ respectively. You should find two nonzero points, in the second row and at the bottom of the first output column, but their magnitudes will be 8 instead of 0.5. However, if you had carefully read the section on FOUR1 in the *Numerical Recipes* you would have seen that you must still provide a normalizing factor, the reciprocal of the number of data points transformed. Here that number is 16, and $8/16 = 0.5$, so that this indeed explains the discrepancy. We should build this division into the macro.

b. Sign: The Fourier transform of $y = \sin(\pi x/8)$ for $x = 0$ (1) 15 should also be two points, of magnitude $-0.5j$ (where $j = \sqrt{-1}$) at $f = +1/8$, and $+0.5j$ at $-1/8$ respectively. You obtained two nonzero points, in the second output column (which contains the imaginary parts of the output), viz. -8 in the second row, and $+8$ in the bottom row. Normalization through division by 16, and realizing that the second column represents the imaginary components, makes these $-0.5j$ and $+0.5j$ respectively. However, upon consulting a standard book on Fourier transformations, you will find that these signs are just the reverse from what they are supposed to be. Another look at the *Numerical Recipes* will show that it uses uncommon definitions of the forward and inverse Fourier transforms, opposite from the usual convention. Consequently the problem is in the subroutine, and is easily fixed by placing a minus sign in front of the term `iSign` in the equation defining `theta`. This correction was already made in the modified version shown.

 c. Driver macros: Now that we have calibrated the macro, it is time to consider some conveniences. We can use the very same macro for inverse transformation if we change the sign of `iSign`. That can of course be done with an input box, but it is easier to make two small macros, ForwardFT and InverseFT, that set `iSign` to +1 and −1 respectively, and then call Fourier as a subroutine. Here are such drivers:

```
Sub ForwardFT()
Dim iSign As Integer
iSign = 1
Call Fourier(iSign)
End Sub

Sub InverseFT()
Dim iSign As Integer
iSign = -1
Call Fourier(iSign)
End Sub
```

 Notes:
 (1) The difference between a macro and a subroutine is that a macro does not exchange information in its (therefore empty) argument (in the space between the brackets). A subroutine does; in the above example both driver macros tell Fourier to use their particular value of iSign. And because the two driver macros are independent, iSign must be dimensioned twice.
 (2) There is slightly more to combining forward and inverse transforms, because (in the common formalism we adopt here) the normalizing factor $1/N$ only applies to the forward transform. (An alternative is to use normalizing factors $1/\sqrt{N}$ for both the forward and inverse transform.)
 (3) The header of the main program must now be changed to `Sub Fourier(iSign)`.

 d. Checking the input block dimensions: The Fourier transform subroutine requires that there are 2^N data points. It is convenient to check ahead of time whether the input range indeed contains such a number of data. We can also make sure that there are only 2 columns, and that there are at least 2 rows. The following code, to be placed immediately below the heading of Fourier(iSign), will accomplish all of these goals.

```
' Check the array width

Dim cMax As Integer
cMax = Selection.Columns.Count

If cMax <> 2 Then
  MsgBox "There must be 2 input columns."
  End
End If

' Check the array length
Dim rMax As Integer, Length As Integer
rMax = Selection.Rows.Count
If rMax < 2 Then
  MsgBox "There must be at least 2 rows."
  End
End If
Length = rMax
Do While length > 1
  Length = Length / 2
Loop
If Length <> 1 Then
  MsgBox "The number of rows must be" _
    & Chr(13) & "an integral power of two."
  End
End If
```

Notes:

(1) `Selection.Columns.Count` finds the number of highlighted columns, which should be 2, one for the real component of the function to be transformed, the other for its imaginary component. Otherwise the macro alerts the user of the problem, and ends.

(2) Similarly, `Selection.Rows.Count` finds the number of rows of the highlighted array, `rMax`. This should be at least 2.

(3) The next check makes sure that `rMax` is an integer power of 2. This is accomplished here by using a second variable, `Length`, that we initially set equal to `rMax`. Then we divide `Length` repeatedly by 2, until it becomes smaller than 1. If there is a nonzero remainder, the number of rows was not an integer power of 2, and the input is rejected.

(4) We here divide `Length` rather than `rMax` in order to keep the latter intact for further use. Alternatively we could use `rMax`, and redetermine it the next time we need it. There are often several ways to get the job done.

e. Checking for overwrite: It is convenient to place the output of the macro immediately to the right of the input data. We now make sure that this region does not contain valuable data that would be lost if overwritten, by letting the macro take a quick look at that area to make sure it can be used for output. Here is an example of code that will do this. It can be inserted just after the code discussed under (d), or before the data output.

```
' Make sure that the output will
' not overwrite valuable data

Dim outputArray As Variant, z As Double
Dim c As Integer, cMax As Integer
```

```
Dim r As Integer, rMax As Integer
Dim n As Integer
n = 0

Selection.Offset(0, 2).Select
OutputArray = Selection.Value
For r = 1 To rMax
  For c = 1 To cMax
    z = outputArray(r, c)
    If IsEmpty(z) Or z = 0 Then
      n = n
    Else
      n = n + 1
    End If
  Next c
Next r

If n > 0 Then
  answer = MsgBox("There are data in the" _
    & Chr(13) & "output space. Can they" _
    & Chr(13) & "be overwritten?", vbYesNo)
  If answer = vbNo Then
    Selection.Offset(0, -2).Select
    End
  End If
End If
```

Notes:

(1) `Selection.Offset(0, 2).Select` moves the highlighted area 2 cells to the right, to the place where the output will be deposited.

(2) The next line makes an output array of the same dimensions as the input array. It is used here only to see whatever is in the cells where the output should come.

(3) Now that we have read what is in the output space, the next lines check every cell in that area. Whenever a cell in this range is found not to be empty or zero, the variable n is incremented by one. Initially, n was set to zero, and at the end we see whether it is still zero. If not, then the message box is activated, asking the user whether the data in the output array can be overwritten. If the answer is no, the highlighted area switches back, and the macro is ended, to give the user time to move the endangered data out of harm's way.

(4) Since Fourier transformation is often applied to fairly large data files, no niceties such as an alternative output via message boxes is provided, since they would be awkward and time-consuming to use.

f. Converting time to frequency etc.: In the Fourier transformation

$$F(f) = \int_{-\infty}^{+\infty} f(t)\, e^{-2\pi j f t}\, dt$$

the product of the parameters f and t must be dimensionless, as it is in the usual pairs of time and frequency, or wavelength and wavenumber. Given t, we can let the computer calculate f, and vice versa. Therefore it is convenient to extend the block to include the independent variable x, to compute its inverse, and to provide that in a third output column.

g. Using a zero-centered scale: A related question is that of the scale to be used for the independent variable. Traditionally, t runs from 0 to t_{max}, while f starts at 0, runs till $f_{max}/2$, has a discontinuity, then continues to run from $-f_{max}/2$ to -0. We here adopt more rational scales that are continuous, and are centered around zero for both t and f. (The final version tolerates both types of input.)

h. Suppressing screen display: Often we will have graphs on the screen in order to visualize the functions. When a macro recalculates a data point, the entire screen will be updated. Usually this is precisely what we want. However, for a computation involving many points, as in a Fourier transformation of a large data set, it is convenient to suppress the screen updating until the entire output set has been computed. This is accomplished with the instruction `Application.ScreenUpdating = False`, which can be placed just before the output statement, `Selection.Value = dataArray`. Screen updating should be suppressed only *after* all input and dialog boxes have been used, since it blocks the convenience of entering ranges into input box windows by the highlight & click method.

i. Modularizing: When you anticipate that a part of the code may also be useful in other macros, it may be convenient to compartmentalize that section of code as a separate subroutine, which can be called by different macros. In the present example, the actual fast Fourier transform algorithm can then be shared with ConvolveFT. On the other hand, ConvolveFT could have used a more efficient fast Fourier transform algorithm that can simultaneously transform *two* real signals rather than one complex one. This illustrates the trade-off between optimizing code for each specific application, or saving development time by using already existing code modules.

j. Dimensioning: By now you will be ready to dimension your parameters. The macro is getting too long to be typed without errors, and dimensioning has other benefits: the user can quickly see to what type each parameter belongs, and the computer can operate more efficiently. Here are some things to keep in mind.

In dimensioning several parameters you need not repeat the dimension statement `Dim` for parameters on one line, but you must repeat the type declaration (as in `Dim A As Double, B As Double, C As Double`) for each and every parameter, even when these statements are on the same line. This is a true nuisance of VBA.

Even if you do not know their dimensions yet, dimension array variables As Variant, and then ReDimension them as soon as the macro knows the corresponding array size. And make sure to distinguish between arrays that start counting at 0 and those that start at 1. If you are unsure about the proper dimension type, just dimension it by name but leave the type unspecified. The program will run fine, though perhaps not optimally efficient. Fortunately, with today's processor speeds, it seldom makes a perceptible difference unless the macros are very computation intensive.

All of the above embellishments have been incorporated in the Fourier transform macro which you already encountered in chapter 5, and which is fully documented in chapter 10. You will now appreciate the difference between a lean-and-mean macro and a well-thought-out but potbellied one. In the latter, more code is usually devoted to embellishments than to the primary function of the macro. One can only hope that the added effort pays off in terms of convenience of use and absence of frustrating program hang-ups.

8.10 Case study 4: specifying a graph

As our next example we will make a macro to generate a graph. Of course you can readily make a graph with the ChartWizard. But if you need to make many graphs for a report or a paper, and want them to be compatible in size and style, it may be convenient to have a standard format available. You can do this by creating a graph just the way you want it to look, and by then making that the default setting, as described in section 1.7.6.

Alternatively, just as an illustration of how much you can manipulate Excel, we will write a macro to specify a simple graph, so that the mouse can stay home for a while. (For another example see the custom macro Mapper.) For the sake of the argument, say that you want to plot the function $2.4 \sqrt{x}$ for $x = 0$ (5) 100, where you have placed values for x in cells A7:A27, and computed the corresponding values for $y = 2.4 \sqrt{x}$ in B7:B27. First reserve the location of the graph on the spreadsheet with

```
Sub MakeGraph()
' Create an embedded graph in the cell grid

Dim ch As ChartObject
Dim cw As Double, rh As Double

cw = Columns(1).Width
rh = Rows(1).Height
Set ch = ActiveSheet.ChartObjects. _
  Add(cw * 2, rh * 1, cw * 5, rh * 5)
```

```
End Sub
```

By setting `cw = Columns(1).Width` and `rh = Rows(1).Height` we make the graph fit the spreadsheet grid, facilitating its subsequent copying into a Word document. Otherwise we need to specify the placement and dimension of the graph in points, where 1 point = 1/72" ≈ 1/3 mm. See what happens when you change the parameter values to, e.g., `Add(cw * 3, rh * 4, cw * 8, rh * 16)`. Now define the data type, and the specific data to be plotted:

```
Sub MakeGraph()
' Create an embedded graph in the cell grid
Dim ch As ChartObject
Dim cw As Double, rh As Double

cw = Columns(1).Width
rh = Rows(1).Height
Set ch = ActiveSheet.ChartObjects. _
  Add(cw * 3, rh * 4, cw * 8, rh * 16)
' Select the graph type:
ch.Chart.ChartType = xlXYScatter
' Insert data series:
ch.Chart.SeriesCollection.Add Source:= _
  ActiveSheet.Range("A7:B27")

End Sub
```

This short macro will give you a graph of the data in A7:B27, at the chosen place on the spreadsheet, with auto-scaled axes. If you want to specify your own axes, add instructions such as:

```
' Insert graph axes:
' (X = "Category", Y = "Value")

With ch.Chart.Axes(xlCategory)
  .MinimumScale = 0
  .MaximumScale = 100
  .MajorUnit = 20
End With
With ch.Chart.Axes(xlValue)
  .MinimumScale = 0
  .MaximumScale = 25
  .MajorUnit = 5
End With
```

Now that the basic choices have been made, the rest is fine-tuning and embellishment. Here are some options:

```
' Define the data range:

ch.Chart.SeriesCollection.Add _
  Source:=ActiveSheet.Range("A7:B27"), _
  RowCol:=xlColumns, _
  SeriesLabels:=True, _
  CategoryLabels:=True
```

```
' Define the axis labels:

With ch.Chart.Axes(xlCategory)
  .MinimumScale = 0
  .MaximumScale = 100
  .MajorUnit = 20
  .HasTitle = True
  With .AxisTitle
    .Caption = "time / s"
    .Font.Size = 12
  End With
End With
With ch.Chart.Axes(xlValue)
  .MinimumScale = 0
  .MaximumScale = 25
  .MajorUnit = 5
  .HasTitle = True
  With .AxisTitle
    .Caption = "signal / A"
    .Font.Size = 12
    .Orientation = xlUpward
  End With
End With

' If you don't want the legend box:

ch.Chart.Legend.Clear

' Specify a graph title

ch.Chart.HasTitle = True
With ch.Chart.ChartTitle
  .Caption = "Sample Chart #1"
  .Font.Name = "Times Roman"
  .Font.Size = 16
  .Font.FontStyle = "Italic"
  .Font.ColorIndex = 4
End With
```

The colors are 1 = black, 2 = reversed (white on black background), 3 = red, 4 = green, 5 = blue, etc., giving you 16 color options. Alternatively you can use the RGB system that lets you select any color combination using 256 shades of red, green and blue, e.g., pure red would be coded by .Font.Color = RGB(255, 0, 0), as illustrated in section 11.7.

```
' Define the points and line in the graph

With ch.Chart.SeriesCollection(1)
  .MarkerBackgroundColorIndex = xlNone
  .MarkerForegroundColorIndex = 1
  .MarkerStyle = xlCircle
  .Smooth = True
  .MarkerSize = 7
  With .Border
    .ColorIndex = 7
    .Weight = xlHairline
    .LineStyle = xlContinuous
  End With
```

```
End With

' Do without gridlines:

ch.Chart.Axes(xlValue).HasMajorGridlines = False
ch.Chart.Axes(xlCategory).HasMajorGridlines _
  = False

' Define the background color of the graph:

ch.Chart.ChartArea.Interior.ColorIndex = 2
ch.Chart.PlotArea.Interior.ColorIndex = xlNone

' Place tickmarks:

ch.Chart.Axes(xlValue).MajorTickMark _
  = xlTickMarkCross
ch.Chart.Axes(xlValue).TickLabelPosition _
  = xlTickLabelPositionNextToAxis
' (and do similarly for xlCategory)

' Introduce a second data set:

ch.Chart.SeriesCollection.Add Range("C7:C27")

' Add a secondary vertical scale:

ch.Chart.SeriesCollection(2).AxisGroup = _
  xlSecondary
With ch.Chart.Axes(xlValue, xlSecondary)
  .HasTitle = True
  .AxisTitle.Caption = "log conc"
End With
With ch.Chart.Axes(xlValue, xlSecondary).AxisTitle
  .Font.Size = 12
  .Orientation = xlUpward
  .Top = 60
End With

' Define markers for a second data set:

With ch.Chart.SeriesCollection(2)
  .MarkerBackgroundColorIndex = 8
  .MarkerForegroundColorIndex = 5
  .MarkerStyle = xlTriangle
  .Smooth = True
  .MarkerSize = 5
End With

' Add a textbox and specify its text
' (note that the numerical values are in points)
With ch.Chart.TextBoxes.Add(164, 116, 96, 50)
  .AutoSize = True
  .Text = "K1=3"
End With
With ch.Chart.TextBoxes
  With .Characters(Start:=1, Length:=4).Font
    .Name = "Times New Roman"
    .Size = 12
  End With
  .Characters(Start:=1, Length:=1) _
```

```
  .Font.FontStyle = "Italic"
 .Characters(Start:=2, Length:=1) _
  .Font.Subscript = True
End With
```

and so on. This is only a sampler of the many possibilities, but you get the idea. You can highlight specific points with different markers and/or colors, add error bars, whatever. Finally, once the macro makes the graph you want, suppress the screen updating during its execution, since this will both clean and speed it up. You can do this by placing the following lines at the beginning of the program:

```
'Suppress screen updating:
Application.ScreenUpdating = False
```

8.11 Case study 5: sorting through permutations

In various areas of science one encounters the problem of permutation, in which exchanging indices makes a difference. A computer is a perfectly suitable tool to sort through this type of problem, and we will here use the example of multivariate least squares analysis to illustrate it. Say that we have block of data organized in rows and columns, where the latter are suggestively labeled y, x_1, x_2, x_3, etc., and further assume that we want to calculate the standard deviation of the fit, s_y, for a least squares fit of the y-values to equation of the type $y = a_0 + a_1x_1 + a_2x_2 + a_3x_3 + ...$ where we may want to see the effect of setting one or more terms a_i equal to zero, as in the problem discussed in section 3.14. Below we will illustrate how this might be approached.

There are several types of possible permutations. Say that we have four numbers, 1, 2, 3, and 4. Then we can ask in how many ways we can order them, as 1234, 1243, 4231, etc., every time using the very same four ingredients but only changing their order. Or we can ask how many possible combinations there are when we disregard their order, and merely delete one or more digits: 1, 12, 123, 124, etc. Here we will illustrate the latter type, in which, e.g., the specific two-digit combinations (from among the four numbers 1 through 4, and disregarding their order) are 12, 13, 14, 23, 24, and 34. The same logic is used in the following for-next loop

```
Sub Permute()

Dim c As Integer, c2 As Integer, cMax As Integer
cMax = 4

For c = 1 To cMax
  For c2 = c + 1 To cMax
    MsgBox c & "," & c2
  Next c2
```

```
  Next c

End Sub
```

Once we have established the principle of using nested for-next loops to do our bidding, the rest is simple. In the custom macro LSPermute1 we write the data in the *y*-column into the yArray, and the contents of the various columns x_1, x_2, x_3, etc., into xArray. We then use the subroutine LLSS (shown in section 9.5) to perform the multiparameter least squares analysis and to return the corresponding s_y values, whereupon we repeat the process for the next permutation.

```
Sub LSPermute1()

Dim c As Integer, c2 As Integer, c3 As Integer
Dim c4 As Integer, cc As Integer, cMax As Integer
Dim ccMax As Integer, Down As Integer
Dim r As Integer, rMax As Integer
Dim StDevY As Double
Dim inputArray As Variant
Dim xArray, yArray, outputArray

' Read and dimension arrays

inputArray = Selection.Value
cMax = Selection.Columns.Count
rMax = Selection.Rows.Count
ReDim yArray(1 To rMax, 1 To 1) As Double
ReDim outputArray(1 To rMax, 1 To cMax)

' Fill the yArray

For r = 1 To rMax
   yArray(r, 1) = inputArray(r, 1)
Next r

' Initialize the outputArray

For r = 1 To rMax
   For c = 1 To cMax
     outputArray(r, c) = ""
   Next c
Next r

Down = 0
Selection.Offset(rMax + 1, 0).Select
Down = Down + rMax + 1

' Write column headings

outputArray(1, 1) = "Indices:"
outputArray(1, 2) = "Sy:"
Selection.Value = outputArray
Selection.Offset(2, 0).Select
Down = Down + 2

' Compute the output for 1 variable:
```

```
ccMax = 4
ReDim xArray(1 To rMax, 1 To ccMax) As Double
For c = 2 To cMax
  For r = 1 To rMax
    xArray(r, 1) = 1
    xArray(r, 2) = inputArray(r, c)
  Next r
  Call LLSS(ccMax, rMax, 1, _
    yArray, xArray, StDevY)
  outputArray(1, 1) = c - 1
  outputArray(1, 2) = StDevY
  Selection.Value = outputArray
  Selection.Offset(1, 0).Select
  Down = Down + 1
Next c
Selection.Offset(1, 0).Select
Down = Down + 1

' Compute the output for 2 variables:

ccMax = 5
ReDim xArray(1 To rMax, 1 To ccMax) As Double
For c = 2 To cMax
  For c2 = c + 1 To cMax
    For r = 1 To rMax
      xArray(r, 1) = 1
      xArray(r, 2) = inputArray(r, c)
      xArray(r, 3) = inputArray(r, c2)
    Next r
    Call LLSS(ccMax, rMax, 1, _
      yArray, xArray, StDevY)
    outputArray(1, 1) = c - 1 & "," & c2 - 1
    outputArray(1, 2) = StDevY
    Selection.Value = outputArray
    Selection.Offset(1, 0).Select
    Down = Down + 1
  Next c2
Next c
Selection.Offset(1, 0).Select
Down = Down + 1

' Compute the output for 3 variables:

ccMax = 6
ReDim xArray(1 To rMax, 1 To ccMax) As Double
For c = 2 To cMax
  For c2 = c + 1 To cMax
    For c3 = c2 + 1 To cMax
      For r = 1 To rMax
        xArray(r, 1) = 1
        xArray(r, 2) = inputArray(r, c)
        xArray(r, 3) = inputArray(r, c2)
        xArray(r, 4) = inputArray(r, c3)
      Next r
      Call LLSS(ccMax, rMax, 1, yArray, xArray, StDevY)
      outputArray(1, 1) = c - 1 & "," & c2 - 1 & _
        "," & c3 - 1
      outputArray(1, 2) = StDevY
      Selection.Value = outputArray
```

```
      Selection.Offset(1, 0).Select
      Down = Down + 1
    Next c3
  Next c2
Next c

Selection.Offset(1, 0).Select
Down = Down + 1

' Compute the output for 4 variables:

ccMax = 7
ReDim xArray(1 To rMax, 1 To ccMax) As Double
For c = 2 To cMax
  For c2 = c + 1 To cMax
    For c3 = c2 + 1 To cMax
      For c4 = c3 + 1 To cMax
        For r = 1 To rMax
          xArray(r, 1) = 1
          xArray(r, 2) = inputArray(r, c)
          xArray(r, 3) = inputArray(r, c2)
          xArray(r, 4) = inputArray(r, c3)
          xArray(r, 5) = inputArray(r, c4)
        Next r
        Call LLSS(ccMax, rMax, 1, yArray, xArray, StDevY)
        outputArray(1, 1) = c - 1 & "," & c2 - 1 & _
          "," & c3 - 1 & "," & c4 - 1
        outputArray(1, 2) = StDevY
        Selection.Value = outputArray
        Selection.Offset(1, 0).Select
        Down = Down + 1
      Next c4
    Next c3
  Next c2
Next c

Selection.Offset(-Down, 0).Select

End Sub
```

Here, as in all the custom least squares macros in the MacroBundle, we assume that the left-most column in the highlighted block of input data is the dependent variable. This convention is used because the usual least squares analysis involves only one dependent variable y but has no limit on the number of independent variables x. Note, however, that this differs from the Excel convention for making graphs, which assumes that the left-most column specifies the abscissa (horizontal axis) normally associated with an independent variable. Simple ways around it are (1) to make a copy of the y-column somewhere to the right of the x-column, and use the latter columns for making the graph, (2) to move the y-column by cutting & pasting before making a graph, and immediately thereafter move it back to where it is required for the custom macro, or (3) to specify the x- and y-columns separately before calling the Chart Wizard or inside it.

At the other end of the macro, we have used a quick-and-dirty output, where we merely move the highlighted block down each time we have a line to write. It is quick because it doesn't take much thought to encode it, and dirty because it takes more space than is needed for the actual output data, and wipes out all data that happen to be in its path. It also takes more time to display its results, because it writes each line sequentially rather than computing all results first, and then displaying them. Section 9.5 contains a cleaned-up version, LSPermute, with more bells and whistles, for up to 6 variables. Still, it is often useful to get a working macro first, and to polish it up later.

A quick-and-dirty approach is still on display in section 9.5 for the treatment of the points near the extremes of the data set. A more compact treatment can be based on Gram polynomials.

8.12 Case study 6: raising the bar

Accompanying this book is the MacroBundle, a collection of custom macros that can be downloaded freely from the web site www.oup-usa/advancedexcel. Having them available on the internet makes them most widely accessible, even to readers who cannot afford to buy this book. The web also makes it possible to correct and upgrade them when necessary, something that neither the printed page nor an enclosed compact disk or floppy will allow. Yet, they are also printed in chapters 9 through 11, for your convenience as well as for the sake of permanence: web sites can and do disappear, disks get lost, and magnetic and optical formats change. Nothing is permanent, but in printed form the longevity of the material in chapters 9-11 is at least linked to that in chapters 1 through 8.

The present section is not about those macros, but about installing them on your machine in an efficient way. These installation procedures apply to all custom macros, not just those of the MacroBundle, and once you understand how this is done you can readily modify the macros in section 11.2 and 11.3 to include your own creations. These procedures will work in Excel 97 and more recent versions, but not in Excel 5 or Excel 95.

When macros are used only occasionally, the standard facilities of Excel are optimal: the custom macros do not usurp monitor 'real estate' but are listed in the macro dialog box accessible with Tools ⇒ Macro ⇒ Macros. To operate them, one merely double-clicks on them, or single-clicks followed by Run. If in doubt about their operation, instead single-click on them and then click <u>E</u>dit, which will get you to the top of the macro text in the Visual Basic Editor. The user instructions should be there, and after reading them you can get back to the spreadsheet with Alt⌣F11 (Mac: Opt⌣F11) and then call the macro into action.

If you need to use the macros frequently, more convenient ways to access them can be provided by embedding them as a menu item in the standard toolbar, or by adding a special toolbar to display them. Here we will illustrate both approaches.

8.12.1 Adding a menu item

As our example we will add a menu item called Custom<u>M</u>acros to the standard toolbar, and give it a submenu listing several macros. The advantage of this approach is that it facilitates access to the custom macros without consuming valuable spreadsheet space, because the standard toolbar has plenty of unused, extra space available, even on a small monitor screen. The code shown below will roughly halve the number of mouse clicks needed for calling custom macros.

```
Sub InsertMenuM()

Dim MenuN As CommandBarControl, Menu1 As CommandBarControl
Dim Menu20 As CommandBarControl, Menu21 As CommandBarControl
Dim MenuM As CommandBarPopup, Menu2 As CommandBarPopup

' Delete possible earlier menu insertions to prevent conflicts

On Error Resume Next
CommandBars(1).Controls("&CustomMacros").Delete

' Locate the new menu item between Tools and Data on the Menu bar

Set MenuN = CommandBars(1).FindControl(ID:=30011)
Set MenuM = CommandBars(1).Controls.Add(Type:=msoControlPopup, _
  Before:=MenuN.Index, Temporary:=True)
MenuM.Caption = "&CustomMacros"

' Create a menu item for SolverAid

Set Menu1 = MenuM.Controls.Add(Type:=msoControlButton)
With Menu1
  .Caption = "&SolverAid "
  .OnAction = "SolverAid"
End With

' Create a menu item for LS

Set Menu2 = MenuM.Controls.Add(Type:=msoControlPopup)
Menu2.Caption = " &LS "
```

```
' Create submenus for LS0 and LS1 respectively

Set Menu20 = Menu2.Controls.Add(Type:=msoControlButton)
With Menu20
  .Caption = "LS&0"
  .OnAction = "LS0"
End With

Set Menu21 = Menu2.Controls.Add(Type:=msoControlButton)
With Menu21
  .Caption = "LS&1"
  .OnAction = "LS1"
End With

End Sub
```

Notes:

(1) In order to avoid inserting multiple copies, we start with deleting pre-existing versions of the added menu item. However, we will then get an error when the menu bar is in its original form, so we add the dodge On Error Resume Next, which bypasses any errors encountered by the delete instruction. However, this trick will not work if your spreadsheet is set to Break on All Errors. You can undo this in the Visual Basic Editor under Tools ⇒ Options, General tab, by setting the Error Trapping to Break on Unhandled Errors instead.

(2) It is also possible to insert the toolbar automatically every time Excel is opened, and to delete it as part of closing Excel down. In fact, the above macro already does the latter, with the instruction Temporary:=True in Set MenuM.

(3) The difference between a Button and a Popup is that the latter refers to further choices: you cannot select a macro LS, but only the specific choices LS0 or LS1. A popup menu shows an arrow.

(4) The ampersand & in the captions is used to indicate that the next letter should be underlined, thereby defining the shortcut hotkeys. You can then select the macro not only by clicking on the toolbar button, but also (and often faster, since your fingers do not have to leave the keyboard to grab the mouse) with Alt‿S or /S for SolverAid, Alt‿L‿0 or /L0 for LS0, etc.

(5) The OnAction instruction does the actual work of calling the macro when you click on that particular menu item.

(6) When you are done experimenting with this macro, remove the inserted menu item with

```
Sub RemoveMenuM()

On Error Resume Next
CommandBars(1).Controls("&CustomMacros").Delete

End Sub
```

The MacroBundle can be configured to use this approach, as can be seen in section 11.3.

8.12.2 Adding a toolbar

At the expense of occupying a row on your monitor screen, even faster access to the custom macros can be provided by creating a new toolbar to display them. In order to emphasize the similarities between these two approaches, we will here illustrate adding a toolbar for the very same macros used in section 8.11.1.

```
Sub InsertToolbarM()

Dim TBar As CommandBar
Dim Button1, Button2, Button20, Button21

' Delete earlier version of M, if it exists, to prevent conflicts

On Error Resume Next
CommandBars("M").Delete

' Create a commandbar

Set TBar = CommandBars.Add
With TBar
  .name = "M"
  .Position = msoBarTop
  .Visible = True
End With

' Create a control button for SolverAid

Set Button1 = CommandBars("M").Controls.Add(Type:=msoControlButton)
With Button1
  .Caption = "&SolverAid "
  .Style = msoButtonCaption
  .OnAction = "SolverAid"
End With

' Create a control button for LS

Set Button2 = CommandBars("M").Controls.Add(Type:=msoControlPopup)
With Button2
  .Caption = " &LS "
  .TooltipText = "Highlight array" & Chr(13) & _
    "before pressing" & Chr(13) & "LS0 or LS1"
  .BeginGroup = True
End With

' Create submenus for LS0 and LS1 respectively

Set Button20 = Button2.Controls.Add(Type:=msoControlButton)
With Button20
  .Caption = "LS&0"
  .Style = msoButtonCaption
  .OnAction = "LS0"
End With

Set Button21 = Button2.Controls.Add(Type:=msoControlButton)
With Button21
```

```
    .Caption = "LS&1"
    .Style = msoButtonCaption
    .OnAction = "LS1"
End With

End Sub
```

Notes:

(1) You will notice that this macro mirrors many aspects of InsertMenuM().

(2) Calling for the installation of an already existing toolbar produces an error. We therefore delete a preexisting toolbar first, using `On Error Resume Next` to avoid problems in case the added toolbar did not already exist. (Again, this will not work if your spreadsheet is set to `Break on All Errors`. In that case go to the Visual Basic Editor and, under <u>T</u>ools ⇒ <u>O</u>ptions, General tab, and set the Error Trapping to `Break on Unhandled Errors`.) Alternatively, we could insert the toolbar automatically when Excel is opened, and let it be deleted just before closing Excel.

(3) ToolTips repeat the caption unless you specify them otherwise.

(4) The instruction `BeginGroup = True` merely inserts a vertical separator in the toolbar.

(5) While it is technically possible to have an inserted menu in the menu bar *and* an extra toolbar (since they work independently of each other), such over-abundance provides no additional benefits.

(6) To remove the added toolbar use

```
Sub RemoveToolbarM()

On Error Resume Next
CommandBars("M").Delete

End Sub
```

Again, the approach illustrated here can readily be extended, as illustrated in section 11.2.

8.13 Tools for macro writing

8.13.1 Editing tools

Visual Basic distinguishes between properties and methods. For every property there is a list of the specific methods you can invoke; likewise, methods only act on specific properties. The available options are not always obvious, but you can get a listing of them displayed on the Visual Basic Editor screen by typing a period behind a property or method, or an equal sign in an assignment, and waiting a few seconds. You can then choose from that list by double-clicking. This feature is especially useful when you need to check the order in which various arguments should be entered, and which ones should be left undefined but given explicit space, as in `MgsBox("Message", ,"Label")` when we do not want to modify the OK button.

The same list will appear when you select Edit ⇒ List Properties/ Methods (Alt⌣e⌣h, /⌣e⌣h) or Ctrl⌣J.

In order to show the proper syntax for an instruction, use Edit ⇒ Quick Info (Alt⌣e⌣q, /⌣e⌣q) or Ctrl⌣I. The proper arguments are displayed with Edit ⇒ Parameter Info (Alt⌣e⌣m, /⌣e⌣m) or Ctrl⌣Shift⌣I.

A list of constants for a particular property is shown with Edit ⇒ List Constants (Alt⌣e⌣s, /⌣e⌣s) or Ctrl⌣Shift⌣J.

In order to finish a word, type Edit ⇒ Complete Word (Alt⌣e⌣w, /⌣e⌣w) or Ctrl⌣space. If Excel knows more than one possible word ending, it will show a list from which you can choose.

8.13.2 The macro recorder

The Macro Recorder records keystroke sequences, so that repetitive operations can be automated. It records all keyboard and mouse actions in VBA notation, and can therefore be useful when you are writing a macro and have no idea how Excel codes some particular action. Macros can do many more things than you can do on the spreadsheet alone, but as long as what you need falls in the latter category, the Macro Recorder can show you a way to do it. It may not be the optimal way, but it will at least get you going, and you can always improve on it later.

In order to record, go to Tools ⇒ Macro ⇒ Record New Macro. This will produce a Record Macro dialog box, in which you can specify the name and a short description of the macro you are going to record, a shortcut key combination, and the file where to store it. All these are optional: the macro will be given a default name and stored in a module. Just click OK and start the Excel operations for which you want to know the VBA code. When you are done, press the Stop Recording button or select Tools ⇒ Macro ⇒ Stop Recording. Then select Tools ⇒ Macro ⇒ Macros, find the latest Macro*n* (they are numbered sequentially), and Edit it. You can now see how Excel codes these instructions.

Say that you don't know how to specify in VBA the color of text, even though you know how to do it in Excel, using the Font Color icon on your formula toolbar or drawing toolbar. The macro recorder lets Excel show you how to do it. On the spreadsheet, point to a cell, call the macro recorder (with Tools ⇒ Macro ⇒ Record New Macro), go to the

Font Color icon, select your color, then stop the macro recorder. Now go to Tools ⇒ Macro ⇒ Macros, with a *single* click select the just-made macro, click on Edit, and voilà, you see how Excel does its own coding. You may find the instruction `Selection.Font.ColorIndex = 3`, which you can incorporate into your own macro. This instruction may be accompanied by other, peripheral information, such as the font used, its size, the absence of underlining, etc. Don't be discouraged by such informational overload, just disregard it: since the MacroRecorder did not know what specific information you were looking for, it simply shows you everything.

8.14 Troubleshooting VBA

Writing functions and macros is not trivial, and the rules governing VBA are sufficiently impenetrable to keep it that way. Consequently you may spend at least as much time trouble-shooting as you will spend writing code in the first place. Before you shoot, it is helpful to look at the trouble you are aiming at.

There are several possible sources of trouble. The most important of these is faulty *logic*, but this you typically find out only while testing or applying the program, and there is little guidance this book can provide to avoid it. (If you don't, Murphy or one of his friends will most likely find it for you.) Instead we will focus on faulty *coding*, a potential sources of trouble that can show up at various times: after writing individual lines, during compilation, or upon running the function or subroutine.

The Visual Basic Editor will often alert you that a line you just typed contains a syntax error. This is helpful because it localizes the problem. Using Option Explicit also operates at the single-line level, and can identify many typos, as long as (1) you dimension variable names to contain capitals, (2) you type your code only in lowercase (except for quotations), and (3) you check whether the necessary caps appear magically as you press Enter at the end of each line.

Some errors the Visual Basic Editor only recognizes upon compiling the code. You typically find out about them when you try to run the program, but you can also test for them without leaving the Visual Basic Editor module, with Debug ⇒ Compile VBAProject on the Visual Basic Editor menu bar.

Then there are the runtime errors, often caused by parameter values that make the program divide by zero, take the logarithm or the square root of a negative number, etc. These depend on the input parameters, and can therefore be caught only by extensive testing over a wide range of input parameters.

Finally, there are the fool's errors, triggered by entering, say, text where numbers or ranges are expected, etc. These are perhaps the hardest errors to anticipate, because it is difficult to imagine what you (or some other user of your macro) might try to put into an input box at some unguarded moment. Perhaps the best way to avoid this type of entry errors is to use dialog boxes, a method we have not used here in order to keep matters simple. Extensive documentation may help to prevent them, but only for those willing to read it. In this book more emphasis has been given to the ideas behind the various methods, and to applying them appropriately, than to the prevention of fool's errors and the generation of 'industrial-strength' macros.

Now that you know what kinds of trouble you are shooting, back to the main topic. Excel contains many aids to troubleshoot VBA code. For yours truly the simplest of these are the most useful: whenever a test run fails, and displays a box with an error message, read (and note down) that message, then click Debug, and (before fixing anything) place the mouse pointer on a variable at or close to where the Visual Basic Editor highlights the code. In recent versions of Excel this will create a yellow ToolTip-like message listing the value of that variable at the moment the procedure bombed, which you write down before moving to the next variable. This will often allow you to identify what went wrong: perhaps an index fell outside its allotted range, a variable value was not specified, etc.

A second, simple method is to insert temporary message boxes at crucial points in the code to see which hurdles are taken, and at the same time report crucial intermediate results. This can be very helpful in programs that allow for various routes, because you can let the program report which choices it has made. However, try *not* to place such message boxes *inside* loops, because this will generate as many message boxes as there are repeats in the loop, and every one of them will have to be acknowledged, manually.

The Visual Basic Editor also contains additional trouble-shooting tools, such as its Code and Immediate windows, which can be helpful in writing and debugging macros. For these see chapter 3 in G. Hart-Davis,

*Mastering VBA6,*Sybex 1999, and/or chapter 7 in J. Walkenbach, *Micro-soft Excel 2000 Power Programming with VBA*, IDG Books, 1999.

Finally a practical hint. While writing a new macro, and while debugging it, you will need to exercise the macro often, in order to check the proper functioning of what you have written. Repeatedly going through the sequence Tools ⇒ Macro ⇒ Macros etc. will soon lose its charm, in which case it may be helpful to make a *button* to activate a macro. Here is how you can do that.

Start with the spreadsheet. Click on View ⇒ Toolbars ⇒ Forms, which will display a set of tool icons. Click on the button icon, which has the shape of a raised rectangle; when you then move the pointer away, the button icon shows that it is activated. Move the pointer (which now shows as a thin +-sign) to where you want the button, depress the left-hand mouse key, and draw a rectangle in the shape of the desired button. Release the mouse key, and the Assign Macro dialog box will appear. Click on the macro name, and from then on the button will call it. If you have not yet saved the macro, you can do the assignment later, by right-clicking on the button (to get its properties) and selecting Assign Macro. The same properties will allow you to change its label (with Edit Text) and its appearance (with Format Control), etc. Note: In earlier incarnations of Excel the button icon was part of the Drawing toolbar.

An alternative to using a button is to assign a *shortcut key-code* to a macro. To do this, select Tools ⇒ Macro ⇒ Macros and, in the Macro dialog box, single-click on the macro name. Click on Options, and assign a lower-case letter or capital as Shortcut key. Exit with OK and Run. Thereafter, the macro is callable with Ctrl‿*n* or Ctrl‿*N* where *n* or *N* is the shortcut key. This is one of a few cases where Excel is case-sensitive. Make sure not to redefine common keystroke combinations you may want to keep, such as Ctrl‿c. (But you could assign Ctrl‿Shift‿c, i.e., Ctrl‿C, to some other purpose.) Use the same procedure to reassign a shortcut key. By erasing the shortcut key, Excel will revert to its default assignment.

8.15 Summary

This chapter has focused on the actual writing of macros. It is one of the best-kept secrets of Excel that you are not restricted to the functional-ities provided, but can make it do your own bidding. Most owners of Excel do not realize that they have a tiger in their tank, a powerful programming language that can readily be learned simply by following, borrowing, modifying, and trying out examples such as those provided here and in the MacroBundle, and by having a few good books on VBA programming handy to consult in case you run into trouble.

The functions and macros in the present book were mostly written by the author, and therefore have a particular style and format. They are somewhat old-fashioned, in that they use subroutines only where that has a clear advantage, e.g., when two or more macros can exploit the same subroutine. You may want to write your own macros in a more modern, modular fashion. At any rate, don't worry, and use them as you might the Macro Recorder: they will get you going, and after you have written several macros yourself you will find your own style and format, which is how it should be.

With today's computer speed and abundant working memory, writing numerically efficient code is no longer as important as it was, e.g., when yours truly bought his first laboratory computer in 1974, a PDP-11 that occupied the space of a clothes cabinet, and boasted all of 32 KB of memory (of which the top 4 KB were reserved for accessories such as the paper tape punch and reader). Then, efficiently written code could save substantial amounts of execution time. Recent personal computers are likely to have gigabytes rather than kilobytes of memory, and the time needed for elementary computer steps is now measured in nanoseconds rather than microseconds. Consequently, almost all computer tasks described in this book can be performed within a fraction of a second, and the most critical aspect of macros is that they work correctly, i.e., give reliable answers. With Excel and VBA, that is eminently feasible even when, as scientists, our main focus is elsewhere. We can therefore leave it to the computer professionals to fret over code efficiency and, yes, elegance.

This is not to suggest that the MacroBundle is only useful as a set of examples, good for cutting and pasting as you assemble your own functions and macros. It can serve that purpose, but it also provides a set of convenient tools that make scientific data analysis much more accessible. In terms of availability, ease of learning, and ease of use, spreadsheets are without peer, and the tools in the MacroBundle (plus the tools you will make yourself) can make the spreadsheet into a quite powerful computational aid, to both aspiring and professional practitioners of science.

8.16 For further reading

There are many books that can help you find your way in VBA Excel. If you have a recent version of Excel, consider the well-organized *Definitive Guide to Excel VBA* by Michael Kofler (2nd ed., Apress/Springer, 2003), the extensive sample codes in John Walkenbach, *Microsoft Excel 200x Power Programming with VBA* (IDG Books, 1999, 2001, 2004), and the compact introduction plus extensive Excel object model appendix of R. Bovey, S. Bullen, J. Green and R. Rosenberg, *Excel 2002 VBA Programmer's Guide*, Wrox 2001. For earlier versions of Excel you may want to consult an older book, such as John Webb, *Using Excel Visual Basic*, Que, 2nd ed. 1996.

For the scientific part of macro writing an excellent source is *Numerical Recipes, the Art of Scientific Computing* by W. H. Press, B. P. Flannery, S. A. Teukolsky & W. T. Vetterling, Cambridge University Press, which comes in several flavors: Fortran, Pascal, C and C^{++}, as well as an update for parallel computing with Fortran90. The original version, for Fortran77, now in its second edition (1992), comes closest to Basic as used in VBA, and should be read for its very clear explanations. A complete set of the software routines (accompanying the first, 1986 edition) was machine-translated into Basic, and is directly usable in Excel. It can be found on the diskette that accompanies J. C. Sprott, *Numerical Recipes, Routines and Examples in Basic*, Cambridge University Press 1991.

Chapter *9*

Macros for least squares & for the propagation of imprecision

This is the first of three chapters that list the custom functions and macros used in this book. These functions and macros can be downloaded freely from the web site www.oup-usa.org/advancedexcel, which is the easiest way to incorporate them into your spreadsheet. Corrections and additions may also appear in the above web site, something the printed page does not allow. Still, web sites as well as magnetic and optical media formats tend to go out of fashion, and the only way to ensure that these programs are available to the readers of this book is to incorporate them in the printed text. Moreover, this is the easiest way to browse for parts that you may want to incorporate into your own creations.

Since these functions and macros were all written or modified by the author, they have a particular style and format. Specifically, they are somewhat old-fashioned, in that they only use subroutines where that has a clear advantage, e.g., when two or more macros can exploit the same, substantial stretch of code. You may want to write your own macros in a more modern, modular fashion. At any rate, don't worry: after you have written several macros yourself you will find your own style and format, which is how it should be. The most critical aspect of macros is that they work properly for you; the second, that they have sufficient transparency and documentation to be usable, maintainable, and modifyable by others.

The macros are listed here roughly in the order in which they appear in this book, see Table 9.0.1. The present chapter contains the macros that deal with least squares analysis, and with the propagation of uncertainty. Chapter 10 covers Fourier transformation and related techniques, such as convolution, deconvolution, and Gabor transformation, while chapter 11 contains a miscellany of macros and functions that do not fit the above two categories, including the terms and conditions for using and distributing these macros, and the toolbar and menu installation tools to make them conveniently available on the spreadsheet.

page name   short description

LS   is a least squares fitting routine for linear, polynomial, and multi-variate fitting, assuming one dependent variable. LS0 forces the fit through the origin, LS1 does not. The output provides the parameter values, their standard deviations, the standard deviation of the fit to the function, the covariance matrix, and (optionally) the matrix of linear correlation coefficients

LSPoly applies LS with a polynomial of gradually increasing order (up to 14)

LSMulti applies LS to an increasing number of terms of a multivariate least squares analysis

LSPermute computes the standard deviation of the fit for all possible permutations of multivariate parameters of up to six terms

Ortho is a Gram-Schmidt orthogonalization alternative to traditional least squares analysis

ELS   provides least squares smoothing and differentiation for an equidistant but otherwise arbitrary function using a 'Savitzky-Golay' moving polynomial fit. ELSfixed uses a fixed-order polynomial, ELSauto self-optimizes the order of the fitting polynomial as it moves along the function

WLS is the equivalent of LS with the inclusion of user-assignable weights

SolverAid provides uncertainty estimates (standard deviations and the covariance matrix) for Solver-derived parameter values

Propagation computes the propagation of uncertainty for a single function, for various independent input parameters with known standard deviations, or for mutually dependent parameters with a known covariance matrix

FT   is a general-purpose Fourier transform macro for forward or inverse Fourier transformation of 2^n data where n is an integer larger than 2

(De)convolve provides general convolution and deconvolution. The convolution macro is generally applicable, the deconvolution macro is not

(De)ConvolveFT yields convolution and deconvolution based on Fourier transformation

DeconvolveIt performs iterative (van Cittert) deconvolution. DeconvolveIt0 has no constraints, DeconvolveIt1 assumes that the function is non-negative

Gabor provides time-frequency analysis

Semi-integrate & semi-differentiate comprises two small macros for cyclic voltammetry assuming planar diffusion

MovieDemos

SolverScan lets Solver scan a two-dimensional array of parameter values

ColumnSolver applies Solver to column-organized data

Mapper generates colored or gray-scale 2-D maps

RootFinder finds a single root by bisection

Table 9.0.1: The macros included in the MacroBundle.

Each macro contains extensive explanatory comments in its heading, and more terse (usually single-line) comments throughout its text to indicate the function of the next block of code, in the style of section headings. The first time you use a macro, or whenever you want to refresh your memory about its function or operation, read the comments in its heading.

The macros are presented here for two applications: (1) as examples of how to write scientific macros, and (2) as directly useful tools to solve common scientific data analysis problems. They are meant to be freely used in science and engineering, by its professional practitioners as well as by students and teachers. They have been copyrighted in order to protect them against commercial exploitation. The copyright gives the individual user explicit freedom to use and copy these macros, or any parts thereof, as long as their use is not linked to any commercial activity, including sale, advertisement, or promotion. Likewise, you may share these macros with others, subject to the same restriction to non-commercial use, as long as the entire warranty and copyright notice is included. When these macros are used in studies that are published, acknowledgment of their use, preferably with reference to this book and/or its web site, will be appreciated.

When shown in their Excel modules, comments will typically be displayed in green. In these final three chapters (printed in monochrome) we have printed all comments in italics, making them readily identifiable as such. Moreover, for the sake of better readability (within the short lines of this book) we have bold-faced the actual code. If these codes are entered into an Excel module, the Visual Basic Editor will ignore these subtleties, and the comment lines will be shown in green (or whatever color you have assigned to comment lines). In order to squeeze the macros on these pages without using an illegibly small or narrow font, more lines of code have been broken up than one would normally do in writing them. But that gives them the benefit that, using a split screen, such a relatively narrow strip of code can be placed conveniently alongside the spreadsheet.

9.1 General comments

(1) Many macros (such as in LS0 and LS1, ForwardFT and InverseFT, ESLfixed and ELSauto, and Mapper0 through Mapper3) use small driver macros to set one parameter in order to get multiple uses from a common subroutine.

(2) All macros shown here are dimensioned, so that they can be used in conjunction with Option Explicit. Some parameters (specifically strings, such as Answer) are dimensioned by name only, because different versions of Excel treat them differently, and they consequently may give trouble in some versions when fully dimensioned.

(3) Where literature routines are used, as with matrix inversion and fast Fourier transformation, the copied code fragment has been converted to double precision by proper dimensioning.

(4) Where convenient we have used the simple input method of highlighting a block of data and *subsequently* calling the macro. This is indicated in the little yellow notes that appear when the pointer dwells on the corresponding MacroBundle Toolbar menu items. However, even when the macro is called first, the user can still use an input box to specify the input data block.

(5) In order to use this method (of highlighting the input data), it is essential that the macro restore the input array to its original form, otherwise formulas might be replaced by numerical results. This is why those macros start by copying both the data and the formulas of the highlighted region, and end by returning the formulas to the spreadsheet.

(6) Because of an early decision to keep macro writing simple by avoiding dialog box construction, these macros do not contain professional-strength input checks, and are in no way foolproof. You can readily trip them up by, e.g., entering letters where they expect numbers. Prevention is built in only for some of the most likely user errors, such as entering input arrays of incorrect size or dimension, or overwriting existing data. If you want more safeguards, put them in, or learn to create your own dialog boxes.

(7) Macros that return data directly to the spreadsheet suppress screen updating during the computations. After executing its instructions but before ending, the macro will automatically reset screen updating and display the results.

(8) Subroutines and functions that are used mostly with one or a few macros are typically shown in combination, while some more general subroutines (e.g., those for matrix operations) are collected at the end of this chapter.

(9) Before first use of one of these macros, read the information in the comment lines immediately following its header. This briefly lists its purpose, its input and output formats, and any required subroutines. If you have loaded the entire MacroBundle, as recommended, all necessary subroutines will be available.

(10) It is also recommended that a first-time user of a macro tests its performance first on a data set for which the answer is known, either because the data were computed according to some formula, or because it

has already been analyzed by a similar analysis elsewhere. Such a test provides familiarity with the macro, and may also indicate its capabilities and limitations.

(11) These macros use the US numerical convention (decimal point) and may need modification when used outside the US.

(12) The Mapper macro partially operates outside Excel, and is therefore more liable than the other macros of this MacroBundle to malfunction in other operating environments.

9.2 LS

The macros LS0 and LS1 serve as the workhorses of least squares analysis in chapters 2 and 3 of this book, fitting data to arbitrary mono- or multivariate functions with linear coefficients. They provide the fitted parameters with their standard deviations, the covariance matrix, and (optionally) the linear correlation coefficient matrix. The covariance matrix can be used with the Propagation macro (see section 9.10) to evaluate the propagation of uncertainty in derived results.

LS has two distinct forms, LS0 for when the fitted curve must pass through the origin, LS1 for when there is no such constraint. The algorithm used is based on the standard statistical matrix formalism described in, e.g., chapter 2 of N. R. Draper & H. Smith, *Applied Regression Analysis*, Wiley, New York 1966, 1981. The specific nomenclature used is explained in blocks of macro comments.

In short, the dependent input variables y_i are collected in the vector $\mathbf{Y}$, and the independent variable(s) x_i in the matrix $\mathbf{X}$, which also contains as its first column a set of zeros (for LS0) or ones (for LS1). The coefficients are then found in the vector $\mathbf{b}$ where

$$\mathbf{b} = (\mathbf{X}^T\mathbf{X})^{-1}\mathbf{X}^T\mathbf{Y} \tag{9.2.1}$$

where the superscript T denotes a transposition, and the superscript -1 a matrix inversion. The covariance matrix $\mathbf{V}$ is calculated from

$$\mathbf{V} = (\mathbf{X}^T\mathbf{X})^{-1}(\mathbf{Y}^T\mathbf{Y} - \mathbf{b}^T\mathbf{X}^T\mathbf{Y})/(N-P) \tag{9.2.2}$$

where N is the number of data points y_i, and P the number of coefficients used in the fitting. Many lines of code are devoted to prevent overwriting spreadsheet data and other standard precautions.

```
'''''''''''''''''''''''''''''''''''''''''''''''''''''''''''''''''''''''''''
'''''''''''''''''''''''''''''''''''''''''''''''''''''''''''''''''''''''''''
''''''''''''''''''^^^^^^^^^^^^^^^^^^^^^^^^^^^^^^''''''''''''''''''''
'''''''''''''''^                                  ^'''''''''''''''''
'''''''''''''''^        LINEAR LEAST SQUARES       ^'''''''''''''''''
'''''''''''''''^                                  ^'''''''''''''''''
''''''''''''''''''^^^^^^^^^^^^^^^^^^^^^^^^^^^^^^''''''''''''''''''''
''''''''''''''''''''''''''''''''''''''''''''''''''''''(c) R. de Levie
'''''''''''''''''''''''''''''''''''''''''''''''''''''v 4.10, Oct. 1, 2004
```

' PURPOSE:
'
' The macros LS1 and LS0 compute the parameters and their
' standard deviations for an unweighted least squares fit
' to data in 2 or more columns. The macros set the input
' parameter p for the subroutine LeastSquares: p = 1 causes
' a general unweighted least squares fit to the data, while
' p = 0 forces the fit to pass through the origin, i.e., it
' assumes that y = 0 for x = 0.
'
' SUBROUTINES:
'
' This macro requires the subroutines Multiply, Invert, and
' Transpose
'
' INPUT:
'
' The input data must be organized in columns, arranged
' as follows. The first column must contain the dependent
' variable y. The second (and any subsequent) column(s)
' must contain the independent variable(s) x.
'
' OUTPUT:
'
' The macro labels the coefficients and standard devi-
' ations, except when there is no space available for
' labels because the first data column is at the left
' edge of the spreadsheet.
'
' PROCEDURE:
'
' Before calling the macro, make sure that the output area
' (two lines below the input data block) does not contain
' valuable data.
'
' In order to start the process, highlight the entire input
' data block, and call LS1 or LS0.
'
' EXAMPLES:
'
' Use of this macro is illustrated starting in sections
' 2.5 and 2.11 of Advanced Excel.
'
''
'
' The function of the following two drivers is merely to
' set the value of one parameter, p, equal to either one or
' zero, in order to choose between a general least squares
' fitting (p = 1) or one that forces the curve through the
' origin (p = 0).

```
Sub LS0()                ' for an unweighted least squares
                         ' fit through the origin
Dim p As Double
p = 0
Call LeastSquares(p)
End Sub


''''''''''''''''''''''''''''''''''''''''''''''''''''''''''''


Sub LS1()                ' for a general unweighted
                         ' least squares fit
Dim p As Double
p = 1
Call LeastSquares(p)
End Sub


''''''''''''''''''''''''''''''''''''''''''''''''''''''''''''


Sub LeastSquares(p)

Dim cMax As Integer, i As Long, j As Integer
Dim jj As Integer, m As Integer, n As Integer

Dim rMax As Long, Root As Double, SSR As Double
Dim StDevF As Double, u As Double, varY As Double

Dim DataArray As Variant, outputArray As Variant
Dim lccArray As Variant, vArray As Variant
Dim v0Array As Variant

Dim myRange As Range

Dim aa, AC, Answer, hAnswer, jAnswer
Dim bArray, btArray, btqArray
Dim pArray, piArray, qArray
Dim XArray, xtArray, YArray, ytArray, ytyArray

' Determination of the array size:

Begin:
rMax = Selection.Rows.Count
cMax = Selection.Columns.Count
u = 1

' If area was not highlighted

If rMax = 1 And cMax = 1 Then
  hAnswer = MsgBox("You forgot to highlight" _
    & Chr(13) & "the block of input data." _
    & Chr(13) & "Do you want to do so now?" _
    , vbYesNo, "Least Squares Fit")
  If hAnswer = vbNo Then End
  If hAnswer = vbYes Then
    Set myRange = Application.InputBox(Prompt:= _
      "The input data are located in:", Type:=8)
    myRange.Select
  End If
  GoTo Begin
End If
```

```
' Check that the number of columns is at least 2:

If cMax < 2 Then
  MsgBox "There must be at least two columns," & _
    Chr(13) & "one for Y, and one or more for X.", _
    , "Least Squares Fit"
  End
End If


' Check that there are more data than coefficients :

If rMax - cMax - p + 1 <= 0 Then
  MsgBox "With " & rMax & " data, LS" & p & _
    " can only deter-" & Chr(13) & "mine " & rMax - 1 & _
    " least squares coefficients." & Chr(13) & Chr(13) _
    & "Add more data, or reduce the re-" & Chr(13) & _
    "quested number of coefficients."
  End
End If


' Dimension the arrays:

ReDim YArray(1 To rMax, 1 To 1) As Double
ReDim XArray(1 To rMax, 1 To cMax) As Double
ReDim ytArray(1 To 1, 1 To rMax) As Double
ReDim ytyArray(1 To 1, 1 To 1) As Double
ReDim xtArray(1 To cMax, 1 To rMax) As Double
ReDim pArray(1 To cMax, 1 To cMax) As Double
ReDim piArray(1 To cMax, 1 To cMax) As Double
ReDim qArray(1 To cMax, 1 To 1) As Double
ReDim bArray(1 To cMax, 1 To 1) As Double
ReDim btArray(1 To 1, 1 To cMax) As Double
ReDim btqArray(1 To 1, 1 To 1) As Double
ReDim vArray(1 To cMax, 1 To cMax) As Double
ReDim v0Array(1 To cMax - 1 + p, 1 To cMax - 1 + p) _
  As Double
ReDim lccArray(1 To cMax, 1 To cMax) As Double


' Read the dataArray, then fill yArray and xArray.

DataArray = Selection.Value

For i = 1 To rMax
  YArray(i, 1) = DataArray(i, 1)
Next i

For i = 1 To rMax
  If IsEmpty(DataArray(i, 1)) Then
    MsgBox "Y-value(s) missing", , "Least Squares Fit"
    End
  End If
Next i
For j = 2 To cMax
  For i = 1 To rMax
    If IsEmpty(DataArray(i, j)) Then
      MsgBox "X-value(s) missing", , "Least Squares Fit"
      End
    End If
```

```
    Next i
Next j

' Fill the first column of xArray with zeroes (for p = 0)
' or ones (for p = 1), the rest with the data in the
' x-column(s)

For i = 1 To rMax
  XArray(i, 1) = CDbl(p)
Next i
For j = 2 To cMax
  For i = 1 To rMax
    XArray(i, j) = DataArray(i, j)
  Next i
Next j

' Compute b = (X' X)" X' Y , where ' or t denote
' transposition, and " or i indicate inversion

' The various arrays and their dimensions (rows,
' columns) are:
'   Y          = yArray        (  rmax,     1)
'   X          = xArray        (  rmax,  cmax)
'   X'         = xtArray       (  cmax,  rmax)
'   X' X       = pArray        (  cmax,  cmax)
'   (X' X)"    = piArray       (  cmax,  cmax)
'   X' Y       = qArray        (  cmax,     1)
'   b          = bArray        (  cmax,     1)

Call Transpose(XArray, rMax, cMax, xtArray)
Call Multiply(xtArray, cMax, rMax, XArray, cMax, pArray)
Call Invert(pArray, cMax, piArray)
Call Multiply(xtArray, cMax, rMax, YArray, 1, qArray)
Call Multiply(piArray, cMax, cMax, qArray, 1, bArray)

' Check against overwriting spreadsheet data

m = 0
If (p = 0 And cMax = 2) Then
  For i = 1 To 3
    Selection.Offset(1, 0).Select
    outputArray = Selection.Value
    For j = 1 To cMax
      If IsEmpty(outputArray(rMax, j)) Then
        m = m
      Else
        m = m + 1
      End If
    Next j
  Next i
  Selection.Offset(-3, 0).Select
  If m > 0 Then Answer = MsgBox("There are data in the " _
    & "three lines below the" & Chr(13) & _
    "input data array. " & "Can they be overwritten?", _
    vbYesNo, "Overwrite?")
  If Answer = vbNo Then End
Else
  For i = 1 To 2 + p + cMax
    Selection.Offset(1, 0).Select
```

```
      outputArray = Selection.Value
      For j = 1 To cMax
        If IsEmpty(outputArray(rMax, j)) Then
          m = m
        Else
          m = m + 1
        End If
      Next j
    Next i
    Selection.Offset(-2 - p - cMax, 0).Select
    If m > 0 Then Answer = MsgBox("There are data in the " _
      & 2 + p + cMax & " lines below the" & Chr(13) & _
      "input data array. " & "Can they be overwritten?", _
      vbYesNo, "Overwrite?")
    If Answer = vbNo Then End
End If

' The additional arrays and their dimensions (rows,
' columns) are:
'   Y'          = ytArray          (    1,   rmax)
'   Y' Y        = ytyArray         (    1,     1)
'   b'          = btArray          (    1,   cmax)
'   b' X' Y     = btqArray         (    1,     1)

Call Transpose(YArray, rMax, 1, ytArray)
Call Transpose(bArray, cMax, 1, btArray)
Call Multiply(ytArray, 1, rMax, YArray, 1, ytyArray)
Call Multiply(btArray, 1, cMax, qArray, 1, btqArray)

' Calculate SSR = Y'Y - b'X'Y; then the variance
' of y as varY = SSR/(rMax-cMax-p+1); and vArray,
' the covariance matrix, as V = (X'X)" times varY.

SSR = ytyArray(1, 1) - btqArray(1, 1)
varY = SSR / (rMax - cMax - p + 1)
StDevF = Sqr(Abs(varY))

For i = 1 To cMax
  For j = 1 To cMax
    vArray(i, j) = varY * piArray(i, j)
  Next j
Next i

Application.ScreenUpdating = False
ActiveCell.Offset(rMax, 0).Select

' Prepare the output format

For j = 1 To cMax
  ActiveCell.Font.Bold = True
  ActiveCell.Font.Italic = True
  ActiveCell.Offset(0, 1).Select
Next j
ActiveCell.Offset(1, -cMax).Select

If (p = 0 And cMax = 2) Then
  For i = 1 To 2
    For j = 1 To cMax
      ActiveCell.Font.Bold = False
```

```
      ActiveCell.Font.Italic = True
      ActiveCell.Offset(0, 1).Select
    Next j
    ActiveCell.Offset(1, -cMax).Select
  Next i
  ActiveCell.Offset(-3, 0).Select
Else
  For i = 1 To 1 + p + cMax
    For j = 1 To cMax
      ActiveCell.Font.Bold = False
      ActiveCell.Font.Italic = True
      ActiveCell.Offset(0, 1).Select
    Next j
    ActiveCell.Offset(1, -cMax).Select
  Next i
  ActiveCell.Offset(-2 - p - cMax, 0).Select
End If

' Prepare the output labels, suppressing them when space
' for them is unavailable or data will be overwritten

aa = ActiveCell.Address
AC = Mid(aa, 2, 1)
If (AC = "A" And p = 1) Then GoTo NoLabel

ActiveCell.Offset(0, -p).Select

If p = 1 Then
  If (IsEmpty(ActiveCell) Or ActiveCell.Value = "Coeff:") _
  Then
    GoTo Step1
  Else
    ActiveCell.Offset(0, p).Select
    GoTo NoLabel
  End If
End If
Step1:
With ActiveCell
  .Value = "Coeff:"
  .Font.Bold = True
  .Font.Italic = True
  .HorizontalAlignment = xlRight
End With

ActiveCell.Offset(1, 0).Select
If p = 1 Then
  If (IsEmpty(ActiveCell) Or ActiveCell.Value = "StDev:") _
  Then
    GoTo Step2
  Else
    ActiveCell.Offset(-1, p).Select
    GoTo NoLabel
  End If
End If
Step2:
With ActiveCell
  .Value = "StDev:"
  .Font.Bold = False
  .Font.Italic = True
```

```
    .HorizontalAlignment = xlRight
End With

ActiveCell.Offset(-1, p).Select
If p = 0 And cMax = 2 Then GoTo NoLabel

ActiveCell.Offset(3, -p).Select
If p = 1 Then
  If (IsEmpty(ActiveCell) Or ActiveCell.Value = "CM:") Then
    GoTo Step3
  Else
    ActiveCell.Offset(-3, p).Select
    GoTo NoLabel
  End If
End If
Step3:
With ActiveCell
  .Value = "CM:"
  .Font.Bold = True
  .Font.Italic = True
  .Font.ColorIndex = 11
  .HorizontalAlignment = xlRight
End With
ActiveCell.Offset(-3, p).Select

NoLabel:

ActiveCell.Offset(0, 1 - p).Select
For j = 2 - p To cMax
  ActiveCell.Value = bArray(j, 1)
  ActiveCell.Offset(0, 1).Select
Next j

ActiveCell.Offset(1, 1 - p - cMax).Select
For j = 2 - p To cMax
  If vArray(j, j) < 1E-40 Then
    ActiveCell.Value = "<1E-20"
  Else
    ActiveCell.Value = Sqr(vArray(j, j))
  End If
  ActiveCell.Offset(0, 1).Select
Next j

ActiveCell.Offset(1, 1 - p - cMax).Select
Selection.Value = StDevF

If p = 0 And cMax = 2 Then GoTo LastLine
ActiveCell.Offset(1, 0).Select
For i = 2 - p To cMax
  For j = 2 - p To cMax
    ActiveCell.Value = vArray(i, j)
    ActiveCell.Font.ColorIndex = 11
    ActiveCell.Offset(0, 1).Select
  Next j
  ActiveCell.Offset(1, 1 - p - cMax).Select
Next i

Application.ScreenUpdating = True
```

```
' Provide as optional output the array of linear
' correlation coefficients. The user specifies
' the cell block in which to write this array

If p = 0 And cMax = 2 Then GoTo LastLine
jAnswer = MsgBox("Do you want to see the " _
  & "matrix of linear correlation" _
  & Chr(13) & "coefficients? It will need a " _
  & "block of " & cMax + p - 1 _
  & " by " & cMax + p - 1 & " cells.", vbYesNo, _
  "Least Squares Fit")

OutlineMatrix:

If jAnswer = vbYes Then
  Set myRange = Application.InputBox(Prompt:= _
    "The array should be located in:", Type:=8)
  myRange.Select

' Make sure that the selected block has the correct size

  If Selection.Rows.Count <> cMax + p - 1 Then
    MsgBox "The selected range does not have " _
      & cMax + p - 1 & " rows. Please correct.", _
      , "Least Squares Fit"
    GoTo OutlineMatrix
  End If
  If Selection.Columns.Count <> cMax + p - 1 Then
    MsgBox "The selected range does not have " _
      & cMax + p - 1 & " columns. Please correct", _
      , "Least Squares Fit"
    GoTo OutlineMatrix
  End If

' Draw a box around the reserved area

    Selection.Borders(xlEdgeTop).LineStyle = xlDashDot
    Selection.Borders(xlEdgeTop).Weight = xlThin
    Selection.Borders(xlEdgeRight).LineStyle = xlDashDot
    Selection.Borders(xlEdgeRight).Weight = xlThin
    Selection.Borders(xlEdgeBottom).LineStyle = xlDashDot
    Selection.Borders(xlEdgeBottom).Weight = xlThin
    Selection.Borders(xlEdgeLeft).LineStyle = xlDashDot
    Selection.Borders(xlEdgeLeft).Weight = xlThin

' Write the array of linear correlation coefficients

  If p = 0 Then
    For i = 1 To cMax - 1
      For j = 1 To cMax - 1
        v0Array(i, j) = vArray(i + 1, j + 1)
      Next j
    Next i
    For i = 1 To cMax - 1
      For j = 1 To cMax - 1
        Root = Sqr(v0Array(i, i) * v0Array(j, j))
        lccArray(i, j) = v0Array(i, j) / Root
    Next j
    Next i
```

```
        Selection.Value = lccArray
      End If

    If p = 1 Then
      For i = 1 To cMax
        For j = 1 To cMax
          v0Array(i, j) = vArray(i, j)
        Next j
      Next i
      For i = 1 To cMax
        For j = 1 To cMax
          Root = Sqr(vArray(i, i) * vArray(j, j))
          lccArray(i, j) = vArray(i, j) / Root
        Next j
      Next i
      Selection.Value = lccArray
    End If
End If

LastLine:

End Sub
```

9.3 LSPoly

This routine is *not* intended for routine fitting of data to a known polynomial such as $y = a_0 + a_1x + a_2x^2$ or $y = a_2x^2 + a_4x^4$, for which LS0 or LS1 should be used instead. LSPoly is meant for use in cases where the length of such a polynomial is not known a priori, and the user wants to screen a number of different polynomial lengths and compare the resulting statistics. LSPoly first fits the data to the lowest-order polynomial in integer powers of x, then automatically adds the next-higher term in the polynomial and repeats the process, until it reaches a user-selected maximum polynomial order.

```
'''''''''''''''''''''''''''''''''''''''''''''''''''''''''''''''
'''''''''''''''''''''''''''''''''''''''''''''''''''''''''''''''
'''''''''''''''''''''^^^^^^^^^^^^^^^^^^^^^^^^^^^^'''''''''''''''
'''''''''''''''''^                              ^'''''''''''''''
''''''''''''''''''^       LEAST SQUARES POLY     ^''''''''''''''
'''''''''''''''''''^                            ^'''''''''''''''
'''''''''''''''''''''^^^^^^^^^^^^^^^^^^^^^^^^^^^^'''''''''''''''
'''''''''''''''''''''''''''''''''''''''''''''''''''(c) R. de Levie
'''''''''''''''''''''''''''''''''''''''''''''''''''v 4.10, Oct. 1, 2004

' PURPOSE:
'
' The macros LSPoly0 and LSPoly1 compute the parameters and
' their standard deviations for an unweighted least squares
' fit of a dependent variable y to a power series in x of
' increasing (positive integer) order m, up to 14. The user
' specifies the highest order to be displayed.
'
```

```
' Use the custom macros Ortho1 or Ortho0 in order to decide
' what polynomial order might be optimal.
'
' SUBROUTINES:
'
' The macros LSPoly0 and LSPoly1 call the subroutine
' LeastSquaresPoly which, in turn, calls the subroutines
' Invert, Multiply, and Transpose.
'
' INPUT:
'
' The input data must be arranged in a block of two adja-
' cent columns, with the dependent variable y in the left-
' most column, and the independent variable x to its right.
' Highlight the data in these two columns, and call the
' macro LSPoly0 or LSPoly1. Then specify the maximum poly-
' nomial order for which you want the results displayed.
'
' OUTPUT:
'
' The macro provides:
' (1) the coefficients of the least squares fit of y to the
'     power series a(1)x + a(2)x^2 + ... = Sum[a(i)x^i] for
'     i = 1(1)m for LSPoly0, or to a(0) + a(1)x + a(2)x^2
'     + ... = Sum[a(i)x^i] for i = 0(1)m for LSPoly1;
' (2) the corresponding standard deviations s
'     for these coefficients;
' (3) the standard deviation of the fit
'     for each value of m;
' (4) the F-ratios for alpha = 0.05 and 0.01
'     for each value of m.
'
' For each order the output consists of three rows. The top
' row lists the order of the polynomial, and the standard
' deviation of the fit. The second row displays the coeffi-
' cients of the fitted polynomial, and the third row the
' corresponding standard deviations. The second and third
' rows also list the values for the F-ratios for 5% and 1%
' respectively. For easy reading the rows are color-coded
' by order.
'
' If you want the output to display more digits, change
' the instruction ActiveCell.NumberFormat = "0.00E+00" to
' ActiveCell.NumberFormat = "0.000E+00", "0.0000E+00", etc.
'
' WARNINGS:
'
' The output is displayed below the highlighted input
' array, and therefore might escape your notice. If
' the macro doesn't seem to respond, look below it.
'
' If you find cells filled with ###### the macro needs
' wider columns to display its results. Click on the
' column letter(s) at the top of the column(s), right-
' click, and insert a larger number in Column Width.
'
' The size of the macro output will be determined by your
' choice of the maximum polynomial order. The output will
' be displayed under the input data, and will gradually
```

```
' expand to the right as results for higher orders occupy
' increasingly more space. The first-order output will
' occupy a block of 3 rows of 5 columns for LSPoly0 (6
' for LSPoly1), and each additional order will use a
' block that is one column wider than its predecessor.
' Please move valuable data from the output region before
' running this macro, lest those data be overwritten.
'
' PROCEDURE:
'
' Before calling the macro, make sure that the output area
' is clear of valuable data (see above under WARNING)
'
' In order to start the process, highlight the (two columns
' wide, and at least 3 rows high) input data block, then
' call LSPoly0 or LSPoly1.
'
' EXAMPLE:
'
' Use of this macro is illustrated in sections 3.12 and
' 3.13 of Advanced Excel.
'
'''''''''''''''''''''''''''''''''''''''''''''''''''''''''''''''
'
' The function of the following two drivers is merely to
' set the value of one parameter, p, equal to either one or
' zero, in order to choose between a general least squares
' fitting (p = 1) or one that forces the curve through the
' origin (p = 0).
'
Sub LSPoly0()                ' for unweighted least squares
                             ' fit through the origin
Dim p As Double
p = 0
Call LeastSquaresPoly(p)
End Sub
'
'''''''''''''''''''''''''''''''''''''''''''''''''''''''''''''''
'
Sub LSPoly1()                ' for general unweighted
                             ' least squares fit
Dim p As Double
p = 1
Call LeastSquaresPoly(p)
End Sub
'
'''''''''''''''''''''''''''''''''''''''''''''''''''''''''''''''
'
Sub LeastSquaresPoly(p)

Dim cMax As Integer, i As Long, j As Integer
Dim m As Integer, n As Integer, rMax As Long
Dim Color(1 To 7) As Integer
Dim MaxOrder As Integer, MaxOrderMax As Integer

Dim FRatio1 As Double, FRatio5 As Double
Dim Root As Double, StDevF As Double
Dim u As Double, z As Double
```

```
Dim DataArray As Variant, F As Variant, lccArray As Variant
Dim outputArray As Variant, SSR As Variant
Dim varY As Variant, vArray As Variant, v0Array As Variant

Dim myRange As Range

Dim bArray, btArray, btqArray, pArray, piArray
Dim qArray, XArray, xtArray, YArray, ytArray, ytyArray

Dim Answer, iAnswer, hAnswer, kAnswer

' Determination of the array size:

Begin:
rMax = Selection.Rows.Count
cMax = Selection.Columns.Count
ReDim F(1 To rMax, 1 To 1) As Double
ReDim SSR(1 To rMax, 1 To 1) As Double
u = 1
z = 0

' If area was not highlighted

If rMax = 1 And cMax = 1 Then
  hAnswer = MsgBox("You forgot to highlight" _
    & Chr(13) & "the block of input data." _
    & Chr(13) & "Do you want to do so now?" _
    , vbYesNo, "LSPoly")
  If hAnswer = vbNo Then End
  If hAnswer = vbYes Then
    Set myRange = Application.InputBox(Prompt:= _
      "The input data are located in:", Type:=8)
    myRange.Select
  End If
  GoTo Begin
End If

' Check that the number of columns is 2:

If cMax <> 2 Then
  MsgBox "There must be two columns," & _
  Chr(13) & "one for Y, and one for X.", _
    , "Least Squares Polynomial Fit"
  End
End If

' Check that rmax > 3, so that the number of data
' points is sufficient to define the problem:

If rMax < 4 Then
  MsgBox "There must be at least 4 input" & _
  Chr(13) & "data pairs to define the problem.", _
    , "Least Squares Polynomial Fit"
  End
End If

MaxOrderMax = 14
If rMax < 16 Then MaxOrderMax = rMax - 2
```

```
DataArray = Selection.Value
Selection.Item(1, 1).Select

' Select the maximum order:

MaxOrder = InputBox _
  ("Select as maximum order an integer" & Chr(13) & _
  "between 3 and " & MaxOrderMax & "." & Chr(13) & _
  Chr(13) & "Enter the maximum order: ", "MaxOrder")
If MaxOrder < 3 Then MaxOrder = 3
If MaxOrder > MaxOrderMax Then MaxOrder = MaxOrderMax

RedimensionArrays:

' Dimension the arrays:

ReDim YArray(1 To rMax, 1 To 1) As Double
ReDim XArray(1 To rMax, 1 To cMax) As Double
ReDim ytArray(1 To 1, 1 To rMax) As Double
ReDim ytyArray(1 To 1, 1 To 1) As Double
ReDim xtArray(1 To cMax, 1 To rMax) As Double
ReDim pArray(1 To cMax, 1 To cMax) As Double
ReDim piArray(1 To cMax, 1 To cMax) As Double
ReDim qArray(1 To cMax, 1 To 1) As Double
ReDim bArray(1 To cMax, 1 To 1) As Double
ReDim btArray(1 To 1, 1 To cMax) As Double
ReDim btqArray(1 To 1, 1 To 1) As Double
ReDim vArray(1 To cMax, 1 To cMax) As Double
ReDim v0Array(1 To cMax - 1 + p, 1 To cMax - 1 + p) _
  As Double
ReDim lccArray(1 To cMax, 1 To cMax) As Double

' Read the dataArray, then fill yArray and xArray.

For i = 1 To rMax
  YArray(i, 1) = DataArray(i, 1)
Next i

If cMax = 2 Then
  For i = 1 To rMax
    If IsEmpty(DataArray(i, 1)) Then
      MsgBox "Y-value(s) missing", _
        , "Least Squares Polynomial Fit"
      End
    End If
  Next i
  For i = 1 To rMax
    If IsEmpty(DataArray(i, 2)) Then
      MsgBox "X-value(s) missing", _
        , "Least Squares Polynomial Fit"
      End
    End If
  Next i
End If

' Fill the first column of xArray with zeroes
' (for p = 0) or ones (for p = 1), the rest
' with the data in the x-column(s)
```

```
For i = 1 To rMax
  XArray(i, 1) = CDbl(p)
Next i
For i = 1 To rMax
  XArray(i, 2) = DataArray(i, 2)
Next i
If cMax > 2 Then
  For j = 3 To cMax
    For i = 1 To rMax
      XArray(i, j) = XArray(i, 2) * XArray(i, j - 1)
    Next i
  Next j
End If

' Compute b = (X' X)" X' Y , where ' or t denote
' transposition, and " or i indicate inversion

' The various arrays and their dimensions (rows,
' columns) are:
'   Y            = yArray       (   rmax,     1)
'   X            = xArray       (   rmax,  cmax)
'   X'           = xtArray      (   cmax,  rmax)
'   X' X         = pArray       (   cmax,  cmax)
'   (X' X)"      = piArray      (   cmax,  cmax)
'   X' Y         = qArray       (   cmax,     1)
'   b            = bArray       (   cmax,     1)
'   Y'           = ytArray      (      1,  rmax)
'   Y' Y         = ytyArray     (      1,     1)
'   b'           = btArray      (      1,  cmax)
'   b' X' Y      = btqArray     (      1,     1)

Call Transpose(XArray, rMax, cMax, xtArray)
Call Multiply(xtArray, cMax, rMax, XArray, cMax, pArray)
Call Invert(pArray, cMax, piArray)
Call Multiply(xtArray, cMax, rMax, YArray, 1, qArray)
Call Multiply(piArray, cMax, cMax, qArray, 1, bArray)
Call Transpose(YArray, rMax, 1, ytArray)
Call Transpose(bArray, cMax, 1, btArray)
Call Multiply(ytArray, 1, rMax, YArray, 1, ytyArray)
Call Multiply(btArray, 1, cMax, qArray, 1, btqArray)

' Calculate SSR = Y'Y - b'X'Y, and then varY, the variance
' of y, as varY = SSR/(rmax-cmax-p+1); and vArray, the co-
' variance matrix, as V = (X'X)" times varY, of which we
' here only use the diagonal elements, i.e., the variances.

SSR(cMax, 1) = ytyArray(1, 1) - btqArray(1, 1)
varY = SSR(cMax, 1) / (rMax - cMax + 1 - p)
StDevF = Sqr(Abs(varY))
If cMax > 2 Then
  F(cMax, 1) = ((SSR(cMax - 1, 1) / SSR(cMax, 1)) - 1) _
    * (rMax - cMax + 1 - p)
  FRatio5 = (F(cMax, 1)) / _
    (Application.FInv(0.05, 1, rMax - cMax + 1 - p))
  FRatio1 = (F(cMax, 1)) / _
    (Application.FInv(0.01, 1, rMax - cMax + 1 - p))
End If
For i = 1 To cMax
  For j = 1 To cMax
```

```
    vArray(i, j) = varY * piArray(i, j)
  Next j
Next i

Application.ScreenUpdating = False

ActiveCell.Offset(rMax + 1, 0).Select

' Paint color bands for up to 14 orders, and set the
' numerical format to scientific with 3 decimal places

Color(1) = 38
Color(2) = 40
Color(3) = 36
Color(4) = 35
Color(5) = 34
Color(6) = 37
Color(7) = 39

For i = 1 To 3
  For j = 1 To cMax + p + 2
    ActiveCell.ClearContents
    If cMax < 9 Then
      ActiveCell.Interior.ColorIndex = Color(cMax - 1)
    Else
      ActiveCell.Interior.ColorIndex = Color(cMax - 8)
    End If
    ActiveCell.Offset(0, 1).Select
    If cMax < 9 Then
      ActiveCell.Interior.ColorIndex = Color(cMax - 1)
    Else
      ActiveCell.Interior.ColorIndex = Color(cMax - 8)
    End If
    ActiveCell.Font.Bold = False
    ActiveCell.Font.Italic = False
    ActiveCell.NumberFormat = "0.00E+00"
  Next j
  ActiveCell.Offset(1, -cMax - p - 2).Select
Next i
ActiveCell.Offset(-3, 0).Select

' Display the top line of the output

With ActiveCell
  .Font.Bold = True
  .Font.Italic = False
  .HorizontalAlignment = xlLeft
  .Value = "Order " & cMax - 1
End With
For j = 1 To cMax + p - 1
  Selection.Offset(0, 1).Select
  With ActiveCell
    .Font.Bold = False
    .Font.Italic = True
    .HorizontalAlignment = xlCenter
    .Value = "term " & j - p
  End With
Next j
Selection.Offset(0, 2).Select
```

```
With ActiveCell
  .Font.Bold = False
  .Font.Italic = True
  .HorizontalAlignment = xlRight
  .Value = "Sf:"
End With
Selection.Offset(0, 1).Select
Selection.HorizontalAlignment = xlLeft
Selection.Value = StDevF
Selection.Offset(1, -cMax - p - 2).Select

' Display the center line of the output

With ActiveCell
  .Font.Bold = False
  .Font.Italic = True
  .HorizontalAlignment = xlRight
  .Value = "Coeff:"
End With
For j = 1 To cMax + p - 1
  Selection.Offset(0, 1).Select
  With ActiveCell
    .Font.Bold = False
    .Font.Italic = False
    .HorizontalAlignment = xlCenter
    .Value = bArray(j + 1 - p, 1)
  End With
Next j
Selection.Offset(0, 2).Select
With ActiveCell
  .Font.Bold = False
  .Font.Italic = True
  .HorizontalAlignment = xlRight
  .Value = "FR5:"
End With
Selection.Offset(0, 1).Select
Selection.HorizontalAlignment = xlLeft
If cMax = 2 Then Selection.Value = "N/A"
If cMax > 2 Then Selection.Value = FRatio5
Selection.Offset(1, -cMax - p - 2).Select

' Display the bottom line of the output

With ActiveCell
  .Font.Bold = False
  .Font.Italic = True
  .HorizontalAlignment = xlRight
  .Value = "StDev:"
End With
For j = 1 To cMax + p - 1
  Selection.Offset(0, 1).Select
  With ActiveCell
    .Font.Bold = False
    .Font.Italic = False
    .HorizontalAlignment = xlCenter
  End With
  If vArray(j - p + 1, j - p + 1) < 1E-40 Then
    ActiveCell.Value = "<1E-20"
  Else
```

```
    ActiveCell.Value = _
        Sqr(Abs(vArray(j - p + 1, j - p + 1)))
  End If
Next j
Selection.Offset(0, 2).Select
With ActiveCell
  .Font.Bold = False
  .Font.Italic = True
  .HorizontalAlignment = xlRight
  .Value = "FR1:"
End With
Selection.Offset(0, 1).Select
Selection.HorizontalAlignment = xlLeft
If cMax = 2 Then Selection.Value = "N/A"
If cMax > 2 Then Selection.Value = FRatio1
Selection.Offset(1, -cMax - p - 2).Select

If cMax < MaxOrder + 2 Then cMax = cMax + 1
ActiveCell.Offset(-rMax - 1, 0).Select
If cMax = MaxOrder + 2 Then End

GoTo RedimensionArrays

End Sub
```

9.4 *LSMulti*

For least squares data fitting to a multivariate expression such as $y = a_1x_1 + a_2x_2 + a_3x_3 + \ldots$, use LS0 or LS1. The macro LSMulti answers a more specialized question, viz. what are the fitting coefficients and their statistical uncertainties when successive terms are added, i.e., when one starts with $y = a_1x_1$, then tries $y = a_1x_1 + a_2x_2$, then $y = a_1x_1 + a_2x_2 + a_3x_3$, etc., while maintaining the order of the terms in the multivariate analysis.

```
'''''''''''''''''''''''''''''''''''''''''''''''''''''''''''''
'''''''''''''''''''''''''''''''''''''''''''''''''''''''''''''
''''''''''''''''''''''^^^^^^^^^^^^^^^^^^^^^^^^^^^''''''''''''''
''''''''''''''''''^                        ^'''''''''''''''''
''''''''''''''''''^     LEAST SQUARES MULTI    ^'''''''''''''''
''''''''''''''''''^                        ^'''''''''''''''''
''''''''''''''''''''''^^^^^^^^^^^^^^^^^^^^^^^^^^^''''''''''''''
''''''''''''''''''''''''''''''''''''''''''''''''''(c) R. de Levie
''''''''''''''''''''''''''''''''''''''''''''''''''v 4.10, Oct. 1, 2004

' PURPOSE:
'
' The macros LSMulti0 and LSMulti1 compute the parameters
' and their standard deviations for an unweighted least
' squares fit of a dependent variable y to a user-specified
' multivariate expression of the form y = a1x1 + a2x2 + ..
' (for LSMulti0) or y = a0 + a1x1 + a2x2 + ...(for
' LSMulti1) by gradually (one term at a time) increasing
' the number of terms included in the least squares
' analysis from left to right
'
```

```
' Note that the macro does NOT rearrange the columns, and
' therefore does not provide all possible permutations.
' If those possible permutations are needed, instead use
' the macros LSPermute0 or LSPermute1.
'
' The macro yields: the fitting coefficients a(j), their
' standard deviations s(j), the standard deviation of the
' over-all fit, sf, and the results of two F-tests, FR5
' and FR1, for 5% and 1% probability respectively.
'
' SUBROUTINES:
'
' The macros LSMulti0 and LSMulti1 call the subroutine
' LSMulti which, in turn, calls the subroutines Invert,
' Multiply, and Transpose.
'
' INPUT:
'
' The input data must be arranged in a block of at least 3
' (for LSMulti0) or 4 (for LSMulti1) adjacent columns, with
' the dependent variable y in the left-most column, and the
' independent variables x to its right. Highlight the data
' in these columns, and call the macro LSMulti0 or LSMulti1
'
' OUTPUT:
'
' The macro provides:
' (1) the coefficients of the least squares fit of y to
'     the series a(1)x(1) + a(2)x^2 + ... + a(j)x(j)
'     = Sum[a(i)x(i)] for j = 1(1)m for LSMulti0, or
'     a(0) + a(1)x(1) + a(1)x(2) + ... = Sum[a(j)x(j)]
'     for j = 0(1)m for LSMulti1;
' (2) the corresponding standard deviations s(j)for these
'     coefficients;
' (3) the corresponding standard deviation Sf of the fit
'     of the function; and
' (4) the corresponding F-ratios for alpha = 0.05 and 0.01.

' For each order the output consists of three rows. The top
' row lists the standard deviation of the fit. The second
' row displays the coefficients of the fitted polynomial,
' and the third row the corresponding standard deviations.
' The second and third rows also list the values for the
' F-ratios for 5% and 1% respectively. For easy reading
' the rows are color-coded.
'
' If you want the output to display more digits, change
' the instruction ActiveCell.NumberFormat = "0.00E+00" to
' ActiveCell.NumberFormat = "0.000E+00", "0.0000E+00", etc.
'
' WARNING:
'
' The macro output will take up much space below and to the
' right of the input data. Please move valuable data from
' the output region before running this macro, lest those
' data be overwritten.
'
' PROCEDURE:
'
```

```
' Before calling the macro, make sure that the output area
' is clear of valuable data (see above under WARNING). The
' macro does NOT check whether that area is free of data.
'
' In order to start the process, highlight the input data,
' which should occupy at least three adjacent columns, then
' call LSMulti0 or LSMulti1.
'
'''''''''''''''''''''''''''''''''''''''''''''''''''''''''''''
'
' The function of the following two drivers is merely to
' set the value of one parameter, p, equal to either one or
' zero, in order to choose between a general least squares
' fitting (p = 1) or one that forces the curve through the
' origin (p = 0).
'
Sub LSMulti0 ()          ' for an unweighted least squares
                         ' fit through the origin
Dim p As Double
p = 0
Call LSMulti (p)
End Sub
'
'''''''''''''''''''''''''''''''''''''''''''''''''''''''''''''
'
Sub LSMulti1 ()          ' for a general, unweighted
                         ' least squares fit
Dim p As Double
p = 1
Call LSMulti (p)
End Sub
'
'''''''''''''''''''''''''''''''''''''''''''''''''''''''''''''
'
Sub LSMulti (p)

Dim cMax As Integer, Color(1 To 7) As Integer, i As Long
Dim j As Integer, m As Integer, MM As Integer
Dim MaxOrder As Integer, n As Integer, rMax As Long

Dim FRatio1 As Double, FRatio5 As Double
Dim Root As Double, StDevF As Double
Dim u As Double, z As Double

Dim DataArray As Variant, F As Variant
Dim lccArray As Variant, outputArray As Variant
Dim SSR As Variant, varY As Variant
Dim vArray As Variant, v0Array As Variant

Dim myRange As Range

Dim bArray, btArray, btqArray, M1, M2, pArray, piArray
Dim qArray, XArray, xtArray, YArray, ytArray, ytyArray

Dim Answer, iAnswer, hAnswer, kAnswer

' Determination of the array size:

Begin:
```

```
rMax = Selection.Rows.Count
cMax = Selection.Columns.Count
ReDim F(1 To rMax, 1 To 1) As Double
ReDim SSR(1 To rMax, 1 To 1) As Double
u = 1
z = 0

' If area was not highlighted

If rMax = 1 And cMax = 1 Then
  hAnswer = MsgBox("You forgot to highlight" _
    & Chr(13) & "the block of input data." _
    & Chr(13) & "Do you want to do so now?" _
    , vbYesNo, "LSMulti")
  If hAnswer = vbNo Then End
  If hAnswer = vbYes Then
    Set myRange = Application.InputBox(Prompt:= _
      "The input data are located in:", Type:=8)
    myRange.Select
  End If
  GoTo Begin
End If

' Check that the number of columns is at least (3+p):

If cMax < 3 + p Then
  MsgBox "There must be at least " & 3 + p & " columns.", _
    , "Least Squares Multivariate Fit"
  End
End If

' Check that rmax > cmax+1, so that the number of data
' points is sufficient to define the problem:

If rMax < cMax + 1 Then
  MsgBox "     There must be at least " & cMax + 1 & _
    Chr(13) & "input data pairs to define the problem.", _
    , "Least Squares Multivariate Fit"
  End
End If

DataArray = Selection.Value
Selection.Item(1, 1).Select
MM = 2

RedimensionArrays:

' Dimension the arrays:

ReDim YArray(1 To rMax, 1 To 1) As Double
ReDim XArray(1 To rMax, 1 To MM) As Double
ReDim ytArray(1 To 1, 1 To rMax) As Double
ReDim ytyArray(1 To 1, 1 To 1) As Double
ReDim xtArray(1 To MM, 1 To rMax) As Double
ReDim pArray(1 To MM, 1 To MM) As Double
ReDim piArray(1 To MM, 1 To cMax) As Double
ReDim qArray(1 To MM, 1 To 1) As Double
ReDim bArray(1 To MM, 1 To 1) As Double
ReDim btArray(1 To 1, 1 To MM) As Double
```

```
ReDim btqArray(1 To 1, 1 To 1) As Double
ReDim vArray(1 To MM, 1 To MM) As Double
ReDim v0Array(1 To MM - 1 + p, 1 To MM - 1 + p) As Double
ReDim lccArray(1 To MM, 1 To MM) As Double

' Read the dataArray, then fill yArray and xArray.

For i = 1 To rMax
  YArray(i, 1) = DataArray(i, 1)
Next i

' Check the input data for contiguity.

If MM = 2 Then
  For i = 1 To rMax
    If IsEmpty(DataArray(i, 1)) Then
      MsgBox "Y-value(s) missing", _
        , "Least Squares Multivariate Fit"
      End
    End If
  Next i
  For i = 1 To rMax
    For j = 2 To cMax
      If IsEmpty(DataArray(i, j)) Then
        MsgBox "X-value(s) missing", _
          , "Least Squares Multivariate Fit"
        End
      End If
    Next j
  Next i
End If

' Fill the first column of xArray with either
' zeros (for p = 0) or ones (for p = 1),
' the rest with the data in the x-column(s)

For i = 1 To rMax
  XArray(i, 1) = CDbl(p)
Next i
For i = 1 To rMax
  XArray(i, 2) = DataArray(i, 2)
Next i
If MM > 2 Then
  For i = 1 To rMax
    For j = 3 To MM
      XArray(i, j) = DataArray(i, j)
    Next j
  Next i
End If

' Compute b = (X' X)" X' Y , where ' or t denote
' transposition, and " or i indicate inversion

' The various arrays and their dimensions (rows,
' columns) are:
'    Y          = yArray        ( rmax,      1)
'    X          = xArray        ( rmax,     mm)
'    X'         = xtArray       ( mm,     rmax)
'    X' X       = pArray        ( mm,       mm)
```

```
'   (X' X)"      = piArray      (   mm,        mm)
'    X' Y        = qArray       (   mm,         1)
'    b           = bArray       (   mm,         1)
'    Y'          = ytArray      (    1,      rmax)
'    Y' Y        = ytyArray     (    1,         1)
'    b'          = btArray      (    1,        mm)
'    b' X' Y     = btqArray     (    1,         1)

Call Transpose(XArray, rMax, MM, xtArray)
Call Multiply(xtArray, MM, rMax, XArray, MM, pArray)
Call Invert(pArray, MM, piArray)
Call Multiply(xtArray, MM, rMax, YArray, 1, qArray)
Call Multiply(piArray, MM, MM, qArray, 1, bArray)
Call Transpose(YArray, rMax, 1, ytArray)
Call Transpose(bArray, MM, 1, btArray)
Call Multiply(ytArray, 1, rMax, YArray, 1, ytyArray)
Call Multiply(btArray, 1, MM, qArray, 1, btqArray)

' Calculate SSR = Y'Y - b'X'Y, and then varY, the variance
' of y, as varY = SSR/(rmax-cmax-p+1); and vArray, the
' covariance matrix, as V = (X'X)" times varY, of which we
' here only use the diagonal elements, i.e., the variances

For i = 1 To MM
  For j = 1 To MM
    vArray(i, j) = varY * piArray(i, j)
  Next j
Next i

Application.ScreenUpdating = False

ActiveCell.Offset(rMax + 1, 0).Select

' Paint color bands for up to 14 orders, and set the
' numerical format to scientific with 3 decimal places

Color(1) = 38
Color(2) = 40
Color(3) = 36
Color(4) = 35
Color(5) = 34
Color(6) = 37
Color(7) = 39

For i = 1 To 3
  For j = 1 To MM + p + 2
    ActiveCell.ClearContents
    If MM < 9 Then
      ActiveCell.Interior.ColorIndex = Color(MM - 1)
    Else
      ActiveCell.Interior.ColorIndex = Color(MM - 8)
    End If
    ActiveCell.Offset(0, 1).Select
    If MM < 9 Then
      ActiveCell.Interior.ColorIndex = Color(MM - 1)
    Else
      ActiveCell.Interior.ColorIndex = Color(MM - 8)
    End If
    ActiveCell.Font.Bold = False
```

```
      ActiveCell.Font.Italic = False
      ActiveCell.NumberFormat = "0.00E+00"
   Next j
   ActiveCell.Offset(1, -MM - p - 2).Select
Next i
ActiveCell.Offset(-3, 0).Select

' Display the top line of the output

With ActiveCell
  .Font.Bold = True
  .Font.Italic = False
  .HorizontalAlignment = xlLeft
  .Value = "Set # " & MM - 1
End With
For j = 1 To MM + p - 1
  Selection.Offset(0, 1).Select
  With ActiveCell
    .Font.Bold = False
    .Font.Italic = True
    .HorizontalAlignment = xlCenter
    .Value = "term " & j - p
  End With
Next j
Selection.Offset(0, 2).Select
With ActiveCell
  .Font.Bold = False
  .Font.Italic = True
  .HorizontalAlignment = xlRight
  .Value = "Sf:"
End With
Selection.Offset(0, 1).Select
Selection.HorizontalAlignment = xlLeft
Selection.Value = StDevF
Selection.Offset(1, -MM - p - 2).Select

' Display the center line of the output

With ActiveCell
  .Font.Bold = False
  .Font.Italic = True
  .HorizontalAlignment = xlRight
  .Value = "Coeff:"
End With
For j = 1 To MM + p - 1
  Selection.Offset(0, 1).Select
  With ActiveCell
    .Font.Bold = False
    .Font.Italic = False
    .HorizontalAlignment = xlCenter
    .Value = bArray(j + 1 - p, 1)
  End With
Next j
Selection.Offset(0, 2).Select
With ActiveCell
  .Font.Bold = False
  .Font.Italic = True
  .HorizontalAlignment = xlRight
  .Value = "FR5:"
```

```
End With
Selection.Offset(0, 1).Select
Selection.HorizontalAlignment = xlLeft
If MM = 2 Then Selection.Value = "N/A"
If MM > 2 Then Selection.Value = FRatio5
Selection.Offset(1, -MM - p - 2).Select

' Display the bottom line of the output

With ActiveCell
  .Font.Bold = False
  .Font.Italic = True
  .HorizontalAlignment = xlRight
  .Value = "StDev:"
End With
For j = 1 To MM + p - 1
  Selection.Offset(0, 1).Select
  With ActiveCell
    .Font.Bold = False
    .Font.Italic = False
    .HorizontalAlignment = xlCenter
  End With
  If vArray(j - p + 1, j - p + 1) < 1E-40 Then
    ActiveCell.Value = "<1E-20"
  Else
    ActiveCell.Value = _
      Sqr(Abs(vArray(j - p + 1, j - p + 1)))
  End If
Next j
Selection.Offset(0, 2).Select
With ActiveCell
  .Font.Bold = False
  .Font.Italic = True
  .HorizontalAlignment = xlRight
  .Value = "FR1:"
End With
Selection.Offset(0, 1).Select
Selection.HorizontalAlignment = xlLeft
If MM = 2 Then Selection.Value = "N/A"
If MM > 2 Then Selection.Value = FRatio1
Selection.Offset(1, -MM - p - 2).Select

If MM < cMax + 1 Then MM = MM + 1
ActiveCell.Offset(-rMax - 1, 0).Select
If MM = cMax + 1 Then End

GoTo RedimensionArrays

End Sub
```

9.5 *LSPermute*

The macro LSPermute computes the standard deviations of the fit, s_y, for all possible combinations and permutations of unweighted least squares fits of a dependent variable y to a user-specified multivariate expression of the form $y = a_1x_1 + a_2x_2 + ...$ (for $a_0 = 0$) or $y = a_0 + a_1x_1 + a_2x_2$ (when a_0 is not constrained), for up to six linear terms x_i. When more terms need to be included, the macro is readily extended to accommodate this by extend the logic used. Again, for a standard multivariate least squares fit, use LS0 or LS1 instead.

```
''''''''''''''''''''''''''''''''''''''''''''''''''''''''''''''''''
''''''''''''''''^^^^^^^^^^^^^^^^^^^^^^^^^^^^^^^^^'''''''''''''''''''
'''''''''''''''^                                ^''''''''''''''''''
'''''''''''''''^      LEAST SQUARES PERMUTE      ^''''''''''''''''''
'''''''''''''''^                                ^''''''''''''''''''
'''''''''''''''''^^^^^^^^^^^^^^^^^^^^^^^^^^^^^^^^^'''''''''''''''''''
'''''''''''''''''''''''''''''''''''''''''''''''''(c) R. de Levie
''''''''''''''''''''''''''''''''''''''''''''''''''v 4.10, Oct. 1, 2004

' PURPOSE:
'
' The macro LSPermute computes the standard deviations of
' the fit, sy, for all possible combinations and permuta-
' tions of unweighted least squares fits of a dependent
' variable y to a user-specified multivariate expression of
' the form y = a1x1 + a2x2 + .. (for "Thru 0", i.e., for a0
' = 0) or y = a0 + a1x1 + a2x2 + .. (for the "General" case
' where the value of a0 is not constrained), for up to six
' linear terms xi.
'
' SUBROUTINES:
'
' The macro LSPermute calls the subroutine LLSS which,
' in turn, calls the subroutines Invert, Multiply, and
' Transpose.
'
' INPUT:
'
' The input data must be arranged in a block of at least 3
' contiguous columns, with the dependent variable y in the
' left-most column, and the independent variables xi to
' its right.
'
' OUTPUT:
'
' In order to keep the output compact, the macro only
' provides three columns of output information:
' (1) in its first column the indices i of the parameters
'     xi considered;
' (2) in its second column the values of the standard
'     deviation of the fit, Sf, assuming a0 = 0; and
' (3) in its third column the values of the standard
'     deviation of the fit Sf for the general case.
' However, the output will sweep clear an area as wide as
' the input array, and extending by rMax lines below the
' bottom line of the output
'
' WARNING:
'
' Make sure that there are no valuable data below the
' input array, because these will be overwritten. This
' macro does NOT check whether that space is empty.
'
```

```
' PROCEDURE:
'
' Before calling the macro, make sure that the space below
' the input data array is clear of valuable data (see above
' under WARNING). The output requires a space as wide as
' the input array, even though that may not be obvious from
' the results displayed.
'
' In order to start the process, highlight the input data
' array, which should occupy at least two adjacent columns,
' then call LSPermute.

Sub LSPermute()

Dim C As Integer, c2 As Integer, c3 As Integer
Dim c4 As Integer, c5 As Integer, c6 As Integer
Dim cc As Integer, cMax As Integer, ccMax As Integer
Dim i As Long, r As Long, rMax As Long
Dim StDevF As Double
Dim inputArray As Variant, outputArray As Variant
Dim hAnswer, XArray, YArray

Dim Down As Integer
Down = 0

' Read input array dataArray

Begin:
inputArray = Selection.Value
cMax = Selection.Columns.Count
rMax = Selection.Rows.Count

' If area was not highlighted

If rMax = 1 And cMax = 1 Then
  hAnswer = MsgBox("You forgot to highlight" _
    & Chr(13) & "the block of input data." _
    & Chr(13) & "Do you want to do so now?" _
    , vbYesNo, "LSPermute")
  If hAnswer = vbNo Then End
  If hAnswer = vbYes Then
    Set myRange = Application.InputBox(Prompt:= _
      "The input data are located in:", Type:=8)
    myRange.Select
  End If
  GoTo Begin
End If

' Check the size of the input array

If cMax < 3 Then
  MsgBox "There should be at least three input columns." _
    , , "LSPermute"
  End
End If
If cMax > 7 Then
  MsgBox "This macro can only handle" & Chr(13) & _
    "six independent parameters.", , "LSPermute"
  End
```

```
End If
If rMax < cMax + 1 Then
  MsgBox "There are too few rows for the num-" & _
  Chr(13) & "ber of independent parameters used.", _
  , "LSPermute"
  End
End If

' Check for missing input data

For i = 1 To rMax
  If IsEmpty(inputArray(i, 1)) Then
    MsgBox "Y-value(s) missing", , "LSPermute"
    End
  End If
Next i
For j = 2 To cMax
  For i = 1 To rMax
    If IsEmpty(inputArray(i, j)) Then
      MsgBox "X-value(s) missing", , "LSPermute"
      End
    End If
  Next i
Next j

' Dimension the data array and the output array

ReDim outputArray(1 To rMax, 1 To cMax)
ReDim YArray(1 To rMax, 1 To 1) As Double
ReDim XArray(1 To rMax, 1 To 1) As Double

' Fill yArray

For r = 1 To rMax
  YArray(r, 1) = inputArray(r, 1)
Next r

' Initialize xArray

For r = 1 To rMax
  For C = 1 To cMax
    outputArray(r, C) = ""
  Next C
Next r

Selection.Offset(rMax + 1, 0).Select
Down = Down + rMax + 1

' Write column headings

outputArray(1, 1) = "Standard deviation of fit"
Selection.Value = outputArray
Selection.Offset(1, 0).Select
outputArray(1, 1) = "Indices:"
outputArray(1, 2) = "Thru 0"
outputArray(1, 3) = "General"
Selection.Value = outputArray
Selection.Offset(2, 0).Select
Down = Down + 3
```

```
' Compute the output for 1 variable:

ccMax = 4
ReDim XArray(1 To rMax, 1 To ccMax) As Double
For C = 2 To cMax
  For r = 1 To rMax
    XArray(r, 1) = 0
    XArray(r, 2) = inputArray(r, C)
  Next r
  Call LLSS(ccMax, rMax, 0, YArray, XArray, StDevF)
  outputArray(1, 1) = C - 1
  outputArray(1, 2) = StDevF
  For r = 1 To rMax
    XArray(r, 1) = 1
  Next r
  Call LLSS(ccMax, rMax, 1, YArray, XArray, StDevF)
  outputArray(1, 3) = StDevF
  Selection.Value = outputArray
  Selection.Offset(1, 0).Select
  Down = Down + 1
Next C

Selection.Offset(1, 0).Select
Down = Down + 1

' Compute the output for 2 variables:

ccMax = 5
ReDim XArray(1 To rMax, 1 To ccMax) As Double
For C = 2 To cMax
  For c2 = C + 1 To cMax
    For r = 1 To rMax
      XArray(r, 1) = 0
      XArray(r, 2) = inputArray(r, C)
      XArray(r, 3) = inputArray(r, c2)
    Next r
    Call LLSS(ccMax, rMax, 0, YArray, XArray, StDevF)
    outputArray(1, 1) = C - 1 & "," & c2 - 1
    outputArray(1, 2) = StDevF
    For r = 1 To rMax
      XArray(r, 1) = 1
    Next r
    Call LLSS(ccMax, rMax, 1, YArray, XArray, StDevF)
    outputArray(1, 3) = StDevF
    Selection.Value = outputArray
    Selection.Offset(1, 0).Select
    Down = Down + 1
  Next c2
Next C

Selection.Offset(1, 0).Select
Down = Down + 1

' Compute the output for 3 variables:

ccMax = 6
ReDim XArray(1 To rMax, 1 To ccMax) As Double
For C = 2 To cMax
```

```
  For c2 = C + 1 To cMax
   For c3 = c2 + 1 To cMax
    For r = 1 To rMax
       XArray(r, 1) = 0
       XArray(r, 2) = inputArray(r, C)
       XArray(r, 3) = inputArray(r, c2)
       XArray(r, 4) = inputArray(r, c3)
    Next r
    Call LLSS(ccMax, rMax, 0, YArray, XArray, StDevF)
    outputArray(1, 1) = C - 1 & "," & c2 - 1 & "," & c3 - 1
    outputArray(1, 2) = StDevF
    For r = 1 To rMax
       XArray(r, 1) = 1
    Next r
    Call LLSS(ccMax, rMax, 1, YArray, XArray, StDevF)
    outputArray(1, 3) = StDevF
    Selection.Value = outputArray
    Selection.Offset(1, 0).Select
    Down = Down + 1
   Next c3
  Next c2
Next C

Selection.Offset(1, 0).Select
Down = Down + 1

' Compute the output for 4 variables:

ccMax = 7
ReDim XArray(1 To rMax, 1 To ccMax) As Double
For C = 2 To cMax
 For c2 = C + 1 To cMax
  For c3 = c2 + 1 To cMax
   For c4 = c3 + 1 To cMax
    For r = 1 To rMax
       XArray(r, 1) = 0
       XArray(r, 2) = inputArray(r, C)
       XArray(r, 3) = inputArray(r, c2)
       XArray(r, 4) = inputArray(r, c3)
       XArray(r, 5) = inputArray(r, c4)
    Next r
    Call LLSS(ccMax, rMax, 0, YArray, XArray, StDevF)
    outputArray(1, 1) = C - 1 & "," & c2 - 1 & _
       "," & c3 - 1 & "," & c4 - 1
    outputArray(1, 2) = StDevF
    For r = 1 To rMax
       XArray(r, 1) = 1
    Next r
    Call LLSS(ccMax, rMax, 1, YArray, XArray, StDevF)
    outputArray(1, 3) = StDevF
    Selection.Value = outputArray
    Selection.Offset(1, 0).Select
    Down = Down + 1
   Next c4
  Next c3
 Next c2
Next C

Selection.Offset(1, 0).Select
```

```
Down = Down + 1

' Compute the output for 5 variables:

ccMax = 8
ReDim XArray(1 To rMax, 1 To ccMax) As Double
For C = 2 To cMax
 For c2 = C + 1 To cMax
  For c3 = c2 + 1 To cMax
   For c4 = c3 + 1 To cMax
    For c5 = c4 + 1 To cMax
      For r = 1 To rMax
         XArray(r, 1) = 0
         XArray(r, 2) = inputArray(r, C)
         XArray(r, 3) = inputArray(r, c2)
         XArray(r, 4) = inputArray(r, c3)
         XArray(r, 5) = inputArray(r, c4)
         XArray(r, 6) = inputArray(r, c5)
      Next r
      Call LLSS(ccMax, rMax, 0, YArray, XArray, StDevF)
      outputArray(1, 1) = C - 1 & "," & c2 - 1 & _
         "," & c3 - 1 & "," & c4 - 1 & "," & c5 - 1
      outputArray(1, 2) = StDevF
      For r = 1 To rMax
         XArray(r, 1) = 1
      Next r
      Call LLSS(ccMax, rMax, 1, YArray, XArray, StDevF)
      outputArray(1, 3) = StDevF
      Selection.Value = outputArray
      Selection.Offset(1, 0).Select
      Down = Down + 1
    Next c5
   Next c4
  Next c3
 Next c2
Next C

Selection.Offset(1, 0).Select
Down = Down + 1

' Compute the output for 6 variables:

ccMax = 9
ReDim XArray(1 To rMax, 1 To ccMax) As Double
For C = 2 To cMax
 For c2 = C + 1 To cMax
  For c3 = c2 + 1 To cMax
   For c4 = c3 + 1 To cMax
    For c5 = c4 + 1 To cMax
     For c6 = c5 + 1 To cMax
      For r = 1 To rMax
         XArray(r, 1) = 0
         XArray(r, C) = inputArray(r, 2)
         XArray(r, c2) = inputArray(r, 3)
         XArray(r, c3) = inputArray(r, 4)
         XArray(r, c4) = inputArray(r, 5)
         XArray(r, c5) = inputArray(r, 6)
         XArray(r, c6) = inputArray(r, 7)
      Next r
```

```
        Call LLSS(ccMax, rMax, 0, YArray, XArray, StDevF)
        outputArray(1, 1) = C - 1 & "," & _
          "," & c2 - 1 & "," & c3 - 1 & "," & _
          c4 - 1 & c5 - 1 & "," & c6 - 1
        outputArray(1, 2) = StDevF
        For r = 1 To rMax
          XArray(r, 1) = 1
        Next r
        Call LLSS(ccMax, rMax, 1, YArray, XArray, StDevF)
        outputArray(1, 3) = StDevF
        Selection.Value = outputArray
        Selection.Offset(1, 0).Select
        Down = Down + 1
      Next c6
    Next c5
   Next c4
  Next c3
 Next c2
Next C

Selection.Offset(-Down, 0).Select

End Sub

''''''''''''''''''''''''''''''''''''''''''''''''''''''''''''''''''
''''''''''''''''''''''''''            ''''''''''''''''''''''''
'''''''''''''''''''''''''''    LLSS    '''''''''''''''''''''''''
'''''''''''''''''''''''''              '''''''''''''''''''''''
''''''''''''''''''''''''''''''''''''''''''''''''''''''''''''''''''

Sub LLSS(ccMax, rMax, p, YArray, XArray, StDevF)

' This subroutine provides the standard deviation StDevF
' of the least squares fit. It calls the subroutines
' Invert, Multiply, and Transpose.

Dim btArray, btqArray
Dim SSR As Double, varY As Double
Dim pArray, piArray, qArray
Dim xtArray, ytArray, ytyArray

ReDim ytArray(1 To 1, 1 To rMax) As Double
ReDim ytyArray(1 To 1, 1 To 1) As Double
ReDim xtArray(1 To ccMax, 1 To rMax) As Double
ReDim pArray(1 To ccMax, 1 To ccMax) As Double
ReDim piArray(1 To ccMax, 1 To ccMax) As Double
ReDim qArray(1 To ccMax, 1 To 1) As Double
ReDim bArray(1 To ccMax, 1 To 1) As Double
ReDim btArray(1 To 1, 1 To ccMax) As Double
ReDim btqArray(1 To 1, 1 To 1) As Double

' Compute the least squares fit

Call Transpose(XArray, rMax, ccMax, xtArray)
Call Multiply(xtArray, ccMax, rMax, XArray, ccMax, pArray)
Call Invert(pArray, ccMax, piArray)
Call Multiply(xtArray, ccMax, rMax, YArray, 1, qArray)
Call Multiply(piArray, ccMax, ccMax, qArray, 1, bArray)
Call Transpose(YArray, rMax, 1, ytArray)
```

```
Call Transpose(bArray, ccMax, 1, btArray)
Call Multiply(ytArray, 1, rMax, YArray, 1, ytyArray)
Call Multiply(btArray, 1, ccMax, qArray, 1, btqArray)

' Compute the standard deviation of the fit

SSR = ytyArray(1, 1) - btqArray(1, 1)
varY = SSR / (rMax - ccMax - p + 3)
StDevF = Sqr(Abs(varY))

End Sub
```

9.6 Ortho

Ortho uses a simple Gram-Schmidt orthogonalization algorithm, as described in, e.g., N. R. Draper & H. Smith, *Applied Regression Analysis*, 2nd ed., Wiley, New York 1981 pp. 266-267 and 275-278. The macro should not be used as a standard alternative to LS because it expresses the function in terms of orthogonal polynomials, instead of as the usual power series in *x*. Rather, Ortho serves as a complement to LS, as illustrated in sections 3.11 through 3.14 of chapter 3. Since the covariance and linear correlation coefficient matrices contain only zero off-diagonal coefficients, they are neither needed nor displayed.

```
'''''''''''''''''''''''''''''''''''''''''''''''''''''''''''''''''''''
''''''''''''''''''''^^^^^^^^^^^^^^^^^^^^^^^^^^^^^''''''''''''''''''''
'''''''''''''''''^                              ^'''''''''''''''''
''''''''''''''''^    ORTHOGONAL POLYNOMIAL FIT   ^'''''''''''''''''
'''''''''''''''''^                              ^'''''''''''''''''
''''''''''''''''''^^^^^^^^^^^^^^^^^^^^^^^^^^^^^''''''''''''''''''''
''''''''''''''''''''''''''''''''''''''''''''''''''(c) R. de Levie
'''''''''''''''''''''''''''''''''''''''''''''v 4.10, Oct. 1, 2004

' PURPOSE:

' This subroutine uses Gram-Schmidt orthogonalization to
' compute and display the orthogonal polynomials correspon-
' ding to one or more independent variables x, which need
' not be equidistant. It also provides the fitting para-
' meters, their standard deviations, and their ratios.
' The latter are convenient for determining which terms
' are statistically significant and should be retained.

' SUBROUTINES:

' This macro requires the subroutines Multiply, Invert,
' and Transpose

' INPUT:

' The input data must be arranged as follows. The first
' column must contain the dependent variable y. The second
' (and subsequent) column(s) must contain the independent
' variable(s) x.
```

```
' The subroutine requires an input parameter p: p = 1
' causes a general unweighted least squares fit to the
' data, while p = 0 forces the fit to pass through the
' origin, i.e., it assumes that Y = 0 for X = 0. The sub-
' routine Ortho is therefore called by a macro, Ortho1 or
' Ortho0, that sets the value of p.

' OUTPUT:

' The macro produces its output to the right of the input,
' separated by one empty column. It therefore repeats the
' y column. It then computes the fitting parameters and
' their standard deviations. Since these are uncorrelated,
' a covariance matrix is neither needed nor provided. The
' standard deviation of the fit is shown directly below the
' label "Coeff:", as in LS1 and LS0. A third row lists the
' ratio of the absolute values of the coefficient and the
' corresponding standard deviation.

' In general you will NOT want to use the listed coeffi-
' cients and standard deviations, which apply to the ortho-
' gonalized independent parameters. The most useful part of
' the output is the row listing their ratios, which indi-
' cates which orders should be considered (green if ratio >
' 5) and which should not be (red if ratio < 1).

' PROCEDURE:

' Before calling the macro, make sure that the output area
' (a block to the right of the input data block, but exten-
' ding one more column and three more rows) contains no
' valuable data, since these will be overwritten.

' In order to start the process, highlight the entire input
' data array, i.e., the rectangular block containing the
' column for y and the adjacent column(s) for the corres-
' ponding values of x, then call either Ortho(1) or
' Ortho(0)

' The function of the following two drivers is merely to
' set the value of one parameter, p, equal to either one or
' zero, in order to choose between a general least squares
' fitting (p = 1) or one that forces the curve through the
' origin (p = 0).

' EXAMPLES:
'
' Use of this macro is illustrated starting in sections
' 3.13 and 3.14 of Advanced Excel.

Sub Ortho0()      ' for unweighted LS fit through the origin

Dim p As Double
p = 0
Call Ortho(p)

End Sub
'
'''''''''''''''''''''''''''''''''''''''''''''''''''''''''''''''
'
```

```
Sub Ortho1()      ' for general unweighted least squares fit

Dim p As Double
p = 1
Call Ortho(p)

End Sub
'
''''''''''''''''''''''''''''''''''''''''''''''''''''''''''''''''
'
Sub Ortho(p)

Dim cMax As Integer, cn As Integer, i As Long
Dim j As Integer, m As Long, MM As Integer
Dim n As Integer, rMax As Long

Dim Num As Double, Resid As Double
Dim Root As Double, SSR As Double, StDevF As Double
Dim Sf As Double, SYZ As Double, SZZ As Double
Dim u As Double, varY As Double

Dim bArray As Variant, coeffArray As Variant
Dim DataArray As Variant, Denom As Variant
Dim lccArray As Variant, orthoArray As Variant
Dim outputArray As Variant, stdevArray As Variant
Dim vArray As Variant, v0Array As Variant
Dim XArray As Variant, YArray As Variant
Dim z As Variant

Dim myRange As Range

Dim Answer, hAnswer, iAnswer, kAnswer

' Determination of the array size:

Begin:
rMax = Selection.Rows.Count
cMax = Selection.Columns.Count
ReDim A(0 To cMax) As Double, s(0 To cMax) As Double
u = 1

' If area was not highlighted

If rMax = 1 And cMax = 1 Then
  hAnswer = MsgBox("You forgot to highlight" _
    & Chr(13) & "the block of input data." _
    & Chr(13) & "Do you want to do so now?" _
    , vbYesNo, "Ortho")
  If hAnswer = vbNo Then End
  If hAnswer = vbYes Then
    Set myRange = Application.InputBox(Prompt:= _
      "The input data are located in:", Type:=8) _
    myRange.Select
  End If
  GoTo Begin
End If

' Check that the number of columns is at least 2:

If cMax < 2 Then
  MsgBox "There must be at least two columns," & _
```

```
      Chr(13) & "one for Y, and one or more for X.", _
        , "Orthogonalization"
  End
End If

' Check that rmax > cmax, so that the number of data
' points is sufficient to define the problem:

If rMax < cMax Then
  MsgBox "There must be at least " & cMax & " input" & _
    Chr(13) & "  data to define the problem.", _
      , "Orthogonalization"
  End
End If

' Dimension the arrays:

ReDim bArray(1 To cMax) As Double
ReDim Denom(1 To cMax)
ReDim vArray(1 To cMax, 1 To cMax) As Double
ReDim XArray(1 To rMax, 1 To cMax) As Double
ReDim YArray(1 To rMax) As Double
ReDim z(1 To rMax, 1 To cMax) As Double

' Read the dataArray, then fill yArray and xArray.

DataArray = Selection.Value

For i = 1 To rMax
  YArray(i) = DataArray(i, 1)
Next i

For i = 1 To rMax
  If IsEmpty(DataArray(i, 1)) Then
    MsgBox "Y-value(s) missing", , "Orthogonalization"
    End
  End If
Next i
For j = 2 To cMax
  For i = 1 To rMax
    If IsEmpty(DataArray(i, j)) Then
      MsgBox "X-value(s) missing", , "Orthogonalization"
      End
    End If
  Next i
Next j

' Fill the first column of xArray with zeroes
' (for p = 0) or ones (for p = 1), the rest with
' the data in the x-column(s)

For i = 1 To rMax
  XArray(i, 1) = CDbl(p)
Next i
For j = 2 To cMax
  For i = 1 To rMax
    XArray(i, j) = DataArray(i, j)
  Next i
Next j
```

```
cn = 1

' Dimension and fill Z, the matrix of column vectors
' already transformed, initially Z is the 1st column of
' xArray if p = 1, the 2nd if p = 0

ReDim z(1 To rMax, 1 To cn) As Double

' Check against overwriting valuable spreadsheet
' data by the output of orthogonal polynomials

Selection.Offset(0, cMax + 1).Select
orthoArray = Selection.Value
outputArray = Selection.Value

m = 0
For i = 1 To rMax
  For j = 1 To cMax
    If IsEmpty(outputArray(i, j)) Then
      m = m
    Else
      m = m + 1
    End If
  Next j
Next i
If m > 0 Then
  Answer = MsgBox("There are data in the highlighted " _
    & "output block to the" & Chr(13) & _
    "right of the input data array. Can they be " _
    & "overwritten? ", vbYesNo, "Overwrite?")
  If Answer = vbNo Then
    End
  End If
End If

' Check against overwriting valuable spreadsheet data
' by the output of coefficients and standard deviations

Selection.Offset(4, 0).Select
outputArray = Selection.Value

MM = 0
For i = rMax - 1 To rMax
  For j = 1 To cMax
    If IsEmpty(outputArray(i, j)) Then
      MM = MM
    Else
      MM = MM + 1
    End If
  Next j
Next i
If MM > 0 Then
  Answer = MsgBox("There are data in the two bottom " _
    & "lines of the " & Chr(13) & "highlighted array. " _
    & "Can they be overwritten? ", vbYesNo, "Overwrite?")
  If Answer = vbNo Then
    End
  End If
End If
```

```
Selection.Offset(-4, 0).Select

For i = 1 To rMax
  orthoArray(i, 1) = DataArray(i, 1)
Next i

Application.ScreenUpdating = False

Do
  For i = 1 To rMax
    For j = 1 To cn
      z(i, cn) = XArray(i, j)
    Next j
  Next i

' Dimension and fill Zi, the next column vector to be
' transformed

  ReDim Zi(1 To rMax, 1 To 1) As Double

  For i = 1 To rMax
    Zi(i, 1) = XArray(i, cn + 1)
  Next i

' Dimension the other vectors and matrices

  ReDim Ztp(1 To cn, 1 To rMax) As Double        ' = Z'
  ReDim ZtpZ(1 To cn, 1 To cn) As Double         ' = Z' Z
  ReDim Z1(1 To cn, 1 To cn) As Double           ' = (Z' Z)"
  ReDim ZtpZi(1 To cn, 1 To 1) As Double         ' = Z' Zi
  ReDim Z2(1 To cn, 1 To 1) As Double
                            ' = Z1 ZtpZi = (Z' Z)" Z' Zi
  ReDim Z3(1 To rMax, 1 To 1) As Double
                            ' = Z Z2 = Z (Z' Z)" Z' Zi

' Compute Z1 = (Z' Z)"

  Call Transpose(z, rMax, cn, Ztp)
  Call Multiply(Ztp, cn, rMax, z, cn, ZtpZ)
  Call Invert(ZtpZ, cn, Z1)
  Call Multiply(Ztp, cn, rMax, Zi, 1, ZtpZi)
  Call Multiply(Z1, cn, cn, ZtpZi, 1, Z2)
  Call Multiply(z, rMax, cn, Z2, 1, Z3)

' Dimension and compute Ztf = Zi - Z3, the transformed
' vector, orthogonal to the vector(s) in Z

  ReDim Ztf(1 To rMax, 1 To 1) As Double
                            ' = Zi - Z (Z' Z)" (Z' Zi)
  For i = 1 To rMax
    Ztf(i, 1) = Zi(i, 1) - Z3(i, 1)
  Next i

  SYZ = 0
  SZZ = 0
  For i = 1 To rMax
    SYZ = SYZ + YArray(i) * Ztf(i, 1)
    SZZ = SZZ + Ztf(i, 1) * Ztf(i, 1)
    orthoArray(i, cn + 1) = Ztf(i, 1)
  Next i
```

```
    If cn < cMax Then cn = cn + 1
    ReDim Preserve z(1 To rMax, 1 To cn) As Double

Loop Until cn = cMax

' Display the orthogonal array

Selection.Value = orthoArray

' Update yArray and xArray.

For i = 1 To rMax
  YArray(i) = orthoArray(i, 1)
Next i

For i = 1 To rMax
  XArray(i, 1) = CDbl(p)
Next i
For j = 2 To cMax
  For i = 1 To rMax
    XArray(i, j) = orthoArray(i, j)
  Next i
Next j

' Compute the coefficients

For j = 2 - p To cMax
  Num = 0
  Denom(j) = 0
  For i = 1 To rMax
    Num = Num + XArray(i, j) * YArray(i)
    Denom(j) = Denom(j) + XArray(i, j) * XArray(i, j)
  Next i
  bArray(j) = Num / Denom(j)
Next j

' Compute the variance of y

SSR = 0
For i = 1 To rMax
  Resid = YArray(i)
  For j = 2 - p To cMax
    Resid = Resid - bArray(j) * XArray(i, j)
  Next j
  SSR = SSR + Resid * Resid
Next i
varY = SSR / (rMax - cMax - p + 1)
StDevF = Sqr(Abs(varY))

' Compute the variances of the coefficients

For j = 2 - p To cMax
  vArray(j, j) = varY / Denom(j)
Next j

ActiveCell.Offset(rMax, 0).Select

' Arrange for the data output

For j = 1 To cMax
  With ActiveCell.Font
```

```
      .Bold = True
      .Italic = True
      .ColorIndex = 1
    End With
    ActiveCell.Offset(0, 1).Select
  Next j
  ActiveCell.Offset(1, -cMax).Select
  For j = 1 To cMax
    ActiveCell.Font.Italic = True
    ActiveCell.Font.ColorIndex = 1
    ActiveCell.Offset(0, 1).Select
  Next j
  ActiveCell.Offset(1, -cMax).Select
  For j = 1 To cMax
    ActiveCell.Font.Italic = True
    ActiveCell.Font.ColorIndex = 1
    ActiveCell.Offset(0, 1).Select
  Next j

  ActiveCell.Offset(-2, -cMax - p).Select
  With ActiveCell
    .Font.Bold = True
    .Font.Italic = True
    .Font.ColorIndex = 1
    .HorizontalAlignment = xlRight
    .Value = "Coeff:"
  End With
  ActiveCell.Offset(0, 1).Select
  For j = 2 - p To cMax
    With ActiveCell.Font
      .Bold = True
      .Italic = True
      .ColorIndex = 1
    End With
    ActiveCell.Value = bArray(j)
    ActiveCell.Offset(0, 1).Select
  Next j

  ActiveCell.Offset(1, -cMax - p).Select
  With ActiveCell.Font
    .Bold = False
    .Italic = True
    .ColorIndex = 1
  End With
  ActiveCell.HorizontalAlignment = xlRight
  ActiveCell.Value = "StDev:"
  ActiveCell.Offset(0, 1).Select
  ActiveCell.Font.ColorIndex = 1
  For j = 2 - p To cMax
    If vArray(j, j) < 1E-40 Then
      ActiveCell.Value = "<1E-20"
    Else
      ActiveCell.Value = Sqr(Abs(vArray(j, j)))
    End If
    ActiveCell.Offset(0, 1).Select
  Next j

  ActiveCell.Offset(1, -cMax - p).Select
  With ActiveCell
```

```
  .Font.Bold = False
  .Font.Italic = True
  .Font.ColorIndex = 1
  .HorizontalAlignment = xlRight
  .Value = "Ratio:"
End With
ActiveCell.Offset(0, 1).Select
For j = 2 - p To cMax
  If vArray(j, j) <= 0 Then
    ActiveCell.Value = "N/A"
    ActiveCell.Font.ColorIndex = 1
  End If
  If vArray(j, j) > 0 Then
    ActiveCell.Font.Bold = False
    ActiveCell.Font.Italic = True
    ActiveCell.Font.ColorIndex = 16
    ActiveCell.Value = Abs(bArray(j) _
      / Sqr(vArray(j, j)))
    If ActiveCell.Value > 5 Then _
      ActiveCell.Font.ColorIndex = 10
    If ActiveCell.Value < 1 Then _
      ActiveCell.Font.ColorIndex = 3
  End If
  ActiveCell.Offset(0, 1).Select
Next j

ActiveCell.Offset(1, -cMax).Select

' Provide the standard deviation of the fit

ActiveCell.Offset(0, -p).Select
With ActiveCell.Font
  .Bold = False
  .Italic = True
  .ColorIndex = 1
End With
ActiveCell.HorizontalAlignment = xlRight
ActiveCell.Value = "Sf:"
ActiveCell.Offset(0, 1).Select
ActiveCell.Font.Italic = True
ActiveCell.Font.ColorIndex = 1
Selection.Value = StDevF

End Sub
```

9.7 ELS

The equidistant least squares macros ELS are based on Gram polynomials, and use a sliding polynomial approach for a piecewise fit to arbitrary functions. The user specifies the length of the moving polynomial and, in ELSfixed, its order. In ELSauto the polynomial order is self-optimized by the macro, using F-tests to mediate between the conflicting requirements of maximal noise rejection and minimal signal distortion. Both macros are based on the work of P. Barak, *Anal. Chem.* 67 (1995) 2758. They will work best when the length of the moving polynomial is smaller than the width of the smallest significant features in the signal.

```
' ' ' ' ' ' ' ' ' ' ' ' ' ' ' ' ' ' ' ' ' ' ' ' ' ' ' ' ' ' ' ' ' ' ' ' ' ' ' ' ' ' ' ' ' ' ' ' ' ' ' ' ' ' ' ' ' ' ' '
' ' ' ' ' ' ' ' ' ' ' ' ' ' ' ' ' ' ' ' ' ' ' ' ' ' ' ' ' ' ' ' ' ' ' ' ' ' ' ' ' ' ' ' ' ' ' ' ' ' ' ' ' ' ' ' ' ' ' '
' ' ' ' ' ' ' ' ' ' ' ' ' ^^^^^^^^^^^^^^^^^^^^^^^^^^^^^^^^^^^^^^^^^^^ ' ' ' ' ' ' ' ' ' ' ' ' ' '
' ' ' ' ' ' ' ' ' ' ' ' ^                                          ^ ' ' ' ' ' ' ' ' ' ' '
' ' ' ' ' ' ' ' ' ' ' ' ^      EQUIDISTANT LEAST SQUARES            ^ ' ' ' ' ' ' ' ' ' ' '
' ' ' ' ' ' ' ' ' ' ' ' ^                                          ^ ' ' ' ' ' ' ' ' ' ' '
' ' ' ' ' ' ' ' ' ' ' ' ' ^^^^^^^^^^^^^^^^^^^^^^^^^^^^^^^^^^^^^^^^^^ ' ' ' ' ' ' ' ' ' ' ' ' '
' ' ' ' ' ' ' ' ' ' ' ' ' ' ' ' ' ' ' ' '© P. Barak, pwbarak@facstaff.wisc.edu
' ' ' ' ' ' ' ' ' ' ' ' ' ' ' ' ' ' ' ' ' ' ' ' ' ' ' ' ' ' ' ' ' 'v 4.6, June 1, 2004
```

```
' PURPOSE:
'
' This program for a least-squares fit to EQUIDISTANT data
' y,x with a moving polynomial uses the approach pioneered
' by Gram [J. reine angew. Math. 94 (1883) 41], extended
' by Sheppard [Proc. London Math. Soc. (2) 13 (1914) 81]
' and Sherriff [Proc. Royal Soc. Edinburgh 40 (1920) 112],
' and subsequently advocated by Whittaker & Robinson [The
' calculus of observations, Blackie & Son, 1924] and by
' Savitzky & Golay [Anal. Chem. 36 (1964) 1627]. It com-
' putes smoothed values of the data set or, if so desired,
' of its first or second derivative.
'
' There are two options: in ELSfixed() the user also
' selects the order of the polynomial, whereas in ELSauto()
' the program optimizes the order of the polynomial (bet-
' ween 1 and an upper limit set by the user) each time the
' moving polynomial slides one data point along the data
' set, using an algorithm described by Barak in Anal. Chem.
' 67 (1995) 2758.
'
' The program compares the ratio of the variances for a
' given order and that for the next-lower order with the
' corresponding F test as its first criterion. Since symme-
' trical functions often contain mostly even powers, a
' single, final comparison is made between the variances of
' the next-higher and the next-lower order. If the latter
' is not desired, simply comment out the section following
' the comment line "Second test for optimum Order".
'
' FUNCTIONS & SUBROUTINES
'
' There are two drivers, ELSfixed and ELSauto, that call
' the main subroutine, ELS(iOrder). The latter uses the
' functions GenFact() and Smooth(). It also calls the sub-
' routine ConvolutionFactors, which calculates the Gram
' polynomials and the corresponding convolution weights.
'
' INPUT
'
' The user must select the moving polynomial length; the
' corresponding value is restricted to odd integers between
' 3 and 31. This choice involves a compromise: the longer
' the polynomial, the more noise is removed, and the more
' the underlying signal is distorted. A useful rule of
' thumb is to make the length such that it encompasses no
' more than the half-width of the most narrow feature in
' the signal that should be preserved.
'
```

```
' Moreover, the length of the moving polynomial, PL, cannot
' exceed the length of the data set, NPts. The selected
' (maximum) order of the polynomial, MaxOrder, must be a
' positive integer, MaxOrder>0. Moreover, for ELSfixed,
' MaxOrder<PL, while for ELSauto we have MaxOrder<(PL-1).
'
' OUTPUT
'
' The output is written in one or two columns to the right
' of the input data. The first output column contains the
' smoothed or differentiated data. The second column, which
' appears only with ELSauto(), displays the order selected
' by the program. Make sure that the output space is free,
' or can be overwritten.
'
' Some of the abbreviations and indices used:
'     DerOrder: the derivative order, selected by the
'         answer to ELS InputBox 4: Derivative Order:
'             DerOrder = 0 for smoothing,
'             DerOrder = 1 for the 1st derivative,
'             DerOrder = 2 for the 2nd derivative.
'     FValueTable: the Fisher criterion, obtained
'         from the Excel function FInv.
'     GP: the Gram Polynomial
'     j: index for the order of the polynomial.
'     k: index for the position of the center of the
'         moving polynomial in the data set;
'         k ranges from m+1 to NPts-m.
'     m: number of points on each side of the central
'         point in the moving polynomial, calculated as
'         m = (PL-1)/2.
'     MaxOrder: the maximum order of the polynomial
'         (from ELS InputBox 3: Polynomial Order) or its
'         maximum value (from ELS InputBox 3: Maximum Poly-
'         nomial Order). MaxOrder must be an integer, > 0,
'         and < PL for ELSfixed, or < (PL-1) for ELSauto.
'     NPts: number of points in the data set, computed by
'         the macro from the data range provided in ELS
'         InputBox 1: Input data.
'     OptOrder: array of optimized Order values.
'     Order: working value of the polynomial order.
'         In ELSfixed, Order = MaxOrder; in ELSauto, Order
'         starts at 1, and has a maximum value of MaxOrder.
'     OutputData: the final (smoothed or derivative) result
'     OutputOrder:  the values of OptOrder used in ELSauto.
'     PL: length (in number of points) of the moving poly-
'         nomial, selected in ELS InputBox 2: Length of Mo-
'         ving Polynomial.
'     s: index for the order of the derivative; s ranges
'         from 0 to DerivOrder.
'     t: index for the individual points in the moving
'         polynomial; t ranges from -m to +m.
'     tries:  number of attempts to enter data in input box
'     Y() and YData(): the input data containing the entire
'         data set.
'
'''''''''''''''''''''''''''''''''''''''''''''''''''''''''''''''
'
```

```
Sub ELSfixed()

' Selects a fixed polynomial order
' by setting iOrder equal to 1

Dim iOrder As Integer
iOrder = 1
Call ELS(iOrder)

End Sub
'
''''''''''''''''''''''''''''''''''''''''''''''''''''''''''''''
'
Sub ELSauto()

' Selects a variable polynomial order (between 1 and a
' user-selectable maximum value,MaxOrder) by setting iOrder
' equal to -1. Note that the high-order polynomials may be
' undesirable for use with, e.g., differentiation or inter-
' polation.

Dim iOrder As Integer
iOrder = -1
Call ELS(iOrder)

End Sub
'
''''''''''''''''''''''''''''''''''''''''''''''''''''''''''''''
'
Sub ELS(iOrder)

Dim A As Integer, B As Integer, DerOrder As Integer
Dim i As Integer, ii As Integer, j As Integer
Dim jj As Integer, k As Integer, m As Integer
Dim MaxOrder As Integer, n As Integer, NPts As Integer
Dim Order As Integer, PL As Integer, q As Integer
Dim s As Integer, t As Integer, Tries2 As Integer
Dim Tries3 As Integer, Tries4 As Integer

Dim GenFact As Double, Percentage As Long

Dim aa As Double, bb As Double, DeltaX As Double
Dim FTest1 As Double, FTest2 As Double, Length As Double
Dim Perc As Double, Sum As Double, SumSq As Double
Dim SumXY As Double, SumY As Double, SumY2 As Double

Dim GP() As Double, SumSquares() As Double
Dim SumX2() As Double, w() As Double, Y() As Double

Dim OptOrder As Variant, outputData As Variant
Dim OutputOrder As Variant, TestContents As Variant
Dim YData As Variant

Dim myRange As Range

Dim Ans As String

Dim z
```

```
' Preliminaries and data input

Set myRange = _
  Application.InputBox(Prompt:="The input data are " _
  & "located in column:", _
  Title:="ELS InputBox 1: Input data", Type:=8)
myRange.Select
If Selection.Columns.Count <> 1 Then
  MsgBox "Only enter a single column of input data."
  End
End If
NPts = Selection.Rows.Count
If NPts = 0 Then End
YData = myRange.Value
outputData = myRange.Value            'defines the array size
OutputOrder = myRange.Value           'defines the array size
OptOrder = myRange.Value              'defines the array size

' Test and prepare the default output range

n = 0
Selection.Offset(0, 1).Select
TestContents = Selection.Value
For i = 1 To NPts
  z = TestContents(i, 1)
  If IsEmpty(z) Then
    n = n
  Else
    n = n + 1
  End If
Next i

If iOrder = 1 Then
  If n > 0 Then
    Ans = MsgBox(" There are data in the " _
      & "column where the output " & Chr(13) & _
      "will be written. Proceed anyway and overwrite " _
      & "those data?", vbYesNo, _
      "Equidistant Least Squares Fit")
    If Ans = vbNo Then
      MsgBox ("Safeguard the data in the highlighted " _
        & "area by" & Chr(13) & "moving them to another " _
        & "place, then try again."), _
        , "Equidistant Least Squares Fit"
    End
    End If
  End If
  Selection.Offset(0, -1).Select
End If

If iOrder = -1 Then
  Selection.Offset(0, 1).Select
  TestContents = Selection.Value
  For i = 1 To NPts
    z = TestContents(i, 1)
    If IsEmpty(z) Then
      n = n
    Else
      n = n + 1
```

```
      End If
    Next i

    If n > 0 Then
      Ans = MsgBox("There are data in the TWO columns " _
        & "where the output " & Chr(13) & "will be " _
        & "written. Proceed anyway and overwrite " _
        & Chr(13) & "those data?", vbYesNo, "Equidistant " _
        & "Least Squares Fit")
      If Ans = vbNo Then
        MsgBox ("Safeguard the data in the highlighted " _
          & "area by" & Chr(13) & "moving them to another " _
          & "place, try again."), _
          , "Equidistant Least Squares Fit"
      End
      End If
    End If
    Selection.Offset(0, -2).Select
End If

' Select the length of the moving polynomial, PL

Tries2 = 0
Line2:
Length = InputBox(Prompt:="The length of the moving " _
  & "polynomial is:", _
  Title:="ELS InputBox 2: Polynomial Length")
PL = CInt(Length)

' Make sure that PL is an odd integer
' larger than 0 and smaller than NPts

If (Length <= 0 Or Length >= NPts Or PL - Length <> 0 _
  Or CInt((PL - 1) / 2) - ((Length - 1) / 2) <> 0) Then
  MsgBox "The length of the moving polynomial must" & _
    Chr(13) & "   be an odd integer larger than zero " _
    & "and " & Chr(13) & "smaller than the length of " & _
    "the input column.", , "Equidistant Least Squares Fit"
  Tries2 = Tries2 + 1
  If Tries2 = 2 Then End
  GoTo Line2
End If

' Select the order of the moving polynomial, MaxOrder

Tries3 = 0
Line3:
If iOrder = 1 Then
  MaxOrder = InputBox(Prompt:="The order of the moving" _
    & "polynomial is:", _
    Title:="ELS InputBox 3: Polynomial Order")
Else
  MaxOrder = InputBox(Prompt:="The maximum order of the " _
    & "moving polynomial is:", _
    Title:="ELS InputBox 3: Polynomial Order")
End If

' Make sure that MaxOrder > 0 and that either MaxOrder < PL
' (for ELSfixed) or MaxOrder < PL - 1 (for ELSauto).
```

```
If iOrder = 1 Then
  If (MaxOrder <= 0 Or MaxOrder >= PL) Then

    MsgBox "The order of the moving polynomial" & Chr(13) _
        & "must be larger than zero, and smaller" & Chr(13) _
        & "than the length of the moving polynomial.", , _
        "Equidistant Least Squares Fit"
    Tries3 = Tries3 + 1
    If Tries3 = 2 Then End
    GoTo Line3
  End If
Else
  If (MaxOrder <= 0 Or MaxOrder >= PL - 1) Then
    MsgBox "The maximum order of the moving polynomial" & _
        Chr(13) & "must be larger than zero, and smaller " _
        & "than" & Chr(13) & "the length of the moving " _
        & "polynomial minus 1.", , _
        "Equidistant Least Squares Fit"
    Tries3 = Tries3 + 1
    If Tries3 = 2 Then End
    GoTo Line3
  End If
End If

' Select smoothing, first derivative, or second derivative

Tries4 = 0
Line4:
DerOrder = InputBox(Prompt:="Select the order of the " _
    & "derivative" & Chr(13) & "(either 1 or 2); for " _
    & "smoothing, select 0." & Chr(13) & Chr(13) _
    & "The order of the derivative is:", _
    Title:="ELS InputBox 4:" & "Derivative Order")

' Make sure that DerOrder has the value 0, 1, or 2

If DerOrder = 0 Then
  GoTo Line6
ElseIf DerOrder = 1 Then
  GoTo Line5
ElseIf DerOrder = 2 Then
  GoTo Line5
Else
  MsgBox " The order of the moving polynomial must be" & _
    Chr(13) & "either 0 (for smoothing), 1 (for the first" _
    & Chr(13) & "derivative), or 2 (for the second " & _
    "derivative).", , "Equidistant Least Squares Fit"
  Tries4 = Tries4 + 1
  If Tries4 = 2 Then End
  GoTo Line4
End If

Line5:
DeltaX = InputBox(Prompt:="The data spacing in x is:", _
  Title:="ELS InputBox 5: X Increment")

Line6:
m = (PL - 1) / 2
```

```
ReDim Y(1 To NPts), OptOrder(1 To NPts, 1)
For i = 1 To NPts
  Y(i) = YData(i, 1)
  OptOrder(i, 1) = MaxOrder
Next i

Call ConvolutionFactors(PL, MaxOrder, DerOrder, GP, w, Y)

' THE FOLLOWING SECTION IS USED ONLY BY ELSauto

If iOrder = -1 Then

  ReDim SumX2(1 To MaxOrder)
  For j = 1 To MaxOrder
    Sum = 0
    For i = -m To m
      Sum = Sum + GP(i, j, 0) ^ 2
    Next i
    SumX2(j) = Sum
  Next j

' Calculate FValueTable(MaxOrder,PL)

  ReDim FValueTable(1 To MaxOrder, 1 To PL)
  jj = 0
  Do
    jj = jj + 1
    For ii = 1 To MaxOrder
      FValueTable(ii, jj) = Application.FInv(0.05, ii, jj)
    Next ii
  Loop Until jj = PL

  For k = m + 1 To NPts - m

    ReDim SumSquares(0 To MaxOrder)

' Calculate SumSquares for Order = 0

    Order = 0
    SumY = 0
    SumY2 = 0
    For t = -m To m
      SumY = SumY + Y(k + t)
      SumY2 = SumY2 + Y(k + t) ^ 2
    Next t
    SumSquares(0) = SumY2 - SumY ^ 2 / (2 * t + 1)

' Calculate SumSquares for Order = 1

    Order = 1
    SumSq = 0
    For t = -m To m
      SumSq = SumSq + (Smooth(PL, k, Order, t, 0, w, Y) _
        - Y(k + t)) ^ 2
    Next t
    SumSquares(1) = SumSq

' Test whether one-higher order satisfies the criterion
```

```
      Do
        Order = Order + 1
        If Order > MaxOrder Then GoTo line10

' Calculate SumSquares for Order > 1

        SumXY = 0
        For t = -m To m
          SumXY = SumXY + Y(k + t) * GP(t, Order, 0)
        Next t
        SumSquares(Order) = SumSquares(Order - 1) _
          - SumXY ^ 2 / SumX2(Order)

' First test for optimum Order

        FTest1 = _
          (SumSquares(Order - 1) - SumSquares(Order)) * _
          (PL - Order) / (SumSquares(Order))
      Loop Until _
        (FTest1 / FValueTable(1, PL - Order - 1)) < 1

' Second test for optimum Order

      If Order < MaxOrder Then
        Order = Order + 1
        SumXY = 0
        For t = -m To m
          SumXY = SumXY + Y(k + t) * GP(t, Order, 0)
        Next t
        SumSquares(Order) = SumSquares(Order - 1) _
          - SumXY ^ 2 / SumX2(Order)
        FTest2 = _
          (SumSquares(Order - 2) - SumSquares(Order)) * _
          (PL - Order) / (SumSquares(Order))
        If (FTest2 / FValueTable(2, PL - Order - 1)) < 1 _
          Then Order = Order - 1
      End If

line10:
      OptOrder(k, 1) = Order - 1

      Perc = 100 * (k / NPts)
      Percentage = Int(Perc)
      Application.StatusBar = _
        "Calculation " & Percentage & "% done."

  Next k

End If

' THIS ENDS THE SECTION USED ONLY BY ELSauto

' Prepare the output files

For k = m + 1 To NPts - m
  If k = m + 1 Then
    For t = -m To -1
      outputData(k + t, 1) = _
        Smooth(PL, k, OptOrder(k + t, 1), _
```

```
        t, DerOrder, w, Y) / (DeltaX ^ DerOrder)
      OutputOrder(k + t, 1) = OptOrder(k, 1)
    Next t
  End If

  outputData(k, 1) = _
    Smooth(PL, k, OptOrder(k, 1), 0, DerOrder, w, Y) _
    / (DeltaX ^ DerOrder)
  OutputOrder(k, 1) = OptOrder(k, 1)

  If k = NPts - m Then
    For t = 1 To m
      outputData(k + t, 1) = _
        Smooth(PL, k, OptOrder(k + t, 1), _
        t, DerOrder, w, Y) / (DeltaX ^ DerOrder)
      OutputOrder(k + t, 1) = OptOrder(k, 1)
    Next t
  End If

Next k

' Write the output files

Selection.Offset(0, 1).Select
Selection.Value = outputData
If iOrder = -1 Then
  Selection.Offset(0, 1).Select
  Selection.Value = OutputOrder
  Selection.Offset(0, -1).Select
End If

Application.StatusBar = False

End Sub
'
''''''''''''''''''''''''''''''''''''''''''''''''''''''''
'
Function GenFact(A, B)

' Computes the generalized factorial

Dim gf As Double, j As Integer

gf = 1
For j = (A - B + 1) To A
  gf = gf * j
Next j
GenFact = gf

End Function
'
''''''''''''''''''''''''''''''''''''''''''''''''''''''''
'
Public Function Smooth(PL, k, j, t, s, w, Y)

' Computes the appropriately weighted sum of the Y-values

Dim i As Integer, m As Integer, Sum As Double
m = (PL - 1) / 2
```

```
Sum = 0
For i = -m To m
  Sum = Sum + w(i, t, j, s) * Y(k + i)
Next i
Smooth = Sum

End Function
'
'''''''''''''''''''''''''''''''''''''''''''''''''''''''''''''''''
'
Sub ConvolutionFactors(PL, MaxOrder, DerOrder, GP, w, Y)

' Calculates tables of GP(i = -m to m, k = -1 to MaxOrder,
' s = 1 to DerOrder), and of W(i = -m to m, t = -m to m,
' k = -1 to MaxOrder, s = -1 to DerOrder)

' Abbreviations used:
'   DerOrder: Derivative Order
'   GP:       Gram Polynomial
'   MaxOrder: Maximum Order,
'   PL:       Polynomial Length
'   W:        Weight

Dim i As Integer, k As Integer, m As Integer
Dim s As Integer, t As Integer
Dim aa As Double, bb As Double

m = (PL - 1) / 2
ReDim GP(-m To m, -1 To MaxOrder, -1 To DerOrder)

'Evaluate the Gram polynomials for DerOrder=0

For i = -m To m
  GP(i, 0, 0) = 1
  GP(i, 1, 0) = 0
Next i
For i = -m To -1
  GP(i, 1, 0) = i / m
Next i
For i = 1 To m
  GP(i, 1, 0) = i / m
Next i
For k = 2 To MaxOrder
  aa = 2 * (2 * k - 1) / (k * (2 * m - k + 1))
  bb = ((k - 1) * (2 * m + k)) / (k * (2 * m - k + 1))
  For i = 0 To m
    GP(i, k, 0) = aa * i * GP(i, k - 1, 0) - _
      bb * GP(i, k - 2, 0)
  Next i
  For i = -m To -1
    If k Mod 2 = 0 Then
      GP(i, k, 0) = GP(-i, k, 0)
    Else
      GP(i, k, 0) = -GP(-i, k, 0)
    End If
  Next i
Next k
```

```
'Evaluate the Gram polynomials for DerOrder>0

If DerOrder > 0 Then
  For s = 1 To DerOrder
    For i = -m To m
      GP(i, -1, s) = 0
      GP(i, 0, s) = 0
    Next i
    For k = 1 To MaxOrder
      aa = 2 * (2 * k - 1) / (k * (2 * m - k + 1))
      bb = ((k - 1) * (2 * m + k)) / (k * (2 * m - k + 1))
      For i = -m To m
        GP(i, k, s) = aa * (i * GP(i, k - 1, s) + _
        s * GP(i, k - 1, s - 1)) - bb * GP(i, k - 2, s)
      Next i
    Next k
  Next s
End If

'Calculate the convolution weights

ReDim w(-m To m, -m To m, -1 To MaxOrder, -1 To DerOrder)

For k = 0 To MaxOrder
  aa = (2 * k + 1) * GenFact(2 * m, k) / _
    GenFact(2 * m + k + 1, k + 1)
  For s = 0 To DerOrder
    For i = -m To m
      For t = -m To m
        w(i, t, k, s) = w(i, t, k - 1, s) _
        + aa * GP(i, k, 0) * GP(t, k, s)
      Next t
    Next i
  Next s
Next k

End Sub
```

9.8 WLS

The macro for weighted least squares is essentially a generalization of the regular linear least squares algorithm LS. In fact, WLS can be used instead of LS by leaving the weights unspecified (while preserving their space), in which case they are all assumed to be unity. The macro implements the mathematical description given in N. R. Draper & H. Smith, *Applied Regression Analysis*, 2nd ed., Wiley, New York 1981 pp. 108-111. In short, the sought coefficients are found in the vector **b** where

$$\mathbf{b} = (\mathbf{X}^T\mathbf{W}\mathbf{X})^{-1}\mathbf{X}^T\mathbf{W}\mathbf{Y} \qquad (9.8.1)$$

where the matrix **W** contains the weights, and the other parameters are the same as in section 9.2, while the covariance matrix **V** is calculated as

$$\mathbf{V} = (\mathbf{X}^T\mathbf{W}\mathbf{X})^{-1}(\mathbf{Y}^T\mathbf{W}\mathbf{Y} - \mathbf{b}^T\mathbf{X}^T\mathbf{W}\mathbf{Y})/(N-P) \qquad (9.8.2)$$

Beyond the involvement of the weight matrix **W** (which reduces to the unit matrix for an unweighted least squares, and is treated differently in order to minimize memory usage), the macro is similar to LS.

```
'''''''''''''''''''''''''''''''''''''''''''''''''''''''''''''''''''''
''''''''''''''''^^^^^^^^^^^^^^^^^^^^^^^^^^^^^^^'''''''''''''''''
''''''''''''''^                                    ^'''''''''''''''''
''''''''''''''^    WEIGHTED LEAST SQUARES     ^'''''''''''''''''
''''''''''''''^                                    ^'''''''''''''''''
'''''''''''''''^^^^^^^^^^^^^^^^^^^^^^^^^^^^^^^'''''''''''''''''
'''''''''''''''''''''''''''''''''''''''''''''' (c) R. de Levie
'''''''''''''''''''''''''''''''''''''''''''''v 4.10, Oct. 1, 2004

' The function of the following two drivers is merely to
' set the value of one parameter, p, equal to either one or
' zero, in order to choose between a general least squares
' fitting (p = 1) or one that forces the curve through the
' origin (p = 0).
'
Sub WLS0()            ' for least squares fit
                      ' through the origin
Dim p As Double
p = 0
Call WeightedLeastSquares(p)
End Sub


'''''''''''''''''''''''''''''''''''''''''''''''''''''''''''''''''''


Sub WLS1()           ' for general least squares fit
Dim p As Double
p = 1
Call WeightedLeastSquares(p)
End Sub


'''''''''''''''''''''''''''''''''''''''''''''''''''''''''''''''''''


Sub WeightedLeastSquares(p)

' PURPOSE:

' The macros WLS1 and WLS0 compute the parameters and their
' standard deviations for a weighted least squares fit to
' data in 2 or more columns. The macros set the input para-
' meter p for the subroutine WeightedLeastSquares: p = 1
' causes a general weighted least squares fit to the data,
' while p = 0 forces the fit to pass through the origin,
' i.e., it assumes that y = 0 for x = 0.

' SUBROUTINES:

' This macro requires the subroutines Multiply, DMult,
' Invert, and Transpose

' INPUT:

' The input data must be organized in columns, arranged as
' follows. The first column must contain the dependent va-
' riable y. The second column should contain the weights w
```

```
' of the individual points. The third (and any subsequent)
' column(s) must contain the independent variable(s) x.

' If an unweighted least squares is desired, leave the
' weights blank, or enter the same number (say, 1, or 13)
' for all individual weights.

' Do NOT delete the second column, as in that case the
' macro will misinterpret the input.

' OUTPUT:

' The macro labels the coefficients and standard devia-
' tions, except when there is no space available for them
' because the first data column is at the left edge of the
' spreadsheet.

' The macro also provides the covariance matrix and,
' optionally, the corresponding linear correlation
' coefficient array.

' If the data to be analyzed are the result of a trans-
' formation (such as taking logarithms of an exponential
' decay), the standard deviation of the overall fit will
' not yield the correct answer with respect to those
' original, untransformed data, because the macro does not
' read those data. If that standard deviation is desired,
' it is best computed separately on the spreadsheet.

' PROCEDURE:

' Before calling the macro, make sure that the output area
' is free of valuable data. To find out the reach of the
' output, try out the macro but, in the "Overwrite?"
' message box, note the number of rows required, answer
' "No" to whether the data can be overwritten, move the
' sensitive data, then try the macro again.

' In order to start the process, highlight the entire input
' data block, then call WLS1 or WLS0.

' EXAMPLES:

' Use of this macro is illustrated starting in sections
' 3.16 through 3.19 of Advanced Excel.

' ''''''''''''''''''''''''''''''''''''''''''''''''''''''''''''''

' NOTATION:
' This subroutine computes the parameters and their
' standard deviations for a weighted or unweighted least
' squares fit to data in 3 or more columns. The columns
' must be arranged as follows:

' The first column must contain the dependent variable y.
' The second column must contain the weights w for y. For
' an unweighted least squares fit, leave this column blank,
' or fill it with ones, but do not omit it. The third (and
' possibly subsequent) column(s) must contain the indepen-
' dent variable(s) x.
```

```
' The subroutine requires an input parameter p: p = 1
' causes a general weighted least squares fit to the data,
' while p = 0 forces the fit to pass through the origin,
' i.e., it assumes that Y = 0 for X = 0. The subroutine is
' therefore called by a driver (WLS0 or WLS1) that sets the
' value of p.

' The weights are placed in a wVector rather than in a
' weight matrix, in order to save memory. This has required
' a separate multiplication subroutine, DMult.

Dim ccMax As Integer, cMax As Integer, i As Long
Dim j As Integer, m As Integer, n As Integer, rMax As Long

Dim Root As Double, SSR As Double
Dim StDevF As Double, sumW As Double
Dim u As Double, varY As Double

Dim DataArray As Variant, outputArray As Variant
Dim lccArray As Variant
Dim vArray As Variant, v0Array As Variant

Dim myRange As Range

Dim Answer, hAnswer, iAnswer, jAnswer, kAnswer, wVector
Dim bArray, btArray, btqArray, pArray, piArray
Dim qArray, XArray, xtArray, YArray, ytArray, ytyArray

' Determination of the array size:

Begin:
rMax = Selection.Rows.Count
cMax = Selection.Columns.Count
ccMax = cMax - 1
u = 1

' If area was not highlighted

If rMax = 1 And cMax = 1 Then
  hAnswer = MsgBox("You forgot to highlight" _
    & Chr(13) & "the block of input data." _
    & Chr(13) & "Do you want to do so now?" _
    , vbYesNo, "Weighted Least Squares")
  If hAnswer = vbNo Then End
  If hAnswer = vbYes Then
    Set myRange = Application.InputBox(Prompt:= _
      "The input data are located in:", Type:=8)
    myRange.Select
  End If
  GoTo Begin
End If

' Check that the number of columns is at least 3:

If cMax < 3 Then
  MsgBox "There must be at least three columns, one" & _
  Chr(13) & "for Y, one for W, and one or more for X.", _
  , "Weighted Least Squares Fit"
  End
```

```
End If

' Check that there are more data than coefficients :

If rMax - cMax - p + 2 <= 0 Then
  MsgBox "With " & rMax & " data, WLS" & p & " can only deter-" & _
    Chr(13) & "mine " & rMax - 1 & " least squares coefficients." & _
    Chr(13) & Chr(13) & "Add more data, or reduce the re-" & _
    Chr(13) & "quested number of coefficients."
  End
End If

' Dimension the arrays:

ReDim wVector(1 To rMax) As Double
ReDim YArray(1 To rMax, 1 To 1) As Double
ReDim XArray(1 To rMax, 1 To ccMax) As Double
ReDim ytArray(1 To 1, 1 To rMax) As Double
ReDim ytwArray(1 To 1, 1 To rMax) As Double
ReDim ytwyArray(1 To 1, 1 To 1) As Double
ReDim xtArray(1 To ccMax, 1 To rMax) As Double
ReDim xtwArray(1 To ccMax, 1 To rMax) As Double
ReDim pArray(1 To ccMax, 1 To ccMax) As Double
ReDim piArray(1 To ccMax, 1 To ccMax) As Double
ReDim qArray(1 To ccMax, 1 To 1) As Double
ReDim bArray(1 To ccMax, 1 To 1) As Double
ReDim btArray(1 To 1, 1 To ccMax) As Double
ReDim btqArray(1 To 1, 1 To 1) As Double
ReDim vArray(1 To ccMax, 1 To ccMax) As Double
ReDim v0Array(1 To ccMax + p - 1, 1 To ccMax + p - 1) _
  As Double
ReDim lccArray(1 To ccMax + p - 1, 1 To ccMax + p - 1) _
  As Double

' Read the dataArray, then fill the various input arrays:
' yArray, wArray, and xArray. The wArray contains zeros
' except that it has the individual, normalized weights as
' its diagonal elements.

DataArray = Selection.Value

For i = 1 To rMax
  YArray(i, 1) = DataArray(i, 1)
Next i

For i = 1 To rMax
  If IsEmpty(DataArray(i, 1)) Then
    MsgBox "Y-value(s) missing", _
      , "Weighted Least Squares"
    End
  End If
Next i
For i = 1 To rMax
  If IsEmpty(DataArray(i, 2)) Then DataArray(i, 2) = u
Next i
For j = 3 To cMax
  For i = 1 To rMax
    If IsEmpty(DataArray(i, j)) Then
```

```
          MsgBox "X-value(s) missing", _
            , "Weighted Least Squares"
          End
        End If
    Next i
  Next j

' Fill wVector with the listed normalized weights,
' where the normalization factor is sumW / rMax

sumW = 0
For i = 1 To rMax
  sumW = sumW + DataArray(i, 2)
Next i
For i = 1 To rMax
  wVector(i) = DataArray(i, 2) * rMax / sumW
Next i

' Fill the first column of xArray with zeroes (for p = 0)
' or ones (for p = 1), the rest with the data in the
' x-column(s)

For i = 1 To rMax
  XArray(i, 1) = p
Next i
For j = 3 To cMax
  For i = 1 To rMax
    XArray(i, (j - 1)) = DataArray(i, j)
  Next i
Next j

' Compute b = (X' W X)" X' W Y , where ' or t denote
' transposition, and " or i indicate inversion

' The various arrays and their dimensions (rows, columns)
' are:
'    Y            = yArray        (  rmax,     1)
'    W            = wVector       (  rmax)
'    X            = xArray        (  rmax, ccmax)
'    X'           = xtArray       ( ccmax,  rmax)
'    X' W         = xtwArray      ( ccmax,  rmax)
'    X' W X       = pArray        ( ccmax, ccmax)
'    (X' W X)"    = piArray       ( ccmax, ccmax)
'    X' W Y       = qArray        ( ccmax,    1)
'    b            = bArray        ( ccmax,    1)

Call Transpose(XArray, rMax, ccMax, xtArray)
Call DMult(xtArray, ccMax, rMax, wVector, xtwArray)
Call Multiply(xtwArray, ccMax, rMax, XArray, ccMax, pArray)
Call Invert(pArray, ccMax, piArray)
Call Multiply(xtwArray, ccMax, rMax, YArray, 1, qArray)
Call Multiply(piArray, ccMax, ccMax, qArray, 1, bArray)

' Check against overwriting spreadsheet data

Selection.Offset(2, 0).Select
outputArray = Selection.Value
Selection.Offset(-2, 0).Select

m = 0
```

```
If (p = 0 And cMax = 3) Then
  For i = 1 To 3
    Selection.Offset(1, 0).Select
    outputArray = Selection.Value
    For j = 1 To cMax
      If IsEmpty(outputArray(rMax, j)) Then
        m = m
      Else
        m = m + 1
      End If
    Next j
  Next i
  Selection.Offset(-3, 0).Select
  If m > 0 Then Answer = MsgBox("There are data in the " _
    & "three lines below the" & Chr(13) & _
    "input data array. " & "Can they be overwritten?", _
    vbYesNo, "Overwrite?")
  If Answer = vbNo Then End
Else
  For i = 1 To 3 + p + cMax
    Selection.Offset(1, 0).Select
    outputArray = Selection.Value
    For j = 1 To cMax
      If IsEmpty(outputArray(rMax, j)) Then
        m = m
      Else
        m = m + 1
      End If
    Next j
  Next i
  Selection.Offset(-3 - p - cMax, 0).Select
  If m > 0 Then Answer = MsgBox("There are data in the " _
    & 1 + p + cMax & " lines below the" & Chr(13) & _
    "input data array. " & "Can they be overwritten?", _
    vbYesNo, "Overwrite?")
  If Answer = vbNo Then End
End If

' The additional arrays and their dimensions (rows,
' columns) are:
'    Y'         = ytArray         (    1,   rmax)
'    Y' W       = ytwArray        (    1,   rmax)
'    Y' W Y     = ytwyArray       (    1,      1)
'    b'         = btArray         (    1,  ccmax)
'    b' X' W Y  = btqArray        (    1,      1)

Call Transpose(YArray, rMax, 1, ytArray)
Call Transpose(bArray, ccMax, 1, btArray)
Call DMult(ytArray, 1, rMax, wVector, ytwArray)
Call Multiply(ytwArray, 1, rMax, YArray, 1, ytwyArray)
Call Multiply(btArray, 1, ccMax, qArray, 1, btqArray)

' Calculate SSR = Y'WY - b'X'WY, and then varY, the vari-
' ance of y, as varY = SSR/(rmax-ccmax); and vArray, the
' covariance matrix, as V = (X'WX)" times varY, of which
' we here only use the diagonal elements, i.e., the vari-
' ances.

SSR = ytwyArray(1, 1) - btqArray(1, 1)
varY = SSR / (rMax - ccMax - p + 1)
```

```
If SSR >= 0 Then StDevF = Sqr(varY)
If SSR < 0 Then
  StDevF = Sqr(-varY)
  MsgBox "SSR is " & SSR & ", which is negative!"
End If

For i = 1 To ccMax
  For j = 1 To ccMax
    vArray(i, j) = varY * piArray(i, j)
  Next j
Next i

Application.ScreenUpdating = False
ActiveCell.Offset(rMax, 0).Select

For j = 1 To cMax
  ActiveCell.Font.Bold = True
  ActiveCell.Font.Italic = True
  ActiveCell.Value = ""
  ActiveCell.Offset(0, 1).Select
Next j
ActiveCell.Offset(0, -cMax).Select
ActiveCell.HorizontalAlignment = xlRight
ActiveCell.Value = "Coeff:"
ActiveCell.Offset(0, 1).Select
For j = 2 - p To ccMax
  ActiveCell.Value = bArray(j, 1)
  ActiveCell.Offset(0, 1).Select
Next j
ActiveCell.Offset(1, 1 - p - cMax).Select
For j = 1 To cMax
  ActiveCell.Font.Bold = False
  ActiveCell.Font.Italic = True
  ActiveCell.Value = ""
  ActiveCell.Offset(0, 1).Select
Next j
ActiveCell.Offset(0, -cMax).Select
ActiveCell.Font.Bold = False
ActiveCell.Font.Italic = True
ActiveCell.HorizontalAlignment = xlRight
ActiveCell.Value = "StDev:"
ActiveCell.Offset(0, 1).Select
For j = 2 - p To ccMax
  If vArray(j, j) < 1E-40 Then
    ActiveCell.Value = "<1E-20"
  Else
    ActiveCell.Value = Sqr(vArray(j, j))
  End If
  ActiveCell.Offset(0, 1).Select
Next j
ActiveCell.Offset(1, 1 - p - cMax).Select
For j = 1 To cMax
  ActiveCell.Font.Bold = False
  ActiveCell.Font.Italic = True
  ActiveCell.Value = ""
  ActiveCell.Offset(0, 1).Select
Next j
ActiveCell.Offset(0, -cMax).Select
ActiveCell.HorizontalAlignment = xlRight
ActiveCell.Value = "Sf:"
ActiveCell.Offset(0, 1).Select
ActiveCell.Value = StDevF
ActiveCell.Offset(1, -1).Select
```

```
' Compute and display the covariance matrix

If (p = 0 And cMax = 3) Then GoTo LastLine

If p = 0 Then
  For i = 1 To cMax - 2
    For j = 1 To cMax
      ActiveCell.Font.Bold = False
      ActiveCell.Font.Italic = True
      ActiveCell.Font.ColorIndex = 1
      ActiveCell.Value = ""
      ActiveCell.Offset(0, 1).Select
    Next j
    ActiveCell.Offset(1, -cMax).Select
  Next i
  ActiveCell.Offset(2 - cMax, 0).Select
  ActiveCell.Font.Bold = True
  ActiveCell.Font.ColorIndex = 11
  ActiveCell.HorizontalAlignment = xlRight
  ActiveCell.Value = "CM:"
  ActiveCell.Offset(0, 1).Select
  For i = 1 To cMax - 2
    For j = 1 To cMax - 2
      ActiveCell.Font.ColorIndex = 11
      ActiveCell.Value = vArray(i, j)
      ActiveCell.Offset(0, 1).Select
    Next j
    ActiveCell.Offset(1, 2 - cMax).Select
  Next i

Else
  For i = 1 To cMax - 1
    For j = 1 To cMax
      ActiveCell.Font.Bold = False
      ActiveCell.Font.Italic = True
      ActiveCell.Font.ColorIndex = 1
      ActiveCell.Value = ""
      ActiveCell.Offset(0, 1).Select
    Next j
    ActiveCell.Offset(1, -cMax).Select
  Next i
  ActiveCell.Offset(1 - cMax, 0).Select
  ActiveCell.Font.Bold = True
  ActiveCell.Font.ColorIndex = 11
  ActiveCell.HorizontalAlignment = xlRight
  ActiveCell.Value = "CM:"
  ActiveCell.Offset(0, 1).Select
  For i = 1 To cMax - 1
    For j = 1 To cMax - 1
      ActiveCell.Font.ColorIndex = 11
      ActiveCell.Value = vArray(i, j)
      ActiveCell.Offset(0, 1).Select
    Next j
    ActiveCell.Offset(1, 1 - cMax).Select
  Next i
End If

Application.ScreenUpdating = True

' Provide as optional output the array of linear
' correlation coefficients. The user specifies
' the cell block in which to write this array
```

```
If p = 0 And cMax = 3 Then GoTo LastLine
jAnswer = MsgBox("Do you want to see the " _
  & "matrix of linear correlation" _
  & Chr(13) & "coefficients? It will need a " _
  & "block of " & cMax + p - 2 _
  & " by " & cMax + p - 2 & " cells.", vbYesNo, _
  "Least Squares Fit")


OutlineMatrix:

If jAnswer = vbYes Then
  Set myRange = Application.InputBox(Prompt:= _
    "The array should be located in:", Type:=8)
  myRange.Select

' Make sure that the selected block has the correct size

  If Selection.Rows.Count <> cMax + p - 2 Then
    MsgBox "The selected range does not have " _
      & cMax + p - 2 & " rows. Please correct.", _
      , "Least Squares Fit"
    GoTo OutlineMatrix
  End If
  If Selection.Columns.Count <> cMax + p - 2 Then
    MsgBox "The selected range does not have " _
      & cMax + p - 2 & " columns. Please correct", _
      , "Least Squares Fit"
    GoTo OutlineMatrix
  End If

' Draw a box around the reserved area

    Selection.Borders(xlEdgeTop).LineStyle = xlDashDot
    Selection.Borders(xlEdgeTop).Weight = xlThin
    Selection.Borders(xlEdgeRight).LineStyle = xlDashDot
    Selection.Borders(xlEdgeRight).Weight = xlThin
    Selection.Borders(xlEdgeBottom).LineStyle = xlDashDot
    Selection.Borders(xlEdgeBottom).Weight = xlThin
    Selection.Borders(xlEdgeLeft).LineStyle = xlDashDot
    Selection.Borders(xlEdgeLeft).Weight = xlThin

' Write the array of linear correlation coefficients

  If p = 0 Then
    For i = 1 To cMax - 2
      For j = 1 To cMax - 2
        v0Array(i, j) = vArray(i + 1, j + 1)
      Next j
    Next i
    For i = 1 To cMax - 2
      For j = 1 To cMax - 2
        Root = Sqr(v0Array(i, i) * v0Array(j, j))
        lccArray(i, j) = v0Array(i, j) / Root
    Next j
    Next i
    Selection.Value = lccArray
  End If

  If p = 1 Then
```

```
   For i = 1 To cMax - 1
     For j = 1 To cMax - 1
       v0Array(i, j) = vArray(i, j)
     Next j
   Next i
   For i = 1 To cMax - 1
     For j = 1 To cMax - 1
       Root = Sqr(vArray(i, i) * vArray(j, j))
       lccArray(i, j) = vArray(i, j) / Root
     Next j
   Next i
   Selection.Value = lccArray
  End If
End If

LastLine:

End Sub
```

9.9 *SolverAid*

SolverAid provides imprecision estimates for the parameters computed by Solver which, typically, minimizes the sum of squares χ^2 between the experimental and calculated functions y, i.e., $\chi^2 = \Sigma\, (y_{n,exp} - y_{n,cal})^2$. SolverAid calculates the standard deviations $s_i = \sqrt{[m_{ii}^{-1}\chi^2/(N-P)]}$ where $m_{ij} = \Sigma\, (\partial y_{n,cal}/\partial a_i)\, (\partial y_{n,cal}/\partial a_j)$, N is the number of data points, and P that of the number of adjustable parameters used. The partial derivatives are obtained by using the VBA instruction Selection.Replace A, B to multiply one adjustable parameter at a time by 1.000001 (i.e., by temporarily incrementing it by 10^{-4}%) and to measure the resulting change in $y_{n,cal}$ before resetting the parameter to its original value. SolverAid also provides the covariance matrix and, optionally, the corresponding linear correlation coefficients.

```
'''''''''''''''''''''''''''''''''''''''''''''''''''''''''''''''
''''''''''''''''^^^^^^^^^^^^^^^^^^^^^^^^^^^^^^^^^^^^'''''''''''''
''''''''''''''^                                   ^'''''''''''''
''''''''''''''^          SOLVER AID               ^'''''''''''''
''''''''''''''^                                   ^'''''''''''''
''''''''''''''^^^^^^^^^^^^^^^^^^^^^^^^^^^^^^^^^^^^^'''''''''''''
'''''''''''''''''''''''''''''''''''''''''''''''''(c) R. de Levie
'''''''''''''''''''''''''''''''''''''''''''''''''v 4.10, Oct. 1, 2004

' PURPOSE:

' SolverAid takes the results of Solver and computes the
' corresponding standard deviations. The macro displays the
' covariance matrix as well, and (optionally) the corres-
' sponding array of linear correlation coefficients.

' REQUIREMENTS:

' This macro requires the subroutine Invert
```

```
' INPUT:

' The input information must be provided in response to
' three input boxes, which ask for (1) the location of the
' row or column containing the parameters determined by
' Solver; (2) the location of the cell containing the para-
' meter to be minimized, such as SSR; and (3) the COLUMN
' containing the y-values calculated with the Solver-deter-
' mined parameters. Note that these data must contain the
' formulas referring to the Solver-determined parameters;
' a column containing merely their numerical values will
' NOT do.

' OUTPUT:

' Provided that these spaces are unoccupied, the standard
' deviations of the fit, and the standard deviation(s) of
' the parameter(s), will be placed directly, in italics, to
' the right of the corresponding parameters (when these
' were entered as a column), or below them (for row input).
' Otherwise, the result(s) will be displayed in message
' boxes. It is therefore most convenient to leave blank
' the spreadsheet cells to the right of (or below) the
' parameters and of SSR.

' Warning: If space to be used for output contains text or
' other non-numerical information (such as time or date),
' the macro will crash.

' The covariance matrix shows the variances on its main
' (top-left to bottom-right) diagonal, and the correspon-
' ding covariances in the off-diagonal positions. The user
' must specify where on the spreadsheet it should be
' displayed.

' The user also specifies the location on the spreadsheet
' of the optional array of the correlation coefficients,
' for which all elements on the main diagonal are 1, and
' all off-diagonal elements are calculated as r(i,j) =
' v(i,j)/sqr[(v(i)*v(j)].

' PROCEDURE:

' In order to start the process, call the macro, and pro-
' vide the requested addresses (either by typing them, or
' by using the 'point & shoot' method) to the input boxes.

' EXAMPLES:

' Use of this macro is illustrated starting in sections
' 4.1 and 4.2 of Advanced Excel.
```

Sub SolverAid()

```
' NOTATION USED:

'    P1:   single Parameter determined by Solver
'    PP:   multiple parameters determined by Solver
```

```
'         These must be in either a single, contiguous row
'         or in a single, contiguous column.
'   SP:   standard deviations on those parameters
'   SSR:  the sum of the residuals squared
'         used to optimize Solver
'   Sf:   the standard deviation on the function
'   YC:   the Y-values computed with the parameters P
'         NOTE: THESE MUST BE IN A SINGLE, CONTIGUOUS COLUMN
'   c:    prefix denoting the number of columns:
'         cP = columns of PP, cX = columns of XE
'         Note: cP and cX should be 1
'   r:    prefix denoting the number of rows:
'         rP = rows of PP, rY = rows of YC


' Dimension all parameters

Dim cP As Integer, cSSR As Integer, cY As Integer
Dim i As Integer, ii As Integer, j As Long
Dim n1 As Integer, n2 As Integer, n3 As Integer
Dim rP As Integer, rY As Long, rrY As Long
Dim rSSR As Integer
Dim P1Value As Double, Root As Double
Dim SDD1 As Double, SP1 As Double
Dim SP1Value As Double, SSRValue As Double
Dim Sf As Double, SYValue As Double, z As Double
Dim CorrelCoeff As Variant, CovarValue As Variant
Dim PPValue As Variant, SPValue As Variant
Dim YCValue As Variant
Dim YYValue As Variant, YYValue1 As Variant
Dim myRange1 As Range, myRange2 As Range
Dim myRange3 As Range, myRange4 As Range
Dim Answer, iAnswer, iiAnswer, SP1Address, SYAddress
Dim TryAgainA, TryAgainB, TryAgainC, TryAgainD


' Select the computed Solver parameter P1 or parameters

Set myRange1 = Application.InputBox(Prompt:= _
   "The parameters determined by Solver are located in:", _
   Title:="SolverAid InputBox 1: Solver parameters", _
   Type:=8)
myRange1.Select
cP = Selection.Columns.Count
rP = Selection.Rows.Count
If cP = 0 Then End
If cP > 1 And rP > 1 Then
  MsgBox "The Solver-determined parameters" & Chr(13) & _
  "must either be in a single contiguous" & Chr(13) & _
  "column, or in a single contiguous row."
  End
End If
If cP = 1 And rP = 1 Then P1Value = Selection.Value
If cP = 1 And rP > 1 Then PPValue = Selection.Value
If cP > 1 And rP = 1 Then PPValue = Selection.Value


' Replace any zeros in the input parameters
' by small non-zero numbers

If cP = 1 And rP = 1 Then
  P1Value = Selection.Value
```

```
      If (IsEmpty(P1Value) Or P1Value = 0) Then P1Value = 1E-20
  ElseIf rP > 1 Then
    PPValue = Selection.Value
    For i = 1 To rP
      If (IsEmpty(PPValue(i, 1)) Or PPValue(i, 1) = 0) Then _
        PPValue(i, 1) = 1E-20
    Next i
  ElseIf cP > 1 Then
    PPValue = Selection.Value
    For i = 1 To cP
      If (IsEmpty(PPValue(1, i)) Or PPValue(1, i) = 0) Then _
        PPValue(1, i) = 1E-20
    Next i
  End If

  ' Test and prepare the default output range for the
  ' standard deviations of the parameters, SP, to the
  ' right of the parameters for a single or columnar
  ' input, below the parameter for a row input.

  n1 = 0
  If cP = 1 And rP = 1 Then
    Selection.Offset(0, 1).Select
    SP1Address = Selection.Address
    SP1Value = Selection.Value
    If IsEmpty(SP1Value) Then
      n1 = n1
    Else
      n1 = n1 + 1
    End If
    Selection.Offset(0, -1).Select
  ElseIf rP > 1 Then
    Selection.Offset(0, 1).Select
    SPValue = Selection.Value
    For i = 1 To rP
      If IsEmpty(SPValue(i, 1)) Then
        n1 = n1
      Else
        n1 = n1 + 1
      End If
    Next i
    Selection.Offset(0, -1).Select
  Else
    Selection.Offset(1, 0).Select
    SPValue = Selection.Value
    For i = 1 To cP
      If IsEmpty(SPValue(1, i)) Then
        n1 = n1
      Else
        n1 = n1 + 1
      End If
    Next i
    Selection.Offset(-1, 0).Select
  End If

  ' Select the computed chi-squared value, SSR

  Set myRange2 = Application.InputBox(Prompt:= _
    "The sum of squares of the residuals is located in:", _
```

```
    Title:="SolverAid InputBox 2: SSR", Type:=8)
myRange2.Select
cSSR = Selection.Columns.Count
rSSR = Selection.Rows.Count
If cSSR <> 1 Then End
If rSSR <> 1 Then End
SSRValue = Selection.Value

' Test the default output range for the standard devi-
' ation of the fit, SY, to the right of SSR for single
' or columnnar parameter input, below SSR for row input

n2 = 0
If cP = 1 Then
   Selection.Offset(0, 1).Select
   SYValue = Selection.Value
   If (IsEmpty(SYValue) Or SYValue = 0) Then
     n2 = n2
     SYAddress = Selection.Address
   Else
     n2 = n2 + 1
   End If
   Selection.Offset(0, -1).Select
End If
If cP > 1 Then
   Selection.Offset(1, 0).Select
   SYValue = Selection.Value
   If (IsEmpty(SYValue) Or SYValue = 0) Then
     n2 = n2
     SYAddress = Selection.Address
   Else
     n2 = n2 + 1
   End If
   Selection.Offset(-1, 0).Select
End If

' Select the computed Y-values, YC

Set myRange3 = Application.InputBox(Prompt:= _
   "The column containing Ycalc is:", _
   Title:="SolverAid InputBox 3: Ycalc", Type:=8)
myRange3.Select
rY = Selection.Rows.Count
cY = Selection.Columns.Count
If cY <> 1 Then
   MsgBox "The Ycalc values should be in" & _
     Chr(13) & "a single, contiguous COLUMN"
   End
End If
If rY <= rP + 1 Then
   MsgBox " The number N of data pairs must be at least" & _
     Chr(13) & "larger by one than the number of " _
     & "parameters P.", , "SolverAid"
   End
End If

YCValue = Selection.Value

Application.ScreenUpdating = False
```

```vba
' Compute the partial differentials and the
' standard deviations for the one-parameter case

If cP = 1 And rP = 1 Then
  myRange1.Select
  P1Value = P1Value * 1.000001
  Selection = P1Value
  myRange3.Select
  YYValue1 = Selection.Value

' The following loop avoids counting empty rows in the
' computation of the variances and standard deviations

  n3 = 0
  For j = 1 To rY
    If IsEmpty(YYValue1(j, 1)) Then n3 = n3 + 1
  Next j
  rrY = rY - n3
  Sf = Sqr(SSRValue / (rrY - rP))

' Resume to compute the partial differentials and
' the standard deviations for the one-parameter case

  ReDim D1(1 To rY) As Double, DD1(1 To rY) As Double
  SDD1 = 0
  For j = 1 To rY
    D1(j) = (YYValue1(j, 1) - YCValue(j, 1)) / _
      (0.000001 * P1Value)
    DD1(j) = D1(j) * D1(j)
    SDD1 = SDD1 + DD1(j)
  Next j
  P1Value = P1Value / 1.000001
  myRange1.Select
  Selection.Value = P1Value
  SP1 = Sf / Sqr(SDD1)
  If n2 = 0 Then
    myRange2.Select
    Selection.Offset(0, 1).Select
    ActiveCell.Font.Italic = True
    Selection.Value = Sf
  Else
    MsgBox "The standard deviation of the fit is ", _
      , "SolverAid" & Sf
  End If
  If n1 = 0 Then
    myRange1.Select
    Selection.Offset(0, 1).Select
    ActiveCell.Font.Italic = True
    Selection.Value = SP1
  Else
    MsgBox "The standard deviation of the parameter is " _
      & SP1, , "SolverAid"
  End If

' Compute the partial differentials in
' case of a multi-parameter COLUMNAR input

ElseIf rP > 1 Then
  ReDim D(1 To rP, 1 To rY) As Double
```

```
For i = 1 To rP
  myRange1.Select
  PPValue(i, 1) = PPValue(i, 1) * 1.000001
  Selection.Value = PPValue
  myRange3.Select
  YYValue = Selection.Value
```

```
' The following loop avoids counting empty rows in the
' computation of the variances and standard deviations
```

```
  n3 = 0
  For j = 1 To rY
    If IsEmpty(YYValue(j, 1)) Then n3 = n3 + 1
  Next j
  rrY = rY - n3
  Sf = Sqr(SSRValue / (rrY - rP))
```

```
' Resume the computation of the partial differentials and
' the standard deviations for the multi-parameter case
```

```
  For j = 1 To rY
    D(i, j) = (YYValue(j, 1) - YCValue(j, 1)) / _
      (0.000001 * PPValue(i, 1))
  Next j
  PPValue(i, 1) = PPValue(i, 1) / 1.000001
Next i
myRange1.Select
Selection.Value = PPValue
```

```
ReDim DD(1 To rP, 1 To rP, 1 To rY) As Double
For i = 1 To rP
  For ii = 1 To rP
    For j = 1 To rY
      DD(i, ii, j) = D(i, j) * D(ii, j)
    Next j
  Next ii
Next i
```

```
ReDim SDD(1 To rP, 1 To rP) As Double
ReDim SDDInv(1 To rP, 1 To rP) As Double
For i = 1 To rP
  For ii = 1 To rP
    SDD(i, ii) = 0
  Next ii
Next i
For i = 1 To rP
  For ii = 1 To rP
    For j = 1 To rY
      SDD(i, ii) = SDD(i, ii) + DD(i, ii, j)
    Next j
  Next ii
Next i
```

```
Call Invert(SDD, rP, SDDInv)
```

```
' Select the option, and the block
' in which to write the matrix
```

```
TryAgainA:
```

```
Application.ScreenUpdating = True
Set myRange4 = Application.InputBox(Prompt:= _
   "The covariance matrix needs a block" & Chr(13) & _
   "of " & rP & " by " & rP & " cells." & _
   " It should be located in:", Type:=8)
myRange4.Select
CovarValue = Selection.Value
CorrelCoeff = Selection.Value
```

```
' Make sure that the selected block has the correct size
```

```
If Selection.Rows.Count <> rP Then
  MsgBox "The selected range does not have " & _
    rP & " rows." & Chr(13) & _
    "Push OK and then select a proper block."
  GoTo TryAgainA
End If
If Selection.Columns.Count <> rP Then
  MsgBox "The selected range does not have " & rP & _
    " columns." & Chr(13) & _
    "Push OK and then select a proper block."
  GoTo TryAgainA
End If
```

```
' Draw a box around the selected block
```

```
Selection.Borders(xlEdgeTop).LineStyle = xlDashDotDot
Selection.Borders(xlEdgeTop).Weight = xlThin
Selection.Borders(xlEdgeRight).LineStyle = xlDashDotDot
Selection.Borders(xlEdgeRight).Weight = xlThin
Selection.Borders(xlEdgeBottom).LineStyle = _
  xlDashDotDot
Selection.Borders(xlEdgeBottom).Weight = xlThin
Selection.Borders(xlEdgeLeft).LineStyle = xlDashDotDot
Selection.Borders(xlEdgeLeft).Weight = xlThin
```

```
' Write the covariance matrix in the selected block
```

```
For i = 1 To rP
  For j = 1 To rP
    CovarValue(i, j) = Sf * Sf * SDDInv(i, j)
  Next j
Next i
For i = 1 To rP
  For j = 1 To rP
    Root = Sqr(CovarValue(i, i) * _
      CovarValue(j, j))
    CorrelCoeff(i, j) = CovarValue(i, j) / Root
  Next j
Next i
Selection.Value = CovarValue
```

```
' Provide the optional display of the
' linear correlation coefficients
```

```
iAnswer = MsgBox("Do you also want to see the" _
  & Chr(13) & "linear correlation coefficients?", _
  vbYesNo, "SolverAid")
```

```
TryAgainB:

  If iAnswer = vbYes Then
    Application.ScreenUpdating = True
    Set myRange4 = Application.InputBox(Prompt:= _
      "The array of linear correlation coefficients" & _
      "also needs" & Chr(13) & "a block of " & rP & _
      " by " & rP & " cells." & _
      " It should be located in:", Type:=8)
    myRange4.Select
```

' Make sure that the selected block has the correct size

```
    If Selection.Rows.Count <> rP Then
      MsgBox "The selected range does not have " & _
        rP & " rows." & Chr(13) & _
        "Push OK and then select a proper block."
      GoTo TryAgainB
    End If
    If Selection.Columns.Count <> rP Then
      MsgBox "The selected range does not have " & rP & _
        " columns." & Chr(13) & _
        "Push OK and then select a proper block."
      GoTo TryAgainB
    End If
```

' Draw a box around the selected block

```
    Selection.Borders(xlEdgeTop).LineStyle = xlDashDotDot
    Selection.Borders(xlEdgeTop).Weight = xlThin
    Selection.Borders(xlEdgeRight).LineStyle = xlDashDotDot
    Selection.Borders(xlEdgeRight).Weight = xlThin
    Selection.Borders(xlEdgeBottom).LineStyle = _
      xlDashDotDot
    Selection.Borders(xlEdgeBottom).Weight = xlThin
    Selection.Borders(xlEdgeLeft).LineStyle = xlDashDotDot
    Selection.Borders(xlEdgeLeft).Weight = xlThin
```

' Write the linear correlation coefficients
' in the selected block

```
    Selection.Value = CorrelCoeff
  End If

  Application.ScreenUpdating = True
```

' Display the standard deviations of the
' Solver parameters

```
  For i = 1 To rP
    SPValue(i, 1) = Sf * Sqr(SDDInv(i, i))
  Next i
  If n1 > 0 Then
    Answer = MsgBox("There are data in the cells to the " _
      & "right of the" & Chr(13) & "Solver parameters. " _
      & "Can they be overwritten?", vbYesNo, "Overwrite?")
    If Answer = vbYes Then n1 = 0
  End If
```

```
If n1 = 0 Then
  myRange1.Select
  Selection.Offset(0, 1).Select
  Selection.Font.Italic = True
  For i = 1 To rP
    Selection.Value = SPValue
  Next i
Else
  For i = 1 To rP
    MsgBox "The standard deviation of parameter #" & _
      i & " is " & SPValue(i, 1), , "SolverAid"
  Next i
End If

' Display the standard deviation of the over-all fit

If n2 > 0 Then
  Answer = MsgBox("There are data in the cells to the" _
    & Chr(13) & "right of the sum of squares of the" _
    & Chr(13) & "residuals. Can they be overwritten?", _
    vbYesNo, "Overwrite?")
  If Answer = vbYes Then n2 = 0
End If
If n2 = 0 Then
  myRange2.Select
  Selection.Offset(0, 1).Select
  ActiveCell.Font.Italic = True
  Selection.Value = Sf
Else
  MsgBox "The standard deviation of the fit is " & Sf
End If
myRange1.Select

' Compute the partial differentials
' in case of a multi-parameter ROW input

ElseIf cP > 1 Then
  ReDim D(1 To cP, 1 To rY) As Double
  For i = 1 To cP
    myRange1.Select
    PPValue(1, i) = PPValue(1, i) * 1.000001
    Selection.Value = PPValue
    myRange3.Select
    YYValue = Selection.Value

' The following loop avoids counting empty rows in the
' computation of the variances and standard deviations

    n3 = 0
    For j = 1 To rY
      If IsEmpty(YYValue(j, 1)) Then n3 = n3 + 1
    Next j
    rrY = rY - n3
    Sf = Sqr(SSRValue / (rrY - cP))

' Resume the computation of the partial differentials and
' the standard deviations for the multi-parameter case

    For j = 1 To rY
```

```
        D(i, j) = (YYValue(j, 1) - YCValue(j, 1)) / _
          (0.000001 * PPValue(1, i))
    Next j
    PPValue(1, i) = PPValue(1, i) / 1.000001
  Next i
  myRange1.Select
  Selection.Value = PPValue

  ReDim DD(1 To cP, 1 To cP, 1 To rY) As Double
  For i = 1 To cP
    For ii = 1 To cP
      For j = 1 To rY
        DD(i, ii, j) = D(i, j) * D(ii, j)
      Next j
    Next ii
  Next i

  ReDim SDD(1 To cP, 1 To cP) As Double
  ReDim SDDInv(1 To cP, 1 To cP) As Double
  For i = 1 To cP
    For ii = 1 To cP
      SDD(i, ii) = 0
    Next ii
  Next i
  For i = 1 To cP
    For ii = 1 To cP
      For j = 1 To rY
        SDD(i, ii) = SDD(i, ii) + DD(i, ii, j)
      Next j
    Next ii
  Next i

  Call Invert(SDD, cP, SDDInv)

' Select the option, and the block
' in which to write the matrix

TryAgainC:

  Application.ScreenUpdating = True
  Set myRange4 = Application.InputBox(Prompt:= _
    "The covariance matrix needs a block" & Chr(13) & _
    "of " & cP & " by " & cP & " cells." & _
    " It should be located in:", Type:=8)
  myRange4.Select
  CovarValue = Selection.Value
  CorrelCoeff = Selection.Value

' Make sure that the selected block has the correct size

  If Selection.Rows.Count <> cP Then
    MsgBox "The selected range does not have " & _
      cP & " rows." & Chr(13) & _
      "Push OK and then select a proper block."
    GoTo TryAgainC
  End If
  If Selection.Columns.Count <> cP Then
    MsgBox "The selected range does not have " & cP & _
      " columns." & Chr(13) & _
```

```
          "Push OK and then select a proper block."
       GoTo TryAgainC
    End If

' Draw a box around the selected block

    Selection.Borders(xlEdgeTop).LineStyle = xlDashDotDot
    Selection.Borders(xlEdgeTop).Weight = xlThin
    Selection.Borders(xlEdgeRight).LineStyle = xlDashDotDot
    Selection.Borders(xlEdgeRight).Weight = xlThin
    Selection.Borders(xlEdgeBottom).LineStyle = _
      xlDashDotDot
    Selection.Borders(xlEdgeBottom).Weight = xlThin
    Selection.Borders(xlEdgeLeft).LineStyle = xlDashDotDot
    Selection.Borders(xlEdgeLeft).Weight = xlThin

' Write the covariance matrix in the selected block

    For i = 1 To cP
      For j = 1 To cP
        CovarValue(i, j) = Sf * Sf * SDDInv(i, j)
      Next j
    Next i
    For i = 1 To cP
      For j = 1 To cP
        Root = Sqr(CovarValue(i, i) * _
          CovarValue(j, j))
        CorrelCoeff(i, j) = CovarValue(i, j) / Root
      Next j
    Next i
    Selection.Value = CovarValue

' Provide the optional display of the
' linear correlation coefficients

    iAnswer = MsgBox("Do you also want to see the" _
      & Chr(13) & "linear correlation coefficients?", _
      vbYesNo, "SolverAid")

TryAgainD:

    If iAnswer = vbYes Then
      Application.ScreenUpdating = True
      Set myRange4 = Application.InputBox(Prompt:= _
        "The array of linear correlation coefficients" & _
        "also needs" & Chr(13) & "a block of " & cP & _
        " by " & cP & " cells." & _
        " It should be located in:", Type:=8)
      myRange4.Select

' Make sure that the selected block has the correct size

      If Selection.Rows.Count <> cP Then
        MsgBox "The selected range does not have " & _
          cP & " rows." & Chr(13) & _
          "Push OK and then select a proper block."
        GoTo TryAgainD
      End If
      If Selection.Columns.Count <> cP Then
```

```
      MsgBox "The selected range does not have " & cP & _
         " columns." & Chr(13) & _
         "Push OK and then select a proper block."
      GoTo TryAgainD
    End If
```

' Draw a box around the selected block

```
   Selection.Borders(xlEdgeTop).LineStyle = xlDashDotDot
   Selection.Borders(xlEdgeTop).Weight = xlThin
   Selection.Borders(xlEdgeRight).LineStyle = xlDashDotDot
   Selection.Borders(xlEdgeRight).Weight = xlThin
   Selection.Borders(xlEdgeBottom).LineStyle = _
      xlDashDotDot
   Selection.Borders(xlEdgeBottom).Weight = xlThin
   Selection.Borders(xlEdgeLeft).LineStyle = xlDashDotDot
   Selection.Borders(xlEdgeLeft).Weight = xlThin
```

' Write the linear correlation coefficients
' in the selected block

```
   Selection.Value = CorrelCoeff
  End If

  Application.ScreenUpdating = True
```

' Display the standard deviations of the
' Solver parameters

```
  For i = 1 To cP
    SPValue(1, i) = Sf * Sqr(SDDInv(i, i))
  Next i
  If n1 > 0 Then
    Answer = MsgBox("There are data in the cells " _
      & "below the" & Chr(13) & "Solver parameters. " _
      & "Can they be overwritten?", vbYesNo, "Overwrite?")
    If Answer = vbYes Then n1 = 0
  End If
  If n1 = 0 Then
    myRange1.Select
    Selection.Offset(1, 0).Select
    Selection.Font.Italic = True
    For i = 1 To cP
      Selection.Value = SPValue
    Next i
  Else
    For i = 1 To cP
      MsgBox "The standard deviation of parameter #" & _
        i & " is " & SPValue(1, i), , "SolverAid"
    Next i
  End If
```

' Display the standard deviation of the over-all fit

```
  If n2 > 0 Then
    Answer = MsgBox("There are data in the cells" _
      & Chr(13) & "below the sum of squares of the" _
      & Chr(13) & "residuals. Can they be overwritten?", _
      vbYesNo, "Overwrite?")
```

```
      If Answer = vbYes Then n2 = 0
    End If
    If n2 = 0 Then
      myRange2.Select
      Selection.Offset(1, 0).Select
      ActiveCell.Font.Italic = True
      Selection.Value = Sf
    Else
      MsgBox "The standard deviation of the fit is " & Sf
    End If
    myRange1.Select
  End If

End Sub
```

9.10 Propagation

This macro is listed here without explanation, since the algorithm for the propagation of experimental imprecision was already discussed in section 8.5.

```
''''''''''''''''''''''''''''''''''''''''''''''''''''''''''''
''''''''''''''''''''''''''''''''''''''''''''''''''''''''''''
'''''''''''''''''^^^^^^^^^^^^^^^^^^^^^^^^^^^^^^^^'''''''''''''
'''''''''''''''^                              ^'''''''''''''
'''''''''''''''^         PROPAGATION          ^'''''''''''''
'''''''''''''''^                              ^'''''''''''''
'''''''''''''''^^^^^^^^^^^^^^^^^^^^^^^^^^^^^^^^'''''''''''''
'''''''''''''''''''''''''''''''''''''''''''''''(c) R. de Levie
'''''''''''''''''''''''''''''''''''''''''''''''v 4.6, June 1, 2004

' PURPOSE:

' This macro computes the propagated standard deviation in
' a single function F based on N input parameters, based on
' their standard deviations or on the corresponding covari-
' ance matrix. When only the standard deviations are given,
' the macro will assume that the input parameters are mutu-
' ally independent. No such assumption will be made when
' the covariance matrix is provided. For a single input
' parameter, there is no distinction between the two ap-
' proaches. For more than one input parameter, the macro
' recognizes which of the two computations to perform
' because the standard deviations will be provided as a
' vector, while the covariance matrix has the form of a
' square data array. The components of the N by N covari-
' ance matrix are assumed to be in the same order as those
' of the N input parameters.

' SUBROUTINES:

' This macro does not require any subroutines

' INPUT:

' The N independent input parameter values must be placed
' either in a contiguous row or in a contiguous column.
```

```
' THEY MUST BE NUMBERS, i.e., they cannot be formulas,
' i.e., equations.

' The N standard deviations must follow the same format,
' again either in a contiguous row or column, consistent
' with the format of the input data, but can be either
' values or formulas.

' The ORDER of the input parameters and of the standard
' deviations must be the same, because the (partial)
' derivative of the function and the corresponding standard
' deviation are combined strictly on the basis of their
' sequential order. The same applies to the covariance
' matrix if this is used instead.

' OUTPUT:
' The standard deviation of the single function F will be
' placed directly to the right of (or below) that function,
' in italics, provided that this cell is either unoccupied
' or its contents can be overwritten. Otherwise, the result
' will be displayed in a message box.

' PROCEDURE:

' In order to start this macro, call it. There is no need
' to highlight anything beforehand.

' You will see an input box in which to place (either
' by typing or by the 'point-and-shoot' method) the
' address(es) of the input parameter(s). After you have
' entered these, a second input box will request the
' addresses of either the standard deviations or the
' covariance matrix. These should have been arranged in
' the same order as the earlier-entered parameters.
' Finally, a third input box will ask for the address of
' the function. The output will be provided either on the
' spreadsheet, or through message box(es).

' NOTATION:

'   N:    the number of input parameters
'   X:    single input parameter (for N=1)
'   S:    the corresponding, single standard deviation of X
'   Xi:   multiple input parameters (for N>1) NOTE: THESE
'         MUST BE IN A SINGLE, CONTIGUOUS ROW OR COLUMN
'   Si:   standard deviations of the multiple input para-
'         meters. NOTE: THESE MUST BE IN A SINGLE, CONTI-
'         GUOUS ROW OR COLUMN
'   CM:   the covariance matrix
'   F:    the single function through which the error(s)
'         propagate(s)
'   VF:   the propagated variance of the function F
'   SF:   the propagated standard deviation of function F

' We distinguish five cases:

' C = 1   one parameter P, one uncertainty U
' C = 2   parameters P and uncertainties U in column format
' C = 3   parameters P and uncertainties U in row format
```

```
' For C = 1 to 3, the uncertainty is the standard deviation

' C = 4   parameters P in column, uncertainty U in matrix
' C = 5   parameters P in row, uncertainty U in matrix

' For C = 4 or 5, the uncertainty must be in the form of
'    a covariance matrix, i.e., the uncertainties are in
'    terms of variances (the squares of the standard
'    deviations) and covariances (which may be zero).

Sub Propagation()

Dim C As Integer        'Case selector
Dim i As Integer, j As Integer, m As Integer
Dim number As Integer, LCCTest As Integer
Dim n As Integer        'Larger dimension of
                        'input parameter set
Dim NCF As Integer      'Number of Columns of output Function
Dim NCP As Integer      'Number of Columns of input Parameters
Dim NCU As Integer      'Number of Columns of the Uncertainty
                        'estimate
Dim NRF As Integer      'Number of Rows of output Function
Dim NRP As Integer      'Number of Rows of input Parameters
Dim NRU As Integer      'Number of Rows in the Uncertainty
                        'estimate

Dim FValue As Double, FFValue As Double
Dim newFiValue As Double, newFValue As Double
Dim newXValue As Double, SFValue As Double
Dim SValue As Double, VFiValue As Double
Dim VFValue As Double, XValue As Double

Dim DelValue As Variant, newXiValue As Variant
Dim SFiValue As Variant, SiValue As Variant
Dim CMValue As Variant, CMiValue As Variant
Dim XiValue As Variant
Dim myRange1 As Range, myRange2 As Range
Dim myRange3 As Range

Dim Answer, Prompt, Title

' Select the input parameters of the function

Prompt = "The input parameters of the" & Chr(13) & _
   "function are located in:"
Title = "Uncertainty Propagation InputBox 1: Input" _
   & " Parameters "
Set myRange1 = Application.InputBox(Prompt, Title, _
   Type:=8)
myRange1.Select
NRP = Selection.Rows.Count
NCP = Selection.Columns.Count

' Check the type of input

If NRP = 0 Then End
If NRP <> 1 And NCP <> 1 Then
   MsgBox "The input parameters should be placed" _
```

```
      & Chr(13) & "either in a single contiguous row," _
      & Chr(13) & "or in a single contiguous column.", _
      , "Propagation of uncertainty"
   End
ElseIf NRP = 1 And NCP = 1 Then
   n = 1
   XValue = Selection.Value
ElseIf NRP > 1 And NCP = 1 Then
   n = NRP
   XiValue = Selection.Value
   DelValue = Selection.Value        ' dimensioning the array
   newXiValue = Selection.Value      ' dimensioning the array
   SFiValue = Selection.Value        ' dimensioning the array
ElseIf NCP > 1 And NRP = 1 Then
   n = NCP
   XiValue = Selection.Value
   DelValue = Selection.Value        ' dimensioning the array
   newXiValue = Selection.Value      ' dimensioning the array
   SFiValue = Selection.Value        ' dimensioning the array
End If

' Select the uncertainty estimates (standard deviations
' or covariance matrix) of the input parameters

A:
Prompt = " The standard deviations, or" _
   & Chr(13) & "the covariance matrix, of the" _
   & Chr(13) & " input parameters are located in:"
Title = "Uncertainty Propagation InputBox 2: " _
   & "Uncertainty estimates"
Set myRange2 = Application _
   .InputBox(Prompt, Title, Type:=8)
myRange2.Select
NRU = Selection.Rows.Count
NCU = Selection.Columns.Count

' Verify that the number of parameters
' matches that of the uncertainty estimates

number = NCP + NRP - 1

If NCU = NRU Then
   If (NCU + NRU) / 2 <> number Then
      MsgBox "The dimension of the covariance matrix does" _
         & Chr(13) & "not match the number of input " _
         & "parameters"
      End
   End If
End If

If NCU <> NRU Then
   If NCU + NRU - 1 <> number Then
      MsgBox "The number of uncertainty estimates does" _
         & Chr(13) & "not match the number of input " _
         & "parameters"
      End
   End If
End If
```

```
' Verify and categorize the inputs,
' then read the uncertainties

If NCU = 0 Then End

If n = 1 And NRU = 1 And NCU = 1 Then
  C = 1      'only one input parameter
  SValue = Selection.Value
End If

If n > 1 Then     'multiple input parameters:

  If n = NRU And NCU = 1 Then
    C = 2   'the independent parameters and
            'their standard deviations are
            'located in single columns
    SiValue = Selection.Value
  End If
  If n <> NRU And NCU = 1 Then
    MsgBox "The number of entries in the two" _
      & Chr(13) & "input columns must be the same.", _
      , "Propagation of uncertainty"
    End
  End If

  If n = NCU And NRU = 1 Then
    C = 3    'the independent parameters and
             'their standard deviations are
             'located in single rows
    SiValue = Selection.Value
    If n <> NCU And NRU = 1 Then
      MsgBox "The number of entries in the two" _
        & Chr(13) & "input rows must be the same.", _
        , "Propagation of uncertainty"
      End
    End If
  End If

  If n = NCU And n = NRU Then
                   'mutually dependent parameters:

    If NCP <> NCU And NRP <> NRU Then
      MsgBox "The number of entries for the " _
        & "uncertainties does" & Chr(13) & _
        "not match the number of input parameters." _
        , , "Propagation of uncertainty"
      End
    End If

    If n = NRP And NCP = 1 Then
      C = 4 'the dependent parameters are located
            'in a single column of N items, and
            'the covariance matrix is N by N
      CMValue = Selection.Value
      CMiValue = Selection.Value
    End If

    If n = NCP And NRP = 1 Then
      C = 5 'the dependent parameters are located
```

```
                        'in a single row of N items, and
                        'the covariance matrix is N by N
             CMValue = Selection.Value
             CMiValue = Selection.Value
          End If
       End If
    End If


    If NCU > 1 And NRU > 1 And NCU <> NRU Then
       MsgBox "The covariance matrix has an" & _
          Chr(13) & " incorrect dimension. Try again.", _
          , "Propagation of uncertainty"
       GoTo A
    End If


    If NCU > 1 And NRU > 1 Then
       LCCTest = 0
       For i = 1 To n
          If CMValue(i, i) > 0.99999 And _
             CMValue(i, i) < 1.00001 Then LCCTest = LCCTest + 1
       Next i
       If LCCTest = n Then
          Answer = MsgBox("You appear to have entered the" _
             & Chr(13) & "array of linear correlation " _
             & "coefficients" & Chr(13) & "rather than the " _
             & "covariance matrix." & Chr(13) _
             & "Do you want to correct the input?", _
             vbYesNo, "Propagation of uncertainty")
          If Answer = vbYes Then GoTo A
       End If
    End If


  ' Select the function

    Set myRange3 = Application.InputBox(Prompt:= _
       "The function is located in:", Title:= _
       "Uncertainty Propagation InputBox 3: Function", Type:=8)
    myRange3.Select
    NRF = Selection.Rows.Count
    NCF = Selection.Columns.Count
    If NRF = 0 Then End
    If NRF = 1 And NCF = 1 Then FValue = Selection.Value
    If NRF <> 1 Or NCF <> 1 Then
       MsgBox "The propagation is computed only for a SINGLE " _
          & "function.", , "Propagation of uncertainty"
       End
    End If


  ' Test and prepare the default output cell for the
  ' standard deviation of the function F

  ' Place the standard deviation to the right of the cell
  ' containing F for a single input parameter, or when the
  ' input parameters are in a single column

    If n = 1 Or NCP = 1 Then
       Selection.Offset(0, 1).Select
       m = 0
       FFValue = Selection.Value
```

```
  If (IsEmpty(FFValue) Or FFValue = 0) Then
    m = m
  Else
    m = m + 1
  End If
  Selection.Offset(0, -1).Select
End If

' Place the standard deviation below F when the
' input parameters are organized in a single row.

If n > 1 And NRP = 1 Then
  Selection.Offset(1, 0).Select
  m = 0
  FFValue = Selection.Value
  If (IsEmpty(FFValue) Or FFValue = 0) Then
    m = m
  Else
    m = m + 1
  End If
  Selection.Offset(-1, 0).Select
End If

Application.ScreenUpdating = False

VFValue = 0
myRange1.Select

' Compute and display the sought standard deviation SFValue

Select Case C

Case 1
  newXValue = XValue * 1.000001
  Selection.Replace XValue, newXValue
  myRange3.Select
  newFValue = Selection.Value
  myRange1.Select
  Selection.Replace newXValue, XValue
  SFValue = Abs(1000000 * (newFValue - FValue) * SValue _
    / XValue)

  myRange3.Select
  If m > 0 Then
    Answer = MsgBox _
      ("The cell to the right of the function is " _
      & "not empty." & Chr(13) & "Can its contents " _
      & "be overwritten?", vbYesNo, "Overwrite?")
    If Answer = vbYes Then m = 0
  End If
  If m = 0 Then
    Selection.Offset(0, 1).Select
    Selection.Font.Italic = True
    Selection.Value = SFValue
  Else
    MsgBox "The standard deviation of the function is ", _
      , "Propagation of uncertainty" & SFValue
  End If
```

```
Case 2
  For i = 1 To n
    newXiValue(i, 1) = XiValue(i, 1) * 1.000001
    Selection.Item(i, 1).Replace XiValue(i, 1), newXiValue(i, 1)
    myRange3.Select
    newFiValue = Selection.Value
    myRange1.Select
    Selection.Item(i, 1).Replace newXiValue(i, 1), XiValue(i, 1)
    VFiValue = 1000000 * (newFiValue - FValue) _
      * SiValue(i, 1) / XiValue(i, 1)
    VFValue = VFValue + VFiValue ^ 2
  Next i
  SFValue = Sqr(VFValue)

  myRange3.Select
  If m > 0 Then
    Answer = MsgBox _
      ("The cell to the right of the function is " _
      & "not empty." & Chr(13) & "Can its contents " _
      & "be overwritten?", vbYesNo, "Overwrite?")
    If Answer = vbYes Then m = 0
  End If
  If m = 0 Then
    Selection.Offset(0, 1).Select
    Selection.Font.Italic = True
    Selection.Value = SFValue
  Else
    MsgBox "The standard deviation of the function is ", _
      , "Propagation of uncertainty" & SFValue
  End If

Case 3
  For j = 1 To n
    newXiValue(1, j) = XiValue(1, j) * 1.000001
    Selection.Item(1, j).Replace XiValue(1, j), newXiValue(1, j)
    myRange3.Select
    newFiValue = Selection.Value
    myRange1.Select
    Selection.Item(1, j).Replace newXiValue(1, j), XiValue(1, j)
    VFiValue = 1000000 * (newFiValue - FValue) _
      * SiValue(1, j) / XiValue(1, j)
    VFValue = VFValue + VFiValue ^ 2
  Next j
  SFValue = Sqr(VFValue)

  myRange3.Select
  If m > 0 Then
    Answer = MsgBox("The cell below the function is " _
      & "not empty." & Chr(13) & "Can its contents be " _
      & "overwritten?", vbYesNo, "Overwrite?")
    If Answer = vbYes Then m = 0
  End If
  If m = 0 Then
    Selection.Offset(1, 0).Select
    Selection.Font.Italic = True
    Selection.Value = SFValue
  Else
  End If
```

```
Case 4
  For i = 1 To n
    newXiValue(i, 1) = XiValue(i, 1) * 1.000001
    Selection.Item(i, 1).Replace XiValue(i, 1), newXiValue(i, 1)
    myRange3.Select
    newFiValue = Selection.Value
    myRange1.Select
    Selection.Item(i, 1).Replace newXiValue(i, 1), XiValue(i, 1)
    DelValue(i, 1) = 1000000 * (newFiValue - FValue) _
      / XiValue(i, 1)
  Next i
  For j = 1 To n
    For i = 1 To n
      VFValue = VFValue + DelValue(i, 1) _
        * DelValue(j, 1) * CMValue(i, j)
    Next i
  Next j
  SFValue = Sqr(VFValue)

  myRange3.Select
  If m > 0 Then
    Answer = MsgBox _
    ("The cell to the right of the function is " _
    & "not empty." & Chr(13) & "Can its contents " _
    & "be overwritten?", vbYesNo, "Overwrite?")
    If Answer = vbYes Then m = 0
  End If
  If m = 0 Then
    Selection.Offset(0, 1).Select
    Selection.Font.Italic = True
    Selection.Value = SFValue
  Else
    MsgBox "The standard deviation of the function is ", _
    , "Propagation of uncertainty" & SFValue
  End If

Case 5
  For i = 1 To n
    newXiValue(1, i) = XiValue(1, i) * 1.000001
    Selection.Item(1, i).Replace XiValue(1, i), newXiValue(1, i)
    myRange3.Select
    newFiValue = Selection.Value
    myRange1.Select
    Selection.Item(1, i).Replace newXiValue(1, i), XiValue(1, i)
    DelValue(1, i) = 1000000 * (newFiValue - FValue) _
      / XiValue(1, i)
  Next i
  For i = 1 To n
    For j = 1 To n
      VFValue = VFValue + DelValue(1, i) _
        * DelValue(1, j) * CMValue(j, i)
    Next j
  Next i
  SFValue = Sqr(VFValue)

  myRange3.Select
  If m > 0 Then
    Answer = MsgBox("The cell below the function is " _
      & "not empty." & Chr(13) & "Can its contents be " _
```

```
              & "overwritten?", vbYesNo, "Overwrite?")
        If Answer = vbYes Then m = 0
      End If
      If m = 0 Then
        Selection.Offset(1, 0).Select
        Selection.Font.Italic = True
        Selection.Value = SFValue
      Else
        MsgBox "The standard deviation of the function is ", _
          , "Propagation of uncertainty" & SFValue
      End If

  End Select

End Sub
```

9.11 Matrix operations

Below are listed the auxiliary subroutines Invert, Multiply, Transpose, and DMult used in matrix manipulations. The inversion subroutine uses Gauss-Jordan elimination, and closely follows many such routines available in the early, open literature. However, rather than making the user look for these or, worse, trying to reinvent the wheel by starting to write these anew, we suggest going to a general source of suitable code, such as the Basic version of the *Numerical Recipes*, in which case only minimal changes (such as declaring non-integer variables in double precision, and some integer variables as Long) are needed. Permission to reproduce some code from the *Numerical Recipes* is gratefully acknowledged.

```
'''''''''''''''''''''''''''''''''''''''''''''''''''''''''''''''''''
'''''''''''''''''''''''''''''''''       '''''''''''''''''''''''''
'''''''''''''''''''''''''''''''     INVERT    '''''''''''''''''''''
'''''''''''''''''''''''''''''''''       '''''''''''''''''''''''''
'''''''''''''''''''''''''''''''''''''''''''''''''''''''''''''''''''
```

```
' The square input and output matrices are Min and Mout
' respectively; nrc is the number of rows and columns in
' Min and Mout

Sub Invert(Min, nrc, Mout)

Dim i As Integer, icol As Integer, irow As Integer
Dim j As Integer, k As Integer, L As Integer, LL As Integer
Dim big As Double, dummy As Double
Dim n As Integer, pivinv As Double
Dim u As Double

n = nrc + 1
ReDim bb(1 To n, 1 To n) As Double
ReDim ipivot(1 To n) As Double
ReDim Index(1 To n) As Double
ReDim indexr(1 To n) As Double
ReDim indexc(1 To n) As Double
u = 1
```

```
' Copy the input matrix in order to retain it

For i = 1 To nrc
  For j = 1 To nrc
    Mout(i, j) = Min(i, j)          'Min rather than M1
  Next j
Next i

' The following is the Gauss-Jordan elimination routine
' GAUSSJ from J. C. Sprott, "Numerical Recipes: Routines
' and Examples in BASIC", Cambridge University Press,
' Copyright (C)1991 by Numerical Recipes Software. Used by
' permission. Use of this routine other than as an integral
' part of the present book requires an additional license
' from Numerical Recipes Software. Further distribution is
' prohibited. The routine has been modified to yield
' double-precision results.

For j = 1 To nrc
  ipivot(j) = 0
Next j
For i = 1 To nrc
  big = 0
  For j = 1 To nrc
    If ipivot(j) <> u Then
      For k = 1 To nrc
        If ipivot(k) = 0 Then
          If Abs(Mout(j, k)) >= big Then
            big = Abs(Mout(j, k))
            irow = j
            icol = k
          End If
          ElseIf ipivot(k) > 1 Then Exit Sub
        End If
      Next k
    End If
  Next j
  ipivot(icol) = ipivot(icol) + 1
  If irow <> icol Then
    For L = 1 To nrc
      dummy = Mout(irow, L)
      Mout(irow, L) = Mout(icol, L)
      Mout(icol, L) = dummy
    Next L
    For L = 1 To nrc
      dummy = bb(irow, L)
      bb(irow, L) = bb(icol, L)
      bb(icol, L) = dummy
    Next L
  End If
  indexr(i) = irow
  indexc(i) = icol
  If Mout(icol, icol) = 0 Then Exit Sub
  pivinv = u / Mout(icol, icol)
  Mout(icol, icol) = u
  For L = 1 To nrc
    Mout(icol, L) = Mout(icol, L) * pivinv
    bb(icol, L) = bb(icol, L) * pivinv
  Next L
```

```
   For LL = 1 To nrc
     If LL <> icol Then
       dummy = Mout(LL, icol)
       Mout(LL, icol) = 0
       For L = 1 To nrc
         Mout(LL, L) = Mout(LL, L) - Mout(icol, L) * dummy
         bb(LL, L) = bb(LL, L) - bb(icol, L) * dummy
       Next L
     End If
   Next LL
Next i
For L = nrc To 1 Step -1
  If indexr(L) <> indexc(L) Then
    For k = 1 To nrc
      dummy = Mout(k, indexr(L))
      Mout(k, indexr(L)) = Mout(k, indexc(L))
      Mout(k, indexc(L)) = dummy
    Next k
  End If
Next L
Erase indexc, indexr, ipivot

End Sub
```

```
'''''''''''''''''''''''''''''''''''''''''''''''''''''''''''
'''''''''''''''''''''''''           '''''''''''''''''''''''
'''''''''''''''''''''''''  MULTIPLY  '''''''''''''''''''''''
'''''''''''''''''''''''''           '''''''''''''''''''''''
'''''''''''''''''''''''''''''''''''''''''''''''''''''''''''
```

```
Sub Multiply(M1, r1, c1, M2, c2, Mout)

' Computes the product of two matrices: Mout = M1 times M2
'    r1: number of rows in M1
'    c1: number of columns in M1
'    c2: number of columns in M2
' M2 must have c1 rows
' Mout will have r1 rows and c2 columns

Dim i As Long, j As Integer, k As Long
For i = 1 To r1
  For j = 1 To c2
    Mout(i, j) = 0
    For k = 1 To c1
      Mout(i, j) = Mout(i, j) + M1(i, k) * M2(k, j)
    Next k
  Next j
Next i
End Sub
```

```
'''''''''''''''''''''''''''''''''''''''''''''''''''''''''''''''
'''''''''''''''''''''''''''''           '''''''''''''''''''''''
'''''''''''''''''''''''''''''  TRANSPOSE  '''''''''''''''''''''''
'''''''''''''''''''''''''''''           '''''''''''''''''''''''
'''''''''''''''''''''''''''''''''''''''''''''''''''''''''''''''
```

```
Sub Transpose(M1, r1, c1, Mout)

' Computes the transpose Mout of matrix M1
```

```
'   r1: number of rows in M1
'   c1: number of columns in M1
' Mout will have c1 rows and r1 columns

Dim i As Integer, j As Long
For i = 1 To c1
  For j = 1 To r1
    Mout(i, j) = M1(j, i)
  Next j
Next i
End Sub
```

```
' ' ' ' ' ' ' ' ' ' ' ' ' ' ' ' ' ' ' ' ' ' ' ' ' ' ' ' ' ' ' ' ' ' ' ' ' ' ' ' ' ' ' ' ' ' ' ' ' ' '
' ' ' ' ' ' ' ' ' ' ' ' ' ' ' ' ' ' ' ' '                 ' ' ' ' ' ' ' ' ' ' ' ' ' ' ' ' ' ' '
' ' ' ' ' ' ' ' ' ' ' ' ' ' ' ' ' ' ' ' '      DMULT      ' ' ' ' ' ' ' ' ' ' ' ' ' ' ' ' ' ' '
' ' ' ' ' ' ' ' ' ' ' ' ' ' ' ' ' ' ' ' '                 ' ' ' ' ' ' ' ' ' ' ' ' ' ' ' ' ' ' '
' ' ' ' ' ' ' ' ' ' ' ' ' ' ' ' ' ' ' ' ' ' ' ' ' ' ' ' ' ' ' ' ' ' ' ' ' ' ' ' ' ' ' ' ' ' ' ' ' ' '
```

```
' Multiplies a matrix Min by a diagonal matrix written as a
' vector, DiagonalVector, in order to keep memory require-
' ments to a minimum
Sub DMult(Min, rin, cin, DiagonalVector, Mout)

'   rin: number of rows in Min
'   cin: number of columns in Min
' DiagonalVector must have cin terms
' Mout will have the dimension of Min

Dim i As Integer, j As Long
For i = 1 To rin
  For j = 1 To cin
    Mout(i, j) = Min(i, j) * DiagonalVector(j)
  Next j
Next i
End Sub
```

Chapter *10*

Fourier transform macros

In this chapter you will find macros that deal with Fourier transformation, convolution and deconvolution, and Gabor transformation, as discussed in chapters 5 and 6. Also listed is a specialized convolution-deconvolution routine called semi-integration & semi-differentiation, useful with problems involving planar heat and mass transport.

10.1 *Fourier transformation*

Section 8.9 already contains extensive comments on this algorithm. Note that the sign convention used here differs from the one used in the *Numerical Recipes*.

```
''''''''''''''''''''''''''''''''''''''''''''''''''''''''''''''''
''''''''''''''''''''''''''''''''''''''''''''''''''''''''''''''''
'''''''''''''''''''^^^^^^^^^^^^^^^^^^^^^^^^^^^^^^^^^^^'''''''''''''''''
'''''''''''''''''^                         ^''''''''''''''''
'''''''''''''''''^      FOURIER TRANSFORMATION      ^''''''''''''''''
'''''''''''''''''^                         ^''''''''''''''''
'''''''''''''''''^^^^^^^^^^^^^^^^^^^^^^^^^^^^^^^^^^^'''''''''''''''''
'''''''''''''''''''''''''''''''''''''''''''''''''''''(c) R. de Levie
'''''''''''''''''''''''''''''''''''''''''''''''''''v 4.6, June 1, 2004
```

```
' PURPOSE:

' The macros ForwardFT and InverseFT perform fast Fourier
' transformations on an array of complex data, arranged in
' a single block of three adjacent columns.

' SUBROUTINES:

' The macros are merely drivers that set iSign to +1 (for
' the forward transform) or to -1 (for inverse transforma-
' tion). The main subroutine Fourier then reads the input
' information, makes a number of checks, and computes the
' output. For the actual Fourier transformation it then
' calls the subroutine FT. This latter part is placed in a
' separate subroutine in order to make it readily available
' to other macros, such as ConvolveFT, DeconvolveFT,
' DeconvolveIt, and Gabor.

' INPUT:

' The first column must contain the variable (e.g., time,
```

```
' or frequency), the second column the real components of
' the input data, the third column their imaginary com-
' ponents. For purely real input data, either leave the
' third column blank, or fill it with zeros. Likewise, for
' purely imaginary input data, the second column should
' only contain zeros, blanks, or combinations thereof.

' The macro accepts two input formats: (1) data with time
' or frequency values centered around zero (jSign = -1),
' and (2) data with time or frequency values starting at
' zero (jSign = 1). The output format is commensurate with
' the input format used.

' OUTPUT:

' The output is written in the three columns to the right
' of the input data block, thereby overwriting any prior
' data in that region. The output columns contain (from
' left to right) frequency or time, the real components
' of the output data, and their imaginary components.

' PROCEDURE:

' To initiate the transform, highlight the three columns
' of the input array, and call one of the two macros,
' ForwardFT() or InverseFT().

'''''''''''''''''''''''''''''''''''''''''''''''''''''''''''

Sub ForwardFT()
Dim iSign As Integer
iSign = 1
Call Fourier(iSign)
End Sub

'''''''''''''''''''''''''''''''''''''''''''''''''''''''''''

Sub InverseFT()
Dim iSign As Integer
iSign = -1
Call Fourier(iSign)
End Sub

'''''''''''''''''''''''''''''''''''''''''''''''''''''''''''

Sub Fourier(iSign)

' Check the array length n, which must be a power of 2,
' and be at least 2

Dim cn As Integer, cnMax As Integer, jSign As Integer
Dim n As Integer, NN As Integer
Dim rn As Integer, rnMax As Integer
Dim Length As Single
Dim Check1 As Double, Check2 As Double
Dim Denom As Double, Interval As Double, z As Double
Dim DataArray As Variant, outputArray As Variant
Dim myRange As Range
Dim Ans, hAnswer
```

```
Begin:
n = 0
rnMax = Selection.Rows.Count
Length = CSng(rnMax)
cnMax = Selection.Columns.Count

' If area was not highlighted

If rnMax = 1 And cnMax = 1 Then
  hAnswer = MsgBox("You forgot to highlight" _
    & Chr(13) & "the block of input data." _
    & Chr(13) & "Do you want to do so now?" _
    , vbYesNo, "Fourier transformation")
  If hAnswer = vbNo Then End
  If hAnswer = vbYes Then
    Set myRange = Application.InputBox(Prompt:= _
      "The input data are located in:", Type:=8)
    myRange.Select
  End If
  GoTo Begin
End If

If Length < 2 Then
  MsgBox "There must be at least two rows."
  End
End If
Do While Length > 1
  Length = Length / 2
Loop
If Length <> 1 Then
  MsgBox "The current number of rows is " & rnMax _
    & "which is not an integer power of two."
  End
End If

' Check that there are three input columns

If cnMax <> 3 Then
  MsgBox "There must be three input columns," _
    & Chr(13) & "one for the variable (time, frequen-," _
    & Chr(13) & "cy, etc.), the next two for the real" _
    & Chr(13) & "and imaginary parts of the input data."
  End
End If

' Read the input data

DataArray = Selection.Value

' Check that the first column has its first two elements

Check1 = VarType(DataArray(1, 1))
If Check1 = 0 Then
  MsgBox "Enter the top left value."
  End
End If
Check2 = VarType(DataArray(2, 1))
If Check2 = 0 Then
  MsgBox "Enter a value in row 2 of the first column."
```

```
   End
End If

' Determine what input convention is used:
' jSign = -1 for input data centered around zero,
' jSign = 1 for input data starting at zero

jSign = 0
Interval = (DataArray(2, 1) - DataArray(1, 1)) * rnMax
If DataArray(1, 1) > (-0.5 * Interval / rnMax) And _
   DataArray(1, 1) < (0.5 * Interval / rnMax) Then jSign = 1
If DataArray(1, 1) < (-0.5 * Interval / rnMax) And _
   DataArray(rnMax / 2 + 1, 1) > (-0.5 * Interval / rnMax) _
   And DataArray(rnMax / 2 + 1, 1) < (0.5 * Interval / _
   rnMax) Then jSign = -1
If jSign = 0 Then
   MsgBox "The input format is incorrect." _
     & Chr(13) & "It should either be centered" _
     & Chr(13) & "around zero, or start at zero."
   End
End If

' Read and rearrange the input data

NN = 2 * rnMax
ReDim Term(NN) As Double
If jSign = 1 Then
   For rn = 1 To rnMax
     Term(2 * rn - 1) = DataArray(rn, 2)
     Term(2 * rn) = DataArray(rn, 3)
   Next rn
End If
If jSign = -1 Then
   For rn = 1 To rnMax / 2
     Term(2 * rn - 1) = DataArray(rnMax / 2 + rn, 2)
     Term(2 * rn) = DataArray(rnMax / 2 + rn, 3)
     Term(rnMax + 2 * rn - 1) = DataArray(rn, 2)
     Term(rnMax + 2 * rn) = DataArray(rn, 3)
   Next rn
End If

' Check that the output does not overwrite valuable data

Selection.Offset(0, 3).Select
outputArray = Selection.Value
For rn = 1 To rnMax
   For cn = 1 To cnMax
     z = outputArray(rn, cn)
     If (IsEmpty(z) Or z = 0) Then
       n = n
     Else
       n = n + 1
     End If
   Next cn
Next rn
If n > 0 Then
   Ans = MsgBox("  There are data in the space where" _
     & Chr(13) & "the output will be written. Proceed " _
     & Chr(13) & "  anyway and overwrite those data?", _
```

```
      vbYesNo)
    If Ans = vbNo Then
      Selection.Offset(0, -3).Select
      End
    End If
  End If
End If

' Calculate and write the frequency or time scale

If jSign = 1 Then
  For rn = 1 To rnMax / 2
    DataArray(rn, 1) = (rn - 1) / Interval
  Next rn
  For rn = (rnMax / 2 + 1) To rnMax
    If iSign > 0 Then
      DataArray(rn, 1) = (rn - rnMax - 1) / Interval
    Else
      DataArray(rn, 1) = (rn - 1) / Interval
    End If
  Next rn
End If

If jSign = -1 Then
  For rn = 1 To rnMax
    DataArray(rn, 1) = (-(rnMax / 2) + rn - 1) / Interval
  Next rn
End If

' Calculate the Fourier transform

Call FT(Term, NN, iSign)

' Arrange and write the output data

Denom = (rnMax + 1 + iSign * (rnMax - 1)) / 2
If jSign = 1 Then
  For rn = 1 To rnMax
    DataArray(rn, 2) = Term(2 * rn - 1) / Denom
    DataArray(rn, 3) = Term(2 * rn) / Denom
  Next rn
End If
If jSign = -1 Then
  For rn = 1 To rnMax / 2
    DataArray(rn, 2) = Term(rnMax + 2 * rn - 1) / Denom
    DataArray(rn, 3) = Term(rnMax + 2 * rn) / Denom
    DataArray((rnMax / 2) + rn, 2) = _
      Term(2 * rn - 1) / Denom
    DataArray((rnMax / 2) + rn, 3) = Term(2 * rn) / Denom
  Next rn
End If

Application.ScreenUpdating = False

Selection.Value = DataArray

End Sub

''''''''''''''''''''''''''''''''''''''''''''''''''''''''''''
```

```
' The following is the Fourier transform routine FOUR1 from
' J. C. Sprott, "Numerical Recipes: Routines and Examples
' in BASIC", Cambridge University Press, Copyright (C)1991
' by Numerical Recipes Software. Used here by permission.
' Use of this routine other than as an integral part of the
' present book requires an additional license from Numeri-
' cal Recipes Software. Further distribution is prohibited.
' The routine has been modified to yield double-precision
' results, and to conform to the standard mathematical sign
' convention for Fourier transformation.

Sub FT(Term, NN, iSign)

Dim i As Integer, istep As Integer, j As Integer
Dim m As Integer, mmax As Integer

Dim tr As Double, ti As Double, theta As Double
Dim wtemp As Double, wi As Double, wr As Double
Dim wpi As Double, wpr As Double

j = 1
For i = 1 To NN Step 2
  If j > i Then
    tr = Term(j)
    ti = Term(j + 1)
    Term(j) = Term(i)
    Term(j + 1) = Term(i + 1)
    Term(i) = tr
    Term(i + 1) = ti
  End If
  m = Int(NN / 2)
  While m >= 2 And j > m
    j = j - m
    m = Int(m / 2)
  Wend
  j = j + m
Next i
mmax = 2
While NN > mmax
  istep = 2 * mmax
  theta = 2 * [Pi()] / (-iSign * mmax)
  wpr = -2 * Sin(0.5 * theta) ^ 2
  wpi = Sin(theta)
  wr = 1
  wi = 0
  For m = 1 To mmax Step 2
    For i = m To NN Step istep
      j = i + mmax
      tr = wr * Term(j) - wi * Term(j + 1)
      ti = wr * Term(j + 1) + wi * Term(j)
      Term(j) = Term(i) - tr
      Term(j + 1) = Term(i + 1) - ti
      Term(i) = Term(i) + tr
      Term(i + 1) = Term(i + 1) + ti
    Next i
    wtemp = wr
    wr = wr * wpr - wi * wpi + wr
    wi = wi * wpr + wtemp * wpi + wi
  Next m
```

```
      mmax = istep
Wend

End Sub
```

10.2 Direct (de)convolution

```
''''''''''''''''''''''''''''''''''''''''''''''''''''''''''''''''''''''
''''''''''''''''''''''''''''''''''''''''''''''''''''''''''''''''''''''
'''''''''''''''∧∧∧∧∧∧∧∧∧∧∧∧∧∧∧∧∧∧∧∧∧∧∧∧∧∧∧∧∧∧∧∧∧''''''''''''''
'''''''''''''∧                                  ∧''''''''''''
'''''''''''''∧      DIRECT (DE)CONVOLUTION       ∧''''''''''''
'''''''''''''∧                                  ∧''''''''''''
'''''''''''''∧∧∧∧∧∧∧∧∧∧∧∧∧∧∧∧∧∧∧∧∧∧∧∧∧∧∧∧∧∧∧∧∧∧∧''''''''''''''
''''''''''''''''''''''''''''''''''''''''''''''''''(c) R. de Levie
''''''''''''''''''''''''''''''''''''''''''''''''''v 4.6, June 1, 2004
```

```
' PURPOSE:

' These macros perform a straightforward (i.e., non-Fourier
' transform) convolution or deconvolution of 2 columns of
' real data, arranged in a single block of 3 adjacent
' columns, the first column containing the variable (time),
' the second column the signals to be convolved, and the
' third column the transfer function. The signal in the
' third column is normalized to have an average of 1.

' The number of points in the data set is arbitrary, but
' the data must be equidistant, since the signal and trans-
' fer functions will be sliding past each other.

' Convolution tends to spread the function. Make sure that
' there is enough space for it to spread into, e.g., by ad-
' ding zeros before and/or after the signal for expansion.
' Likewise, for a symmetrical transfer function, signal
' shifting can be prevented by centering the transfer
' function at t = 0.

' The deconvolution routine works well when the deconvol-
' ving function (in the third column) is a monotonically
' decreasing function of time, but otherwise may lead to
' oscillations.

' SUBROUTINES:

' The macros Convolve and Deconvolve set the value of d
' to +1 (for convolution) or -1 (for deconvolution), then
' call the subroutine Convolution. The latter requires no
' further subroutines.

' INPUT:

' The macro accepts any number of input data, but requires
' that they be equidistant. The output is independent of
' the starting value of the time scale, but does depend on
' the phase relationship between the two input signals.

' OUTPUT:
```

```
' The output is written in one column, immediately to the
' right of the input data block, thereby overwriting any
' prior data in that region. After writing the output, the
' activated area returns to its original position and
' contents.

' PROCEDURE:

' Before starting the macro, make sure that the column to
' the right of the input data block contains no valuable
' data.

' To initiate the transform, highlight the three columns of
' the input array, and call the macro.

''''''''''''''''''''''''''''''''''''''''''''''''''''''''''''

Sub Convolve()

Dim d As Integer
d = 1
Call Convolution(d)
End Sub
'
''''''''''''''''''''''''''''''''''''''''''''''''''''''''''''
'
Sub Deconvolve()
Dim d As Integer
d = -1
Call Convolution(d)
End Sub
'
''''''''''''''''''''''''''''''''''''''''''''''''''''''''''''
'
Sub Convolution(d)

Dim cMax As Integer, rM As Integer, rMax As Integer
Dim i As Integer, j As Integer, n As Integer

Dim Incr As Double, mySum As Double
Dim Sum As Double, z As Double

Dim Inp As Variant, myInput As Variant
Dim myInput2 As Variant, myOutput As Variant
Dim Outp As Variant, Trans As Variant

Dim Ans, hAnswer

' Read the input

Begin:
cMax = Selection.Columns.Count
rMax = Selection.Rows.Count

' If area was not highlighted

If rMax = 1 And cMax = 1 Then
  hAnswer = MsgBox("You forgot to highlight" _
    & Chr(13) & "the block of input data." _
```

```
        & Chr(13) & "Do you want to do so now?" _
        , vbYesNo, "(De)Convolution")
    If hAnswer = vbNo Then End
    If hAnswer = vbYes Then
      Set myRange = Application.InputBox(Prompt:= _
        "The input data are located in:", Type:=8)
      myRange.Select
    End If
    GoTo Begin
  End If

' Check that there are three input columns

  If cMax <> 3 Then
    MsgBox "There must be three input columns," _
      & Chr(13) & "one each for time, signal s, and" _
      & Chr(13) & "transfer function t, in that order."
    End
  End If

' Read the input data

  myInput = Selection.Value
  myInput2 = Selection.Formula
  Incr = myInput(2, 1) - myInput(1, 1)

  rM = rMax - 1
  ReDim Inp(-rM To rM)
  ReDim Outp(-rM To rM)
  ReDim Trans(-rM To rM)

' Check whether the fourth column can be overwritten

  n = 0
  Selection.Offset(0, 1).Select
  myOutput = Selection.Value
  For i = 1 To rMax
    z = myOutput(i, 3)
    If (IsEmpty(z) Or z = 0) Then
      n = n
    Else
      n = n + 1
    End If
  Next i
  If n > 0 Then
    Ans = MsgBox("There are data in the space where" _
      & Chr(13) & "the output will be written. Proceed" _
      & Chr(13) & "anyway and overwrite those data?", vbYesNo)
    If Ans = vbNo Then
      Selection.Offset(0, -1).Select
      End
    End If
  End If
  Selection.Offset(0, -1).Select

' Normalize and invert the transfer function

  Sum = 0
  For i = 1 To rMax
```

```
    Sum = Sum + myInput(i, 3)
  Next i

  For i = 1 To rMax
    Inp(1 - i) = 0
    Inp(i - 1) = myInput(i, 2)
    Trans(i - 1) = 0
    Trans(1 - i) = myInput(i, 3)
    Outp(1 - i) = 0
    Outp(i - 1) = 0
  Next i

  ' Compute the convolution (for d = 1)

  If d = 1 Then
    For j = 0 To rM
      mySum = 0
      For i = 0 To rM
        mySum = mySum + Inp(j - i) * Trans(-i)
      Next i
    Outp(j) = mySum / Sum
    myOutput(j + 1, 3) = Outp(j)
    Next j
  End If

  ' Compute the deconvolution (for d = -1)

  If d = -1 Then
    For j = 0 To rM
      mySum = Inp(j)
      For i = 1 To rM
        mySum = mySum - Outp(j - i) * Trans(-i)
      Next i
    Outp(j) = mySum
    Next j
    For j = 1 To rMax
      myOutput(j, 3) = Outp(j - 1) * Sum
    Next j
  End If

  ' Output the result

  Selection.Offset(0, 1).Select
  Selection.Value = myOutput
  Selection.Offset(0, -1).Select
  Selection.Formula = myInput2

End Sub
```

10.3 *Fourier transform (de)convolution*

```
''''''''''''''''''''''''''''''''''''''''''''''''''''''''''''
''''''''''''''''''''''''''''''''''''''''''''''''''''''''''''
'''''''''^^^^^^^^^^^^^^^^^^^^^^^^^^^^^^^^^^^^^^^^^^^'''''''''
'''''''^                                            ^'''''''
'''''''^       FOURIER TRANSFORM (DE)CONVOLUTION     ^'''''''
'''''''^                                            ^'''''''
'''''''''^^^^^^^^^^^^^^^^^^^^^^^^^^^^^^^^^^^^^^^^^^^^'''''''''
'''''''''''''''''''''''''''''''''''''''''''''(c) R. de Levie
''''''''''''''''''''''''''''''''''''''''''''''v 4.6, June 1, 2004
```

```
' PURPOSE:

' These macros perform either a convolution or a deconvolu-
' tion of two sets of real data, arranged in a single block
' of three adjacent columns, the first column containing
' their common variable (e.g., time), and the next columns
' the data sets to be convolved or deconvolved.

' For convolution the order of the second and third column
' does not matter, and interchanging the data sets in the
' second and third column will yield the same result.

' For deconvolution, the second column should contain the
' data to be deconvolved, and the third column the data set
' with which the data in the second column are to be decon-
' volved. In this case, exchanging the second and third
' column will in general yield quite different results.

' For deconvolution the macro incorporates an adjustable
' von Hann window with a single, continually adjustable
' positive parameter, w. The default, w = 0, yields a
' rectangular window (i.e., the absence of filtering), but
' allows the user to select a sharp high-frequency cut-off.
' Setting w = 1 selects the traditional von Hann window,
' while other w-values >0 produce filtering that is less
' severe (0 < w < 1) or more severe (w > 1) than the stan-
' dard von Hann filter. Note that the filters have not been
' normalized.

' SUBROUTINES:

' The macros Convolve and Deconvolve require the subroutine
' Convolution which, in turn, calls the subroutine FT.

' INPUT:

' The macro accepts any input format in which the time
' scale contains 2^n equidistant values (where n is a posi-
' tive integer larger than 1), regardless of its starting
' value. While the output is independent of the starting
' value of the time scale, it does depend on the phase
' relationship between the two input signals.

' Provided that the function in the third column is symme-
' trical, such phase shifts can be avoided by starting that
' function at its point of symmetry (typically: at its
' maximum), and placing the part before that point of
' symmetry at the very end of the column. What makes this
' 'wrap-around' method work is the assumption of the
' Fourier transform method that the functions are self-
' repeating.

' OUTPUT:

' The output is written in one column, immediately to the
' right of the input data block, thereby overwriting any
' prior data in that region. After writing the output,
' the activated area returns to its original position and
' contents.
```

```
' PROCEDURE:

' Before starting the macro, make sure that the column to
' the right of the input data block contains no valuable
' data.

' To initiate the transform, highlight the three columns
' of the input array, and call the macro.

'''''''''''''''''''''''''''''''''''''''''''''''''''''''''

' The following are the two drivers for the (de)convolution
' subroutine. They set kSign to either +1 (for convolution)
' or -1 (for deconvolution).

Sub ConvolveFT()
Dim kSign As Integer
kSign = 1
Call ConvolutionFT(kSign)
End Sub
'
'''''''''''''''''''''''''''''''''''''''''''''''''''''''''
'

Sub DeconvolveFT()
Dim kSign As Integer
kSign = -1
Call ConvolutionFT(kSign)
End Sub
'
'''''''''''''''''''''''''''''''''''''''''''''''''''''''''
'

Sub ConvolutionFT(kSign)

Dim cn As Integer, cnMax As Integer
Dim n As Integer, NN As Integer, nfZ As Integer
Dim rn As Integer, rnMax As Integer, rrn As Integer

Dim nfZero As Single, q As Single

Dim Average3 As Double, Check1 As Double, Check2 As Double
Dim d As Double, dataSpacing As Double, Length As Double
Dim Min As Double, Norm As Double, Pi As Double
Dim Ratio As Double, Rnm2 As Double, s As Double
Dim Sum As Double, Sum3 As Double
Dim WindowFunction As Double, z As Double

Dim DataArray As Variant, inputArray As Variant
Dim outputArray As Variant

Dim Answer, hAnswer, vAnswer, Default1, Default2
Dim Message1, Message2, Title1, Title2

' Read the input

Begin:
n = 0
z = 0
rnMax = Selection.Rows.Count
NN = 2 * rnMax
```

```
cnMax = Selection.Columns.Count
Length = CDbl(rnMax)

' If area was not highlighted

If rMax = 1 And cMax = 1 Then
  hAnswer = MsgBox("You forgot to highlight" _
    & Chr(13) & "the block of input data." _
    & Chr(13) & "Do you want to do so now?" _
    , vbYesNo, "Fourier transform (de)convolution")
  If hAnswer = vbNo Then End
  If hAnswer = vbYes Then
    Set myRange = Application.InputBox(Prompt:= _
      "The input data are located in:", Type:=8)
    myRange.Select
  End If
  GoTo Begin
End If

' Check the array length n, which must be a power of 2,
' and be at least 2

If Length < 2 Then
  MsgBox "There must be at least two rows."
  End
End If
Do While Length > 1
  Length = Length / 2
Loop
If Length <> 1 Then
  MsgBox "The number of rows must be a power of two."
  End
End If

' Check that there are three input columns

cnMax = Selection.Columns.Count
If cnMax <> 3 Then
  If kSign = 1 Then
    MsgBox " There must be 3 input columns," _
      & Chr(13) & "one for the independent variable" _
      & Chr(13) & " (e.g., time), the next for the" _
      & Chr(13) & " two functions to be convolved."
    End
  End If
  If kSign = -1 Then
    MsgBox " There must be 3 input columns," _
      & Chr(13) & "one for the independent variable" _
      & Chr(13) & " (e.g., time), the next for the" _
      & Chr(13) & " two functions to be deconvolved."
    End
  End If
End If

' Read the input data

DataArray = Selection.Value
inputArray = Selection.Formula
```

```
' Check that the first column has its first two elements

Check1 = VarType(DataArray(1, 1))
If Check1 = 0 Then
  MsgBox "Enter the top left value."
  End
End If
Check2 = VarType(DataArray(2, 1))
If Check2 = 0 Then
  MsgBox "Enter a value in row 2 of the first column."
  End
End If
dataSpacing = DataArray(2, 1) - DataArray(1, 1)

' Read and rearrange the input data
' from the second and third columns

ReDim Term2(NN) As Double, Term3(NN) As Double
ReDim Term4(NN) As Double
For rn = 1 To rnMax
  Term2(2 * rn - 1) = DataArray(rn, 2)
  Term2(2 * rn) = z
  Term3(2 * rn - 1) = DataArray(rn, 3)
  Term3(2 * rn) = z
Next rn

' Normalize the data in the third column

Sum = 0
For rn = 1 To rnMax
  Sum = Sum + Term3(2 * rn - 1)
Next rn
For rn = 1 To rnMax
' If normalization is NOT desired,
' comment out the next line:
  Term3(2 * rn - 1) = Term3(2 * rn - 1) * rnMax / Sum
Next rn

' Check that the output does not overwrite valuable data.

Selection.Offset(0, 1).Select
outputArray = Selection.Value
For rn = 1 To rnMax
  q = outputArray(rn, 3)
  If (IsEmpty(q) Or q = 0) Then
    n = n
  Else
    n = n + 1
  End If
Next rn
Selection.Offset(0, -1).Select
If n > 0 Then
  Answer = MsgBox(" There are data in the column where" _
    & Chr(13) & "the output will be written. Proceed" & _
    Chr(13) & " anyway and overwrite those data?", vbYesNo)
  If Answer = vbNo Then End
End If

' Transform the data from the second and third columns
```

```
Call FT(Term2, NN, 1)
Call FT(Term3, NN, 1)

' Multiply in the frequency domain for convolution, or
' divide in the frequency domain for deconvolution. For
' deconvolution, a minimum value "min" (arbitrarily set
' here to 1E-6) prevents division by zero. Moreover, an
' input box is provided for optional noise filtering.

Rnm2 = CDbl(rnMax) * CDbl(rnMax)

' For convolution, multiply in the frequency domain:
' (a + jb) (c + jd) = (ac - bd) + j(ad + bc)

If kSign = 1 Then

  For rn = 1 To rnMax
    Term4(2 * rn - 1) = _
      (Term2(2 * rn - 1) * Term3(2 * rn - 1) _
      - Term2(2 * rn) * Term3(2 * rn)) / rnMax
    Term4(2 * rn) = _
      (Term2(2 * rn - 1) * Term3(2 * rn) _
      + Term2(2 * rn) * Term3(2 * rn - 1)) / rnMax
  Next rn

End If

' For deconvolution, select the window parameter s

If kSign = -1 Then

 Min = 0.000001
 Pi = [Pi()]
 Message1 = "Enter the window parameter, a " & _
   "non-negative number." & Chr(13) & "The default " & _
   "is 0, which corresponds to no filtering," & Chr(13) & _
   "but allows you to insert a sharp frequency cut-off." _
   & Chr(13) & Chr(13) & "For the standard von Hann " _
   & "filter select 1." & Chr(13) & Chr(13) _
   & "For an adjustable von Hann / Tukey window," _
   & Chr(13) & " select a value other than 0 or 1."
 Title1 = "Adjustable von Hann / Tukey window"
 Default1 = "0"
 s = InputBox(Message1, Title1, Default1)
 If s < Min Then s = 0

' Provide the option of removing
' high-frequency data for M1 = 0

  If s = 0 Then
    Message2 = "Enter the number of frequencies" _
      & Chr(13) & "(an integer smaller than " _
      & rnMax & ") for which" & Chr(13) _
      & "you want the signal to be set to zero." & _
      Chr(13) & Chr(13) & "Press ENTER or OK for the " _
      & "default, 0," & Chr(13) & "in which case no " _
      & "data will be set to zero."
    Title2 = "Zeroing out high frequencies"
    Default2 = "0"
```

```
       nfZero = InputBox(Message2, Title2, Default2)
       If nfZero < 0 Then nfZ = 0
       If nfZero > 0 And nfZero < rnMax / 2 Then _
         nfZ = CInt(nfZero)
       If nfZero > rnMax / 2 Then nfZ = rnMax / 2
       If nfZ > 0 Then
         For rn = (rnMax / 2 + 2 - nfZ) To (rnMax / 2 + nfZ)
           Term4(2 * rn - 1) = 0
           Term4(2 * rn - 2) = 0
         Next rn
       End If
     End If

' For deconvolution, divide in the frequency domain:
' (a+jb)/(c+jd) = (a+jb)(c-jd)/(cc+dd)
'    = [(ac+bd)+j(bc-ad)]/(cc+dd)

     For rn = 1 To rnMax
       d = (Term3(2 * rn - 1) * Term3(2 * rn - 1) + _
         Term3(2 * rn) * Term3(2 * rn)) * dataSpacing / rnMax
       If d < Min Then d = Min
       Term4(2 * rn - 1) = _
         (Term2(2 * rn - 1) * Term3(2 * rn - 1) _
         + Term2(2 * rn) * Term3(2 * rn)) / d
       Term4(2 * rn) = (Term2(2 * rn) * Term3(2 * rn - 1) _
         - Term2(2 * rn - 1) * Term3(2 * rn)) / d

' Compute and apply the window function

       Ratio = 2 * CDbl(rn - 1) / CDbl(rnMax)
       If s < 1 Then WindowFunction = 1
       If s > 0 And s < 1 Then
         If Abs(Ratio - 1) < s Then WindowFunction = _
           0.5 + 0.5 * Cos(Pi * (Abs(Ratio) - 1 + s) / s)
       End If
       If s >= 1 Then
         WindowFunction = (0.5 + 0.5 * Cos(Pi * Ratio)) ^ s
       End If
       Term4(2 * rn - 1) = Term4(2 * rn - 1) * WindowFunction
       Term4(2 * rn) = Term4(2 * rn) * WindowFunction
     Next rn

End If

' Calculate output data

Call FT(Term4, NN, -1)

' Arrange and write the output data

For rn = 1 To rnMax
  outputArray(rn, 3) = Term4(2 * rn - 1) / rnMax
Next rn

Application.ScreenUpdating = False
Selection.Offset(0, 1).Select
Selection.Value = outputArray
Selection.Offset(0, -1).Select
Selection.Value = inputArray
```

`End Sub`

10.4 Iterative deconvolution

This macro follows the approach of van Cittert as described in section 6.6. For the optional least squares filtering between successive iteration steps we use equidistant least squares, similar to those used in ELSfixed, and described in section 3.15, using the recursive relations given by Gorry in *Anal. Chem.* 62 (1990) 570.

```
''''''''''''''''''''''''''''''''''''''''''''''''''''''''''''''
''''''''''''''''''''''''''''''''''''''''''''''''''''''''''''''
'''''''''''''''^^^^^^^^^^^^^^^^^^^^^^^^^^^^^^^^^^^^^''''''''''''
'''''''''''''^                                    ^'''''''''''''
'''''''''''''^        ITERATIVE DECONVOLUTION     ^'''''''''''''
'''''''''''''^                                    ^'''''''''''''
'''''''''''''^^^^^^^^^^^^^^^^^^^^^^^^^^^^^^^^^^^^^^^''''''''''''
''''''''''''''''''''''''''''''''''''''''''''''''(c) R. de Levie
''''''''''''''''''''''''''''''''''''''''''''''''v 4.6, June 1, 2004

' PURPOSE:

' This macro performs an iterative deconvolution along the
' lines of the van Cittert approach. It convolves (rather
' than deconvolves) the data in the second (signal) column
' with the filter function in the third column, then
' corrects the signal by the difference between it and its
' convolution. The macro provides the option of smoothing
' intermediate results with a moving quadratic of selec-
' table length, using the recursive expressions given by
' Gorry in Anal. Chem. 62 (1990) 570. The iteration stops
' when the sum of the squares of the residuals has reached
' a minimum, or the number of iterations has reached a pre-
' set limit.

' There are two choices: DeconvolveIt0 involves no
' constraints, while DeconvolveIt1 assumes one constraint,
' namely that the function is always positive. It therefore
' replaces all negative intermediate results by zero.

' INPUT:

' The input requires three adjacent columns of equal
' length. The first column should contain the independent
' parameter, such as time, wavelength, etc. The second
' column should contain the (real) input data that need to
' be deconvolved with the (real) filter data in the third
' column.

' The macro accepts any number of input data, but requires
' that they be equidistant. The output is independent of
' the starting value of the time scale, but does depend on
' the phase relationship between the two input signals.
```

```
' An optional parabolic noise filter is provided to reduce
' the effect of noise. Use of such a filter introduces its
' own distortion, the more so the longer the length of the
' moving parabola. If used at all, the parabola length
' should therefore be kept to a minimum.

' INTERRUPT:

' Because the iteration can take more time than you may
' have available or care to spend, the process can be
' interrupted, by pressing either the Escape key or the     '
' Control+Break key combination. A message box then
' provides the option of ending the computation and
' displaying the result obtained so far, or of resuming
' the calculation where it was interrupted.

' OUTPUT:

' The output is written in one column, immediately to the
' right of the input data block, thereby overwriting any
' prior data in that region. After writing the output,
' the activated area returns to its original position and
' contents. Moreover, the number of iterations used, and
' the value of the termination criterion are shown at the
' bottom of the data set.

' SUBROUTINES AND FUNCTIONS:

' The macros DeconvIt0 and DeconvolveIt1 require the
' subroutine DeconvolveIteratively which, in turn, calls
' the subroutine FT. Moreover, when filtering is used,
' the functions ConvolutionWeight, GramPolynomial, and
' GenFact are also required.

' PROCEDURE:

' Before starting the macro, make sure that the column to
' the right of the input data block contains no valuable
' data.

' To initiate the macro, highlight the three columns of the
' input array, and call the macro. The macro will then ask
' you to specify the maximum number of iterations; its
' default value is 10, and its maximum value has been set
' at 100,000. (If that takes you too long, interrupt the
' iterations with Esc.) The iterations will stop whenever
' the sum of the squares of the residuals has reached a
' minimum, or the set maximum number of iterations has been
' performed, whichever comes first.

'''''''''''''''''''''''''''''''''''''''''''''''''''''''''''

' For iterative deconvolution without constraints:
'
Sub DeconvolveIt0()

Dim zz As Integer
zz = 0
Call DeconvolveIteratively(zz)
```

```
End Sub
'
''''''''''''''''''''''''''''''''''''''''''''''''''''''''''''''
'
' For iterative deconvolution constrained at x = 0:
'
Sub DeconvolveIt1()
Dim zz As Integer
zz = 1
Call DeconvolveIteratively(zz)
End Sub
'
''''''''''''''''''''''''''''''''''''''''''''''''''''''''''''''
'
Sub DeconvolveIteratively(zz)

Dim C As Integer, cn As Integer, cnMax As Integer
Dim ItNo As Integer, n As Integer
Dim NN As Integer, nfZ As Integer
Dim rn As Integer, rnMax As Integer, rrn As Integer

Dim nfZero As Single, q As Single

Dim Average3 As Double, Check1 As Double, Check2 As Double
Dim d As Double, dataSpacing As Double, Delta As Double
Dim Factor As Double, Length As Double, MaxItNo As Double
Dim Min As Double, myScale As Double, Norm As Double
Dim p As Double, Pi As Double, previousSSR As Double
Dim Ratio As Double, Rnm2 As Double, SSR As Double
Dim s As Double, Sum As Double
Dim Sum3 As Double, WindowFunction As Double, z As Double

Dim DataArray As Variant, inputArray As Variant
Dim outputArray As Variant

Dim aa, bb, cc, Answer, hAnswer, vAnswer, ContinueHere
Dim Default, InterruptHandler, Message, myFilter
Dim myFunction, Reply, Title, TryAgain

' Read the input

Begin:
n = 0
z = 0
rnMax = Selection.Rows.Count
NN = 2 * rnMax
cnMax = Selection.Columns.Count
Length = CDbl(rnMax)
Pi = [Pi()]

' If area was not highlighted

If rnMax = 1 And cnMax = 1 Then
  hAnswer = MsgBox("You forgot to highlight" _
    & Chr(13) & "the block of input data." _
    & Chr(13) & "Do you want to do so now?" _
    , vbYesNo, "Iterative (de)convolution")
  If hAnswer = vbNo Then End
```

```
  If hAnswer = vbYes Then
    Set myRange = Application.InputBox(Prompt:= _
      "The input data are located in:", Type:=8)
    myRange.Select
  End If
  GoTo Begin
End If
On Error GoTo InterruptHandler

' Check the array length n, which must
' be a power of 2, and be at least 2

If Length < 2 Then
  MsgBox "There must be at least two rows."
  End
End If
Do While Length > 1
  Length = Length / 2
Loop
If Length <> 1 Then
  MsgBox "The number of rows must be a power of two."
  End
End If

' Check that there are three input columns

If cnMax <> 3 Then
  MsgBox "There must be three input columns, one for " _
    & "the" & Chr(13) & "   independent variable (e.g., " _
    & "time), the next" & Chr(13) _
    & "   two for the two functions to be deconvolved."
  End
End If

' Read the input data

DataArray = Selection.Value
inputArray = Selection.Formula

' Check that the first column has its first two elements

Check1 = VarType(DataArray(1, 1))
If Check1 = 0 Then
  MsgBox "Enter the top left value."
  End
End If
Check2 = VarType(DataArray(2, 1))
If Check2 = 0 Then
  MsgBox "Enter a value in row 2 of the first column."
  End
End If
dataSpacing = DataArray(2, 1) - DataArray(1, 1)

' Check that the output does not overwrite valuable data.

Selection.Offset(0, 1).Select
outputArray = Selection.Value
For rn = 1 To rnMax
  q = outputArray(rn, 3)
```

```
    If (IsEmpty(q) Or q = 0) Then
      n = n
    Else
      n = n + 1
    End If
Next rn
Selection.Offset(0, -1).Select
If n > 0 Then
  Answer = MsgBox("There are data in the column where" & _
    Chr(13) & "the output will be written. Proceed" & _
    Chr(13) & " anyway and overwrite those data?", vbYesNo)
  If Answer = vbNo Then End
End If

' Select a filter

TryAgain:
Message = "You can select a moving parabola to filter" & _
Chr(13) & "the data. Specify a moving parabola with an" & _
Chr(13) & "odd integer number of data points, at least" & _
Chr(13) & "5 but always much smaller than the number" & _
Chr(13) & "of points in your data set, or select the" & _
Chr(13) & "default, 0, if you do NOT want any filtering."
Title = "Deconvolve Iteratively: Select moving polynomial length"
Default = "0"
myFilter = InputBox(Message, Title, Default)
If myFilter = 0 Then GoTo aa
m = CInt((myFilter - 1) / 2)
If (m <> 0 And m < 2) Then
  MsgBox "Select either 0 (for no filtering)," & _
  Chr(13) & "or an odd number larger than 3 for" & _
  Chr(13) & "the length of the moving parabola."
  GoTo TryAgain
End If
If rnMax < 2 * m + 3 Then
  MsgBox "Select a shorter moving parabola length."
  GoTo TryAgain
End If

aa:

' Save the input signal

ReDim signal(1 To rnMax) As Double
ReDim newSignal(1 To rnMax) As Double
For rn = 1 To rnMax
  signal(rn) = DataArray(rn, 2)
Next rn

' Read and rearrange the input data from the third column

ReDim Term3(1 To NN) As Double
For rn = 1 To rnMax
  Term3(2 * rn - 1) = DataArray(rn, 3)
  Term3(2 * rn) = z
Next rn

' Normalize the data in the third column
```

```
Sum = 0
For rn = 1 To rnMax
  Sum = Sum + DataArray(rn, 3)
Next rn
myScale = rnMax / Sum

' Select the maximum number of iterations; the
' default value is 10, and its maximum value is
' limited at 10000 to prevent an endless loop.

Message = "Select the maximum number of iterations"
Title = _
  "Deconvolve Iteratively: Select max. # of iterations"
Default = "10"
MaxItNo = InputBox(Message, Title, Default)
If MaxItNo > 10000 Then MaxItNo = 10000

' Make code uninterruptible for next section

Application.EnableCancelKey = xlDisabled

' Set the iteration number and start the iteration loop

ItNo = 1

bb:

previousSSR = SSR

' Read and rearrange the input data from the second column

ReDim Term2(NN) As Double, Term4(NN) As Double
For rn = 1 To rnMax
  Term2(2 * rn - 1) = DataArray(rn, 2)
  Term2(2 * rn) = z
  Term3(2 * rn - 1) = DataArray(rn, 3) * myScale
  Term3(2 * rn) = z
Next rn

' Transform the data from the second and third columns

Call FT(Term2, NN, 1)
Call FT(Term3, NN, 1)

' Multiply in the frequency domain for convolution

Rnm2 = CDbl(rnMax) * CDbl(rnMax)

' Multiply in the frequency domain, using
' (a + jb) * (c + jd) = (ac - bd) + j(ad + bc)
' where j is the square root of -1

For rn = 1 To rnMax
  Term4(2 * rn - 1) = _
    (Term2(2 * rn - 1) * Term3(2 * rn - 1) _
    - Term2(2 * rn) * Term3(2 * rn)) / rnMax
  Term4(2 * rn) = (Term2(2 * rn - 1) * Term3(2 * rn) _
    + Term2(2 * rn) * Term3(2 * rn - 1)) / rnMax
Next rn
```

```
' Inverse transform to obtain the convolution

Call FT(Term4, NN, -1)
For rn = 1 To rnMax
  outputArray(rn, 3) = Term4(2 * rn - 1) / rnMax
Next rn

' Compute the corrected signal value

If zz < 2 Then
  For rn = 1 To rnMax
    p = 1
    If zz = 1 And signal(rn) < 0 Then p = 0
    newSignal(rn) = p * signal(rn) + _
      DataArray(rn, 2) - outputArray(rn, 3)
  Next rn
ElseIf zz = 2 Then
  For rn = 1 To rnMax
    newSignal(rn) = signal(rn) + (1 - 2 * _
      Abs(signal(rn) - 0.5)) * (DataArray(rn, 2) - _
      outputArray(rn, 3))
  Next rn
End If

' Compute SSR

SSR = 0
For rn = 1 To rnMax
  SSR = SSR + (outputArray(rn, 3) - signal(rn)) ^ 2
Next rn

If myFilter = 0 Then GoTo cc

' Apply the filter

ReDim SmoothedArray(rnMax) As Double
For rn = 1 To rnMax
  SmoothedArray(rn) = DataArray(rn, 2)
Next rn
k = 2              ' for a parabola
s = 0              ' for smoothing

For rn = 1 To m
  SmoothedArray(rn) = 0
  For i = -m To m
    SmoothedArray(rn) = SmoothedArray(rn) _
    + ConvolutionWeight(i, rn - m - 1, m, k, s) _
    * DataArray(i + m + 1, 2)
  Next i
Next rn

For rn = m + 1 To rnMax - m
  SmoothedArray(rn) = 0
  For i = -m To m
    SmoothedArray(rn) = SmoothedArray(rn) _
    + ConvolutionWeight(i, 0, m, k, s) _
    * DataArray(rn + i, 2)
  Next i
Next rn
```

```
For rn = rnMax - m + 1 To rnMax
  SmoothedArray(rn) = 0
  For i = -m To m
    SmoothedArray(rn) = SmoothedArray(rn) _
    + ConvolutionWeight(i, rn - rnMax + m, m, k, s) _
    * DataArray(rnMax - m + i, 2)
  Next i
Next rn

For rn = 1 To rnMax
  DataArray(rn, 2) = SmoothedArray(rn)
Next rn

cc:

' Set negative values equal to zero for DeconvolveIt1

If zz = 1 Then
  For rn = 1 To rnMax
    If DataArray(rn, 2) < 0 Then DataArray(rn, 2) _
      = -DataArray(rn, 2)
  Next rn
End If

ContinueHere:

' Make code briefly interruptible

Application.EnableCancelKey = xlErrorHandler

' Update the second (signal) column of dataArray

For rn = 1 To rnMax
  DataArray(rn, 2) = signal(rn) _
    + DataArray(rn, 2) - outputArray(rn, 3)
Next rn

' increment ItNo and loop back

If ItNo = 1 Then previousSSR = SSR
ItNo = ItNo + 1

Application.StatusBar = "Iteration # " & _
  ItNo & ", SSR = " & SSR
If (ItNo < MaxItNo And previousSSR >= SSR) Then GoTo bb

Output:

' Prepare for landing

For rn = 1 To rnMax
  outputArray(rn, 3) = signal(rn) _
    + DataArray(rn, 2) - outputArray(rn, 3)
Next rn

If zz > 0 Then
  For rn = 1 To rnMax
    If outputArray(rn, 3) < 0 Then _
      outputArray(rn, 3) = 0
```

```
  Next rn
End If

' Summarize the parameters used

' If you do not want a reminder of the parameters chosen,
' and a display of the final score on the status bar, place
' the apostrophe before the word MsgBox

MsgBox "The program DeconvolveIt" & zz & "," & _
  Chr(13) & "using a " & myFilter & _
  "-point parabolic filter," & Chr(13) & _
  "found an answer after " & ItNo & " iterations" & _
  Chr(13) & "with an SSR value of " & SSR & "."

Application.StatusBar = False
Application.ScreenUpdating = False

Selection.Offset(0, 1).Select
Selection.Value = outputArray
Selection.Offset(0, -1).Select
Selection.Value = inputArray
End

InterruptHandler:
If Err.number = 18 Then
  Reply = MsgBox("Do you want to terminate the" & _
    vbCr & "computation? If so, press Yes", vbYesNo, _
    "DeconvolveIt:   Stop iteration?")
  If Reply = vbYes Then GoTo Output
  If Reply = vbNo Then
    Resume ContinueHere
  End If
End If
End Sub

Function ConvolutionWeight(i, t, m, k, s) As Double
Dim h As Integer
Dim Sum As Double
Sum = 0
For h = 0 To k
  Sum = Sum + (2 * h + 1) * (GenFact(2 * m, h) _
  / GenFact(2 * m + h + 1, h + 1)) _
  * GramPolynomial(i, m, h, 0) _
  * GramPolynomial(t, m, h, s)
Next h
ConvolutionWeight = Sum
End Function

Function GramPolynomial(i, m, k, s) As Double
If k > 0 Then
  GramPolynomial = ((4 * k - 2) / (k * (2 * m - k + 1))) _
  * (i * GramPolynomial(i, m, k - 1, s) _
  + s * GramPolynomial(i, m, k - 1, s - 1)) _
  - ((k - 1) / k) * ((2 * m + k) / (2 * m - k + 1)) _
  * GramPolynomial(i, m, k - 2, s)
ElseIf k = 0 And s = 0 Then
  GramPolynomial = 1
Else
```

```
  GramPolynomial = 0
End If
End Function
```

10.5 Time-frequency analysis

```
' ' ' ' ' ' ' ' ' ' ' ' ' ' ' ' ' ' ' ' ' ' ' ' ' ' ' ' ' ' ' ' ' ' ' ' ' ' ' ' ' ' ' ' ' ' ' ' ' ' ' ' ' ' '
' ' ' ' ' ' ' ' ' ' ' ' ' ' ' ' ' ' ' ' ' ' ' ' ' ' ' ' ' ' ' ' ' ' ' ' ' ' ' ' ' ' ' ' ' ' ' ' ' ' ' ' ' ' '
' ' ' ' ' ' ' ' ' ' ' ' ' ' ^^^^^^^^^^^^^^^^^^^^^^^^^^^^^^^^^ ' ' ' ' ' ' ' ' ' ' ' ' ' '
' ' ' ' ' ' ' ' ' ' ' ' ' ^                                ^ ' ' ' ' ' ' ' ' ' ' ' ' ' '
' ' ' ' ' ' ' ' ' ' ' ' ' ^     GABOR TRANSFORMATION        ^ ' ' ' ' ' ' ' ' ' ' ' ' ' '
' ' ' ' ' ' ' ' ' ' ' ' ' ^                                ^ ' ' ' ' ' ' ' ' ' ' ' ' ' '
' ' ' ' ' ' ' ' ' ' ' ' ' ' ' ^^^^^^^^^^^^^^^^^^^^^^^^^^^^^^^^ ' ' ' ' ' ' ' ' ' ' ' ' ' '
' ' ' ' ' ' ' ' ' ' ' ' ' ' ' ' ' ' ' ' ' ' ' ' ' ' ' ' ' ' ' ' ' ' ' ' ' ' ' ' ' ' ' ' ' ' ' ' ' ' ' ' ' ' '
' ' ' ' ' ' ' ' ' ' ' ' ' ' ' ' ' ' ' ' ' ' ' ' ' ' ' ' ' ' ' ' ' ' ' ' ' ' ' ' ' ' ' ' ' ' ' ' ' ' ' ' ' ' '
' ' ' ' ' ' ' ' ' ' ' ' ' ' ' ' ' ' ' ' ' ' ' ' ' ' ' ' ' ' ' ' ' ' ' ' ' ' '(c) R. de Levie
' ' ' ' ' ' ' ' ' ' ' ' ' ' ' ' ' ' ' ' ' ' ' ' ' ' ' ' ' ' ' ' ' ' ' ' ' ' 'v 4.6, June 1, 2004
```

```
' PURPOSE:

' Gabor transformation analyzes a time-dependent signal in
' terms of its frequency content as a function of time. It
' does this by multiplying the time-dependent signal by a
' moving Gaussian window, and by then Fourier-transforming
' the resulting product. The result is stored in two
' arrays, ReOut() and ImOut(), which contain the real and
' imaginary parts of the Fourier transform as a function of
' time and frequency. The contents of one of these arrays,
' or of the corresponding magnitude or phase angle, can
' then be displayed in a color map (using Mapper) or a 3-D
' plot.

' SUBROUTINES:

' This macro requires the subroutine FT.

' INPUT:

' In input information should be placed in two adjacent
' columns, with the left-most column containing time, the
' right-most the corresponding signal. The macro is re-
' stricted to equidistant data, and the time increments
' must therefore be equal. The width of the moving window
' must be an odd power of 2 (here set to be at least a
' factor 2 smaller than the number of data in the set),
' and is selected with an input box.

' OUTPUT:

' The result is displayed with a time axis on top, and a
' frequency axis to the left, ready for immediate visuali-
' zation with Mapper.

' PROCEDURE:

' In order to start the Gabor transform, call the macro
' and enter the requested information in the input boxes.

' WARNING:
```

```
' This macro produces a large output array to the right of
' the input data. It does NOT check whether that array
' contains any information that should not be overwritten.
' Therefore make sure that there is no valuable information
' on the spreadsheet to the right of the input columns.

' dataArray    input data set, two columns wide, the left-
'                 most for time, the rightmost for signal
' M            the number of data in the set, i.e., the
'                 number of rows in dataArray
' N            the number of data used for the window,
'                 smaller than about half of M
' Gaussian     the window function used, containing N points
' ReOut        the real component of the output signal,
'                 as a function of time and frequency
' ImOut        the imaginary component of the output signal,
'                 as a function of time and frequency
' MagOut       the magnitude (absolute value) of the output
'                 signal, as a function of time and frequency
' LogOut       the 10-based logarithm of the magnitude of
'                 the output signal, as a function of time
'                 and frequency
' PhaseOut     the phase angle (in radians) of the output
'                 signal, as a function of time and frequency

Sub Gabor()

Dim i As Integer, j As Integer, jj As Integer
Dim m As Integer, MM As Integer, n As Integer
Dim NN As Integer, MinSpacing As Integer
Dim p As Integer, Spacing As Integer

Dim Gaussian() As Double, ImOut() As Double
Dim Interval As Double, LogOut() As Double
Dim MagOut() As Double, Norm As Double
Dim PhaseOut() As Double, Pi As Double, ReOut() As Double
Dim s As Double, Term() As Double

Dim DataArray As Variant, freqArray As Variant
Dim outputArray As Variant

Dim myRange As Range

Dim Message1, Message3, Title1, Title3, Default3

' Read the time interval

Message1 = "The time interval between successive data is:"
Title1 = "Gabor InputBox 1: Time interval"
Interval = InputBox(Message1, Title1)

' Read the input data

Set myRange = Application.InputBox(Prompt:= _
  "The input data are located in column:", Title:= _
  "Gabor InputBox 2: Input data", Type:=8)
myRange.Select

' Check that there is only one data input column
```

```
If Selection.Columns.Count <> 1 Then
  MsgBox "There can only be ONE data input column."
  End
End If

DataArray = Selection.Value
freqArray = Selection.Value
outputArray = Selection.Value

m = Selection.Rows.Count

' Determine the size of the window width N

MM = m / 4
n = 2
Do
n = 2 * n
Loop Until n > MM

' Set the minimum sample spacing

MinSpacing = Int((m - n + 1) / 125)
jj = MinSpacing

' Select a sample spacing

Message3 = "The minimum sample spacing is:"
Title3 = "Gabor InputBox 3: Sample spacing"
Default3 = MinSpacing
Spacing = InputBox(Message3, Title3, Default3)

If Spacing >= MinSpacing Then jj = Spacing

' Compute the frequency scale

For i = 1 To n
   freqArray(i, 1) = " "
Next i

For i = 1 + n / 2 To n
   freqArray(i, 1) = (-n + 2 * i - 2) / (2 * n * Interval)
Next i

For i = n + 1 To n + 1
   freqArray(i, 1) = (-n + 2 * i - 2) / (2 * n * Interval)
Next i

' Display the frequency scale

Selection.Offset(0, 1).Select
Selection.Value = freqArray

Application.ScreenUpdating = False

' Compute the window function Gaussian()

ReDim Gaussian(1 To n)
Pi = [Pi()]
s = n / 6
```

```
Norm = 12 / Sqr(2 * Pi)
For i = 1 To n
  Gaussian(i) = _
    Norm * Exp(-(i - (n + 1) / 2) ^ 2 / (2 * s * s))
Next i

' The main loop, repeating the analysis M-N+1 times

For j = jj To m - n + 1 Step jj

' Window the input data fragment and rearrange it for FFT

  NN = 2 * n
  ReDim Term(NN) As Double
  For i = 1 To n
    Term(2 * i - 1) = DataArray(i + j - 1, 1) * Gaussian(i)
    Term(2 * i) = 0
  Next i

'  Call the forward Fourier transform subroutine

  Call FT(Term, NN, 1)

' Compute the output data. The following section presents
' several output options, of which only one combination can
' be selected at any one time. For general visualization of
' the result, MagOut is usually the preferred output format

  ReDim MagOut(n, m - n + 1)
'  ReDim ReOut(N, M - N + 1)
'  ReDim ImOut(N, M - N + 1)
'  ReDim LogMagOut(N, M - N + 1)
'  ReDim PhaseOut(N, M - N + 1)
  For i = 1 To n
    MagOut(i, j) = _
      (Sqr(Term(2 * i - 1) ^ 2 + Term(2 * i) ^ 2)) / n
'    ReOut(i, j) = Term(2 * i - 1) / N
'    ImOut(i, j) = Term(2 * i) / N
'    LogMagOut(i, j) = 0.5 * Log((Term(2 * i - 1) ^ 2 _
      + Term(2 * i) ^ 2) / N)
'    PhaseOut(i, j) = Atn(Term(2 * i) / Term(2 * i - 1))
  Next i
  p = Int(100 * (j / (m - n + 1)))
  Application.StatusBar = "Calculation " & p & "% done"

' Data output
' (shown here for MagOut; modify by replacing MagOut
' by alternative output file name XXX(i, j) if so desired)

  For i = 1 To n / 2 - 1
    outputArray(i, 1) = " "
  Next i

  For i = n / 2 To n / 2
    outputArray(i, 1) = j
  Next i

  For i = 1 + n / 2 To n
    outputArray(i, 1) = MagOut(i, j)
```

```
Next i

For i = n + 1 To n + 2
  outputArray(i, 1) = MagOut(1, j)
Next i

For i = n + 2 To m
  outputArray(i, 1) = " "
Next i

  Selection.Offset(0, 1).Select
  Selection.Value = outputArray

Next j

Application.StatusBar = False

End Sub
```

10.6 Semi-integration & semi-differentiation

This short macro is based on an algorithm developed by Keith Oldham (see K. B. Oldham & J. C. Myland, *Fundamentals of Electrochemical Science*, Academic Press 1994) for convolution and deconvolution in cyclic voltammetry, a popular electrochemical method.

```
''''''''''''''''''''''''''''''''''''''''''''''''''''''''''''
'''''''''''''''^^^^^^^^^^^^^^^^^^^^^^^^^^^^^'''''''''''''''''
'''''''''''''''^                           ^''''''''''''''''
'''''''''''''''^    SEMI-INTEGRATION AND    ^''''''''''''''''
'''''''''''''''^    SEMI-DIFFERENTIATION    ^''''''''''''''''
'''''''''''''''^                           ^''''''''''''''''
'''''''''''''''^^^^^^^^^^^^^^^^^^^^^^^^^^^^^'''''''''''''''''
''''''''''''''''''''''''''''''''''''''''''''''(c) R. de Levie
'''''''''''''''''''''''''''''''''''''''''''''v 4.6, June 1, 2004
```

```
' PURPOSE:

' This macro performs semi-integration and semi-differen-
' tiation, specialized (de)convolution methods applicable
' to problems of planar heat conduction, planar diffusion,
' and signal transmission along a cable with uniformly
' distributed resistance and capacitance, see K. B. Oldham,
' Anal. Chem. 41 (1969) 1121; 44 (1972) 196.

' The macro uses a simple semi-integration algorithm; for
' more sophisticated algorithms see K. B. Oldham & J. C.
' Myland, Fundamentals of electrochemical science, Academic
' Press 1994. The semi-differential is then found by taking
' first differences.

' In the context of linear sweep voltammetry or cyclic
' voltammetry (which are both methods used in electro-
' chemical analysis), semi-integration can convert a
' current-time-voltage curve into the corresponding
' steady-state current-voltage curve, which is often
```

```
' much easier to interpret quantitatively. For a discussion
' of such an application, see any modern electrochemical
' textbook, or consult my How to use Excel in analytical
' chemistry, Cambridge Univ. Press, 2001, pp. 257-263.

' SUBROUTINES:

' The drivers SemiIntegrate() and SemiDifferentiate()
' call the subroutine Semi

' INPUT:

' The input data must be equidistant, and should be
' stored in a single, continuous column.

' OUTPUT:

' The resulting transformed output data will be written
' in the column immediately to the right of the input
' data. That column is therefore best left free.

' PROCEDURE:

' Call the macro, and input the data by following the
' instructions with its input boxes.
```

```
Sub SemiIntegrate()
Dim iIntDif As Integer
iIntDif = 1
Call Semi(iIntDif)
End Sub

Sub SemiDifferentiate()
Dim iIntDif As Integer
iIntDif = -1
Call Semi(iIntDif)
End Sub

Sub Semi(iIntDif)
```

```
' The macro uses a simple semi-integration algorithm due
' to Oldham which is adequate to illustrate the approach.
' The semi-differential is then found by taking first
' differences.

' The input data should be stored in a single, continuous
' column. The resulting transformed output data will be
' written in the column immediately to the right of the
' input data. That column is therefore best left free.

' Parameter names used:
'     cnmax          number of columns in
'                    highlighted data block
'     rnmax          number of rows in
'                    highlighted data block
'     dataArray      array of all input data
'     rn             index specifying row number
'                    in input data array
```

```
Dim cnMax As Integer, iIntDif As Integer
Dim j As Integer, k As Integer
Dim n As Integer, rnMax As Integer

Dim A As Double, s As Double, deltaTime As Double
Dim myRange As Range

Dim inputData As Variant, semiInt As Variant
Dim outputData As Variant, testValue As Variant
Dim z As Variant

Dim myAddress, Ans

n = 0

' Input the time increment and use it
' to compute the parameter s

If iIntDif = 1 Then
  deltaTime = _
    InputBox("Enter the time increments, in seconds.", _
    "SemiIntegration InputBox 1: Time increments")
Else
  deltaTime = _
    InputBox("Enter the time increments, in seconds.", _
    "SemiDifferentiation InputBox 1: Time increments")
End If
s = Sqr(Abs(deltaTime))

' Enter the input data

If iIntDif = 1 Then
  Set myRange = Application.InputBox(Prompt:= _
  "The current values are located in:", Title:= _
  "SemiIntegration InputBox 2: Input data", Type:=8)
Else
  Set myRange = Application.InputBox(Prompt:= _
  "The current values are located in:", Title:= _
  "SemiDifferentiation InputBox 2: Input data", Type:=8)
End If
myRange.Select
If Selection.Columns.Count <> 1 Then
  End
Else
  rnMax = Selection.Rows.Count
  inputData = Selection.Value
  semiInt = Selection.Value
  outputData = Selection.Value
  myAddress = Selection.Address
End If

' Check that the output will not overwrite valuable data

Selection.Offset(0, 1).Select
testValue = Selection.Value
For j = 1 To rnMax
  z = testValue(j, 1)
  If IsEmpty(z) Then
    n = n
  Else
```

```
      n = n + 1
   End If
Next j

If n > 0 Then
   Ans = MsgBox("There are data in the space where " _
      & "the output will be" & Chr(13) & " written. " _
      & "Proceed anyway and overwrite those data?", _
   vbYesNo)
   If Ans = vbNo Then
      Selection.Offset(0, -1).Select
      End
   End If
End If
```

```
' Compute the semi-integration
```

```
ReDim p(1 To rnMax) As Double
p(1) = 1
```

```
For j = 2 To rnMax
   p(j) = p(j - 1) * (j - 1.5) / (j - 1)
Next j
For k = 1 To rnMax
   A = 0
   For j = 1 To k
      A = A + p(k - j + 1) * inputData(j, 1)
   Next j
   semiInt(k, 1) = A * s
Next k
```

```
If iIntDif = -1 Then
   For k = 2 To rnMax
      outputData(k, 1) = _
         (semiInt(k, 1) - semiInt(k - 1, 1)) / deltaTime
   Next k
   semiInt(1, 1) = ""
Else
   For k = 1 To rnMax
      outputData(k, 1) = semiInt(k, 1)
   Next k
End If
```

```
' Write the result
```

```
Selection.Value = outputData
```

```
End Sub
```

Chapter 11

Miscellaneous macros

This final chapter lists the macros and functions that could not find a proper home in either chapter 9 or 10, and therefore encompasses the entire range from relatively simple to rather complicated code.

11.1 Terms & conditions

```
'''''''''''''''''''''''''''''''''''''''''''''''''''''''''''''''''
''''''''''''''^^^^^^^^^^^^^^^^^^^^^^^^^^^^^^^^^^^^^^''''''''''''''
''''''''''''''^                                  ^''''''''''''''
''''''''''''''^            MACROBUNDLE            ^''''''''''''''
''''''''''''''^                                  ^''''''''''''''
''''''''''''''^^^^^^^^^^^^^^^^^^^^^^^^^^^^^^^^^^^^^^''''''''''''''
''''''''''''''''''''''''''''''''''''''''''''''''''''(c) R. de Levie
'''''''''''''''''''''''''''''''''''''''''''''''''''v 4.6, June 1, 2004

' PURPOSE

' The macros in this MacroBundle are primarily offered
' as examples of macro writing. They can also be used as
' such in scientific data analysis. Moreover, they can
' be modified by the user (under his responsibility,
' at his own risk, and subject to the conditions
' specified below) for more specialized applications

' WARRANTY

' Because of the inherent complexity of this software,
' and the consequent likelihood of undetected errors, the
' programs in this MacroBundle are made available without
' any warranty whatsoever. There is no guarantee that these
' programs will work, or will be error-free. Always verify
' your answers independently if decisions of possible
' consequence will be based on them. Neither implicit nor
' explicit warranty is made regarding this software,
' including (but not limited to) implied warranties of
' fitness for any particular purpose or application.

' COPYRIGHT

' The material in this MacroBundle is copyrighted.
' Commercial use without specific, written permission from
' the copyright holder is strictly prohibited. However,
' permission is hereby granted for private or educational
' use, provided that such use is strictly non-commercial
```

```
' and/or is neither tied to nor combined with any sale,
' rental, advertisement, promotion, or other commercial
' activity.

' It will be appreciated if, where appropriate, reference
' is made to this software by listing the web site http://
' www.oup-usa.org/advancedexcel where it can be found, and
' /or the book "Advanced Excel for scientific data analy-
' sis" where these macros and functions are explained and
' illustrated.

' INSTALLATION

' The macros in this MacroBundle are written in VBA (Visual
' BASIC for Applications) and will not work in versions of
' Excel preceding Excel 5, because those early versions did
' not use VBA as their macro language. They have been
' developed in Excel 97 and Excel 2000, and are expected to
' work equally well in more recent versions of Excel. Many
' of them will also work in Excel 5 and Excel 95.
'
' The installation procedure is slightly different for
' Excel 5 and Excel 95 on the one hand, and for more
' recent versions on the other. However, all such instal-
' lation procedures start with selecting this text (e.g.,
' with Edit -> SelectAll), copying it to the clipboard,
' and subsequently opening Excel. Thereafter follow the
' instructions under either (A) or (B) as appropriate.

' (A) For installation in Excel 97 or more recent versions,
' use the function key F11 or Tools -> Macro -> Visual
' Basic Editor, followed by (in the VBEditor menu) Insert
' -> Module. Then paste the MacroBundle into that module.

' (B) For installation in Excel 5 or Excel 95, after Excel
' has been opened, use Insert -> Macro -> Module to open a
' module, then paste the MacroBundle text from the clip-
' board into the module. Note: most but not all of these
' programs have been tested to run properly in Excel 5 and
' Excel 95. Therefore, some may occasionally use instruc-
' tions that were not included in these versions of Excel.

' With the above you will have access to all macros of this
' MacroBundle via Alt+F8 (Mac: Opt+F8) or Tools -> Macro ->
' Macros. For more convenient access, first install the
' MacroBundle Toolbar or the MacroBundle Menu. To install,
' e.g., the Toolbar, select Tools, Macro, Macros, then
' double-click on InstallMBToolbar. For the Menu, instead
' double-click on InstallMBMenu. There is no benefit in
' installling both. The Toolbar is the more convenient,
' the Menu takes up less space but requires an additional
' keystroke anytime a macro is selected.

' The MacroBundle Toolbar or MacroBundle Menu can be saved
' with your spreadsheet, and they can be removed with
' RemoveMBToolbar and RemoveMBMenu respectively. You can
' also add your own custom macros to that Toolbar or Menu.

' If you want these macros to be available every time you
```

```
' open a spreadsheet, you can incorporate them in the
' Personal.xls file, which is automatically opened whenever
' you open Excel. However, only place well-tested macros in
' Personal.xls. A poor instruction during macro develop-
' ment, if done in Personal.xls, may get it to 'hang up',
' in which case you may need expert help to extricate you.

' On any given line, all text to the right of an apostrophe
' (such as in this instroduction) is considered a comment,
' and is therefore ignored by the VBEditor. Consequently
' it is not necessary to remove them.

' UPDATE

' Minor corrections have been made in several macros. In
' addition, the following major updates have been made in
' the macros since October 1, 2002:

' *  A new macro, ColumnSolver, has been added. It applies
' Solver sequentially to all cells in a given column rather
' than to just one cell. It takes one target cell, one or
' more parameter cells (which mist be in the same row), and
' (for EqualTo) one parameter value (again in that same
' row), applies Solver, then moves on to the next row. It
' is useful for, e.g., inverse interpolation of algebraic
' functions. Like SolverScan, it requires that Solver.xla
' has been activated, so that the macro can control Solver.

' *  RootFinder has been modified, so that it now has two
' input boxes, allowing input from two independent columns
' (of equal-length), one containing the function F(x), the
' other the parameter x.
```

11.2 Insert a toolbar

The macro shown below is InsertMBToolbar, designed specifically to insert the MacroBundle toolbar. However, once you see how it is done, the principle is easily applied to any other set of macros you may want to make readily accessible. Note that the items shown can (and often have) secondary choices, which appear as submenus by dwelling or clicking on the primary items.

Most of the commands are rather self-explanatory: Popup buttons have secondary menu items, a TooltipText inserts a text note, and BeginGroup a vertical icon divider. The ampersand & in the Caption indicates the character to be underlined, for use as shortcut key. OnAction calls the macro.

The list of items included in the toolbar is readily expanded. You could, e.g., add an item such as Misc, or Whatever, to call a custom macro you are developing. Or you might want to delete some items that you will not use, replace them by others, or whatsoever. This toolbar is now yours to play with.

In order to remove the toolbar, use RemoveMBToolbar, a four-line macro that can be found at the very end of this section.

```
''''''''''''''''''''''''''''''''''''''''''''''''''''''''''''''''
''''''''''''''''''''''''''''''''''''''''''''''''''''''''''''''''
'''''''''''''^^^^^^^^^^^^^^^^^^^^^^^^^^^^^^^^^^^^^^'''''''''''''''
''''''''''''^                                     ^'''''''''''''''
''''''''''''^       INSERT MACROBUNDLE TOOLBAR     ^'''''''''''''''
''''''''''''^                                     ^'''''''''''''''
'''''''''''''^^^^^^^^^^^^^^^^^^^^^^^^^^^^^^^^^^^^^^'''''''''''''''
'''''''''''''''''''''''''''''''''''''''''''''''''''(c) R. de Levie
''''''''''''''''''''''''''''''''''''''''''''''''''v 4.6 June 1, 2004
```

```
' PURPOSE:
'
' This subroutine places an extra toolbar in the Excel
' spreadsheet in order to facilitate access to the custom
' macros of this MacroBundle.
'
' SUBROUTINES:
'
' All the custom macros of the MacroBundle are callable
' with this toolbar. It also establishes the shortcut hot-
' keys to call these macros directly from the keyboard with
' Alt or / followed by the underlined character(s).
'
' LIMITATIONS:
'
' This subroutine works in Excel 97 and in more recent
' versions of Excel; it will not work in Excel 95 or
' earlier versions, which handled toolbars differently.
'
' NOTE:
'
' It is possible to insert a pull-down menu in the standard
' toolbar also, using the macro InsertMBMenu. Although it
' does not lead to any malfunction, there is no advantage
' to installing both the extra menu in the menu bar, and
' the extra toolbar.

Sub InsertMBToolbar()

Dim TBar As CommandBar
Dim Button1 As CommandBarButton
Dim Button2 As CommandBarPopup
Dim Button20 As CommandBarButton
Dim Button21 As CommandBarButton
Dim Button3 As CommandBarPopup
Dim Button30 As CommandBarButton
Dim Button31 As CommandBarButton
Dim Button4 As CommandBarPopup
Dim Button40 As CommandBarButton
Dim Button41 As CommandBarButton
Dim Button5 As CommandBarPopup
Dim Button50 As CommandBarButton
Dim Button51 As CommandBarButton
Dim Button6 As CommandBarPopup
Dim Button60 As CommandBarButton
```

```
Dim Button61 As CommandBarButton
Dim Button7 As CommandBarPopup
Dim Button70 As CommandBarButton
Dim Button71 As CommandBarButton
Dim Button8 As CommandBarButton
Dim Button9 As CommandBarPopup
Dim Button90 As CommandBarButton
Dim Button91 As CommandBarButton
Dim Button92 As CommandBarButton
Dim Button10 As CommandBarButton
Dim Button11 As CommandBarPopup
Dim Button110 As CommandBarButton
Dim Button111 As CommandBarButton
Dim Button12 As CommandBarPopup
Dim Button120 As CommandBarButton
Dim Button121 As CommandBarButton
Dim Button13 As CommandBarPopup
Dim Button130 As CommandBarButton
Dim Button131 As CommandBarButton
Dim Button14 As CommandBarPopup
Dim Button140 As CommandBarButton
Dim Button141 As CommandBarButton
Dim Button15 As CommandBarButton
Dim Button16 As CommandBarPopup
Dim Button160 As CommandBarButton
Dim Button161 As CommandBarButton
Dim Button162 As CommandBarButton
Dim Button163 As CommandBarButton
Dim Button17 As CommandBarButton


' Delete earlier version of MacroBundle,
' if existing, to prevent conflicts

On Error Resume Next
CommandBars("MacroBundle").Delete

' Create a commandbar

Set TBar = CommandBars.Add
With TBar
  .Name = "MacroBundle"
  .Position = msoBarTop
  .Visible = True
End With

' Create Button1 for &Propagation

Set Button1 = CommandBars("MacroBundle").Controls _
  .Add(Type:=msoControlButton)
With Button1
  .Caption = "&Propagation"
  .Style = msoButtonCaption
  .OnAction = "Propagation"
End With

' Create Button2 for &LS

Set Button2 = CommandBars("MacroBundle").Controls _
  .Add(Type:=msoControlPopup)
```

```
With Button2
  .Caption = "&LS"
  .TooltipText = "Highlight array" & Chr(13) & _
    "before pressing" & Chr(13) & "LS0 or LS1"
  .BeginGroup = True
End With

' Create submenus for LS&0 and LS&1 respectively

Set Button20 = Button2.Controls.Add(Type:=msoControlButton)
With Button20
  .Caption = "LS&0"
  .Style = msoButtonCaption
  .OnAction = "LS0"
End With

Set Button21 = Button2.Controls.Add(Type:=msoControlButton)
With Button21
  .Caption = "LS&1"
  .Style = msoButtonCaption
  .OnAction = "LS1"
End With

' Create Button3 for &WLS

Set Button3 = CommandBars("MacroBundle").Controls _
  .Add(Type:=msoControlPopup)
Button3.Caption = "&WLS"
Button3.TooltipText = "Highlight array" & Chr(13) & _
    "before pressing" & Chr(13) & "WLS0 or WLS1"

' Create submenus for WLS&0 and WLS&1 respectively

Set Button30 = Button3.Controls.Add(Type:=msoControlButton)
Button30.Caption = "WLS&0"
Button30.OnAction = "WLS0"

Set Button31 = Button3.Controls.Add(Type:=msoControlButton)
Button31.Caption = "WLS&1"
Button31.OnAction = "WLS1"

' Create Button4 for &ELS

Set Button4 = CommandBars("MacroBundle").Controls _
  .Add(Type:=msoControlPopup)
Button4.Caption = "&ELS"

' Create submenus for ELS&auto and ELS&fixed respectively

Set Button40 = Button4.Controls.Add(Type:=msoControlButton)
Button40.Caption = "ELS&auto"
Button40.OnAction = "ELSauto"

Set Button41 = Button4.Controls.Add(Type:=msoControlButton)
Button41.Caption = "ELS&fixed"
Button41.OnAction = "ELSfixed"

' Create Button5 for LSMul&ti
```

```
Set Button5 = CommandBars("MacroBundle").Controls _
  .Add(Type:=msoControlPopup)
With Button5
  .Caption = "LSMul&ti"
  .BeginGroup = True
  .TooltipText = "Highlight array" & Chr(13) & _
    "before pressing" & Chr(13) & _
    "LSMulti0 or LSMulti1"
End With

' Create submenus for LSMulti&0 and LSMulti&1 respectively

Set Button50 = Button5.Controls _
  .Add(Type:=msoControlButton)
Button50.Caption = "LSMulti&0"
Button50.OnAction = "LSMulti0"

Set Button51 = Button5.Controls.Add(Type:=msoControlButton)
Button51.Caption = "LSMulti&1"
Button51.OnAction = "LSMulti1"

' Create Button6 for LSPol&y

Set Button6 = CommandBars("MacroBundle").Controls _
  .Add(Type:=msoControlPopup)
Button6.Caption = "LSPol&y"
Button6.TooltipText = "Highlight array" & Chr(13) & _
  "before pressing" & Chr(13) & "LSPoly0 or LSPoly1"

' Create submenus for LSPoly&0 and LSPoly&1 respectively

Set Button60 = Button6.Controls.Add(Type:=msoControlButton)
Button60.Caption = "LSPoly&0"
Button60.OnAction = "LSPoly0"

Set Button61 = Button6.Controls.Add(Type:=msoControlButton)
Button61.Caption = "LSPoly&1"
Button61.OnAction = "LSPoly1"

' Create Button7 for &Ortho

Set Button7 = CommandBars("MacroBundle").Controls _
  .Add(Type:=msoControlPopup)
Button7.Caption = "&Ortho"
Button7.TooltipText = "Highlight array" & Chr(13) & _
  "before pressing" & Chr(13) & "Ortho0 or Ortho1"

' Create submenus for Ortho&0 and Ortho&1 respectively

Set Button70 = Button7.Controls.Add(Type:=msoControlButton)
Button70.Caption = "Ortho&0"
Button70.OnAction = "Ortho0"

Set Button71 = Button7.Controls.Add(Type:=msoControlButton)
Button71.Caption = "Ortho&1"
Button71.OnAction = "Ortho1"

' Create Button8 for Solver&Aid
```

```
Set Button8 = CommandBars("MacroBundle").Controls _
  .Add(Type:=msoControlButton)
With Button8
  .Caption = "Solver&Aid"
  .Style = msoButtonCaption
  .BeginGroup = True
  .OnAction = "SolverAid"
End With

' Create Button9 for ColSolver

Set Button9 = CommandBars("MacroBundle").Controls _
  .Add(Type:=msoControlPopup)
Button9.Caption = "Col&umnSolver"

' Create submenus for ColSolverM&ax, ColSolverM&in,
' and ColSolver&Value respectively

Set Button90 = Button9.Controls.Add(Type:=msoControlButton)
Button90.Caption = "ColumnSolverM&ax"
Button90.OnAction = "ColumnSolverMax"

Set Button91 = Button9.Controls.Add(Type:=msoControlButton)
Button91.Caption = "ColumnSolverM&in"
Button91.OnAction = "ColumnSolverMin"

Set Button92 = Button9.Controls.Add(Type:=msoControlButton)
Button92.Caption = "ColumnSolver&Value"
Button92.OnAction = "ColumnSolverValue"

' Create Button10 for Solver&Scan

Set Button10 = CommandBars("MacroBundle").Controls _
  .Add(Type:=msoControlButton)
With Button10
  .Caption = "Solver&Scan"
  .Style = msoButtonCaption
  .OnAction = "SolverScan"
End With

' Create Button11 for &FT

Set Button11 = CommandBars("MacroBundle").Controls _
  .Add(Type:=msoControlPopup)
With Button11
  .Caption = "&FT"
  .BeginGroup = True
  .TooltipText = "Highlight array" & Chr(13) & _
    "before pressing" & Chr(13) & "ForwardFT or" & _
    Chr(13) & "InverseFT"
End With

' Create submenus for &ForwardFT
' and &InverseFT respectively

Set Button110 = _
  Button11.Controls.Add(Type:=msoControlButton)
With Button110
  .Caption = "&ForwardFT"
```

```
  .Style = msoButtonCaption
  .OnAction = "ForwardFT"
End With

Set Button111 = _
  Button11.Controls.Add(Type:=msoControlButton)
With Button111
  .Caption = "&InverseFT"
  .Style = msoButtonCaption
  .OnAction = "InverseFT"
End With

' Create Button11 for (De)&Convolve

Set Button12 = CommandBars("MacroBundle").Controls _
  .Add(Type:=msoControlPopup)
With Button12
  .Caption = "(De)&Convolve"
  .BeginGroup = True
  .TooltipText = "Highlight array" & Chr(13) & _
    "before pressing" & Chr(13) & "Convolve or" & _
    Chr(13) & "Deconvolve"
End With

' Create submenus for &Convolve
' and &Deconvolve respectively

Set Button120 = _
  Button12.Controls.Add(Type:=msoControlButton)
With Button120
  .Caption = "&Convolve"
  .Style = msoButtonCaption
  .OnAction = "Convolve"
End With

Set Button121 = _
  Button12.Controls.Add(Type:=msoControlButton)
With Button121
  .Caption = "&Deconvolve"
  .Style = msoButtonCaption
  .OnAction = "Deconvolve"
End With

' Create Button13 for (De)Con&volveFT

Set Button13 = CommandBars("MacroBundle").Controls _
  .Add(Type:=msoControlPopup)
Button13.Caption = "(De)Con&volveFT"
Button13.TooltipText = "Highlight array" & Chr(13) & _
    "before pressing" & Chr(13) & "ConvolveFT or" & _
    Chr(13) & "DeconvolveFT"

' Create submenus for &ConvolveFT
' and &DeconvolveFT respectively

Set Button130 = Button13.Controls _
  .Add(Type:=msoControlButton)
Button130.Caption = "&ConvolveFT"
Button130.OnAction = "ConvolveFT"
```

```
Set Button131 = Button13.Controls _
  .Add(Type:=msoControlButton)
With Button131
  .Caption = "&DeconvolveFT"
  .Style = msoButtonCaption
  .OnAction = "DeconvolveFT"
End With

' Create Button14 for Deconvolve&It

Set Button14 = CommandBars("MacroBundle").Controls _
  .Add(Type:=msoControlPopup)
Button14.Caption = "Deconvolve&It"
Button14.TooltipText = "Highlight array" & Chr(13) _
  & "before pressing" & Chr(13) & "DeconvolveIt0," _
  & Chr(13) & "or DeconvolveIt1."

' Create submenus for DeconvolveIt&0 and DeconvolveIt&1

Set Button140 = Button14.Controls _
  .Add(Type:=msoControlButton)
With Button140
  .Caption = "DeconvolveIt&0"
  .Style = msoButtonCaption
  .OnAction = "DeconvolveIt0"
End With

Set Button141 = Button14.Controls _
  .Add(Type:=msoControlButton)
With Button141
  .Caption = "DeconvolveIt&1"
  .Style = msoButtonCaption
  .OnAction = "DeconvolveIt1"
End With

' Create Button15 for &Gabor

Set Button15 = CommandBars("MacroBundle").Controls _
  .Add(Type:=msoControlButton)
With Button15
  .Caption = "&Gabor"
  .BeginGroup = True
  .Style = msoButtonCaption
  .OnAction = "Gabor"
End With

' Create Button16 for &Mapper

Set Button16 = CommandBars("MacroBundle").Controls _
  .Add(Type:=msoControlPopup)
Button16.TooltipText = "Select Mapper0 for grayscale" _
  & Chr(13) & "or either Mapper1, Mapper2" & Chr(13) & _
  "     or Mapper3 for color"
Button16.Caption = "&Mapper"
Button16.BeginGroup = True

' Create submenus for Mapper&0 through Mapper&3

Set Button160 = Button16.Controls _
```

```
    .Add(Type:=msoControlButton)
With Button160
   .Caption = "Mapper&0"
   .Style = msoButtonCaption
   .OnAction = "Mapper0"
End With

Set Button161 = Button16.Controls _
   .Add(Type:=msoControlButton)
With Button161
   .Caption = "Mapper&1"
   .Style = msoButtonCaption
   .OnAction = "Mapper1"
End With

Set Button162 = Button16.Controls _
   .Add(Type:=msoControlButton)
With Button162
   .Caption = "Mapper&2"
   .Style = msoButtonCaption
   .OnAction = "Mapper2"
End With

Set Button163 = Button16.Controls _
   .Add(Type:=msoControlButton)
With Button163
   .Caption = "Mapper&3"
   .Style = msoButtonCaption
   .OnAction = "Mapper3"
End With

' Create Button17 for &RootFinder

Set Button17 = CommandBars("MacroBundle").Controls _
   .Add(Type:=msoControlButton)
With Button17
   .Caption = "&RootFinder"
   .BeginGroup = True
   .Style = msoButtonCaption
   .OnAction = "RootFinder"
End With

End Sub
```

' '

```
Sub RemoveMBToolbar()

On Error Resume Next
CommandBars("MacroBundle").Delete

End Sub
```

11.3 Insert a menu

If you don't want to flaunt the MacroBundle toolbar, or wish to save a row of screen space, insert a menu instead. The coding is quite similar to that of section 11.2. To delete, use RemoveMBMenu. Note that this macro will only insert MacroBundle menus in the *main* menu toolbar, not in the toolbar CommandBars(2) that replaces it when you activate a chart.

```
''''''''''''''''''''''''''''''''''''''''''''''''''''''''''''''''''''''''''
''''''''''''''''''''''''''''''''''''''''''''''''''''''''''''''''''''''''''
'''''''''''''''''''^^^^^^^^^^^^^^^^^^^^^^^^^^^^^^^^^^'''''''''''''''''''''
''''''''''''''^                                    ^'''''''''''''''
'''''''''''''''^        INSERT MACROBUNDLE MENU     ^'''''''''''''''
'''''''''''''''^                                    ^'''''''''''''''
'''''''''''''''''''^^^^^^^^^^^^^^^^^^^^^^^^^^^^^^^^^^'''''''''''''''''''''
''''''''''''''''''''''''''''''''''''''''''''''''''''''(c) R. de Levie
''''''''''''''''''''''''''''''''''''''''''''''''''''''v 4.6, June 1, 2004

' PURPOSE:
'
' This subroutine places an extra pull-down menu in the
' Excel menu bars, between Tools and Data (or Chart), in
' order to make it easier to access the custom macros of
' the MacroBundle.
'
' SUBROUTINES:
'
' Many custom macros of the MacroBundle are callable with
' this extra menu. It also establishes the shortcut hotkeys
' to call these macros directly from the keyboard with Alt
' or / followed by the underlined character(s).
'
' LIMITATIONS:
'
' This subroutine works for Excel 97 and more recent ver-
' sions; it will not work in Excel 5 or Excel 95, which
' handle menus quite differently. For example, in Excel 95
' you can insert menu items using the menu editor, but not
' with VBA.
'
' This macro inserts the extra CustomMacros menu in the
' standard toolbar, CommandBars(1), between Tools and
' Data, but NOT in the chart toolbar, CommandBars(2).
'
' NOTE:
'
' The InsertMBMenu macro is offered as an alternative to
' the InsertMBToolbar macro. Although it does not lead to
' any malfunction, there is no advantage to having both
' the extra menu in the menu bar, and the extra toolbar,
' available simultaneously in the same workbook.

Sub InsertMBMenu()

Dim Menu As CommandBarPopup
Dim Menu0 As CommandBarControl
Dim Menu1 As CommandBarControl
Dim Menu2 As CommandBarPopup
Dim Menu20 As CommandBarControl
Dim Menu21 As CommandBarControl
```

```
Dim Menu3 As CommandBarPopup
Dim Menu30 As CommandBarControl
Dim Menu31 As CommandBarControl
Dim Menu4 As CommandBarPopup
Dim Menu40 As CommandBarControl
Dim Menu41 As CommandBarControl
Dim Menu5 As CommandBarPopup
Dim Menu50 As CommandBarControl
Dim Menu51 As CommandBarControl
Dim Menu6 As CommandBarPopup
Dim Menu60 As CommandBarControl
Dim Menu61 As CommandBarControl
Dim Menu7 As CommandBarPopup
Dim Menu70 As CommandBarControl
Dim Menu71 As CommandBarControl
Dim Menu8 As CommandBarControl
Dim Menu9 As CommandBarPopup
Dim Menu90 As CommandBarControl
Dim Menu91 As CommandBarControl
Dim Menu92 As CommandBarControl
Dim Menu10 As CommandBarControl
Dim Menu11 As CommandBarPopup
Dim Menu110 As CommandBarControl
Dim Menu111 As CommandBarControl
Dim Menu12 As CommandBarPopup
Dim Menu120 As CommandBarControl
Dim Menu121 As CommandBarControl
Dim Menu13 As CommandBarPopup
Dim Menu130 As CommandBarControl
Dim Menu131 As CommandBarControl
Dim Menu14 As CommandBarPopup
Dim Menu140 As CommandBarControl
Dim Menu141 As CommandBarControl
Dim Menu15 As CommandBarControl
Dim Menu16 As CommandBarPopup
Dim Menu160 As CommandBarControl
Dim Menu161 As CommandBarControl
Dim Menu162 As CommandBarControl
Dim Menu163 As CommandBarControl
Dim Menu17 As CommandBarControl

' Delete possible earlier menu insertions to prevent
' conflicts and position the new menu on the Menu bar
' just before Data

On Error Resume Next
CommandBars(1).Controls("Custom&Macros").Delete

On Error Resume Next
Set Menu0 = CommandBars(1).FindControl(ID:=30011)
Set Menu = CommandBars(1).Controls _
  .Add(Type:=msoControlPopup, _
  Before:=Menu0.Index, Temporary:=True)
Menu.Caption = "Custom&Macros"

' Create a menu item for Propagation

Set Menu1 = Menu.Controls.Add(Type:=msoControlButton)
Menu1.Caption = "&Propagation "
```

```
Menu1.OnAction = "Propagation"

' Create a menu item for LS

Set Menu2 = Menu.Controls.Add(Type:=msoControlPopup)
Menu2.Caption = "&LS "

' Create submenus for LS0 and LS1 respectively

Set Menu20 = Menu2.Controls.Add(Type:=msoControlButton)
Menu20.Caption = "LS&0"
Menu20.OnAction = "LS0"

Set Menu21 = Menu2.Controls.Add(Type:=msoControlButton)
Menu21.Caption = "LS&1"
Menu21.OnAction = "LS1"

' Create a menu item for WLS

Set Menu3 = Menu.Controls.Add(Type:=msoControlPopup)
Menu3.Caption = "&WLS"

' Create submenus for WLS0 and WLS1 respectively

Set Menu30 = Menu3.Controls.Add(Type:=msoControlButton)
Menu30.Caption = "WLS&0"
Menu30.OnAction = "WLS0"

Set Menu31 = Menu3.Controls.Add(Type:=msoControlButton)
Menu31.Caption = "WLS&1"
Menu31.OnAction = "WLS1"

' Create Button4 for ELS

Set Menu4 = Menu.Controls.Add(Type:=msoControlPopup)
Menu4.Caption = "&ELS"

' Create submenus for ELSauto and ELSfixed respectively

Set Menu40 = Menu4.Controls.Add(Type:=msoControlButton)
Menu40.Caption = "ELS&auto"
Menu40.OnAction = "ELSauto"

Set Menu41 = Menu4.Controls.Add(Type:=msoControlButton)
Menu41.Caption = "ELS&fixed"
Menu41.OnAction = "ELSfixed"

' Create Menu5 for LSMulti

Set Menu5 = Menu.Controls.Add(Type:=msoControlPopup)
Menu5.Caption = "LSMul&ti"
Menu5.TooltipText = "Highlight array" & Chr(13) & _
  "before pressing" & Chr(13) & "LSMulti0 or LSMulti1"

' Create submenus for LSMulti0 and LSMulti1 respectively

Set Menu50 = Menu5.Controls.Add(Type:=msoControlButton)
Menu50.Caption = "LSMulti&0"
Menu50.OnAction = "LSMulti0"
```

```
Set Menu51 = Menu5.Controls.Add(Type:=msoControlButton)
Menu51.Caption = "LSMulti&1"
Menu51.OnAction = "LSMulti1"

' Create Menu6 for LSPoly

Set Menu6 = Menu.Controls.Add(Type:=msoControlPopup)
Menu6.Caption = "LSPol&y"
Menu6.TooltipText = "Highlight array" & Chr(13) & _
  "before pressing" & Chr(13) & "LSPoly0 or LSPoly1"

' Create submenus for LSPoly0 and LSPoly1 respectively

Set Menu60 = Menu6.Controls.Add(Type:=msoControlButton)
Menu60.Caption = "LSPoly&0"
Menu60.OnAction = "LSPoly0"

Set Menu61 = Menu6.Controls.Add(Type:=msoControlButton)
Menu61.Caption = "LSPoly&1"
Menu61.OnAction = "LSPoly1"

' Create Menu7 for Ortho

Set Menu7 = Menu.Controls.Add(Type:=msoControlPopup)
Menu7.Caption = "&Ortho"
Menu7.TooltipText = "Highlight array" & Chr(13) & _
  "before pressing" & Chr(13) & "Ortho0 or Ortho1"

' Create submenus for Ortho0 and Ortho1 respectively

Set Menu70 = Menu7.Controls.Add(Type:=msoControlButton)
Menu70.Caption = "Ortho&0"
Menu70.OnAction = "Ortho0"

Set Menu71 = Menu7.Controls.Add(Type:=msoControlButton)
Menu71.Caption = "Ortho&1"
Menu71.OnAction = "Ortho1"

' Create Menu8 for SolverAid

Set Menu8 = Menu.Controls.Add(Type:=msoControlButton)
Menu8.Caption = "Solver&Aid"
Menu8.OnAction = "SolverAid"

' Create Menu9 for ColSolver

Set Menu9 = Menu.Controls.Add(Type:=msoControlPopup)
Menu9.Caption = "Col&umnSolver"

' Create submenus for ColSolverMax, ColSolverMin, and
' ColSolverValue respectively

Set Menu90 = Menu9.Controls.Add(Type:=msoControlButton)
Menu90.Caption = "ColumnSolverM&ax"
Menu90.OnAction = "ColumnSolverMax"

Set Menu91 = Menu9.Controls.Add(Type:=msoControlButton)
Menu91.Caption = "ColumnSolverM&in"
Menu91.OnAction = "ColumnSolverMin"
```

```
Set Menu92 = Menu9.Controls.Add(Type:=msoControlButton)
Menu92.Caption = "ColumnSolver&Value"
Menu92.OnAction = "ColumnSolverValue"

' Create Menu10 for SolverScan

Set Menu10 = Menu.Controls.Add(Type:=msoControlButton)
Menu10.Caption = "Solver&Scan"
Menu10.OnAction = "SolverScan"

' Create Menu11 for FT

Set Menu11 = Menu.Controls.Add(Type:=msoControlPopup)
Menu11.Caption = "&FT"
Menu11.TooltipText = "Highlight array" & Chr(13) & _
  "before pressing" & Chr(13) & "ForwardFT or" & _
  Chr(13) & "InverseFT"

' Create submenus for ForwardFT and InverseFT respectively

Set Menu110 = Menu11.Controls.Add(Type:=msoControlButton)
With Menu110
  .Caption = "&ForwardFT"
  .Style = msoButtonCaption
  .OnAction = "ForwardFT"
End With

Set Menu111 = Menu11.Controls.Add(Type:=msoControlButton)
With Menu111
  .Caption = "&InverseFT"
  .Style = msoButtonCaption
  .OnAction = "InverseFT"
End With

' Create Menu12 for (De)Convolve

Set Menu12 = Menu.Controls.Add(Type:=msoControlPopup)
Menu12.Caption = "(De)&Convolve"
Menu12.TooltipText = "Highlight array" & Chr(13) & _
  "before pressing" & Chr(13) & "Convolve or" & _
  Chr(13) & "Deconvolve"

' Create submenus for Convolve and Deconvolve respectively

Set Menu120 = Menu12.Controls.Add(Type:=msoControlButton)
With Menu120
  .Caption = "&Convolve"
  .Style = msoButtonCaption
  .OnAction = "Convolve"
End With

Set Menu121 = Menu12.Controls.Add(Type:=msoControlButton)
With Menu121
  .Caption = "&Deconvolve"
  .Style = msoButtonCaption
  .OnAction = "Deconvolve"
End With

' Create Menu13 for ConvolveFT
```

```
Set Menu13 = Menu.Controls.Add(Type:=msoControlPopup)
Menu13.Caption = "Con&volveFT"
Menu13.TooltipText = "Highlight array" & Chr(13) & _
  "before pressing" & Chr(13) & "ConvolveFT or" & _
  Chr(13) & "DeconvolveFT"

' Create submenus for ConvolveFT
' and DeconvolveFT respectively

Set Menu130 = Menu13.Controls.Add(Type:=msoControlButton)
With Menu130
  .Caption = "&ConvolveFT"
  .Style = msoButtonCaption
  .OnAction = "ConvolveFT"
End With

Set Menu131 = Menu13.Controls.Add(Type:=msoControlButton)
With Menu131
  .Caption = "&DeconvolveFT"
  .Style = msoButtonCaption
  .OnAction = "DeconvolveFT"
End With

' Create Menu14 for DeConvolveIt

Set Menu14 = Menu.Controls.Add(Type:=msoControlPopup)
Menu14.Caption = "Deconvolve&It"
Menu14.TooltipText = "Highlight array" & Chr(13) & _
  "before pressing" & Chr(13) & "DeconvolveIt0" _
  & Chr(13) & "or DeconvolveIt1."

' Create submenus for DeconvolveIt0
' and DeconvolveIt1 respectively

Set Menu140 = Menu14.Controls.Add(Type:=msoControlButton)
With Menu140
  .Caption = "DeconvolveIt&0"
  .Style = msoButtonCaption
  .OnAction = "DeconvolveIt0"
End With

Set Menu141 = Menu14.Controls.Add(Type:=msoControlButton)
With Menu141
  .Caption = "&DeconvolveIt&1"
  .Style = msoButtonCaption
  .OnAction = "DeconvolveIt1"
End With

' Create Menu15 for Gabor

Set Menu15 = Menu.Controls.Add(Type:=msoControlButton)
With Menu15
  .Caption = "&Gabor"
  .Style = msoButtonCaption
  .OnAction = "Gabor"
End With

' Create Menu16 for Mapper
```

```
Set Menu16 = Menu.Controls.Add(Type:=msoControlPopup)
Menu16.Caption = "&Mapper"

' Create submenus for Mapper

Set Menu160 = Menu16.Controls.Add(Type:=msoControlButton)
With Menu160
  .Caption = "Mapper&0"
  .Style = msoButtonCaption
  .OnAction = "Mapper0"
End With

Set Menu161 = Menu16.Controls.Add(Type:=msoControlButton)
With Menu161
  .Caption = "Mapper&1"
  .Style = msoButtonCaption
  .OnAction = "Mapper1"
End With

Set Menu162 = Menu16.Controls.Add(Type:=msoControlButton)
With Menu162
  .Caption = "Mapper&2"
  .Style = msoButtonCaption
  .OnAction = "Mapper2"
End With

Set Menu163 = Menu16.Controls.Add(Type:=msoControlButton)
With Menu163
  .Caption = "Mapper&3"
  .Style = msoButtonCaption
  .OnAction = "Mapper3"
End With

' Create Menu17 for RootFinder

Set Menu17 = Menu.Controls.Add(Type:=msoControlButton)
With Menu17
  .Caption = "&RootFinder"
  .Style = msoButtonCaption
  .OnAction = "RootFinder"
End With

End Sub

''''''''''''''''''''''''''''''''''''''''''''''''''''''''''''

Sub RemoveMBMenu()

On Error Resume Next
CommandBars(1).Controls("Custom&Macros").Delete

End Sub
```

11.4 Movie demos

These small demonstration programs graphically illustrate how to manipulate the spreadsheet with VBA. Notice in MovieDemo4 the instruction `Application.Volatile True`, which forces the function to update not only when one of its inputs is changed, but whenever *any* spreadsheet cell is recalculated.

```
''''''''''''''''''''''''''''''''''''''''''''''''''''''''''''''
''''''''''''''''''''''''''''''''''''''''''''''''''''''''''''''
'''''''''''''^^^^^^^^^^^^^^^^^^^^^^^^^^^^^^^^^^^^^^^^'''''''''''''
''''''''''''^                                      ^'''''''''''''
''''''''''''^      MOVIE DEMONSTRATION MACROS       ^'''''''''''''
''''''''''''^                                      ^'''''''''''''
'''''''''''''^^^^^^^^^^^^^^^^^^^^^^^^^^^^^^^^^^^^^^^^'''''''''''''
''''''''''''''''''''''''''''''''''''''''''''''''''''(c) R. de Levie
''''''''''''''''''''''''''''''''''''''''''''''''''''v 4.6, June 1, 2004
```

```
' The following macros merely demonstrate how to make
' simple Excel 'movies'
```

```
''''''''''''''''''''''' MOVIEDEMO 1 '''''''''''''''''''''''
```

```
' This demonstration macro requires that you enter the
' number 0 in cells A1 and B1, and the number 10 in A2 and
' B2. Then highlight the area A1:B2, and make a correspon-
' ding graph. Format both axes to have manual scales from 0
' to 10. Make sure that the graph displays B1:B2 vs. A1:A2
' as individual points ('markers'). Then call the macro,
' and enjoy the show.
```

```
Sub MovieDemo1()

Range("A1") = 0
Range("A2") = 0

For i = 1 To 400
  Range("A1") = 10 - 0.05 * Abs(i - 200)
  Range("A2") = 10 * Exp(-0.001 * (i - 300) ^ 2)
  Application.ScreenUpdating = True
Next i

Range("A1") = 0
Range("A2") = 0

End Sub
```

```
''''''''''''''''''''''' MOVIEDEMO 2 '''''''''''''''''''''''
```

```
' This demonstration macro requires that you enter the num-
' ber 0 in cells H1 and I1, and the number 10 in H2 and I2.
' Then highlight the area H1:I2, and make a corresponding
' graph. Format both axes to have manual scales from 0 to
' 10. Make sure that the graph displays I1:I2 vs. H1:H2 as
' individual points ('markers') connected by a line. Then
' call the macro.
```

```
Sub MovieDemo2()

Range("H1") = 5: Range("I1") = 1
Range("H2") = 5: Range("I2") = 5

'Application.ScreenUpdating = True
```

```
For i = 1 To 1000
  Range("H1") = 5 - 5 * Sin(0.06 * i)
  Range("I1") = 5 - 5 * Cos(0.07 * i)
  Application.ScreenUpdating = True
Next i

Range("H1") = 5: Range("I1") = 1
Range("H2") = 5: Range("I2") = 5


End Sub
```

'''''''''''''''''''''''' **MOVIEDEMO 3** '''''''''''''''''''''''''''

```
' This demonstration macro requires that you enter the
' numbers 0 through 10 in cells A15 through A25, and the
' number 5 in cells B15:B25. Again use a graph with manual
' scales from 0 to 10, and display the data in B15:B25 vs.
' A15:A25 as markers plus (smoothed) connecting lines.

Sub MovieDemo3()

Range("A15") = 0: Range("B15") = 5
Range("A16") = 1: Range("B16") = 5
Range("A17") = 2: Range("B17") = 5
Range("A18") = 3: Range("B18") = 5
Range("A19") = 4: Range("B19") = 5
Range("A20") = 5: Range("B20") = 5
Range("A21") = 6: Range("B21") = 5
Range("A22") = 7: Range("B22") = 5
Range("A23") = 8: Range("B23") = 5
Range("A24") = 9: Range("B24") = 5
Range("A25") = 10: Range("B25") = 5
Application.ScreenUpdating = True

For i = 1 To 100
  Application.ScreenUpdating = False
  Range("B15") = 5 + 0.04 * i * Sin(0.01 * i)
  Range("B16") = 5 + 0.04 * i * Sin(0.01 * i - 100)
  Range("B17") = 5 + 0.04 * i * Sin(0.01 * i - 200)
  Range("B18") = 5 + 0.04 * i * Sin(0.01 * i - 300)
  Range("B19") = 5 + 0.04 * i * Sin(0.01 * i - 400)
  Range("B20") = 5 + 0.04 * i * Sin(0.01 * i - 500)
  Range("B21") = 5 + 0.04 * i * Sin(0.01 * i - 600)
  Range("B22") = 5 + 0.04 * i * Sin(0.01 * i - 700)
  Range("B23") = 5 + 0.04 * i * Sin(0.01 * i - 800)
  Range("B24") = 5 + 0.04 * i * Sin(0.01 * i - 900)
  Range("B25") = 5 + 0.04 * i * Sin(0.01 * i - 1000)
  Application.ScreenUpdating = True
Next i

For i = 101 To 900
  Application.ScreenUpdating = False
  Range("B15") = 5 + 4 * Sin(0.01 * i)
  Range("B16") = 5 + 4 * Sin(0.01 * i - 100)
  Range("B17") = 5 + 4 * Sin(0.01 * i - 200)
  Range("B18") = 5 + 4 * Sin(0.01 * i - 300)
  Range("B19") = 5 + 4 * Sin(0.01 * i - 400)
  Range("B20") = 5 + 4 * Sin(0.01 * i - 500)
  Range("B21") = 5 + 4 * Sin(0.01 * i - 600)
```

```
  Range("B22") = 5 + 4 * Sin(0.01 * i - 700)
  Range("B23") = 5 + 4 * Sin(0.01 * i - 800)
  Range("B24") = 5 + 4 * Sin(0.01 * i - 900)
  Range("B25") = 5 + 4 * Sin(0.01 * i - 1000)
  Application.ScreenUpdating = True
Next i


For i = 901 To 1000
  Application.ScreenUpdating = False
  Range("B15") = 5 + 0.04 * (1000 - i) * Sin(0.01 * i)
  Range("B16") = _
    5 + 0.04 * (1000 - i) * Sin(0.01 * i - 100)
  Range("B17") = _
    5 + 0.04 * (1000 - i) * Sin(0.01 * i - 200)
  Range("B18") = _
    5 + 0.04 * (1000 - i) * Sin(0.01 * i - 300)
  Range("B19") = _
    5 + 0.04 * (1000 - i) * Sin(0.01 * i - 400)
  Range("B20") = _
    5 + 0.04 * (1000 - i) * Sin(0.01 * i - 500)
  Range("B21") = _
    5 + 0.04 * (1000 - i) * Sin(0.01 * i - 600)
  Range("B22") = _
    5 + 0.04 * (1000 - i) * Sin(0.01 * i - 700)
  Range("B23") = _
    5 + 0.04 * (1000 - i) * Sin(0.01 * i - 800)
  Range("B24") = _
    5 + 0.04 * (1000 - i) * Sin(0.01 * i - 900)
  Range("B25") = _
    5 + 0.04 * (1000 - i) * Sin(0.01 * i - 1000)
  Application.ScreenUpdating = True
Next i


Range("A15") = 0: Range("B15") = 5
Range("A16") = 1: Range("B16") = 5
Range("A17") = 2: Range("B17") = 5
Range("A18") = 3: Range("B18") = 5
Range("A19") = 4: Range("B19") = 5
Range("A20") = 5: Range("B20") = 5
Range("A21") = 6: Range("B21") = 5
Range("A22") = 7: Range("B22") = 5
Range("A23") = 8: Range("B23") = 5
Range("A24") = 9: Range("B24") = 5
Range("A25") = 10: Range("B25") = 5


End Sub


''''''''''''''''''''''''' MOVIEDEMO 4 '''''''''''''''''''''''''

' This demonstration macro requires that you enter the
' numbers 0, 0, 5, 5, 5, 5, 10 in cells A29:A36, and the
' number 0,1,7,5,5,5,5,0 in cells B29:B36. Again use a
' graph with manual scales from 0 to 10, and display the
' data as individually distinct points, each of a different
' type and/or color. For example, point A32,B32 might be a
' hollow black circle of size 18, point A33,B33 a hollow
' red circle of size 14, point A34,B34 a hollow black cir-
' cle of size 9, and point A35,B35 be a solid red circle of
' size 6. Also make the other data markers distinct.
```

```
Sub MovieDemo4()

Range("A1") = 0: Range("B1") = 0
Range("A2") = 0: Range("B2") = 1
Range("A3") = 5: Range("B3") = 9
Range("A4") = 5: Range("B4") = 5
Range("A5") = 5: Range("B5") = 5
Range("A6") = 5: Range("B6") = 5
Range("A7") = 5: Range("B7") = 5
Range("A8") = 10: Range("B8") = 0

Application.ScreenUpdating = True
Application.Volatile True

For i = 1 To 1000
  Application.ScreenUpdating = False
  Range("A1") = 5 - 5 * Sin(0.01 * (i - 500))
  Range("B1") = 5 - 5 * Sin(0.01 * (i - 500))
  Range("A2") = Range("A2") + 0.01
  Range("B2") = 5 - 4 * Cos(0.03 * i)
  Range("A3") = 5 + 4 * Sin(0.2 * i)
  Range("B3") = 5 - 4 * Cos(0.2 * i)
  If CDbl(i) / 160 - CInt(i / 160) = 0 Then
    Range("A4") = 5 + (5 * Rnd() - 2.5)
    Range("B4") = 5 + (5 * Rnd() - 2.5)
  End If
  If CDbl(i) / 170 - CInt(i / 170) = 0 Then
    Range("A5") = Range("A4")
    Range("B5") = Range("B4")
  End If
  If CDbl(i) / 180 - CInt(i / 180) = 0 Then
    Range("A6") = Range("A4")
    Range("B6") = Range("B4")
  End If
  If CDbl(i) / 190 - CInt(i / 190) = 0 Then
    Range("A7") = Range("A4")
    Range("B7") = Range("B4")
  End If
  If CDbl(i) / 10 - CInt(i / 10) = 0 Then
    Range("A8") = 5 + 5 * Sin(0.01 * (i - 500))
  End If
  Range("B8") = Range("B8") + 0.01
  Application.ScreenUpdating = True
Next i

Range("A1") = 0: Range("B1") = 0
Range("A2") = 0: Range("B2") = 1
Range("A3") = 5: Range("B3") = 9
Range("A4") = 5: Range("B4") = 5
Range("A5") = 5: Range("B5") = 5
Range("A6") = 5: Range("B6") = 5
Range("A7") = 5: Range("B7") = 5
Range("A8") = 10: Range("B8") = 0
End Sub
```

'''''''''''''''''''''' **MOVIEDEMO 5** ''''''''''''''''''''''''

```
' This demonstration macro requires that you enter the
' numbers 4, 4, 4, 4, 6, 6, 6, and 6 in cells H15:H22,
```

```
' and the number 5 in cells I15:I22. Again use a graph
' with manual scales from 0 to 10, and display the points
' H15, I15, and H19:I19 as small solid circles, preferably
' of different color, and the others as larger, hollow
' (concentric) rings around them.

Sub MovieDemo5()

Range("H15") = 4: Range("I15") = 5
Range("H16") = 4: Range("I16") = 5
Range("H17") = 4: Range("I17") = 5
Range("H18") = 4: Range("I18") = 5
Range("H19") = 6: Range("I19") = 5
Range("H20") = 6: Range("I20") = 5
Range("H21") = 6: Range("I21") = 5
Range("H22") = 6: Range("I22") = 5

For i = 1 To 252
  Range("H15") = 4 + 0.2 * Sin(0.1 * i)
  Range("H16") = 4 + 0.3 * Sin(0.1 * i)
  Range("H17") = 4 + 0.4 * Sin(0.1 * i)
  Range("H18") = 4 + 0.5 * Sin(0.1 * i)
  Range("H19") = 6 - 0.2 * Sin(0.1 * i)
  Range("H20") = 6 - 0.3 * Sin(0.1 * i)
  Range("H21") = 6 - 0.4 * Sin(0.1 * i)
  Range("H22") = 6 - 0.5 * Sin(0.1 * i)
  Application.ScreenUpdating = True
Next i

For i = 253 To 502
  Range("H15") = _
    5 + Cos(0.025 * i) * (-1 + 0.2 * Sin(0.1 * i))
  Range("I15") = _
    5 + Sin(0.025 * i) * (-1 + 0.2 * Sin(0.1 * i))
  Range("H16") = _
    5 + Cos(0.025 * i) * (-1 + 0.3 * Sin(0.1 * i))
  Range("I16") = _
    5 + Sin(0.025 * i) * (-1 + 0.3 * Sin(0.1 * i))
  Range("H17") = _
    5 + Cos(0.025 * i) * (-1 + 0.4 * Sin(0.1 * i))
  Range("I17") = _
    5 + Sin(0.025 * i) * (-1 + 0.4 * Sin(0.1 * i))
  Range("H18") = _
    5 + Cos(0.025 * i) * (-1 + 0.5 * Sin(0.1 * i))
  Range("I18") = _
    5 + Sin(0.025 * i) * (-1 + 0.5 * Sin(0.1 * i))
  Range("H19") = _
    5 + Cos(0.025 * i) * (1 - 0.2 * Sin(0.1 * i))
  Range("I19") = _
    5 + Sin(0.025 * i) * (1 - 0.2 * Sin(0.1 * i))
  Range("H20") = _
    5 + Cos(0.025 * i) * (1 - 0.3 * Sin(0.1 * i))
  Range("I20") = _
    5 + Sin(0.025 * i) * (1 - 0.3 * Sin(0.1 * i))
  Range("H21") = _
    5 + Cos(0.025 * i) * (1 - 0.4 * Sin(0.1 * i))
  Range("I21") = _
    5 + Sin(0.025 * i) * (1 - 0.4 * Sin(0.1 * i))
  Range("H22") = _
```

```
     5 + Cos(0.025 * i) * (1 - 0.5 * Sin(0.1 * i))
   Range("I22") = _
     5 + Sin(0.025 * i) * (1 - 0.5 * Sin(0.1 * i))
   Application.ScreenUpdating = True
Next i

For i = 503 To 630
   Range("H15") = 4 + 0.2 * Sin(0.1 * i)
   Range("H16") = 4 + 0.3 * Sin(0.1 * i)
   Range("H17") = 4 + 0.4 * Sin(0.1 * i)
   Range("H18") = 4 + 0.5 * Sin(0.1 * i)
   Range("H19") = 6 - 0.2 * Sin(0.1 * i)
   Range("H20") = 6 - 0.3 * Sin(0.1 * i)
   Range("H21") = 6 - 0.4 * Sin(0.1 * i)
   Range("H22") = 6 - 0.5 * Sin(0.1 * i)
   Application.ScreenUpdating = True
Next i

Range("H15") = 4: Range("I15") = 5
Range("H16") = 4: Range("I16") = 5
Range("H17") = 4: Range("I17") = 5
Range("H18") = 4: Range("I18") = 5
Range("H19") = 6: Range("I19") = 5
Range("H20") = 6: Range("I20") = 5
Range("H21") = 6: Range("I21") = 5
Range("H22") = 6: Range("I22") = 5
Application.ScreenUpdating = True

End Sub
```

11.5 Lagrange interpolation

This *function* is provided here and in the MacroBundle because you may want to insert it in some other spreadsheet. As a function it must be repeated in every cell that uses it, but it updates automatically.

The code contains the Match function, which has the syntax Match (*Value*, *Array*, *Type*). It returns a ranking number indicating the location of *Value* in the searched *Array*. *Type* can have one of three values, 1, 0, and –1, which defines what it will look for. The default, 1, looks for the largest number that is smaller than or equal to ($\leq$) *Value*, assuming that *Array* has been sorted in ascending order. Its mirror image, with *Type* is specified as –1, recovers the smallest number $\geq$ *Value*, provided *Array* is organized in descending order. When *Type* is set to 0, the function looks for an exact match, and can also be used to search text, including single-character (?) and multicharacter (*) wildcards.

```
'''''''''''''''''''''''''''''''''''''''''''''''''''''''''''''''''
'''''''''''''''''''''''''''''''''''''''''''''''''''''''''''''''''
'''''''''''''''^^^^^^^^^^^^^^^^^^^^^^^^^^^^^^^'''''''''''''''''''
'''''''''''''''^                             ^'''''''''''''''''''
'''''''''''''''^    LAGRANGE INTERPOLATION    ^'''''''''''''''''''
'''''''''''''''^                             ^'''''''''''''''''''
```

```
' ' ' ' ' ' ' ' ' ' ' ' ' ' ' ' ^^^^^^^^^^^^^^^^^^^^^^^^^^^^^^^^^ ' ' ' ' ' ' ' ' ' ' ' ' ' ' ' ' '
' ' ' ' ' ' ' ' ' ' ' ' ' ' ' ' ' ' ' ' ' ' ' ' ' ' ' ' ' ' ' ' ' ' ' '(c)  R.  de  Levie
' ' ' ' ' ' ' ' ' ' ' ' ' ' ' ' ' ' ' ' ' ' ' ' ' ' ' ' ' ' ' 'v 4.6, June 1, 2004

Function Lagrange(XArray, YArray, x, m)

' m denotes the order of the polynomial used,
' and must be an integer between 1 and 14

Dim Row As Integer, i As Integer, j As Integer
Dim Term As Double, Y As Double

Row = Application.Match(x, XArray, 1)
If Row < (m + 1) / 2 Then Row = (m + 1) / 2
If Row > XArray.Count - (m + 1) / 2 Then _
  Row = XArray.Count - (m + 1) / 2
For i = Row - (m - 1) / 2 To Row + (m + 1) / 2
  Term = 1
  For j = Row - (m - 1) / 2 To Row + (m + 1) / 2
    If i <> j Then Term = Term * (x - XArray(j)) / _
      (XArray(i) - XArray(j))
  Next j
  Y = Y + Term * YArray(i)
Next i
Lagrange = Y

End Function
```

11.6 SolverScan

As described in section 4.17, SolverScan lets Solver determine two adjustable parameters by searching the corresponding, two-dimensional parameter space of initial conditions with a user-specified grid size, and then displays the corresponding value of the optimization criterion used, such as SSR, the sum of squares of the residuals. When the optimization criterion is single-valued throughout the sampled parameter domain, the latter apparently does not contain 'false' optima (i.e., minima with SSR) unless these are so narrow that they escaped detection, in which case they are of relatively little consequence anyway.

Depending on the complexity of the problem posed, Solver may take one or more seconds for each determination, and a fine search grid may therefore take a long time. The grid size for each parameter has been limited to 251 steps (which will also ensure that the results can be displayed on the spreadsheet), but that limit involves more than 63,000 repeat operations of Solver, and will be quite time-consuming. A much more limited search grid is therefore advisable.

While it is possible to run Solver with all its bells and whistles in SolverScan, it is advisable to use it in its fastest form, i.e., without any unnecessary constraints in Solver and, likewise, without unneeded nonlinear functions such as IF or LOOKUP embedded in the adjustable function. Also make sure that, in the Solver Parameters dialog box under Options, the Show Iteration Results is turned off.

The input to SolverScan is somewhat awkward, since (in order to stay within the self-imposed constraints of this book) it contains ten separate input boxes, four for each of the two input parameters, and one each to specify the location of the target cell and of the output, instead of a single dialog box. This might make it rather laborious to make input corrections. We have therefore included default values in the input boxes, so that data that were earlier entered correctly need not be reentered.

The bottom line shows the progress of the macro. Operation can be interrupted by pushing the Esc key, but will not display the output data computed at that point.

11.6.1 Calling Solver with VBA

Solver can be driven with a VBA call provided that Solver.xla is properly referenced in the VBAProject. To see whether it is, go to the spreadsheet, select the module (e.g., with Alt∪F11), and look under Tools ⇒ References to see whether Solver has been activated. It should be part of the contiguous, check-marked top items in the list. If it is check-marked but not adjacent to the other check-marked items, move it up. If it is not check-marked at all, follow the procedure given in the heading of SolverScan. Some specific commands to specify the parameters used by Solver are listed below. They fall in four categories that follow the layout of the Solver dialog boxes.

The basic Solver parameters, otherwise specified in the top of the Solver Parameters dialog box, are defined with `SolverOK`. The advanced features of the Solver Options dialog box are set with the command `SolverOptions`, and any constraints with `SolverAdd`, `SolverChange`, or `SolverDelete`. Finally, the output is specified with `SolverFinish`, and the status of all these parameters can be probed with `SolverGet`. Finally, the command `SolverSolve` starts Solver; it is equivalent to the Solve command in the Solver Parameters dialog box. If you want VBA to read the status of Solver, use `SolverGet`.

Information on all these commands is listed in the VBA Help file, accessible from the VBA module with F1 or Help ⇒ Microsoft Visual Basic Help under the Index tab. Note that you can only call that help file in the module, but that it will sometimes appear in the spreadsheet, in which case you should quickly move back to the spreadsheet with Alt∪F11.

The syntax of `SolverOK` is `SolverOK`(*SetCell, MaxMinValue, By Change*), where *SetCell* specifies the target cell containing the optimization criterion, *MaxMinVal* has the value 1 for <u>M</u>ax, 2 for Mi<u>n</u>, and 3 for <u>V</u>alue of: (in which case you must also give the specific value), and *ByChange* lists the parameters that Solver should adjust. Such an instruction might therefore read

```
SolverOK SetCell:="F5", MaxMinVal:=2, ByChange:="D2:D4,D6"
```

if the criterion (e.g., SSR) is listed in cell F5, and the adjustable parameters are located in cells D2 through D4 and D6.

To initiate action you need to use the command `SolverSolve`. Its syntax is `SolverSolve`(*UserFinish, ShowRef*), where `UserFinish:=True` simply performs the Solver operation, whereas `UserFinish:=False` (or absence of this part of the instruction) ensures that the Solver Results dialog box appears, letting you choose to either accept or reject it. The second item, *ShowRef*, is also optional, and lets Solver call another macro after each trial solution.

A complete, working subroutine might therefore look like

```
Sub TestSolverDriver()
SolverOK SetCell:="F5", MaxMinVal:=2, ByChange:="D2:D4,D6"
SolverSolve UserFinish:=True
End Sub
```

11.6.2 Programming details

A user who is turned back by one of the built-in checks at, say, the ninth input box will not appreciate having to reenter all the data. Default values are therefore incorporated in the later input boxes. That user is therefore sent back only partway. Moreover, default values are set on first data entry, and are shown when subsequent input corrections must be made. Another way to achieve this is by dimensioning a parameter as `Static` (instead of `Dim`), in which case its last-assigned value will be remembered by the program.

ScreenUpdating is suppressed while the program checks for possible data overwrite, turned back on briefly to allow input for a possible query, and turned off again during the main calculation. This speeds up the computation, and also yields a quieter screen. Just before the program ends, ScreenUpdating is automatically restored.

Solver uses the StatusBar. In order to avoid a conflict, the StatusBar is turned off while Solver is working, then turned back on to display the progress of the calculation. Because the status bar remains until removed or overwritten, the user will not notice any discontinuities.

11.6.3 Possible extensions

If you must adjust n parameters simultaneously (where $n > 2$), you can modify the macro to accommodate this, but the output must then be stored as an n-dimensional array, of which only two-dimensional 'slices' can be displayed by Mapper.

If you require a random or pseudorandom search, you can modify the macro by using the Randomize statement to generate random numbers. In that case the individual coordinates of all initial values must be saved (since they cannot be reconstructed), and Mapper (which requires equidistant points) cannot be used.

```
'''''''''''''''''''''''''''''''''''''''''''''''''''''''''''''''
'''''''''''''''''''''''''''''''''''''''''''''''''''''''''''''''
''''''''''''''''''''''''^^^^^^^^^^^^^^^^^^^^^^^^''''''''''''''''
'''''''''''''''''''''^                     ^''''''''''''''''''''
''''''''''''''''''''^        SOLVER  SCAN    ^'''''''''''''''''''
'''''''''''''''''''''^                     ^'''''''''''''''''''''
''''''''''''''''''''''''^^^^^^^^^^^^^^^^^^^^^^^''''''''''''''''''
''''''''''''''''''''''''''''''''''''''''''''''''''(c) R.  de Levie
''''''''''''''''''''''''''''''''''''''''''''''''''v 4.6, June 1, 2004

' PURPOSE:
'
' SolverScan uses Solver to scan possible combinations of
' two adjustable parameters, P and Q, by changing the
' initial guess values that Solver uses as its points of
' departure. Its output displays the value of the criterion
' (such as SSR) used to optimize P and Q.
'
' The user specifies the initial values, the step sizes to
' be used to vary those initial values, and the numbers of
' such steps. The output is presented as an array suitable
' for display with Mapper or as a 3-D plot.
'
' Selecting a fine search grid (i.e., many small steps)
' increases the execution time of the macro. The macro has
' built-in limits of 251 steps per parameter, but using far
' fewer steps is usually sufficient, and certainly makes
' the macro complete its task much faster.
'
' INPUT:
'
' Set up Solver as if for a single operation, including
' all necessary specifications of constraints and options,
' if any. Then call SolverScan and answer the questions in
' the input boxes. SolverScan will start once the output
' area has been specified.
'
' OUTPUT:
'
' The user selects the location where the output array will
```

```
' appear, complete with top and left-hand axis labels for
' subsequent visual display with Mapper or as a 3-D plot
' of SSR as a function of P and Q, where P and Q are the
' two Solver-adjusted parameters, and where P is plotted
' in the X-direction, and Q in the Y-direction.
'
' SUBROUTINES:
'
' SolverScan requires that both Solver and Solver.xla
' have been installed.
'
' ONE-TIME PROCEDURE FOR INSTALLING SOLVER.XLA
'
' SolverScan can only call Solver as a subroutine, when
' Solver.xla is properly referenced in the VBAProject.
' To see whether this is the case, go to the spreadsheet,
' select its VBA module, and look under Tools ->
' References to see whether SOLVER has been activated.
' It should be part of the contiguous, check-marked top
' items in the listed References - VBAProject. If it is
' not, first prepare your computer to make Solver callable.
' The procedure to do so is outlined below, and is needed
' only once until the operating system and/or Excel is
' re-installed or updated.
'
' Click on the Start button, and in the resulting menu, on
' Search, For Files or Folders...(or Find > Files or
' Folders). In the Find: All Files dialog box, under the
' tab Name & Location, in the Name: window type Solver.xla,
' and, if necessary, enter Systemdisk[C:] in the Look in:
' window, activate Include subfolders, and click on Find
' now. Note down where Solver.xla is located. (If you have
' Microsoft Office, it most likely is in Systemdisk[C:],
' Program Files\Microsoft Office\Office\Library\Solver.)
' Exit the Search or Find dialog box, which will bring you
' back to the spreadsheet, select the VBEditor with
' Alt+F11, then go to Tools -> References, which will
' display the References - VBAProject dialog box. Click on
' Browse, select Filers of type: Microsoft Excel Files
' (*.xls, *.xla), and now that you know where to find it,
' navigate your way to Solver.xla, and Open it. This
' will return you to the References - VBAProject dialog
' box, where you now use the Priority up button to move
' it up, so that it is listed contiguously with the other,
' already activated add-ins. Click OK; from then on (i.e.,
' until you reload or upgrade Excel) VBA will know how to
' find Solver when it is called from a macro.

Sub SolverScan()

Dim nc As Integer, ns As Integer, nz As Integer
Dim p As Integer, PassOut As Integer, PassP As Integer
Dim PassQ As Integer, PassTarget As Integer, q As Integer
Dim StepNumberP As Integer, StepNumberQ As Integer
Dim InitialValueP As Double, InitialValueQ As Double
Dim StepSizeP As Double, StepSizeQ As Double
Dim SSR As Variant, z As Variant
Dim RangeOut As Range, RangeP As Range
Dim RangeQ As Range, RangeTarget As Range
```

```
Dim AddressOut, AddressP, AddressQ, AddressTarget
Dim Answer, Default, Prompt, Title

' Specify the location of the Target criterion

Prompt = "Enter a CELL ADDRESS:" & Chr(13) & Chr(13) & _
  "The target cell (containing the opti-" _
  & Chr(13) & "mization criterion) is located in:"
Title = "SolverScan: Address of target cell"
Set RangeTarget = Application.InputBox(Prompt, Title, Type:=8)
RangeTarget.Select
AddressTarget = RangeTarget.Address
SSR = RangeTarget.Value

PassP = 1
AP:

' Read the address of the first adjustable parameter, P

Prompt = "Enter a CELL ADDRESS:" & Chr(13) & Chr(13) & _
  "The first adjustable parameter, P, is located in:"
Title = "SolverScan: Address of P"
If PassP = 1 Then Default = " "
If PassP > 1 Then Default = RangeP.Address
Set RangeP = Application.InputBox(Prompt, Title, Default, Type:=8)
RangeP.Select
AddressP = RangeP.Address

' Specify the initial guess value for P

Prompt = "Enter a value:" & Chr(13) & Chr(13) & _
  "The initial value of P is:"
Title = "SolverScan: Initial value of P"
If PassP = 1 Then Default = " "
If PassP > 1 Then Default = InitialValueP
InitialValueP = InputBox(Prompt, Title, Default)

' Specify the step size for P

Prompt = "Enter a value:" & Chr(13) & Chr(13) & _
  "The step size for P is:"
Title = "SolverScan: Step size for P"
If PassP = 1 Then Default = " "
If PassP > 1 Then Default = StepSizeP
StepSizeP = Application.InputBox(Prompt, Title, Default)

' Specify the number of steps for P

Prompt = "Enter a value:" & Chr(13) & Chr(13) & _
  "The number of steps for P is:"
Title = "SolverScan: Step number for P"
If PassP = 1 Then Default = " "
If PassP > 1 Then Default = StepNumberP
StepNumberP = Application.InputBox(Prompt, Title, Default)
PassP = PassP + 1

' Check that StepNumberP is smaller than 252

If StepNumberP > 251 Then
```

```
    MsgBox "The number of steps cannot be larger than 251."
    GoTo AP
End If

PassQ = 1
AQ:

' Read the address of the first adjustable parameter, Q

Prompt = "Enter a CELL ADDRESS:" & Chr(13) & Chr(13) & _
  "The first adjustable parameter, Q, is located in:"
Title = "SolverScan: Address of Q"
If PassQ = 1 Then Default = ""
If PassQ > 1 Then Default = RangeQ.Address
Set RangeQ = Application.InputBox(Prompt, Title, _
  Default, Type:=8)
RangeQ.Select
AddressQ = RangeQ.Address

' Specify the initial guess value for Q

Prompt = "Enter a value:" & Chr(13) & Chr(13) & _
  "The initial value of Q is:"
Title = "SolverScan: Initial value of Q"
If PassQ = 1 Then Default = ""
If PassQ > 1 Then Default = InitialValueQ
InitialValueQ = InputBox(Prompt, Title, Default)

' Specify the step size for Q

Prompt = "Enter a value:" & Chr(13) & Chr(13) & _
  "The step size for Q is:"
Title = "SolverScan: Step size for Q"
If PassQ = 1 Then Default = " "
If PassQ > 1 Then Default = StepSizeQ
StepSizeQ = Application.InputBox(Prompt, Title, Default)

' Specify the number of steps for Q

Prompt = "Enter a value:" & Chr(13) & Chr(13) & _
  "The number of steps for Q is:"
Title = "SolverScan: Step number for Q"
If PassQ = 1 Then Default = " "
If PassQ > 1 Then Default = StepNumberQ
StepNumberQ = Application.InputBox(Prompt, Title, Default)
PassQ = PassQ + 1

' Check that StepNumberQ is smaller than 252

If StepNumberQ > 251 Then
  MsgBox "The number of steps cannot be larger than 251."
  GoTo AQ
End If

' Specify the top left-hand corner of the Output array

PassOut = 1
AOut:
```

```
Prompt = "The output array, including its axes, " _
   & "will be" & Chr(13) & StepNumberP + 1 _
   & " columns wide, and " & StepNumberQ + 1 _
   & " rows high." & Chr(13) & _
   "                    Enter a CELL ADDRESS:" & Chr(13) _
   & "The top left-hand corner of the output" & Chr(13) _
   & "array should be located at:"
Title = "SolverScan: Top left-hand corner of output array"
If PassOut = 1 Then Default = " "
If PassOut > 1 Then Default = RangeOut.Address
Set RangeOut = Application.InputBox(Prompt, Title, Type:=8)
RangeOut.Select
AddressOut = RangeOut.Address
PassOut = PassOut + 1

' Count the number of columns nc to the left of RangeOut

nc = 0
AEdge:
On Error GoTo OnEdge
Selection.Offset(0, -1).Select
nc = nc + 1
GoTo AEdge

OnEdge:
RangeOut.Select

' Make sure that there is enough space for the output array

If nc + StepNumberP > 254 Then
  MsgBox "Move the left-hand corner of the" & _
     Chr(13) & "output array to the left, in order" & _
     Chr(13) & "to accommodate its projected size."
  GoTo AOut
End If

' Verify that the output will not overwrite valuable data

Application.ScreenUpdating = False
nz = 0
RangeOut.Select
For p = 0 To StepNumberP + 1
  Selection.Offset(0, 1).Select
  For q = 0 To StepNumberQ + 1
    Selection.Offset(1, 0).Select
    z = Selection.Value
    nz = nz + 1
    If (IsEmpty(z) Or z = Null) Then nz = nz - 1
  Next q
Next p

Application.ScreenUpdating = True
If nz > 0 Then
  Answer = MsgBox("There are data in the array in which" _
     & Chr(13) & "the output data will be written. " _
     & "Proceed" & Chr(13) _
     & "anyway and overwrite those data?", vbYesNo)
  If Answer = vbNo Then GoTo AOut
End If
```

```
Application.ScreenUpdating = False
ReDim SSR(StepNumberQ + 1, StepNumberP + 1) As Double

' Enter the initial guess values,
' run Solver, and write output file

ns = 0
For p = 0 To StepNumberP
  RangeP.Select
  RangeP.Value = InitialValueP + p * StepSizeP
  For q = 0 To StepNumberQ
    RangeQ.Select
    RangeQ.Value = InitialValueQ + q * StepSizeQ

    Application.DisplayStatusBar = False
    SolverOK SetCell:="addressTarget", MaxMinVal:=2, _
      ByChange:="addressP, addressQ"
    SolverSolve UserFinish:=True

    RangeTarget.Select
    SSR(q, p) = RangeTarget.Value
    ns = ns + 1
    Application.DisplayStatusBar = True
    Application.StatusBar = "SolverScan has completed " & _
      ns & " out of " & (StepNumberP + 1) * _
      (StepNumberQ + 1) & " calculations."
  Next q
Next p

' Write the axis scale labels

RangeOut.Select
For p = 1 To StepNumberP + 1
  Selection.Offset(0, p).Select
  Selection.Value = InitialValueP + (p - 1) * StepSizeP
  ActiveCell.Font.Italic = True
  ActiveCell.Font.Bold = True
  Selection.Offset(0, -p).Select
Next p
For q = 1 To StepNumberQ + 1
  Selection.Offset(q, 0).Select
  ActiveCell.Font.Italic = True
  ActiveCell.Font.Bold = True
  Selection.Value = InitialValueQ + (q - 1) * StepSizeQ
  Selection.Offset(-q, 0).Select
Next q

' Output the SSR data

RangeOut.Select
For p = 0 To StepNumberP
  For q = 0 To StepNumberQ
    Selection.Offset(q + 1, p + 1).Select
    Selection.Value = SSR(q, p)
    Selection.Offset(-q - 1, -p - 1).Select
  Next q
Next p

End Sub
```

11.7 Mapper

Mapper complements the 3-D graphing capabilities of Excel, by providing a colored (or gray-scale) map of a function with equidistant *x*- and *y*-axes. Other color schemes can readily be added, and/or the existing schemes modified. Linear scales are used, but you can of course modify this. For example, the map on the cover of this book was made by inserting, immediately following the line `Application.ScreenUpdating = False`, a nested double For...Next loop with the instruction `input Array(rn, cn) = Sqr(inputArray(rn, cn))` for `rn = 2 To rnMax` and `cw = 2 To cwMax`, in order to accentuate the signal. Using its logarithm rather than its square root would have emphasized the signal even more over its background.

Both Mapper and Excel's 3-D plots are limited to display single-valued functions of *x* and *y*. For more complicated three-dimensional shapes, more sophisticated software is needed.

Mapper briefly takes you outside Excel, and therefore may need some fine-tuning for a particular computer. It converts the values of a data set into RGB color code, then writes a file to a bitmap, which is subsequently re-imported into Excel as the background of a graph. It uses several subroutines. Of most direct interest to the user are the subroutines BitMap*n*(), which define the color schemes used. You can modify them or, better yet, add similar subroutines of your own making in order to broaden your palette. The samples amply illustrate how to do this. Leave the rest alone unless you are comfortable with computer code at this level.

William H. Craig of Georgetown University wrote most of the special code for this macro, generous help that is gratefully acknowledged.

```
''''''''''''''''''''''''''''''''''''''''''''''''''''''''''''''''''''''
''''''''''''''''''''''''''''''''''''''''''''''''''''''''''''''''''''''
''''''''''''''''''''''''''^^^^^^^^^^^^^^^^^^^''''''''''''''''''''''''''
''''''''''''''''''''''''^                 ^'''''''''''''''''''''''''''
''''''''''''''''''''''''^     MAPPER      ^'''''''''''''''''''''''''''
''''''''''''''''''''''''^                 ^'''''''''''''''''''''''''''
''''''''''''''''''''''''''^^^^^^^^^^^^^^^^^^^''''''''''''''''''''''''''
''''''''''''''''''''''''''''''''''''''''''''''''''''(c) R. de Levie
''''''''''''''''''''''''''''''''''''''''''''''''''''v 4.6, June 1, 2004

' PURPOSE:
'
' This macro reads a highlighted block of data, including
' axis labels at its top and left-hand side. This format
' was chosen in order to be compatible with that of Excel
' 2-D graphs and 3-D surface plots. The macro separates
```

```
' these labels, converts the remaining data into RGB colors
' with either a gray scale (for iColor = 0) or one of three
' sample color schemes provided (iColor = 1 to 3), and uses
' these to make a graph. If you wish, look at the subrou-
' tines BitMap0 through BitMap3 to see how it is done, then
' add your own color scheme.
'
' This macro is most useful when there are many data points
' in both directions. If not, Excel's 3-D plot may well be
' the more satisfactory. Both of them require the input
' data to be equidistant in x as well as in y. When the
' plot contains relatively few data points, the simple, bi-
' linear interpolation to generate pixel values can cause
' star-like artifacts, as if one looks at a street lamp
' through a finely woven cloth. This could be remedied by
' using a more sophisticated interpolation scheme.
'
' The resulting figure can be moved, enlarged or reduced,
' annotated, and modified as any other XY graph. Data
' points, curves, and text can be added, scales can be
' modified or deleted, etc.
'
' In order to facilitate displaying scales, the macro
' checks whether the top left cell in the highlighted
' array is empty, and the cells below it and to its right
' are filled. Note, however, that the scales displayed
' merely reflect the numbers provided in the top row and
' the left column, and are NOT functional, so that modi-
' fying them afterwards will not rescale or otherwise
' affect the map. Moreover, the map does not respond to
' subsequent changes in the input data until the macro
' is called again to update the input information.
'
' SUBROUTINES:
'
' The drivers Mapper0 through Mapper3 call the main routine
' Mapper, which in turn calls on a number of subroutines:
' BitmapHeader, WriteAWord, WriteALong, WriteAPixel,
' WriteAByte, and Bitmap0 through Bitmap3. If you want to
' add a different color scheme, just add one as Bitmap4
' with a corresponding driver (Mapper4), using the existing
' code as example. If you use the MBToolbar or MBMenu, make
' sure to include the new driver(s) there.
'
' INPUT:
'
' The macro requires an input array together with the
' corresponding scales, which must be placed in the top
' row and in the left-hand column, leaving the top left-
' hand cell empty.
'
' OUTPUT:
'
' The resulting map can be resized, rescaled, moved, and
' otherwise manipulated as any graph. You can also insert
' text, overlay curves, add inserts, etc.
'
' PROCEDURE:
'
```

```
' Highlight the array to be mapped together with the
' corresponding scales, which must be placed in the
' top row and in the left-hand column, leaving the
' top left-hand cell empty. Then call the macro.
'
' WARNING:
'
' This macro goes OUTSIDE OF Excel in order to write
' a bitmap, which is then re-imported as 'background'
' for the graph. Depending on how the rest of the Office
' bundle is configured (or in its absence, when only
' Excel is loaded) the macro may not always run properly.

Sub Mapper0()

Dim iColor As Integer
iColor = 0
Call Mapper(0)

End Sub
Sub Mapper1()

Dim iColor As Integer
iColor = 1
Call Mapper(1)

End Sub
Sub Mapper2()

Dim iColor As Integer
iColor = 2
Call Mapper(2)

End Sub
Sub Mapper3()

Dim iColor As Integer
iColor = 3
Call Mapper(3)

End Sub
```

' '

```
Sub Mapper(iColor As Integer)

' Nomenclature used:
'
' inputArray     the highlighted block containing the data
'                plus (at its top and left-hand side)
'                either axis labels or space for them.
' scaledArray    the input array scaled to fit the range
'                from 0 to 255.
' valueArray     the interpolated array. It has as many
'                terms as there are pixels in the plotting
'                area. All terms are double precision, in
'                the range from 0 to 255
' pixelArray     the value array expressed in terms of
'                integers.
```

```
' rn              input data height.
' ph              pixel (instead or row) height, starting at
'                     the bottom with 0.
' cw              input data width.
' pw              pixel (instead of column) width, starting
'                     at the left with 0.
' cwMax-1, rhMax-1      number of input data, in terms of
'                     columns and rows respectively.
' hMax, wMax      number of pixels, in terms of height and
'                     width respectively.
' HH, WW          number of pixels per input data point, in
'                     terms of height and width respectively.

Dim cn As Integer, cw As Integer, cwMax As Integer
Dim ph As Integer, pw As Integer
Dim rh As Integer, rn As Integer, rhMax As Integer
Dim i As Integer, iH As Integer, iW As Integer
Dim j As Integer
Dim OutputFileNumber As Integer
Dim maxValue As Double, minValue As Double
Dim Product As Long
Dim XLabelMax As Double, XLabelMin As Double
Dim YLabelMax As Double, YLabelMin As Double
Dim a1 As Integer, a2 As Integer, b1 As Integer
Dim h As Integer, HH As Integer, hScale As Integer
Dim hMax As Integer, hMax0 As Integer         ' plot pixel height
Dim wMax As Integer, wMax0 As Integer    ' plot pixel width
Dim ns As Integer                        ' number of data series
Dim p As Integer
Dim w As Integer, WW As Integer, wScale As Integer
Dim h1 As Double, h2 As Double
Dim w1 As Double, w2 As Double
Dim inputArray As Variant, scaledArray As Variant
Dim pixelArray As Variant, ValueArray As Variant
Dim OutputFileName As String, Sheetname As String
Dim hAnswer, myRange, ThisSheet

' Read the inputArray

Begin:
inputArray = Selection.Value
cwMax = Selection.Columns.Count
rhMax = Selection.Rows.Count

' If input area was not highlighted

If rhMax = 1 And cwMax = 1 Then
  hAnswer = MsgBox("You forgot to highlight" _
    & Chr(13) & "the block of input data." _
    & Chr(13) & "Do you want to do so now?" _
    , vbYesNo, "Mapper")
  If hAnswer = vbNo Then End
  If hAnswer = vbYes Then
    Set myRange = Application.InputBox(Prompt:= _
      "The input data are located in:", Type:=8)
    myRange.Select
  End If
  GoTo Begin
End If
```

```
Application.ScreenUpdating = False

If rhMax < 3 Then
  MsgBox "The block, including (space for)" & _
    Chr(13) & "a scale at the top row," & _
    Chr(13) & "should be at least 3 cells high."
End
End If
If cwMax < 3 Then
  MsgBox "The block, including (space for)" & _
    Chr(13) & "a scale at the left-most column," & _
    Chr(13) & "should be at least 3 cells wide."
  End
End If

' Make sure that the top left cell is empty, but that
' its two nearest neighbors are not. Note: the top column
' and the left-most column will be used for creating the
' map scales, and will NOT be plotted.

p = 0
If IsEmpty(inputArray(1, 1)) Or IsNull(inputArray(1, 1)) _
  Then p = p + 1
If p = 0 Then
  MsgBox "Make sure that the top left cell" & _
  Chr(13) & "of the highlighted area is empty."
  End
End If
If IsEmpty(inputArray(2, 1)) Or IsNull(inputArray(2, 1)) _
  Then p = p + 1
If IsEmpty(inputArray(1, 2)) Or IsNull(inputArray(1, 2)) _
  Then p = p + 1
If p <> 1 Then
  MsgBox "  Make sure that the top row and the" & _
  Chr(13) & "left-hand column contain the plot scales," & _
  Chr(13) & "while leaving the left top cell empty."
  End
End If

' Find maximum and minimum values in XLabels and YLabels

YLabelMax = inputArray(2, 1)
YLabelMin = inputArray(2, 1)
For rn = 3 To rhMax
  If inputArray(rn, 1) > YLabelMax Then YLabelMax = _
    inputArray(rn, 1)
  If inputArray(rn, 1) < YLabelMin Then YLabelMin = _
    inputArray(rn, 1)
Next rn

XLabelMax = inputArray(1, 2)
XLabelMin = inputArray(1, 2)
For cn = 3 To cwMax
  If inputArray(1, cn) > XLabelMax Then XLabelMax = _
    inputArray(1, cn)
  If inputArray(1, cn) < XLabelMin Then XLabelMin = _
    inputArray(1, cn)
Next cn
```

```
' Find maximum and minimum values in inputArray

maxValue = inputArray(2, 2)
minValue = inputArray(2, 2)
For rn = 2 To rhMax
  For cn = 2 To cwMax
    If inputArray(rn, cn) > maxValue Then maxValue = _
      inputArray(rn, cn)
    If inputArray(rn, cn) < minValue Then minValue = _
      inputArray(rn, cn)
  Next cn
Next rn

' Scale the inputArray on a scale from 0 to 255

ReDim scaledArray(0 To rhMax, 0 To cwMax)
For rn = 2 To rhMax
  For cn = 2 To cwMax
    scaledArray(rn, cn) = 255 * (inputArray(rn, cn) _
      - minValue) / (maxValue - minValue)
  Next cn
Next rn

' Draw graph

cw = Columns(1).Width
rh = Rows(1).Height
Sheetname = ActiveSheet.Name
Charts.Add
ActiveChart.ChartType = xlXYScatter
ActiveChart.Location Where:=xlLocationAsObject, Name:=Sheetname
ActiveChart.Axes(xlValue).Select
With ActiveChart.Axes(xlValue)
  .MinimumScaleIsAuto = True
  .MaximumScaleIsAuto = True
  .MajorUnitIsAuto = True
  .MinorUnitIsAuto = True
  .Crosses = xlAutomatic
  .MajorTickMark = xlCross
  .MinorTickMark = xlNone
  .TickLabelPosition = xlLow
End With
Selection.TickLabels.NumberFormat = "General"
ActiveChart.Axes(xlCategory).Select
With ActiveChart.Axes(xlCategory)
  .MinimumScaleIsAuto = True
  .MaximumScaleIsAuto = True
  .MajorUnitIsAuto = True
  .MinorUnitIsAuto = True
  .Crosses = xlAutomatic
  .MajorTickMark = xlCross
  .MinorTickMark = xlNone
  .TickLabelPosition = xlLow
End With
With Selection.Border
  .Weight = xlHairline
  .LineStyle = xlAutomatic
End With
```

```
' Round plot area height and width to integer
' multiples of the data in the input array

wScale = 1
If wMax > cwMax - 1 Then wScale = Int(wMax0 / (cwMax - 2))
hScale = 1
If hMax > rhMax - 1 Then hScale = Int(hMax0 / (rhMax - 2))
wMax = (cwMax - 2) * wScale
hMax = (rhMax - 2) * hScale
HH = hMax / (rhMax - 2)
WW = wMax / (cwMax - 2)


' Calculate valueArray for cn = 2 to cwMax

ReDim ValueArray(0 To hMax, 0 To wMax) As Double
ReDim pixelArray(0 To hMax, 0 To wMax) As Integer
For cn = 2 To cwMax
  h = hMax
  iH = Int(h / HH)
  h1 = (iH + 1) - h / HH
  h2 = h / HH - iH
  ValueArray(hMax, (cn - 2) * WW) = _
    h1 * scaledArray(iH + 2, cn)
Next cn

For cn = 2 To cwMax
  For h = 0 To hMax - 1
    iH = Int(h / HH)
    h1 = (iH + 1) - h / HH
    h2 = h / HH - iH
    ValueArray(h, (cn - 2) * WW) = _
      h1 * scaledArray(iH + 2, cn) _
      + h2 * scaledArray(iH + 3, cn)
  Next h
Next cn

' Calculate all of valueArray

For h = 0 To hMax
  For w = 1 To wMax - 1
    iW = Int(w / WW)
    w1 = (iW + 1) - w / WW
    w2 = w / WW - iW
    ValueArray(h, w) = w1 * ValueArray(h, iW * WW) + _
      w2 * ValueArray(h, (iW + 1) * WW)
  Next w
Next h

' Convert pixel values to integers

For h = 0 To hMax
  For w = 0 To wMax
    pixelArray(h, w) = CInt(ValueArray(h, w))
  Next w
Next h

'Create, write, and close the bitmap file

OutputFileName = "ColorMap.BMP"
```

```
OutputFileNumber = 1
Open OutputFileName For Binary Access Write As _
  #OutputFileNumber

Call BitmapHeader(hMax, wMax)

If iColor = 0 Then Call BitMap0(hMax, wMax, pixelArray)
If iColor = 1 Then Call BitMap1(hMax, wMax, pixelArray)
If iColor = 2 Then Call BitMap2(hMax, wMax, pixelArray)
If iColor = 3 Then Call BitMap3(hMax, wMax, pixelArray)

Close #OutputFileNumber
ThisSheet = ActiveSheet.Name
ActiveChart.PlotArea.Fill.UserPicture OutputFileName

' Maximize the plot area

ActiveChart.PlotArea.Select
Selection.Fill.Visible = True

' Set the axis labels

ActiveChart.Axes(xlCategory).Select
ActiveChart.Axes(xlCategory).MinimumScale = XLabelMin
ActiveChart.Axes(xlCategory).MaximumScale = XLabelMax
ActiveChart.Axes(xlValue).Select
ActiveChart.Axes(xlValue).MinimumScale = YLabelMin
ActiveChart.Axes(xlValue).MaximumScale = YLabelMax

' Remove all markers

ns = ActiveChart.SeriesCollection.Count
For i = 1 To ns
  ActiveChart.SeriesCollection(i).Select
  ActiveChart.SeriesCollection(i).MarkerStyle = xlNone
Next i

ActiveChart.ChartArea.Select

End Sub

'''''''''''''''''''''''''''''''''''''''''''''''''''''''''''''''''

' This routine writes a minimal 54 byte bitmap file header.

Private Sub BitmapHeader(ph As Integer, pw As Integer)

' Values for pixel width pW, pixel height pH, ImageSize-
' InByte and TotalFileSize change with the image size.

Dim RowLengthInBytes  As Long
Dim ImageSizeInByte As Long
Dim TotalFileSize As Long

' Calculate three values needed write header. In
' particular, row length is the number of bytes
' rounded up to the next DWORD (4 byte) boundary.

RowLengthInBytes = (((pw + 1) * 3) \ 4) * 4
```

```
ImageSizeInByte = RowLengthInBytes * ph
TotalFileSize = 54 + (ph * RowLengthInBytes)

' Write the BitmapFileHeader

WriteAWord 19778          ' bfType    The two characters BM
WriteALong TotalFileSize            ' bfSize    Headers + image
WriteALong 0             ' bfReserved1&2  Two words of zero.
WriteALong 54            ' bfOffBits      Byte offset to image.

' Write the BitmapInfoHeader

WriteALong 40    ' biSize        BITMAPINFOHEADER size = 40.
WriteALong pw      ' biWidth          Image width.
WriteALong ph      ' biHeight         Image width.
WriteAWord 1       ' biPlanes         Always 1.
WriteAWord 24      ' biBitCount   Always 24 bits per pixel.
WriteALong 0       ' biCompression   No compression = 0
WriteALong ImageSizeInByte
                ' biSizeImage      Image size in bytes
WriteALong 3000      ' biXPelsPerMeter  A safe value
WriteALong 3000      ' biYPelsPerMeter  A safe value
WriteALong 0         ' biClrUsed        Always 0
WriteALong 0         ' biClrImportant   Always 0

End Sub

''''''''''''''''''''''''''''''''''''''''''''''''''''''''''''''''''''

Private Sub BitMap0(hMax As Integer, _
  wMax As Integer, pixelArray As Variant)

Dim h As Integer, w As Integer, RedVal As Integer
Dim GreenVal As Integer, BlueVal As Integer

For h = hMax To 0 Step -1
  For w = 0 To wMax - 1
    RedVal = pixelArray(h, w)
    GreenVal = pixelArray(h, w)
    BlueVal = pixelArray(h, w)
    WriteAPixel RedVal Mod 256, GreenVal Mod 256, _
      BlueVal Mod 256
  Next w
' Do not change the following, essential row padding
  w = wMax * 3
  Do While (w Mod 4) <> 0
    WriteAByte 0
    w = w + 1
  Loop
Next h

End Sub

''''''''''''''''''''''''''''''''''''''''''''''''''''''''''''''''''''

Private Sub BitMap1(hMax As Integer, _
  wMax As Integer, pixelArray As Variant)

Dim h As Integer, w As Integer, RedVal As Integer
```

```
Dim GreenVal As Integer, BlueVal As Integer

For h = hMax To 0 Step -1
  For w = 0 To wMax - 1

' from black to dark gray

    If pixelArray(h, w) < 32 Then
      RedVal = Int(4 * pixelArray(h, w))
      GreenVal = Int(4 * pixelArray(h, w))
      BlueVal = Int(4 * pixelArray(h, w))

' from dark gray to dark brown

    ElseIf pixelArray(h, w) < 64 Then
      RedVal = 128
      GreenVal = Int(192 - 2 * pixelArray(h, w))
      BlueVal = Int(192 - 2 * pixelArray(h, w))

' from dark brown to dark purple

    ElseIf pixelArray(h, w) < 96 Then
      RedVal = 128
      GreenVal = 64
      BlueVal = Int(-64 + 2 * pixelArray(h, w))

' from dark purple to dark blue

    ElseIf pixelArray(h, w) < 128 Then
      RedVal = Int(320 - 2 * pixelArray(h, w))
      GreenVal = 64
      BlueVal = Int(-64 + 2 * pixelArray(h, w))

' from dark blue to light blue

    ElseIf pixelArray(h, w) < 160 Then
      RedVal = Int(192 - pixelArray(h, w))
      GreenVal = Int(-576 + 5 * pixelArray(h, w))
      BlueVal = Int(64 + pixelArray(h, w))

' from light blue to green

    ElseIf pixelArray(h, w) < 192 Then
      RedVal = Int(192 - pixelArray(h, w))
      GreenVal = 224
      BlueVal = Int(864 - 4 * pixelArray(h, w))

' from green to yellow green

    ElseIf pixelArray(h, w) < 208 Then
      RedVal = Int(-1152 + 6 * pixelArray(h, w))
      GreenVal = 224
      BlueVal = 96

' from yellow green to brown yellow

    ElseIf pixelArray(h, w) < 224 Then
      RedVal = Int(-1568 + 8 * pixelArray(h, w))
      GreenVal = 224
```

```
          BlueVal = 96

' from brown yellow to bright yellow

    ElseIf pixelArray(h, w) < 240 Then
      RedVal = Int(-224 + 2 * pixelArray(h, w))
      GreenVal = Int(-224 + 2 * pixelArray(h, w))
      BlueVal = 96

' from bright yellow to white

    ElseIf pixelArray(h, w) >= 240 Then
      RedVal = 255
      GreenVal = 255
      BlueVal = Int(-864 + 10 * pixelArray(h, w))

    End If
    WriteAPixel RedVal Mod 256, GreenVal Mod 256, _
      BlueVal Mod 256
  Next w
' Do not change the following, essential row padding
  w = wMax * 3
  Do While (w Mod 4) <> 0
    WriteAByte 0
    w = w + 1
  Loop
Next h

End Sub

''''''''''''''''''''''''''''''''''''''''''''''''''''''''''''

Private Sub BitMap2(hMax As Integer, _
  wMax As Integer, pixelArray As Variant)

Dim h As Integer, w As Integer, RedVal As Integer
Dim GreenVal As Integer, BlueVal As Integer

For h = hMax To 0 Step -1
  For w = 0 To wMax - 1

' from black to red

    If pixelArray(h, w) < 64 Then
      RedVal = Int(4 * pixelArray(h, w))
      GreenVal = 0
      BlueVal = 0

' from red to orange

    ElseIf pixelArray(h, w) < 128 Then
      RedVal = 255
      GreenVal = Int(2 * (pixelArray(h, w) - 64))
      BlueVal = 0

' from orange to yellow

    ElseIf pixelArray(h, w) < 192 Then
      RedVal = 255
```

```
        GreenVal = Int(2 * (pixelArray(h, w) - 64))
        BlueVal = 0

' from yellow to white

    Else
        RedVal = 255
        GreenVal = 255
        BlueVal = Int(4 * (pixelArray(h, w) - 192))

    End If
    WriteAPixel RedVal Mod 256, GreenVal Mod 256, _
        BlueVal Mod 256
  Next w
' Do not change the following, essential row padding
  w = wMax * 3
  Do While (w Mod 4) <> 0
    WriteAByte 0
    w = w + 1
  Loop
Next h

End Sub

' ' ' ' ' ' ' ' ' ' ' ' ' ' ' ' ' ' ' ' ' ' ' ' ' ' ' ' ' ' ' ' ' ' ' ' ' ' ' ' ' ' ' ' ' ' ' ' ' ' ' ' '

Private Sub BitMap3(hMax As Integer, _
  wMax As Integer, pixelArray As Variant)

Dim h As Integer, w As Integer, RedVal As Integer
Dim GreenVal As Integer, BlueVal As Integer

For h = hMax To 0 Step -1
  For w = 0 To wMax - 1

' from black to dark blue

    If pixelArray(h, w) < 64 Then
        RedVal = 0
        GreenVal = 0
        BlueVal = Int(4 * pixelArray(h, w))

' from dark blue to light blue

    ElseIf pixelArray(h, w) < 192 Then
        RedVal = 0
        GreenVal = Int(2 * (pixelArray(h, w) - 64))
        BlueVal = 255

' from light blue to white

    Else
        RedVal = Int(4 * (pixelArray(h, w) - 192))
        GreenVal = 255
        BlueVal = 255

    End If
    WriteAPixel RedVal Mod 256, GreenVal Mod 256, _
        BlueVal Mod 256
```

```
  Next w
' Do not change the following, essential row padding
  w = wMax * 3
  Do While (w Mod 4) <> 0
    WriteAByte 0
    w = w + 1
  Loop
Next h

End Sub
```

'''

```
Private Sub WriteAWord(ByVal WordValue As Integer)

' Write a two byte short word to the binary data stream.

Dim OutputFileNumber As Integer
OutputFileNumber = 1
Put #OutputFileNumber, , WordValue

End Sub
```

'''

```
Private Sub WriteALong(ByVal LongValue As Long)

' Write a four-byte long word to the binary data stream.

Dim OutputFileNumber As Integer
OutputFileNumber = 1
Put #OutputFileNumber, , LongValue

End Sub
```

'''

```
Private Sub WriteAPixel(ByVal RedValue As Byte, _
  ByVal GreenValue As Byte, ByVal BlueValue As Byte)

' Write a three-byte pixel color value to
' the binary data stream. Note that there is
' no padding up to a word or long boundary.

Dim OutputFileNumber As Integer
OutputFileNumber = 1
Put #OutputFileNumber, , BlueValue
Put #OutputFileNumber, , GreenValue
Put #OutputFileNumber, , RedValue

End Sub
```

'''

```
Private Sub WriteAByte(ByVal ByteValue As Byte)

' Write a byte.

Dim OutputFileNumber As Integer
```

```
OutputFileNumber = 1
Put #OutputFileNumber, , ByteValue

End Sub
```

11.8 RootFinder

The following macro is is an expanded version of the bisection algorithm described in section 8.6.

```
'''''''''''''''''''''''''''''''''''''''''''''''''''''''''''
'''''''''''''''^^^^^^^^^^^^^^^^^^^^^^^^^^^^''''''''''''''''''
''''''''''''''^                            ^''''''''''''''''
''''''''''''''^      ROOT  FINDER           ^''''''''''''''''
''''''''''''''^                            ^''''''''''''''''
'''''''''''''''^^^^^^^^^^^^^^^^^^^^^^^^^^^^''''''''''''''''''
'''''''''''''''''''''''''''''''''''''''''''(c) R. de Levie
'''''''''''''''''''''''''''''''''''''''''''v 4.6, June 1, 2004

' PURPOSE:

' This macro finds the real root of a function F(x) of a
' single variable x by bisection inside a user-defined
' range. Note: because the macro looks for a sign change
' in F(x), it will also find singularities, such as with
' tan(x) for x = pi/2.

' The value of the resolution criterion FRes can be changed
' depending on the requirements of the problem. For simple
' functions, a high resolution (i.e., a small value of
' FRes, such as 1E-12) may be desired, while complicated
' expressions may require a lower resolution. For functions
' that reach values much larger than 1, a relative rather
' than an absolute resolution may be more appropriate.

' SUBROUTINES:

' This macro does not require any subroutines.

' INPUT:

' The locations of the function F(x) and the independent
' variable x must be in columns of equal length, and are
' entered into the macro via input boxes.

' The parameter x must change monotonically (i.e., either
' ascend or descend continuously) in its column, while
' the function F(x) should have one and only one zero
' crossing in the selected column or column fragment.
' The parameter x can be a value or a function of some
' other parameters.

' If the function on the spreadsheet exhibits more than one
' zero crossing, restrict the size of the block so that it
' will contain only one of them.

' OUTPUT:

' The root is displayed in a message box.
```

```
' PROCEDURE:

' Call the macro, then enter the column ranges for F(x) and
' x in the input boxes.

Sub RootFinder()

Dim i As Integer, n As Integer
Dim nc As Integer, nr As Integer

Dim FFirst As Double, FLast As Double, FNew As Double
Dim FRes As Double
Dim XFirst As Double, XLast As Double, XNew As Double

Dim FFormula As Variant, FValue As Variant
Dim XFormula As Variant, XValue As Variant
Dim FFormulaSave As Variant, XFormulaSave As Variant

Dim FRange As Range, XRange As Range

Dim FPrompt, XPrompt, FTitle, XTitle

' Input the function F(x) and its associated files

FPrompt = "The function F(x) is in column:"
FTitle = "RootFinder: Input F(x)"
Set FRange = Application.InputBox(FPrompt, FTitle, Type:=8)
FRange.Select
FFormula = Selection.Formula
FValue = Selection.Value
FFormulaSave = Selection.Formula

' Test the F(x) input

nc = Selection.Columns.Count
If nc <> 1 Then
  MsgBox "The function should be in a single column."
  End
End If

nr = Selection.Rows.Count
If nr < 3 Then
  MsgBox "The column should have at least three rows."
  End
End If

' Input the variable x and its associated files

XPrompt = "The variable x is in column:"
XTitle = "RootFinder: Input x"
Set XRange = Application.InputBox(XPrompt, XTitle, Type:=8)
XRange.Select
XFormula = Selection.Formula
XValue = Selection.Value
XFormulaSave = Selection.Formula

' Test the x input

nc = Selection.Columns.Count
If nc <> 1 Then
  MsgBox "The variable should be in a single column."
  End
End If
```

```
If nr <> Selection.Rows.Count Then
  MsgBox "The F(x) and x columns must have equal lengths."
  End
End If

' Check for one root
' Note: an odd number of roots will also pass this test

FFirst = FValue(1, 1)
FLast = FValue(nr, 1)

If FFirst * FLast >= 0 Then
  MsgBox "The array should encompass a single root."
  End
End If

' Set the resolution; FRes must be positive

FRes = 0.0000000000001

' Suppress screen updating

Application.ScreenUpdating = False

' Bisection

n = 0
Do
  XRange.Select
  XFirst = XValue(1, 1)
  XLast = XValue(nr, 1)
  XNew = (XFirst + XLast) / 2
  XValue(2, 1) = XNew
  Selection.Value = XValue

  FRange.Select
  FValue = Selection.Value
  FFirst = FValue(1, 1)
  FLast = FValue(nr, 1)
  FNew = FValue(2, 1)

  XRange.Select
  If FFirst * FNew = 0 Then GoTo A
  If FFirst * FNew > 0 Then
    For i = 1 To nr
      XValue(i, 1) = XNew + _
        (XLast - XNew) * (i - 1) / (nr - 1)
    Next i
  End If
  If FFirst * FNew < 0 Then
    For i = 1 To nr
      XValue(i, 1) = XFirst + _
        (XNew - XFirst) * (i - 1) / (nr - 1)
    Next i
  End If
  n = n + 1
  Selection.Value = XValue
Loop Until Abs(FLast - FFirst) < FRes Or n = 100

' Restore data input area and display the found root

A:
```

```
XRange.Select
Selection.Formula = XFormulaSave
FRange.Select
Selection.Formula = FFormulaSave
MsgBox "Root at x = " & XNew

End Sub
```

11.9 ColumnSolver

Here is a macro that drives Solver to work, one row at a time, on data organized in columns, as described in section 4.18. As with SolverScan, make sure that Solver is callable by incorporating a reference to Solver.xla.

```
''''''''''''''''''''''''''''''''''''''''''''''''''''''''''''''''''
''''''''''''''''''''''''''''''''''''''''''''''''''''''''''''''''''
''''''''''''''''''''''''^^^^^^^^^^^^^^^^^^^^^^'''''''''''''''''''''
''''''''''''''''''''^                    ^'''''''''''''''''''''
''''''''''''''''''^     COLUMN  SOLVER    ^'''''''''''''''''''''
''''''''''''''''''^                    ^'''''''''''''''''''''
''''''''''''''''''''''''^^^^^^^^^^^^^^^^^^^^^^'''''''''''''''''''''
''''''''''''''''''''''''''''''''''''''''''''''''''''(c) R. de Levie
'''''''''''''''''''''''''''''''''''''''''''''''''''v 4.6 June 1, 2004
```

```
' PURPOSE:

' ColumnSolver allows the user to apply Solver sequentially
' to data located within in single row, whereupon it moves
' to the next row and repeats the procedure.

' The user specifies the location of the target cells, and
' the location of the adjustable parameter(s). Moreover,
' for ColumnSolverValue, the location of the wanted target
' values must be specified. All input information must be
' in columns and blocks of the same length, with all input
' information for any individual Solver application
' confined to a single row. When there are several
' adjustable parameters, these must be in a single
' contiguous block.

' ColumnSolverMax maximizes the value in the target cell,
' ColumnSolverMin minimizes the value in the target cell,
' while ColumnSolverValue makes the values of the target
' cells equal to the values specified in the WantedValue
' column. The column or block of parameter values should
' contain appropriate initial values for Solver, which
' ColumnSolver then changes into the final parameter values
' computed by Solver.

' The level of precision, tolerance, and convergence of
' Solver, and all other preferences and constraints, should
' be set in the Solver Options before calling ColumnSolver.

' INPUT:

' Set up Solver as if for a single operation, including all
' necessary specifications of constraints and options, if
' any. Then call ColumnSolver and answer the questions in
```

```
' its input boxes. ColumnSolver will start once the needed
' input information has been entered.

' OUTPUT:

' ColumnSolver adjusts the parameters so that the target cells
' yield the specified criterion, Min, Max, or EqualToValue.

' REQUIREMENTS:

' ColumnSolver requires that both Solver and Solver.xla have
' been installed.

' ONE-TIME PROCEDURE FOR INSTALLING SOLVER.XLA

' ColumnSolver can only call Solver as a subroutine when
' Solver.xla is properly referenced in the VBAProject.
' To see whether this is the case, go to the spreadsheet,
' select its VBA module, and look under Tools -> References
' to see whether SOLVER has been activated. It should be
' part of the contiguous, check-marked top items in the
' listed References - VBAProject.
'
' If it is not, first prepare your computer to make Solver
' callable. The procedure to do so is outlined below, and
' is needed only once until the operating system and/or
' Excel is re-installed or updated.

' Click on the Start button, and in the resulting menu, on
' Search, under For Files or Folders...(or Find > Files or
' Folders), search for Solver.xla. Note down where
' Solver.xla is located. If you have Microsoft Office, it
' most likely is in C:\Program Files\MicrosoftOffice\Office
' \Library\Solver.

' Exit the Search or Find dialog box, which will bring you
' back to the spreadsheet, select the VBA editor with
' Alt+F11, then go to Tools -> References, which will
' display the References - VBAProject dialog box. Click on
' Browse, select Filers of type: Microsoft Excel Files
' (*.xls, *.xla), and now that you know where to find it,
' navigate your way to Solver, and Open it. This will
' return you to the References - VBAProject dialog box,
' where you now use the Priority Up button to move it up,
' so that it is listed contiguously with the other, already
' activated add-ins. Click OK; from then on (i.e., until
' you reload or upgrade Excel) VBA will know how to find
' Solver when it is called from a macro.

Sub ColumnSolverMax()
Dim d As Integer
d = 1
Call ColumnSolver(d)
End Sub

Sub ColumnSolverMin()
Dim d As Integer
d = 2
Call ColumnSolver(d)
End Sub

Sub ColumnSolverValue()
```

```
Dim d As Integer
d = 3
Call ColumnSolver(d)
End Sub

Sub ColumnSolver(d)

Dim i As Integer, nc As Integer, nr As Integer
Dim PositionOf2ndDollar As Integer
Dim ParameterAddress As Variant, RowNumber As Variant
Dim TargetAddress As Variant, WantedValue As Variant
Dim myRow As Range, ParameterRange As Range
Dim TargetRange As Range, WantedValues As Range
Dim AAA, Cell, EqualTo, Prompt, Title

' Read the location of the target column

A:
Prompt = "The target cells are located in:" & Chr(13) _
    & "(Highlight a column or enter its address)"
Title = "ColumnSolver: Address of target column"
Set TargetRange = Application.InputBox(Prompt, Title, _
    Type:=8)
TargetRange.Select
nr = Selection.Rows.Count
i = 0
ReDim TargetAddress(1 To nr)
For Each Cell In TargetRange
  i = i + 1
  TargetAddress(i) = Cell.Address
Next Cell

ReDim outputArray(1 To nr)

' Verify that the target range is a single column

nc = Selection.Columns.Count
If nc <> 1 Then
  MsgBox "There can be only one single Target column"
  GoTo A
End If

' Read the column containing the target values

B:
If d = 3 Then
  Prompt = "The wanted target values are located in:" & Chr(13) _
      & "(Highlight a column or enter its address)"
  Title = "ColumnSolver: Wanted target values"
  Set WantedValues = Application.InputBox(Prompt, Title, _
      Type:=8)
  WantedValues.Select
  ReDim WantedValue(1 To nr) As Double
  i = 0
  For Each Cell In WantedValues
    i = i + 1
    WantedValue(i) = Cell.Value
  Next Cell

' Verify that the target range is a single column

  nc = Selection.Columns.Count
```

```
   If nc <> 1 Then
     MsgBox "There can be only one single" & _
        Chr(13) & " column with target values"
     GoTo B
   End If
End If

' Verify that the target range has the correct length

If nr - Selection.Rows.Count <> 0 Then
  MsgBox "The column of target values must have the" _
     & Chr(13) & "same number of rows as the target column."
  GoTo B
End If

' Read the location of the adjustable parameter column

C:
Prompt = "The location of the adjustable parameter(s) is:" & _
  Chr(13) & "(Highlight a column or block, or enter its address)"
Title = "ColumnSolver: Address of parameter range"
Set ParameterRange = Application.InputBox(Prompt, Title, _
  Type:=8)
ParameterRange.Select
nc = Selection.Columns.Count
If nc < 1 Then
  MsgBox "There must be at least one" _
     & Chr(13) & "column of adjustable parameters."
  GoTo C
End If

' Verify that the parameter range has the correct length

If nr - Selection.Rows.Count <> 0 Then
  MsgBox "The parameter block must have the same" _
     & Chr(13) & "number of rows as the target column."
  GoTo C
End If

ReDim ParameterAddress(1 To nr)
Application.ScreenUpdating = False

' For one parameter per row

If nc = 1 Then
  i = 0
  For Each Cell In ParameterRange
    i = i + 1
    ParameterAddress(i) = Cell.Address
  Next Cell

' Run Solver

  For i = 1 To nr
    If d < 3 Then EqualTo = " "
    If d = 3 Then EqualTo = WantedValue(i)
    SolverOK SetCell:=TargetAddress(i), MaxMinVal:=d, _
      valueof:=EqualTo, ByChange:=ParameterAddress(i)
    SolverSolve UserFinish:=True
  Next i
  GoTo E
```

```
' For multiple parameters per row

Else

' Find the parameter range for the proper row
' at the intersection of ParameterRange and myRow

  ReDim ParameterAddress(1 To nr)
  ReDim RowNumber(1 To nr)
  For i = 1 To nr
    PositionOf2ndDollar = InStr(2, TargetAddress(i), "$")
    RowNumber(i) = Mid(TargetAddress(i), PositionOf2ndDollar)
    AAA = "$A" & RowNumber(i) & ":" & "$IV" & RowNumber(i)
    Set myRow = Range(AAA)
    Intersect(ParameterRange, myRow).Select
    ParameterAddress = Selection.Address

' Run Solver

    If d < 3 Then EqualTo = " "
    If d = 3 Then EqualTo = WantedValue(i)
    SolverOK SetCell:=TargetAddress(i), MaxMinVal:=d, _
      valueof:=EqualTo, ByChange:=ParameterAddress
    SolverSolve UserFinish:=True
  Next i
End If

E:
End Sub
```

Appendix

A.1 The basic spreadsheet operations

Symbol	Description	Notes	Precedence[1]

Numeric operators:

Symbol	Description	Notes	Precedence
^	Exponentiation	** will not work; e or E may work[2]	1
*	Multiplication	×, · or . will not work[3]	2
/	Division		2
\	Integer division		3
Mod	Modulus	the remainder of a division	4
+	Addition		6
−	Subtraction		6
=	Assignment		8

String operators:

Symbol	Description	Notes	Precedence
&	Concatenation		7
=	Assignment		8
:	Range	as in `SUM(B3:B15)`	
,	Union	as in `SUM(B3:B15,A7:F9)`	
	Intersection	as in `SUM(B3:B15 A7:F9)`	

Comparison operators:

Symbol	Description	Notes	Precedence
=	Equal to	as in: `If x = 3 Then`	1
<>	Unequal to	as in: `If x <> 3 Then`	2
<	Smaller than		3
>	Larger than		4
<=	Smaller than or equal to		5
>=	Larger than or equal to		6
Like	Pattern match	as in: `If top Like t?p Then`	7
Is	Object comparison		7
=	Assignment	as in: `x = 3`	8

Symbol	Description	Precedence[1]

Logical operators:

Not	Negation	1
And	Conjunction	2
Or	Disjunction	3
Xor	Exclusion	4
Eqv	Equivalence	5
Imp	Implication	6
=	Assignment	8

Notes: **1**: Precedence (ranging from 1 for highest to 8 for lowest) indicates the order in which operations will be performed *in the absence of brackets*. **2**: E-notation *only* works for integer exponents. **3**: Multiplication *always* requires the explicit multiplication sign *.

A.2 Some common mathematical functions

Function	Description

Function	Description
ABS(*x*)	Absolute value:
AVERAGE(*range*)	Average of the range specified
COUNT(*range*)	Counts number of entries in given range
COUNTA(*range*)	Counts number of non-blank values in range
COUNTBLANK(*range*)	Counts number of blank cells in specified range
COUNTIF(*range, criterion*)	Counts only those values in the range that satisfy a given criterion
DEGREES(*angle in radians*)	Converts radians to degrees
EVEN(*x*)	Rounds a number to the nearest even integer away from zero
EXP(*x*)	Exponentiates
FACT(*n*)	Factorial of a non-negative integer
FACTDOUBLE(*n*)	Double factorial of a non-negative number
INT(*x*)	Rounds a number down to the nearest integer

LN(x)	Natural logarithm of positive number
LOG(x,n)	Logarithm of base n, where n is optional, with a default value of 10
LOG10(x)	Ten-based logarithm
MAX(*range*)	Finds the maximum value in a specified range, or in up to 30 ranges
MDETERM(*array*)	Yields the determinant of a square array of numbers
MEDIAN(*range*)	The median of a set of numbers
MIN(*range*)	Finds the smallest number in a range or number of ranges
MOD(x,y)	The remainder of the division x/y
ODD(x)	Rounds away from zero to the nearest odd number
PI( )	The number $\pi = 3.14159265358979$
POWER(x,y)	$= x^{\wedge}y$
PRODUCT(*range*)	Product of numbers in specified rage
RADIANS(*angle*)	Converts from degrees to radians
RAND( )	Yields a random number between 0 and 1
ROUND(x,n)	Rounds x to n decimal places
ROUNDDOWN(x,n)	Rounds away from zero
ROUNDUP(x,n)	Rounds towards zero
SIGN(x)	Sign of (x)
SQRT(x)	Square root of non-negative number
SUM(*range*)	Sums values in specified range or ranges
SUMPRODUCT(*array*1,*array*2, …)	Computes the sums of the products of two or more arrays of equal dimensions
SUMSQ(*range*)	Sum of squares of specified range or ranges
SUMX2MY2(*xaray*,*yarray*)	$= \Sigma\,(x^2 - y^2)$
SUMX2PY2(*xaray*,*yarray*)	$= \Sigma\,(x^2 + y^2)$
SUMXMY2(*xaray*,*yarray*)	$= \Sigma\,(x - y)^2$
TRUNC(x)	Truncates a number to an integer

A.3 Trigonometric and related functions

Function	Description
ACOS(x)	The inverse cosine, arccos, in radians
ACOSH(x)	The inverse hyperbolic cosine, arcosh, in radians
ASIN(x)	The inverse sine, arcsin, in radians
ASINH(x)	The inverse hyperbolic sine, arsinh, in radians
ATAN(x)	The inverse tangent, arctan, in radians
ATAN2(x,y)	=ATAN(y/x)
ATANH(x)	The inverse hyperbolic tangent, artanh, in radians
COS(x)	The cosine, in radians
COSH(x)	The hyperbolic cosine, cosh, in radians
SIN(x)	The sine, in radians
SINH(x)	The hyperbolic sine, in radians
TAN(x)	The tangent, in radians
TANH(x)	The hyperbolic tangent, in radians

A.4 Some engineering functions

These functions require the Data Analysis Toolpak.

Function	Description
BESSELI(x,n)	The modified Bessel function $I_n(x) = i^{-1} J_n(ix)$
BESSELJ(x,n)	The Bessel function $J_n(x)$
BESSELK(x,n)	The modified Bessel function $K_n(x)$
BESSELY(x,n)	The Bessel function $Y_n(x)$
CONVERT($n,fromUnit,toUnit$)	Converts a number from one measurement system to another
DELTA(n,m)	Kronecker delta
ERF(n)	The error function
ERFC(n)	The complementary error function
GESTEP($n,step$)	Tests whether a number n exceeds a threshold value *step*

RANDBETWEEN(n,m)   Generates a random integer between the integer values n and m; it will change every time a spreadsheet calculation is performed.

A.5 *Functions involving complex numbers*

These functions require that the Analysis Toolpak has been loaded.

Function	Description and example
COMPLEX(a,b)	Converts the real numbers a and b into the complex number $a+bi$
IMABS($"a+bi"$)	$= (a^2+b^2)^{1/2}$, the absolute value (modulus) of a complex number
IMAGINARY($"a+bi"$)	$= b$, the imaginary component of a complex number
IMARGUMENT($"a+bi"$)	$= \arctan(b/a)$, the argument of a complex number, in radians
IMCONJUGATE($"a+bi"$)	$= a-bi$, the complex conjugate of a complex number
IMCOS($"a+bi"$)	The cosine of a complex number
IMDIV($"a+bi"$, $"c+di"$)	The quotient of two complex numbers
IMEXP($"a+bi"$)	The exponential of a complex number
IMLN($"a+bi"$)	The natural logarithm of a complex number
IMLOG10($"a+bi"$)	The base-10 logarithm of a complex number
IMLOG2($"a+bi"$)	The base-2 logarithm of a complex number
IMPOWER($"a+bi"$, n)	$= (a^2+b^2)^n$, the complex number raised to an integer power
IMPRODUCT($"a+bi"$, $"c+di"$)	The product of two complex numbers
IMREAL($"a+bi"$)	$= a$, the real component of a complex number
IMSIN($"a+bi"$)	The sine of a complex number

IMSQRT("*a* + *bi*")	The square root of a complex number
IMSUB("*a* + *bi*", "*c* + *di*")	The difference between two (or more) complex numbers
IMSUM("*a* + *bi*","*c* + *di*")	The sum of two (or more) complex numbers

Notes: Operations on complex numbers all start with IM, and use text strings to squeeze the two components of a complex number into one cell. In order to use the results of complex number operations, you must therefore first *extract* its real and imaginary components, using IMREAL() and IMAGINARY(). Instead of i you can use j to denote the square root of minus one (which you must then *specify* as such), but you *cannot* use the corresponding capitals, I or J.

A.6 *Matrix operations*

Function	**Description**
INDEX(*array,row#,column#*)	Yields an individual matrix element in given array
MDETERM(*array*)[1]	The determinant of a square array
MINVERSE(*array*)[1]	The matrix inverse of a square array
MMULT(*array*) [1]	The matrix product of two arrays; the number of columns in the first array must be equal to the number of rows in the second array

Note **1**: Matrix inversion and matrix multiplication work only on data *arrays*, i.e., rectangular blocks of cells, but not on single cells. To enter these instructions, enter the array with Ctrl‿Shift‿Enter (on the MacIntosh: Command‿Return).

A fourth matrix operation, Transpose, is performed as part of the Edit ⇒ Paste Special operation.

A.7 Excel error messages

Error message	Problem
#DIV/0!	Division by zero or by the contents of an empty cell
#NAME?	Excel does not recognize the name; perhaps it has been deleted
#N/A	Some needed data are not available
#NULL!	The formula refers to a non-existing intersection of two ranges
#NUM!	The number is of incorrect type, e.g., it is negative when a positive number is expected
#REF!	The reference is not valid; it may have been deleted
#VALUE!	The argument or operand is of the wrong type

A.8 Some shortcut keystrokes for pc & Mac

Excel operation	common to pc & Mac	
	pc	Mac
Copy	Ctrl⌣c	
Paste	Ctrl⌣v	
Cut	Ctrl⌣x	
Bold toggle	Ctrl⌣b	
Italics toggle	Ctrl⌣i	
Underline toggle	Ctrl⌣u	
Find	Ctrl⌣f	
Replace	Ctrl⌣h	
Fill down	Ctrl⌣d	
Fill right	Ctrl⌣r	

	pc & Mac	
	pc	**Mac**
Repeat		Ctrl␣y
Undo		Ctrl␣z
Open new workbook		Ctrl␣n
Select next worksheet		Ctrl␣PageDown
Select previous worksheet		Ctrl␣PageUp
Display Formula dialog box		Ctrl␣a

(after typing a formula name in a cell or in the formula bar)

	pc	**Mac**
Display Find dialog box		Ctrl␣f
Display Replace dialog box		Ctrl␣h
Display GoTo dialog box		Ctrl␣g
Display Define Name dialog box		Ctrl␣F3
Insert a Cell Comment		Shift␣F2
Display Paste Function dialog box		Shift␣F3
Display Macro dialog box	**Alt␣F8**	**Opt␣F8**
Toggle between Excel and VBA	**Alt␣F11**	**Opt␣F11**

VBA operation	**pc & Mac**	
	pc	**Mac**
Run macro	F5	
Stop macro	Esc	
Step through macro	F8	
Toggle breakpoint	F9	
Toggle between Excel and VBA	**Alt␣F11**	**Opt␣F11**

Some other differences between pc & Mac

Excel operation	**pc**	**Mac**
Enter / end of line	**Enter**	**Return**
Get properties	**right-click**	**Ctrl␣click**
Specify a matrix	**Ctrl␣Shift␣Enter**	**Command␣Return**

A.9 Installation requirements & suggestions

In order to make full use of the methods described in this book, you will *need* the following:

(1) Excel 97 or a more recent version of Excel, installed on your computer. If you start by installing Excel, load its full version rather than its 'typical' or 'small' option in order to avoid having to add the items under (2) separately.

(2) The items listed below, automatically included when installing the full version of Excel. If you do not find them installed on a computer with preinstalled Excel, the following items should be added from the original Microsoft Windows or Excel installation disk:

Data Analysis ToolPak	see section 1.7.1
Data Analysis ToolPak - VBA	see section 1.7.1
Solver add-in	see section 1.7.2
Solver.xla	see section 1.7.2
VBA Help file	see section 1.7.3

(3) The MacroBundle contains the custom macros used in this book. It should be downloaded as a Word text file (.doc) from the web site www.oup-usa.org/advancedexcel, and entered into a VBA module, see section 1.7.4. For most convenient access, then install the MBToolbar.

The following *optional* files, in Word format, and downloadable from the same web site that contains the MacroBundle, are not needed, but are made available for your convenience:

(4) To refresh your command of Excel before starting to use this book, download and practice with the file Getting up to speed.

(5) If you write some sample macros, but want to avoid typing them, download the SampleMacros file, copy a sample macro from there, and paste it into your spreadsheet.

(6) Likewise, if you want to check a particular exercise based on an external data set, but wish to avoid the (tedious as well as error-prone) manual data entry, copy the data set from the SampleData file, then paste it into your spreadsheet.

Epilogue

Science begins and ends with contemplation. Behind each experiment lies a question, and the experiment must be designed to answer that question. A crucial first part of the experiment is sampling, i.e., finding or selecting the proper object(s) of your study. If one would want to 'prove' that whites have larger brains than blacks (even apart from the question whether brain size correlates with brain power), one might compare the cranial volumes of tall white males with those of petite black females and, voilà, find what one is looking for. No, I am not making this up: Stephen Jay Gould, in his *Mismeasure of Man*, amply documents this type of self-serving pseudo-science.

A second part of the experiment involves the measurement of the sought information, a process usually called data acquisition, especially if it is done automatically, by an instrument. The data so generated are just numbers, often reams of them, that are useful only within a given context. Again, measurements can introduce distortion that, as discussed in chapter 6, can sometimes be corrected, at least partially.

The present book deals with the third stage, in which those data are organized and analyzed, thereby making them available for interpretation, which is again an introspective, contemplative activity. If the sampling is biased or the measurements systematically distorted, no amount of subsequent analysis will overcome those initial handicaps, although it may more effectively conceal them with an overlayer of sophistication.

*****

Data analysis can be achieved in many different ways, but in modern science it often involves computer assistance, because of the ease and speed with which computers can execute laborious and often iterative analysis protocols. Many software packages are available for data analysis. The focus of this book has been Excel, mainly for the following reasons:

(1) Since Excel is included in the Microsoft Office bundle sold with many personal computers, it is the most widely available software package suitable for numerical data analysis. Thus, using Excel often avoids the hurdle of having to select, buy, and master more specialized data analysis software packages.

(2) The macros described and used here are written in a relatively easy-to-read language, Visual Basic, and the code remains fully accessible and modifiable. Thus the user can judge what the underlying assumptions are, and can even alter the macros if so desired. To the conscientious scientist, that may be enough justification for preferring an open glass case to the usually sealed black box.

(3) Excel is quite intuitive and easy to learn. In teaching this is important, because spreadsheets offer a method to get students to treat data numerically with a relatively low activation energy barrier. The use of custom functions and macros can then be introduced gradually, thereby providing a gentle learning slope that, eventually, can lead to a quite high level of competence in data analysis.

(4) Because Excel is so widely used in different areas, such as science, commerce, and administration, novices will often be more willing to learn it than to invest time and energy in familiarizing themselves with specialized software useful only in a particular field of study.

*****

The ready availability of sophisticated algorithms has made it very easy to apply least squares to experimental data, so that this method is no longer restricted to statisticians. However, there is a need to understand what these algorithms do, and to know what tacit assumptions are made, otherwise Mark Twain's ordering of untruths as lies, damned lies, and statistics may still apply. In this book I have therefore tried to focus not only on the mechanics of applying these methods, but also on their inherent limitations. While the spreadsheet can perform the numerical operations, the user must contribute both the context and the value judgment.

*****

New tools often lead to the development of more efficient approaches. Once users have become familiar with nonlinear least squares, they can often replace linearizing approximations with the real thing. Math no longer needs to get in the way of science in, say, the undergraduate physical chemistry lab, which generations of students have come to hate because of its emphasis on lengthy computations of 'error' propagation, a task that distracts from the real topic, and that can now be accomplished with a few clicks on a spreadsheet. When books on statistics mention the covariance, it tends to remain an unused concept unless convenient tools are available to calculate it; when texts exhort the advantages of orthogonalization, it helps to have an easy way to implement it. If you have a similar pet peeve, remember first to look for a helping hand at the end of your own arm. Having come this far in reading this book, you can often retire that peeve by writing your own macro.

New tools can also lead to new questions. By emphasizing the rather open-ended possibilities of Excel, I hope that you, my reader, will see ways to analyze your data in a more satisfactory way, and perhaps will even design novel experiments to formulate new questions and to find novel answers.

Orr's Island
October 1, 2002

Index